W9-ATV-879

To Know the Past

Ancient Landmarks

Heritage Studies 6

for Christian Schools®

TEACHER'S EDITION

Second Edition

Bob Jones University Press, Greenville, SC 29614

**HERITAGE STUDIES 6 for Christian Schools® Teacher's Edition
Second Edition**

Coordinating Writers
Peggy Davenport
Eileen M. Berry

Contributing Writers
Sharon Hambrick
Stephanie Ralston
Maggie D. Sloan
E. Anne Smith
Dawn L. Watkins
Karen Wooster

Computer Formatting
Peggy Hargis

Project Editor
Manda Cooper

Graphics Coordinator
Mary Ann Lumm

Graphics
Timothy Banks
Vincent Barnhart
Johanna Berg
John Bjerk
Paula Cheadle
Barbara Gladin
Jim Hargis

Joyce Landis
Sam Laterza
Dick Mitchell
Duane Nichols
Kathy Pflug
John Roberts
Lynda Slattery
Joe Tyrpak
Dan Van Leeuwen

Photo Acquisition
Rachel Carper
Drew Fields
Terry Latini

ISBN 1-57924-085-2

15 14 13 12 11 10 9 8 7 6 5

CONTENTS

SUMMARY OF CORRELATED SKILLS AND INSTRUCTIONAL MATERIALS

	Chapters and Lessons	Suggested teaching days	Lesson pages	Text pages	Notebook pages
1	**BETWEEN GREAT RIVERS: MESOPOTAMIA**				
	1 The Days of Abraham	1	3-4	2-3	1
	2 Seeking the Past	2	5-7	4-6	2
	3 Sumer of Mesopotamia	2	8-10	7-11	
	4 Artisans and Craftsmen	2	11-13	12-14	3
	5 Religion and Royalty	2	14-16	15-17	4-5
	6 At School or Home	2	17-20	18-22	6
2	**THE GIFT OF THE NILE: ANCIENT EGYPT**				
	7 Gift of the Nile	1	31-33	24-27	7
	8 Storehouse of the World	1	34-36	28-30	8
	9 Pharaohs, Pyramids, and Papyrus	2	37-40	31-34	9
	10 Ancient Symbols and Secrets	2	41-43	35-37	10
	11 Hebrews and Hyksos	2	44-46	38-41	11
	12 Relics and Rituals	2	47-50	42-45	12
	13 A Taste of Culture	2	51-53	46-48	13

Bible Action Truths; Bible Promises	Heritage Studies skills
BATs: 8a Faith in God's promises, 8b Faith in the power of the Word of God	summarizing data, inferring relationships, identifying sources of information, working with maps
BAT: 8b Faith in the power of the Word of God	sequencing events, summarizing data, inferring relationships, formulating opinions, identifying sources of information, showing respect for heritage
BAT: 1a Understanding Jesus Christ; Bible Promise: D. Identified in Christ	summarizing data, inferring relationships, formulating opinions, identifying sources of information
BAT: 7e Humility; Bible Promises: H. God as Father, I. God as Master	summarizing data, inferring relationships, making decisions, formulating opinions
BAT: 6c Spirit-filled; Bible Promises: F. Christ as Intercessor, I. God as Master	sequencing events, summarizing data, inferring relationships, making decisions, formulating opinions, identifying sources of information, valuing the rights of citizenship, showing respect for heritage
BATs: 2a Authority, 2e Work, 5d Communication	summarizing data, inferring relationships, making decisions, formulating opinions
BATs: 7b Exaltation of Christ, 7c Praise; Bible Promise: I. God as Master	summarizing data, making decisions, formulating opinions, working with maps, working with time lines
BAT: 5b Giving	summarizing data, making decisions, formulating opinions, working with maps
BATs: 1b Repentance and faith, 7d Contentment, 8a Faith in God's promises	summarizing data, formulating opinions, identifying sources of information, working with maps
BATs: 2c Faithfulness, 2e Work	sequencing events, summarizing data, working with time lines, identifying sources of information
BATs: 2c Faithfulness, 5a Love, 6e Forgiveness	sequencing events, summarizing data, making decisions
BAT: 1b Repentance and faith; Bible Promise: E. Christ as Sacrifice	summarizing data, inferring relationships, making decisions, formulating opinions
BATs: 1b Repentance and faith, 4b Purity; Bible Promise: B. Guiltless by the Blood	summarizing data, making decisions, showing respect for heritage

3

4

Bible Action Truths; Bible Promises	Heritage Studies skills
BAT: 8a Faith in God's promises	sequencing events, formulating opinions, identifying sources of information, working with maps, using cardinal directions, showing respect for heritage
BAT: 1a Understanding Jesus Christ; Bible Promise: B. Guiltless by the Blood	sequencing events, summarizing data, inferring relationships, formulating opinions, working with maps, using cardinal directions, showing respect for heritage
BATs: 2a Authority, 2c Faithfulness	inferring relationships, making decisions, formulating opinions, showing respect for heritage
BAT: 1c Separation from the world; Bible Promise: B. Guiltless by the Blood	inferring relationships, making decisions, formulating opinions, working with maps, using cardinal directions, showing respect for heritage
BAT: 8d Courage	inferring relationships, formulating opinions, working with maps, using cardinal directions, showing respect for heritage
BATs: 1a Understanding Jesus Christ, 1b Repentance and faith; Bible Promises: B. Guiltless by the Blood, E. Christ as Sacrifice, H. God as Father, I. God as Master	sequencing events, inferring relationships, formulating opinions, working with time lines, showing respect for heritage
BAT: 5c Evangelism and missions	sequencing events, summarizing data, inferring relationships, formulating opinions, working with time lines, working with maps, using cardinal directions, showing respect for heritage
BAT: 7d Contentment	summarizing data, inferring relationships, making decisions, working with maps, using cardinal directions, showing respect for heritage
BAT: 5c Evangelism and missions; Bible Promises: H. God as Father, I. God as Master	inferring relationships, making decisions, formulating opinions, working with maps, using cardinal directions, showing respect for heritage
BAT: 1a Understanding Jesus Christ	inferring relationships, formulating opinions, showing respect for heritage
BATs: 2b Servanthood, 5a Love, 7a Grace, 7e Humility; Bible Promise: I. God as Master	inferring relationships, making decisions, formulating opinions, working with time lines, showing respect for heritage

Bible Action Truths; Bible Promises	Heritage Studies skills
Bible Promise: I. God as Master	summarizing data, making predictions, inferring relationships, making decisions, working with time lines, working with maps, showing respect for heritage
BATs: 1b Repentance and faith, 6a Bible study, 6b Prayer; Bible Promise: A. Liberty from Sin	summarizing data, making decisions, formulating opinions, showing respect for heritage
BAT: 2a Authority	summarizing data, making decisions, formulating opinions, working with maps, showing respect for heritage
BAT: 7d Contentment	summarizing data, making decisions, showing respect for heritage
BAT: 1b Repentance and faith	summarizing data, making decisions, formulating opinions, working with maps, showing respect for heritage
BATs: 7b Exaltation of Christ, 7c Praise	summarizing data, inferring relationships, formulating opinions, working with maps
BATs: 8b Faith in the power of the Word of God, 8c Fight, 8d Courage	summarizing data, making decisions, formulating opinions, valuing the rights of citizenship, showing respect for heritage
BAT: 7e Humility	summarizing data, making predictions, formulating opinions, working with maps
BAT: 5b Giving	summarizing data, making predictions, formulating opinions, showing respect for heritage
BATs: 1a Understanding Jesus Christ, 7a Grace; Bible Promises: A. Liberty from Sin, B. Guiltless by the Blood, D. Identified in Christ, E. Christ as Sacrifice	summarizing data, inferring relationships, formulating opinions, identifying sources of information, working with maps, showing respect for heritage
BATs: 3a Self-concept, 7c Praise, 7e Humility	summarizing data, inferring relationships, formulating opinions, identifying sources of information
BATs: 5c Evangelism and missions, 8b Faith in the power of the Word of God, 8c Fight, 8d Courage	sequencing events, summarizing data, working with maps, identifying key documents, showing respect for heritage
BATs: 2a Authority, 2b Servanthood, 7e Humility; Bible Promise: I. God as Master	sequencing events, summarizing data, inferring relationships, formulating opinions, working with time lines, working with maps and globes, showing respect for heritage

7

8

Bible Action Truths; Bible Promises	Heritage Studies skills
BATs: 1a Understanding Jesus Christ, 2b Servant-hood, 6c Spirit-filled, 7a Grace, 7e Humility, 8b Faith in the power of the Word of God, 8c Fight, 8d Courage; Bible Promise: E. Christ as Sacrifice	summarizing data, inferring relationships, making decisions, formulating opinions, working with maps, using cardinal directions, identifying key documents, valuing the rights of citizenship, showing respect for heritage
BATs: 1b Repentance and faith, 1c Separation from the world, 3e Unity of Christ and the church, 4b Purity, 7a Grace, 7c Praise; Bible Promise: F. Christ as Intercessor	sequencing events, summarizing data, inferring relationships, making decisions, formulating opinions, identifying sources of information, identifying key documents, valuing the rights of citizenship, showing respect for heritage
BATs: 2a Authority, 4d Victory; Bible Promise: A. Liberty from Sin	summarizing data, inferring relationships, formulating opinions, working with maps, using cardinal directions, valuing the rights of citizenship, showing respect for heritage
BATs: 2a Authority, 3d Body as a temple, 4b Purity, 4d Victory, 5a Love, 6c Spirit-filled; Bible Promises: D. Identified in Christ, I. God as Master	sequencing events, summarizing data, making predictions, inferring relationships, making decisions, formulating opinions, working with maps, valuing the rights of citizenship, showing respect for heritage
BATs: 3b Mind, 5d Communication; Bible Promise: H. God as Father	summarizing data, inferring relationships, formulating opinions, working with maps, showing respect for heritage
BATs: 1a Understanding Jesus Christ, 1b Repentance and faith, 1c Separation from the world, 2e Work, 2f Enthusiasm, 5c Evangelism and missions, 8d Courage; Bible Promise: E. Christ as Sacrifice	sequencing events, summarizing data, inferring relationships, making decisions, formulating opinions, working with time lines, working with maps and globes, using cardinal directions, showing respect for heritage
BATs: 6d Clear conscience, 6e Forgiveness	sequencing events, summarizing data, making decisions, formulating opinions, working with maps, using cardinal directions, showing respect for heritage
BATs: 6a Bible study, 8b Faith in the power of the Word of God	sequencing events, summarizing data, making decisions, working with time lines, identifying sources of information, working with maps, showing respect for heritage
BATs: 4b Purity, 5a Love, 5c Evangelism and missions, 7e Humility	summarizing data, formulating opinions, working with time lines, identifying sources of information, showing respect for heritage
BATs: 2c Faithfulness, 2e Work	summarizing data, inferring relationships, making decisions, formulating opinions
Bible Promise: I. God as Master	summarizing data, formulating opinions, working with diagrams, showing respect for heritage
BATs: 1a Understanding Jesus Christ, 2a Authority, 2c Faithfulness; Bible Promise: E. Christ as Sacrifice	summarizing data, inferring relationships, making decisions, formulating opinions, identifying sources of information, showing respect for heritage

Bible Action Truths; Bible Promises	Heritage Studies skills
Bible Promise: I. God as Master	summarizing data, inferring relationships, working with maps, using cardinal directions
BAT: 8b Faith in the power of the Word of God	summarizing data, formulating opinions, identifying sources of information, showing respect for heritage
BAT: 7d Contentment; Bible Promise: G. Christ as Friend	summarizing data, formulating opinions, working with maps, using cardinal directions
BATs: 5a Love, 5b Giving, 6a Bible study, 6b Prayer; Bible Promises: H. God as Father, I. God as Master	summarizing data, making decisions, formulating opinions, working with maps and globes
BATs: 1a Understanding Jesus Christ, 5c Evangelism and missions; Bible Promises: B. Guiltless by the Blood, D. Identified in Christ	summarizing data, making decisions, formulating opinions, working with maps
BAT: 6a Bible study	summarizing data, inferring relationships, formulating opinions, showing respect for heritage
BAT: 7b Exaltation of Christ	summarizing data, showing respect for heritage
BATs: 7b Exaltation of Christ, 7e Humility	summarizing data, inferring relationships, showing respect for heritage
Bible Promise: I. God as Master	summarizing data, formulating opinions, showing respect for heritage
BAT: 3a Self-concept	summarizing data, formulating opinions, working with maps, showing respect for heritage
BAT: 6a Bible study	summarizing data, inferring relationships, working with maps, showing respect for heritage
BATs: 3a Self-concept, 7c Praise	summarizing data, formulating opinions, showing respect for heritage
BAT: 7b Exaltation of Christ	summarizing data, making predictions, formulating opinions, showing respect for heritage

Bible Action Truths; Bible Promises	Heritage Studies skills
BAT: 1a Understanding Jesus Christ	summarizing data, inferring relationships, formulating opinions, working with maps, showing respect for heritage
BATs: 1b Repentance and faith, 2a Authority; Bible Promise: I. God as Master	sequencing events, making decisions, formulating opinions, working with time lines, working with maps, valuing the rights of citizenship, showing respect for heritage
BAT: 8a Faith in God's promises	sequencing events, summarizing data, making predictions, making decisions, formulating opinions, working with time lines, valuing the rights of citizenship, showing respect for heritage
BATs: 4c Honesty, 5c Evangelism and missions	sequencing events, summarizing data, making decisions, formulating opinions, valuing the rights of citizenship, showing respect for heritage
BATs: 1a Understanding Jesus Christ, 1b Repentance and faith, 8b Faith in the power of the Word of God	sequencing events, summarizing data, making predictions, inferring relationships, making decisions, working with time lines, identifying key documents, valuing the rights of citizenship, showing respect for heritage
BAT: 8b Faith in the power of the Word of God	sequencing events, summarizing data, formulating opinions, valuing the rights of citizenship, showing respect for heritage
BATs: 4c Honesty, 8b Faith in the power of the Word of God	sequencing events, summarizing data, making decisions, formulating opinions, working with maps, valuing the rights of citizenship, showing respect for heritage
Bible Promises: H. God as Father, I. God as Master	summarizing data, making predictions, formulating opinions, working with maps, valuing the rights of citizenship, showing respect for heritage
BATs: 1b Repentance and faith, 2a Authority	summarizing data, inferring relationships, formulating opinions, working with maps, showing respect for heritage
BAT: 3a Self-concept	sequencing events, summarizing data, showing respect for heritage
BATs: 2c Faithfulness, 2d Goal setting, 2e Work	sequencing events, summarizing data, showing respect for heritage
BAT: 7b Exaltation of Christ	summarizing data, inferring relationships, working with maps, showing respect for heritage
BATs: 8c Fight, 8d Courage	sequencing events, summarizing data, formulating opinions, showing respect for heritage
BATs: 1c Separation from the world, 8c Fight, 8d Courage	summarizing data, formulating opinions, showing respect for heritage
BAT: 8b Faith in the power of the Word of God	summarizing data, inferring relationships, formulating opinions, valuing the rights of citizenship, showing respect for heritage

INTRODUCTION

HERITAGE STUDIES 6 for Christian Schools is part of a developmental social studies program. In the hands of a skillful teacher, these materials can be used to teach history, geography, economics, culture, and government skills as well as a knowledge of God and Christian character. You, the teacher, have a choice in scheduling the teaching of Heritage Studies. Some suggested methods follow:

- You may choose to use the scheduling plan provided by the Day symbols in the lessons. Each Day symbol represents a class period of 30-40 minutes and gives logical starting and stopping points for discussions and activities. (*NOTE:* Since supplemental lessons are optional, they have not been included in the Day symbol plan.) Following the Day symbol plan and teaching Heritage Studies every day, you can complete the curriculum in 167 days.
- Or you may choose to teach an entire lesson each day, enabling you to complete Heritage Studies in a semester. (*NOTE:* There are seventy-six lessons in Heritage Studies 6. Some teachers alternate the teaching of Heritage Studies and science, devoting a semester to each subject.)

Remember, as always, you should arrange the lessons to accommodate your class and school schedules. Many lessons offer several procedures and activities. The creative teacher may choose to use all of one lesson but only parts of another, or he may adapt the material to his own methods.

Major Goals

1. Developing a knowledge of God

Creation tells us about God (Ps. 19:1; Rom. 1:20). By studying the history of the world and the features of the earth, we can see illustrations of God's wisdom, omnipotence, sovereignty, and benevolence.

2. Encouraging Christian growth

What a student learns in Heritage Studies class can affect his spiritual growth and ministry. He should learn discipline in his approach to and his execution of responsibilities. He should be prepared to evaluate and reject false philosophies. He should have a better testimony among unbelievers.

3. Promoting historic and geographic literacy

The current trend in social studies education is to return to an emphasis on historical fact and geography. While this series includes many history concepts and geography skills, it also emphasizes Christian philosophy, character, and attitudes, promoting a balanced approach to social studies instruction.

- Historic and Geographic Knowledge

History and geography can be defined as a body of knowledge. History can also be defined as a way of thinking. The study of these topics, therefore, is a product (body of knowledge) and a process (way of investigating and thinking). The Bob Jones University Press elementary Heritage Studies series continually interweaves the product and process aspects of history and geography.

The products of history and geography are stated in several forms. For example, knowledge can be expressed as a fact. A *fact* is an event that has been observed and recorded by more than one person, the records showing no disagreement among the observers. (This does not mean that a fact cannot be in error.) Knowledge can also be expressed as a *concept,* a mental set of ideas, objects, or events. Finally, knowledge can be expressed as a *principle,* a statement predicting interrelationships among concepts. The Bob Jones University Press elementary Heritage Studies program uses the words *main idea* to include all three forms of knowledge. Note the following examples of each form of knowledge:

- □ *Fact:* Abraham obeyed God by taking Isaac to the altar to be sacrificed.

- □ *Concept:* Faith allowed Abraham to make this step of obedience.

- □ *Principle:* The monotheism of the Hebrews separated them from all other nations and made their values and lifestyle unique.

The product of Heritage Studies is organized according to a scope and sequence. The scope is *what* knowledge will be covered in the program, and the sequence is *when* that knowledge will be presented. There is disagreement among educators about the scope of knowledge that should be presented on the elementary level. Some still hold to the post-1920s experiment in "socializing" the study of history, organizing the material around the child and his environment. Recent research recommends, however, that true historic and geographic understanding rests on the more traditional emphasis on skills, such as working with maps and sequencing events.

There are several ways to sequence Heritage Studies knowledge. For example, it can be organized around a unifying framework of themes (referred to in literature as conceptual themes) that subsume all branches of Heritage Studies. Another approach is a spiral pattern in which the same general topics are taken up periodically—every year, or two or three times in a program. Another option, supported by research and experience, is to study history chronologically, exploring eras in order, thereby helping students see connections between events. The Bob Jones University Press elementary Heritage Studies program combines the two latter organizations.

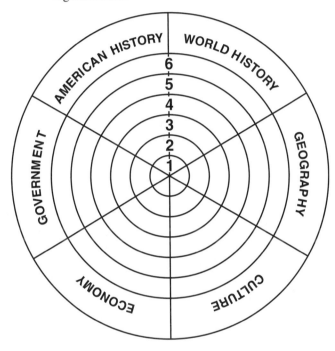

• History and Geography Skills

Students should be deriving knowledge through practical experiences that involve action—"hands-on" or "learning-by-doing" activities. Christians can use the inductive method in good conscience provided that they remember that historical recording is fallible and changeable and that it often disregards many biblical truths. It would be helpful to all Christian teachers to study the principles discussed in *The Christian Teaching of History,* available from Bob Jones University Press.

The inductive method does not require following a certain set of steps, but there are *process skills* employed in this method of teaching. The following is a list of the process skills in the Bob Jones University Press elementary Heritage Studies program.

☐ Sequencing events
☐ Summarizing data
☐ Making predictions
☐ Inferring relationships
☐ Making decisions

☐ Formulating opinions
☐ Working with time lines
☐ Identifying sources of information
☐ Working with maps and globes
☐ Using cardinal directions
☐ Working with tables, graphs, charts, diagrams
☐ Identifying key documents
☐ Valuing the rights of citizenship
☐ Showing respect for heritage

• Heritage Studies Attitudes

The dictionary defines *attitude* as "a state of mind or feeling with regard to some matter." Heritage Studies attitudes develop as students learn about their history. Some of the attitudes that you will see developed by the Bob Jones University Press Heritage Studies program fall into the following broad categories.

Attitudes Toward Classwork
The students will be able to do the following:
a. Cooperatively share responsibilities and tasks.
b. Demonstrate proper care and handling of maps, globes, and other equipment.
c. Stay with the task in search of comprehension and evaluation of ideas.

Attitudes Toward Interests and Careers
The students will be able to do the following:
a. Pursue history- or geography-related leisure activities.
b. Voluntarily seek additional information about history and related studies.
c. Seek information about careers in research, history, and geography.

Attitudes Toward Personal Application of Heritage Studies Principles
The students will be able to do the following:
a. Use an objective approach in problem solving.
b. Display a willingness to consider other points of view.
c. Demonstrate divergent thinking when solving problems.
d. Demonstrate curiosity about history, geography, and related subjects.
e. Show an appreciation for their heritage.
f. Uphold the foundational principles of their government.
g. Counteract influences detrimental to the perpetuation of their heritage.
h. Reflect a knowledge of history in everyday decision making.

Attitudes Toward Oneself

The students will be able to do the following:

a. Display confidence in their ability to use geographic skills successfully.
b. Demonstrate a scriptural view of themselves through the study of history.

Attitudes Toward History and Society

The students will be able to do the following:

a. Select cause-and-effect relationships to explain contemporary problems.
b. Identify historical precedent as a way of solving some current problems.
c. Describe historians as persons sensitive to normal human concerns.
d. Demonstrate an awareness of the need for conservation, preservation, and the wise use of natural resources.
e. Demonstrate patriotism.
f. Explain how the study of history and geography can have positive (or, if unbalanced, negative) effects on one's personal life.

The goal of historic literacy is to emphasize God's plan for the individual, the family, and the nation. Although history is the study of man's actions, it is essentially the record of God's dealing with men. The Christian teacher must be able to distinguish God's leading in historical events and to impress upon the students the significance of the study. Learning history well helps students more fully appreciate and comprehend their own times. They gain understanding and an ability to discern connections among events. This broad perspective, then, helps them make better decisions and helps them become responsible Christian citizens.

Instructional Materials

Student materials

- **Text** The *HERITAGE STUDIES 6 Student Text* is a four-color text containing historical surveys of Mesopotamia, Egypt, Israel, India, China, Greece, Rome, the Mayas (Americas), Africa, the Orient's Golden Age, the Byzantine Empire, and the Middle Ages.

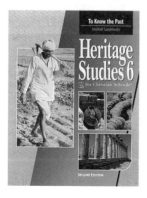

- **Notebook** The *HERITAGE STUDIES 6 Student Notebook* is a consumable companion tool for the text. It is used primarily to evaluate the students' understanding of the material. The Notebook will also save the teacher time. The pages are designed to be used in a notebook binder.

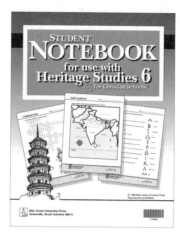

- **Tests** *Tests for Use with HERITAGE STUDIES 6 for Christian Schools* contains a chapter test for each of the twelve chapters in the student text. A separate answer key is available.

- **Miscellaneous school supplies** Each student will need standard school supplies: crayons, colored pencils, or felt-tip pens; pencils; scissors; and so on.

- **Library trade books** No history program can provide enough information for enthusiastic young readers. A collection of trade books (library books) must be available to students. Be careful of books that slant the history of certain events. For example, library books about ancient Mesopotamia are generally written by people who do not believe in the God of the Bible. In these instances, try to find books that present a truthful and objective account of these people.

Teacher materials

- **Teacher's edition** The *HERITAGE STUDIES 6 Teacher's Edition* (this volume) is the foundation of the program from which all the activities originate. This volume contains the parts labeled below.

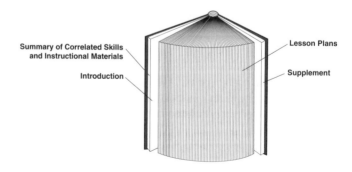

Summary of Correlated Skills and Instructional Materials

Lesson Plans

Introduction

Supplement

Each lesson plan in the teacher's edition contains the following parts.

□ Preview

- *Subject Box* lists the main topics of the lesson.
- *Objectives* describe the outcome of instruction in terms of student behavior.
- *Materials* lists items to be obtained or prepared.
- *Notes* presents helpful hints and any necessary clarification of information.

□ Lesson

- *Introducing the Lesson* suggests a way to start the lesson.
- *Teaching the Lesson* suggests ways to direct the reading of the text as well as a procedure for instruction.

- *Discussion Questions* evaluate students' understanding of the text.
- *Application Box* relates spiritual truths to lesson topics and includes Scripture references, Bible Action Truths, and Bible Promises.
- *Evaluating the Lesson* gives ideas to evaluate, not test, the students' grasp of the material presented.

□ Going Beyond

- *Enrichment* includes activities and games that students can do independently. These activities may occasionally require adult supervision.
- *Additional Teacher Information* provides the teacher with extra information to help him expand his knowledge of the related topics. It is not necessary to understand or even read the information in this section to teach the lesson.

LESSON 16
Out of Egypt, into Canaan

Text, pages 56-59
Notebook, page 17

- Into Canaan
- Smelting Iron
- Family Life

Preview

□ **Objective**
Given proper instruction, the students will be able to do the following:
- Identify correct statements about the Israelites' early years in Canaan.

□ **Materials**
Have available:
- An overhead projector.
- A blank overhead transparency.

Prepare an overhead transparency of the "Name of God" page. (*NOTE:* See the reproducible material at the end of Lesson 19.)

□ **Notes**
See the books of Joshua and Judges for scriptural accounts of the events discussed in this lesson.

Day 26

Lesson

□ **Introducing the Lesson**
The tetragrammaton—Display the overhead transparency of the "Name of God" page. Tell the students that these four Hebrew letters are called the *tetragrammaton* and are the Hebrew word for God. In English these letters are written YHWH or JHVH. When vowels are added to the tetragrammaton, the name for God is written *Jehovah*. Explain to the students that Jews do not pronounce the tetragrammaton. To a Jew, the name of God is so holy that it should not even be spoken.

□ **Teaching the Lesson**
Into Canaan—Instruct the students to read pages 56-57 silently to find out what God told the Israelites to do when they entered the land of Canaan. *(to destroy all the Canaanites)*

ECHOES FROM THE PAST
The Law of God

The thing that set the Israelites apart from all other people was their belief in the true God, Yahweh or Jehovah. God ruled His people directly. Direct rule by God is called a *theocracy*, from the Greek words *theos* meaning "god" and *kratos* meaning "power."

In most ancient cultures, the laws were made by the king or ruler. In Israel, the laws were made by God. The best known part of the law is the Ten Commandments, found in Exodus 20. How many do you know?

Today, the laws of many Western countries are "echoes" of the law given to Moses. Why do you think the laws of the Israelites have had such an effect on the laws of other lands? Unlike laws written by man, God's laws are perfect.

Modern tourists visit the traditional site of Mt. Sinai, the place where God gave the law to Moses.

56

Discussion Questions
➤ Why do you think God wanted the Canaanites destroyed? *(Answers will vary but should include that the Canaanites were idolaters.)*
➤ Did the Israelites obey God and destroy all the Canaanites? *(no)*
➤ How did God punish the people when they worshiped the Canaanite gods? *(He made them subjects of the people they had not destroyed.)*
➤ What happened when the Israelites called on God to help them? *(He sent judges to deliver them.)*
➤ What is direct rule by God called? *(theocracy)*
➤ Where in the Bible can we read the Ten Commandments? *(Exodus 20)*

The last judge, Samuel, was appointed by God to replace Eli. Eli lost the blessing of God because he did not restrain his sons' wicked behavior. Samuel, on the other hand, served the Lord faithfully throughout his long life, and God's blessing was upon him. (BAT: 2c Faithfulness)

—Lesson 16   69

Inhabiting the Promised Land

After Moses died in about 1400 B.C., Joshua led the Israelites into the land of Canaan. God commanded the Israelites to destroy all the Canaanites. Joshua assigned each of the twelve tribes of Israel a portion of the land. Each tribe was supposed to destroy the Canaanites in its part of the land. Many Canaanites were destroyed or driven away, but some were left alone. Do you think God was pleased?

The Hebrews began to worship Canaanite gods. God punished the Israelites for this idolatry by making them subjects of the people they had not destroyed. In defeat, God's people called to Him for deliverance. God sent deliverers, called *judges*. Even when the judges brought peace to the land, the people did not remain faithful to God.

The pattern of disobedience and punishment followed by repentance and deliverance continued for more than three hundred years. Finally, the people of Israel began to believe that the problems with their enemies could be solved only one way. They asked the last judge, Samuel, to give them a king like the other nations.

Samson, one of the judges of Israel, personally killed many of the Philistines during his lifetime.

57

Smelting iron—Instruct the students to read page 58 silently to find out why the Israelites had to purchase iron implements from the Philistines before 1100 B.C. *(The Philistines controlled the iron industry.)* Elicit from the students reasons that being able to work with iron would be valuable to a growing nation. *(The people would be able to make their own farm tools, weapons, etc.)*

Discussion Questions
➤ How was iron separated from the ore? *(The ore was heated; then other substances were added to the ore to separate the iron.)*
➤ How was the iron purified? *(with intense heat)*
➤ How was the hot metal formed? *(It was poured into molds or hammered into the desired shape.)*

Family life—Instruct the students to read page 59 silently to find out what skills Israelite parents taught their children. *(Boys were taught a trade and how to work the farm and tend the animals; girls were taught to cook, make clothing, tend a garden, and make goods to sell.)*

Discussion Questions
➤ What do you think is the most important thing parents can teach their children? *(Answers will vary, but lead the students to understand that Christian parents seek to teach their children about Christ, the Savior.)*
➤ What skills have your parents taught you? *(Answers will vary.)*
➤ What skills would you like to learn that you have not yet learned? *(Answers will vary.)*

Remind the students that even if they do not understand why their parents are teaching them a particular skill, they should submit to their parents' leadership in their lives. Tell them that God often uses things later in our lives that we did not appreciate learning when we were young. (BAT: 2a Authority)

□ **Evaluating the Lesson**
Into Canaan (Notebook page 17)—Instruct the students to write the letter of the correct choice in each blank. Discuss the answers with the students.

Going Beyond

□ **Enrichment**
Hebrew letters—Set up an AREA with paper, pencils, and a copy of the Hebrew alphabet. (*NOTE:* See the reproducible material at the end of Lesson 19.) Encourage students to practice writing Hebrew letters.

□ **Additional Teacher Information**
The word *Jehovah* is combined with a number of other words in the Old Testament to indicate specific traits of the one true God. *Jehovah* indicates the one "which is, and which was, and which is to come," and particularly signifies the covenant relationship of God to His people. Other titles of God using the word *Jehovah* include the following: Jehovah-jireh (Jehovah will provide), Jehovah-ropheca (Jehovah will heal), Jehovah-shalom (Jehovah our peace), and Jehovah-tsidkenu (Jehovah our righteousness).

When a Hebrew of ancient times read the Torah, he did not speak aloud the name of God. Instead, he read *Adonai,* the word for "master." When Hebrew vowel markings were added to the text (ancient Hebrew was written without vowels), the vowel markings for the word *Adonai* were inserted. Transliterated into English, the pronunciation of the name of God is *Jehovah.* Jews, however, still read it as *Adonai.* Because the name of God is so holy, pronouncing it is considered an improper, degrading use of the name.

70   Heritage Studies 6 TE

• **History TimeLine** The TimeLine is a visual, working chart with figures representing important events or people. It enhances the students' chronology skills.

• **Maps and More** *Maps and More* is a package of $12\frac{1}{2}"\times18"$ charts, featuring enlargements of maps and pictures for teaching concepts and skills.

• **Listening Cassette B** The cassette tape contains songs and readings that will enhance the students' enjoyment of, understanding of, and participation in the study of history.

• **Heritage Studies supplies** Refer to the list in the Supplement of this book.

Student Text Format

The student book presents for the student an outline of the more detailed study that the lessons will offer. It reinforces with grade-level text the concepts developed in class. Although it contains much information, it is only part of the complete package of learning provided by the combination of teacher's edition, History TimeLine, Maps and More, student text, and Student Notebook.

The student book has twelve chapters, each emphasizing one ancient civilization.

In addition, some chapters have special sections. *Famous People* highlights important or influential people. *Things People Did* focuses on common trades, skills, or practices of the past. The *Discovering How* sections provide hands-on activities that enliven the lesson and allow students to experience some flavor of the times, as well as develop thinking skills.

Sections entitled *Then and Now* relate the ancient world to our modern world. Comparing the ancient map of each region studied to its modern-day counterpart, these sections point out specific geographical and cultural details. These sections enhance not only the students' understanding of the ancient civilization but also their knowledge of modern geography. *In the Bible* sections point out biblical references to ancient civilizations, showing their significance in God's plan for world history.

Bible Action Truths

The quality and consistency of a man's decisions reflect his character. Christian character begins with justification, but it grows throughout the lifelong process of sanctification. God's grace is sufficient for the task, and a major part of God's gracious provision is His Word. The Bible provides the very "words of life" that instruct us in salvation and Christian living. By obeying God's commands and making godly decisions based on His Word, Christians can strengthen their character.

Too often Christians live by only vague guidance—for instance, that we should "do good" to all men. While doing good is desirable, more specific guidance will lead to more consistent decisions.

Consistent decisions are made when man acts on Bible principles—or Bible Action Truths. The thirty-seven Bible Action Truths (listed under eight general principles) provide Christians with specific goals for their actions and attitudes. Study the Scriptures indicated for a fuller understanding of the principles in Bible Action Truths.

Thousands have found this format helpful in identifying and applying principles of behavior. Yet, there is no "magic" in this formula. As you study the Word, you likely will find other truths that speak to you. The key is for you to study the Scriptures, look for Bible Action Truths, and be sensitive to the leading of the Holy Spirit.

1. Salvation—Separation Principle

Salvation results from God's direct action. Although man is unable to work for this "gift of God," the Christian's reaction to salvation should be to separate himself from the world unto God.

a. Understanding Jesus Christ (Matthew 3:17; 16:16; I Corinthians 15:3-4; Philippians 2:9-11) Jesus is the Son of God. He was sent to earth to die on the cross for our sins. He was buried but rose from the dead after three days.

b. Repentance and faith (Luke 13:3; Isaiah 55:7; Acts 5:30-31; Hebrews 11:6; Acts 16:31) If we believe that Jesus died for our sins, we can accept Him as our Savior. We must be sorry for our sins, turn from them, confess them to God, and believe that He will forgive us.

c. Separation from the world (John 17:6, 11, 14, 18; II Corinthians 6:14-18; I John 2:15-16; James 4:4; Romans 16:17-18; II John 10-11) After we are saved, we should live a different life. We should try to be like Christ and not live like those who are unsaved.

2. Sonship—Servant Principle

Only by an act of God the Father could sinful man become a son of God. As a son of God, however, the Christian must realize that he has been "bought with a price"; he is now Christ's servant.

a. Authority (Romans 13:1-7; I Peter 2:13-19; I Timothy 6:1-5; Hebrews 13:17; Matthew 22:21; I Thessalonians 5:12-13) We should respect, honor, and obey those in authority over us.

b. Servanthood (Philippians 2:7-8; Ephesians 6:5-8) Just as Christ was a humble servant while He was on earth, we should also be humble and obedient.

c. Faithfulness (I Corinthians 4:2; Matthew 25:23; Luke 9:62) We should do our work so that God and others can depend on us.

d. Goal setting (Proverbs 13:12, 19; Philippians 3:13; Colossians 3:2; I Corinthians 9:24) To be faithful servants, we must set goals for our work. We should look forward to finishing a job and going on to something more.

e. Work (Ephesians 4:28; II Thessalonians 3:10-12) God never honors a lazy servant. He wants us to be busy and dependable workers.

f. Enthusiasm (Colossians 3:23; Romans 12:11) We should do *all* tasks with energy and with a happy, willing spirit.

3. Uniqueness—Unity Principle

No one is a mere person; God has created each individual a unique being. But because God has an overall plan for His creation, each unique member must contribute to the unity of the entire body.

a. Self-concept (Psalm 8:3-8; 139; II Corinthians 5:17; Ephesians 2:10; 4:1-3, 11-13; II Peter 1:10) We are special creatures in God's plan. He has given each of us special abilities to use in our lives for Him.

b. Mind (Philippians 2:5; 4:8; II Corinthians 10:5; Proverbs 23:7; Luke 6:45; Proverbs 4:23; Romans 7:23, 25; Daniel 1:8; James 1:8) We should give our hearts and minds to God. What we do and say really begins in our minds. We should try to think of ourselves humbly as Christ did when He lived on earth.

c. Emotional control (Galatians 5:24; Proverbs 16:32; 25:28; II Timothy 1:7; Acts 20:24) With the help of God and the power of the Holy Spirit, we should have control over our feelings. We must be careful not to act out of anger.

d. Body as a temple (I Corinthians 3:16-17; 6:19-20) We should remember that our bodies are the dwelling place of God's Holy Spirit. We should keep ourselves pure, honest, and dedicated to God's will.

e. Unity of Christ and the Church (John 17:21; Ephesians 2:19-22; 5:23-32; II Thessalonians 3:6, 14-15) Since we are saved, we are now part of God's family and should unite ourselves with others to worship and grow as Christians. Christ is the head of His Church, which includes all believers. He wants us to work together as His Church in carrying out His plans, but He forbids us to work in fellowship with disobedient brethren.

4. Holiness—Habit Principle

Believers are declared holy as a result of Christ's finished action on the cross. Daily holiness of life, however, comes from forming godly habits. A Christian must consciously establish godly patterns of action; he must develop habits of holiness.

a. Sowing and reaping (Galatians 6:7-8; Hosea 8:7; Matthew 6:1-8) We must remember that we will be rewarded according to the kind of work we have done. If we are faithful, we will be rewarded. If we are unfaithful, we will not be rewarded. We cannot fool God.

b. Purity (I Thessalonians 4:1-7; I Peter 1:22) We should try to live lives that are free from sin. We should keep our minds, words, and deeds clean and pure.

c. Honesty (II Corinthians 8:21; Romans 12:17; Proverbs 16:8; Ephesians 4:25) We should not lie. We should be honest in every way. Even if we could gain more by being dishonest, we should still be honest. God sees all things.

d. Victory (I Corinthians 10:13; Romans 8:37; I John 5:4; John 16:33; I Corinthians 15:57-58) If we constantly try to be pure, honest, and Christlike, with God's help we will be able to overcome temptations.

5. Love—Life Principle

We love God because He first loved us. God's action of manifesting His love to us through His Son demonstrates the truth that love must be exercised. Since God acted in love toward us, believers must act likewise by showing godly love to others.

a. Love (I John 3:11, 16-18; 4:7-21; Ephesians 5:2; I Corinthians 13; John 15:17) God's love to us was the greatest love possible. We should, in turn, show our love for others by our words and actions.

b. Giving (II Corinthians 9:6-8; Proverbs 3:9-10; Luke 6:38) We should give cheerfully to God the first part of all we earn. We should also give to others unselfishly.

c. Evangelism and missions (Psalm 126:5-6; Matthew 28:18-20; Romans 1:16-17; II Corinthians 5:11-21) We should be busy telling others about the love of God and His plan of salvation. We should share in the work of foreign missionaries by our giving and prayers.

d. Communication (Ephesians 4:22-29; Colossians 4:6; James 3:2-13; Isaiah 50:4) We should have control of our tongues so that we will not say things displeasing to God. We should encourage others and be kind and helpful in what we say.

e. Friendliness (Proverbs 18:24; 17:17; Psalm 119:63) We should be friendly to others, and we should be loyal to those who love and serve God.

6. Communion—Consecration Principle

Because sin separates man from God, any communion between man and God must be achieved by God's direct action of removing sin. Once communion is established, the believer's reaction should be to maintain a consciousness of this fellowship by living a consecrated life.

a. Bible study (I Peter 2:2-3; II Timothy 2:15; Psalm 119) To grow as Christians, we must spend time with God daily by reading His Word.

b. Prayer (I Chronicles 16:11; I Thessalonians 5:17; John 15:7, 16; 16:24; Psalm 145:18; Romans 8:26-27) We should bring all our requests to God, trusting Him to answer them in His own way.

c. Spirit-filled (Ephesians 5:18-19; Galatians 5:16, 22-23; Romans 8:13-14; I John 1:7-9) We should let the Holy Spirit rule in our hearts and show us what to say and do. We should not say and do just what we want to do, for those things are often wrong and harmful to others.

d. Clear conscience (I Timothy 1:19; Acts 24:16) To be good Christians, we cannot have wrong acts or thoughts or words bothering our consciences. We must confess them to God and to those people against whom we have sinned. We cannot live lives close to God if we have guilty consciences.

e. Forgiveness (Ephesians 4:30-32; Luke 17:3-4; Colossians 3:13; Matthew 18:15-17; Mark 11:25-26) We must ask forgiveness of God when we have done wrong. Just as God forgives our sins freely, we should forgive others when they do wrong things to us.

7. Grace—Gratitude Principle

Grace is unmerited favor. Man does not deserve God's grace. However, after God bestows His grace, believers should react with an overflow of gratitude.

a. Grace (I Corinthians 15:10; Ephesians 2:8-9) Without God's grace we would be sinners on our way to hell. He loved us when we did not deserve His love and provided for us a way to escape sin's punishment by the death of His Son on the cross.

b. Exaltation of Christ (Colossians 1:12-21; Ephesians 1:17-23; Philippians 2:9-11; Galatians 6:14; Hebrews 1:2-3; John 1:1-4, 14; 5:23) We should realize and remember at all times the power, holiness, majesty, and perfection of Christ, and we should give Him the praise and glory for everything that is accomplished through us.

c. Praise (Psalm 107:8; Hebrews 13:15; I Peter 2:9; Ephesians 1:6; I Chronicles 16:23-36; 29:11-13) Remembering God's great love and goodness toward us, we should continually praise His name.

d. Contentment (Philippians 4:11; I Timothy 6:6-8; Psalm 77:3; Proverbs 15:16; Hebrews 13:5) Money, houses, cars, and all things on earth will last only for a little while. God has given us just what He meant for us to have. We should be happy and content with what we have, knowing that God will provide for us all that we need. We should also be happy wherever God places us.

e. Humility (I Peter 5:5-6; Philippians 2:3-4) We should not be proud and boastful but should be willing to be quiet and in the background. Our reward will come from God on Judgment Day, and men's praise to us here on earth will not matter at all. Christ was humble when He lived on earth, and we should be like Him.

8. Power—Prevailing Principle

Believers can prevail only as God gives the power. "I can do all things through Christ." God is the source of our power used in fighting the good fight of faith.

a. Faith in God's promises (II Peter 1:4; Philippians 4:6; Romans 4:16-21; I Thessalonians 5:18; Romans 8:28; I Peter 5:7; Hebrews 3:18–4:11) God always remains true to His promises. Believing that He will keep all the promises in His Word, we should be determined fighters for Him.

b. Faith in the power of the Word of God (Hebrews 4:12; Jeremiah 23:29; Psalm 119; I Peter 1:23-25) God's Word is powerful and endures forever. All other things will pass away, but God's Word shall never pass away because it is written to us from God, and God is eternal.

c. Fight (Ephesians 6:11-17; II Timothy 4:7-8; I Timothy 6:12; I Peter 5:8-9) God does not have any use for lazy or cowardly fighters. We must work and fight against sin, using the Word of God as our weapon against the Devil. What we do for God now will determine how much He will reward us in heaven.

d. Courage (I Chronicles 28:20; Joshua 1:9; Hebrews 13:6; Ephesians 3:11-12; Acts 4:13, 31) God has promised us that He will not forsake us; therefore, we should not be afraid to speak out against sin. We should remember that we are armed with God's strength.

Bible Promises

A. Liberty from Sin—Born into God's spiritual kingdom, a Christian is enabled to live right and gain victory over sin through faith in Christ. (Romans 8:3-4—"For what the law could not do, in that it was weak through the flesh, God sending his own Son in the likeness of sinful flesh, and for sin, condemned sin in the flesh: that the righteousness of the law might be fulfilled in us, who walk not after the flesh, but after the Spirit.")

B. Guiltless by the Blood—Cleansed by the blood of Christ, the Christian is pardoned from the guilt of his sins. He does not have to brood or fret over his past because the Lord has declared him righteous. (Romans 8:33—"Who shall lay any thing to the charge of God's elect? It is God that justifieth." Isaiah 45:24—"Surely, shall one say, in the Lord have I righteousness and strength: even to him shall men come; and all that are incensed against him shall be ashamed.")

C. Basis for Prayer—Knowing that his righteousness comes entirely from Christ and not from himself, the Christian is free to plead the blood of Christ and to come before God in prayer at any time. (Romans 5:1-2—"Therefore being justified by faith, we have peace with God through our Lord Jesus Christ: by whom also we have access by faith into this grace wherein we stand, and rejoice in hope of the glory of God.")

D. Identified in Christ—The Christian has the assurance that God sees him as a son of God, perfectly united with Christ. He also knows that he has access to the strength and the grace of Christ in his daily living. (Galatians 2:20—"I am crucified with Christ: nevertheless I live; yet not I, but Christ liveth in me: and the life which I now live in the flesh I live by the faith of the Son of God, who loved me, and gave himself for me." Ephesians 1:3—"Blessed be the God and Father of our Lord Jesus Christ, who hath blessed us with all spiritual blessings in heavenly places in Christ.")

E. Christ as Sacrifice—Christ was a willing sacrifice for the sins of the world. His blood covers every sin of the believer and pardons the Christian for eternity. The purpose of His death and resurrection was to redeem a people to Himself. (Isaiah 53:4-5—"Surely he hath borne our griefs, and carried our sorrows: yet we did esteem him stricken, smitten of God, and afflicted. But he was wounded for our transgressions, he was bruised for our iniquities: the chastisement of our peace was upon him; and with his stripes we are healed." John 10:27-28—"My sheep hear my voice, and I know them, and they follow me: and I give unto them eternal life; and they shall never perish, neither shall any man pluck them out of my hand.")

F. Christ as Intercessor—Having pardoned them through His blood, Christ performs the office of High Priest in praying for His people. (Hebrews 7:25—"Wherefore he is able also to save them to the uttermost that come unto God by him, seeing he ever liveth to make intercession for them." John 17:20—"Neither pray I for these alone, but for them also which shall believe on me through their word.")

G. Christ as Friend—In giving salvation to the believer, Christ enters a personal, loving relationship with the Christian that cannot be ended. This relationship is understood and enjoyed on the believer's part through fellowship with the Lord through Bible reading and prayer. (Isaiah 54:5—"For thy Maker is thine husband; the Lord of hosts is his name; and thy Redeemer the Holy One of Israel; The God of the whole earth shall he be called." Romans 8:38-39—"For I am persuaded, that neither death, nor life, nor angels, nor principalities, nor powers, nor things present, nor things to come, nor height, nor depth, nor any other creature, shall be able to separate us from the love of God, which is in Christ Jesus our Lord.")

H. God as Father—God has appointed Himself to be responsible for the well-being of the Christian. He both protects and nourishes the believer, and it was from Him that salvation originated. (Isaiah 54:17—"No weapon that is formed against thee shall prosper; and every tongue that shall rise against thee in judgment thou shalt condemn. This is the heritage of the servants of the Lord, and their righteousness is of me, saith the Lord." Psalm 103:13—"Like as a father pitieth his children, so the Lord pitieth them that fear him.")

I. God as Master—God is sovereign over all creation. He orders the lives of His people for His glory and their good. (Romans 8:28—"And we know that all things work together for good to them that love God, to them who are the called according to his purpose.")

LESSON PLANS

Between Great Rivers: Mesopotamia

This chapter focuses on the people, land, and culture of ancient Mesopotamia, concentrating on the biblical city of Ur. Sir Leonard Woolley's archaeological discoveries in the valley between the Tigris and Euphrates Rivers yielded evidence that supports the existence of many people and places in the Old Testament. Ur, the city of Abraham, was a sophisticated and innovative society, leaving thousands of clay tablets in cuneiform that chronicle ancient life. Located in the fertile river valley, Ur was a city of farmers, artisans, and scribes. Sumerian students, instilled with the values of discipline and hard work, helped to perpetuate this advanced society. By studying about ancient Mesopotamia, students will gain an appreciation for the people of the land between two rivers—the home of great men such as Abraham.

☐ Materials

Lessons 1-4 require certain items that must be obtained or prepared several days to several weeks before the presentation of the lessons. These items are labeled with an asterisk (*) in each lesson and in the Materials List in the Supplement. Occasionally, items not commonly found in the classroom as well as items needed in large quantities may also be labeled with an asterisk. For further information, see the individual lessons.

☐ Chapter Bulletin Board

For the bulletin board *Between Great Rivers,* mount Maps and More 1, the map of Mesopotamia. Enlarge the cuneiform sheet to the size desired and mount it to the right of Maps and More 1. (*NOTE:* See the reproducible material at the end of Lesson 6.)

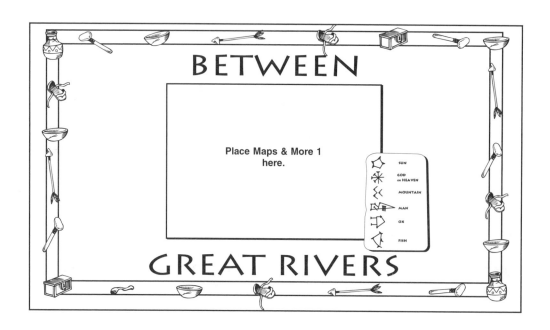

Place Maps & More 1
here.

✧	SUN
✳	GOD or HEAVEN
	MOUNTAIN
	MAN
	OX
	FISH

Between Great Rivers:
Mesopotamia

1

LESSON 1
The Days of Abraham

Text, pages 2-3
Notebook, page 1

> - Sumer
> - Then and Now

━━━━━ Preview ━━━━━

☐ Objectives
Given proper instruction, the students will be able to do the following:
- Match related words about Mesopotamia.
- Label a map of the region of Mesopotamia.

☐ Materials
Have available:
- A Bible.
- Maps and More 1.*
- A *HERITAGE STUDIES 6 Student Notebook* for each student.*
- A three-ring binder for each student.*

☐ Notes
The *HERITAGE STUDIES 6 Student Notebook* will be used for the first time during this lesson. Each student should have a Student Notebook and a three-ring binder in which to put the pages.

This lesson also uses for the first time materials from *Maps and More,* a collection of large posters, featuring maps, visuals, charts, graphs, and other helps for teaching Heritage Studies. Occasionally, a chart may contain more than one visual; you may wish to cut apart such charts as indicated.

Lesson 2 requires students to bring items from home that reveal something about their daily lives. Suggest that the students bring items such as a hair dryer, a purse, a baseball bat, or a book.

Lesson 4 requires either a field trip to a pottery shop, an in-class demonstration, or a video showing the use of a potter's wheel. You may need to make arrangements to visit a shop or to invite an artist to demonstrate the use of a potter's wheel. (*NOTE:* If you invite an artist to your classroom, request that he bring some finished samples of his work as well as any needed materials to work with on site.)

Day 1

━━━━━ Lesson ━━━━━

☐ Introducing the Lesson
Abraham—Select a volunteer to read Nehemiah 9:7 from page 2. Review the story of Abraham and Sarah. (*NOTE:* If you have available flannelgraph figures, flash card pictures, or Bible storybook pictures illustrating this story, show them

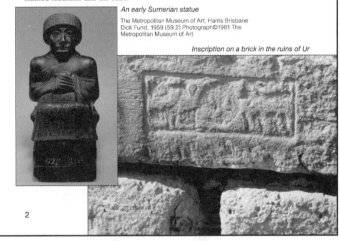

The Days of Abraham

> "Thou art the Lord the God, who didst choose Abram, and broughtest him forth out of Ur of the Chaldees, and gavest him the name of Abraham."
>
> Nehemiah 9:7

Perhaps you have read about Abraham many times and know his story well. But some people doubt his existence—and the truth of most of the Bible. They prefer to trust in science and their own understanding. Scientific discoveries, however, support the Bible accounts.

In the 1850s English explorers proved that an ancient ruin in the Middle East was the biblical city of Ur. In 1922 Sir Leonard Woolley, a British archaeologist, began extensive digging at the site. In *Mesopotamia,* the land between the Tigris and Euphrates Rivers (in modern Iraq), Woolley uncovered many treasures from Ur and the land it belonged to, called Sumer.

These writings and objects, long hidden under the sand, tell us about the Sumerians, whose kingdoms lasted one thousand years. We know, for instance, that Ur, like other Sumerian cities, was a grand place surrounded by high walls and boasting huge palaces and plazas. People of Abraham's day used canals to irrigate their fields; they grew grain and vegetables and sold wool to other countries. They were weavers and metalworkers; they studied medicine and the stars.

An early Sumerian statue
The Metropolitan Museum of Art, Harris Brisbane Dick Fund, 1959 (59.2) Photograph©1981 The Metropolitan Museum of Art

Inscription on a brick in the ruins of Ur

2

to the students as part of the review. Read Genesis 17:4-5 to the students, reminding them that Abraham's name was changed from its original form, *Abram*.) Allow the students to help you recount the story. Explain that Abraham was from the city of Ur, a place located in ancient Mesopotamia.

☐ Teaching the Lesson
Sumer—Point out Maps and More 1 on the bulletin board. Select a volunteer to point to Iraq. Instruct the students to read page 2 silently to find what city in the Bible was probably located here. *(Ur)*

Discussion Questions
➤ **Which Bible character came from Ur?** *(Abraham)*
➤ **What famous archaeologist conducted a dig in 1922, searching for the ancient city of Ur?** *(Sir Leonard Woolley)*
➤ **Why was Sir Woolley's discovery important?** *(It proved that Abraham's people existed.)* (*NOTE:* Some historians and theologians dispute whether the site discovered by Woolley was truly the Ur of Abraham's time.)

Explain that some people do not believe what the Bible says unless science specifically supports it. Remind the students that Christians should accept God's Word as truth. Explain that the Christian faith is based on God's promises, not human understanding. (BATs: 8a Faith in God's promises, 8b Faith in the power of the Word of God)

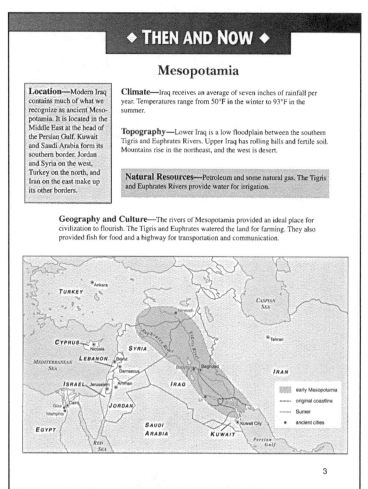

Mesopotamia

Location—Modern Iraq contains much of what we recognize as ancient Mesopotamia. It is located in the Middle East at the head of the Persian Gulf. Kuwait and Saudi Arabia form its southern border. Jordan and Syria on the west, Turkey on the north, and Iran on the east make up its other borders.

Climate—Iraq receives an average of seven inches of rainfall per year. Temperatures range from 50°F in the winter to 93°F in the summer.

Topography—Lower Iraq is a low floodplain between the southern Tigris and Euphrates Rivers. Upper Iraq has rolling hills and fertile soil. Mountains rise in the northeast, and the west is desert.

Natural Resources—Petroleum and some natural gas. The Tigris and Euphrates Rivers provide water for irrigation.

Geography and Culture—The rivers of Mesopotamia provided an ideal place for civilization to flourish. The Tigris and Euphrates watered the land for farming. They also provided fish for food and a highway for transportation and communication.

3

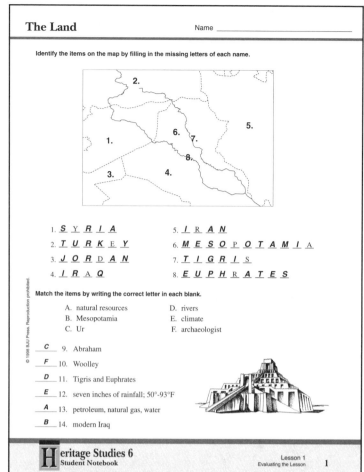

The Land   Name _____

Identify the items on the map by filling in the missing letters of each name.

1. **S Y R I A**   5. **I R A N**
2. **T U R K E Y**   6. **M E S O P O T A M I** A
3. **J O R D A N**   7. **T I G R I** S
4. **I R A Q**   8. **E U P H R** A **T E S**

Match the items by writing the correct letter in each blank.

A. natural resources   D. rivers
B. Mesopotamia   E. climate
C. Ur   F. archaeologist

__C__   9. Abraham
__F__ 10. Woolley
__D__ 11. Tigris and Euphrates
__E__ 12. seven inches of rainfall; 50°–93°F
__A__ 13. petroleum, natural gas, water
__B__ 14. modern Iraq

Heritage Studies 6
Student Notebook

Lesson 1
Evaluating the Lesson   1

© 1996 BJU Press. Reproduction prohibited.

Explain that the land between the Tigris and Euphrates Rivers was called Mesopotamia. Point to Mesopotamia on Maps and More 1. Point to the southeastern region of Iraq. Explain that this area was called Sumer. Tell the students that Ur was a city in the region of Sumer.

➤ **How long did the Sumerian civilization last?** *(one thousand years)*
➤ **What kind of place was Ur according to archaeological discoveries?** *(a grand place that was surrounded by high walls and that had huge palaces and plazas)*
➤ **What kinds of things did the people of Abraham's day do?** *(They used canals to irrigate their fields; they grew grain and vegetables; they sold wool to other countries. They were weavers, metalworkers, and students of medicine and the stars.)*

Then and Now—Instruct the students to read page 3 silently to find how the Tigris and Euphrates Rivers affected the Mesopotamian lifestyle. *(They watered the land for farming, provided fish for food, and served as a means of transportation and communication.)* Direct the students' attention to the Then and Now map, noting ancient cities, changes in boundary lines, and so on.

□ Evaluating the Lesson

The Land (Notebook page 1)—Instruct the students to identify the items on the map by filling in the missing letters of each name. Then tell them to match the items by writing the correct letter in each blank.

━━━ Going Beyond ━━━

□ Enrichment

Landforms and lifestyles—Give a copy of the Landforms and Lifestyles page to each student. (*NOTE:* See the reproducible material at the end of Lesson 6.) Instruct the students to follow the directions given on the page. (*NOTE:* Landforms that affect lifestyle include areas such as deserts, forests, mountains, lakes, and cities.)

□ Additional Teacher Information

Sir Charles Leonard Woolley, one of England's leading archaeologists, began his study of antiquities with a job as assistant keeper of a museum. His first archaeological expedition was to Nubia, in the Nile valley, from 1907 to 1911.

Woolley is best known for excavating the ancient city of Ur. Beginning work in 1922, he and his associates traced Ur's development from its last days in the fourth century B.C. to its beginnings in the time before written history. The great riches unearthed at Ur's royal cemetery drew much attention to Woolley's work. Woolley published a ten-volume series on the findings at Ur as well as books on Egypt, Syria, and Turkey. During his investigations, Woolley found geological evidence supporting the Genesis Flood. He was knighted for his work.

LESSON 2
Seeking the Past

Text, pages 4-6
Notebook, page 2

> - Archaeology
> - On a Dig
> - Archaeological Evidence

═══ Preview ═══

☐ Objectives
Given proper instruction, the students will be able to do the following:
- Use key words to write sentences about archaeology.
- Sequence the activities of a dig in chronological order.

☐ Materials
Have available the items that the students have brought from home.*

Day 2

═══ Lesson ═══

☐ Introducing the Lesson
Modern artifacts—Display the items that the students have brought. Select a volunteer to explain what an artifact is. *(an object from the past that people study to learn more about people from the past)* Allow each student to explain how his item reveals something about modern life.

☐ Teaching the Lesson
Archaeology—Instruct the students to read page 4 silently to find how archaeologists learn about people who lived nearly five thousand years ago. *(by studying artifacts)*

Discussion Questions
➤ **What is an archaeologist?** *(a person who studies objects from the past to learn about who made and used them)*
➤ **What benefits do you think come from studying the past?** *(We can learn about our heritage and about ancient peoples who provided important foundations in literature, science, technology, etc.)*
➤ **What types of artifacts are studied by archaeologists?** *(clay tablets, pottery, jewelry, sculpture, coins, etc.)*
➤ **How do artifacts reveal information about the past?** *(They often give clues about a person's lifestyle or character traits.)*
➤ **How do archaeologists usually find artifacts?** *(by digging)*
➤ **What is an *excavation*?** *(an archaeological dig)*

How We Find Out About the Past

Look at the pictures on this page. What do you think they look like? Like a chicken left its footprints in wet clay? Although those marks may look like hen scratchings, they are really words written nearly five thousand years ago in Sumer.

Such writings have often puzzled *archaeologists,* men and women who study objects from the past to learn about the people who made and used them. Manmade objects, called *artifacts*—such as clay tablets, pottery, jewelry, sculptures, and coins—often give clues about a person's lifestyle or character traits. A woman's jewelry could reveal whether she was rich and powerful or poor but inventive.

Archaeologists usually find artifacts by digging. An archaeological *dig* or excavation may be small or large. Every dig needs experts in photography, architecture, translation, and drawing to interpret and preserve what is found. Archaeologists sometimes choose an excavation site by the presence of a *tell,* or mound. *Tell* comes from the Arabic word for "high" and refers to a hill built up over the centuries. Such mounds result from drifting sand settling in layers over cities that have been destroyed and rebuilt time and again.

Sumerian writing on a relief carving (left), small tablets (right), and a drum-shaped document (below)

Document and tablets, Bob Jones University Bible Lands Museum

4

➤ **What kinds of experts are needed on a dig?** *(experts in photography, architecture, translation, and drawing)*
➤ **Why is it important to have these experts on a dig?** *(They help interpret and preserve what is found.)*
➤ **What is a *tell*?** *(a hill built up over the centuries)*
➤ **How are some mounds formed?** *(from drifting sand settling in layers over cities that have been destroyed and rebuilt time and again)*

Tags mark the locations of artifacts found at this archaeological dig.

Work on the tell begins with air and ground surveys. From this information the archaeologists draw a map and section off the area into squares. Today archaeologists often use computers to help keep records and make calculations. The actual digging is done slowly, a layer at a time. Everyone must work carefully to avoid damaging fragile objects. When an object is found, it is photographed, recorded, and tagged.

The clues and information, thus patiently uncovered, are the source for much of what you will read in this book. You will not have to decipher ancient writing, but you may be asked to draw conclusions about the people of the past.

5

◄▌ IN THE BIBLE ▐►

Archaeology and the Old Testament

Because they reject the Bible and a worldwide flood, many secular archaeologists and historians assume that Sumer was one of the first civilizations. Although there are no written records or other artifacts from before the Flood, we know that the earlier civilizations were quite advanced. Genesis 4 says that the people before Noah built cities, were skilled musicians and workers in brass and iron, and knew much about agriculture. The fact that we have no physical evidence of pre-Flood civilization is no reason to doubt the Bible.

Other assumptions researchers have made about the events in the Bible have been proved wrong in many archaeological sites. For example, some people used to reject the story of Abraham as a myth because they assumed that camels, such as the one Rebekah rode to meet Isaac, would not have been used as beasts of burden in Abraham's time. But Sumerian tablets not only record that indeed camels were ridden then but also tell how: behind the hump.

Furthermore, discoveries of skeletons in caves around Ur explain the Bible phrase "gathered to his people." The same burial caves were used by Sumerians for generations. Thus, Abraham's sons were following a common custom when they buried him.

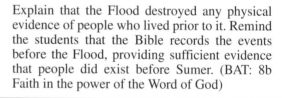

Day 3

On a dig—Instruct the students to read page 5 silently to find the first steps of a dig. *(surveying from the air and on the ground, drawing a map, and sectioning the area into squares)*

Discussion Questions

➤ **What do some archaeologists use today to help them on a dig?** *(computers)*

➤ **Why is work on a dig slow?** *(Workers must be careful not to damage any fragile artifacts.)*

➤ **What happens to an artifact after it is found?** *(It is photographed, recorded, and tagged.)*

➤ **Do you think archaeologists can always interpret the artifacts accurately? Why or why not?** *(No, they do not always have all the pieces or facts, so they can only speculate about some artifacts.)*

Archaeological evidence—Instruct the students to read page 6 silently to find what some secular archaeologists assume about Sumer and the Flood. *(They believe that Sumer was one of the first civilizations and that there was no worldwide flood.)*

Discussion Questions

➤ **How do we know that people lived before the Flood?** *(The Bible discusses people who built advanced cities, were skilled musicians, worked with brass and iron, and knew much about agriculture.)*

Explain that the Flood destroyed any physical evidence of people who lived prior to it. Remind the students that the Bible records the events before the Flood, providing sufficient evidence that people did exist before Sumer. (BAT: 8b Faith in the power of the Word of God)

➤ **Why did people reject the story of Abraham?** *(They assumed that camels, such as the one Rebekah rode to meet Isaac, would not have been used as beasts of burden in Abraham's time.)*

➤ **How was this assumption proved incorrect?** *(Sumerian tablets record the use of camels.)*

➤ **How does the discovery of skeletons in caves around Ur explain the Bible phrase "gathered to his people"?** *(Abraham's burial is similar to the Sumerian practice in which several generations of a family were buried in a cave.)*

On a Dig

Name _____

Write a sentence using the word given.

1. archaeologists _____*Answers will vary.*_____

2. artifacts _____*Answers will vary.*_____

3. dig _____*Answers will vary.*_____

4. tell (*NOTE:* Use this term to mean "mound.") _____*Answers will vary.*_____

Number the steps of the excavation process in order from 1 through 6.

4	The actual digging begins.
1	Air and ground surveys are made.
6	Objects are photographed, recorded, and tagged.
2	The archaeologist draws a map and sections off the chosen area into squares.
5	Everyone must work carefully to avoid damaging fragile objects.
3	The archaeologist may use computers to help keep records and do calculations.

Heritage Studies 6
Student Notebook

Lesson 2
Evaluating the Lesson   **2**

□ Evaluating the Lesson

On a Dig (Notebook page 2)—Instruct the students to write a sentence using each word given. Encourage the students to write their sentences so that the meaning of each word is understood. Then tell them to number the steps of the excavation process in the correct order.

▬▬▬ Going Beyond ▬▬▬

□ Enrichment

Student archaeologists—Set up a research AREA with encyclopedias and a variety of books about different countries. Distribute one research page, one map page, and one artifact page to each student. (*NOTE:* See the reproducible material at the end of Lesson 6.) Assign a different Middle East country for each student to research. Instruct each student to turn in his completed research pages.

□ Additional Teacher Information

Sir Leonard Woolley wrote a detailed account of his archaeological work in a book titled *Excavations at Ur.* Woolley's discoveries have yielded evidence supporting various parts of the Old Testament. Woolley and his men discovered large deposits of silt and dirt, such as those left by a large flood. He writes that Sumerian records note the Flood, using it as a dating reference. For example, Sumerian records note events about their kings in relation to the Flood, saying, "The Flood came. After the Flood came, kingship was sent down from on high."

On these ancient Flood deposits, Woolley found bits of bitumen, a sticky substance used by the Sumerians for waterproofing. This bitumen had weaving imprints, suggesting that it was used in a basket or possibly in a boat. Woolley notes that the height of the Flood deposits is about the same as the height of the waters mentioned in Genesis.

Woolley himself did not believe the Flood was universal, but he did believe it to be the most devastating disaster to hit the Sumerians. Woolley also believed that biblical accounts were based on history but embellished by poets to provide a moral. Although Woolley did not believe in the complete truth of the Bible, his work provides evidence that the biblical account is indeed true.

LESSON 3
Sumer of Mesopotamia

Text, pages 7-11

- Farmers and Fishermen
- Merchants and Traders

━━━━ Preview ━━━━

□ Objective
Given proper instruction, the students will be able to do the following:
- Make and use a cylinder seal.

□ Materials
Have available:
- An overhead projector.
- A blank overhead transparency.
- Modeling clay for each student.*
- A wooden craft stick for each student.*

Prepare an overhead transparency of the pictowords page. (*NOTE: See the reproducible material at the end of Lesson 6.*)

□ Notes
A distinction must be made between pictographs and hieroglyphs. Pictographs are literal representations of an object or activity, whereas hieroglyphs represent a word, an idea, or even a syllable or a sound. Pictographs are believed to be the earliest form of writing. Hieroglyphs, usually associated only with ancient Egyptian writing, may have begun as a form of pictographs. Sumerian pictographs were altered by the addition of wedge-shaped designs and became known as *cuneiform*.

Day 4

━━━━ Lesson ━━━━

□ Introducing the Lesson
Pictowords—Display an overhead transparency of the pictowords page. Invite the students to guess the word represented by each picture. (*cowboy, flagpole, cupcake, basketball, and brainstorm*) Explain that early writing consisted of pictures, or *pictographs*. Point to each cuneiform figure and its meaning on the bulletin board. Tell the students that the Sumerians added little wedge shapes to their pictographs, developing their own form of writing.

Sumer of Mesopotamia
The land around Ur has changed little since Abraham's day. It is still dry and dusty, the clay soil often made hard by the sun. The Tigris and Euphrates Rivers still wind their way slowly through the flat plains, and the people practice many of the same skills and professions as their ancestors.

Farmers and Fishermen
Outside the great city of Ur, farmers worked hard in their fields. Irrigation canals crisscrossed the fields, bringing water from the river to the soil. Mesopotamia had few natural resources, but the Sumerians made good use of the crucial natural resource of water. Modern farmers also use irrigation to grow crops in places too dry for agriculture.

Sumerian farmers may have been the first people to use the wheel. You can imagine that pulling a heavy load on a cart with wheels was much easier than dragging that same load along on a skid. Sumerian farmers also used plows pulled by oxen. The oxen were hitched to the plow with a yoke, another implement first recorded in Sumer. The yoke helped the oxen to pull a plow or a heavy wagonload.

7

□ Teaching the Lesson
Farmers and fishermen—Instruct the students to read page 7 silently to find what the land of Ur is like today. (*It is still dry and dusty with sun-hardened clay soil.*)

Discussion Questions
➤ **How did Sumerian farmers water their crops?** (*by using irrigation canals that brought water from the river to the soil*)
➤ **What do modern farmers do like ancient Mesopotamian farmers?** (*also use irrigation to grow crops in places too dry for agriculture*)
➤ **Who were probably the first people in Mesopotamia to use the wheel?** (*the farmers*)

Explain that a *skid* is an object like a log that is used as a track to move heavy objects.
➤ **Why do you think a wheel would be better to use than a skid?** (*It would take less effort; there would be less resistance so that the object could move more easily.*)
➤ **How did Sumerian farmers plow their fields?** (*They used oxen hitched to a yoke to pull the plows.*)
➤ **What did a *yoke* do?** (*helped the oxen to pull a plow or a heavy wagonload*)

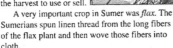
Dates were one of the common food crops of early Sumer.

The farmers of Sumer grew nearly all that the people needed: barley, wheat, peas, onions, garlic, leeks, lettuce, turnips, cucumbers, sesame seeds, dates, and figs. The farmers who owned their own land sold their harvests in the city market. Many farmers did not own their own land but worked on land owned by the temple or by wealthy individuals. They received part of the harvest to use or sell.

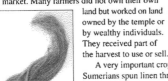

A very important crop in Sumer was *flax*. The Sumerians spun linen thread from the long fibers of the flax plant and then wove those fibers into cloth.

The farmers also raised animals, such as donkeys and oxen, to work in the fields and transport heavy loads. Goats, pigs, and sheep supplied meat as well as hides and wool. Sheep were so important to the Sumerians that they had over two hundred different words to describe all the breeds.

Fibers of flax (above) and wool shorn from sheep (below) were used in Sumerian clothing.

8

On the Euphrates, which ran along the eastern side of Ur, sailed many boats. Some were trading ships that had come from faraway places. Many, however, were fishing boats owned by local fishermen. Every day the fishermen went to the river and then returned home to sell their catches at the city market. Fish and bread were the most important foods of the Sumerians' diet.

Merchants and Traders

At the edge of the city, on the Euphrates River, stood the docks where trading ships and fishing boats anchored. Dockworkers, merchants, traders, and sailors carried on their business there. Ships brought goods from as far away as India in the east and Egypt in the west. Their holds were loaded with stone, wood, gems, and metals—goods for the workshops of Ur. Why do you think Sumer imported these goods? It had none of them as natural resources.

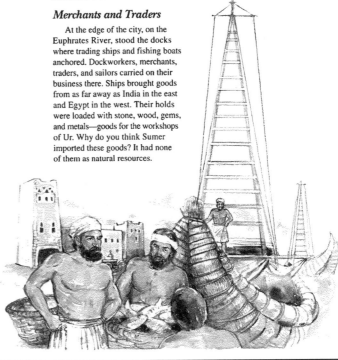

Instruct the students to read page 8 silently to find where the farmers sold their harvests. *(in the city market)*

Discussion Questions

➤ **What kinds of crops did Sumerian farmers grow?** *(barley, wheat, peas, onions, garlic, leeks, lettuce, turnips, cucumbers, sesame seeds, dates, and figs)*

➤ **Did all farmers have their own land?** *(No, some worked on land owned by the temple or by wealthy individuals, receiving part of the harvest to use or sell.)*

➤ **What is *flax,* and why was it an important crop for the Sumerians?** *(It is a plant with long fibers; it was used to spin linen thread to weave cloth.)*

➤ **How do we know that sheep were important to the Sumerians?** *(The Sumerians had over two hundred different words to describe all the types of sheep.)*

Instruct the students to read silently the first paragraph on page 9 to find along which side of Ur the Euphrates River ran. *(the eastern side)*

Discussion Questions

➤ **How was the Euphrates used by the Sumerians?** *(for trading with other countries and for fishing to make a living)*

➤ **What were the most important foods in the Sumerian diet?** *(fish and bread)*

Day 5

Merchants and traders—Instruct the students to read silently the last paragraph on page 9 and all of page 10 to find where the merchants and traders conducted their business. *(on the docks where trading ships and fishing boats anchored)*

Discussion Questions

➤ **What distant places sent ships to Sumer?** *(India and Egypt)*

➤ **What kinds of goods did Sumer import?** *(stone, wood, gems, and metals)*

➤ **Why did Sumer import these goods?** *(It had none of them as natural resources.)*

➤ **Who wrote down every sale?** *(scribes)*

➤ **What is a *stylus?*** *(a reed instrument used to write records on a tablet made of soft clay)*

➤ **What is *cuneiform?*** *(the Sumerian writing made of wedge-shaped characters)*

➤ **How many characters did the Sumerian language have?** *(over six hundred symbols that stood for words, numbers, or syllables)*

➤ **What did the scribe do with the tablet after he wrote the records?** *(wrapped the tablet in another piece of clay that served as an envelope and stored it in the temple with other legal records)*

➤ **How have these records helped modern archaeologists learn about the Sumerians?** *(The careful records reveal much about Sumerian economics.)*

The Sumerians kept careful records of all their business dealings. *Scribes* wrote down every sale with a reed *stylus* on a tablet made of soft clay. The writing, one of the greatest accomplishments of Sumer, is called *cuneiform* from the Latin words for "wedge-shaped." The Sumerian language had over six hundred symbols that stood for words, numbers, or syllables. After a scribe recorded a transaction, he wrapped the tablet in another piece of clay that served as an envelope. When the tablet dried, it was stored in the temple with other legal records. From these careful records we have learned much about Sumerian economics.

When two merchants finished a business deal and the scribe put his last marks on the tablet, each man had to sign it. They did not use the scribe's stylus to write their names. Rather they used clay seals shaped like cylinders. The *cylinder seal* was small, only about one to two inches high and about a half-inch in diameter. It had carvings that identified the owner. The carvings included plants, animals, gods, and wedge-shaped symbols. Each man rolled his seal across the wet clay tablet to approve the sale. The cylinder seal was a fast, simple way to sign one's name. The mark of a cylinder seal stood either for approval, as on a legal document, or for ownership, as on goods ready to be shipped.

> *"He that hath received his testimony hath set to his seal that God is true."*
> **John 3:33**

Cylinder seals (right) and impressions from seals (above), Bob Jones University Bible Lands Museum

10

To Make a Cylinder Seal

1. Decide what design would best represent you on the seal.

2. Get the clay and styling tool from your teacher. Shape the clay into a cylinder about two inches long and one inch wide. With your styling tool, create your signature picture or design around the clay cylinder. Let the clay harden.

3. On another day make small tablets with the remaining clay. Roll your cylinder seal over a clay tablet to imprint your signature.

11

➤ **What is a *cylinder seal*?** *(a small, clay seal with carvings of plants, animals, gods, or wedge-shaped symbols that identifies the owner)*

➤ **How did each merchant sign the tablet to complete a business deal?** *(He rolled his cylinder seal across the wet clay tablet.)*

➤ **How was the cylinder seal important to Sumerian life?** *(It was a fast, simple way to sign one's name, and the cylinder mark was recognized for approval or for ownership.)*

Remind the students that those who trust in Jesus Christ as their Savior become identified in Christ. Christians are under the Lord's seal, or ownership. (BAT: 1a Understanding Jesus Christ; Bible Promise: D. Identified in Christ)

□ **Evaluating the Lesson**

Cylinder seals—Direct a *Discovering How* activity on page 11. Distribute a portion of modeling clay and a wooden craft stick to each student. Read aloud the first two steps on page 11. Instruct each student to make a cylinder seal, creating with his stylus a picture or word that will serve as his signature. On another day, complete Step 3. Display the students' cylinder seals and tablets in the classroom.

Going Beyond

□ **Enrichment**

Wheels—Set up a weaving AREA with some raw fibers (flax, cotton, and wool) as well as clothing or fabric of linen, cotton, and wool. Also have available books about these fibers and how weaving is done. To give students opportunities to weave, have available small looms and enough potholder loops for each student to weave a potholder to take home.

□ **Additional Teacher Information**

Linguists believe that pictographs preceded cuneiform as a means of writing. Eventually, the pictographs developed into a wedge-shaped writing, each character consisting of between one and thirty wedges. The stylus used to write cuneiform was made of reed, bone, or wood.

Since the 1800s, over a hundred thousand cuneiform tablets have been found. Most modern knowledge of ancient Mesopotamia comes from these clay tablets. When cuneiform was first found, however, historians and linguists could not decipher it. In 1835 archaeologists found a message on a rock in the Zagros Mountains in Iran. The message was carved in three languages and provided the link to deciphering cuneiform. This written language provides insight into a lifestyle of long ago.

LESSON 4
Artisans and Craftsmen

Text, pages 12-14
Notebook, page 3

- ■ Exports
- ■ Pottery
- ■ Jewelry

▬▬▬ Preview ▬▬▬

□ Objective
Given proper instruction, the students will be able to do the following:
- • Identify key words through the use of context clues.

□ Materials
Have available either a potter with a potter's wheel and clay or a video showing the use of a potter's wheel.*

Day 6

▬▬▬ Lesson ▬▬▬

□ Introducing the Lesson
Pottery demonstration—Invite an artist or show a video to demonstrate the use of a potter's wheel. (*NOTE:* You may choose to take a field trip to a pottery shop instead.) As time permits, allow the students to ask questions. Explain to the students that thousands of years ago, the Sumerians used a similar method to make pottery.

Day 7

□ Teaching the Lesson
Exports—Instruct the students to read page 12 silently to find out what *artisans* are. *(skilled craftsmen)*

Discussion Questions
- ➤ **What was the job of Sumerian artisans?** *(to turn raw materials into finished goods)*
- ➤ **What are *exports*?** *(goods sold to foreign traders)*
- ➤ **What kinds of things produced by artisans have archaeologists found in Ur?** *(records and remains of jewelry, pottery, clothing, etc.)*

Artisans and Buyers
Unloaded goods did not stay long at the docks. Workers gathered them up and took them into the city. In the center of Ur, skilled craftsmen, also called *artisans,* turned raw materials into finished goods. These products made up most of Sumer's *exports,* goods sold to foreign traders. Archaeologists have found both records and remains of jewelry, pottery, clothing, and other objects fashioned in the artisans' shops.

Many of the workshops in Ur produced goods for everyday use. Some of the busiest shops in the city were those that sold cloth. The cloth makers employed many women to spin thread from flax or wool and then weave it into cloth. The people of Ur bought their cloth at one shop, had it dyed at another, and then took it home to make clothing.

12

- ➤ **What did women do for the cloth makers?** *(spun thread from flax or wool and then wove it into cloth)*
- ➤ **What did the people of Ur do with cloth after they bought it?** *(had it dyed at another shop and then took it home to make clothing)*
- ➤ **How is this process of getting clothes different from or similar to the way we get clothes today?** *(Most people today buy clothes already made, or if they make their own clothes, the fabric they buy is usually already dyed.)*

After leaving the cloth maker's shop, a shopper might have stopped at a pottery workshop. Clay was one of the few raw materials plentiful in the river valley. While the potters busily threw clay onto their wheels and formed pots, the shopper ordered his goods. Sumerians were possibly the first to use a potter's wheel to make clay pots. Before that time, pots had to be molded or coiled by hand, but the wheel allowed a potter to produce pots of uniform size and shape faster than before. Potters in Ur made all sorts of containers for storing and serving food. The potters added carvings and decorations to make the pots attractive as well as useful.

Potters still work at their wheels. The potters' wheels have changed little over the centuries. The potters' designs of pitchers, bowls, cups, and plates are also much the same. But now tourists can buy this beautiful pottery as souvenirs, and huge ships can carry these lovely works of art to countries that had not been imagined when Abraham left Ur.

A modern potter shapes the neck of a vase as it rotates on his potter's wheel.

Pottery on the docks in modern Kuwait

13

The Standard of Ur, Sumerian art made of shell inlay with red limestone and lapis lazuli set in bitumen on a wooden case

The city also had shops that made luxury goods. The artisans of these shops trained for many years to learn the skills for making beautiful objects. Several workshops made jewelry and fine dishes from the gold, silver, copper, and precious jewels imported into Sumer. The finished pieces, intricately and beautifully designed, were either sold in Ur or shipped to other lands.

A special craft in Ur was *shell inlay*. An artisan used white shells from the river and arranged them into a design. He had to make sure the pieces fit together well, almost like pieces of a puzzle. Once satisfied with his design, he pressed the pieces into softened tar on another surface, such as metal. After the main design was finished, he may have surrounded it with a bright blue stone called *lapis lazuli*. A shell inlay artisan had to be patient and careful. Some works of sparkling white shells and lapis lazuli inlay still exist and show us the high quality of Sumerian workmanship.

14

Pottery—Instruct the students to read page 13 silently to find out where Sumerian potters found their clay. *(in the river valley)* Select a volunteer to explain what a potter's wheel is and how it works. *(It is a flat, smooth surface that rotates. The potter places a lump of clay on the wheel and then shapes it with his hands as the wheel turns.)*

Discussion Questions

➤ **How did the potter shape clay before the use of the potter's wheel?** *(molded or coiled it by hand)*

➤ **How did the wheel help a potter's production of pots or other items made from clay?** *(It allowed a potter to produce pots of uniform size and shape faster than by hand.)*

➤ **How are modern potters and their work similar to those of Abraham's day?** *(The potters' wheels have changed little over the centuries, and their pottery designs are much the same.)*

Remind the students of the biblical illustration of the potter and the clay. Explain that Christians should be like clay in the Potter's hand, willing to be used and shaped by the Lord. Remind the students of God's sovereignty and His ability to make Christians beautiful vessels, useful and fit for His service. (BAT: 7e Humility; Bible Promises: H. God as Father, I. God as Master)

Jewelry—Instruct the students to read page 14 silently to find out what types of luxury goods were made in Ur. *(jewelry and fine dishes from the gold, silver, copper, and precious jewels imported to Sumer)*

Discussion Questions

➤ **What happened to the finished pieces of jewelry?** *(They were either sold in Ur or shipped to other lands.)*

➤ **What is a *shell inlay*?** *(a design made from white river shells pressed into softened tar on another surface, such as metal)*

➤ **What is *lapis lazuli*?** *(a bright blue stone)*

➤ **What do the works found by archaeologists reveal about the Sumerian artisans?** *(Their workmanship was of high quality.)*

□ Evaluating the Lesson

Shopping Day (Notebook page 3)—Instruct the students to read the paragraphs, noting the italicized phrases. Tell them to write the word or phrase from the list that has the same meaning as the italicized phrase.

━━━━ Going Beyond ━━━━

□ Enrichment

Shell inlay—Set up an art AREA with blue construction paper, glue, an 8"×8" square of cardboard, clay, and small white shells or pebbles for each student. Instruct each student to cut the blue construction paper to size and then to glue it to the cardboard to make a lapis lazuli background. Then tell him to smooth out a fist-sized lump of clay on top of the construction paper. Instruct the students to make a design, pressing the shells into the clay. Display the students' shell inlays.

□ Additional Teacher Information

In his excavations at Ur, Sir Woolley uncovered one of the oldest machines in the world—the potter's wheel. He described it as "a heavy disc of baked clay about three feet in diameter."

Clay was an important part of Sumerian society, used in making utensils, keeping records, and building homes. The clay used for making pottery had to be sifted and refined until all the coarse materials were eliminated. In order to do this, the Sumerians added water to the clay and stirred it. The heavier objects, such as pebbles, settled on the bottom while the lighter particles, such as leaves and twigs, remained on top. Eventually, the water was drained, leaving a layer of clean clay. Once the pot was shaped on the wheel, it was fired to create a smooth, strong vessel.

LESSON 5
Religion and Royalty

Text, pages 15-17
Notebook, pages 4-5

- Priests and Worshipers
- Kings and Subjects

Preview

□ Objectives

Given proper instruction, the students will be able to do the following:

- Create laws determining punishment for certain crimes.
- Compare and contrast Sumerian beliefs with biblical truths.

□ Materials

Have available a Bible for each student.

Day 8

Lesson

□ Introducing the Lesson

Royal Legislation (Notebook page 4)—Instruct the students to imagine that they are kings or queens. Tell them that for each crime listed on Notebook page 4, they should write a law that would provide punishment for offenders. (For example, anyone caught stealing will have to repay the debt and provide ten hours of public service.) As time permits, discuss the laws decreed by the students. Explain that even thousands of years ago, laws existed in Mesopotamia.

□ Teaching the Lesson

Priests and worshipers—Instruct the students to read page 15 silently to find what a *ziggurat* is. *(a temple tower)*

Royal Legislation   Name _____

For each crime listed, decree a law that would provide punishment for offenders.

1. stealing   *Answers will vary.*
   _____
   _____

2. lying   *Answers will vary.*
   _____
   _____

3. cheating   *Answers will vary.*
   _____
   _____

4. fighting   *Answers will vary.*
   _____
   _____

Heritage Studies 6
Student Notebook

Lesson 5
Introducing the Lesson   **4**

Discussion Questions

➤ **How big was the ziggurat and its other buildings?** *(It took up one-fourth of the city.)*

➤ **How many levels did the ziggurat have, and what was on them?** *(three levels with gardens planted on each terrace and with a shrine on the top)*

➤ **What was in the temple complex?** *(a few other large structures containing shrines, homes for the high priestess and many temple workers, a storehouse, and additional chambers)*

➤ **Where does the word *polytheism* come from?** *(Greek words meaning "many gods")*

➤ **What were the Sumerian gods like?** *(false gods made up by men and acting like men)*

Remind the students that there is only one true God and that He is holy and sovereign. (Bible Promise: I. God as Master)

Priests and Worshipers

In the center of Ur, both four thousand years ago and today, stands the temple tower, called a *ziggurat*. The ziggurat and surrounding temple buildings took up about one-fourth of the city. People approaching the city could see the ziggurat while they were still a long distance away. It rose in three levels with gardens planted on each terrace and with a shrine on the top. An area beside the ziggurat formed a temple complex, complete with a few other large structures containing shrines, homes for the high priestess and many temple workers, a storehouse, and additional chambers.

The Sumerians were polytheistic in their worship. The word *polytheism* comes from the Greek words meaning "many gods." The gods the Sumerians worshiped were false gods made up by men and acting like men.

View looking up the steps of the ziggurat

The reconstructed ziggurat in Ur

15

Each Sumerian city had one god in particular whom the people worshiped. In Ur the people worshiped the moon god *Nanna*. They believed that the god lived in the ziggurat, in a little shrine at the very top. His statue was kept there and food was offered to him daily. The priests and priestesses who lived at the temple used these offerings to perform magic rituals or to meet their own needs. The priests held powerful positions in Sumer because the Sumerians believed that the priests had more power with the gods than did the common people.

The Sumerians did not believe that their city-god cared about their everyday problems. They thought that he had larger concerns dealing with other gods and earthly kings. Instead, they trusted lesser gods whose statues they worshiped at home. They thought that these gods acted as go-betweens to gods of greater power.

The Sumerians worshiped their gods by praying to them, giving them gifts, and performing rituals. They believed that if the gods were pleased, the people would prosper. If the gods were not pleased, disaster would strike. Religious rituals and prayers accompanied all the Sumerians' activities, no matter how ordinary.

Stone statue from Tell Asmar, Iraq. (detail) Early dynastic (Sumerian), 2600 B.C

Iraq Museum, Baghdad, Iraq

16

Day 9

Instruct the students to read page 16 silently to find the name of the god worshiped by the people of Ur. *(Nanna)*

Discussion Questions

➤ **What did the people of Ur believe about Nanna?** *(that he lived in the ziggurat in a little shrine at the very top)*

➤ **How was Nanna treated?** *(People offered food daily to his statue.)*

➤ **What did the priests and priestesses do with these food offerings?** *(used them to perform magic rituals or to meet their own needs)*

➤ **Why were the priests powerful people in Sumer?** *(The Sumerians believed that the priests had more power with the gods than did the common people.)*

➤ **Why did the Sumerians think that their city-god did not care about their everyday problems?** *(They thought that he had larger concerns dealing with other gods and earthly kings.)*

➤ **How was Nanna different from the God of the Bible?** *(The God of the Bible is real and cares about every aspect of the lives of His people. He is omnipotent, able to handle all things.)*

➤ **Whom did the Sumerians worship at home?** *(lesser gods who they thought acted as go-betweens to gods of greater power)*

Remind the students that Christ intercedes for those who trust in Him. Explain that the Holy Spirit also serves as a Comforter and Guide to those who are saved. (BAT: 6c Spirit-filled; Bible Promise F. Christ as Intercessor)

➤ **How did the Sumerians worship their gods?** *(by praying to them, giving them gifts, and performing rituals)*

➤ **What did the Sumerians believe about pleasing their gods?** *(If the gods were pleased, the people would prosper; if the gods were not pleased, disaster would strike.)*

➤ **How much of the Sumerians' lives were focused on religious activities?** *(Religious rituals and prayers accompanied all the Sumerians' activities, no matter how ordinary.)*

Kings and Subjects

The temple was important not only as the center of religion but also as the seat of the Sumerian government. Sumer was made up of several city-states. A *city-state* is an independent city and its surrounding land. The Sumerian city-states often fought against each other, with kings trying to gain more land and power from the other city-states. During Abraham's lifetime, Ur was the most powerful Sumerian city-state.

Every city-state had its own king and its own god. The king was the god's highest representative on earth. The people looked on him as a god too. He lived in a lavish palace within the temple complex, and he ruled from his throne. Slaves and other servants waited upon him; court musicians played instruments and sang his praises.

Whatever the kings demanded, citizens did. Some kings wrote down laws and ruled by them. In Ur a lawbreaker often had to pay fines as punishment. For example, if a man cut off another man's foot or nose, he paid the injured man a certain amount of silver. Legal records were required on all business transactions, contracts, marriages, adoptions, and wills. Archaeologists have found many of Sumer's records, still in their clay envelopes, filed in the temple.

Ruins of the palace/temple complex in Ur

17

Compare and Contrast   Name _____

Use your textbook and the Bible references given to complete each statement.

The Sumerian Religion	The Bible
1. The Sumerians were **polytheistic**. They believed in many gods.	The Bible teaches that there is **one God** (I Corinthians 8:6).
2. The Sumerians had **statues** of their gods in the temple.	In the Bible, God says not to make **idols** or any graven image (Leviticus 26:1).
3. The Sumerians thought that their city-god did not care about their **everyday** problems.	The Bible teaches us to cast **all** our **cares** upon the Lord (I Peter 5:7).
4. The Sumerians believed that lesser gods acted as **go-betweens** to gods of greater power.	The Bible teaches that there is only one God and one **mediator** between God and men (I Timothy 2:5).
5. Religious **rituals** and **prayers** accompanied all the Sumerians' activities, no matter how **ordinary**.	The Bible tells us to do all to the **glory** of **God** (I Corinthians 10:31).

© 1998 BJU Press. Reproduction prohibited.

Heritage Studies 6
Student Notebook

Lesson 5
Evaluating the Lesson   **5**

Kings and subjects—Instruct the students to read page 17 silently to find what a *city-state* is. *(an independent city and its surrounding land)*

Discussion Questions

➤ **Why did the Sumerian city-states fight against each other?** *(Kings tried to gain more land and power from other city-states.)*

➤ **Which city-state was the most powerful during Abraham's time?** *(Ur)*

➤ **What kind of government did each city-state have?** *(its own king and its own god)*

➤ **How did the people view the king?** *(as the god's highest representative on earth or as a god too)*

➤ **How did the king live?** *(in a lavish palace with slaves and servants and with court musicians praising him)*

➤ **What were lawbreakers required to do as punishment?** *(pay fines)*

➤ **What types of legal records were Sumerians forced to keep?** *(all business transactions, contracts, marriages, adoptions, and wills)*

➤ **Where were many of these Sumerian records kept?** *(in the temple)*

□ Evaluating the Lesson

Compare and Contrast (Notebook page 5)—Instruct the students to use their textbooks and the Bible references given to complete the statements on Notebook page 5. As time permits, discuss the differences and similarities between Sumerian religion and biblical truths.

Going Beyond

□ Enrichment

The Tower of Babel—Explain that some archaeologists believe the Tower of Babel was a ziggurat. Give a copy of the Tower of Babel page to each student. (*NOTE:* See the reproducible material at the end of Lesson 6.) Instruct the students to explain in their own words the biblical account of the Tower of Babel in Genesis 11:1-9.

□ Additional Teacher Information

Sumerian ziggurats were made of either sun-dried or kiln-baked mud bricks. The Sumerians decorated the plain brick by embedding painted clay stones into the wet mud plaster to form geometrical designs. The inside of the temple was decorated with frescoes or motifs, such as humans or animals.

Archaeologists believe that certain parts of the temple were waterproofed since bitumen was found on various temple remains. Archaeological digs have revealed several layers of temples, some dating from different eras. Archaeologists believe that temple ground was considered holy; therefore, if a temple was destroyed, only another temple could be built in its place. Thus, through the years ziggurats remained in the same area of the city. The temple found at Eridu, a city south of Ur, was built over the remains of at least seventeen other temples.

LESSON 6
At School or Home

Text, pages 18-22
Notebook, page 6

- School-Fathers and Students
- Proverbs
- Parents and Children
- The Years

Preview

□ Objective
Given proper instruction, the students will be able to do the following:
- Identify people and items of the Sumerian school system.

Day 10

Lesson

□ Introducing the Lesson
School terms—On the chalkboard, write the following terms used in reference to the Sumerian school system: *the man in charge of the whip; tablet-house; school-father; big brother.* Invite volunteers to guess what functions these items or people had in the Sumerian schools. Explain that the students will find out the meanings of these terms in this lesson.

□ Teaching the Lesson
School-fathers and students—Instruct the students to read page 18 silently to find how archaeologists knew that the building near the ziggurat was a school. *(Two thousand clay tablets were found in the building.)*

Discussion Questions
➤ **Who do archaeologists believe operated the school?** *(a scribe)*
➤ **Who was able to attend school in Ur?** *(usually only boys from wealthy families)*
➤ **What were the boys taught?** *(how to become good scribes)*
➤ **How could Sumerian students earn the respect of others?** *(by writing well)*
➤ **How many free days did the students have each month?** *(only six)*
➤ **Who helped the students discipline themselves to study?** *("the man in charge of the whip")*
➤ **Who helps discipline students in your school?** *(Possible answers include the teacher, the principal, and the vice principal.)*

School-fathers and Students

Near the ziggurat in Ur was a large house with an unusual guest room and courtyard. This building puzzled archaeologists for a while until they realized it was the home of a scribe who operated a school. (The chief clue was two thousand clay tablets found in the building.)

Usually only boys from wealthy families were able to attend school in Ur. The instruction helped them learn to become good scribes. Students who learned to write well became highly respected in Sumer. They practiced making the wedge-shaped symbols of Sumerian writing during the long school days, with only six free days each month. To help the students discipline themselves to study, the school had a teacher called "the man in charge of the whip."

The Sumerians called the school building the *tablet-house.* All day the *school-father,* or chief teacher, gave students lessons to practice. They wrote lists, did mathematical problems, and learned grammar. An assistant, called a "big brother," wrote out assignments for the young students to copy and then checked their work. To practice reading, the students recited their tablets aloud both at school and home.

18

➤ **What did the Sumerians call the school building?** *(the tablet-house)*
➤ **Why do you think the school had this name?** *(Answers will vary but may include because the students practiced writing on tablets.)*
➤ **What was the chief teacher called?** *(the school-father)*
➤ **What kinds of assignments did the Sumerian students have?** *(writing lists, working mathematical problems, and learning grammar)*
➤ **What did the "big brother" do?** *(wrote out assignments for the young students to copy and then checked their work)*

Making Up Proverbs

"Into an open mouth, a fly enters."

This was a saying many schoolboys often heard. The Sumerians liked *proverbs*, or wise sayings. Proverbs give bits of wisdom in a short, easy-to-remember form. Sometimes Sumerian proverbs expressed a simple truth: "A sweet word is everybody's friend." Other proverbs showed a contrast between two types of behavior: "A loving heart builds the home; a hating heart destroys the home." Some offered commonsense observations on life: "A scribe whose hand moves as fast as the mouth, that's a scribe for you."

19

Parents and Children

Ur was a bustling city of perhaps fifty thousand people. Simple houses crowded the narrow, winding streets and alleys. Most of these houses had only one outside door and no windows. The thick mud walls kept the houses cool in the hot Mesopotamian climate.

Wealthy families lived in two-story houses. Each house had a large central courtyard, off which smaller rooms for cooking, sleeping, and entertaining opened. There was a special room for the family's statue of their personal god. The furniture was a few low tables and perhaps some chairs and a bed. Woolen and reed mats lined the walls and floors. Often the family slept and entertained guests outdoors on the flat roof, where the air was cooler in the evenings.

The families in Ur were small for ancient times. Most families had four or five children. Girls stayed at home and learned housekeeping skills from their mothers. Boys learned trades or skills from their fathers or went to school. When children reached marrying age, the parents arranged the marriages for them. They tried to choose a hard-working partner for each child.

20

Proverbs—Instruct the students to read page 19 silently to find what a *proverb* is. *(a wise saying)* Select a volunteer to explain the meaning of the Sumerian proverb "Into an open mouth, a fly enters." *(It means that it is good for a person to be quiet and not say too much. People who talk a lot often get into trouble.)* (BAT: 5d Communication)

Discussion Questions
➤ **Why are proverbs good forms of instruction?** *(They give bits of wisdom in a short, easy-to-remember form.)*
➤ **What types of Sumerian proverbs were there?** *(Some proverbs expressed a simple truth; some showed a contrast between two types of behavior; and some offered commonsense observations on life.)*

Discuss with the students the Sumerian proverbs mentioned on page 19. Select a different volunteer to explain each one. (*NOTE:* As time allows, you may choose to read several proverbs from the Bible.)

Parents and children—Instruct the students to read page 20 silently to find how many people probably lived in Ur. *(about fifty thousand people)*

Discussion Questions
➤ **How many doors and windows did the typical Sumerian house have?** *(only one outside door and no windows)*
➤ **What were the walls made from?** *(thick mud)*
➤ **What kinds of rooms were in each Sumerian house?** *(a central courtyard; smaller rooms for cooking, sleeping, and entertaining; and a special room for the family's statue of their personal god)*
➤ **What kinds of furniture did the Sumerians have?** *(a few low tables and perhaps some chairs and a bed)*
➤ **What were the families like in Sumer?** *(usually small for ancient times, with four or five children)*
➤ **What did Sumerian girls do?** *(stayed at home and learned housekeeping skills from their mothers)*
➤ **What did Sumerian boys do?** *(learned trades or skills from their fathers or went to school)*
➤ **How were marriages in ancient Sumer different from marriages today?** *(Marriages in ancient Sumer were usually arranged by the parents. Today a person usually chooses his own spouse.)*

A bull-headed harp found in a royal grave in Sumer

Parents encouraged their children to work and to study hard. In the evenings fathers listened to their sons recite their daily lessons. Families also spent the evenings singing and playing musical instruments, such as harps, lyres, drums, tambourines, and pipes (instruments similar to flutes). Music was important to religious rituals and daily work as well.

Parents in Sumer believed in strong discipline. They taught their children obedience and respect. A child who disobeyed might even be disowned or disinherited by his father. The values of hard work and discipline instilled in these Sumerian children helped them to become industrious adults and to maintain an impressive civilization.

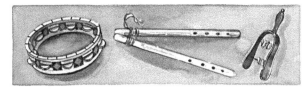

21

Numbering the Years

Nearly fifteen hundred years ago people stopped using the old system of numbering years from the founding of Rome. Instead they decided to number years from the birth of Jesus Christ.

Scholars decided that if events were earlier than Christ's birth, the year would be labeled B.C. (*before Christ.*) If they were after Christ's birth, the year would be labeled A.D. (short for *anno Domini,* the Latin words for "in the year of the Lord").

Usually we do not use the letters A.D. unless we think there will be some confusion. For example, if someone lived from 43 B.C. until A.D. 25, we include the letters to show that he lived sixty-eight years rather than eighteen.

Every time someone writes a date—whether referring to Sumer in 2500 B.C. or an event last year in New York City—he is really "echoing" the most important event in human history.

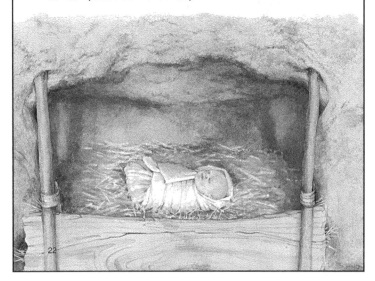

22

Day 11

Instruct the students to read page 21 silently to find what Sumerian families did in the evenings. *(Boys recited their lessons to their fathers, or the entire family spent the evenings singing and playing harps, lyres, drums, tambourines, and pipes.)*

Discussion Questions

➤ **In what other ways was music important?** *(as part of religious rituals and daily work)*
➤ **What did parents in Sumer teach their children?** *(obedience and respect through strong discipline)*
➤ **What happened to a child who disobeyed?** *(He might be disowned or disinherited by his father.)*
➤ **How did the values instilled in Sumerian children influence the kinds of adults they became?** *(They became industrious adults who helped maintain an impressive civilization.)*

Remind the students that Christians need to obey those in authority over them. Encourage them to work hard now so that they will become responsible, mature adults. Explain that obedience and discipline are part of a Christian's testimony. (BATs: 2a Authority, 2e Work)

The years—Instruct the students to read page 22 silently to find how long ago the numbering of years changed. *(nearly fifteen hundred years ago)*

Discussion Questions

➤ **What does B.C. mean in reference to a date?** *("before Christ")*
➤ **What abbreviation do we use for years after Christ's birth?** *(A.D.)*
➤ **What does A.D. represent?** *(anno Domini, which is Latin for "in the year of the Lord")*
➤ **When do we usually include the letters A.D.?** *(when they are needed to avoid confusion)*

Word Circle   Name _____

Circle the word that completes each statement.

1. The chief teacher, or the ____, gave students lessons to practice.

   principal   (school-father)   tutor

2. The "man in charge of the whip" maintained ____.

   the school   the finances   (discipline)

3. "A sweet word is everybody's friend" is an example of a(n) ____.

   (proverb)   song   essay   story

4. An assistant, known as the ____, wrote out assignments for the young students to copy and then checked their work.

   helper   aide   (big brother)

5. The time period in which you were born is ____.

   (A.D.)   B.C.

6. The time period during which people lived in the land of Ur is ____.

   A.D.   (B.C.)

7. The place where Sumerian students attended school was the ____.

   learning center   (tablet house)   courtyard

© 1998 BJU Press. Reproduction prohibited.

Heritage Studies 6
Student Notebook

Lesson 6
Evaluating the Lesson   **6**

□ Evaluating the Lesson

Word Circle (Notebook page 6)—Instruct the students to circle the word that completes each statement.

Going Beyond

□ Enrichment

Houses—Set up an art AREA with blank drawing paper and colored pencils. Instruct each student to draw the layout of the house he lives in. As time permits, discuss the differences between the students' houses and the Sumerian houses described in this chapter.

□ Additional Teacher Information

Among the clay writing tablets uncovered in Sumer were several essays about the Sumerian school system. Three of these essays were given the following titles that summarize their contents: *Schooldays, School Rowdies,* and *A Scribe and His Perverse Son.*

The *Schooldays* essay consisted of an older man's account of his years as a young student. He writes about the many problems that one particular day held, resulting in canings from various school officials. Great emphasis was placed on responsibility and discipline in Sumerian schools.

The essay *School Rowdies* contains a discourse between two scribes that appears to be a repartee in which each student first disparages the other and then praises himself. Modern scholars believe that the first usage of the word *sophomore* occurs here. The English word *sophomore,* which means "clever fool," comes from the Greek and first appeared in English in 1688.

The essay *A Scribe and His Perverse Son* is an account of a father admonishing his son to be diligent, to behave, to seek higher things than the material, and to succeed. This essay contains one of the earliest uses of the word *humanity,* referring to both mankind as a whole and to human kindness. This essay reveals the values held by the Sumerian family. Although all three essays have gaps in their content, they nonetheless provide insight into the workings of Sumerian society.

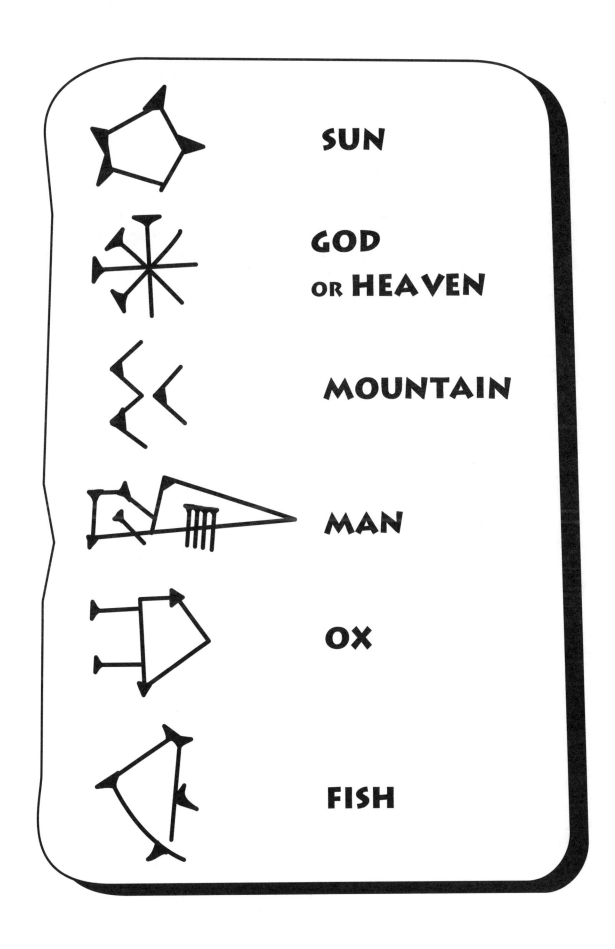

SUN

GOD OR HEAVEN

MOUNTAIN

MAN

OX

FISH

Landforms and Lifestyles

Read the description of the rivers of Mesopotamia. On the lines provided, explain in your own words how the rivers were important to the people of Mesopotamia.

Enkri listened as Father told of the great rivers. Enkri had been to the edge of the rivers many times, but he had never seen the water as Father had. Father spoke of the fish pulled from the rivers, of the grain grown from fields watered by the rivers, and of the beauty of the water itself as the sun shone on its wrinkled surface. Father spoke of the water with respect. He taught Enkri to be thankful for the rivers, for he knew that the people depended on the water for food, for trade, and for life itself.

_____

_____

_____

_____

_____

_____

Think about where you live. What landforms are there? How do they affect the way you or other people live?

_____

_____

_____

_____

_____

_____

Research Page

Use this page to keep records of your research "dig." Answer each question or follow the instructions.

1. What country are you researching? _____

2. What language is spoken in this country? _____

3. What foods are important to the people there? _____

   _____

   _____

4. Give a brief description of the main religion practiced there. _____

   _____

   _____

   _____

   _____

5. What sources have you used in research? _____

   _____

   _____

   _____

Map Page

Draw a map of the area you are surveying. Include the capital and any major landforms, such as mountain ranges, deserts, rivers, or lakes.

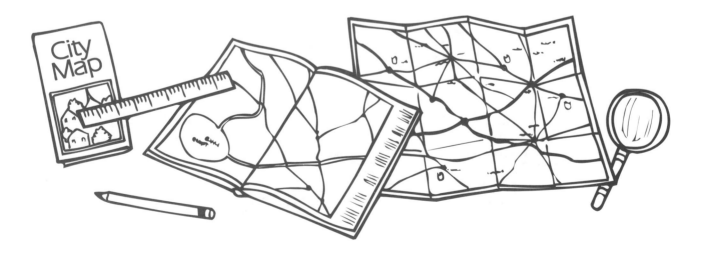

Artifact Page

Draw an "artifact," such as a product or typical clothing, housing, or artwork, that is unique to the country you are researching.

+   =

_____

+   =

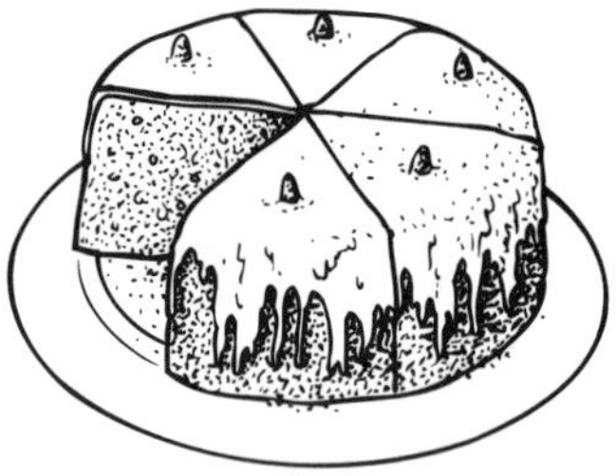

_____

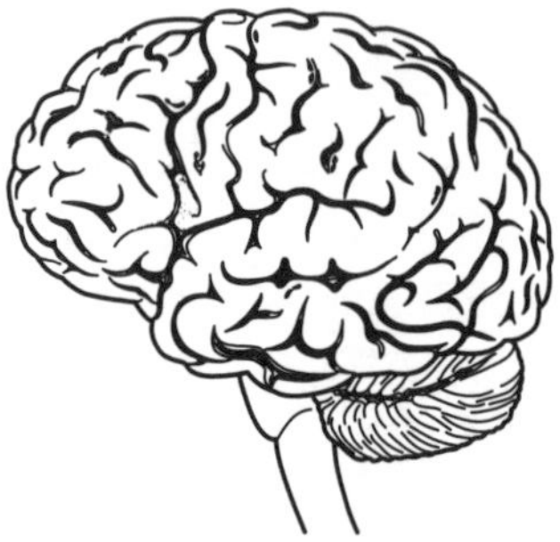

+   =

_____

+   =

_____

+   =

_____

Use with Lesson 3. Heritage Studies 6 TE

Tower of Babel

Read Genesis 11:1-9. Explain what the Tower of Babel was, why it was built, and what happened to those who built it.

_____

_____

_____

_____

_____

_____

_____

_____

_____

_____

_____

_____

_____

_____

2 LESSONS 7-13

The Gift of the Nile: Ancient Egypt

This chapter explores the land, history, and culture of ancient Egypt. The students will learn why Egypt was given the name "the Gift of the Nile" as they study the important role the Nile River played in the land's economy, agriculture, and religion. They will survey the history of Egypt's Old, Middle, and New Kingdoms, focusing on the pharaohs who made significant contributions to each era. The chapter also reveals how the history of the Hebrew people mingles with Egyptian history, highlighting the lives of Joseph and Moses. The students will unlock ancient secrets of the pyramids, hieroglyphics, and mummies. Special activities allow them to make an Egyptian wig and to design and decode hieroglyphs. The board game Find the Pharaoh in Lesson 12 provides an opportunity for students to review what they have learned.

□ Materials

Lessons 7-9 and 13 require certain items that must be obtained or prepared several days to several weeks before the presentation of the lessons. These items are labeled with an asterisk (*) in each lesson and in the Materials List in the Supplement. Occasionally, items not commonly found in the classroom as well as items needed in large quantities may also be labeled with an asterisk. For further information, see the individual lessons.

□ Chapter Bulletin Board

Under the title *Egypt: The Gift of the Nile,* pin a long strand of blue yarn on the board to represent the Nile River. Use more strands of yarn to make a fan-shaped delta at one end. Add pictures or photographs of Egypt's sights and artifacts from old magazines, calendars, travel brochures, or books. As you progress through the chapter, place these pictures at various spots along the "Nile."

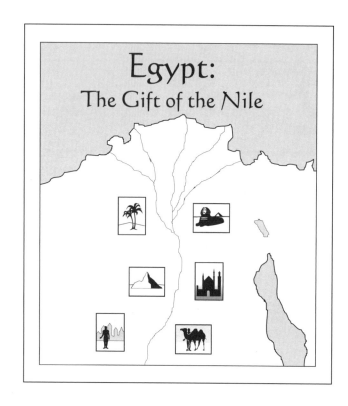

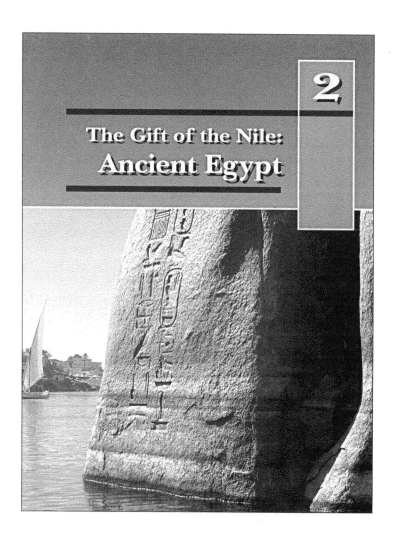

LESSON 7
Gift of the Nile

Text, pages 24-27
Notebook, page 7

- **Rami's Egypt**
- **The Nile River**
- **Then and Now**

Rami lowered the *shadoof* one last time. That should be enough water, he thought. I'm so tired! He stretched his arms over his head to ease his cramped muscles and nearly tumbled over backward. He looked out over his family's fields. The grain was almost ready to harvest. It waved in the hot winds blowing in from the desert.

Rami smiled. He was glad he had the important job of keeping his father's irrigation canals full of water. Without the water of the Nile, no crops could grow. Without those crops, he would not have a lunch to eat.

Soon the men from the village would cut the grain. Rami would help again this year by tying the sheaves of grain into bundles. After harvest, the villagers would spread the bundles of grain on the threshing floor and drive the farm animals over them. The trampling hooves would shake the ripe grain from the stalks, and then each family would store its grain in a silo for the next year's bread.

Rami sat down and leaned against a large palm tree. "It won't be long," he said aloud, "and there will be feasting and giving thanks to the gods for such a good harvest." He stretched and yawned. "Then all we'll have to do is wait for the season of flooding."

24

━━━ Preview ━━━

☐ Objective
Given proper instruction, the students will be able to do the following:
- Complete statements about ancient Egypt and the Nile River.

☐ Materials
Have available:
- Maps and More 2.
- The figure representing the Early Egyptians (3800 B.C.) from the History TimeLine Packet.*

☐ Notes
If you have purchased the History TimeLine, you will refer to it for the first time in this lesson. A time line is a simple way to organize the important events in history. It can easily be used to establish a sequence of events, and it will also help you to illustrate relationships between the events pictured. You will want to post the TimeLine before beginning this lesson. Figures from the History TimeLine Packet for grade 6 will be added throughout the year. You may also choose to add pictures of your own to the TimeLine as opportunities arise.

Day 12

━━━ Lesson ━━━

☐ Introducing the Lesson
Irrigation methods—Ask for a show of hands of the students whose parents grow a garden or a crop of some kind. Allow several students to describe the plants their families grow and the tools and methods they use to water the crops or the gardens. Display Maps and More 2 and allow several volunteers to guess how the tool works. Explain that this lesson will tell them what this tool is called and how it watered the crops of the ancient Egyptians in an unusual way.

☐ Teaching the Lesson
Rami's Egypt—Instruct the students to read page 24 silently to find out what Rami's job is. *(keeping his father's irrigation canals full of water)* Explain that Rami and his family are fictional characters but that many families like Rami's lived in ancient Egypt.

Discussion Questions
➤ **What details does this story give about how farmers irrigated their crops in ancient Egypt?** *(They used water from the Nile; they used special tools called shadoofs.)*

Display Maps and More 2 again and select a student to describe a shadoof as if to someone who had never seen one before. Explain that a bucket or a bag made from animal skin was lowered into the river, filled with water, lifted and swung around to be emptied into the irrigation canals. Explain that the shadoof is still sometimes used in Egypt today.

➤ **Do you think you would have liked Rami's job? Why or why not?** *(Answers will vary.)*
➤ **How did the ancient Egyptians thresh their grain?** *(They drove the farm animals over the grain on the threshing floor so that the trampling hooves would shake the ripe grain from the stalks.)*
➤ **What clues does the story give about Rami's religious beliefs?** *(He does not worship the true God; he worships many gods.)*

Ancient Egypt and the Nile

Egypt has been called "The Gift of the Nile." Why do you think Egypt was given this name? Without the Nile River, it would not have existed. The great civilization that lasted for more than three thousand years would not have developed. The great pyramids, the Sphinx, and the temples of Egypt would not have been built.

No one knows just when the Egyptians settled along the Nile River. They may have arrived as early as thirty-eight hundred years before the birth of Christ. Imagine how these early travelers to Egypt felt after their long trip. Suddenly, right in front of them flowed a mighty river. What do you think these people thought about the river?

All Egyptians throughout history honored and gave thanks to the Nile. They gave it the nickname *Hapi*, which means "well-fed" or "fat." They worshiped the Nile as a god. The following lines are from the "Hymn to the Nile":

Hail to thee, O Nile, that issues from the earth and comes to keep Egypt alive! . . . The bringer of food, rich in provision, creator of all good, lord of majesty, sweet of fragrance.

25

If you were to fly over Egypt and look out the window of the airplane, you would see desert in all directions. This is the great Sahara, a desert that covers most of North Africa. Soon you would see a thin ribbon of green cutting the desert into two parts. In the middle of that green ribbon would be a silver thread, the mighty Nile River.

The early settlers in Egypt soon discovered that wherever the Nile River flowed, plants grew. Where there was no water, all was desert. At the edge of Egyptian farms like Rami's, a person could stand with one foot in green grass and the other foot in yellow desert sand.

26

The Nile River—Instruct the students to read page 25 silently to learn why Egypt is called "the Gift of the Nile." *(because the Egyptian civilization depended on the Nile for its survival and development)* Ask the students about what year the first Egyptians may have settled along the Nile River. *(3800 B.C.)* Add the figure representing the Early Egyptians to the History TimeLine at the year 3800 B.C. Tell the students that the delta region of the Nile was the most fertile area for farming.

Discussion Questions

➤ **How did the early Egyptians view the Nile?** *(They honored it and gave thanks to it; they worshiped it as a god.)*
➤ **What name was given to the Nile, and what does the name mean?** (Hapi, *meaning "well fed" or "fat"*)
➤ **Name several ways the Nile is described in the "Hymn to the Nile."** *(bringer of food, rich in provision, creator of all good, lord of majesty, sweet of fragrance)*

> Remind the students that God alone, not a river, can be truly described in this way. Allow the students to give other names and descriptions of God from the Bible. (BATs: 7b Exaltation of Christ, 7c Praise; Bible Promise: I. God as Master)

Instruct the students to read page 26 silently to find through which desert the Nile River flows. *(the Sahara)*

Discussion Questions

➤ **If you were to fly over Egypt, which would you see more of, desert or water?** *(desert)*
➤ **What did the early settlers in Egypt discover about the Nile?** *(Wherever its water flowed, plants grew. Where there was no water, all was desert.)*
➤ **Would you like to have lived on the desert's edge so that you could see the dramatic change between the two types of land?** *(Answers will vary.)*

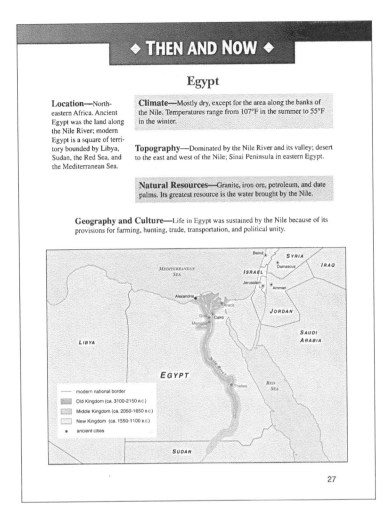

◆ THEN AND NOW ◆

Egypt

Location—Northeastern Africa. Ancient Egypt was the land along the Nile River; modern Egypt is a square of territory bounded by Libya, Sudan, the Red Sea, and the Mediterranean Sea.

Climate—Mostly dry, except for the area along the banks of the Nile. Temperatures range from 107°F in the summer to 55°F in the winter.

Topography—Dominated by the Nile River and its valley; desert to the east and west of the Nile; Sinai Peninsula in eastern Egypt.

Natural Resources—Granite, iron ore, petroleum, and date palms. Its greatest resource is the water brought by the Nile.

Geography and Culture—Life in Egypt was sustained by the Nile because of its provisions for farming, hunting, trade, transportation, and political unity.

— modern national border
▨ Old Kingdom (ca. 3100-2150 B.C.)
▨ Middle Kingdom (ca. 2050-1650 B.C.)
▨ New Kingdom (ca. 1550-1100 B.C.)
• ancient cities

27

Nile Exploration   Name _____

Find the appropriate word to complete each sentence and write the word in the blank.

3,000	fat	irrigation
silo	Sahara Desert	Hapi
transportation	shadoof	hooves
plants	gift	farmers
political	creator	200

shadoof 1. Egyptians used a _____ to draw water from the Nile.

farmers 2. Many ancient Egyptians were _____ by trade.

irrigation 3. Egyptians used water from the Nile for _____ of their crops.

hooves 4. The grain was threshed by the trampling of animals' _____.

gift 5. Egypt is the "_____ of the Nile."

silo 6. After threshing, Egyptians stored their grain in a _____.

Hapi 7. Egyptians named the Nile River "_____."

3,000 8. The first settlers in Egypt may have arrived more than _____ years before Christ.

creator 9. Egyptians thought that the Nile was the _____ of all good.

fat 10. *Hapi* means "_____."

plants 11. Wherever the Nile flows, _____ grow.

Sahara Desert 12. The Nile flows through the _____.

political 13. The Nile River helped Egypt to maintain _____ unity.

transportation 14. The Nile River provided _____ from one part of Egypt to another.

© 1998 BJU Press. Reproduction prohibited.

Heritage Studies 6
Student Notebook

Lesson 7
Evaluating the Lesson   **7**

Then and Now—Instruct the students to read page 27 silently to find several provisions the Nile made for Egypt. *(provisions for farming, hunting, trade, transportation, and political unity)* Direct the students' attention to the Then and Now map, noting ancient cities, changes in boundary lines, and so on.

□ Evaluating the Lesson

Nile Exploration (Notebook page 7)—Instruct the students to find the appropriate word to complete each sentence. Tell them to write the correct word in each blank.

══ Going Beyond ══

□ Enrichment

Hymn writing—Set up an AREA with some hymnbooks. Encourage the students to read the words to several hymns and then to write words for another verse of a hymn of their choice. Remind them that the words of a hymn do not have to rhyme but that the hymn should be worshipful and reverent.

□ Additional Teacher Information

The ancient Egyptians believed the Nile was a gift from the gods. They did not look for its source because they believed that a god poured the waters out for them.

However, many explorers later looked for the Nile's source. Early expeditions encountered obstacles, such as cataracts, rugged mountains, and dense jungles, and they never finished their search. An expedition sent by the Roman emperor Nero was stopped by a huge swamp called the Sudd.

In the sixteenth century, explorers discovered that two rivers joined to form the Nile. In 1602, a Spanish missionary found the source of the smaller of these branches, the Blue Nile, in Lake Tana in Ethiopia.

The larger branch, the White Nile, was more difficult to trace to its source. Finally, in the mid-1800s, an English explorer named John Speke found a huge lake in the mountains of central Africa and named it "Victoria" after the queen of England. He announced to the world that he had discovered the source of the Nile.

Later explorers traced the White Nile even farther into the African interior. In 1937 in the remote country of Burundi, a German discovered a mountain spring that was believed to be the Nile's southernmost headwater. Although many other trickles of water in central Africa contribute to the Nile, a plaque on a small stone pyramid by this spring declares it to be "the Source of the Nile." From that point the great river begins a 4,160-mile journey to the Mediterranean Sea.

LESSON 8
Storehouse of the World

Text, pages 28-30
Notebook, page 8

- **Flooding and Farming**
- **The Delta**
- **Egypt's Prosperity**

Preview

□ Objectives

Given proper instruction, the students will be able to do the following:

- Match activities with the appropriate season from the Egyptian calendar.
- Draw a picture of Rami doing a seasonal activity.

□ Materials

Have available:

- A tray.
- An overhead projector.
- A blank overhead transparency.
- Watermelon slices for each student.*
- Cantaloupe slices for each student.*
- Cucumber slices for each student.*
- A date for each student.*
- A fig for each student.*

Prepare an overhead transparency of the map of the Nile delta. (*NOTE:* See the reproducible material at the end of Lesson 13.)

□ Notes

The various food items in the Materials List may be changed or omitted at your preference. Some other foods of ancient Egypt were wheat, barley, onions, garlic, fish, and waterfowl.

Day 13

Lesson

□ Introducing the Lesson

Egyptian food—Place the food items on a tray and circulate among the students, allowing them to taste each item. Ask them which ones are new to them. Allow several students to tell which of the foods is their favorite and which is their least favorite. Then ask them what they think all of these foods have in common. (*Each was grown in ancient Egypt.*)

Each summer in ancient Egypt, the Nile overflowed its banks. Melting snows in African mountains and heavy spring rains far to the south caused the river to rise dramatically. The water rushed down the mountains and across the flat land of Egypt. Soon everything except the tallest palm trees was under water. The flood lasted for four months. During that time, the water soaked into the land. It also deposited a layer of rich soil on top of the land.

When the land was nearly dry, Egyptian farmers like Rami's father went into their fields. They did not have to plow but simply scattered their seeds onto the damp ground. After that, they walked the farm animals back and forth across the field. The animals' hooves pushed the seeds into the soil.

All that families had to do after that was to water the crops. Remember the shadoof that Rami used? It is a long pole with a weight on one end and a bucket on the other. Rami dipped the bucket into the Nile River, pulled it up, and emptied it into the irrigation canals. It was hard work and had to be done every day until the crops were ready to harvest. If a family had a donkey or an ox, they could use it to turn a water wheel to raise water to the fields. But few could afford such luxuries.

28

□ Teaching the Lesson

Flooding and farming—Instruct the students to read page 28 silently to find out what characteristic of the Nile River made it especially helpful to the land. (*It overflowed its banks every summer.*)

Discussion Questions

➤ **What caused the flooding of the Nile?** (*melting snows in the mountains and heavy spring rains*)

➤ **What was the advantage of the heavy flooding?** (*Water soaked into the land and deposited a layer of rich soil on top of the land.*)

➤ **In what way was planting similar to threshing for the Egyptians?** (*They walked the farm animals back and forth across the fields to push the seeds into the soil.*)

➤ **Where was water raised by the shadoof used?** (*in the irrigation canals*)

➤ **How did wealthy families raise water to their fields?** (*They used a donkey or an ox to turn a water wheel.*)

cucumbers

garlic

figs

pomegranate

onions

dates

Egyptians who lived long before Rami's time built irrigation canals so that they could plant more crops. The strip of fertile land along the Nile River was only about ten miles wide. But it stretched the whole length of the river.

At the north end of the Nile, where it flows into the Mediterranean Sea, the early settlers found a much larger area to farm. The waters of the Nile separated into many smaller rivers and flowed out into a fan shape. This fan shape is called a *delta*. It looks a bit like a flower on a long stem. Egyptians who settled here did not have to worry about water because the land was low and swampy. They grew cucumbers, melons, and date palms.

When everything went well, the people ate very well. They had wheat and barley, melons and cucumbers, onions and garlic, dates and figs. The river supplied them with many kinds of fish and waterfowl. They also raised animals for meat.

29

Egypt was the storehouse of the ancient world. Large harvests allowed Egyptians to store food for times of famine when the Nile River did not rise to soak the land and leave its rich soil behind. Because of their careful planning, the Egyptians usually had more than enough to eat.

Foreigners knew of Egypt's bounty, and many traveled there when in need. As you will soon see, God used Egypt as a temporary place of safety and prosperity for His chosen people.

In this Egyptian wall painting, the colorfully-clad people in the middle band may be Hebrews being presented to the pharaoh.

All of Egypt depended on the Nile River. Government officials kept detailed records of when the river flooded and how high the water rose. They used a device called a *nilometer.* From these measurements, they calculated the taxes the people owed. Egyptians paid taxes according to how good their crops were, and those crops depended on the waters of the Nile.

Because of the importance of the Nile floods, the priests developed a calendar that would tell them the exact days that the Nile was supposed to flood. This calendar had only three seasons: Flood (Akhit), Planting (Perit), and Harvest (Shemu).

30

The delta—Instruct the students to read page 29 silently to discover the dimensions of the strip of fertile land around the Nile. *(about ten miles wide, stretching the whole length of the river)*

Discussion Questions

➤ **Where was the delta region located?** *(at the north end of the Nile where it flows into the Mediterranean Sea)*

➤ **Describe the shape of the delta.** *(like a fan or like a flower on a long stem)*

Display the overhead transparency of the Nile delta. (*NOTE:* See the reproducible material at the end of Lesson 13.) Point out that the Nile separates into smaller rivers at this point. Explain to the students that this land has a low elevation compared to the other land around the Nile. Remind them that the reason this region was so fertile was that every time the Nile flooded, a new layer of rich soil would settle over this region.

➤ **What kinds of crops did the Egyptians grow in the delta?** *(cucumbers, melons, and date palms)*

➤ **What other foods did the people eat?** *(wheat, barley, onions, garlic, figs, fish, waterfowl, meat)*

Egypt's prosperity—Instruct the students to read page 30 silently to find what name is given to Egypt. *(the storehouse of the ancient world)*

Discussion Questions

➤ **What did Egypt's large harvests enable it to do?** *(store food for times of famine)*

➤ **Did Egypt consume all of its own food? If not, what was done with the food?** *(No, the food was shared with foreigners in need.)*

Point out to the students that Egypt's willingness to share its food with foreigners was used by God to provide for His chosen people, Israel, during a famine. Remind them that Christians, too, need to be willing to share what God has given them with people in need. (BAT: 5b Giving)

➤ **What instrument did government officials in Egypt use to measure and record the Nile's flooding?** *(a nilometer)*

➤ **What did these measurements help them to do?** *(calculate the taxes that the people owed)*

➤ **On what basis did the Egyptians pay taxes?** *(according to how good their crops were)*

➤ **Describe the ancient Egyptian calendar.** *(The ancient Egyptian calendar had only three seasons: Flood [Akhit], Planting [Perit], and Harvest [Shemu]. It told the exact days that the Nile was supposed to flood.)*

Rami's Yearly Planner

Name _____

Read the following entries from Rami's yearly planner. In the blank beside each entry, write the name of the season during which he will do that activity: Akhit (Flood), Perit (Planting), or Shemu (Harvest).

Perit	1. Scatter seeds in fields.
Shemu	2. Take grain to family silo.
Akhit	3. Play with brother in deep puddles.
Shemu	4. Celebrate the harvest.
Perit	5. Walk donkey over seeds in fields.
Akhit	6. Rest while the fields are under water.
Perit	7. Empty shadoof into irrigation canals.
Shemu	8. Help the men tie grain into bundles.
Akhit	9. Watch the men measure floodwater with nilometer.
Shemu	10. Help the men drive oxen over the grain at threshing floor.

Now draw a picture of Rami doing one of the above activities.

Heritage Studies 6
Student Notebook

Lesson 8
Evaluating the Lesson   8

□ Evaluating the Lesson

Rami's Yearly Planner (Notebook page 8)—Instruct the students to read each entry from Rami's yearly planner. Tell them to write in the blank beside each entry the name of the calendar season during which Rami will do that activity. Instruct them to draw a picture of Rami doing one of the activities.

Going Beyond

□ Enrichment

Farming today—In an AREA, place a stack of note cards with a different aspect of farming or gardening written on each one (e.g., planting, irrigation, harvesting, threshing, weeding). Allow each student to choose a note card and use reference books or encyclopedias to research modern methods of doing that task, writing on the back of the card a short description of at least one modern method. As time permits, allow the students to tell the class what they found out.

□ Additional Teacher Information

The Aswan High Dam was built in Egypt in the 1960s to control the Nile's flooding. The dam retains a large amount of water in Lake Nasser instead of allowing the water to flow over the land during flooding season as it once did. The water stored in Lake Nasser is used to irrigate the land during the dry seasons, and it also provides electricity for factories and villages. Egypt can now irrigate its land all year around.

But the Aswan High Dam has also brought with it some disadvantages. Because the dam keeps the layer of rich soil from spreading over the land, Egyptian farmers now have to use expensive fertilizers. Parts of the land around the Nile have eroded because of the lack of silt. The dam also causes land drainage problems in some areas. In addition, medical experts have noted an increase in an intestinal and urinary disease called *schistosomiasis,* thought to be carried by the snails of the Nile River. Before the dam was built, these snails died during the dry season. But now the abundance of water in the canals has caused them to thrive year-round.

LESSON 9
Pharaohs, Pyramids, and Papyrus

Text, pages 31-34
Notebook, page 9

- ■ **The Old Kingdom**
- ■ **Mummies and Pyramids**
- ■ **Buildings and Artifacts**

Preview

☐ Objective

Given proper instruction, the students will be able to do the following:
- Complete a word puzzle about ancient Egypt using the clues given.

☐ Materials

Have available:
- Maps and More 3.
- A roll of bathroom tissue for each group of four students.*
- Small prizes for four students.*
- The figure representing Egypt United (3100 B.C.) from the History TimeLine Packet.

☐ Notes

During this lesson, you will work with Heritage Studies partners for the first time. As mentioned in the Supplement, you will want to assign Heritage Studies partners who will work together for group activities. This idea will help organize the class quickly into even-numbered groups of students no matter where they are sitting in the room. Also, as mentioned in the Supplement, you may want to change the members in each group from time to time.

Old sheets may be torn into strips and used in place of bathroom tissue if this is more convenient.

Day 14

Lesson

☐ Introducing the Lesson

Making mummies—Display Maps and More 3 and ask the students what the figure is called. *(a mummy)* Point out the way the mummy is carefully wrapped in linen bandages. Instruct the students to get with their Heritage Studies partners and to join with another set of partners to form groups of four. Give each group a roll of bathroom tissue and tell them to decide which student will be the mummy. Tell them that at your signal, the embalmers should completely wrap

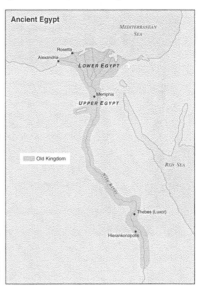

Old Kingdom (ca. 3100-2150 B.C.)

In the first centuries after the early settlers came, Egypt was divided into two kingdoms. The area around the Nile delta was called the Lower Kingdom, and the area along the rest of the river was the Upper Kingdom.

About the year 3100 B.C., the ruler of the city Hierankonopolis conquered all of the villages and cities along the Nile River. His name was Narmer. Do you think this sounds like a royal name? It really means "catfish." Narmer was the first king, or pharaoh, of a united Egypt. Historians call this the Old Kingdom of Egypt. Although Egypt was one kingdom, people still recognized Lower and Upper Egypt as two separate geographical regions.

31

the mummies in the tissue. Give a prize to the group that finishes first.

☐ Teaching the Lesson

Old Kingdom—Instruct the students to read page 31 silently to learn the names of the two divisions of Egypt. *(Lower Kingdom and Upper Kingdom)*

Discussion Questions
- ➤ **What particular region of Egypt was called the Lower Kingdom?** *(the area around the Nile delta)*
- ➤ **What region was called the Upper Kingdom?** *(the area along the rest of the Nile River)*

Direct the students' attention to these two divisions on the map on page 31. Instruct them to find the city of Memphis in Lower Egypt and the city of Thebes in Upper Egypt. Explain that these were the most important cities in each kingdom.
- ➤ **What event around 3100 B.C. caused the two kingdoms to be united?** *(Narmer conquered all of the villages and cities along the Nile River.)*

Making Mummies and Pyramids

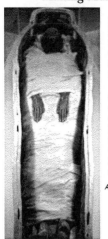

Although the Egyptians did not believe in the true God, they were firm believers in life after death. They believed that without a body, a person could not exist in the next world. Immediately after a person died, his family paid an *embalmer* to preserve his body.

Dressed in the jackal-headed costume of the embalming god, Anubis, the embalmer cleaned out the body's skull and abdominal cavities and filled them with spices. The body was then soaked for seventy days in a salt solution called *natron*. Afterward, it was washed and wrapped in linen bandages. Bodies preserved in this way were called *mummies*.

An Egyptian mummy

Cross-section of the Great Pyramid at Giza

The embalmer returned the preserved mummy to the family for burial. If the family was wealthy enough, they purchased several coffins that fit one inside another in which to place the mummy. The coffins were made of metal, wood, and stone.

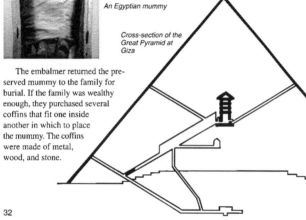

32

The Egyptian pharaoh was a man of great power. During the Old Kingdom, Egyptians began to believe that the pharaoh was a god. Pharaohs had large burial chambers built and filled with food, clothing, furniture, and even games and toys. The pharaohs thought that they would need these things to bring them pleasure and ease in the next life. They thought that small statues of gods placed in the tombs would act as servants and that scenes of daily life painted on the walls would make them feel at home. All other Egyptians who could afford to do so followed this practice.

The most famous of these tombs are Khufu's three pyramids at Giza. Khufu had the largest of these pyramids, the Great Pyramid, built around 2500 B.C. It covers 13 acres and measures about 756 feet on each side. The house you live in would fit inside it, along with several of your neighbors' houses.

Khufu also ordered the building of the Sphinx, a large stone statue near the pyramids. He is said to have seen a huge rock while working on his pyramid and thought that it looked like a lion lying in the desert. He had his workers finish the sculpture and make the lion's head look like him.

The Sphinx and the Great Pyramid at Giza

33

Add the figure representing Egypt United to the History TimeLine at 3100 B.C.

➤ **What does Narmer's name mean?** *(catfish)*
➤ **What title was Narmer given?** *(king or pharaoh)*
➤ **What do historians call this period of a united Egypt?** *(the Old Kingdom)*

Mummies and pyramids—Instruct the students to read page 32 silently to find out what the Egyptians believed about life after death. *(They believed that a person traveled to another world after death but that he could not exist in that world without a body.)*

Discussion Questions

➤ **What did the family of a dead person do to ensure that their loved one would have a body in the next world?** *(They paid an embalmer to preserve the dead body.)*
➤ **What did the embalmer wear while he did his job?** *(the jackal-headed costume of Anubis, the embalming god)*
➤ **Describe the process of embalming.** *(The embalmer cleaned out the body's skull and abdominal cavities and filled them with spices. Then the body was soaked for seventy days in a salt solution after which it was washed and wrapped in linen bandages.)*
➤ **What was the preserved body called?** *(a mummy)*
➤ **How did wealthy families bury their dead?** *(They purchased several coffins that fit one inside another in which to place the mummy.)*

Point out that the Bible teaches that Christians will be given new, glorified bodies in heaven after death. (Phil. 3:20-21). Choose a volunteer to explain how a person can be sure he will go to heaven after death and receive this new body. (BATs: 1b Repentance and faith, 8a Faith in God's promises)

Day 15

Instruct the students to read page 33 silently to learn what the ancient Egyptians believed about the pharaoh. *(that he was a god)*

Discussion Questions

➤ **What kinds of things were placed in the tombs of the pharaohs?** *(food, clothing, furniture, games, toys, and small statues of gods)*
➤ **Why did the Egyptians put these things into their tombs?** *(They thought that they would need them to bring pleasure and ease in the next life. They thought the statues would act as servants for them.)*
➤ **What items bring you pleasure and make life easier?** *(Answers will vary.)*

The pharaohs built other things besides pyramids. In the cities of Memphis and Thebes, they constructed beautiful palaces, storehouses, and many temples to their gods. The pharaohs' slaves dug irrigation canals for the farmers along the Nile so that new fields could be planted. The canals also helped control the floodwaters of the Nile.

Much of our information about the Old Kingdom comes from artifacts left behind by the Egyptians. The largest artifacts are the great pyramids and the Sphinx. The colorful paintings inside the pyramids tell us a great deal about the daily life of Egyptians in the Old Kingdom. What other artifacts might have been left behind by these early Egyptians?

Papyrus is the most important artifact. It is a paper made from the stalk of the papyrus plant, a reed that grows along the banks of the Nile. This paper was light and thin and could be stored easily. The Egyptians used it for thousands of years to keep records, write letters, and tell stories. When the apostle Paul dictated his letter to the Romans, his scribe, Tertius, probably wrote on a scroll of papyrus. People of Europe continued using papyrus until the Middle Ages.

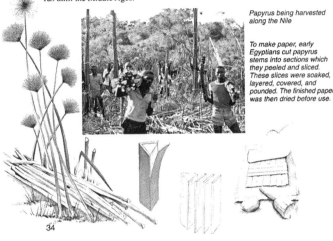

Papyrus being harvested along the Nile

To make paper, early Egyptians cut papyrus stems into sections which they peeled and sliced. These slices were soaked, layered, covered, and pounded. The finished paper was then dried before use.

34

Fill in the blanks using the clues given. When you are finished, the boxed letters will spell a word that applies to pyramids and papyrus.

1. H I E R A N K O N O P O L I S
2. N A T R O N
3. T E R T I U S
4. S P H I N X
5. K H U F U
6. E M B A L M E R
7. J A C K A L
8. T W O
9. S T A T U E S

1. Narmer's city
2. mummy-preserving solution
3. a scribe who wrote on papyrus
4. lion with a pharaoh's head
5. pyramid builder
6. a person who made mummies
7. Anubis had the head of this animal.
8. the number of geographical regions in Egypt
9. placed in tombs to act as "servants"

Hidden Word: _____ **artifacts**

Heritage Studies 6
Student Notebook   Lesson 9
Evaluating the Lesson   **9**

Remind the students that riches are only temporary and that we cannot take them with us after we die. Read Matthew 6:20 and Colossians 3:2, pointing out that these verses exhort Christians to lay up treasures in heaven and to set their affections on things above. (BAT: 7d Contentment)

➤ **Who built the largest pyramid and where is it located?** *(Khufu; located at Giza)*

Explain that Khufu was a pharaoh during the Old Kingdom of Egypt. He is recorded as being selfish and tyrannical during his reign, but the monuments he left behind are magnificent.

➤ **What are the dimensions of the largest pyramid?** *(covers 13 acres and measures about 756 feet on each side)*
➤ **How did Khufu get the idea to build the Sphinx?** *(He is said to have seen a huge rock and thought it looked like a lion lying in the desert. He had his workers finish the sculpture, making the lion's head look like his.)*

Buildings and artifacts—Instruct the students to read page 34 silently to find in which cities the pharaohs built most of their buildings. *(Memphis and Thebes)*

Discussion Questions

➤ **Name several items the pharaohs and their slaves constructed.** *(palaces, storehouses, temples, irrigation canals)*

➤ **From what does much of our information about the Old Kingdom of Egypt come?** *(from artifacts)*
➤ **What particular artifacts tell us a great deal about the daily life of the ancient Egyptians?** *(the colorful paintings inside the pyramids)*
➤ **What is *papyrus*?** *(paper made from the stalk of the papyrus reed)*
➤ **What were some advantages of this type of paper?** *(It was light and thin and could be stored easily.)*
➤ **What kinds of documents were written on papyrus?** *(letters, records, stories)*
➤ **What other artifacts might the Egyptians have left behind?** *(Answers will vary.)*

□ Evaluating the Lesson

Word Sculpture (Notebook page 9)—Instruct the students to fill in the blanks, using the clues given. When they are finished, the boxed letters will spell a word that applies to pyramids and papyrus. *(artifacts)*

═══ Going Beyond ═══

□ Enrichment

Papyrus scrolls—Set up an AREA with thin parchment paper; felt-tip pens or calligraphy pens; dowel rods or unsharpened, round pencils; and glue. Encourage each student to design his own papyrus scroll by gluing the ends of the paper to the dowel rods or pencils so that the scroll rolls up. Tell each student to write on the scroll something important that he would want people to read if they were to find it. Suggest that the students write their favorite Bible verse or a personal testimony. If time allows, let the students hide their scrolls around the classroom and at a later time, direct a search for the hidden scrolls with all the students participating.

□ Additional Teacher Information

The Great Pyramid is made of 2.3 million blocks. The average weight of each block is 2.5 tons. Workmen cut the blocks from quarries up the Nile, moved them to the river, rafted them downstream, and dragged them from the Nile to the work site. The only known tools that they used to cut, move, and position the blocks were copper saws, rollers, sleds, ramps, and wooden levers. But they built the pyramid with great precision. The corners of the Great Pyramid point almost exactly to the four compass points. This pyramid is the largest building in the world.

We get information about daily life in ancient Egypt both from art and from papyrus records. Making the papyrus plant into paper took time and skill. First, workers gathered the papyrus reeds, and then the paper makers peeled the bark off the stem and cut the stem into very thin strips, about a foot long and an inch wide. The strips were placed side by side on a cloth. Another row of papyrus strips was placed on top of the first layer, running the opposite way.

The Egyptians then wet the papyrus strips with water, covered them with a cloth, and pounded them with a mallet to bind their fibers. The newly made sheets were laid out in the sun to dry. Later, the paper makers smoothed the surface of the papyrus with a stone or shell. Finally, they joined the sheets together with glue and rolled them into a scroll.

The Egyptians used the papyrus plant for more than just writing paper. They burned the thick roots of the plants as fuel or carved them into tools or containers. They wove the fibers of the plants into ropes, sails, and blankets. They even made chewing gum out of part of the plant. Sometimes they built boats by weaving papyrus strips together. The "ark of bulrushes" in which Moses' mother hid him (Exod. 2:3) may have been made of papyrus.

LESSON 10
Ancient Symbols and Secrets

Text, pages 35-37
Notebook, page 10

- **The Rosetta Stone**
- **Drawing and Reading Hieroglyphics**
- **The Middle Kingdom**

━━━━ Preview ━━━━

□ Objective
Given proper instruction, the students will be able to do the following:
- Write a journal entry from the perspective of the person who discovered the Rosetta stone.

□ Materials
Have available:
- A sheet of notebook paper for each student.
- Maps and More 4.
- The figure of the Rosetta stone (A.D. 1799) from the History TimeLine Packet.

Day 16

━━━━ Lesson ━━━━

□ Introducing the Lesson
Hieroglyphic word race—Display Maps and More 4. Explain that in ancient Egypt, pictures, rather than letters, represented different sounds. Some pictures could be used to represent more than one sound.

After giving the students a few moments to study the hieroglyphic alphabet (Maps and More 4), divide the class into two teams. Choose one student on each team to come to the chalkboard. Quietly tell these students the same word (e.g., *pyramid*), instructing them that when you give the signal, they are to write out the word on the chalkboard as fast as they can, using pictures from the hieroglyphic alphabet. Instruct their teammates to raise their hands as soon as they know the word. Call on each volunteer to guess the word. The first team to guess the correct word wins that round of the word race. Continue the game, using words such as *mummy, Nile, shadoof, flood,* and *artifact,* until each student has had a chance to draw. Keep track of the scores of each team and leave the alphabet on display for reference throughout the game.

Point out to the students that without the translation of the alphabet on Maps and More 4, they could not have

The Rosetta Stone
Egyptian writing is called *hieroglyphics,* or picture writing. People drew pictures of the ideas they wanted to express. This kind of writing was used from 3100 B.C. to A.D. 1100— longer than any other kind in the world.

For many centuries after the Egyptian civilization declined, no one could read hieroglyphs. In 1799, a large, black stone was found in the sand of the Nile delta. The message carved on the stone was written in two important languages. One of them was Egyptian hieroglyphs. The other was Greek, a language read by many educated Europeans.

The Rosetta stone

Have you ever tried to decipher a coded message? To break the code, you have to compare it to a language that is familiar to you. A Frenchman named Jean Champollion worked many years to decipher the hieroglyphs by comparing them with the Greek. Finally, in 1822, he succeeded. People interested in Egypt could now read letters and books over four thousand years old.

Modern restorers at work repairing and preserving hieroglyphics in the tomb of Queen Nefertari, wife of Rameses II

35

figured out the code. Explain that in this lesson they will learn how the secret code of hieroglyphics was broken after thousands of years.

Day 17

□ Teaching the Lesson
The Rosetta stone—Add the figure of the Rosetta stone to the History TimeLine at the year A.D. 1799. Instruct the students to read page 35 silently to find out what happened in this year. *(The Rosetta stone was found.)*

Discussion Questions
➤ **What was Egyptian writing called, and what did it look like?** *(It was called hieroglyphics; it used pictures to express ideas.)*
➤ **Where was the Rosetta stone found?** *(in the sand of the Nile delta)*
➤ **In what two important languages was the message on the stone written?** *(Egyptian hieroglyphs and Greek)*

Explain that the message on the Rosetta stone was actually written three times. It included another type of writing called *demotic* writing, the popular language of Egypt during the centuries before Christ's birth. This language, however, was not important to Champollion's deciphering of the hieroglyphs.
➤ **Why was the Rosetta stone such an important discovery?** *(Because many people could read Greek, the hieroglyphs could be deciphered for the first time.)*

➤ **Who decoded the hieroglyphs on the Rosetta stone?** *(Jean Champollion)*

➤ **How many years after the stone was found did he complete his translation work and publish it?** *(twenty-three years later, in 1822)*

> Point out that Jean Champollion worked patiently for many years before finally decoding the Rosetta stone's message. Encourage the students to be diligent in their work at home and at school and never to give up on a task that the Lord has given them. (BATs: 2c Faithfulness, 2e Work)

Drawing and reading hieroglyphics—Direct a *Discovering How* activity on page 36. Read aloud Step 1. Direct the Heritage Studies partners to form teams of four. Give them time to work together to make up a hieroglyphic alphabet. Instruct them to write the letters *A-Z* and then to draw a picture beneath each letter.

When each team has finished making the hieroglyphic alphabet, read Steps 2 and 3 aloud and allow time for each team to write a team message and its English translation.

Read Step 4 aloud, giving time for the teams to exchange messages and to try to decipher the codes. When all the teams have finished, allow a member of each team to read aloud the message they decoded.

The Middle Kingdom—Instruct the students to read page 37 silently to learn how long the Old Kingdom of Egypt lasted. *(over nine hundred years)*

Discussion Questions

➤ **Who finally reunited Egypt after more than a century of fighting?** *(Amenemnes of Thebes)*

➤ **In what ways did he help Egypt?** *(He set up a new system of government, built a wall to protect his people from invasion, encouraged trade up and down the Nile, and conquered part of Sudan.)*

➤ **What kinds of structures did the pharaohs of the Middle Kingdom build?** *(temples, small pyramids, forts, palaces, and tombs)*

Imagine that you are the engineer who discovered the Rosetta stone while digging in the mud near Alexandria, Egypt. Write a journal entry describing your experience.

□ Evaluating the Lesson

Journal Entry (Notebook page 10)—Instruct each student to imagine that he is the engineer who discovered the Rosetta stone in the mud near Alexandria, Egypt. Tell each student to write a journal entry about his experience.

Going Beyond

□ Enrichment

Creating cartouches—In an AREA, display pictures and photographs of *cartouches,* groups of Egyptian hieroglyphs which represented names of individuals enclosed in oval rings. Encourage each student to create a cartouche for his own name, using symbols that represent things they like to do or personality traits that they have. Display the cartouches on the classroom wall and allow the students to guess who created each one.

□ Additional Teacher Information

The message on the Rosetta stone is a decree to commemorate the coronation of an Egyptian king, Ptolemy V Epiphanes. Ptolemy was king of Egypt from 203 to 181 B.C. The black basalt stone is 3 feet 9 inches long, 2 feet 4½ inches wide, and nearly 11 inches thick. Today, the Rosetta stone is on display in the British Museum in London.

LESSON 11
Hebrews and Hyksos

Text, pages 38-41
Notebook, page 11

- Joseph
- Rewards
- The Hyksos
- The New Kingdom

═══ Preview ═══

☐ Objectives
Given proper instruction, the students will be able to do the following:
- Associate specific words with either Joseph or Moses.
- Answer questions about Joseph and Moses.

☐ Materials
Have available:
- A Bible for each student.
- The figure of Joseph (1897 B.C.) from the History Time-Line Packet.

Day 18

═══ Lesson ═══

☐ Introducing the Lesson
Bible drill—For this drill, use the following Scripture references: Genesis 13:1, Genesis 15:18, Genesis 45:8, Exodus 3:20, Exodus 12:51, II Kings 18:21, Isaiah 19:21, Joel 3:19, Matthew 2:13, and Revelation 11:8. Instruct the students to keep their Bibles closed on their desks as you read a Scripture reference. Tell them that after you read each reference and give the signal "Go!" they are to find the reference in their Bibles as quickly as possible. Instruct them to stand when they have found the passage and allow the first person who stands to read it aloud. When you have finished the drill, ask them what word all of the passages have in common. *(Egypt)* Point out that the land of Egypt figured prominently in the events of the Bible. Explain that in this lesson, the students will discover how two very familiar biblical events fit into their study of ancient Egypt.

◄▓ IN THE BIBLE ▓►

Joseph (Genesis 37-50)
Sold to merchants by his jealous brothers, Joseph was taken to Egypt around 1897 B.C., during the reign of Sesostris II. He was bought as a slave by Potiphar, the captain of the pharaoh's guard.

Joseph had already made up his mind that, no matter where he was, he would serve God. Potiphar soon trusted his new slave with all he owned. One day Potiphar's wife told a lie about Joseph because she wanted to get even with him. Potiphar believed his wife and put Joseph into prison.

But even there, God blessed Joseph for his faithfulness. When the keeper of the prison discovered that he could trust Joseph, he put him in charge of the prison. During this time, Pharaoh Sesostris II learned that Joseph could interpret dreams, and he told him his dream of starving cows and withered ears of corn. Joseph explained to the pharaoh that this dream

38

☐ Teaching the Lesson
Joseph—Instruct the students to read page 38 and the first two lines of page 39 silently to find out what year Joseph arrived in Egypt. *(around 1897 B.C.)*

Add the figure of Joseph to the History TimeLine at 1897 B.C.

Discussion Questions
➤ **Who was the pharaoh at this time in Egypt?** *(Sesostris II)*
➤ **Who bought Joseph as a slave?** *(Potiphar, the captain of the pharaoh's guard)*
➤ **What decision had Joseph already made when he arrived in Egypt?** *(that no matter where he was, he would serve God)*
➤ **What difficult thing happened to Joseph while he was serving Potiphar?** *(Potiphar's wife lied about Joseph, and Potiphar put Joseph in prison.)*
➤ **How might Joseph have been tempted to respond to this treatment?** *(Answers will vary but may include that he might have become bitter and angry.)*
➤ **How did he respond, and how was he rewarded?** *(He remained faithful to God in prison, and the prison keeper put him in charge of the prison.)*
➤ **What did Joseph do to help Sesostris II?** *(He interpreted his dream.)*

was God's message about a famine that would last for seven years but that Sesostris II would have seven years of good harvests to save food and prepare.

How do you think Sesostris felt about Joseph now? Sesostris was so grateful to be able to understand his dream that he gave Joseph his royal ring and made him the *vizier*, or the second highest official in government. Joseph saved one-fifth of all the crops for the next seven years to prepare for the famine. He also collected taxes and served as Egypt's chief judge.

When the famine years came, the Egyptians went to Joseph to buy food. He opened the storehouses. There was enough for everyone. In Canaan, Jacob's family also suffered from the famine. He sent his sons to Egypt to purchase food.

When Joseph saw the strangers from Canaan, he recognized his brothers. He forgave them and gave them food. Soon after, Jacob moved his family to Egypt. They settled in the land of Goshen near the Nile delta.

39

The last years of the Middle Kingdom were not peaceful. The pharaohs were more interested in riches than in ruling. They did not strengthen the borders of Egypt or keep the walls repaired. A people called the *Hyksos* invaded Egypt. They attacked the cities and countryside and took whatever they wanted. The Egyptian army could not stop them because the Hyksos had a new weapon: the horse-drawn chariot.

In 1630 B.C., the Hyksos conquered Egypt and made Avaris their capital city. They tried to live and rule like the pharaohs. They even worshiped Egyptian gods. They dressed in Egyptian clothes, lived in Egyptian houses, and ate Egyptian food.

The Hebrews, the descendants of Joseph and his brothers, held important positions in Egypt at this time. The Hyksos feared that the Hebrews might become powerful enough to take over the government. To keep this from happening, the Hyksos forced the Hebrews into slavery. They made the Hebrews farm their fields, build cities for them, and make all the bricks for the buildings.

Finally, Ahmose, an Egyptian prince of Thebes, raised an army. He attacked the Hyksos, captured their capital city, and drove them out of the land. Egypt was once again united, but Ahmose did not free the Hebrews.

A North African man using a brick-making process similar to that used by Hebrew slaves in ancient Egypt

An Egyptian-style illustration of slaves making bricks

40

Day 19

Rewards—Instruct the students to read the rest of page 39 silently to find out what Sesostris did to reward Joseph for his help. *(He gave him his royal ring and made him vizier of Egypt.)*

Discussion Questions

➤ **What did Joseph do to prepare for Egypt's famine?** *(He saved one-fifth of all the crops for the next seven years.)*

➤ **What other duties did he have?** *(He collected taxes and served as Egypt's chief judge.)*

➤ **Who came to buy food from Joseph during the famine?** *(his brothers)*

➤ **How might he have been tempted to treat them?** *(Answers will vary but may include that he could have refused to give them food or treated them rudely to punish them for selling him as a slave.)*

➤ **How did Joseph respond to his brothers?** *(He forgave them and gave them food.)*

Point out that Joseph's responses to his trials are good examples for Christians to follow when the Lord takes them through difficult experiences. Joseph was kind and forgiving toward those who had wronged and hurt him. He remained faithful to God through all of his trials. (BATs: 2c Faithfulness, 5a Love, 6e Forgiveness)

The Hyksos—Instruct the students to read page 40 silently to learn what new weapon the Hyksos used to attack Egypt. *(the horse-drawn chariot)*

Discussion Questions

➤ **What circumstances in Egypt made it easy for the Hyksos to conquer it?** *(The pharaohs did not strengthen Egypt's borders or keep its walls repaired.)*

➤ **What city became the new capital during the reign of the Hyksos?** *(Avaris)*

➤ **In what ways were the Hyksos pharaohs similar to the Egyptian pharaohs?** *(They ruled like the Egyptians had, worshiped Egyptian gods, wore Egyptian clothes, ate Egyptian food, and lived in Egyptian houses.)*

➤ **How do you think the Egyptians felt about the Hyksos?** *(Answers will vary.)*

Explain that the Hyksos were from an area northeast of Egypt. The Hyksos' name meant "peoples of the uplands" or "chieftains of foreign countries."

➤ **What people did the Hyksos fear and why?** *(the Hebrews; because the Hebrews held important positions in the land)*

➤ **What did the Hyksos do to keep the Hebrews from becoming too powerful?** *(forced the Hebrews into slavery)*

➤ **What did the Hebrew slaves have to do?** *(farm fields, build cities, and make all the bricks for the buildings)*

➤ **Who finally conquered the Hyksos?** *(Ahmose)*

➤ **What did Ahmose do about the slaves?** *(Nothing; he did not free them.)*

New Kingdom (ca. 1550-1100 B.C.)

In 1550 B.C., Ahmose became the first pharaoh of the New Kingdom. He and his successors made Egypt mightier than it had ever been. They used the horse-drawn chariot to invade Palestine and Syria. Egypt's empire soon stretched all the way to the upper Euphrates River. The people of southern Egypt traded with the Sudan for gold and ivory. It was the greatest period of Egyptian history, but the Egyptians kept the Hebrew people enslaved.

It was during the New Kingdom, probably under Amenhotep II's reign, that God raised up Moses to free His chosen people from slavery in Egypt. Moses, a Hebrew child, was given the privilege of being brought up in the pharaoh's household. He learned to read and write and studied history, arithmetic, and science. As an adult, Moses left Egypt and became a shepherd in Midian.

From a burning bush in the desert, the Lord called Moses to return to Egypt and lead the Hebrews to freedom. Moses went before Amenhotep II to ask him to free the slaves. When Amenhotep refused, God sent a series of ten plagues on the Egyptians. After the last plague, when all the first-born sons of the Egyptians were dead, Amenhotep finally agreed to let the Hebrews go.

A few days later, after the Hebrews had left, Amenhotep changed his mind again. He chased the Hebrews with six hundred chariots and an army of men, but the Lord protected His chosen ones. He destroyed all of Amenhotep's army in the waters of the Red Sea.

41

Hebrews in Egypt   Name _____

Draw a line to match each word in the list with either Joseph or Moses.

Joseph   Moses

1800s B.C.
1500s B.C.
Amenhotep II
Sesostris II
slave
adopted son
chief judge
shepherd
vizier
prisoner
before the Hyksos
after the Hyksos
educated
interpreted dreams
freed his people
fed his people

© 1998 BJU Press. Reproduction prohibited.

Name four ways in which God blessed Joseph for his faithfulness.   *Possible answers include the following: he was made keeper of the prison, a vizier, and Egypt's chief judge. He helped prepare Egypt for famine by collecting food in storehouses. (See Genesis 37-50 for additional answers.)*

Name three miracles God did through Moses.   *Possible answers include changing the rod to a serpent, making water flow out of the rock, speaking through the burning bush, and parting the Red Sea. (See Exodus for additional answers.)*

Heritage Studies 6
Student Notebook

Lesson 11
Evaluating the Lesson   **11**

The New Kingdom—Instruct the students to read page 41 silently to find out how Egypt prospered during the New Kingdom. *(Egypt invaded Palestine and Syria and stretched its empire all the way to the upper Euphrates River. Egypt traded with the Sudan for gold and ivory.)*

Discussion Questions

➤ **What important event for the Hebrew people occurred during the New Kingdom?** *(They were freed from slavery.)*

➤ **Whom did God raise up to free His people from slavery?** *(Moses)*

➤ **What happened early in Moses's life to prepare him for his task?** *(He was brought up and educated in the pharaoh's household.)*

➤ **Where was Moses when God called him?** *(in Midian at a burning bush in the desert)*

➤ **Whose permission did Moses have to receive to free the slaves?** *(Amenhotep II's)*

➤ **What finally convinced Amenhotep to let the Hebrews go?** *(the tenth plague)*

➤ **What finally happened to Amenhotep?** *(He changed his mind and chased the Hebrews with his men and his chariots, but God destroyed all of Amenhotep's army in the Red Sea.)*

□ Evaluating the Lesson

Hebrews in Egypt (Notebook page 11)—Instruct the students to draw a line to match each word in the list with either Joseph or Moses. Then instruct them to answer the questions at the bottom of the page.

⬛ Going Beyond ⬛

□ Enrichment

Copying Egyptian dress—Set up an AREA with large pieces of felt, glue, safety pins, gold braid, small plastic beads or jewels, and cardboard circles in various sizes to use as tracing patterns. Encourage the students to copy Egyptian fashions by making decorative collars or bracelets for themselves as the Hyksos did.

□ Additional Teacher Information

The Hyksos came from Palestine and nearby regions. After the Babylonian Empire dissolved around 1700 B.C., Hittites and Hurrians invaded the land and forced the Hyksos down into Egypt. They ruled only northern Egypt, while native Egyptian pharaohs continued to rule from Thebes in the south. The Theban pharaohs struggled to drive the Hyksos from Egypt and finally expelled them in 1565 B.C.

The Hyksos were the first to bring horses into Egypt. Horse-drawn chariots soon became popular among the Egyptians rich enough to afford them. With the help of swift chariots, hunting for ostriches and gazelles became a favorite sport. The Hyksos also brought new weapons of bronze into Egypt. Before this time, Egyptians had used copper weapons, which were not as sturdy.

LESSON 12
Relics and Rituals

Text, pages 42-45
Notebook, page 12

- **Tutankhamen's Treasure**
- **Rameses II**
- **Religion in Ancient Egypt**

—— Preview ——

□ Objective
Given proper instruction, the students will be able to do the following:
- Determine whether sentences about Egypt are true or false.

□ Notes
The board game Find the Pharaoh is introduced in the Enrichment section. (*NOTE:* See the reproducible material at the end of Lesson 13.) If you choose to use the game, take the following steps to prepare the game pieces.

First, to assemble the **game board,** make one copy of each game board sheet and affix the copies side by side to the inside of a manila file folder. (*NOTE:* You may need to trim the inside edges to make the paths line up.) You may want to add color with colored pencils or felt-tip pens before laminating the boards.

Next, make one copy of the **game cards** (front and back) and affix them to stiff backing, such as tagboard. After laminating them, cut the cards apart.

Finally, make one copy of the **spinner** sheet. Affix the copy to a stiff backing. After laminating it, cut out the numbered dial and the arrow. Place the end of the arrow over the center of the numbered dial. Add an adhesive paper reinforcement to the arrow for extra durability around the hole and then push the brad through to assemble the spinner. To let the arrow spin freely, bend the prongs of the brad approximately $\frac{1}{8}$" from the head. Tape the prongs to the back of the dial to keep the brad from spinning with the arrow. For additional spinning ease, bend the dial slightly away from the arrow. The dial will curve downward, and the arrow will spin freely.

Put the spinner, game cards, and game markers (eight buttons of different colors) in a resealable plastic bag or an envelope. Attach the bag or envelope to the back of the game board folder.

—— Lesson ——

□ Introducing the Lesson
The child king—Instruct the students to listen as you read aloud the following story.

The boy sat on the large golden chair, his feet dangling just above the floor. Nearby, a servant waved an ostrich feather fan, keeping a steady rhythm. On the boy's head was the red-and-white crown of United Egypt. It was heavy and made him want to droop his chin a little. But Amthose, his chief adviser, had said, "With all due respect, my lord, you must hold your head high as becomes the dignity and honor of your office."

The boy stole a sideways glance at Amthose, seated beside him. Then he lifted his chin and stifled a yawn. At a cue from Amthose, he extended his scepter to the gray-haired man who bowed before the throne.

The man rose slowly, keeping his head bowed. "Your majesty," he began, "I have an important matter to bring before you for your decree. Rains have been plentiful during this growing season, and the delta farmers have produced a harvest of exceptional bounty. The people are in need of funds for building more storehouses. . . ."

The boy's gaze moved to the open palace door, and his mind wandered. He knew he did not really have to listen to such matters of business. Amthose and his other advisers would take care of them. His presence in the court was just a formality.

Besides, there were more interesting things to think about today. He had been given a new chariot and a swift black horse, and one of his servants had promised to take him for a ride this very afternoon. He could almost imagine the sounds of the wind whistling past his ears and the horse's hooves thundering over the earth. He loved chariot rides. The only part he did not like was seeing the other boys playing games by the roadside. The sight of them always made him wish—just for a moment—that he did not have to be a king.

Discussion Questions
➤ **What is the setting of this story?** *(the palace of Egypt)*
➤ **What is the boy-king doing?** *(listening to matters of business about his kingdom)*
➤ **What does he wish he were doing?** *(riding in his new chariot; playing games)*
➤ **How do you think the boy feels about being king?** *(Answers will vary.)*

Tutankhamen (ca. 1358-1339 B.C.)

Would you like to be the ruler of a kingdom at the age you are now? What kinds of decisions would you have to make? Whom would you consult for advice?

Tutankhamen was only about ten years old when he became pharaoh of Egypt. He died when he was only nineteen. He did not do anything of importance during his short reign. The world would not have paid him any attention at all, except that his tomb was discovered intact on November 4, 1922, by British archaeologist Howard Carter.

Inside King Tut's tomb, Carter found wonderful treasure. It took him over eight years to catalog all the statues, furniture, toys, pottery, and precious objects he found. Because King Tut's tomb was found, we now know a great deal about how the pharaohs lived and died.

42

Rameses II was one of the last pharaohs who kept the empire strong. He defeated the Hittites, a warrior people from Asia Minor. He also built some of the greatest temples in Egypt. Karnak is the most famous. Rameses also had many colossal statues made of himself.

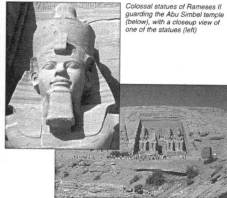

Colossal statues of Rameses II guarding the Abu Simbel temple (below), with a closeup view of one of the statues (left)

Statue of Rameses II

Rameses II deserves to be called great. He was a great warrior. He worked hard at being a wise and good pharaoh, and he was kind to his subjects. When he died, he was buried in a beautiful tomb. Although this tomb was broken into by grave robbers, Rameses II's mummy was not destroyed. Today it is in the Cairo Museum.

After the death of Rameses II around 1213 B.C., Egypt grew weaker. The pharaohs were not able to protect the empire from invaders. Barely two hundred years after Rameses's death, people from the west invaded Egypt. From then on, Egyptians were ruled by foreigners until the twentieth century, when the modern state of Egypt was formed.

43

□ Teaching the Lesson

Tutankhamen's treasure—Instruct the students to read page 42 silently to find out about how old King Tut was when he became pharaoh of Egypt. *(ten)*

Discussion Questions

➤ **Why do we remember King Tut today?** *(His tomb was discovered intact, and a great deal of treasure was found inside.)*

➤ **In what year was the tomb discovered and by whom?** *(in 1922 by Howard Carter, a British archaeologist)*

➤ **Name some items found in King Tut's tomb.** *(statues, furniture, toys, pottery)*

➤ **How was the finding of King Tut's tomb beneficial to the world?** *(It taught us a great deal about how the pharaohs lived and died.)*

➤ **Would you like to have been a king or a queen at the age of ten?** *(Answers will vary.)*

Rameses II—Instruct the students to read page 43 silently to find out what people Rameses conquered. *(the Hittites)*

Discussion Questions

➤ **What did Rameses build?** *(temples and statues of himself)*

➤ **What is his most famous temple?** *(Karnak)*

➤ **Why does Rameses deserve to be called great?** *(He was a great warrior, a wise and good pharaoh, and kind to his subjects.)*

➤ **What do you think the Egyptian people thought of Rameses?** *(Answers will vary; probably many liked him.)*

➤ **What happened to Rameses' tomb?** *(Grave robbers broke into it and stole most of its valuables.)*

➤ **What item from Rameses' tomb still exists today?** *(his mummy)*

➤ **What happened to Egypt after the death of Rameses?** *(Egypt grew weaker and eventually fell to invaders.)*

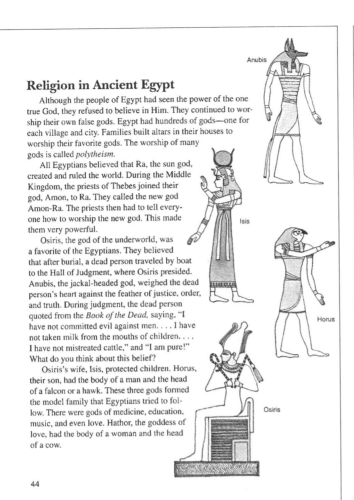

Religion in Ancient Egypt

Although the people of Egypt had seen the power of the one true God, they refused to believe in Him. They continued to worship their own false gods. Egypt had hundreds of gods—one for each village and city. Families built altars in their houses to worship their favorite gods. The worship of many gods is called *polytheism.*

All Egyptians believed that Ra, the sun god, created and ruled the world. During the Middle Kingdom, the priests of Thebes joined their god, Amon, to Ra. They called the new god Amon-Ra. The priests then had to tell everyone how to worship the new god. This made them very powerful.

Osiris, the god of the underworld, was a favorite of the Egyptians. They believed that after burial, a dead person traveled by boat to the Hall of Judgment, where Osiris presided. Anubis, the jackal-headed god, weighed the dead person's heart against the feather of justice, order, and truth. During judgment, the dead person quoted from the *Book of the Dead,* saying, "I have not committed evil against men. . . . I have not taken milk from the mouths of children. . . . I have not mistreated cattle," and "I am pure!" What do you think about this belief?

Osiris's wife, Isis, protected children. Horus, their son, had the body of a man and the head of a falcon or a hawk. These three gods formed the model family that Egyptians tried to follow. There were gods of medicine, education, music, and even love. Hathor, the goddess of love, had the body of a woman and the head of a cow.

Anubis

Isis

Horus

Osiris

44

Egyptians believed that the pharoah was the son of Horus. This made the pharaoh a god and the high priest of Egypt. Every morning, after washing and dressing, the pharaoh went to the temple to "awaken" the idol of Horus. He washed and clothed the idol, gave it food, and put makeup on it. Now, everyone believed, the day could proceed with the god's blessing.

Only one pharaoh tried to change the religion of Egypt. His name was Amenhotep IV (1356-1340 B.C.). He believed there was only one great god, Aton. The pharaoh even changed his name to Akhenaton to show that he worshiped the god Aton.

How do you think the people felt about this change? The priests of the old gods did not like losing their influence. The Egyptians did not want to give up the old gods either. Akhenaton was murdered, and his successor, Tutankhamen, returned to the old religion.

An Egyptian relief carving showing Akhenaton and his wife with the sun god Aton

45

Day 21

Religion in ancient Egypt—Instruct the students to read page 44 silently to learn what the worship of many gods is called. *(polytheism)*

Discussion Questions

➤ **Give some examples of how the Egyptians witnessed the power of the one true God.** *(through Joseph's ability to interpret dreams, through the ten plagues, through the parting of the Red Sea, etc.)*

➤ **Who did the Egyptians believe had created the world?** *(Ra, the sun god)*

➤ **What happened to Ra during the Middle Kingdom?** *(The priests of Thebes joined their god, Amon, to Ra, making a new god, Amon-Ra.)*

➤ **Who was the god of the underworld?** *(Osiris)*

➤ **What was Anubis's role in the Hall of Judgment?** *(He weighed the dead person's heart against the feather of justice, order, and truth.)*

➤ **How did the dead person defend himself before Osiris?** *(He quoted from the* Book of the Dead, *citing examples of his good works.)*

➤ **What do you think about this Egyptian belief?** *(Answers will vary.)*

Ask the students what the Bible says about the relationship between good works and salvation. *(People cannot be saved by doing good things; people can be saved only by accepting Christ's sacrifice on the cross as a payment for their sin.)* (BAT: 1b Repentance and faith; Bible Promise: E. Christ as Sacrifice)

➤ **Which god protected Egyptian children?** *(Isis, Osiris's wife)*

➤ **Why do you think the Egyptians felt that they needed so many gods?** *(Answers will vary.)*

Instruct the students to read page 45 silently to learn whose son the pharaoh of Egypt was thought to be. *(Horus's son)*

Discussion Questions

➤ **Describe the ritual the pharaoh had to go through every morning.** *(He had to "awaken" the idol of Horus, wash and clothe it, give it food, and put makeup on it.)*

➤ **Which pharaoh tried to change the religion of Egypt?** *(Amenhotep IV)*

➤ **What one god did he want Egypt to worship?** *(Aton)*

➤ **How did Amenhotep show that he worshiped this god?** *(He changed his name to Akhenaton.)*

➤ **How do you think the people felt about the change of religion?** *(Answers will vary.)*

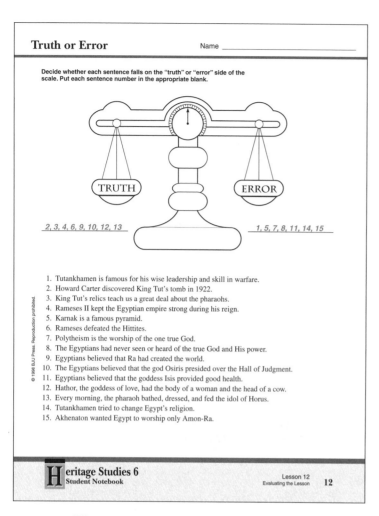

Truth or Error   Name _____

Decide whether each sentence falls on the "truth" or "error" side of the scale. Put each sentence number in the appropriate blank.

TRUTH   ERROR

2, 3, 4, 6, 9, 10, 12, 13   1, 5, 7, 8, 11, 14, 15

1. Tutankhamen is famous for his wise leadership and skill in warfare.
2. Howard Carter discovered King Tut's tomb in 1922.
3. King Tut's relics teach us a great deal about the pharaohs.
4. Rameses II kept the Egyptian empire strong during his reign.
5. Karnak is a famous pyramid.
6. Rameses defeated the Hittites.
7. Polytheism is the worship of the one true God.
8. The Egyptians had never seen or heard of the true God and His power.
9. Egyptians believed that Ra had created the world.
10. The Egyptians believed that the god Osiris presided over the Hall of Judgment.
11. Egyptians believed that the goddess Isis provided good health.
12. Hathor, the goddess of love, had the body of a woman and the head of a cow.
13. Every morning, the pharaoh bathed, dressed, and fed the idol of Horus.
14. Tutankhamen tried to change Egypt's religion.
15. Akhenaton wanted Egypt to worship only Amon-Ra.

© 1998 BJU Press. Reproduction prohibited.

Heritage Studies 6
Student Notebook   Lesson 12
Evaluating the Lesson   **12**

➤ **What eventually happened to Akhenaton and to the religion?** *(Akhenaton was murdered and his successor returned to the old religion.)*

▢ Evaluating the Lesson

Truth or Error (Notebook page 12)—Instruct the students to read each sentence, decide whether it falls on the "truth" or "error" side of the scale, and put its number in the appropriate blank beneath the weights.

━━━ Going Beyond ━━━

▢ Enrichment

Find the Pharaoh game—Set up an AREA with the board game Find the Pharaoh. Show the students the game board and point out the instructions or pictures on each space. Call special attention to the six spaces throughout the board marked "CLUE!" Tell the students that the object of the game is for each player to reach the Burial Chamber space to find the pharaoh's mummy.

Show the students the Clue cards, pointing out that these are used when a player lands on a CLUE! space on the game board.

Show the students the spinner and the buttons. Explain that each player will move one button around the game board.

Give directions for playing the game. Play begins with all the buttons on the Start space and the Clue cards placed in a stack facedown. Each player spins the spinner. The player spinning the highest number goes first. That player spins again and moves his button the number of spaces indicated. The player must follow any instructions on each space on which he lands. If a player lands on a CLUE! space, another player selects the top Clue card from the pile and asks him the question printed on it. If the player answers correctly, he may spin again. If he answers incorrectly, play proceeds to the next player. If a player lands on a space with a hieroglyph, he leaves his marker there until his next turn. The next player then spins and follows any instructions on the space on which he lands. Play continues until one player reaches the Burial Chamber to find the pharaoh's mummy.

▢ Additional Teacher Information

Akhenaton's wife, Nefertiti, is thought to have been Egypt's most beautiful woman. She was a favorite subject for sculptors and portrait artists, and many representations of her exist in museums today. Nefertiti was a strong supporter of her husband's new monotheistic religion. Not only did she assist Akhenaton in religious ceremonies, but she probably had a great influence on his political ideas and decisions as well. Near the time of Akhenaton's death, the name *Nefernefruaton* began to appear with his on documents, probably indicating a joint rule.

Akhenaton and Nefertiti moved the capital of Egypt to el'Amarna. They brought a new style of art into popularity—a realistic style that focused on details, showing people's facial expressions and even reproducing physical imperfections. The time of their reign is called the *Amarna Revolution* because they created so many changes in art, religion, and social life.

LESSON 13
A Taste of Culture

Text, pages 46-48
Notebook, page 13

- Music and Fashion
- Celebrations
- Home and Family

Preview

□ Objectives

Given proper instruction, the students will be able to do the following:
- Make an Egyptian wig.
- Answer questions about Egyptian culture.

□ Materials

Have available:
- A tape measure for each group of four students.*
- A sheet of construction paper for each student.
- A ruler for each student.
- Scissors for each student.
- Glue for each student.
- Several staplers.*
- Enough black yarn for each student to have 5-6 yards.*
- A circle of black felt (about 9 inches in diameter) for each student.*

Day 22

Lesson

□ Introducing the Lesson

Making an Egyptian wig—Direct the students to get with their Heritage Studies partners and to join with other partners to form groups of four. Explain to the students that both men and women in ancient Egypt wore wigs. Give a tape measure to each group. Instruct the students to assist each other in measuring with the tape measure the circumference of each student's head about an inch above his eyebrows. Then instruct each student to cut out of colored construction paper a two-inch-wide headband one inch longer than the circumference of his head. Distribute five to six yards of black yarn to each student. Tell each student to cut the yarn into eight-inch lengths and to glue the yarn close together side-by-side along the length of his headband, leaving a six-inch gap for the face in the center.

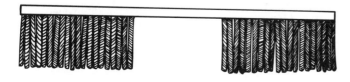

Culture in Ancient Egypt

The ancient Egyptians loved music. It was part of everyday life, not just for celebrations. They sang praises to the Nile. They sang while they worked in the fields. Children sang while they played. Craftsmen and traders sang as they worked in their shops or sailed up and down the Nile. Slaves made their chores less tedious by singing. Religious ceremonies used many songs, both of praise and of prayer to the gods. The pharaoh and nobles often had musicians to entertain them.

Egyptians were known for their cleanliness. They wore fresh clothing of linen, cotton, or wool. Both men and women used cosmetics and wore wigs made from human hair and beeswax. Women usually wore their hair long, while men were bald or cropped their hair just above their shoulders. The Egyptians washed frequently and put on clean clothes often, not just for special occasions. The plagues of frogs, lice, and flies sent by God were a terrible trial for the Egyptians.

razor

child's hairstyle

female hairstyle with perfume cone

mirror

male hairstyle

makeup kit

46

When they have finished, instruct them to staple the two ends of the headband together. Then tell them to glue or staple the circle of black felt to the inside of the headband so that it will cover the top of the head when the wig is in place. Allow the students to wear their wigs during the remainder of this lesson if they wish.

□ Teaching the Lesson

Music and fashion—Instruct the students to read page 46 silently to find two things the Egyptians valued. *(music and cleanliness)*

Discussion Questions

➤ **What part did music play in the lives of the Egyptians?** *(Music and singing were part of everyday life, not just for celebrations. People sang at work and at play.)*

Rami lay on the soft ground. The harvest was over, and now he could rest. All that mattered to him was that there was no more work until after the next flood of the Nile. It was good to be a farmer in Egypt.

The harvest celebration would be tomorrow night. Everyone would eat, sing, and play games. Rami knew many songs, and he had his own flute to play when others sang. His sister played a small harp that she held in her lap. One of the older boys had a *sistrum*, an instrument made of metal rods attached to a metal frame. It was like a huge rattle.

Rami's mother had made new clothing and purchased cosmetics for the whole family. Rami knew his sister had a new wig to wear. His mother would wear a small cone of perfumed oil on her head. During the evening the melting cone would cover her head and shoulders in fragrant oil.

47

Rami glanced down at his dirty clothes. Mother will never let me in the house looking like this, he thought. He knew his mother would leave fresh clothes for him near the water bucket.

Rami thought of the little three-room house made of mud brick where he lived. The animals stayed in the first room, and the family lived in the other two. Maybe if it were cool this evening, he and his family would go up to the flat roof to enjoy the breezes.

Rami stood up and stretched his weary body. He walked toward home through the shorn fields, the Nile waters gleaming behind him in the last rays of sun.

"And the Lord shall be known to Egypt, and the Egyptians shall know the Lord in that day, and shall do sacrifice and oblation; yea, they shall vow a vow unto the Lord, and perform it. And the Lord shall smite Egypt: he shall smite and heal it: and they shall return even to the Lord, and he shall be intreated of them, and shall heal them."

Isaiah 19:21-22

48

➤ **To whom did the Egyptians direct their songs of praise?** *(to the Nile or to the gods)*
➤ **What special privilege did the pharaohs and nobles have?** *(musicians to entertain them)*
➤ **What kinds of cloth did Egyptians use for clothing?** *(linen, cotton, wool)*
➤ **What were Egyptian wigs made of?** *(human hair and beeswax)*
➤ **What kinds of hairstyles were popular among Egyptians?** *(All wore wigs; women usually had long hair; men were bald or had long hair cropped just above their shoulders.)*
➤ **Why were the plagues of frogs, lice, and flies such a terrible trial for the Egyptians?** *(because the Egyptians placed a high value on cleanliness)*

Remind the students that although outward cleanliness is important, inward cleanliness is much more important to God. Emphasize that people can only be inwardly clean by having their sins washed away by the blood of Christ. (BATs: 1b Repentance and faith, 4b Purity; Bible Promise: B. Guiltless by the Blood)

Day 23

Celebrations—Instruct the students to read page 47 silently to find out which celebration Rami is anticipating. *(harvest celebration)*

Discussion Questions
➤ **How do you think Rami is feeling at the time of this story?** *(Answers will vary but may include tired after the harvest and excited about the celebration.)*
➤ **What activities went on at the harvest celebration?** *(eating, singing, and playing games)*
➤ **What musical instruments are mentioned?** *(flute, harp, sistrum)*
➤ **What details confirm that the celebration is a very important occasion for Rami's family?** *(New clothes, cosmetics, and wigs will be worn; his mother will wear a special perfumed cone on her head.)*
➤ **Would you like to use the Egyptian method of applying perfume or cologne today?** *(Answers will vary.)*

Home and family—Instruct the students to read page 48 silently to find out what makes Rami decide to go home. *(He knows his clothes are dirty and he needs to change them; he is excited about going up on the roof to enjoy the breezes.)*

Discussion Questions
➤ **What details does the story give about Rami's home?** *(It is small; it has three rooms; it is made of mud brick; one room is used by the animals; it has a flat roof; Rami's mother probably keeps it very clean.)*
➤ **Would you like to share your home with farm animals, such as donkeys or oxen?** *(Answers will vary.)*
➤ **What can you learn about Egyptian families from Rami's story?** *(They were close-knit; they enjoyed doing things together.)*

Egyptian Culture   Name _____

Answer the following questions about the Egyptian way of life.

1. Name two things the ancient Egyptians loved. *music, cleanliness*
   _____

2. Name three occasions during which the Egyptians used music. *at work, at*
   religious ceremonies, at celebrations

3. Describe an Egyptian woman's appearance at a harvest celebration. *She would*
   wear a wig, clean clothing, and a perfumed cone on her head.

4. Describe three sounds you might hear at a harvest celebration. *Possible answers*
   are flute, harp, sistrum, singing, and laughter.

5. Describe a typical Egyptian home. *It was made of mud-brick, was small with a*
   flat roof, was shared with animals, and had two or three rooms.

© 1998 BJU Press. Reproduction prohibited.

Heritage Studies 6
Student Notebook

Lesson 13
Evaluating the Lesson   **13**

Read aloud the passage from Isaiah on the page. Encourage the students to think for a few moments about what it means.

➤ **Whom does the passage say the Egyptians will one day worship?** *(the Lord)*
➤ **What does it say that the Lord will do for the Egyptians when they return to Him?** *(heal them)*

□ Evaluating the Lesson

Egyptian Culture (Notebook page 13)—Instruct the students to read and answer the questions about the Egyptian way of life.

Going Beyond

□ Enrichment

A harvest celebration—Set up an AREA with samples of Egyptian food, such as melon and cucumber slices, dates, figs, and garlic bread. If possible, obtain some of the musical instruments mentioned in this lesson, such as a flute (or a recorder), a small harp, and a sistrum (or a tambourine). Allow the students to eat the food and try to play the instruments. If convenient, allow the students to invite another class to share their celebration.

□ Additional Teacher Information

Egyptian men wore linen cloths tied at the waist, while women usually wore long, straight dresses with shoulder straps. Children often wore no clothing at all. Hairstyles varied, depending on age and economic status. Many children had completely shaved heads except for a ponytail on the side of the head. Long, plaited hair on men was a symbol of rank, and an elaborate wig on a woman indicated her wealth.

One of Egypt's most popular domestic animals was the cat, but the cat was not just a pet to the Egyptians. Both male and female cats were thought to represent pagan deities, and they were considered sacred animals. Egyptian law forbade the killing of cats or even the taking of cats out of Egypt. Sometimes special agents were commissioned to travel to other countries to buy back cats that had been taken from the land.

The Nile Delta

Nile River

Nile Delta

MEDITERRANEAN SEA

Use with Lesson 8. Heritage Studies 6 TE

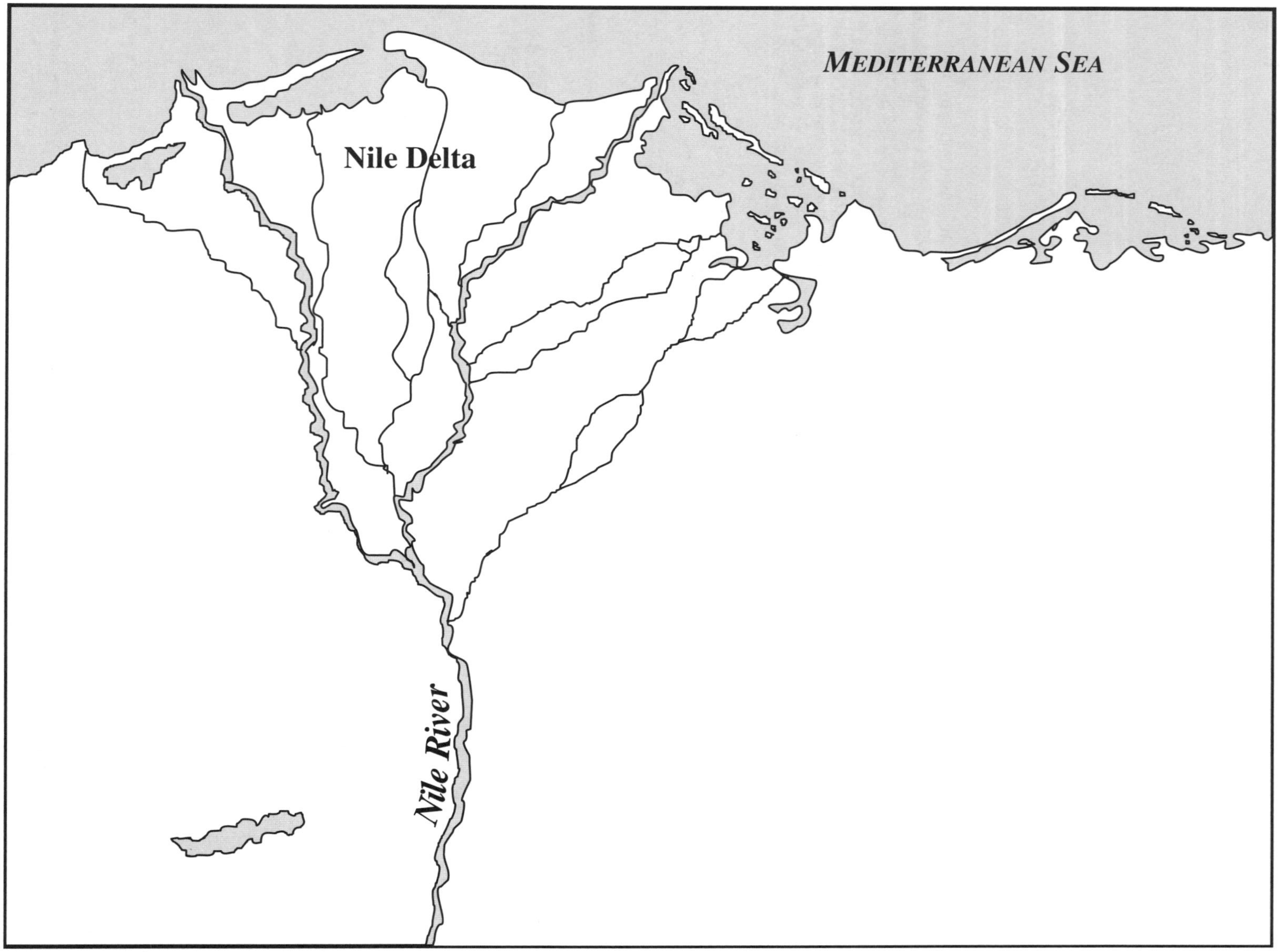

FIND the PHARAOH

Burial Chamber

Grave robbers have been here. Move back 4 spaces.

Clue!

Unearth a papyrus scroll. Move forward 3 spaces.

Discover a new passageway. Move forward 3 spaces.

Clue!

Find a golden statue of the pharaoh's queen. Move forward 3 spaces.

Clue!

Find a jade crocodile. Move forward 2 spaces.

START

Photograph a wall painting. Move forward 2 spaces.

Clue!

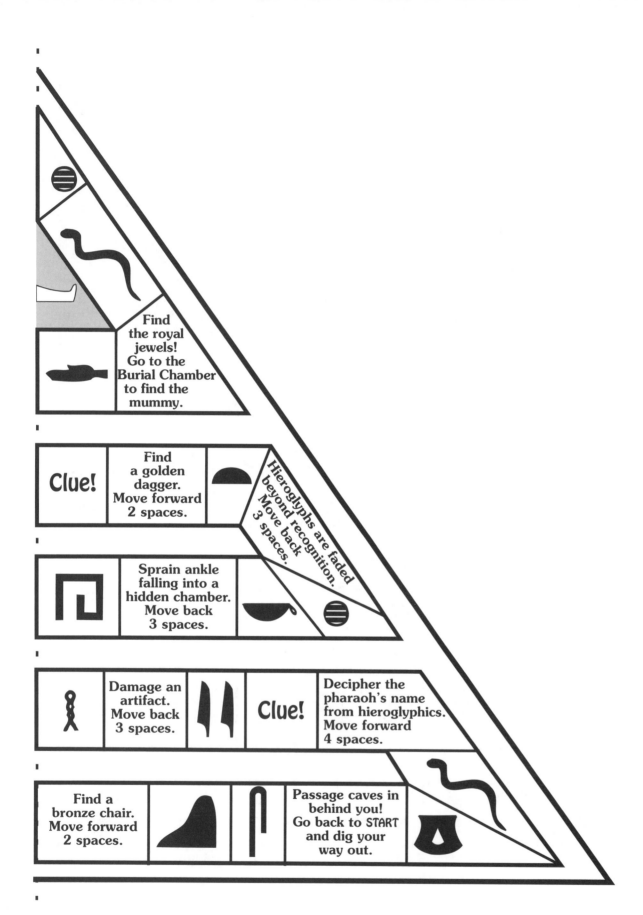

Find
the royal
jewels!
Go to the
Burial Chamber
to find the
mummy.

Clue!

Find
a golden
dagger.
Move forward
2 spaces.

Hieroglyphs are faded
beyond recognition.
Move back
3 spaces.

Sprain ankle
falling into a
hidden chamber.
Move back
3 spaces.

Damage an
artifact.
Move back
3 spaces.

Clue!

Decipher the
pharaoh's name
from hieroglyphics.
Move forward
4 spaces.

Find a
bronze chair.
Move forward
2 spaces.

Passage caves in
behind you!
Go back to START
and dig your
way out.

Q	A	Q	A	Q	A
Q: Name the pharaoh who united Egypt and began the Old Kingdom.	A: Narmer	Q: Name the instrument used to measure the flooding of the Nile River.	A: nilometer	Q: Name the tool used to water Egyptian crops.	A: shadoof
Q: Name the pharaoh who built the three Giza pyramids and the Sphinx.	A: Khufu	Q: Name the plant used by Egyptians to make paper.	A: papyrus	Q: Tell in what year the Rosetta stone was found.	A: 1799
Q: Tell what the preserved pharaohs were called.	A: mummies	Q: Tell Joseph's title after he was promoted by Sesostris.	A: vizier	Q: Tell Egypt's most famous nickname.	A: Gift of the Nile
Q: Name the people from the north who invaded Egypt in 1630 B.C.	A: Hyksos	Q: Name the people who were slaves in Egypt for centuries.	A: Hebrews	Q: Name the pharaoh whose army was drowned in the Red Sea.	A: Amenhotep II
Q: Name the man who discovered King Tut's tomb.	A: Howard Carter	Q: Name whom the Egyptians worshiped as the god of the underworld.	A: Osiris	Q: Tell whose mummy is in the Cairo Museum today.	A: Rameses II
Q: Name the pharaoh who tried to change Egypt's religion.	A: Amenhotep IV (Akhenaton)	Q: Tell the nickname given to the Nile River.	A: Hapi	Q: Name the continent on which Egypt is located.	A: Africa

Clue	Clue	Clue
Clue	Clue	Clue
Clue	Clue	Clue
Clue	Clue	Clue
Clue	Clue	Clue
Clue	Clue	Clue

Use with Lesson 12.

Heritage Studies 6 TE

FIND the PHARAOH

The People of One God: Ancient Israel

This chapter focuses on the history of ancient Israel, from the call of Abraham around 2000 B.C. to the destruction of Masada in A.D. 73. Particular emphasis is paid to the biblical accounts of the Exodus, the judges, the time of the kings, and the time of captivity. Extra-biblical history, such as the Maccabean deliverance and the siege of Masada, are included. By studying the geography, culture, and history of ancient Israel, students will gain a sense of connection to both biblical history and current events in the Middle East. By incorporating the figure of Abraham and the figure of the Cross of Christ on the History TimeLine, students will gain historical perspective of the work of God in the world of men.

□ Chapter Bulletin Board

Entitle the bulletin board *Captivity and Deliverance: The History of the Jews.* On a solid background, place five sheets of blue construction paper and five sheets of white construction paper next to each other to make five sets. Entitle the blue sheets of paper *Captivity* and the white sheets *Deliverance.* Throughout the lessons, allow students to contribute drawings to place on the bulletin board to illustrate the captivity and deliverance of the Jews. Place a drawing of the Egyptian captivity on the first Captivity sheet and a drawing of Moses on the first *Deliverance* sheet and so on. For the last white sheet of paper, explain to the students that the Jews were not delivered from the Romans but that they dispersed throughout the world. This dispersion is called the *diaspora.* For this space, a student drawing might include a modern-day Jew who does not live in Israel. Depending upon the interest of your students, more captivity/deliverance sets could be placed on the bulletin board, representing later struggles of the Jewish people. You might want to include the German "captivity" of the Jews (the Holocaust), the deliverance for which might be attributed to the liberating Allied armies or the establishment of the nation of Israel.

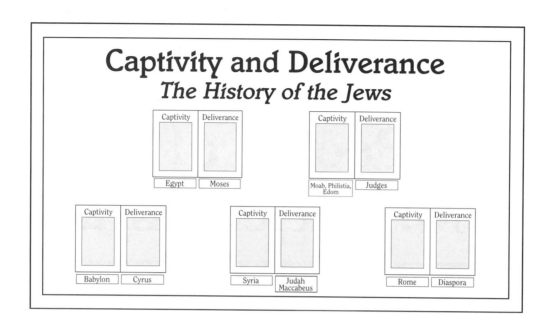

Captivity and Deliverance
The History of the Jews

Captivity	Deliverance
Egypt	Moses

Captivity	Deliverance
Moab, Philistia, Edom	Judges

Captivity	Deliverance
Babylon	Cyrus

Captivity	Deliverance
Syria	Judah Maccabeus

Captivity	Deliverance
Rome	Diaspora

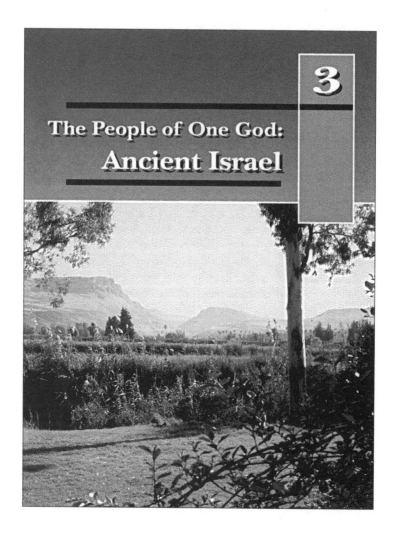

3

The People of One God:
Ancient Israel

LESSON 14
A New Nation

Text, pages 50-52
Notebook, page 14

- A New Nation
- Then and Now
- Israel in Egypt

━━━━━━━ **Preview** ━━━━━━━

☐ Objective
Given proper instruction, the students will be able to do the following:
- Match statements about early Hebrew history.

☐ Materials
Have available:
- A wall map of the world.
- The figure of Abraham (2000 B.C.) from the History Time-Line Packet.

☐ Notes
See Genesis 12 (the call of Abraham) through Exodus 2:10 (the rescue of Moses from the Nile) for scriptural accounts of the events discussed in this lesson.

Day 24

━━━━━━━ **Lesson** ━━━━━━━

☐ Introducing the Lesson
Map activity—Point out Israel on the world map. Use the following questions to familiarize students with Israel's location.

Discussion Questions
➤ **What countries are located around Israel?** *(Egypt, Jordan, Syria, Lebanon, etc.)*
➤ **How far is Israel from where you live?** *(Answers will vary.)*
➤ **By what water route could you travel to Israel from where you live?** *(Answers will vary.)*

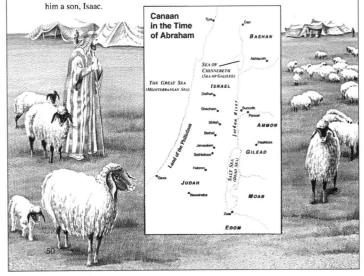

A New Nation
The history of Israel begins with God's *covenant*, or special agreement, with Abraham. In about 2100 B.C., God called Abraham to leave his country. God promised to make Abraham's descendants into a great nation.

God led Abraham to the land of *Canaan*. Although there were a few cities in Canaan, many Canaanites were *nomads*. They wandered about the land, grazing their animals. Nomads lived in tents that could be moved easily from place to place. Do you think your family would like to live in a tent? Abraham and his family lived as nomads in Canaan.

God blessed Abraham with many servants and large flocks of sheep and herds of cattle. When Abraham was one hundred years old, God gave him a son, Isaac.

> "And I will bless them that bless thee, and curse him that curseth thee: and in thee shall all families of the earth be blessed."
> *Genesis 12:3*

Canaan in the Time of Abraham

☐ Teaching the Lesson
A new nation—Instruct the students to read page 50 silently to find out what type of people lived in Canaan. *(nomads)* Choose students to tell how nomads lived.

Discussion Questions
➤ **Whom did God choose to be the father of a great nation?** *(Abraham)*
➤ **How did God bless Abraham?** *(by promising to make Abraham's descendants into a great nation; by giving him many servants and large flocks of sheep and herds of cattle; by giving him a son, Isaac)*

Place the figure of Abraham on the TimeLine at 2000 B.C. Emphasize that the call of God to Abraham marked the beginning of the Jewish nation.

◆ THEN AND NOW ◆

Israel

Location—In the Middle East, on the eastern shore of the Mediterranean Sea. The ancient territory of Canaan is now held by four nations: Israel, Lebanon, Jordan, and Syria.

Climate—Temperate; mild winters and warm summers. Temperatures range from 48°F in the winter to 90°F in the summer. In the northern mountains, annual precipitation may reach 40 inches, while in the southern deserts little or no rain falls.

Topography—Five major land regions run north to south. The lowland coastal plain lies along the Mediterranean Sea. Rolling hills and valleys lead to the Lebanon Mountains in the northeast. The valley of the Jordan River lies to the east of these hills, and further east yet is a large plateau. A desert, the final region, is found in the southeast.

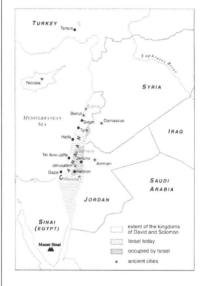

Natural Resources—Modern Israel has few natural resources. Some petroleum and natural gas are available, and salt is mined near the Dead Sea. In ancient times, forests of cedar and other hardwoods were abundant.

Geography and Culture—Part of an area known as the Fertile Crescent, a crescent-shaped region surrounding the Tigris, Euphrates, and Jordan Rivers, provides rich soil for farming. There are few other sources of water; famine often followed times when rain was scarce. Because Canaan lay between Assyria and Egypt, it became both a trading route and a target for expansion for both of these ancient empires.

51

God blessed Isaac and his son Jacob as He had blessed Abraham. Do you know how this group came to be known as the children of Israel? When Jacob surrendered to God's will, God gave him a new name: Israel.

One of Jacob's twelve sons was Joseph. Joseph became a slave in Egypt when his brothers sold him to passing merchants. God blessed Joseph by causing the pharaoh to put him in charge of Egypt's grain storehouses. In this position, Joseph was second to the pharaoh in the land of Egypt. When famine drove the rest of Joseph's family from Canaan, Joseph gave them food and a home in Egypt. They would not return to Canaan for four hundred years.

Eventually, a pharaoh who had not known Joseph became ruler of Egypt. He grew angry with the Israelites, or *Hebrews*, because they were more in number and mightier than the Egyptians. He made them his slaves.

Then the pharaoh decreed that all Hebrew boy babies must be killed. One boy was saved when his mother put him into a basket on the Nile River. The pharaoh's daughter took him from the river and named him *Moses*, which means "drawn from the water."

52

Then and Now—Instruct the students to read page 51 silently to find out what nations today make up the land of Canaan. *(Israel, Lebanon, Jordan, and Syria)* Direct the students' attention to the Then and Now map, noting ancient cities, changes in boundary lines, and so on.

Israel in Egypt—Instruct the students to read page 52 silently to find out why one of the pharaohs of Egypt did not like the Hebrews. *(They were more in number and mightier than the Egyptians.)*

Discussion Questions

➤ **Why are the Hebrews called the "children of Israel"?** *(God changed Jacob's name to Israel. The "children of Israel" are Israel's [Jacob's] descendants.)*

➤ **What did pharaoh decree that caused Moses' mother to put him in a basket in the Nile River?** *(He decreed that all Hebrew baby boys be killed.)*

➤ **Why do you think pharaoh wanted to kill the Hebrew boy babies?** *(Answers will vary, but elicit the idea that pharaoh was afraid the Hebrews would become too strong for him to enslave.)*

➤ **How did Moses receive his name?** *(Pharaoh's daughter named him Moses because she drew him out of the water.)*

Explain that Moses' parents showed great faith in God when they placed their son in a basket on the Nile River. God blessed them by saving the life of their son and using him to deliver the Hebrews from slavery. Moses' parents are mentioned in the list of "great heroes of faith" in Hebrews 11:23. (BAT: 8a Faith in God's promises)

64   Heritage Studies 6 TE

Canaan Match

Name _____

Match each name with its correct description by writing the corresponding letter in the blank.

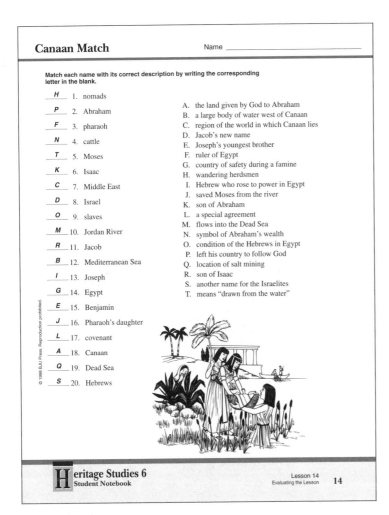

_H_ 1. nomads	A. the land given by God to Abraham
_P_ 2. Abraham	B. a large body of water west of Canaan
_F_ 3. pharaoh	C. region of the world in which Canaan lies
_N_ 4. cattle	D. Jacob's new name
_T_ 5. Moses	E. Joseph's youngest brother
_K_ 6. Isaac	F. ruler of Egypt
_C_ 7. Middle East	G. country of safety during a famine
_D_ 8. Israel	H. wandering herdsmen
_O_ 9. slaves	I. Hebrew who rose to power in Egypt
_M_ 10. Jordan River	J. saved Moses from the river
_R_ 11. Jacob	K. son of Abraham
_B_ 12. Mediterranean Sea	L. a special agreement
_I_ 13. Joseph	M. flows into the Dead Sea
_G_ 14. Egypt	N. symbol of Abraham's wealth
_E_ 15. Benjamin	O. condition of the Hebrews in Egypt
_J_ 16. Pharaoh's daughter	P. left his country to follow God
_L_ 17. covenant	Q. location of salt mining
_A_ 18. Canaan	R. son of Isaac
_Q_ 19. Dead Sea	S. another name for the Israelites
_S_ 20. Hebrews	T. means "drawn from the water"

© 1998 BJU Press. Reproduction prohibited.

Heritage Studies 6
Student Notebook

Lesson 14
Evaluating the Lesson   **14**

□ Evaluating the Lesson

Canaan Match (Notebook page 14)—Direct the students to match each name with its correct description by writing the corresponding letter in the blank on Notebook page 14.

■ Going Beyond ■

□ Enrichment

Bible search—Set up an AREA with Bibles, a concordance, notebook paper, and pencils. Invite the students to use the concordance to find and list Bible verses about Syria, Lebanon, and Egypt. Lead the students to understand that these countries—which still exist today—have existed for thousands of years.

□ Additional Teacher Information

There are approximately thirteen million Jews in the world today. About half of these live in the United States. There are large Jewish communities in America's largest cities, such as New York and Los Angeles. Some American Jews hold citizenship in both Israel and the United States and travel to Jerusalem to vote in important elections.

Jews have distinguished themselves throughout history and in many countries around the world. The British prime minister Benjamin Disraeli was a Jew, as was Felix Mendelssohn, the great composer. Other famous Jews include the musicians Isaac Stern, Leonard Bernstein, and George Gershwin; escape artist Harry Houdini; political philosopher Karl Marx; and scientist Albert Einstein. Today in America, many prominent leaders in science, entertainment, and business are Jewish.

LESSON 15
A Spotless Lamb

Text, pages 53-55
Notebook, pages 15-16

- Ten Plagues
- The Law and the Tabernacle

━━━━ Preview ━━━━

□ Objectives

Given proper instruction, the students will be able to do the following:

- Build a model of the tabernacle.
- Complete a crossword puzzle about the Passover and the wilderness wanderings.

□ Materials

Have available:

- Maps and More 5.
- An overhead projector.
- A blank overhead transparency.
- A Bible for each group.

Prepare an overhead transparency of the "Path to Sinai" page. (*NOTE:* See the reproducible material at the end of Lesson 19.)

□ Notes

See Exodus 2 and 3 (call of Moses), Exodus 11 and 12 (death of the first-born and the Passover), Exodus 20 (giving of the Law), and Exodus 25 through 27 (the Tabernacle) for scriptural accounts of the events discussed in this lesson.

Day 25

━━━━ Lesson ━━━━

□ Introducing the Lesson

Discussing names—Ask the students what names are applied to people who live in the United States or soldiers who have fought for the United States. (*Americans, Yankees, GI's, doughboys, etc.*) Tell the students that there are also a number of different names used to refer to the descendants of Abraham, Isaac, and Jacob. Choose students to tell these names. List them on the chalkboard as the students say them. (*Israelites, children of Israel, Israelis, Jews, Hebrews*)

□ Teaching the Lesson

Ten plagues—Instruct the students to read page 53 silently to find out how the first-born children of Israel escaped death in the tenth plague. (*They were saved when their fathers put blood on the doorposts of their houses.*)

When Moses was eighty years old, God told him that he would be the one to lead the Israelites back into the land He had promised to Abraham, Isaac, and Jacob.

Do you think the pharaoh was willing to let the people of Israel go? No, he said that he did not know Moses' God, and he would not obey Him. God sent terrible diseases and destruction upon Egypt. The story of these *plagues* can be read in the Bible, beginning in Exodus 7:20.

The tenth plague—death of the first-born of every family—was the most terrible. Moses instructed the Hebrews to spread the blood of a lamb on the doorposts of each house. In every house not covered by blood, the first-born child died. Pharaoh's first-born son died in the plague. At last, pharaoh agreed to let the Hebrews go.

Jews celebrate Passover each year to commemorate the deliverance from slavery in Egypt.

53

Lead a discussion of how the blood of Christ saves people from eternal death. (Bible Promise: B. Guiltless by the Blood)

Discussion Questions

➤ **Why do you think pharaoh did not willingly let the Israelites go?** (*Answers may vary but may include that he wanted the Israelites to stay in Egypt and work for him.*)

➤ **Why did pharaoh let the Israelites go at last?** (*His son was killed.*)

➤ **What was the Passover?** (*the celebration of the night the death angel passed over the first-born children of the Israelites*)

Point out that the Passover lamb is a picture of Christ, whose blood was shed for the redemption of His people. Those who stand "under the blood" are confident that their lives have been purchased by the spotless Lamb of God. There is no need to fear eternal death when a person has placed his trust in the Savior. (BAT: 1a Understanding Jesus Christ)

God led the Israelites across the desert toward the land of Canaan. At Mount Sinai, God gave Moses the *law.* He told the Israelites to build a place for worship called the *tabernacle.* The tabernacle was a symbol of God's presence with His people.

Daily the priests sacrificed animals on the altar of the tabernacle. And once each year, the high priest entered the most holy place to sprinkle blood on the mercy seat. Why was the blood sacrifice necessary? It was a picture of Christ's blood that would be shed on the cross.

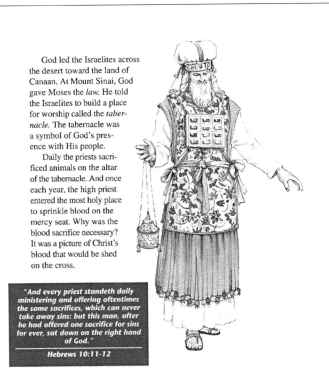

> *"And every priest standeth daily ministering and offering oftentimes the same sacrifices, which can never take away sins: but this man, after he had offered one sacrifice for sins for ever, sat down on the right hand of God."*
>
> **Hebrews 10:11-12**

In a short time, the Israelites reached the edge of the land of Canaan. Along the way the people complained about God's care of them. They did not believe God's promise to help them take the land from the Canaanites. Because they did not trust God, they wandered for forty years in the desert between Egypt and Canaan.

54

◆ DISCOVERING HOW ◆

To Work with a Research Team

1. You and your research team will need a Bible, a pencil, a ruler, and a sheet of drawing paper.

2. Read the passage your teacher assigns you about one of the furnishings of the tabernacle. Take notes as you read, writing down details of the item's appearance, as well as its dimensions and location in the tabernacle if given.

3. With your research team, compare notes and make a drawing of the piece of furniture, keeping it as close as possible to the biblical description.

4. Choose one member of your research team to show your team's drawing to the rest of the class and to give any details you found.

55

The Law and the tabernacle—Instruct the students to read page 54 silently to find out what happened to the Israelites when they did not believe the promises of God. *(They wandered for forty years in the desert between Egypt and Canaan.)* Display the overhead transparency of the "Path to Sinai" page. Point out the path of the Israelites as they left Rameses (also called Raamses) in Egypt, crossed the Red Sea, and moved into the Sinai Desert. Display Maps and More 5. Point out the court, the Holy Place, and the Holy of Holies. Point out the furniture and special articles used in the worship ceremony. Discuss each section of the tabernacle as desired.

Discussion Questions

➤ **What did God instruct the Israelites to build?** *(the tabernacle)*

➤ **Did the Israelites believe God's promise to take care of them?** *(no)*

Working with a research team—Direct a *Discovering How* activity on page 55. Select a student to read aloud the steps. Assign the students to work with their Heritage Studies partners and to join with other partners to form groups of four to research the furnishings of the tabernacle. Instruct each group to write a description of one of the furnishings of the tabernacle based on the Bible's description. Then instruct them to make a drawing of the item based on their research. Encourage the groups to share the information they gathered and the drawing they made with the rest of the class. Write the following references on the chalkboard to aid the students with their research.

ark of the covenant—Exodus 25:10-16

mercy seat—Exodus 25:17-21

table of showbread (shewbread)—Exodus 25:23-30

candlestick—Exodus 25:31-39

brazen altar—Exodus 27:1-8

altar of incense—Exodus 30:1-5

laver—Exodus 30:18-21

Use the clues to complete the puzzle on page 16.

Across

1. Canaan was the land God ____ to Abraham.
4. The Israelite fathers put the blood here on the night of the Passover.
5. The high priest put blood here once a year. (two words)
6. The first-born of all the Egyptians ____.
10. The Passover lamb pictures the __ ____ ____. (three words)
11. The ____ ____ resulted in many deaths. (two words)
14. ____ is celebrated every year by Jews.
16. The Ten Commandments are part of the ____.
18. where the Israelites wandered
19. Moses' age at the time of the Exodus
20. ruler of Egypt

Down

2. Hebrew people enslaved in Egypt
3. leader of the Israelites
7. center for worship in the wilderness
8. where the Law was given (two words)
9. entered once a year (three words)
12. He placed blood on the mercy seat. (two words)
13. Each family killed one ____.
14. When the Israelites complained, God ____ them.
15. what the high priest did with the lamb's blood
17. length of time the Israelites wandered in the wilderness (two words)

© 1998 BJU Press. Reproduction prohibited.

Heritage Studies 6
Student Notebook   Lesson 15
Evaluating the Lesson   **15**

Use the clues on page 15 to complete the puzzle.

Crossword puzzle answers:

1. PROMISED
3. MOSES (down)
4. DOORPOSTS
2. MISSAL (down) / SA...
5. MERCYSEAT
6. DIED
7. TABERNACLE (down)
8. MOUNTSINAI (down)
9. MOSTHOLYPLACE (down)
10. BLOODOFCHRIST
11. TENTHPLAGUE
12. HIGHPRIEST (down)
13. LAMB (down)
14. PASSOVER
15. SPRINKLED (down)
16. LAW
17. FORTYYEARS (down)
18. WILDERNESS
19. EIGHTY
20. PHARAOH

© 1998 BJU Press. Reproduction prohibited.

Heritage Studies 6
Student Notebook   Lesson 15
Evaluating the Lesson   **16**

☐ Evaluating the Lesson

Israelites Puzzle (Notebook pages 15-16)—Direct the students to use the clues to complete the crossword puzzle.

——— Going Beyond ———

☐ Enrichment

Researching Passover—Set up an AREA with books about Passover celebrations. Encourage the students to read the books and then to share what they learned with their classmates by giving short talks or by drawing pictures of Passover observances.

☐ Additional Teacher Information

Passover, known as *Pesach* to the Jews, is celebrated each spring to commemorate the deliverance of the first-born. The entire family gathers for a traditional dinner called the *seder.* Songs and prayers are offered to God; the father tells the story of the Hebrews' deliverance from Egypt. Unleavened bread, called *matzo,* is eaten to remind the family of the unleavened bread eaten with the Passover lamb. Other traditional dishes include roast lamb and a roasted egg. Bitter herbs are served as a reminder of the harsh conditions under which the Hebrews lived in Egypt. Also, a ground-up mixture of apples, raisins, almonds, and cinnamon is formed into a patty to represent the bricks the Jews were forced to make for their Egyptian taskmasters.

"The Four Questions," asked by the youngest child, inquire how and why Passover is celebrated. The father answers the child's questions carefully to make sure the memory of Passover is passed on faithfully to the next generation.

LESSON 16
Out of Egypt, into Canaan

Text, pages 56-59
Notebook, page 17

- Into Canaan
- Smelting Iron
- Family Life

Preview

☐ Objective
Given proper instruction, the students will be able to do the following:
- Identify correct statements about the Israelites' early years in Canaan.

☐ Materials
Have available:
- An overhead projector.
- A blank overhead transparency.

Prepare an overhead transparency of the "Name of God" page. (*NOTE:* See the reproducible material at the end of Lesson 19.)

☐ Notes
See the books of Joshua and Judges for scriptural accounts of the events discussed in this lesson.

Day 26

Lesson

☐ Introducing the Lesson
The tetragrammaton—Display the overhead transparency of the "Name of God" page. Tell the students that these four Hebrew letters are called the *tetragrammaton* and are the Hebrew word for God. In English these letters are written YHWH or JHVH. When vowels are added to the tetragrammaton, the name for God is written *Jehovah.* Explain to the students that Jews do not pronounce the tetragrammaton. To a Jew, the name of God is so holy that it should not even be spoken. When the King James Version of the Bible was translated, the tetragrammaton was translated as LORD, with all capital letters. Encourage students to find instances of this spelling in their Bibles.

☐ Teaching the Lesson
Into Canaan—Instruct the students to read pages 56-57 silently to find out what God told the Israelites to do when they entered the land of Canaan. *(to destroy all the Canaanites)*

The Law of God

The thing that set the Israelites apart from all other people was their belief in the true God, *Yahweh* or *Jehovah.* God ruled His people directly. Direct rule by God is called a *theocracy,* from the Greek words *theos* meaning "god" and *kratos* meaning "power."

In most ancient cultures, the laws were made by the king or ruler. In Israel, the laws were made by God. The best known part of the law is the Ten Commandments, found in Exodus 20. How many do you know?

Modern tourists visit the traditional site of Mt. Sinai, the place where God gave the law to Moses.

Today, the laws of many Western countries are "echoes" of the law given to Moses. Why do you think the laws of the Israelites have had such an effect on the laws of other lands? Unlike laws written by man, God's laws are perfect.

56

Discussion Questions

➤ **Why do you think God wanted the Canaanites destroyed?** *(Answers will vary but should include that the Canaanites were idolaters.)*
➤ **Did the Israelites obey God and destroy all the Canaanites?** *(no)*
➤ **How did God punish the people when they worshiped the Canaanite gods?** *(He made them subjects of the people they had not destroyed.)*
➤ **What happened when the Israelites called on God to help them?** *(He sent judges to deliver them.)*
➤ **What is direct rule by God called?** *(theocracy)*
➤ **Where in the Bible can we read the Ten Commandments?** *(Exodus 20)*

The last judge, Samuel, was appointed by God to replace Eli. Eli lost the blessing of God because he did not restrain his sons' wicked behavior. Samuel served the Lord faithfully throughout his long life. (BAT: 2c Faithfulness)

Inhabiting the Promised Land

After Moses died in about 1400 B.C., Joshua led the Israelites into the land of Canaan. God commanded the Israelites to destroy all the Canaanites. Joshua assigned each of the twelve tribes of Israel a portion of the land. Each tribe was supposed to destroy the Canaanites in its part of the land. Many Canaanites were destroyed or driven away, but some were left alone. Do you think God was pleased?

The Hebrews began to worship Canaanite gods. God punished the Israelites for this idolatry by making them subjects of the people they had not destroyed. In defeat, God's people called to Him for deliverance. God sent deliverers, called *judges*. Even when the judges brought peace to the land, the people did not remain faithful to God.

The pattern of disobedience and punishment followed by repentance and deliverance continued for more than three hundred years. Finally, the people of Israel began to believe that the problems with their enemies could be solved only one way. They asked the last judge, Samuel, to give them a king like the other nations.

Samson, one of the judges of Israel, personally killed many of the Philistines during his lifetime.

Israel's Twelve Tribes

57

◆ THINGS PEOPLE DID ◆

Smelting Iron

Swords, javelins, arrowheads, and spearheads hung on the smithy's blackened walls. Nails, knives, sickles, and axes decorated the crude shelves in the small Israeli shop. But it had not always been so.

Before 1100 B.C., the Philistines controlled the iron industry. Anyone in Canaan who wanted an iron weapon or tool had to purchase it from a Philistine ironsmith. The Philistines kept the secret of smelting iron from those around them.

In later years the Israelites made their own weapons by smelting the iron. They had to mine *ore*—a rock or mineral that contains something valuable, such as a metal. Then they smelted the iron by heating the ore and adding different substances to separate the iron from the ore. After purifying the iron with intense heat, the ironsmiths poured the liquefied metal into a clay or stone mold. On other occasions they would hammer it into the desired shape.

> "Behold, I have created the smith that bloweth the coals in the fire, and that bringeth forth an instrument for his work; . . . No weapon that is formed against thee shall prosper; . . . This is the heritage of the servants of the Lord."
>
> Isaiah 54:16-17

No longer did the Philistines limit Israel's use of weapons or tools. The Israelites could now mine the ore and smelt the iron themselves. But even with this advantage over their enemies, ultimately God was their protector.

58

Smelting iron—Instruct the students to read page 58 silently to find out why the Israelites had to purchase iron implements from the Philistines before 1100 B.C. *(The Philistines controlled the iron industry.)* Elicit from the students reasons that being able to work with iron would be valuable to a growing nation. *(The people would be able to make their own farm tools, weapons, etc.)*

Discussion Questions

➤ **How was iron separated from the ore?** *(The ore was heated; then other substances were added to the ore to separate the iron.)*

➤ **How was the iron purified?** *(with intense heat)*

➤ **How was the hot metal formed?** *(It was poured into molds or hammered into the desired shape.)*

Family life—Instruct the students to read page 59 silently to find out what skills Israelite parents taught their children. *(Boys were taught a trade and how to work the farm and tend the animals; girls were taught to cook, make clothing, tend a garden, and make goods to sell.)*

Discussion Questions

➤ **What do you think is the most important thing parents can teach their children?** *(Answers will vary, but lead the students to understand that Christian parents seek to teach their children about Christ, the Savior.)*

➤ **What skills have your parents taught you?** *(Answers will vary.)*

➤ **What skills would you like to learn that you have not yet learned?** *(Answers will vary.)*

> Remind the students that even if they do not understand why their parents are teaching them a particular skill, they should submit to their parents' leadership in their lives. Tell them that God often uses things later in our lives that we did not appreciate learning when we were young. (BAT: 2a Authority)

☐ Evaluating the Lesson

Into Canaan (Notebook page 17)—Instruct the students to write the letter of the correct choice in each blank.

Life in the Promised Land

God commanded the Israelite parents to teach their children. What things do your parents teach you? The most important thing Israelite parents taught their children was the law of God.

Parents also taught their children practical skills. Fathers taught their sons a trade and how to work the farm and tend the animals. Mothers taught their daughters to cook, make clothing, tend a garden, and make goods to sell.

> *"And these words, which I command thee this day, shall be in thine heart: and thou shalt teach them diligently unto thy children, and shalt talk of them when thou sittest in thine house, and when thou walkest by the way, and when thou liest down, and when thou risest up."*
>
> **Deuteronomy 6:6-7**

Gerrit van Honthorst, *Holy Family in the Carpenter Shop, The Bob Jones University Collection*

59

━━━ **Going Beyond** ━━━

□ Enrichment

Hebrew letters—Set up an AREA with paper, pencils, and a copy of the Hebrew alphabet for each student. (*NOTE:* See the reproducible material at the end of Lesson 19.) Encourage students to practice writing Hebrew letters.

□ Additional Teacher Information

The word *Jehovah* is combined with a number of other words in the Old Testament to indicate specific traits of the one true God. *Jehovah* indicates the one "which is, and which was, and which is to come," and particularly signifies the covenant relationship of God to His people. Other titles of God using the word Jehovah include the following: Jehovah-jireh (Jehovah will provide), Jehovah-ropheca (Jehovah will heal), Jehovah-shalom (Jehovah our peace), and Jehovah-tsidkenu (Jehovah our righteousness).

When a Hebrew of ancient times read the Torah, he did not speak aloud the name of God. Instead, he read *Adonai,* the word for "master." When Hebrew vowel markings were added to the text (ancient Hebrew was written without vowels), the vowel markings for the word *Adonai* were inserted. Transliterated into English, the pronunciation of the name of God is *Jehovah.* Jews, however, still read it as *Adonai.* Because the name of God is so holy, pronouncing it is considered an improper, degrading use of the name.

Into Canaan
Name _____

Write the letter of the correct choice in each blank.

B 1. *theocracy*
  A. Greek power
  B. rule by God
  C. type of food eaten in the wilderness
  D. Greek for "Ten Commandments"

C 2. This man led the Israelites after the death of Moses.
  A. Aaron
  B. Samuel
  C. Joshua
  D. Samson

A 3. what God asked the Israelites to do to the Canaanites
  A. Destroy them.
  B. Make friends with them.
  C. Learn their religion.
  D. Convert them to Judaism.

C 4. deliverers sent by God
  A. economists
  B. juries
  C. judges
  D. kingmakers

D 5. why God allowed His people to be defeated by other nations
  A. The Israelites moved back to Egypt.
  B. The Israelites made iron weapons.
  C. The Israelites forced Joshua to be their king.
  D. The Israelites worshiped heathen gods.

A 6. people who controlled the iron industry
  A. Philistines
  B. Canaanites
  C. Judges
  D. Javelinites

Heritage Studies 6
Student Notebook

Lesson 16
Evaluating the Lesson   **17**

D 7. Smelting was a process of
  A. making and selling idols.
  B. defending against an enemy.
  C. baking in Canaanite ovens.
  D. shaping tools from iron.

B 8. The Ten Commandments are found in
  A. Genesis 5.
  B. Exodus 20.
  C. John 3.
  D. Numbers 10.

D 9. the last judge of Israel
  A. Gideon
  B. Saul
  C. Eli
  D. Samuel

A 10. how iron weapons were formed
  A. Iron was melted and poured into molds.
  B. Iron bars were carved into the desired shape.
  C. Wooden arrowheads were fastened onto iron bars.
  D. Men looked in the ground for iron already shaped like weapons.

17a

LESSON 17
Land of Kings

Text, pages 60-63
Notebook, page 18

- ■ Kings of Israel
- ■ Solomon
- ■ Phoenicians
- ■ Two Kingdoms

══ Preview ══

□ Objectives

Given proper instruction, the students will be able to do the following:
- Decide whether statements about Israel are true or false.
- Rewrite false statements about Israel to make them true.

□ Materials

Have available:
- An overhead projector.
- 2 light-colored overhead transparency pens.
- 2 blank overhead transparencies.

Prepare:
- An overhead transparency of the "Kings of Israel and Judah" page. (*NOTE:* See the reproducible material at the end of Lesson 19.)
- An overhead transparency of the "Divided Kingdom" page. (*NOTE:* See the reproducible material at the end of Lesson 19.)

□ Notes

See I Samuel 10 through 31 (the reign of King Saul), II Samuel (the reign of King David), I Kings 1 through 11 (the reign of King Solomon), and II Kings 17 and 18 (the captivity of Israel) for scriptural accounts of the events discussed in this lesson.

Day 27

══ Lesson ══

□ Introducing the Lesson

Kings of Israel and Judah—Display the overhead transparency of the "Kings of Israel and Judah" page. Use an overhead transparency marking pen to circle the names David, Solomon, Asa, Jehoshaphat, Joash, Amaziah, Uzziah, Jotham, Hezekiah, and Josiah. Tell the students that these were the kings who honored the Lord. Ask what they notice about the list of the kings of Israel. *(None of the names are circled; none of the kings were righteous.)* Choose students to tell what qualities God would desire in a king. *(trust in God, honesty, integrity, worship of God, obedience to the Law, etc.)*

God warned the Israelites that a king would take their sons for his armies. He would take their daughters to work in his palace. He would take their land and their crops to feed his servants and armies. Still, the people wanted a king.

God chose Saul to be Israel's first king about 1020 B.C. At first it seemed that Saul would defeat the *Philistines,* Israel's worst enemies. Then Saul disobeyed the instructions of the Lord. Although Saul was king for many more years, he never led the Israelites to victory as the people had hoped.

60

□ Teaching the Lesson

Kings of Israel—Instruct the students to read page 60 silently to find out who Israel's first king was. *(Saul)*

Discussion Questions

- ➤ **Did the people believe God's warning about how a king would treat them?** *(no)*
- ➤ **What happened when Saul disobeyed God?** *(He never led Israel to victory as the people had hoped.)*

Solomon—Direct the students to read page 61 silently to find out how Solomon made treaties with other nations. *(He married the daughters of foreign kings.)*

Discussion Questions

- ➤ **Who was appointed king after Saul?** *(David)*
- ➤ **When did Israel finally have peace?** *(during the reign of Solomon)*
- ➤ **What buildings did Solomon build in Israel?** *(storehouses, palaces, forts, and the temple in Jerusalem)*
- ➤ **How many wives did Solomon have?** *(seven hundred)*
- ➤ **What problems do you think Solomon had with so many wives?** *(Answers will vary but will include that each wife brought with her a false god.)*

God appointed a new king—David—in the place of Saul. Under King David, the Philistine armies were finally defeated. David also captured the Canaanite city of Jerusalem. At David's death in 961 B.C., his son Solomon became king. Solomon made *treaties*, or peace agreements, with many other countries. During Solomon's reign, the people of Israel had peace.

Solomon built storehouses, palaces, and forts throughout Israel. His most impressive project was the temple in Jerusalem. It was built from huge stones and cedar timbers from the Lebanon Mountains. Decorations were made from ivory, gold, and precious stones.

Solomon made peace treaties with other countries by marrying the daughters of foreign kings. Solomon had seven hundred wives, including Ammonite, Phoenician, and Egyptian princesses. Each wife brought with her a false god.

61

The Phoenicians

One Canaanite group was the *Phoenicians*. Tyre, Sidon, and Byblos are Phoenician cities mentioned in the Bible. The Phoenicians were prosperous traders, craftsmen, and businessmen.

The hills of Phoenicia were covered with forests—the famous cedars of Lebanon. David used wood from these forests when he built his palace, and Solomon included Lebanon cedar in the construction of the temple in Jerusalem.

The wicked Queen Jezebel, daughter of a Phoenician king, brought idol worship to Israel after her marriage to Ahab. She supported 450 priests of Baal, the storm god. Many Israelites turned to the worship of Baal.

The prophet Ezekiel warned that the Phoenician city of Tyre would be destroyed and thrown into the sea. Can you guess what happened to Tyre? Nebuchadnezzar destroyed it in 571 B.C. Years later, the remains were thrown into the sea to build a *causeway*, or land bridge, to the new island city of Tyre. The old city of Tyre was never rebuilt and is even today "like the top of a rock" (Ezekiel 26:14).

Ruins of Tyre

62

Remind the students that although many Israelites, especially wealthy ones, had more than one wife, this was not the plan of God. God's plan, as illustrated in Genesis 2:21-24, is that one man and one woman be married to each other as long as both of them are living. (BAT: 2c Faithfulness) Emphasize that God used many people, including David and Solomon, who, though they were not perfect, sought to please the Lord and trusted Him to save them. (BAT: 1c Separation from the world; Bible Promise: B. Guiltless by the Blood)

Phoenicians—Instruct the students to read page 62 silently to find out whether the Phoenicians feared the Lord. (*No, they were idolaters.*)

Discussion Questions

➤ **How did the daughter of a Phoenician king influence Israel?** (*Jezebel married King Ahab of Israel. She brought idol worship with her and convinced many Israelites to turn to Baal worship.*)

➤ **How did God judge the Phoenician city of Tyre?** (*He caused it to be destroyed and never rebuilt.*)

The Kingdom Divided

God required one thing of Solomon: to serve and worship Him. But Solomon's wives had turned his heart away from the Lord. At Solomon's death in 922 B.C., the ten northern tribes followed Jeroboam, one of Solomon's officials. The two southern tribes, Judah and Benjamin, were ruled by Solomon's son Rehoboam.

> *"And if thou wilt walk before me, as David thy father walked, in integrity of heart, and in uprightness, to do according to all that I have commanded thee, and wilt keep my statutes and my judgments: then I will establish the throne of thy kingdom upon Israel for ever, as I promised to David thy father, saying, There shall not fail thee a man upon the throne of Israel."*
>
> **I Kings 9:4-5**

Divided Kingdom

The northern tribes took the name *Israel*. Jeroboam established his capital at *Samaria*. To keep his people from returning to Jerusalem to worship, he made two golden calves and proclaimed them the gods of Israel. None of Israel's nineteen kings over the next two hundred years served the Lord. In 722 B.C. Israel was conquered by Assyria.

63

Kings of the People   Name _____

If the statement is true, write *true* on the blank. If the statement is false, rewrite the statement to make it true.

Wording may vary.

1. God told the people that a king would be good for them and would treat them well. **God warned the people that a king would treat them harshly.**

2. Saul, Israel's first king, soundly defeated the Philistine army. **King David defeated the Philistines.**

3. David captured the city of Jerusalem and made it his capital. **true**

4. After the death of King David, his son Jeroboam became king. **Solomon became king after King David died.**

5. Solomon had many wives, and they turned his heart away from God. **true**

6. After Solomon's death, Israel was divided into three kingdoms—Samaria, Israel, and Judah. **Israel was divided into two kingdoms, Israel and Judah.**

7. All of Israel's nineteen kings served the Lord. **None of Israel's kings served the Lord.**

8. The cities of Tyre and Sidon were part of the Philistine kingdom. **Tyre and Sidon were Phoenician cities.**

Heritage Studies 6
Student Notebook

Lesson 17
Evaluating the Lesson **18**

Two kingdoms—Instruct the students to read page 63 silently to find out what happened to the nation of Israel after the death of Solomon. (*The nation was divided into two kingdoms.*)

Discussion Questions

➤ **Who ruled the separate kingdoms?** (*Jeroboam ruled the ten northern tribes, and Rehoboam ruled the two southern tribes.*)

➤ **What was the capital of Israel?** (*Samaria*)

Display the overhead transparency of the Divided Kingdom. Color in the kingdom of Israel, pointing out its capital, Samaria; then color the kingdom of Judah a different color, point out its capital, Jerusalem.

➤ **How did Jeroboam keep the people of Israel from traveling to Jerusalem to worship?** (*He made two golden calves and told the people to worship them.*)

➤ **How did God punish the people of Israel for their idolatry?** (*The Israelites were ruled by nineteen wicked kings over the next two hundred years, and then they were conquered by the Assyrians in 722 B.C.*)

□ Evaluating the Lesson

Kings of the People (Notebook page 18)—Direct the students to read each statement. Tell them to write *true* if the statement is true. If the statement is false, tell them to rewrite the statement to make it true.

━━ Going Beyond ━━

□ Enrichment

Writing a journal entry—Set up a writing AREA with notebook paper and pencils. Instruct the students to think about how it might have been to be a servant in Solomon's palace. Encourage each student to write a journal entry about a day in the life of a servant of King Solomon.

□ Additional Teacher Information

Built of hewn stone, the Temple in Jerusalem was about one hundred twenty feet long, forty feet wide, and sixty feet high. The glory of the Temple's beauty was its interior, which was overlaid with gold. The detailed work on the Temple continued for seven years.

Animal sacrifices were made in the courtyard of the Temple every day. Priests went in and out of the Holy Place in the regular course of their duties. The Most Holy Place, however, was entered just once each year and only by the High Priest. On *Yom Kippur,* the Day of Atonement, the High Priest carried into the Most Holy Place the blood of an unblemished lamb. The High Priest sprinkled the blood on the mercy seat, prefiguring the once-for-all offering of God's perfect Lamb, the Lord Jesus Christ.

LESSON 18
The Maccabees

Text, pages 64-67
Notebook, page 19

- God's People in Exile
- Antiochus IV and Judah Maccabeus

——— Preview ———

□ Objective
Given proper instruction, the students will be able to do the following:
- Complete a puzzle about the Babylonian exile.

□ Materials
Have available:
- A cassette player.
- *HERITAGE STUDIES Listening Cassette B.*
- An overhead projector.
- 2 blank overhead transparencies.
- A Bible.

Prepare overhead transparencies of the "Exile Map" and the Babylonian Empire map overlay. (*NOTE:* See the reproducible material at the end of Lesson 19.)

□ Notes
See II Kings 24 (the captivity of Judah), II Chronicles 36 (Cyrus's decree), and the Book of Esther (the celebration of Purim) for scriptural accounts of the events discussed in this chapter.

HERITAGE STUDIES Listening Cassette B includes songs and readings for grades 4, 5, and 6. This is the first use of *Listening Cassette B* for grade 6.

Day 28

——— Lesson ———

□ Introducing the Lesson
Listening activity—Play the song "See, the Conqu'ring Hero Comes" from *HERITAGE STUDIES Listening Cassette B*. Tell the students that this song comes from the oratorio *Judas Maccabaeus*. Written by George Frederick Handel, *Judas Maccabaeus* describes the struggle of the Maccabees against the foreign rule of Israel. Explain that today's lesson will include discussion of the Jewish fighter Judah Maccabeus, who delivered the Jews from the Syrians in 165 B.C.

The Southern Kingdom took the name *Judah*. Judah's kings were all descendants of King David. Some of these kings were wicked, but a few of Judah's rulers did "that which was right in the sight of the Lord."

In 586 B.C., Nebuchadnezzar, king of Babylon, conquered Judah. He destroyed Jerusalem, including the temple. He took more than ten thousand people away to *exile* in Babylonia. Daniel and his friends Shadrach, Meshach, and Abednego were among the Babylonian exiles. Many of those who were left behind fled into Egypt, Moab, Samaria, and other countries. This scattering of the Judeans—or Jews as they became known—into many other nations is known as the dispersion, or *diaspora*.

God's People in Exile
In Babylon the Jews had no temple. Small groups met together in *synagogues*, where priests instructed them in the *Torah*, the first five books of the Bible.

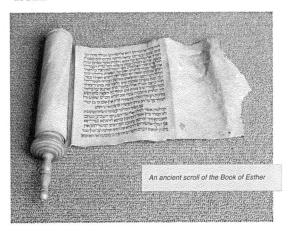
An ancient scroll of the Book of Esther

64

□ Teaching the Lesson
God's people in exile—Instruct the students to read pages 64-65 silently to find out what the *diaspora* is. (*the dispersion, or scattering, of the Jews into many other nations*) Remind the students that they read in Lesson 17 about the northern tribes being taken captive by the Assyrians.

Discussion Questions
➤ **Who conquered Judah and took more than ten thousand people away to exile?** (*Nebuchadnezzar, king of Babylon*)
➤ **How do you think you would feel if you were one of the Judean captives?** (*Answers will vary.*)
➤ **How did the Jews meet together since they had no temple in Babylon?** (*They met in small groups in synagogues.*)

Display the overhead transparency of the "Exile Map." Position the Babylonian Empire map on top of the "Exile Map." Point out the Assyrian Empire and the Babylonian Empire. Ask the students which group of Jews were in Assyria and which were taken captive to Babylon. (*Jews from the northern tribes of Israel were in Assyria, and Jews from Judah were taken captive to Babylon.*) Point out Israel and Judah on the "Exile Map."
➤ **What Jewish girl became queen of Babylon?** (*Esther*)
➤ **How did Esther show courage?** (*She pleaded with the king to save her people from destruction.*)

During the reign of King Ahasuerus, Haman, a greedy palace official, grew angry with a Jew named Mordecai. Haman decided to take revenge on Mordecai by plotting to kill all the Jews of Babylon. But Esther, a Jew, had become queen. Esther risked her life to plead with the king to save her people from destruction. King Ahasuerus gave the Jews the right to defend themselves from anyone who would try to hurt or kill them. He also ordered the execution of Haman.

"And in every province, and in every city, whithersoever the king's commandment and his decree came, the Jews had joy and gladness, a feast and a good day."

Esther 8:17

After Haman's death, the Jews held a great feast, sent each other presents, and gave gifts to poor people. Today this holiday is called *Purim* and is celebrated by Jews around the world.

65

Rebuilding the Nation

Cyrus the Great of Persia conquered Babylon in 539 B.C. He allowed the Jews to return to Judah. Do you think all the Jews returned to their homeland? Not all did. Many stayed in Babylon where they had made their homes.

The first group that returned to Judah was discouraged by what it found. The Jews who had remained in Judah during the exile were not willing to help rebuild Jerusalem. Not until 515 B.C. was the temple finally rebuilt.

Alexander the Great defeated the Persians in 331 B.C., and the land of Judea became part of Alexander's empire. Greek rulers brought new ideas and laws to the Jews. Many Jews felt that as long as they were allowed to worship God, the changes in culture would not matter.

Alexander the Great

In 176 B.C. Antiochus IV became ruler of Judea. He outlawed obedience to God's law. Keeping the Sabbath became punishable by death. It was against the law to own a copy of the Torah. Antiochus even set up idols in the temple and sacrificed pigs on the altar of God.

66

➤ **What happened to the man who desired the destruction of the Jews?** *(Haman was killed.)*

Antiochus IV and Judah Maccabeus—Instruct the students to read pages 66-67 to find out why the Jewish festival of Hanukkah began. *(to celebrate the rededication of the temple in 164 B.C.)* Explain that Jews celebrate Hanukkah in December each year.

Discussion Questions

➤ **What did Antiochus IV do that angered many Jews?** *(He outlawed obedience to God's law and practiced pagan worship in the temple.)*
➤ **How would you feel if the government made it illegal to obey the commands of God?** *(Answers will vary.)*

Tell the students that God expects Christians to obey the government. However, if obeying a government order would cause a Christian to disobey a command of God, he must choose to obey God rather than the government. Read Acts 5:29 aloud. Tell the students that the government had forbidden Christians from speaking about Jesus and that the Christians replied that they would not disobey God but would continue to preach the gospel. (BAT: 8d Courage)

Discussion Questions

➤ **Why did Mattathias and his sons flee to the mountains?** *(Mattathias had killed a man for bowing down to the pagan altar.)*
➤ **Why did Judah Maccabeus fight the Syrians?** *(The Syrians were persecuting the Jews.)*
➤ **Why did Judah Maccabeus capture Jerusalem?** *(Pagan gods were being worshiped in the temple.)*
➤ **What did Judah Maccabeus establish to commemorate the rededication of the temple?** *(the festival of Hanukkah, to be celebrated every year with gladness and joy)*

Altars to false gods were set up in many Jewish cities, including the small town of Modin. As the people of Modin watched to see what would happen, a Syrian official commanded a Jew to bow down to the altar. When he bowed, the priest Mattathias jumped out of the crowd and killed the man. He also killed the Syrian official and destroyed the altar. Mattathias knew his life was in danger. He and his five grown sons escaped to the mountains, where they gathered a group of three thousand fighting men.

Mattathias died in 166 B.C. His third son, Judah, took his place of leadership. Judah, called Judah Maccabeus ("the hammer"), led surprise attacks throughout the countryside. In one battle, he defeated the Syrians and burned their camp. Finally, in 164 B.C., the Syrians stopped persecuting the Jews. However, pagan gods were still worshiped in the temple.

In December 164 B.C. the Maccabees took Jerusalem. They destroyed the idols and all evidence of pagan worship. Exactly three years after the first pagan sacrifice was offered, the priests again offered an unblemished lamb to God. The rededication of the temple was celebrated for eight days. Judah Maccabeus declared that this festival, Hanukkah, should be celebrated every year with gladness and joy.

The Menorah is featured during the celebration of the Jewish holiday Hanukkah.

67

Use the clues to fill in the blanks.

1. city destroyed in 586 B.C.
2. king of Babylon
3. land of the Jews
4. a scattering of the Jews
5. Jewish queen of Babylon
6. celebration of deliverance
7. center of worship during the exile
8. Esther's uncle
9. friend of Daniel
10. celebration of rededication
11. land of exile
12. defeated by Alexander the Great
13. king who defeated Babylon in 539 B.C. (three words)
14. empire that conquered Israel in 722 B.C.

1. J E R U S A L E M
2. N E B U C H A D N E Z Z A R
3. J U D E A
4. D I A S P O R A
5. E S T H E R
6. P U R I M
7. S Y N A G O G U E
8. M O R D E C A I
9. M E S H A C H
10. H A N U K K A H
11. B A B Y L O N I A
12. P E R S I A N S
13. C Y R U S T H E G R E A T
14. A S S Y R I A

The letters in the shaded boxes spell the name of a great Jewish leader. (two words)

Judah Maccabeus

H eritage Studies 6
Student Notebook

Lesson 18
Evaluating the Lesson   **19**

□ Evaluating the Lesson

Exile and Deliverance (Notebook page 19)—Instruct the students to use the clues to complete the puzzle.

━━ Going Beyond ━━

□ Enrichment

News reporting—Allow the students to work with their Heritage Studies partners to write simulated news reports about events in the Book of Esther from the Bible. Possible events to report about would include the removal of Vashti as queen, the choosing of Esther, the humiliation of Haman, Esther pleading for her people, the death of Haman, the deliverance of the Jews, and the celebration of Purim. Encourage students to perform their "newscasts" for the class.

□ Additional Teacher Information

The Festival of Purim celebrates the defeat of the Jews' enemies during the time of Queen Esther. A happy occasion, Purim is celebrated with songs and merriment. Children shout and clap their hands at the mention of Haman during the reading of the Book of Esther. Jewish children dress up as Queen Esther, Mordecai, and King Ahasuerus. Families give gifts to their neighbors and to the poor people in the community.

The festival of Hanukkah was decreed by Judah Maccabeus at the time of the temple's rededication. Hanukkah commemorates the Maccabean victory against the Syrians and is a symbol of the irrepressible spirit of the Jew—his determination to preserve his people in the face of seemingly overwhelming enemies. The celebration of Hanukkah lasts for eight days during which families sing hymns, offer prayers, eat special foods, play games, and give gifts to one another. Hanukkah is called the "Festival of Lights" because of the miraculous preservation of the temple's oil during the rededication in 165 B.C. Tradition records that the priests were able to find only one night's supply of holy oil to light the temple lamps. Miraculously, the oil kept the lamps burning for eight days. In memory of this miracle, Jews place candles in a special candlestick, the *menorah,* during the celebration of Hanukkah. The first night one candle is lit, the second night two candles are lit, and so on, for the entire eight days. Hanukkah is celebrated during December each year.

Judas Maccabaeus, an oratorio by Handel, includes the song "See, the Conqu'ring Hero Comes." The song was written to honor an English general recently returned from a victorious military campaign.

The *synagogue* came into existence during the exile. Before exile, Jews gathered at the temple for formal worship. With the temple destroyed, there were no sacrifices and no sanctified priesthood. Judaism came to be centered more on teaching and studying the Scripture. Synagogues now exist all over the world as the religious gathering places of Jewish people.

LESSON 19
Salvation and Destruction

Text, pages 68-72
Notebook, pages 20-21

- **Jesus in Israel**
- **Destruction of the Temple**
- **Masada**

Preview

□ Objective
Given proper instruction, the students will be able to do the following:
- Use clues to complete a word search puzzle about ancient Israel.

□ Materials
Have available:
- A Bible.
- An overhead projector.
- A blank overhead transparency.
- The figure representing the crucifixion of Christ (c. A.D. 30) from the History TimeLine Packet.

□ Notes
The incarnation of Christ is discussed in this lesson. See the New Testament books of Matthew, Mark, Luke, and John for pertinent scriptural accounts.

Day 29

Lesson

□ Introducing the Lesson
Reading a story—Read the following story aloud to the class.

> As I walked along the dusty roads of Jerusalem today, I passed some merchants who called out to me. I did not stop to look at their fruits and vegetables. I was too absorbed in my own thoughts to think about eating. I had spent the morning with an old rabbi, my grandfather's friend. The rabbi had agreed with my grandfather to teach me from the Torah, so every week I went to his house with a fresh loaf of bread that my mother had baked.

> On this day, the rabbi had spoken to me of the coming Messiah, the redeemer of Israel who would save us from all oppression. He read to me from the great prophet Isaiah, who said the Messiah would be wounded and afflicted and bruised for the iniquities of His people. I wondered how such a thing could be—how could Messiah be powerful enough to save us and yet weak enough to be bruised and stricken?

> As I continued down the dirt roads, I passed a group of men who were shouting excitedly. I was deep in thought, but even so I heard a few of their words. "A baby is born," one said. I thought another man said something about angels, but perhaps I misunderstood him, since I wasn't really listening. Instead, I was thinking about the Messiah—who He would be, when He might come to deliver us from the Romans. I did not pay attention to the rough looking men who might, I thought, be shepherds. What could shepherds have to say, anyway?

Placing a figure on the TimeLine—Place the figure representing the crucifixion of Christ on the TimeLine at approximately A.D. 30. Invite a student to explain how the Messiah could be strong enough to save and yet weak enough to be bruised for His people. *(Jesus was Almighty God, yet He humbled Himself to come to earth to become the sacrifice for the sins of mankind.)*

> Explain to the students that God Himself entered into the story of man in order to make a way for man to be saved from his sinful condition. Take this opportunity to explain God's plan of redemption. Emphasize that anyone who repents of his sin and trusts Christ to save him will be saved. (BATs: 1a Understanding Jesus Christ, 1b Repentance and faith; Bible Promises: B. Guiltless by the Blood, E. Christ as Sacrifice)

□ Teaching the Lesson
Jesus in Israel—Instruct the students to read pages 68-69 silently to find out what two groups of religious leaders were influential in Israel at the time Jesus was born. *(the Pharisees and the Sadducees)*

Discussion Questions
➤ **What was the political situation in Israel at the time Christ was born?** *(The Roman Empire ruled Israel.)*
➤ **Why did many Jews not recognize Jesus as the Messiah?** *(They were looking for political salvation from the oppressive government, not salvation for their eternal souls.)*

During this time, two groups of scholars became important in Judea, the Pharisees and the Sadducees. The Pharisees stressed complete obedience to the law. The Sadducees were more willing to accept the ideas and customs of the secular rulers of Israel—first the Greeks and then the Romans.

Which of these groups do you think was more popular with the common people in Israel? Many thought of the Pharisees as the perfect example of holiness. But Jesus condemned both groups. He knew their good works were nothing more than rituals, and their hearts were cold.

"Woe unto you, scribes and Pharisees, hypocrites! for ye are like unto whited sepulchers, which indeed appear beautiful outward, but are within full of dead men's bones, and of all uncleanness. Even so ye also outwardly appear righteous unto men, but within ye are full of hypocrisy and iniquity."

Matthew 23:27-28

68

By the time Jesus was born, the Greek Empire had been overthrown by the Roman Empire. Although some Jews in Judea had become used to the idea of foreign rule, many wanted independence. Some of these people spoke against the Roman government. Some—the Zealots—actually planned to rebel against the government.

Jesus Christ preached and performed miracles throughout Judea, proving that He was the Son of God. He kept the entire law of God and died a perfect death on the cross. In His death, He paid the penalty of the law for the sins of His people. Looking for salvation from the oppressive government, most of the Jews did not recognize Jesus as Messiah. They continued to hope for an earthly Messiah to free them from the Romans, not a heavenly Redeemer to save them from their sins.

"He came unto his own, and his own received him not."

John 1:11

Possible site of the Crucifixion

69

Lead the students to understand that although God often does provide temporal blessings for His children, the primary blessings of God that the believer has in Christ are the spiritual blessings—the presence of the Holy Spirit, the comfort of the Word of God, access to the Father by prayer in the name of Christ, and eternal life. (Bible Promise: H. God as Father)

Destruction of the temple—Instruct the students to read page 70 silently to find out why Emperor Vespasian decided to destroy the Jews. *(They would not become like Romans.)* Lead a discussion about ways that the Jews differed from the Romans. Emphasize the fact that the greatest difference between the Jews and the Romans was the Jews' insistence on the worship of the one true God and adherence to the Law of Moses.

Discussion Questions

➤ **Why did the Jews feel secure when Titus began his siege of Jerusalem?** *(They believed God would send the Messiah to save them.)*

➤ **What did the Jews endure during this time?** *(famine)*

➤ **What happened to the temple when the Romans attacked it?** *(The temple was looted and burned.)*

In A.D. 70, Emperor Vespasian looked out from his palace in Rome and considered his empire. He ruled lands as far away as Britain and India. Only the Jews refused to adopt Roman ways and worship Roman gods. Vespasian decided to destroy the Jews.

Led by Vespasian's son Titus, the Roman army surrounded Jerusalem and waited. At first the Jews within the city felt secure. They believed God would send them a deliverer, that perhaps now Messiah would come. Then famine set in. Many Jews ate grass and gnawed on leather shoes to keep from dying.

The Wailing Wall (left) is all that remains of the temple complex in Jerusalem.

At last the Romans broke down the wall and marched through Jerusalem, killing all the Jews they met and destroying building after building. Many Jews still hoped that Messiah would save them, but when they saw the temple in flames, they despaired. Old men wept as the building burned. Soldiers looted the temple, stealing the golden candlesticks, the table of showbread, and thousands of gold and silver coins from the temple treasury. Jerusalem was destroyed. The Romans had conquered all of Judea with one exception—Masada.

70

Masada still sits atop its hill in Israel.

Masada

Nearly one thousand Jews lived at Masada, a fort city overlooking the Dead Sea. They believed they were safe from the Romans because they had plenty of food and water, and the Roman army could not attack them. The only trail up to Masada was narrow and winding. If the Roman soldiers attempted to come up this trail, the Jews could kill them one by one. And, although they could see soldiers camped below them, the Jews knew that the summer heat would soon force the Romans to leave.

But the Romans did not give up. Using tons of earth, they built a huge ramp up to the walls of Masada. Then they used a battering ram to break down the outer wall. The soldiers then shot fiery arrows against the timbers of the inner wall. At first the wind caused the flames to blow back against the Roman invaders. Then, as evening set in, the wind shifted and the wall caught fire. The Jews despaired. Their cause was lost.

The Roman soldiers decided to attack in the morning. That night, the Jews of Masada met together around a fire. Their leader told them it would be better to die in freedom than to be killed by the Romans. The Jews agreed. The Jews chose ten men to carry out the executions. When only the ten men were left alive, they chose one man to kill the other nine. How do you think that man felt as he looked on his family and friends lying dead around him? Do you think he changed his mind about dying? He did not.

The next morning the Romans burst in upon Masada, expecting a fight. They were met by silence. Then two women crept out of a cellar. They told the Romans what had happened and led them to the bodies. The Romans stood in silence at the sight of 960 Jews who died on the last day of Masada's defense.

71

Read aloud Mark 13:1-2. Tell the students that when Jesus' disciples pointed out the greatness of the temple to Him, He prophesied that the temple would be destroyed. (Bible Promise: I. God as Master)

Masada—Instruct the students to read page 71 silently to find out how the Jews of Masada evaded capture by the Romans. *(They killed themselves.)* Point out the photograph of Masada as you discuss its siege and capture.

Discussion Questions

➤ **Do you think the Jews did the right thing by killing themselves rather than giving themselves up to torture and slavery?** *(Answers will vary.)*

➤ **Can you imagine a situation similar to this in which Christians would be in danger? If so, what might your family do?** *(Answers will vary.)*

The Jews' resistance ended with the defeat of Masada. But the life of Israel, in the study of the Torah and the ancient worship of God, went on as Jews settled all over the world. They also took with them the hope of a coming Messiah. So long the servants of other nations, the Jews anxiously awaited His coming. Unfortunately, most Jews had formed their own ideas of what Messiah should be like, and they did not recognize Him when He came.

Today, not one of ancient Israel's beautiful buildings remains. The gifts of Israel to the world are far greater than mere arts and crafts, monuments, language, or ideas. Israel's gifts are God's gifts: His Word, the Bible, and the Word, God's precious Son.

Scenes of Israel, including a source of the Jordan River (left)

72

Early Israel Word Search
Clues

Name _____

Write the correct answer in each blank. Then find the words in the word search puzzle on page 21.

Abraham	1.	father of the Jews
Isaac	2.	Abraham's promised son
Jacob	3.	father of twelve sons
Joseph	4.	sold by his brothers into slavery
pharaoh	5.	ruler of Egypt
Judah Maccabeus	6.	delivered the Jews and instituted Hanukkah (two words)
Antiochus	7.	Syrian ruler who offered pigs on the altar of God
Nebuchadnezzar	8.	king of Babylon in 586 B.C.
Cyrus	9.	Persian king who defeated Babylon in 539 B.C.
Ezekiel	10.	prophet who foretold the destruction of Tyre
Masada	11.	fort in which 960 Jews died
Purim	12.	celebration of the deliverance of the Jews from Haman
Hanukkah	13.	celebration of the rededication of the temple
Romans	14.	soldiers who defeated Jerusalem in A.D. 70
Pharisees	15.	Jews who stressed obedience to the Law
Sadducee	16.	a Jew who was open to Greek ideas
Vespasian	17.	Roman emperor who ordered the destruction of Jerusalem
Torah	18.	first five books of the Bible
Messiah	19.	Jesus Christ
Passover	20.	celebration of the deliverance of the first-born son
Egypt	21.	land of the Hebrews' slavery
Canaan	22.	the Promised Land
Philistines	23.	enemies of the Jews defeated by King David
Saul	24.	first king of Israel

Heritage Studies 6
Student Notebook

Lesson 19
Evaluating the Lesson   **20**

Instruct the students to read page 72 to find out what great gifts Israel has given to the world. *(the Bible and Jesus the Messiah, God's Son)* Discuss page 72 as desired.

□ Evaluating the Lesson

Early Israel Word Search (Notebook pages 20-21)—Instruct the students to use the clues to identify the words in the word search puzzle on Notebook page 20 and then to find those words in the puzzle on Notebook page 21.

═══ Going Beyond ═══

□ Enrichment

For Christ—Show the students the video *Wine of Morning* available from ShowForth Videos, Bob Jones University Press. A fictional story based around the time of the crucifixion of Christ, the story tells of Joel, a young man who turns outlaw to free his people from Roman tyranny.

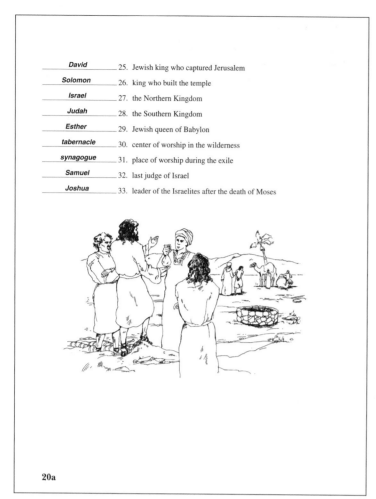

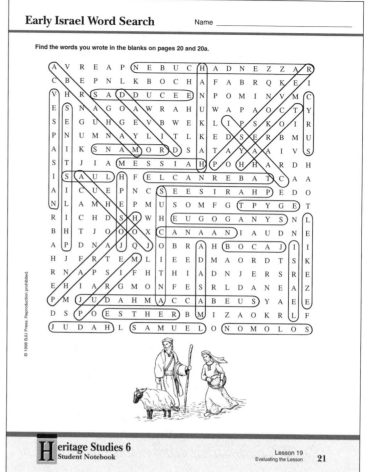

Left worksheet (page 20a):

David	25. Jewish king who captured Jerusalem
Solomon	26. king who built the temple
Israel	27. the Northern Kingdom
Judah	28. the Southern Kingdom
Esther	29. Jewish queen of Babylon
tabernacle	30. center of worship in the wilderness
synagogue	31. place of worship during the exile
Samuel	32. last judge of Israel
Joshua	33. leader of the Israelites after the death of Moses

20a

Right worksheet (page 21):

Early Israel Word Search   Name _____

Find the words you wrote in the blanks on pages 20 and 20a.

Heritage Studies 6 Student Notebook

Lesson 19 Evaluating the Lesson   21

Additional Teacher Information

The fire that destroyed the temple was started by an excited soldier in defiance of Titus's order to keep the building intact. The soldier, disobeying orders, threw a burning torch through an open window. When Titus heard that the temple was aflame, he shouted orders to put out the fire, but by that time the soldiers had been aroused to a destructive pitch and were doing all they could to hasten the ruin of God's house. Old Jewish men stood around the burning building quoting Scripture, while tears streamed down their faces.

Masada had been built by Herod as a defensive palace about one hundred years before its siege. Herod had provisioned it with great stores of food, which, in the end, were used to feed his enemies the Jews.

Little is known about the two women who survived Masada and reported its events to the Roman soldiers. They had rescued a few children along with themselves, and apparently the group had remained hidden in the cellar throughout the massacre.

Excavations at Masada uncovered the remains of twenty-seven Jewish defenders. These men, women, and children were buried with full military honors on July 7, 1969, by the nation of Israel.

Herod the Great ruled the land of Palestine with an iron hand. So heinous were his crimes that the "Massacre of the Innocents," in which all the children unto two years old were murdered, was—although deeply mourned in Palestine—not considered one of his worst acts. It was seen by the Romans as an attempt to keep the local people submissive.

Herod died in 4 B.C. This would place the birth of Christ somewhat earlier.

The ninth day of the Hebrew month Ab is remembered yearly. On this day in 586 B.C., the temple was destroyed by the Babylonians. And on this day in the year A.D. 70, the temple was destroyed by the Romans. For four hundred years after A.D. 70, no Jews were allowed into Jerusalem except on the ninth of Ab to mourn the loss of the temple.

Josephus, a writer whose work is important as supplemental history to the Bible, was a Jewish military general. At the time of the Roman siege of Jerusalem, Josephus turned traitor and joined the Romans. At one point he approached the Jews who were suffering in Jerusalem and told them to give up the fight. They rejected his advice and continued to hold out against massive opposition. Josephus remained in the pay of the Romans while writing his famous histories.

Path to Sinai

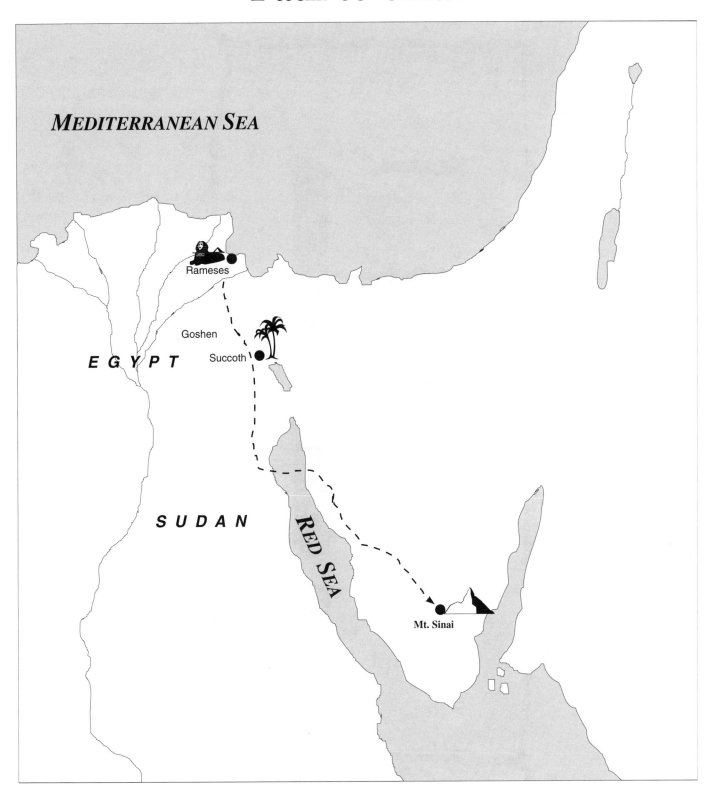

MEDITERRANEAN SEA

Rameses

Goshen

Succoth

E G Y P T

S U D A N

RED SEA

Mt. Sinai

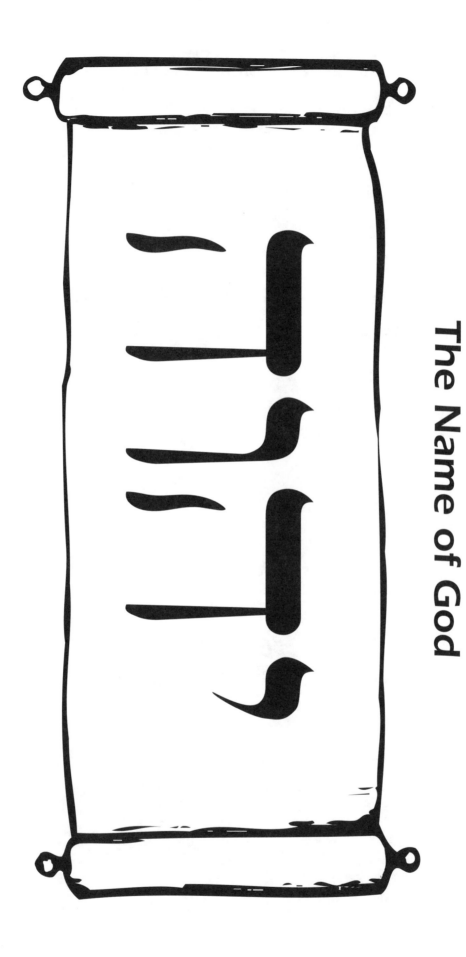

The Name of God

Hebrew Alphabet

א Aleph	ב Beth	ב Veth
ג Gimel	ד Daleth	ה He
ו Waw	ז Zayin	ח Heth
ט Teth	י Yod	כ Kaph
כ Khaph	ל Lamed	מ Mem
נ Nun	ס Samekh	ע Ayin
פ Peh	פ Feh	צ Tsadi
ק Koph	ר Resh	ש Shin
ש Sin	ת Taw	

Kings of Israel and Judah

The United Kingdom

Saul

David

Solomon

The Divided Kingdom

Israel	Judah
Jeroboam	Rehoboam
Nadab	Abijam
Baasha	Asa
Elah	Jehoshaphat
Zimri	Jehoram
Tibni	Ahaziah
Omri	Athaliah (queen)
Ahab	Joash
Ahaziah	Amaziah
Jehoram	Uzziah
Jehu	Jotham
Jehoahaz	Ahaz
Joash	Hezekiah
Jeroboam II	Manasseh
Zechariah	Amon
Shallum	Josiah
Menahem	Jehoahaz
Pekahiah	Jehoiakim
Pekah	Jehoiachin
Hoshea	Zedekiah

Divided Kingdom

Tyre

PHOENICIA

Dan

SYRIA (ARAM)

Kedesh

Hazor

SEA OF GALILEE

Bashan

THE GREAT SEA
(MEDITERRANEAN SEA)

Megiddo

Jezreel

Dothan

Jabesh-gilead

ISRAEL

Jordan River

Samaria

Shechem

Succoth

AMMON

Shiloh

Joppa

Bethel

Gilgal

Jericho

Jerusalem

Heshbon

Ashdod

Bethlehem

DEAD SEA

Ashkelon

PHILISTIA

Hebron

Gaza

En-gedi

JUDAH

MOAB

Beersheba

EDOM

Exile Map

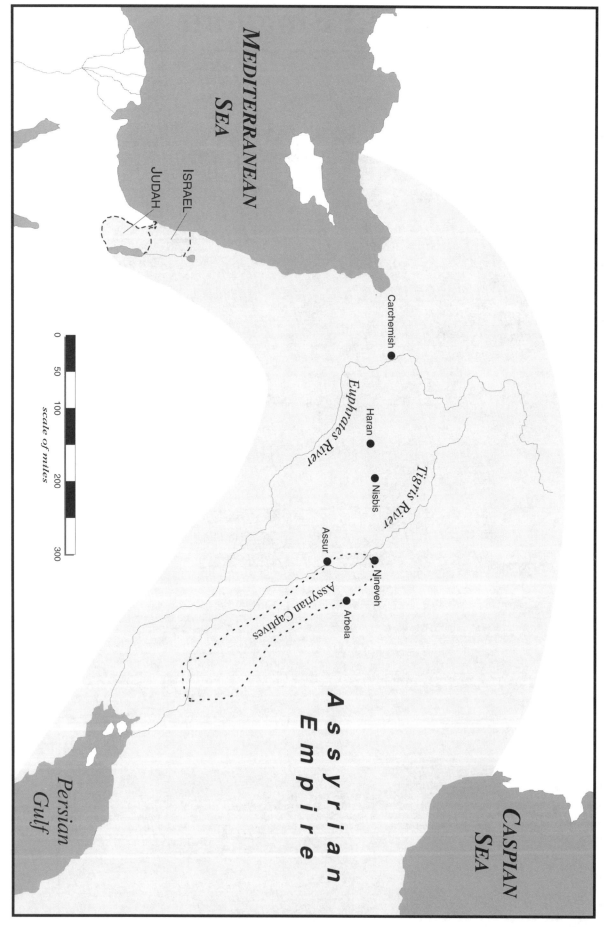

MEDITERRANEAN SEA

ISRAEL

JUDAH

Carchemish

Euphrates River

Tigris River

Haran

Nisbis

Assur

Nineveh

Arbela

Assyrian Captives

A s s y r i a n
E m p i r e

Persian Gulf

CASPIAN SEA

0
50
100
200
300
scale of miles

Use with Lesson 18. Heritage Studies 6 TE

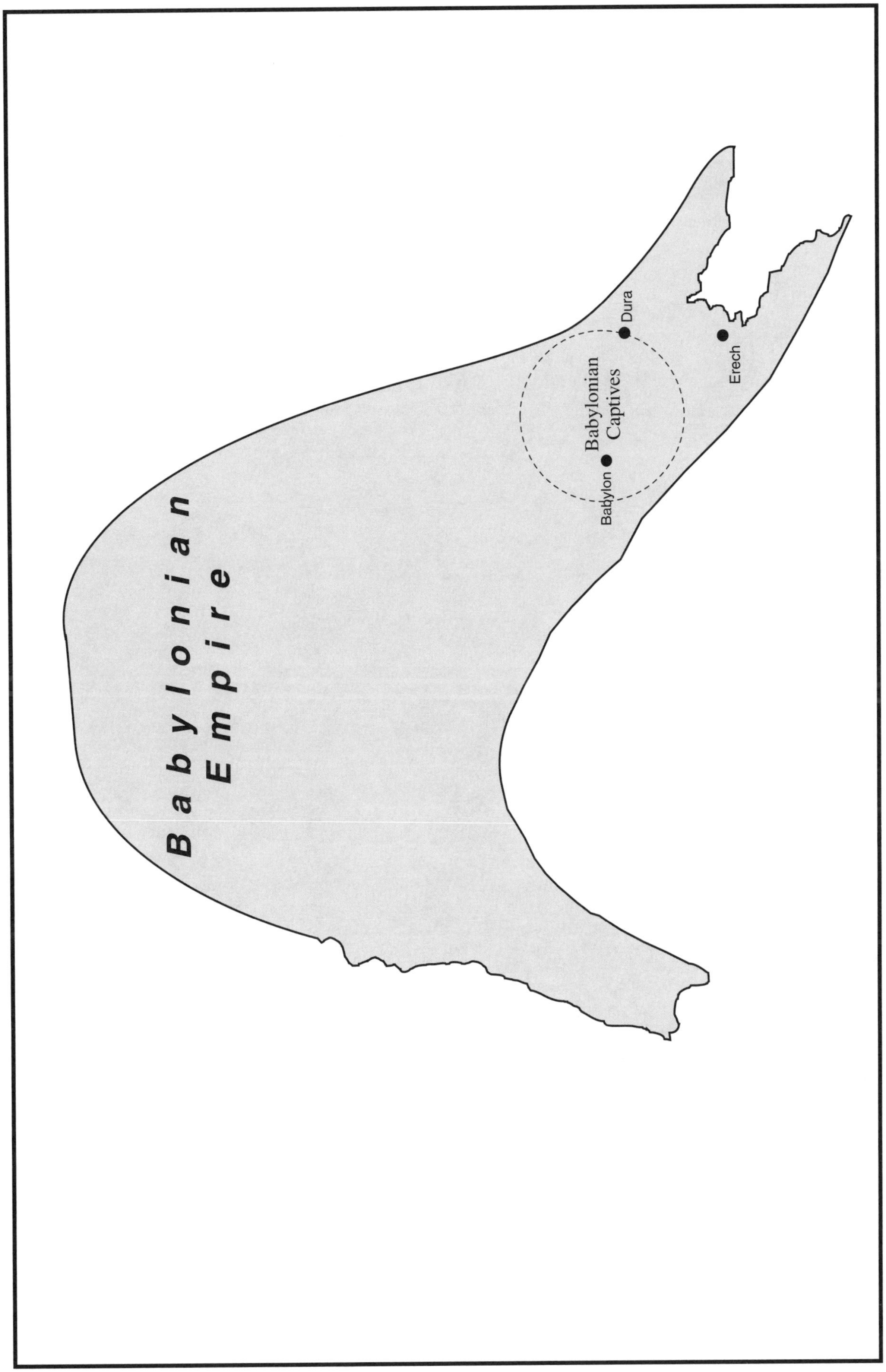

Babylonian
Empire

Dura

Erech

Babylonian
Captives

Babylon

Mysteries of the Indus: Ancient India

This chapter highlights the first two civilizations of India, the Indus and the Aryan. The Indus Valley civilization is presented through a series of fictitious letters between a young man who is helping at an archaeological dig in Mohenjo-Daro and his younger sister at home in England. Through this exchange, the students learn about the activities of an archaeologist. The *Discovering How* activity in Lesson 21 provides valuable hands-on experience for the students as they record information about an artifact. Understanding the value of written records is an important historical concept developed throughout the lessons. The study of the Aryans begins the foundation for later studies of India by covering the basis of Indian life—Hinduism. Contrasting Hinduism and Buddhism with biblical truth exposes the students to the error of mystical Eastern religions.

□ Materials

Lessons 20 and 21 require certain items that must be obtained or prepared several days to several weeks before the presentation of the lesson. These items are labeled with an asterisk (*) in each lesson and in the Materials List in the Supplement. Occasionally, items not commonly found in the classroom as well as items needed in large quantities may also be labeled with an asterisk. If you plan to do the Enrichment activities in Lessons 22 and 24, allow time to obtain the additional items necessary. For further information, see the individual lessons.

□ Chapter Bulletin Board

Place a background of brightly colored paper on the bulletin board. Prepare a figure of the globe and place it in the center of the board. (*NOTE:* See the reproducible material at the end of Lesson 24.) Display the Question Cards on the bulletin board after the students write their questions. (NOTE: See the reproducible material at the end of Lesson 24.) Place the title *Ask Me About India!* in the top center of the bulletin board. For further instructions about the interactive bulletin board activity, refer to Evaluating the Lesson in Lesson 20.

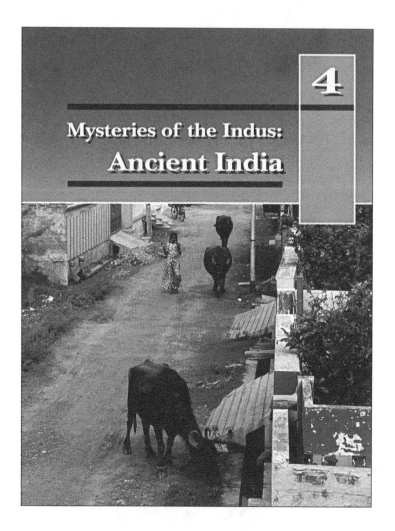

Mysteries of the Indus:
Ancient India

4

LESSON 20

A Moment in Time

Text, pages 74-78
Notebook, pages 22-23

- Discovery of Ancient India
- Description of India
- Then and Now

━━━ Preview ━━━

□ Objectives

Given proper instruction, the students will be able to do the following:

- Locate India on a map or globe.
- Label the major landforms on a map of India.
- Answer questions about India's major landforms.

□ Materials

Have available:

- *Just So Stories* by Rudyard Kipling (optional).
- Crayons or colored pencils for each student: blue, green, orange, and purple.
- A hand mirror.*
- A Bible.
- A globe or a wall map of the world.
- Maps and More 6.
- The figure representing the Indus Valley civilization (2500 B.C.) from the History TimeLine Packet.
- 4 stickers for each student.*

Prepare:

- A *Question Card* for each student. (*NOTE:* See the reproducible material at the end of Lesson 24.)
- An *Ask Me Answer Card* for each student. (*NOTE:* See the reproducible material at the end of Lesson 24.)

□ Notes

The *Discovering How* activity in Lesson 21 requires an item for each student. Allow time to collect the items needed.

If you plan to do the Enrichment activities in Lessons 22 and 24, allow time to obtain samples of breads made with a variety of grains and a copy of the book *With Daring Faith: A Biography of Amy Carmichael,* available through Bob Jones University Press.

The modern border between India and Pakistan along Jammu and Kashmir is shown on the maps according to the Simia Agreement of 1972.

━━━ Lesson ━━━

□ Introducing the Lesson

The Elephant's Child—Read aloud the following story. (*NOTE:* This selection is adapted from Rudyard Kipling's *Just So Stories.* You may prefer to read the entire story from a copy of the book.)

Once long ago, there was an Elephant's Child whose 'satiable curiosity moved him to ask many questions. His first and foremost question was, "What does the Crocodile have for dinner?" Twitching his blackish, bulgy nose that was only as big as a boot, the Elephant's Child persisted with this question until one day the Kolokolo Bird simply said, "Go to the banks of the great grey-green, greasy Limpopo River, and find out."

And so, the Elephant's Child sojourned to the great Limpopo to discover what the Crocodile has for dinner. At the brink of the grey-green water, the Elephant's Child trod on what he thought was a log of wood. But it was really the Crocodile.

"'Scuse me," said the Elephant's Child most politely, "but did you happen to have seen a Crocodile in these promiscuous parts, and if so, could you kindly tell me what he has for dinner?"

"Come hither, Little One," said the Crocodile, "for I am the Crocodile," and he wept crocodile tears to show it was quite true. The Elephant's Child breathlessly kneeled on the bank to hear the raspy whisper of the Crocodile.

"I think," whispered the Crocodile, "that I will start with the Elephant's Child!" and with that, his jaws clamped down upon the blackish, bulgy nose of the Elephant's Child.

At this, the Elephant's Child was much 'nnoyed, and he said through his nose, "Led go! You are hurtig be!" But the Crocodile was determined to have dinner, and a great tug-of-war followed in which the Elephant's Child's nose stretched and stretched. Now, the Elephant's Child planted his feet in the mud and pulled until the Crocodile, really a little bored now, released the nose with a great 'plop!' that echoed all along the Limpopo. The Crocodile then slithered away to find another entree.

The Elephant's Child sat in the cool mud and looked mournfully down upon his now long nose. Perhaps some banana leaves would cool it, he thought. Before he knew it, he reached with his now long nose and picked a few leaves. Later, as he felt the warmth of the setting sun, he cooled himself by using his now long nose to schloop a schloop of mud atop his head. Finally, it dawned on the Elephant's Child what a wonderful thing his now long nose was. He could pick fruit and trumpet songs—and all because of his 'satiable curiosity. And that is how the Elephant's Child got his long nose, and elephants thereafter have had long, useful noses and have been happy, happy creatures.

Ask the students whether the story is true. *(no)* Tell them that the story is included in the *Just So Stories,* a collection of fanciful stories written by Rudyard Kipling. Ask whether the students know another well-known Kipling story about

The sun is starting to rise over a distant hill. It is a sandy hill that stands behind the scene below. Dark-skinned men in flowing robes murmur in the hush of the early morning as they swing shovels rhythmically into the earth. Suddenly—like a rush of wind—the murmur rises to an excited buzz. They have found something!

The supervisor walks slowly to the spot where the helpers have dug. Each step is calm and deliberate. He cannot get too excited—it could be a false alarm. He kneels beside the hard brick that one of the nationals has uncovered. The supervisor removes a small, delicate brush from the satchel that is slung over his shoulder. He gently sweeps the brick. Terra cotta! He leans closer, using his magnifying glass to examine the terra cotta piece.

Slowly, so slowly, the supervisor's eyes swing upward. He stares at the distant hill, the air blurring with the sun's now bright heat. "It is Mohenjo-Daro," he whispers to the distant hill. "We have found the Indus."

74

One of the greatest archaeological finds occurred in India during the 1920s. This find was the discovery of *Mohenjo-Daro* and its sister city, *Harappa*. These cities have been dated to approximately 2500 B.C. Do you know how long ago that was?

Archaeological digs do not always uncover secrets from the past. Archaeologists may spend years studying and searching for ancient civilizations. They may excavate site after site, only to end up empty-handed. Mohenjo-Daro and Harappa were different, however. The discovery of these two ancient cities opened the door to a world long forgotten—the world of the Indus Valley civilization. Why do you think this discovery was so important to archaeologists and historians? The discovery of artifacts belonging to these ancient peoples began the unraveling of the mystery that envelopes our past.

Ruins of Mohenjo-Daro

75

an Indian child named Mowgli who is lost in the jungle. *(The Jungle Book)* Tell the students that Rudyard Kipling was born in India in 1865, but his parents sent him to England for schooling at age five. At age seventeen Kipling returned to India and wrote short stories, poems, and novels that tell about India during British rule. He was awarded the Nobel Prize for Literature in 1913. His personal experiences of living in India influenced his perspective and artful writing. Tell the students that they will learn more of Kipling's India in this chapter.

□ Teaching the Lesson

Discovery of ancient India—Instruct the students to read pages 74-75 silently to find out other names for ancient India. *(the Indus, the Indus Valley civilization)* Add the figure representing the Indus Valley civilization to the History TimeLine at the year 2500 B.C. Tell the students that the picture is an example of a seal found by archaeologists in the Indus Valley area.

Discussion Questions

➤ **What is an *artifact*?** *(an object from the past that people study to learn more about the past)*
➤ **What two Indian cities did archaeologists discover in 1920?** *(Mohenjo-Daro and Harappa)*
➤ **Why was the discovery of these cities important?** *(It provided information about the people and culture of the Indus Valley civilization.)*

➤ **Do you think the owner of the terra cotta piece thought it was valuable?** *(probably not)*
➤ **Why is a brush used to uncover artifacts?** *(so that the artifacts are not damaged as they are unearthed)*
➤ **In approximately what year did the cities of Mohenjo-Daro and Harappa exist?** *(2500 B.C.)*

Ask the students how many years have elapsed since these cities were built. *(about four thousand five hundred years)* Point out that in the entire perspective of time, the people of the Indus portray only a small segment of history.

Remind the students that life is brief. Select a volunteer to read aloud James 4:14. Illustrate the brevity of life by blowing onto a mirror. Allow the students to observe how quickly the mirror returns to clearness. Point out that our time on the earth is short, but the decisions we make affect our souls for eternity. Christians should be busy telling others about God's plan of salvation. (BAT: 5c Evangelism and missions)

The year is 1925. A young man sits at a makeshift desk made of empty crates. The flap of his tent stirs with a sudden breeze. His pen scratches the paper at a furious pace. Occasionally, he stops and stares thoughtfully at a small photograph propped against a dusty hat.

"My dear Lucy," he writes, smiling at the name that brings so many memories to mind. "I do miss you and Mother and the children. Though I yearn to be with you all, my trip here to India is necessary for my ancient history studies. The exciting discoveries by Sir John Marshall here make this site one of the most desirable places for study. He is a very knowledgeable man to work for. Five officers work under him, including my supervisor, Mr. Hargreaves."

76

"You asked me about some of the strange sights I have seen. No, I haven't seen any cobras or men on beds of nails since we left the big city of Karachi where we first docked. Here in Mohenjo-Daro we are far away from any big cities. But I rather like this peaceful area with its rolling hills. The hills remind me of southern England. Yet everything here is dry and yellow with dust—how I miss green England!"

William pauses and gazes between the tent flaps at the late afternoon sky. "The weather here has been perfect for the dig," he writes. "Now is the dry, cool season in India. Our temperatures are in the fifties, which is perfect for outdoor work. The Indians tell me that during the hot season, temperatures rise to over 100°. Quite warm, wouldn't you say? At any rate, Mohenjo-Daro is a splendid place to excavate. I must leave off for now to prepare for tomorrow's work. Do write again. Give my love to Mother and the others."

77

Day 32

Description of India—Explain to the students that they will be reading a series of letters. These letters are fictitious, but the material within them about the Indus civilization is accurate. Tell them that India (including the Indus River Valley) was part of the British Empire during the 1920s when the initial archaeological work was being done at Mohenjo-Daro. Instruct the students to read pages 76-77 silently to find out why the writer is in India. *(William is a student who is part of an archaeological dig.)*

Discussion Questions

➤ **What year is the setting for the letters?** *(1925)*
➤ **How did the writer travel to India?** *(by boat)*
➤ **How far do you think it is from England to India?** *(Answers will vary; it is about four thousand miles by air.)* **From the United States to India?** *(Answers will vary; it is about seven thousand miles by air.)*
➤ **What sights would you expect to see in India?** *(Answers will vary.)*
➤ **What do you learn about India from the letter?** *(There are hills; it is dusty, dry, and cool. The hot season is over 100°.)*

◆ THEN AND NOW ◆

India

Location—A large peninsula in south-central Asia, jutting out into the Indian Ocean above the equator. Modern India is bordered by Pakistan in the northwest. China, Nepal, Bhutan, Burma, and Bangladesh are on the eastern and northeastern borders.

Climate—Primarily temperate, with patches of tropical and dry climates. Affected by yearly *monsoons*, or winds that bring wet air in the summer and dry air in the winter. Temperatures are above 70°F most of the year, except in the north. Annual precipitation ranges from zero to over four hundred inches.

Topography—Contains three major land regions. The Himalaya Mountains stretch across northeastern India, cutting off India and some of her neighbors from the rest of the continent. In so doing, they create what is called the Indian subcontinent. South of the mountains is the northern plain, watered by three rivers: the Indus, the Ganges, and the Brahmaputra. Southern India is a large plateau called Deccan.

Natural Resources—Large deposits of iron ore and some coal. Small amounts of other minerals, including uranium, diamonds, emeralds, gold, and silver. There is also much fertile land.

Geography and Culture—The Indus and Ganges riverbanks provided the first homes for the ancient civilizations of India. The rivers supplied water, fish, and transportation. The mountains of northern India have also influenced India's history. Only through the passes in the northwest could foreigners invade India, which they have done regularly throughout history. Because desert and rough terrain lie south of the river valleys, invaders rarely penetrated farther south. Most of India's history has taken place in northern India.

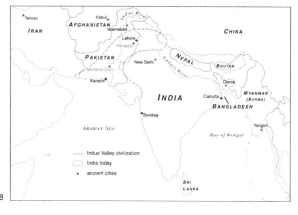

78

Map Activity   Name _____

Complete the following statements by writing the answer in the blank or by labeling and coloring the map on page 23.

1. Label the countries of India, Pakistan, Nepal, and China.

2. What are the three main rivers of India? *Indus, Ganges, and Brahmaputra*
   _____ Color the rivers blue.

3. Label the ocean off the southern coast of India. *Indian Ocean*

4. What mountains are a northern boundary to India? *Himalayan Mountain Range*
   Color the mountain system purple.

5. What is the tallest mountain in the world? *Mount Everest*

6. What is the plateau in southern India called? *Deccan Plateau*
   Color the plateau orange.

7. What is one of India's major cities? *New Delhi, Mumbai (Bombay), or Calcutta*

8. In which area of India do most of the people live? *northern India (Northern Plains)*
   Color this part of India green.

9. Which direction is India from the equator? *north*

10. Explain how the Himalayas have affected India's history. *The mountains have cut off India to the north, allowing invaders only through passes in the mountains to the northwest.*
    _____

© 1998 BJU Press. Reproduction prohibited.

Heritage Studies 6
Student Notebook

Lesson 20
Evaluating the Lesson   **22**

Then and Now—Instruct the students to read page 78 silently to find out what mountains in northern India have affected India's history. *(the Himalaya Mountains)* Point out that Mount Everest, the highest mountain in the world, lies in the Himalayas north of India in the neighboring country of Nepal.

Point to India on a globe or a wall map of the world. Explain that the country's name, *India,* and its dominant religion, *Hinduism,* are derived from the name of the Indus River. Direct attention to the Then and Now map on page 78. Direct the students' attention to ancient cities, changes in boundary lines, and so on.

Display Maps and More 6. Point out that on a modern map of the area, the Indus River lies mostly in the nation of Pakistan rather than India. Explain that this region was a part of the traditional area of the Indian subcontinent and is a part of the same culture region. Historically, the Indus is an Indian river, but new boundaries established in 1947 place the river within the modern country of Pakistan.

Discussion Questions

➤ **Is India north or south of the equator?** *(north)*
➤ **What ocean lies to the south of India?** *(Indian Ocean)*
➤ **What is the large plateau in southern India called?** *(Deccan)*
➤ **What other countries border India to the east?** *(China, Nepal, Bhutan, Bangladesh, and Burma [now called Myanmar])*

➤ **What are *monsoons?*** *(winds that bring wet air in the summer and dry air in the winter)*
➤ **What modern city is located in the Indus delta area about 150 miles south of Mohenjo-Daro's remains?** *(Karachi, Pakistan)*
➤ **The site of Harappa is located near what other large city in northeastern Pakistan?** *(Lahore)*
➤ **Why did the ancient civilization of India settle by the Indus and Ganges Rivers?** *(The rivers provided water, fish, and transportation.)*

☐ Evaluating the Lesson

Map of India (Notebook pages 22-23)—Instruct the students to read each statement. Tell them to complete the page by writing the answer in the blank or by labeling and coloring the map on Notebook page 23.

Writing questions—Give each student a copy of the *Question Card,* telling him to write a question about India. Collect the *Question Cards* and display them on the bulletin board. Give each student an *Ask Me Answer Card,* instructing him to fold it on the dotted lines accordion style. Throughout the study of this chapter, challenge each student to choose four *Question Cards* from the bulletin board. On his *Answer Card,* the student should write in each section the name of the person asking the question and the answer to the question. If a student wishes to check his answers, allow him to ask the person who wrote each of the questions he chose. Provide stickers for the students to place over the question

96

Heritage Studies 6 TE

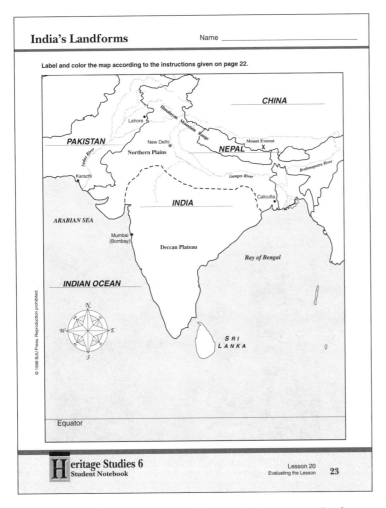

India's Landforms   Name _____

Label and color the map according to the instructions given on page 22.

CHINA

Himalayan Mountain Range

Lahore

PAKISTAN   New Delhi
                  Northern Plains   NEPAL

Indus River   Mount Everest
                                       X

Karachi   Ganges River   Brahmaputra River

                    INDIA   Calcutta

ARABIAN SEA

Mumbai
(Bombay)   Deccan Plateau

                                Bay of Bengal

INDIAN OCEAN

N
W   E
S   S R I
                         L A N K A

Equator

Heritage Studies 6
Student Notebook   Lesson 20
                                    Evaluating the Lesson   23

© 1998 BJU Press. Reproduction prohibited.

marks on the four sections of their *Ask Me Answer Cards* to represent each correct response. As the chapter progresses, you may want to encourage the students to write additional questions. Display the *Ask Me Answer Cards* below the bulletin board if you wish.

━━━ Going Beyond ━━━

□ Enrichment

Research activity—Set up an AREA with books about India, encyclopedias, felt-tip pens, and colored pencils. Have available a copy of the "Picture This" page for each student. (*NOTE:* See the reproducible material at the end of Lesson 24.) Instruct the students to follow the directions given on the page. Display the papers in the classroom.

□ Additional Teacher Information

In addition to the two ancient cities of Mohenjo-Daro and Harappa, five towns and over one hundred smaller villages belonging to the civilization have been found. These sites are spread over a wide area in the Indus Valley and along the coast of the Arabian Sea. Harappa is not as well preserved as Mohenjo-Daro because railroad builders in the 1800s removed large quantities of the baked bricks from that city's ruins for use as filler in their nearby roadbeds. Nevertheless, both cities seem to have been built on an almost identical, well-organized plan. Streets were laid out in parallel fashion, and the dwellings were equipped with an impressive system of sewers and drains.

Pakistan was established on August 14, 1947, as a Muslim nation. India gained independence the next day as a Hindu nation. Turmoil and unrest have been characteristic of the government of Pakistan throughout the years. Today Pakistan remains a rural society.

LESSON 21
Pieces of the Past

Text, pages 79-83
Notebook, page 24

- Indus Valley Civilization
- Ancient Artifacts
- House VIII

━━━ Preview ━━━

☐ Objective
Given proper instruction, the students will be able to do the following:
- Record and catalog an artifact.

☐ Materials
Have available:
- A triangular-bladed mason's trowel (optional).
- Several soft-bristled utility brushes (optional).
- A camera (optional).
- A sheet of paper for each student.
- A permanent marking pen for each student.*
- A self-adhesive label for each student.*
- A resealable plastic bag for each student.*
- A meter stick or metric ruler for each student.*
- A postal scale.*
- An artifact for each student.* (*NOTE:* See the Notes section below for specific ideas.)
- A box of sand (optional).
- An overhead projector.
- A blank overhead transparency.

Prepare an overhead transparency of the map of the Indus and Ganges deltas. (*NOTE:* See the reproducible material at the end of Lesson 24.)

☐ Notes
You may choose to expand the Enrichment activities in Lessons 23 and 24 for study during the entire chapter.

Measurements for the *Discovering How* activity should be done with metric measurement. However, the students may use customary measurement and convert the information to metric terms if you wish.

Items for the *Discovering How* activity should be unusual but useful. Some suggestions include the following: a saltcellar, an eight-track cassette tape, game markers, a nail punch, a wood chisel, a sawtooth picture hanger, tweezers, and a slide for use with a microscope. Other possibilities include a mirror, a cork, a citrus peeler, a drawer knob, marbles, a ring, a button, a rubber band, or a key. Be sure to use items made of varying materials, such as wood, glass, stone, or metal.

William wrote his letters in 1925, but his work took him back through time, placing him in a civilization that existed thousands of years ago. Locate Mohenjo-Daro on the map on page 78. Can you guess the name of the ancient civilization that lived there? It is sometimes called the *Harappan* civilization after the Pakistani town of Harappa—the site where archaeological evidence was first found.

Historians believe that the people of Harappa were very similar to those who lived nearly four hundred miles away at Mohenjo-Daro. Similar artifacts were found in both locations, indicating that both cities were part of the same civilization. Why do you think this is true? For about eight hundred years these ancient Indians flourished in the fertile river valley.

The Indus River

79

Day 33

━━━ Lesson ━━━

☐ Introducing the Lesson
Spelling challenge—Give each student a sheet of paper. Tell the students that they will be writing words that relate to archaeology in some way. Direct each student to write the word *excavate* on his paper. Select a volunteer to spell the word correctly as you write it on the chalkboard; direct the students to check whether they spelled the word correctly. Continue the activity, using the words *artifacts, historians, civilization, ancient, linguistics, terra-cotta, geography, pictographs,* and *photograph.* Tell the students that these words are used in this lesson.

☐ Teaching the Lesson
Indus Valley civilization—Instruct the students to read page 79 silently to find out why the Indus Valley civilization is also called the *Harappan* civilization. (*Archaeological evidence was first found in the city of Harappa.*) Instruct the students to locate Mohenjo-Daro and Harappa on the map on page 78.

Discussion Questions
➤ In what modern-day country are Mohenjo-Daro and Harappa located? (*Pakistan*)
➤ What is the approximate distance between the two cities? (*four hundred miles*)

At first, historians and archaeologists could only speculate about this ancient civilization. Later, artifacts found in the 1920s indicated that the Indus people were highly sophisticated. Because of its closeness to the river, the land was good for farming and raising animals. Around 2500 B.C. some of the first communities were formed in the Indus Valley. Archaeologists have found in these villages well-organized, two-story houses that included a bathing area and a drainage system that ran throughout the entire city. How is this design similar to your town or city?

More artifacts, such as gold ornaments, bronze utensils, and bronze pots, led archaeologists to believe that the Indus people were artistic and skilled craftsmen. Many of these ornaments contain pictographs, but these ancient writings remain an unsolved mystery even today.

In this view of Mohenjo-Daro, the large area at the center left is called the Great Bath.

80

William watches the helpers record and label each artifact that has been found. It is getting to be late afternoon. He wipes his damp forehead, leaving a smudge of yellow dust. He sits down at the corner table to jot a few lines to his sister. "Dear Lucy," he writes. "I'm glad to hear your schoolwork is going better. Keep studying hard. I'm also pleased that you are reading about India. We have many native boys and girls about your age working for us. They carry away baskets of soil from the dig. The carriers often search the dirt in their baskets in hopes of finding more artifacts for which they will receive an extra reward above their usual wage."

William smiles. "I bet you would enjoy that job as well! I am taking a short break now, but our work here at Mohenjo-Daro continues. Mr. Hargreaves assigned me to help excavate a particular house. We believe there is an entire city buried in this area, but my house is House VIII on what we call High Lane. It seems that Mohenjo-Daro had two main streets. Much of the remains we have found appear to have been middle-class houses owned by merchants and craftsmen. It must have been a prosperous city."

81

➤ **What indication is there that the two cities were once part of the same civilization?** *(Similar artifacts were found in both locations.)*

➤ **About how long did the area prosper?** *(eight hundred years)*

➤ **Why do you think the particular site was chosen for your city?** *(Answers will vary. Possible answers include access to railroads and nearness to natural resources, such as a body of water.)*

Display the transparency of the Indus and Ganges deltas. Point to the Indus River. Explain that a delta forms where a main stream separates into smaller rivers. Select a volunteer to locate the mouth of the Ganges River and the mouth of the Indus River.

➤ **Where is the source of the Indus, Ganges, and Brahmaputra Rivers?** *(the Himalaya Mountains)*

➤ **Why are there so many rivers in northern India?** *(The melting snow in the Himalayas forms many rivers.)*

Ancient artifacts—Instruct the students to read pages 80-81 silently to find out what the artifacts indicate about the Indus people. *(They were highly sophisticated, artistic, and skilled.)*

Discussion Questions

➤ **What three occupations are mentioned?** *(farmers, craftsmen, merchants)*

➤ **What did the first Indus villages contain?** *(well-organized, two-story houses that included a bathing area and a drainage system that ran throughout the entire city)*

➤ **How do we know that the Indus people were artistic and skilled craftsmen?** *(Gold ornaments, bronze pots and utensils, and pictographs have been found.)*

Remind the students that money, houses, and all other material goods on earth last only a little while. Point out that a Christian can be happy, knowing that God provides what is needed. (BAT: 7d Contentment)

William pauses, watching the helpers tag a bronze pot. "When I come home," he writes, continuing his letter, "I'll bring sketches of House VIII. The first floor is made of red brick. We believe at one time it had a second story of wood. We think that because of the charred bits of wood we have found along the top of the brick. The house has an open courtyard to let in light.

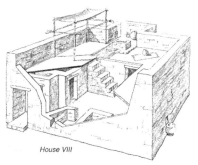

House VIII

There are small rooms off the courtyard, one for the well and the other for a bathroom. The Indus people had advanced plumbing! Other rooms were probably used as kitchens and guest rooms. The family's sleeping quarters were in the back and upstairs."

William pauses. The helpers have moved on to tagging shell-like utensils. "House VIII contained some interesting artifacts," he continues. "Some of our finds from it include a spoon made from a shell, a small clay ball, a pretty ring, and some grain kernels. We also found several pieces of sculpted alabaster. Putting them together, we discovered they formed the figure of a man. We don't know whether it was used as an idol for worship or as a piece of art. Right now, it is one of the earliest Indian sculptures we have."

"Each artifact must first be photographed where it was found, then labeled, and then removed. Then we record all our artifacts to keep track of them."

The helpers stir, putting the artifacts carefully away. William glances at his watch. "I must leave off for now, Lucy. I had meant for this to be only a brief letter. As you can see, we are very busy, but it is so exciting to uncover pieces of the past. It is like catching glimpses of a secret and silent world. Keep up with your studies like a good girl! I shall write again soon."

82

◆ DISCOVERING HOW ◆

To Catalog an Artifact

1. Get Notebook page 24 and the following supplies: a resealable plastic bag, a self-adhesive label, a pencil, a permanent marking pen, a postal scale, a meter stick, and a metric ruler.

2. Carefully examine the "artifact" your teacher has given you.

3. Complete the catalog sheet based on your study of the artifact.

4. Follow your teacher's instructions for safe storage of the artifact.

83

Day 34

House VIII—Instruct the students to read page 82 silently to find out how House VIII in Mohenjo-Daro is described. *(It was a two-story house of red brick and wood with an open courtyard. There were small rooms off the courtyard, one for the well and the other for a bathroom. Other rooms were probably used as kitchens and guest rooms. The family's sleeping quarters were in the back and upstairs.)* Ask the students how the Harappan house is similar to or different from houses today. *(Answers will vary.)*

Discussion Questions

➤ **What were some artifacts of interest found in the house?** *(a spoon made from a shell, a small clay ball, a pretty ring, grain kernels, and pieces of sculpted alabaster)*

➤ **What happens to an artifact when it is found at an archaeological site?** *(It is photographed where it is found, labeled, removed, and recorded.)*

➤ **Why were the pieces of alabaster of interest?** *(They formed the figure of a man.)*

➤ **Are there any written records to explain the meaning of the sculpture?** *(no)*

Explain that because there are no decipherable written records from the Indus civilization, it can be referred to as a "prehistoric" civilization, meaning "before written history."

☐ Evaluating the Lesson

Catalog for Artifacts (Notebook page 24)—Instruct the students to read the steps for *Discovering How* on page 83. Tell the students that they will be "discovering" an artifact and recording information about it. Then explain the following guidelines for using the Notebook page.

> **Collection of:** *(student's name)*
> **Date:** *(the date the student does the cataloging)*
> **Number:** *(Create a number to give the artifact; use the permanent marking pen to write the number on the self-adhesive label; attach the label to the outside of the plastic bag.)*
> **Description:** *(Be as specific as possible.)*
> **Material:** *(what the artifact is made of—whether it is wood, metal, shell, etc.)*
> **Dimensions:** *(Measure with a meter stick or metric ruler.)*
> **Weight:** *(Use a postal scale to determine weight; convert customary measurement to metric terms.)*
> **Remarks:** *(Notice the object's condition—broken, chipped, etc.)*

Give each student a self-adhesive label, a resealable plastic bag, and an artifact. Instruct the students to place the artifact inside the plastic bag and seal it tightly when they have completed the cataloging. Assist the students as needed while they analyze and record the objects.

You may expand the *Discovering How* activity by placing each small artifact in a box of sand. Allow the students to use a triangular-bladed mason's trowel and brushes to

□ Additional Teacher Information

Mohenjo-Daro covers an area of about two hundred forty acres, but only small portions of it have been uncovered for study. Both Mohenjo-Daro and Harappa have a large mound, thought to have been a citadel, beside the larger and lower main residential area of the city. The most impressive structure excavated on Mohenjo-Daro's mound was a public bath. The bath contains a large, watertight pool that measures thirty-nine by twenty-three feet, is eight feet deep, and has a drain. A number of small rooms, one with a well, adjoined the pool area. The bath may have served a religious function for the people or priests of the city. Also on the citadel were a large granary, two pillared halls, a large residence, and fortification walls and towers. In addition to these structures, the ruins of a two-thousand-year-old Buddhist *stupa* (shrine) stand atop the citadel, possibly covering the remains of a temple or other significant Mohenjo-Daro buildings.

"find" the item. A camera could also be used to photograph each item as it is revealed.

Writing questions—Allow time for the students to answer questions from the bulletin board throughout the day. You may also want the students to write new questions.

═══ Going Beyond ═══

□ Enrichment

Interview—Challenge the students to interview a grandparent or another older person to find out what life was like when he or she was a child and about inventions that changed his or her life. Instruct them to record the interview on an audio cassette tape. Place the cassette tapes and a tape player in a listening AREA. Encourage the students to listen to the various accounts given on the cassette tapes.

LESSON 22
Mysteries of a Forgotten World

Text, pages 84-88
Notebook, pages 25-26

- Seals and Skeletons
- Disappearance of the Indians
- Village Life
- Aryans Throughout History

▬▬▬ Preview ▬▬▬

□ Objectives
Given proper instruction, the students will be able to do the following:
- Get information from circle graphs.
- Determine whether sentences about the Indus civilization are true or false.

□ Materials
Have available Maps and More 1 and 6.

□ Notes
The Enrichment activity requires samplings of breads that are made from a variety of grains. You may also want to include other grain products such as banana bread and tortillas. You may choose to extend the Enrichment activity to the end of this chapter.

Day 35

▬▬▬ Lesson ▬▬▬

□ Introducing the Lesson
Standing in Contrast (Notebook page 25)—Direct the students to examine the graphs and to read the information. Point out that the Census Bureau defines *urban* as "any community with twenty-five hundred or more people." Ask the students which term, *rural* or *urban*, describes a farming community. *(rural)* Call on a volunteer to identify what part of India's population lives in rural areas. *(about ¾)* Direct the students to complete the remaining questions. Point out that the land size of India is about one-third the land size of the United States.

Remind the students that at one time most people in the United States lived on farms rather than in cities. Read to the students the paragraphs on the bottom of page 25, directing them to fill in the blanks as you give them the answers. Tell the students that the current average farm size in the United States is 468 acres, but in India the average farm size is about two and one-half acres.

Standing in Contrast   Name _____

Statistics

rural ☐   urban ▨

population   India 926,317,000   United States 258,120,000

population density (people per square mile)   730   71

Answer the following questions.

1. Do most people in the United States today live in rural or urban areas? __urban__

2. Which country, the United States or India, has more people? __India__

3. What would it be like if all of the people in the United States lived east of the Mississippi River and the population were four times larger? __crowded__

Fill in the blanks as directed by your teacher.

Turning Around

Until about 1920 the United States was a rural society. In __1870__ the U.S. population was 74 percent rural and 26 percent urban. Most people lived on small farms. To prepare the soil, plant the seed, and harvest one acre of wheat required __sixty-four__ hours. Today the same process takes less than __three__ hours.

Modernization

U.S. agriculture changed dramatically with the introduction of __modern machines__ in the 1800s. With equipment such as the __combine__, __tractor__, and __plow__, a farm family could cultivate one thousand acres of wheat. Before these advances, a farm family's wheat production was about two and one-half acres.

Heritage Studies 6
Student Notebook
Lesson 22
Introducing the Lesson   **25**

Stress the need for a farmer to plan carefully and work hard; however, it is God alone who controls the harvest. Point out that a Christian is God's laborer to tell others about salvation. (BAT: 5c Evangelism and missions)

□ Teaching the Lesson
Seals and skeletons—Direct attention to the drawings of Indus seals on page 84. Ask the students what they think the pictographs mean. *(Answers will vary.)* Instruct the students to read pages 84-85 silently to find out what discoveries were made at Mohenjo-Daro. *(jewelry, toys, standard weights, pottery fragments, seals, and skeletons)*

Discussion Questions
➤ **What is *terra cotta*?** *(a type of clay)*
➤ **How were the Indus seals used?** *(probably to identify an owner's goods)*
➤ **What ancient civilization of Mesopotamia (from Chapter 1) used seals?** *(Sumer)*
(NOTE: See Lesson 3 in Chapter 1 for further information.)

Some time has passed since William's last letter. The dig uncovers more and more artifacts that tell about the ancient Indus. "Dear Lucy," writes William. "It has been some time since I last wrote. Our finds are increasing almost every day, it seems. Since my last letter, we have found more artifacts. We have pieces of jewelry made from gold and precious stones. We also have children's toys, several standard weights made of stone, and of course, many pottery fragments."

Drawings of Indus seals

"Several interesting items in the collection are small seals carved with pictures and the Indus script. They are made from *terra cotta,* a type of clay, or from *steatite,* a type of soapstone. The seals were probably used to identify an owner's goods. Unfortunately, we have been unable to decipher the script. A man here who specializes in *linguistics,* the study of languages, thinks it may be a long time before the Indus pictographs can be translated. We would know much more about these people if we could read their writing. One thing we would know is the purpose of a large building excavated by Sir John. We call it the Great Bath because it is a hall with a large sunken pool. We think it may have been used for religious purposes or for bathing. Until we can read the Indus script, we will not know for certain."

84

William's lamp flickers, causing shadows to shiver on the side of his tent. "One of our most interesting discoveries was a group of skeletons that we found in one room. There were fourteen in all. Although this may have been a burial room, it is more likely the scene of a tragedy—perhaps an indication that they were invaded by another people. Finding those bones reminded me that there was more to the ancient Indus civilization than just interesting artifacts. Real people walked these streets and cooked in these pots."

William pauses, thoughtfully rubbing his chin. "I often wonder what they were really like—these dwellers of Mohenjo-Daro. Sometimes I walk on the ancient streets—just dirt paths now—and wonder whether there was a young man my age who walked this same way long ago. And if there was, what made him and his people vanish so quickly as the evidence seems to indicate?" William shakes himself a little as his lamp grows dimmer.

He glances at his lamp and writes quickly. "But, Lucy, this must remain one of those unsolved mysteries of the past. We must content ourselves with what we do know. I must go now and fetch more oil for my lamp—it shall soon be out. I will write again if we uncover any more interesting things. Take care."

85

Point to the southeastern region of Iraq on Maps and More 1. Ask the students what this area was called. *(Sumer)* Explain that the Indus area is east of Sumer. Tell them that stone, wood, gems, and metal were sent from India to Sumer. The seals used in Sumer as a signature were probably adapted by the Indians.

➤ **What is *linguistics?* (the study of languages)**
➤ **Why is little known today about the Indus people?** *(There are no written records that we can understand.)*
➤ **What interpretations were given to explain why so many skeletons were in one room?** *(It may have been a burial room or the scene of a tragedy.)*

The mystery that surrounds the ancient Indus people deepened as archaeologists uncovered more and more artifacts. It seems that this civilization came to a sudden halt between 1700 and 1500 B.C. Archaeologists believe that the Indus people suddenly disappeared from India. There could be a variety of reasons for the disappearance of these sophisticated, well-organized people. Flood, famine, or invasion by other peoples could have driven the inhabitants of Mohenjo-Daro from their homes.

One major cause for the disappearance of the Indians may have been an invasion by another people from the north. These people were *nomads,* or wanderers, and called themselves *Arya,* which means "noble."

The Aryans were warlike people who came into India with horses, chariots, and weapons. They spread across northern India and settled down into villages. Their way of life became the characteristic culture of ancient—and modern—India.

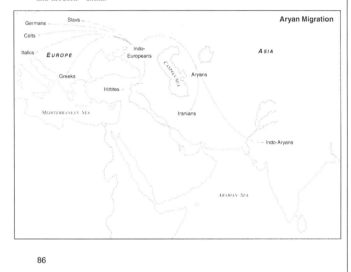

Village Life

The Aryans in India did not form a strong central government. Rather, India was made up of many independent villages first settled by the Aryans. Each settlement had a village council of the leading men of the village. The most important man in the village held the office of headman. The council and headman governed the village.

Every village had farmers and craftsmen. The craftsmen made necessary tools and household items for the villagers. They also produced artwork, much of which reflected religion. Sculptures of gods and goddesses were very common and were probably used in worship.

Modern Indian farmers grow much of the world's rice.

Most ancient Indians farmed for a living. Their success depended upon the yearly rains of the wet season—June to September. In India the rains come with the *monsoons,* yearly winds that blow from the west and bring moisture off the ocean. Once over land, the water vapor in the air condenses and falls as rain. If the rains are late or small, drought and famine may occur.

86   87

Disappearance of the Indians—Instruct the students to read page 86 silently to find out why the Indus civilization disappeared. *(flood, famine, or invasion)*

Discussion Questions

➤ **What people invaded the Indus area from the north?** *(the Aryans)*
➤ **What is the meaning of the name *Arya?*** *(noble)*
➤ **How have the Aryans influenced modern India?** *(The Aryan way of life became the characteristic culture of India.)*
➤ **What words describe the Aryan people?** *(nomads, or wanderers, and warlike)*

Day 36

Village life—Instruct the students to read page 87 silently to find out what weather factor is very important in India. *(monsoons)*

Discussion Questions

➤ **Why are monsoons important to India?** *(The winds bring rain during the wet season.)*
➤ **Why did the ancient Indians rely on yearly rains?** *(Most ancient Indians farmed for a living.)*
➤ **When does a famine or drought occur?** *(when the rains are late or too small)*
➤ **Would too much rain also be a problem? Why?** *(Yes; too much rain would cause flooding.)*

Point to the Indian Ocean and the equator on Maps and More 6. Explain that the monsoons bring the warm, moist air from the Indian Ocean to India.

➤ **What type of government developed as the Aryans settled?** *(independent villages)*
➤ **Who governed the villages?** *(Each village was led by a headman and a council.)*
➤ **What types of smaller governing units exist on the local level in the United States?** *(Possible answers include a village, a township, a city or a county council, and a parish.)*
➤ **Who are some of the government leaders in your area?** *(Possible answers include mayor, trustees, council members, or any individual by name.)*
➤ **How was the work of the craftsmen important to Indian villages?** *(They made necessary tools and household items for the villagers. They also produced artwork and sculptures of gods and goddesses.)*

Aryans throughout history—Instruct the students to read page 88 silently to find out what leader in the twentieth century used the term *Aryan. (Adolf Hitler)*

Discussion Questions

➤ **What country was Hitler from?** *(Germany)*
➤ **In what major war was Hitler involved?** *(World War II)*
➤ **What symbol did Hitler borrow from the ancient Indians?** *(the swastika)*
➤ **What is the Indian language called?** *(Sanskrit)*

ECHOES FROM THE PAST

Aryans Throughout History

Throughout history, the term *Aryan* has assumed different meanings. The original Aryans were those light-skinned people who invaded India from the north. We can trace the echoes of these ancient peoples' name even in modern times. Thousands of years later—in the twentieth century—the term *Aryan* came to describe the people of Hitler's Germany.

Adolf Hitler borrowed from a French philosopher the idea that there is a master race. He believed that the northern European people were the most important race. Hitler called them Aryans. He believed that other races—particularly the Jews—did not deserve to live, so he started executing them. Today, the term *Aryan* is associated with Hitler and the racist ideas he represented. Do you remember what major war Hitler was involved in?

The Aryan name was not all that Hitler borrowed from the ancient Indians. He also borrowed one of their symbols. This symbol, the swastika, has been found on buildings and artifacts from ancient India as well as in places such as Turkey and Egypt. The term *swastika* in the Indian language, Sanskrit, means "a sign of good luck."

The swastika prominently displayed at one of Hitler's Nazi rallies

88

Is It True?   Name _____

Circle *true* if the statement is true or *false* if the statement is false.

1. *Monsoons* bring rain for the crops in India. (**true**) false	2. Villages were settled by the Aryans and ruled by a king. true (**false**)	3. The Indian language is called *Sanskrit*. (**true**) false
4. There are no written records about the Indus people. true (**false**)	5. *Linguistics* is the study of languages. (**true**) false	6. The craftsmen bought the necessary tools for the villages. true (**false**)
7. Many ancient Indians farmed for a living. (**true**) false	8. The Aryans brought horses, chariots, and weapons. (**true**) false	9. Some possible reasons for the disappearance of the Indus people include flood, famine, and invasion. (**true**) false
10. Seals of terra cotta were probably used to identify an owner's goods. (**true**) false	11. Adolf Hitler was the first to use the *swastika* symbol. true (**false**)	12. The current southeastern region of Iraq was once called Sumer. (**true**) false

© 1998 BJU Press. Reproduction prohibited.

Heritage Studies 6
Student Notebook

Lesson 22
Evaluating the Lesson   **26**

➤ **Why do you think people in Turkey and Egypt also used the swastika?** *(Answers will vary; the term* swastika *means "a sign of good luck.")*

> Remind the students that God orders the lives of Christians. A Christian does not need to fear the future or to rely on "good luck" symbols. (Bible Promises: H. God as Father, I. God as Master)

☐ Evaluating the Lesson

Is It True? (Notebook page 26)—Instruct the students to read each statement on Notebook page 26 and to circle *true* if the statement is true or *false* if the statement is false.

Writing questions—Allow time for the students to answer questions from the bulletin board throughout the day. You may also want the students to write new questions.

Going Beyond

☐ Enrichment

Samples of breads—Set up an AREA with samples of breads made from a variety of grains. Label each type of bread. Explain that bread is made from barley, oats, corn, rice, rye, wheat, or a combination of several of these grains. Point out that some breads contain yeast. Allow the students to taste the bread samples.

☐ Additional Teacher Information

The average annual rainfall in India varies from less than 10 inches in the Thar Desert to 71.2 inches in Bombay to over 400 inches in the Assam Hills of northeast India. The city of Cherrapunji holds the world's record for the most rainfall in one year. From August 1860 to July 1861, this city in northeast India recorded 1,042 inches of rain.

Artifacts without written records generally leave the historical record incomplete. For instance, the skeletons found at Mohenjo-Daro still puzzle historians. These people apparently met a violent death, but it is impossible to tell whether it was wrought by natural disaster, civil disorder, or an outside attack. Sir Mortimer Wheeler, a leading archaeologist involved in the excavations, believed that the civilization fell to Aryan invaders, as some passages in the Rig-Veda may indicate. However, other archaeological evidence seems to indicate that the Indus civilization fell because of floods, droughts, and declining agricultural production. Whatever the situation, the existing archaeological evidence is simply too sparse to draw firm conclusions.

Mysteries of the Indus—Lesson 22   105

LESSON 23
Religions and Rituals

Text, pages 89-91
Notebook, page 27

- Hindu Beliefs
- Hindu Practices
- Families and Castes

Preview

☐ Objective

Given proper instruction, the students will be able to do the following:
- Match Hindu beliefs with Bible verses that refute them.

☐ Materials

Have available:
- A Bible for each student.
- An overhead projector.
- A blank overhead transparency.

Prepare an overhead transparency of "Christianity and Hinduism Contrasted." (*NOTE:* See the reproducible material at the end of Lesson 24.)

☐ Notes

You may choose to extend the Enrichment activity to the end of this chapter.

The Indian subcontinent is traditionally all part of the same culture region. However, new boundaries were made in 1947 to include the Muslim nation of Pakistan and the Hindu nation of India. Chapter 11 will discuss the religion of Islam.

Hinduism is, admittedly, a very complex religion that cannot be covered comprehensively on this grade level. Thus, only a few of the major beliefs are described here. Hindu beliefs and practices vary widely within the basic framework of the religion. The Vedas and other sacred writings of Hinduism do not establish a firm set of doctrines for followers to observe. Neither is there an organized religious hierarchy to govern Hinduism as a whole. Therefore, priests and practitioners find great freedom in this manmade religion to adapt its worship to their own interests.

Day 37

Lesson

☐ Introducing the Lesson

Review—Write the following names on the chalkboard: *Sumerians, Egyptians,* and *Hebrews.* Allow the students to tell what they remember about each civilization. Ask the students which people believed in the one true God. (*Hebrews*) Point out that the Sumerians and Egyptians wor-

Religions of Ancient India

Hinduism

The Aryans, because they were nomads, probably encountered many different people and cultures in their travels. How do you think this interaction with other people affected the Aryans? As they settled in India, they adopted many beliefs and customs. The Aryans developed a religion that would soon spread across India and that still exists today. Although this religion, *Hinduism*, was not formulated fully until after the time of Christ, its beliefs and practices quickly grew to influence the Indians' entire way of life.

Like many other ancient religions, Hinduism is *polytheistic*, or having many gods. The Hindus worship thousands of gods although they consider three gods to be the most important. These three gods are *Brahma*, the Creator; *Shiva*, the Destroyer; and *Vishnu*, the Preserver.

Hindus believe that these three gods, in addition to thousands of others, are only different forms of the *World Soul*, a great spirit to which everything in the world—plants, animals, and gods—belongs. This belief is a form of *pantheism*, or the idea that there is deity in nature. How does this view of nature differ from the biblical description of God and creation?

> "Thou shalt have no other gods before me. Thou shalt not make unto thee any graven image, or any likeness of any thing that is in heaven above, or that is in the earth beneath, or that is in the water under earth: Thou shalt not bow down thyself to them, nor serve them."
>
> ——————
> Exodus 20:3-5

Vishnu

Lakshmi, goddess of beauty, wealth, and good fortune

89

shiped many gods and were ruled by priests. Explain that this lesson will discuss Hinduism, the dominant religion of India.

☐ Teaching the Lesson

Hindu beliefs—Instruct the students to read page 89 silently to find out whether Hinduism teaches that there is one God or many gods. (*many gods*) Read aloud Exodus 20:3-5 from page 89. Call on a volunteer to read aloud Psalm 135:15-18. Ask the students what the Bible says about idols. (*They cannot see, hear, speak, or breathe. They are not to be worshiped.*)

Discussion Questions

➤ **What is *polytheistic* religion?** (*the worship of many gods*)
➤ **What are the three most important gods in Hinduism?** (*Brahma, Shiva, Vishnu*)
➤ **What is the name of the great spirit that Hindus believe plants, animals, and gods belong to?** (*the World Soul*)
➤ **What is *pantheism*?** (*the idea that there is deity in nature*)
➤ **What does the Bible say about creation?** (*God created all things.*)

Call on a student to recite Genesis 1:1. Remind the students that God controls His creation. Tell the students that Hinduism establishes no distinction between man, God, and the natural world in which we live. The Hindu belief says

Hindus follow their religious practices diligently. They worship at Hindu temples and shrines, bring sacrifices and money to the priests, pray, and perform rituals. Some Hindus discipline their bodies to try to become holier. They seclude, starve, and inflict pain on themselves in an attempt to make their souls purer for the World Soul.

By following these practices, the Hindu hopes to be good enough to obtain salvation. Because these practices are part of a long process, another part of Hinduism is *reincarnation*. The Hindus believe that a reincarnated person lives more than

A Hindu temple

once in different bodies—even in animals. Because of their belief in reincarnation, many Hindus will not eat certain animals, such as cattle. In some instances, they would rather starve than eat this type of meat.

These Indians and their livestock, including many sacred cows, have gathered for the Pushkar Fair, a religious occasion.

90

Families and Castes

Hinduism concerns itself not only with man's relationship to the gods but also with his relationship to other people. Because it teaches that everything is a part of the World Soul, Hinduism emphasizes the group above the individual. Social relationships in Hinduism center on the group. The two basic groups in India since the rise of Hinduism have been the family and the *caste,* or social class.

The core of Indian life was the family. When the Aryans settled in India, they encouraged large families. Families included more than just parents and their children. Grandparents, parents, sons, daughters-in-law, unmarried daughters, and grandchildren lived together in family *compounds* made up of several huts or houses.

The ancient Indians generally married when they were adults, not children. The oldest man in the family had complete authority over the other members. Everyone had to follow his orders. Hinduism teaches that complete obedience in the family is an important part of earning salvation.

Scenes from a Hindu wedding

91

that man can become a god by his good works and that many gods exist in nature. Explain that without accountability to God, this religion focuses on man and his works. (Bible Promise: I. God as Master)

Display the overhead transparency entitled "Christianity and Hinduism Contrasted." Discuss the first three points as desired. Emphasize that each individual either accepts God by faith or accepts his own ideas by faith.

> Remind the students that God provides salvation through the blood of Jesus on the cross. (BATs: 1a Understanding Jesus Christ, 1b Repentance and faith; Bible Promise: I. God as Master)

Day 38

Hindu practices—Instruct the students to read page 90 silently to find out why many Hindus will not eat the meat from cattle. *(Hindus believe in reincarnation, the idea that a person can live more than once in different bodies, even in the bodies of animals.)*

Discussion Questions

> **What are some Hindu practices?** *(worship at temples and shrines; bring sacrifices and money to the priest; pray; perform rituals; discipline their bodies by seclusion, starvation, and infliction of pain; and refuse to eat certain animals)*

> **Why does a Christian pray?** *(to ask forgiveness of God, to maintain fellowship with God, to bring requests to God)*
> **Why do the Hindus follow their religious practices diligently?** *(They hope to earn salvation by good works.)*
> **What does the Bible say about salvation by works?** *(A person cannot earn salvation by good works.)*

Call on a volunteer to read aloud Ephesians 2:8-10. Emphasize that salvation is a gift of God. (BAT: 1b Repentance and faith) Discuss the fourth and fifth points on the overhead transparency as desired.

> Point out that once a person repents and accepts Jesus as Savior, he should show his love for God through obedience to Him. (BATs: 2b Servanthood, 5a Love)

Families and castes—Instruct the students to read page 91 silently to find out why the family is important in Indian life. *(Indians believe that complete obedience in the family is an important part of earning salvation.)*

Discussion Questions

> **Is the emphasis in Hinduism centered more on the group or the individual?** *(the group)*
> **What are the two most important categories of social relationships in India?** *(families and castes)*

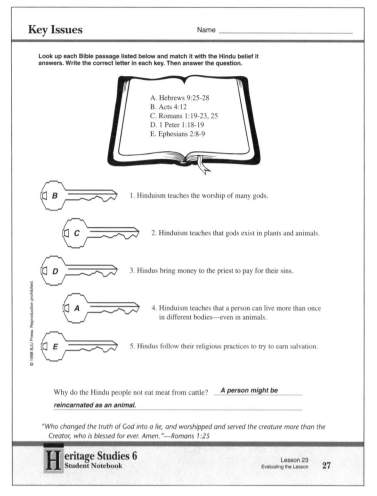

Key Issues Name _____

Look up each Bible passage listed below and match it with the Hindu belief it answers. Write the correct letter in each key. Then answer the question.

A. Hebrews 9:25-28
B. Acts 4:12
C. Romans 1:19-23, 25
D. 1 Peter 1:18-19
E. Ephesians 2:8-9

B 1. Hinduism teaches the worship of many gods.

C 2. Hinduism teaches that gods exist in plants and animals.

D 3. Hindus bring money to the priest to pay for their sins.

A 4. Hinduism teaches that a person can live more than once in different bodies—even in animals.

E 5. Hindus follow their religious practices to try to earn salvation.

Why do the Hindu people not eat meat from cattle?   *A person might be*

reincarnated as an animal.

"Who changed the truth of God into a lie, and worshipped and served the creature more than the Creator, who is blessed for ever. Amen."—Romans 1:25

Heritage Studies 6
Student Notebook

Lesson 23
Evaluating the Lesson   **27**

➤ **What were the living arrangements like for Aryan families?** *(Extended families lived together in family compounds.)*

Explain that families composed of simply parents and children are called *nuclear families,* while families with additional family members (such as grandparents and uncles and aunts) living together with the parents and children are called *extended families.* Traditional Indian families are extended families. Most modern American families are nuclear families.

➤ **What advantages or disadvantages would there be to living as part of an extended family?** *(Answers will vary. Unity would be essential.)*

➤ **Which family member had authority among the ancient Indians?** *(the oldest man)*

☐ **Evaluating the Lesson**

Key Issues (Notebook page 27)—Instruct the students to look up each Bible passage listed and to match it with the Hindu belief it answers, writing the correct letter in each key. Then direct them to answer the question.

Writing questions—Allow time for the students to answer questions from the bulletin board throughout the day. You may also want the students to write new questions.

Going Beyond

☐ **Enrichment**

Memorizing Bible verses—Set up a listening and writing AREA at the back of the classroom. Prepare a cassette tape of the following Bible verses: Ephesians 2:8-9, Titus 3:5-7, John 14:6, Galatians 2:16, and I Peter 1:18-19. Provide a Bible, 3"×5" cards, pencils, and a cassette player. Instruct the students to listen to each verse on the cassette tape, locate it in the Bible, write the verse on a 3"×5" card, and then say the verse to a partner. You may also use a role-playing activity, allowing partners to practice witnessing to a Hindu person or to any other person who relies on works for salvation.

☐ **Additional Teacher Information**

It is important to note the parallels between ancient Indian beliefs and more modern philosophical movements, such as Transcendentalism (nineteenth century) and New Age beliefs (twentieth century). Ralph Waldo Emerson, often referred to as the Father of Transcendentalism, studied ancient Indian writings. Walt Whitman, a follower of Emerson, was also interested in ancient Indian writings. Emerson and Whitman cultivated the idea of the Oversoul, which greatly resembles the Hindu concept of the World Soul. Other American writers during the Romantic era (1800s) that referred to themselves as the Brahman were Longfellow, Lowell, Whittier, and Holmes.

In God's plan there is no second chance for salvation after death. The Hindus recognize man's sinfulness and inability to do good. Yet they have tried to make their own plan of salvation by doing the good works prescribed by Hinduism. And because of reincarnation the Hindus expect to have many lives in which to try to earn their salvation. The Bible, however, clearly refutes reincarnation (Eccles. 9:4-6 and Heb. 9:27).

Hindus usually have at least one idol set up in an honored place in their houses for private worship. However, they are quick to recognize other gods for fear of offending them. For this reason, Hindus may be outwardly open to the gospel message for fear of offending the "Christian God." Hindus thus may appear very amiable and inoffensive, yet man without the Savior is lost no matter how affable his religion may be.

A disregard for the value of human life is a key element of Hinduism. This aspect can be seen not only in the emphasis on caste rather than individual character and accomplishment but also in the preferences Hindus place on animal life regardless of the effect on humans.

LESSON 24

Threads Woven in Time

Text, pages 92-96
Notebook, pages 28-29

- Social Status
- Sacred Writings
- Search for Answers
- Silhouettes

Preview

□ Objectives

Given proper instruction, the students will be able to do the following:

- Match statements about ancient India.
- Contrast the differences between Hinduism and Buddhism with biblical truth.

□ Materials

Have available:

- A Bible for each student and the teacher.
- A red crayon, colored pencil, or felt-tip pen for each student.
- A green crayon, colored pencil, or felt-tip pen for each student.
- The figure of the Rig-Veda (1500 B.C.) from the History TimeLine Packet.

□ Notes

You may choose to extend the Enrichment activity to the completion of the novel.

Titus 3:5 can be used to refute both Hinduism and Buddhism. You will notice that the common feature of false religions is that they assume man can somehow save himself through his own works. The Bible makes it clear that this is impossible, and it sets forth the true way of salvation through accepting God's perfect sacrifice for sins (Rom. 3:24-25).

Both Hinduism and Buddhism have attracted a wider following in recent years through the popularity of the New Age movement. In the process, unwary people have embraced the meditational exercises of yoga, the veneration of animal life as the equal of human life, and even the idea of reincarnation. The Christian should beware of these false religions. The religious teachings of these mystical faiths are clearly contrary to Scripture, and the practices (particularly the inwardly focused meditation) often open the way for satanic influence.

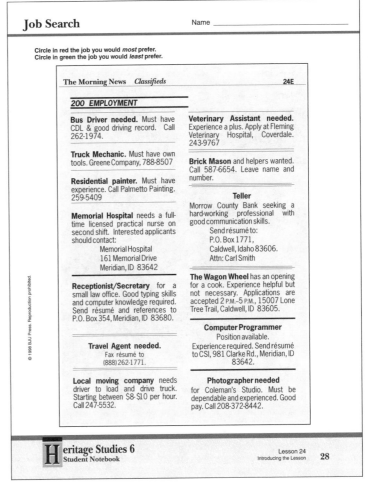

Day 39

Lesson

□ Introducing the Lesson

Job Search (Notebook page 28)—Direct each student to indicate which job he would *most* prefer and which job he would *least* prefer. As time permits, call on volunteers to tell their most preferred and least preferred jobs. Point out that the caste system in India determined each person's occupation.

The second important social group that every Indian belonged to was the *caste*. Castes were the classes of Indian society. Hindus believed that the higher a person was in the caste system, the closer he was to reuniting with the World Soul. Every Hindu hoped that his next rebirth would put him into a higher caste.

Hindu priests

There were four main caste divisions in Indian society. The highest was the priestly caste. When a member of this caste died, he supposedly reunited immediately with the World Soul. In this life, the priests held much power over the people because they directed most religious worship.

92

The caste of warriors and rulers came after the priestly caste. Farmers, traders, and laborers made up the third caste. Servants belonged to the lowest caste. Some Indians were outside the caste system. They were called *untouchables*, or *outcastes*. How do we use the word *outcast* today? Untouchables included any non-Hindu, anyone who worked with meat, and anyone who was expelled from his own caste. Within these four main castes there were hundreds of subcastes.

The caste had rules governing its members. The caste rules dictated whom one married, what clothing one wore, with whom one could eat, and what one's occupation was. In order to be reborn into a higher caste, a Hindu had to accept his present caste and the caste rules. A Hindu who did more or less than his caste demanded was unlikely to be reborn on a higher level. The caste system made Indian society very rigid. Today the caste system still exists in India, although it is not as rigid as it once was.

93

□ Teaching the Lesson

Social status—Instruct the students to read pages 92-93 silently to find out the four main caste divisions in Indian society. *(priests; warriors and rulers; farmers, traders, and laborers; servants)*

Discussion Questions

➤ **What is a *caste*?** *(a class in Indian society)*
➤ **Why would an Indian desire a higher rank in the caste system?** *(to be closer to reuniting with the World Soul)*
➤ **According to Hinduism, how could a person attain a higher caste?** *(possibly in his next rebirth)*
➤ **Which caste level was considered the highest?** *(priestly)*
➤ **Who belonged to the lowest caste?** *(servants)*

Remind the students that Jesus came to earth as a servant (Phil. 2:3-10). Realizing man's sinfulness and God's grace, a Christian should also be a humble servant who is willing to think of others ahead of himself. (BATs: 2b Servanthood, 7a Grace, 7e Humility)

➤ **What were the people called who were outside the caste system?** *(untouchables, or outcastes)*
➤ **Who were the *untouchables*?** *(any non-Hindu, anyone who worked with meat, anyone expelled from his own caste)*
➤ **Why did it matter what caste one belonged to?** *(Caste rules determined one's job, marriage, clothing, and eating habits.)*
➤ **What do you think about this caste system?** *(Answers will vary.)*

Point out that the caste system would tend to make some people proud, thinking themselves better than another simply because they were born into a prestigious group. In contrast to this prejudice of Hinduism, the Bible clearly teaches that God is no respecter of persons. Choose volunteers to read aloud Psalms 138:6, Acts 10:34, James 2:1-9, and I Peter 1:17. Remind the students that God loves each individual and gave His Son to provide salvation to all who will believe (John 3:16). Just as God demonstrated His great love to man, a Christian should show godly love to others (Rom. 5:8). (BAT: 5a Love)

The Written Legacy

How do we know so much about early Hinduism? The early Indians left a written legacy called the *Vedas.* The Indian word *Veda* means "knowledge." The Vedas are the sacred books of Hinduism. The oldest Veda, the *Rig-Veda,* is believed to be one of the earliest known books, dating around the sixteenth century B.C.

The Rig-Veda, though difficult for modern man to understand, is a collection of the knowledge of the day. It includes hymns, prayers, poems, rituals, and philosophy. The existence of the Vedas, particularly the Rig-Veda, helps us to know that the people of the ancient Indus were sophisticated and enjoyed beauty and artistry.

In this Indian illustration, Brahma is shown at center left holding the Vedas.

94

Siddhartha Gautama

Not all Indians agreed with Hindu teachings, however. Near the end of the sixth century B.C., a man began to question Hindu beliefs. He disliked the caste system and the priests who ruled the people. He could not accept the Hindu belief that only members of the priestly caste were ready to reunite with the World Soul. This man, *Siddhartha Gautama,* decided that he was going to change Hinduism.

Gautama was born into a ruling family as a member of the warrior caste. Although he had many of the luxuries this world could offer, he was not satisfied. The poverty and pain he saw in the world bothered him. At the age of twenty-nine, he left his home to find a remedy for his own unhappiness and that of the world.

For six years he lived in seclusion and near starvation but found no satisfactory answers. Then, according to the story, one day while meditating, Gautama became *enlightened* about the meaning of life. He assumed the name, *Buddha,* meaning "Enlightened One." Buddha developed his view of life through introducing what he called the *Four Noble Truths.* In these writings he proposed the concept that suffering can be overcome if a person does good works and ignores his desires. Buddhism also includes steps called *The Eightfold Path,* a list of good works that will help a person to achieve happiness and peace. Buddhism remains an important religion in India even today.

An Indian carving of the sleeping Buddha

95

Day 40

Sacred writings—Instruct the students to read page 94 silently to find out the name of the sacred books of Hinduism. *(Vedas)* Add the figure of the Rig-Veda to the History TimeLine at approximately 1500 B.C.

Discussion Questions

➤ **What does the word *Veda* mean?** *(knowledge)*

➤ **What does the Rig-Veda tell about the people of the ancient Indus?** *(They were sophisticated people who enjoyed beauty and artistry.)*

➤ **Why was the finding of the Rig-Veda important?** *(It is believed to be one of the earliest books in the history of civilization.)*

➤ **What is the source of God's truth?** *(the Bible)*

> Tell the students that knowing God's truth is more important than acquiring knowledge. Read aloud II Timothy 3:7. Many people today continue to search for knowledge but reject the truth of God's Word. (BAT: 8b Faith in the Power of the Word of God)

Search for answers—Instruct the students to read page 95 silently to find out how Buddhism developed. *(Siddhartha Gautama sought to find a remedy for unhappiness.)*

Discussion Questions

➤ **Why was Gautama not satisfied although he had many luxuries?** *(He was bothered by the poverty and pain that he saw.)*

➤ **What is the meaning of the name *Buddha?*** *(Enlightened One)*

➤ **What were the *Four Noble Truths?*** *(Buddha's view of life)*

➤ **What is Buddha's list of good works called?** *(The Eightfold Path)*

➤ **According to a Buddhist, how does a person achieve happiness and peace?** *(by doing good and ignoring personal desires)*

➤ **How does this belief differ from what the Bible says?** *(The Holy Spirit brings peace to those who put their faith in Jesus Christ.)*

Silhouettes—Instruct the students to read page 96 silently to find out what William longs to do someday. *(return to India to find more about its ancient peoples)*

Discussion Questions

➤ **What have you learned about the Indus civilization?** *(Answers will vary.)*

➤ **What would you still like to know about the ancient Indians?** *(Answers will vary.)*

William sits at his desk, scribbling away. "Dear Lucy," he writes, "My time here at Mohenjo-Daro is almost over. Though I long to be in England once more, a part of me wants to stay excavating out on the field. I know I shall miss this place." He pauses and looks at the soft walls of his tent.

"I have learned so much here—so much about the ancient people who lived along the Indus, but how I want to learn more! There are many things we do not know—not just about the people at Mohenjo-Daro, but about ancient peoples around the world. Maybe someday—when you are older— you and I can return to India to find more about these ancient people. We could at least try. I must go for now and catch one last glimpse of the Indus. I shall see you soon. Love, William."

William rises from his desk and stands at his tent door. The buildings at the dig site are silhouettes against the reds and oranges of the setting sun. He takes a deep breath, listening to murmurings of the men who are finishing up at the site—or are those sounds voices from long ago? William smiles at his fancy. He will remember Mohenjo-Daro. He will never forget the mysteries of the Indus.

96

Write the letter of the correct choice in each blank.

A.	caste	G.	servants
B.	Four Noble Truths	H.	Buddha
C.	priest	I.	The Eightfold Path
E.	untouchables	J.	reincarnation
F.	*Vedas*	K.	*Rig-Veda*

B   1. Buddha's view of life

A   2. social class

F   3. Hindu religious writings

I   4. list of good works

J   5. the Hindu belief that a person lives more than once in different bodies

E   6. Indians outside of the social-class system, outcasts

C   7. considered the highest level in ancient India's social-class system

K   8. one of the earliest books in the history of civilization

G   9. belonged to the lowest class in India's society

H   10. a name that means "Enlightened One"

Complete the sentences below, using the following choices.

     Buddhism   Christianity   Hinduism

Hinduism   11. Man seeks spiritual purity through his good works.

Buddhism   12. Man seeks happiness and peace by doing good works and ignoring his desires.

Christianity   13. God seeks men who would be saved through faith in the blood of Jesus as the payment for sin.

Heritage Studies 6
Student Notebook   Lesson 24
Evaluating the Lesson   **29**

☐ Evaluating the Lesson

India Match (Notebook page 29)—Direct the students to write the letter of each correct choice in the blank. Then direct them to complete the statements at the bottom of the page.

Writing questions—Allow time for the students to answer questions from the bulletin board throughout the day.

——— Going Beyond ———

☐ Enrichment

Read a missionary biography—Read aloud *With Daring Faith: A Biography of Amy Carmichael,* a missionary to India. This book is available from Bob Jones University Press.

☐ Additional Teacher Information

The Aryans who settled in India esteemed their fair skin while looking down upon the peoples around them with darker skin. This prejudice probably led to the caste system. In addition, the Aryans developed a complicated collection of rituals to be performed in worship to their gods. Their concern with performing these rituals led to the exaltation of the priestly class of religious experts over the warriors and other classes.

Buddhism and Hinduism are products of India. Both religions teach that man achieves salvation by being reunited with or absorbed by the World Soul. Both religions also teach that people earn salvation by suffering and doing good works. Buddhism gained wide popularity in several areas outside India, but it never gained a stronghold in India itself.

Traditionally, the untouchables held unclean occupations and were scorned by caste members. They were required to use noisemakers to warn others of their approach. Even the touch of an outcaste's shadow could pollute a member of a caste. Modern India has outlawed untouchability and has attempted to lessen the stigma placed upon this group. Nonetheless, the social pressures related to caste at all levels are still very evident in Indian culture.

Modern Hindus associate with members of other castes at the workplace but maintain a much stricter separation in their homes. Villagers continue to be much stricter in following caste traditions than are city dwellers.

The Vedas consist of four parts, the oldest and best-known of which is the Rig-Veda ("Veda of praise"). It is a collection of hymns to the Aryan gods. Most of the hymns, chants, stories, magical spells, and other contents of the Vedas were passed on orally from one generation to the next by the Aryans until late in their era, when the works began to be written down. Hindus consider the Vedas to be inspired writings. Other writings, called the *Upanishads,* were written around 700 B.C. The Upanishads are commentaries on the Vedas and are also included as Hindu sacred writings.

Ask me about

INDIA!

Question:

Name:

Ask Me
Answer Cards
for

Name _____

Name _____

Name _____

Name _____

Name _____

Ask Me
Answer Cards
for

Name _____

Name _____

Name _____

Name _____

Name _____

Use with the chapter bulletin board.

Heritage Studies 6 TE

Picture This

Select one of the following topics about India. Research to find information in the encyclopedia.

Climate	Wildlife
Landforms	Vegetation
Bodies of water	Religions

Write three sentences below about your topic.

_____

_____

_____

_____

_____

_____

_____

Illustrate the sentences in the picture frame below.

Indus and Ganges Deltas

Indus

Jhelum

Chenab

Ravi

Sutlei

● Harappa

Himalayas

Brahmaputra River

Jumna

Sarda

Thar Desert
(Indian Desert)

Indus River

● Mohenjo-Daro

● Chanhu-Daro

Amri ●

Chambal

Ganges

Ghaghra

Gandak

Sapt Kosi

Himalayas

Brahmaputra River

Betwa

Ancient
Hakra River

Ganges   River

Son

Mouth
of the
Indus

Mouth
of the
Ganges

ARABIAN SEA

INDIA

Deccan Plateau

Bay of Bengal

N

NW   NE

W   E

SW   SE

S

SRI
LANKA

INDIAN OCEAN

Equator

Christianity and Hinduism Contrasted

1. Hinduism teaches *polytheism*—the worship of many gods.

    The Bible says, "I am the Lord, and there is none else, there is no God beside me: I girded thee, though thou hast not known me: that they may know from the rising of the sun, and from the west, that there is none beside me. **I am the Lord, and there is none else."** Isaiah 45:5-6

    Read also Isaiah 43:10.

2. Hinduism teaches *creation by Brahma.*

    The Bible says, "In the beginning **God created** the heaven and the earth." Genesis 1:1

    Read also John 1:1-3.

3. Hinduism teaches *pantheism*—that gods exist in plants and animals.

    The Bible says, "For by him were all things created, that are in heaven, and that are in the earth, visible and invisible, whether they be thrones, or dominions, or principalities, or powers: all things were created by him, and for him: and he is before all things, and by him all things consist." Colossians 1:16-17

    Read also Isaiah 45:12.

    Psalm 104 reminds us that God controls the world.

4. Hinduism teaches *reincarnation*—that a person can live more than once in different bodies, even in the bodies of animals.

    The Bible says, "And as it is appointed unto men **once** to die, but after this the judgment." Hebrews 9:27

5. Hinduism teaches that *man achieves holiness by suffering and doing good works.*

    The Bible says, "For by **grace** are ye saved through faith; and that not of yourselves: it is the gift of God: **Not of works,** lest any man should boast." Ephesians 2:8-9

    Read also John 14:6 and Romans 3:24-25, 28.

5 LESSONS 25-29

Dynasties in Seclusion: Ancient China

In this chapter, the students will explore the world of ancient China—a world of artistry, scholarship, and invention. Against a religious backdrop of ancestor worship and Confucianism, the ancient people of China worked, studied, and thought. The students will learn how this secluded civilization made great progress on its own, apart from the influences of trade or contact with other cultures. A separate look at each dynasty from the Shang to the Han offers students an opportunity to evaluate the ideas and appreciate the contributions of each. Special activities include learning to decipher and draw Chinese pictographs and making paper in the ancient Chinese tradition by collecting fibers on a screen and drying them.

□ Materials

Lessons 25-26 and 29 require certain items that must be obtained or prepared several days to several weeks before the presentation of the lessons. These items are labeled with an asterisk (*) in each lesson and in the Materials List in the Supplement. Occasionally, items not commonly found in the classroom as well as items needed in large quantities may also be labeled with an asterisk. For further information, see the individual lessons.

□ Chapter Bulletin Board

In the center of the bulletin board, place the words *Ancient China* along with the dates 1766 B.C.–A.D. 220. In each corner place a piece of brightly colored paper labeled with the name of one of the dynasties: Shang, Chou, Ch'in, and Han. Provide paper of different colors, textures, and shapes for the students to write accomplishments or ideas associated with each dynasty as they study it. Allow the students to surround the name of each dynasty on the bulletin board with words that relate to it. See the bulletin board illustration for examples.

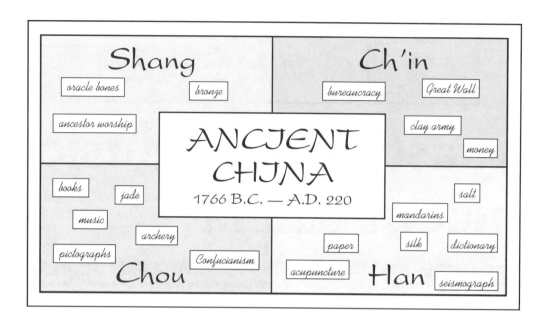

Shang
oracle bones
bronze
ancestor worship

Ch'in
bureaucracy
Great Wall
clay army
money

ANCIENT
CHINA
1766 B.C. — A.D. 220

books
jade
music
archery
pictographs
Confucianism
Chou

salt
mandarins
paper
silk
dictionary
acupuncture
Han
seismograph

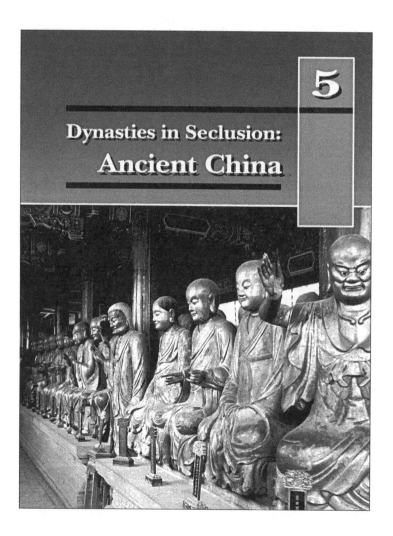

5

Dynasties in Seclusion:
Ancient China

LESSON 25
Progress Behind Barriers

Text, pages 98-101
Notebook, page 30

- **Natural Barriers and Dynasties**
- **Then and Now**
- **The Shang Dynasty**
- **Bronze Making**

Look back through the mist of thousands of years—back to an ancient civilization concealed among several mountain ranges, a large desert, and jungles. It is the ancient Chinese civilization, hidden from the rest of the world by *natural barriers*.

Throughout history, these barriers, or landforms that isolate a country from outside influence, kept the Chinese from having contact with other countries. How do you think this isolation affected China's culture? The Chinese were in no way behind the times. In fact, they were an advanced people, more skilled than other peoples of their day.

The ancient Chinese were ruled by several *dynasties*. A dynasty is a line of kings or rulers who belong to the same family. China, under these dynasties and in seclusion, began to flourish as a sophisticated society.

98

Preview

☐ Objective
Given proper instruction, the students will be able to do the following:
- Complete sentences about China with appropriate words from the lesson.

☐ Materials
Have available:
- A penny.
- A tin can.*
- A lead pipe or a mechanical pencil.*
- An object made of bronze or of a metal that looks like bronze.*
- The figure of the Shang art (1176 B.C.) from the History TimeLine Packet.

Day 41

Lesson

☐ Introducing the Lesson
Metal objects—Place the penny, tin can, and lead pipe (or mechanical pencil) on a table and ask the students what these three objects have in common. *(Answers will vary but should include that they are all made from metal.)* Invite the students to name the type of metal that each is made of. *(penny—copper; can—tin; pipe or pencil—lead)* Ask the students what they think would happen if a person combined these three metals. *(A new metal would be formed.)*

Show the students the bronze object you have brought. Explain that the new metal formed when copper, tin, and lead are melted down is called *bronze*. Pass the bronze object among the students. Ask them whether they have any bronze objects in their homes. *(Answers will vary.)* Explain that this lesson will reveal how the ancient Chinese used bronze.

☐ Teaching the Lesson
Natural barriers and dynasties—Instruct the students to read page 98 silently to learn what the term *natural barrier* means. *(a landform that isolates a country from outside influence)*

Discussion Questions
➤ **What are some examples of natural barriers that isolated ancient China?** *(mountain ranges, a large desert, jungles)*
➤ **How was the effect of these barriers on China's culture different from what we might have expected?** *(They did not cause China's culture to be behind the times; they were an advanced people, more skilled than other peoples of their day.)*
➤ **What type of government did the ancient Chinese have?** *(They were ruled by dynasties.)*
➤ **What is a *dynasty*?** *(a line of kings or rulers who belong to the same family)*

China

Location—Asia, or the Far East. China faces the Pacific Ocean in the east and Russia and Mongolia in the north. Pakistan, India, Nepal, Bhutan, Burma, Laos, and Vietnam border China on the west and south. North Korea also shares an eastern border with China.

Natural Resources—Large amounts of coal and oil, but both are under-developed. Contains deposits of tungsten, bauxite, iron ore, tin, lead, and mercury. The land has been heavily farmed and many of the original forests destroyed.

Climate—Most of China has a temperate climate. The northern regions are snowy. Climate is affected by yearly *monsoons*, or winds that bring rain. Annual precipitation ranges from twenty to eighty inches. Temperatures vary widely from region to region.

Topography—Three main land regions. The eastern region is the lowlands where the Huang He and Yangtze Rivers flow to the sea. In central China the land becomes rolling hills. The western third of China is hilly and mountainous. Tibet, in southwest China, has some of the highest mountain peaks in the world.

Geography and Culture—Civilization began along the major rivers, the Huang He and the Yangtze. Natural borders isolate China, limiting its contact with other countries in ancient times. Because of this isolation, the Chinese thought of themselves as the Central Kingdom, the only civilized kingdom on earth. This attitude affected much of China's culture.

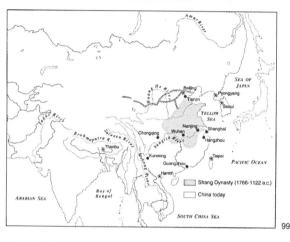

99

The Shang

One of the earliest dynasties in China was the Shang, ruling from 1766-1122 B.C. The Shang lived along the Huang He, or Yellow River, in northern China. Most of the common people in Shang China were farmers. The grains and vegetables they grew, especially rice, were necessary to feed the people. The Huang He was often called "China's Sorrow" because its many floods killed thousands of people and ruined many harvests.

The Shang people, particularly the royal family, practiced a religion that involved *ancestor worship*. The Shang believed that the spirits of their dead ancestors had power over them. When the weather was good, the Shang believed their ancestors were pleased. If *drought* or *famine* swept the land, the Shang thought they had angered their ancestors in some way. How do these beliefs differ from what the Bible teaches? The Bible teaches that there is only one God, and He has control over all things.

What do you think the Shang did to try to please their dead ancestors? They would make ornate bronze vessels called *tings* to cook meat as a sacrifice. Royal families had special ceremonies just to prepare and serve their sacrifices.

Ancestor worship shrines in modern China

100

Then and Now—Instruct the students to read page 99 silently to find out how China's isolation made them view themselves. *(They thought of themselves as the Central Kingdom, the only civilized kingdom on earth.)* Direct the students' attention to the Then and Now map, noting ancient cities, changes in boundary lines, and so on.

Day 42

The Shang dynasty—Instruct the students to read page 100 silently to find out when the Shang ruled in China. *(1766-1122 B.C.)* Add the figure of the Shang art to the History TimeLine at 1176 B.C. as a representation of the Shang dynasty.

Discussion Questions

➤ **Along what river did the Shang live?** *(Huang He, or Yellow River)*
➤ **What was the occupation of the common people in China at that time?** *(farmer)*
➤ **What valuable crop was grown for food?** *(rice)*
➤ **What was the Huang He called and why?** *("China's Sorrow" because its floods killed people and ruined harvests)*

➤ **Describe some religious practices and beliefs of the Shang people.** *(They worshiped their ancestors and believed that the spirits of their dead ancestors had power over them; good weather meant that the ancestors were pleased, but drought or famine meant that the ancestors had been angered.)*
➤ **How do these beliefs differ from what the Bible teaches?** *(The Bible says there is only one God, and He has control over all things.)*
➤ **What did the Shang do to try to please their dead ancestors?** *(made special vessels called tings to cook meat in as a sacrifice; performed special ceremonies as they prepared and served the meat)*

> Remind the students that God alone is to be worshiped and that He, not dead ancestors or any other god, controls the elements of nature. (Bible Promise: I. God as Master)

Bronze making—Instruct the students to read page 101 silently to learn what tings, ornaments, and statues were made from. *(bronze)*

Discussion Questions

➤ **For how many years before Europeans made bronze were the Chinese making it?** *(over two thousand years)*

The Bronze Age

Bronze Making

The tings were usually made from bronze as were ornaments and statues. Well over two thousand years before people in Europe made bronze, the Chinese developed special techniques in bronze smithing. Their skill as craftsmen has not been equalled, even today. Why do you think the Chinese did not share their knowledge of bronze making with other countries? For centuries, the natural barriers prevented trade and the spread of ideas.

Shang dynasty bronze ting (left) and another type of vessel, a kuang (above)

The Shang used a difficult process of bronze casting used by no other ancient people. First they made a mold of clay pieces that fit together into the shape of the piece to be cast. The detailed designs of the vessel were carved carefully into the clay. Some bronze smiths used ceramic molds.

After the molds were made, the bronze smith poured the molten bronze, consisting of copper, tin, and lead, into the molds. The smith had to work carefully to keep any air bubbles from entering the mixture. When the bronze hardened, the craftsman removed the mold pieces cautiously so that he could use them again. Once polished, the bronze vessel was ready to be used.

101

Fill in the blanks with words from this lesson.

natural barriers	1. Mountains, deserts, and jungles are some of China's ____ ____.
dynasty	2. A ____ was a line of kings or rulers who belonged to the same family.
monsoons	3. Each year, heavy winds that bring rain, called ____, affect China's climate.
Tibet	4. The region of ____ in southwest China has some of the world's highest peaks.
North Korea	5. ____ ____ borders China on the east.
coal	6. China contains large deposits of ____ and ____.
oil	
Huang He	7. China's two major rivers are the ____ ____ and the ____.
Yangtze	
China's Sorrow	8. The Huang He was nicknamed ____ ____ because of its frequent floods.
Shang	9. The ____ dynasty ruled China from 1766-1122 B.C.
ancestors	10. The Shang people worshiped their ____.
tings	11. The Shang cooked meat as sacrifices in vessels called ____.
bronze	12. Tings were made of ____.
smith	13. A maker of bronze is a bronze ____.
molds	14. The Shang made special clay ____ into which the molten bronze was poured.
ceramic	15. Some bronze smiths used ____ molds.
polish	16. The last step in the bronze-making process was to ____ the bronze.

© 1996 BJU Press. Reproduction prohibited.

Heritage Studies 6
Student Notebook

Lesson 25
Evaluating the Lesson   **30**

➤ **Why were the Chinese skills in bronze making not shared with other countries?** *(because the natural barriers prevented trade and the spread of ideas)*

➤ **What was a person who made bronze called?** *(a bronze smith)*

➤ **What was the first step in the bronze casting process used by the Shang?** *(making a mold of clay in the shape of the piece to be cast)*

➤ **How did the bronze smith use the molds?** *(He poured the molten bronze into them to harden.)*

➤ **What did molten bronze consist of?** *(copper, tin, and lead)*

➤ **What did the smith have to be careful of when pouring the bronze into the mold?** *(not to let any air bubbles enter the mixture)*

➤ **What were the final two steps in the process after the bronze hardened?** *(removing the mold pieces to be used again and polishing the vessel)*

□ Evaluating the Lesson

Tings and Things (Notebook page 30)—Instruct the students to fill in the blanks with the appropriate words from this lesson.

━━━ Going Beyond ━━━

□ Enrichment

Identifying natural barriers—Display in an AREA a detailed world map that shows landforms. Have available a copy of the "Natural Barriers of the World" page for each student. (*NOTE:* See the reproducible material at the end of Lesson 29.) Encourage each student to complete the sheet with information from the map.

□ Additional Teacher Information

The Shang dynasty built many beautiful structures in China. Bronze statues, fine palaces, and entire walled cities were part of their heritage. Much of what we know about the Shang dynasty has come from the discovery of royal tombs near Anyang. The Shang buried their dead in deep, cross-shaped pits with slanted ramps leading to the center of each grave, allowing them to carry the body and funerary offerings to the bottom. Valuables, pottery, and sometimes even chariots were buried with the Shang rulers. Some tombs contained the remains of human and animal sacrifices.

The Shang seem to have had a feudal society consisting of two main classes—commoners and nobles. At the head of the society were the priests and the king.

Shang religion centered on rituals and superstition. In addition to ancestor worship, the Shang had a polytheistic system in which there were two chief gods: the Ruler Above and the God of Earth.

LESSON 26
An Era of Excellence

Text, pages 102-5
Notebook, page 31

- Oracle Bones
- The Chou Dynasty
- Confucius and the Classical Age

———— Preview ————

□ Objectives

Given proper instruction, the students will be able to do the following:
- Write a sentence that uses two or more Chinese characters.
- Complete paragraphs about Shang priests, Chinese writing, and Confucius's teachings.

□ Materials

Have available:
- An overhead projector.
- A blank overhead transparency.
- A blank sheet of paper for each student.
- A black felt-tip pen for each student.*

Prepare an overhead transparency of the Chinese pictographs. (*NOTE:* See the reproducible material at the end of Lesson 29.)

□ Notes

For the Introducing the Lesson activity, felt-tip calligraphy pens with square tips could be used instead of regular felt-tip pens if convenient. Calligraphy pens come in several colors and are available through Bob Jones University Press and at most art supply stores.

———— Lesson ————

□ Introducing the Lesson

Chinese pictographs—Ask for a show of hands of the students who have seen Chinese writing. Explain that Chinese writing has changed over the centuries. Display the overhead transparency of the pictographs, but cover it so that only the first pictograph is showing. Explain that this is one of the earliest Chinese characters, used as early as 1500 B.C. Allow several students to guess what idea they think it represents and then tell them that this character means "sun."

Uncover the second pictograph on the overhead transparency and point out the more intricate brush strokes involved in writing this character. Tell the students that it represents "eternity."

Uncover the third pictograph. Point out that this pictograph combines two separate parts, and explain that it is called a *compound character.* One part shows the idea being represented, and the other part shows how to pronounce it. Explain that this character means "butterfly."

Uncover the fourth pictograph and explain that some compound characters combine two different words, rather than a word and a pronunciation guide. Tell the students that this pictograph joins the characters for "man" and "speech." (*NOTE:* The pictograph representing "speech" literally stands for "mouth" and is used whenever the mouth is part of the action being described [e.g., talking, drinking, eating, quarreling, agreeing].) Allow two or three students to guess what this pictograph means; then tell the class that it means "trust," pointing out that a person who means what he says and says what he means is a person to trust.

Review the four pictographs and their meanings—sun, eternity, butterfly, and trust. Explain that the ancient Chinese used small paintbrushes to write these characters. Instruct each student to write a sentence with his felt-tip pen that uses at least two of these words, substituting the Chinese pictograph for the word it represents. Encourage them to copy the characters from the overhead transparency as accurately as possible. When they have finished, allow them to exchange papers and read what a classmate has written.

Besides using tings in ancestor worship, the Chinese also used *oracle bones.* An *oracle* was a message given by a person who the Chinese thought was a prophet or a god. Kings consulted priests and oracles before making decisions about planting, fighting, and building.

Oracle bones were pieces of bone or shell that priests heated with a hot metal rod. Cracks appeared, which supposedly revealed the ancestors' wishes. The priests then interpreted these cracks and reported the answers to the king. They also wrote the question and answer on the oracle bones and kept them for future reference.

The priests, who were also government officials, kept close watch on political and economic affairs. They made most of their interpretations in light of these current events. The priests had great power in the Shang dynasty because of the religious beliefs of the ancient Chinese. Oracle bones found by archaeologists today provide historical information about the Shang dynasty.

The Chou

The Shang dynasty ruled until 1122 B.C. At this time, a new family came into power—the Chou (jō). The Chou dynasty ruled for about eight hundred years, lasting longer than any other dynasty in Chinese history.

Under the Chou, the Chinese developed an interest in education and literature. Chinese writing also developed in this period. Early writing in China consisted of *pictographs,* or pictures that are used in place of words. Pictographs were brushed on with fine strokes so that writing became a form of art.

The different pictographs used by the Chinese changed over time. Some pictographs combined to form a new word. A more common name for a pictograph is a *character.* What do we use to form words? We use letters. How many letters are in our alphabet? Our alphabet of twenty-six letters is simple compared to the Chinese system of writing. Chinese writing is not based on an alphabet but has about fifty thousand characters. Most Chinese today, however, know only about four thousand of these characters.

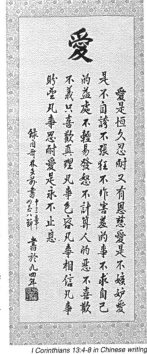

I Corinthians 13:4-8 in Chinese writing

□ Teaching the Lesson

Oracle bones—Instruct the students to read page 102 silently to learn what an *oracle* was. *(a message given by a person who the Chinese thought was a prophet or a god)*

Discussion Questions

➤ **For what types of decisions did kings consult priests and oracles?** *(decisions about planting, fighting, and building)*

➤ **What were *oracle bones?*** *(pieces of bone or shell that cracked after the priests heated them with a metal rod)*

➤ **What did the Chinese think was significant about the cracks in oracle bones?** *(They thought the cracks revealed the ancestors' wishes.)*

➤ **Who interpreted the meanings of the cracks in the bones?** *(priests)*

➤ **Where did the priests record the questions they asked and the answers they interpreted?** *(on the oracle bones)*

➤ **In addition to religion, what other matters interested the priests?** *(political and economic affairs)*

➤ **How did the priests use their knowledge of these subjects to their advantage?** *(They used this knowledge to help them make interpretations of oracle bones.)*

➤ **How were priests viewed by the Shang dynasty?** *(They had great power.)*

➤ **How are oracle bones helpful today?** *(They provide historical information about the Shang dynasty.)*

➤ **What do you think of the Shang method of seeking guidance?** *(Answers will vary.)*

Remind the students that Christians should seek guidance from God through praying and studying His Word. (BATs: 6a Bible study, 6b Prayer)

Day 44

The Chou dynasty—Instruct the students to read page 103 silently to find out in what year the Shang dynasty ended. *(1122 B.C.)*

Discussion Questions

➤ **What new family came into power after the Shang?** *(the Chou)*

➤ **How long did the Chou rule?** *(about eight hundred years)*

➤ **In what two fields did the Chinese become interested during this period?** *(education and literature)*

➤ **What style of Chinese writing developed during the Chou period?** *(pictographs)*

➤ **How did pictographs affect the method of writing?** *(Pictographs were brushed on with fine strokes so that writing became a form of art.)*

➤ **What is a more common name for a pictograph?** *(character)*

➤ **Do the Chinese today use the same pictographs as the ones used during the Chou period?** *(no)*

➤ **How is Chinese writing different from the English way of writing?** *(Chinese writing is not based on an*

The Classical Age

Another name for the rule of the Chou is the *Classical Age*. A *classic* is something that is thought to be the best of its kind and sets a standard of excellence. What do you think a Classical Age is, then? The Classical Age of China was a period that marked a high point in its cultural development. During this time, many important ideas and attitudes were formed that continue to affect the Chinese people today.

One man, Confucius, was a great influence in China during the Classical Age. He was a scholar and a teacher. His teachings were the most important ideas to come out of the Chinese Classical Age.

Confucius thought the key to having a peaceful society was to have every person know his place and act accordingly. He believed that society should be divided into classes, from peasants to nobility, and that this system would help people get along better. Do you think that following Confucius's teachings completely can create a perfect society? Man, alone, cannot be perfect.

Confucius

"Not by works of righteousness which we have done, but according to his mercy he saved us, by the washing of regeneration, and renewing of the Holy Ghost."

Titus 3:5

104

Confucian beliefs may be considered a code of behavior. For example, Confucius taught about five important human relationships: (1) between king and subject, (2) between father and son, (3) between husband and wife, (4) between elder and younger brother, and (5) between friends.

In these relationships the younger and inferior person must always obey the elder and superior person. For example, a citizen must always obey the king, and a son must always obey his father. Can you think of verses in the Bible that teach similar values? Those who were the elder and superior, however, had to set a good example for those beneath them. The two main principles of Confucius's teaching, then, were being obedient and setting a good example.

Confucian teaching also emphasized the importance of the family. Several generations would live in one home. It was not uncommon for children to have grandparents or aunts and uncles living with them. Do you have any grandparents or aunts or uncles living in your home?

105

---

alphabet; symbols represent whole words or are combined to form new words.)

➤ **How many characters does Chinese writing have all together?** *(about fifty thousand)*

➤ **How many characters do most Chinese people actually know today?** *(four thousand)*

➤ **Would you like to learn how to write in Chinese? Why or why not?** *(Answers will vary.)*

Confucius and the Classical Age—Instruct the students to read pages 104-5 silently to find out why the rule of the Chou is called the Classical Age of China. *(A classic sets a standard of excellence; this period was a high point in China's cultural development.)*

Discussion Questions

➤ **What Chinese scholar's teachings were influential during the Classical Age?** *(Confucius)*

➤ **What did Confucius teach about Chinese society?** *(He thought society should be divided into classes with everyone knowing his place and acting accordingly. He believed this would create a perfect and peaceful society.)*

➤ **What was wrong with this teaching?** *(It left out God; man cannot be perfect by himself.)*

Read Titus 3:5 from the page. Ask the students what is really needed in order for men to be considered righteous in God's eyes. *(salvation)* (BAT: 1b Repentance and faith; Bible Promise: A. Liberty from Sin)

➤ **What five human relationships did Confucius teach about?** *(relationships between king and subject, between father and son, between husband and wife, between elder and younger brother, and between friends)*

➤ **According to Confucius, what two principles were true for each of these relationships?** *(The younger and inferior person must obey the elder and superior person; the elder and superior person must set a good example.)*

➤ **What are some Bible verses that sound similar to these teachings?** *(Answers will vary but may include I Peter 5:2-3 and I Timothy 5:1, 17.)*

➤ **What else was important in Confucius's teachings?** *(family)*

➤ **Describe a typical Chinese family.** *(several generations—children, grandparents, aunts and uncles—in one home)*

➤ **How many generations live in your home?** *(Answers will vary.)*

Paragraph Project

Name _____

長 象 轉
軍 贈
膾 民
耔

Read each topic sentence below and then write three or four sentences in your own words to complete each paragraph.

1. The Shang priests had important religious responsibilities. _____

   Answers will vary.

   _____
   _____
   _____
   _____

2. Writing in Chinese is very different from writing in English. _____

   Answers will vary.

   _____
   _____
   _____
   _____

耔
民
膾
軍
轉 象 長

3. Confucius's teachings greatly influenced China's Classical Age. _____

   Answers will vary.

   _____
   _____
   _____
   _____

Heritage Studies 6
Student Notebook

Lesson 26
Evaluating the Lesson   **31**

□ Evaluating the Lesson

Paragraph Completion (Notebook page 31)—Instruct the students to read each topic sentence and to compose three or four sentences in their own words to complete each paragraph.

■ Going Beyond ■

□ Enrichment

Bible search—Set up an AREA with a Bible concordance, notebook paper, and pencils. Invite the students to use the concordance to find Bible verses that teach about the human relationships they discussed in this lesson. Encourage them to keep a list of the references and what they teach, and allow them to share their findings with the other students.

□ Additional Teacher Information

In China today, the Chinese language is written the same way throughout the country. But the spoken language varies from one part of China to another. China has seven major dialects, and pronunciation differs so greatly among dialect groups that people from different areas of the country may have difficulty understanding one another. In some cases, people from two different parts of China might not be able to communicate verbally at all.

Although no one is certain of the exact dates of Confucius's life, he lived during the 500s-400s B.C. He was born Kong Qiu, and he was called *Kongfuzi,* meaning "Great Master Kong," by his followers. The name *Confucius* is the Latin form of *Kongfuzi.* During his lifetime, Confucius was a rather obscure figure, failing in his attempt to secure an important government position and later receiving only a few minor appointments. However, his teachings gained him a following of loyal supporters. After Confucius's death, his followers published his teachings and wise sayings.

LESSON 27
Scholars, Artists, and Builders

Text, pages 106-9
Notebook, page 32

- Classical Education
- Classical Art
- The Ch'in Dynasty
- Great Wall

━━━ Preview ━━━

☐ Objective
Given proper instruction, the students will be able to do the following:
- Match words about China with their descriptions.

☐ Materials
Have available:
- A cassette player.
- *HERITAGE STUDIES Listening Cassette B.*
- Maps and More 7.

Day 45

━━━ Lesson ━━━

☐ Introducing the Lesson
Chinese music—Play the recording of the classical Chinese music from *HERITAGE STUDIES Listening Cassette B.* Explain that although no one is sure exactly how the ancient Chinese music sounded, it might have been similar to this recording. Probably some of the same types of instruments were used. Ask the students what they like or dislike about this music. *(Answers will vary.)* Ask them what the music makes them think of. *(Answers will vary.)* Explain that music was a very important part of Chinese life and that in this lesson they will discover some of the ways music was used.

☐ Teaching the Lesson
Classical education—Instruct the students to read page 106 silently to learn what the book published by Confucius's students was called. *(Confucian Classics)*

Discussion Questions
➤ **What do you think Confucius's quotation about learning and thought means?** *(Learning without thought is a snare because it will only make a person proud. Knowledge alone will not benefit a person if he does not evaluate what he has learned and thoughtfully apply it to his behavior. Thought without learning is a*

Classical Education
Confucius's teachings told people how to live a good life. After his death, his students collected their master's teachings and put them into a collection of sayings called the Confucian *Classics.*

One saying was "Learning without thought is a snare; thought without learning is a danger." What do you think this means? Confucius emphasized education as one way people could improve themselves and live better lives. During the Chou period, education became important. Chinese students spent many years learning the difficult Chinese language. Scholars held positions in government and were respected by the people.

Scholars during the Chou dynasty wrote many books. In addition to the Confucian *Classics,* these books are considered to be the classics of Chinese literature. Poetry, history, rituals, conduct, and music are some of the subjects found in books from this period. To be considered a true scholar in China, one had to have a thorough knowledge of these books. Many ancient Chinese books are based on Confucian teaching.

106

danger because a person lacking proper understanding of truth will come to wrong conclusions about life.)
➤ **What did Confucius emphasize as a way of improving one's life?** *(education)*
➤ **How were educated people treated during the Chou period?** *(They were highly valued; they were given important government positions and were respected by the people.)*
➤ **What did many scholars do to advance education during the Chou period?** *(wrote many books)*
➤ **What subjects did these books include?** *(poetry, history, rituals, conduct, and music)*
➤ **Upon what were many of these books based?** *(Confucian teaching)*
➤ **Which of these subjects would you most like to study?** *(Answers will vary.)*

Classical art—Instruct the students to read page 107 silently to learn what material many Chou artisans used. *(bronze)*

Discussion Questions
➤ **How was Chou bronze work different from the Shang artists' work?** *(It was simpler.)*
➤ **How did the Chou decorate their bronze work?** *(with Chinese writing and carvings of real and imaginary animals)*
➤ **What were these bronze works used for?** *(mainly for religious ceremonies; often placed in tombs of ancestors)*
➤ **What other material did the Chou artists carve to create decorative pieces of art?** *(jade)*

Classical Art

Artisans of the Chou dynasty continued to work with bronze. Chou bronze smiths, however, used a simpler method than the Shang used. The Chou produced fine works that still exist today. Much of their bronze work is covered with Chinese writing and intricate carvings of both real and imaginary animals.

The Chou, like the Shang, used their bronze works mainly in religious ceremonies, which often included placing the vessels in the tombs of ancestors. They also carved pieces of jade to create decorative pieces of art.

Late Chou dynasty ritual vessels

The Metropolitan Museum of Art, Rogers Fund, 1947 (47.27ab) Photograph©1979 The Metropolitan Museum of Art

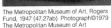

Modern Chinese jade objects

As with other ancient peoples, music was important to the ancient Chinese. Music accompanied worship, work, and pleasure—even archery contests held by Chou nobles. One event used music to keep time for the shooting. If a contestant failed to shoot on the beat, the shot was disqualified.

107

The Ch'in

Government

After the Chou, the Ch'in dynasty was the next to rule, beginning about 221 B.C. Also spelled "Qin," the Ch'in dynasty was begun by the fierce emperor, Qin Shi Huangdi *(chĭn' shē' hwäng'dē')*. Under his rule, China experienced many changes.

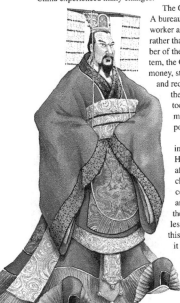

The Ch'in set up a *bureaucracy.* A bureaucracy is a system that gives a worker a job and then trains him for it, rather than passing on the job to a member of the family. In addition to this system, the Ch'in established one kind of money, standardized all measurements, and required all Chinese people to use the same writing. The emperor also took away land from the nobles, making it possible for both the poor and the rich to own land.

There were many changes in the Ch'in society at this time. How do you think these changes affected China? Although the changes helped to unify the country, Shi Huangdi used cruel and harsh methods to implement them. The Ch'in dynasty lasted less than thirty years. The reign of this powerful dynasty was short, yet it left a lasting monument, the name *China.* Can you see how China got its name?

Qin Shi Huangdi

108

➤ **What other art form was important during the Chou period?** *(music)*

➤ **In what three activities was music used?** *(worship, work, and pleasure)*

➤ **What sport involved using music to keep time?** *(archery)*

➤ **What happened to players who missed shooting on the beat of music?** *(Their shots were disqualified.)*

Day 46

The Ch'in dynasty—Instruct the students to read page 108 silently to learn when the Ch'in dynasty began its reign. *(about 221 B.C.)*

Discussion Questions

➤ **Who was the first emperor of the Ch'in dynasty?** *(Qin Shi Huangdi)*

➤ **What is a *bureaucracy*?** *(a system that gives a worker a job and then trains him for it, rather than passing on the job to a member of the family)*

➤ **Besides adopting a bureaucratic system, what were some other changes that took place in China under Shi Huangdi's leadership?** *(established one kind of money, standardized all measurements, standardized writing, and made land ownership possible for the poor)*

➤ **What effect did these changes have on China?** *(helped to unify the country)*

➤ **How do you think the Chinese people felt about the changes?** *(Answers will vary, but probably many were happy with the changes and some were not.)*

➤ **What kind of ruler was Shi Huangdi?** *(cruel and harsh)*

➤ **How long did the Ch'in dynasty last?** *(less than thirty years)*

➤ **What lasting monument came out of this dynasty?** *(the country's name, China)*

Point out that it was probably hard for the Chinese to respect a leader who was harsh and cruel. Remind them that the Bible commands Christians to submit to their authorities even when they do not treat them well. (BAT: 2a Authority)

Great Wall—Instruct the students to read page 109 silently to find out how long the Great Wall of China was during the Ch'in dynasty. *(more than fifteen hundred miles long)*

Display Maps and More 7. Point out the three maps that show the changes in the Great Wall over the years. Ask the students what difference they notice between the earliest map and the map during the barbarian invasions. *(The wall was expanded farther west.)* Tell them that by the time of the Ming dynasty, much of the Great Wall was in ruin. To protect itself from invasion, the Ming government ordered some major changes in the building and repair of the Great Wall. Direct attention to the map during the Ming dynasty. *(NOTE: Throughout the centuries, much restoration has taken place on the Great Wall. The current length given for the Great Wall is about 4,000 miles, making the wall the longest structure ever built. The main part of the Great Wall is about 2,150 miles long, and additional branches make up the*

The Great Wall

Perhaps the greatest accomplishment of the Ch'in period was the construction of the Great Wall. Shi Huangdi ordered the wall to be built by connecting a series of walls that were already standing. Stretching for more than fifteen hundred miles, the wall was designed to keep out invaders from the north, but it also served to keep discontented citizens busy.

Thousands, perhaps even millions, of men built the wall, using stone, brick, dirt, or whatever materials happened to be near the section that was being worked on. The wall was actually designed as two walls with packed dirt in between so that a road could be built on top. The construction of the wall was a long and often dangerous process. Many men died during construction, and legends say that thousands of dead laborers lie buried under the wall.

Although much of the Great Wall was erected during the Ch'in period, it was reconstructed during the reign of the dynasties that followed.

The Great Wall of China

109

The Great Wall Matchup   Name _____

Match the terms with their descriptions by writing the correct letter in each blank.

A. road	H. the Great Wall
B. Confucian *Classics*	I. unification
C. writing	J. archery
D. Ch'in dynasty	K. snare
E. music	L. jade
F. bureaucracy	M. Ming dynasty
G. danger	N. Shi Huangdi

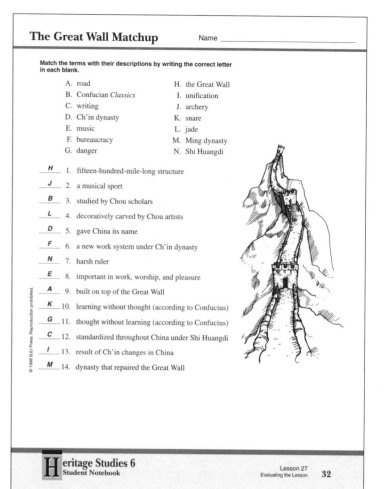

__H__ 1. fifteen-hundred-mile-long structure

__J__ 2. a musical sport

__B__ 3. studied by Chou scholars

__L__ 4. decoratively carved by Chou artists

__D__ 5. gave China its name

__F__ 6. a new work system under Ch'in dynasty

__N__ 7. harsh ruler

__E__ 8. important in work, worship, and pleasure

__A__ 9. built on top of the Great Wall

__K__ 10. learning without thought (according to Confucius)

__G__ 11. thought without learning (according to Confucius)

__C__ 12. standardized throughout China under Shi Huangdi

__I__ 13. result of Ch'in changes in China

__M__ 14. dynasty that repaired the Great Wall

Heritage Studies 6
Student Notebook

Lesson 27
Evaluating the Lesson   **32**

---

remainder.) Call attention to the inset photo of the watchtower. Ask the students what they think watchtowers were used for. *(Answers will vary.)* Explain that one purpose of the wall was military defense and that the watchtowers were manned with soldiers in times of war.

Discussion Questions

➤ **Who ordered the construction of the wall?** *(Shi Huangdi)*

➤ **From what was the wall built?** *(a series of walls that were already standing)*

➤ **What was the wall designed to do?** *(keep out invaders from the north)*

➤ **What other purpose did the building of the wall serve?** *(to keep discontented citizens busy)*

➤ **How many people helped to construct the wall?** *(thousands, or perhaps even millions)*

➤ **How was the wall constructed?** *(Workers used stone, brick, dirt, or material that was available near their construction site; it was designed as two walls with packed dirt between so that a road could be built on top.)*

➤ **What happened to many of the workers?** *(They died; legend says thousands lie buried under the wall.)*

□ Evaluating the Lesson

The Great Wall Matchup (Notebook page 32)—Instruct the students to match the terms at the top of the page with their descriptions, writing the correct letter in each blank.

Going Beyond

□ Enrichment

Researching the history of names—Set up an AREA with a set of encyclopedias or other resource materials about various countries of the world. Remind the students that China received its name from the Ch'in dynasty. Encourage each student to use the resource materials to discover the history behind the names of at least two other countries and to share his findings with the class.

□ Additional Teacher Information

Qin Shi Huangdi burned many of the books in the empire, including all privately owned books. He wanted every piece of literature in the empire to belong to the state. For the Chinese people, who loved their literary tradition, this was a great atrocity. But Shi Huangdi went even further. Believing that literate men and their ideas were a threat to his power, he had many scholars buried alive. Toward the end of his life, he further revealed his mental unsoundness by seeking help from magicians to try to make himself immortal.

LESSON 28
Discoveries and Inventions

Text, pages 110-14
Notebook, pages 33-34

- **The Clay Army**
- **The Han Dynasty**
- **Progress and Inventions**

═══ Preview ═══

□ Objectives
Given proper instruction, the students will be able to do the following:
- Complete a crossword puzzle about China.
- Draw an invention that is both decorative and useful.

□ Materials
Have available:
- A dictionary.
- A small piece of paper for each student.
- A container in which to collect the paper.
- A sticker or small trinket for one student.

Day 47

═══ Lesson ═══

□ Introducing the Lesson
Dictionaries—Show the dictionary, allowing several students to guess how many words the dictionary contains. *(Answers will vary.)* Ask them how long they think it would take to compile a dictionary of all the words in the English language. *(Answers will vary.)*

Play the game Dictionary with the students. Allow one student to choose an unfamiliar word from the dictionary and to write it on the chalkboard. Instruct each of the remaining students to make up a definition for that word and to write it on their pieces of papers, making it sound as close as possible to a real dictionary definition. The student who chose the word should write the true dictionary definition on the paper. When they have finished, collect all the papers in a container and read them one by one, instructing each student to vote on the definition he thinks is the true one. Keep a record of the number of votes for each definition. Give an award to the student whose made-up definition receives the most votes.

Explain that the people of the Han dynasty were the first to compile a dictionary of the Chinese language. Tell the students to pay special attention to this lesson to find out

A Clay Army
It was common practice among the ancient Chinese as well as other ancient peoples to bury the dead with supplies, such as food, weapons, and money. The Chinese believed in life after death but not as the Bible teaches. Like the Egyptians, they thought that their dead ancestors would live on into the next world, needing those supplies to survive.

In 1974, some Chinese peasants were digging for a well when they made an incredible discovery—an entire clay army keeping a silent guard over the tomb of the emperor Qin Shi Huangdi. Each life-sized statue of this clay army was uniquely carved with great detail, including the weapons in its hands. The clay army included over six thousand soldiers, horses, and chariots and was probably designed to protect the emperor as he lived on into the next world.

Artifacts like this clay army reveal the way people in the ancient world lived and died. One journalist, Audrey Topping, wrote after looking at the clay figures, "Looking into the pit . . . was like looking back more than two thousand years at an ancient battlefield."

Part of the army of life-sized figures found at the tomb of Qin Shi Huangdi

110

how the Chinese dictionary was different from the English dictionary.

□ Teaching the Lesson
The clay army—Instruct the students to read page 110 silently to find out what the common burial practice of the ancient Chinese was. *(to bury the dead with supplies, such as food, weapons, and money)*

Discussion Questions
➤ **What was the Chinese belief about life after death?** *(that their dead ancestors would live on into the next world and that they would need the supplies to survive)*
➤ **What discovery was made in 1974?** *(While digging a well, Chinese peasants found an army of clay statues keeping watch over the tomb of Qin Shi Huangdi.)*
➤ **How big were the soldiers in this clay army?** *(life-sized)*
➤ **How many soldiers, horses, and chariots did the army include?** *(over six thousand)*
➤ **What was the builders' purpose in making this army?** *(to protect the emperor in the next world)*
➤ **What do you think the clay figures revealed about ancient military customs?** *(Answers will vary but may include how the soldiers dressed, the types of weapons they used, the type of armor their horses wore, and what their chariots looked like.)*

The Han

Compared with other Chinese dynasties, Ch'in rule was very brief. After the Ch'in emperor died, another dynasty, the Han, rose to power around 200 B.C. Replacing the harsh Ch'in, the Han provided a strong, but fair, government.

The Han rulers needed officials to help govern the country. These officials, or *mandarins*, were chosen according to their abilities. A man wanting to be a mandarin had to spend long years studying the Confucian *Classics*. At the end of those years, when he was almost thirty, the candidate had to take some very difficult government tests that involved being locked in a small room for days on end.

If a man passed the upper levels of the test, he was allowed to have the title of a mandarin. A mandarin could be identified by his special robes. He was highly respected for his superior intelligence and education.

The mandarins were not just a group of scholars, however. They were vital to the running of the Chinese government. They supervised government activities that included the building of roads, the dealings of merchants, and the collecting of taxes. Mandarins remained an important part of the Chinese government for more than two thousand years. Today the term *mandarin* refers to a dialect that is spoken by many Chinese people.

112

Remind the students that earthly treasures cannot be taken beyond the grave. Point out that the Bible commands Christians to lay up treasures in heaven where they will never decay. God wants Christians to be content with the things He has given them here on earth, but not to treasure those things above heavenly riches. (BAT: 7d Contentment)

Day 48

The Han dynasty—Instruct the students to read pages 111-12 silently to find out when the Han dynasty began. *(around 200 B.C.)*

Discussion Questions

➤ **How was the Han rule different from the rule of the Ch'in?** *(The Han were strong, but they were fair rather than harsh.)*

➤ **What were the Han rulers' officials called?** *(mandarins)*

➤ **What did a man have to do to become a mandarin?** *(spend long years studying the Confucian* Classics *and take government tests that involved being locked in a small room for days)*

➤ **How was a mandarin identified?** *(by his special robes)*

➤ **How were mandarins viewed?** *(highly respected)*

➤ **Name some duties of mandarins besides being scholars.** *(They supervised the building of roads, the dealings of merchants, and the collecting of taxes.)*

➤ **For how long did mandarins remain an important part of Chinese government?** *(more than two thousand years)*

➤ **What does the term** *mandarin* **refer to today?** *(a dialect spoken by many Chinese people)*

The era of the Han proved a glorious period in Chinese history. The Chinese were far ahead of other countries, making progress in writing, medicine, and science. During this period, the first Chinese dictionary was completed with about nine thousand words and their meanings. Included in these early dictionaries were the different ways to write each word.

A common medical treatment was *acupuncture*, a method of relieving pain by sticking needles into certain points of the body. The Chinese also used special herbs as medicine.

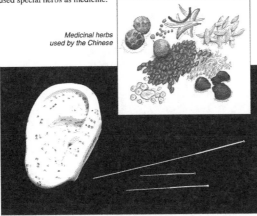

Medicinal herbs used by the Chinese

A model of the ear with acupuncture points labeled (left) and three different sizes of acupuncture needles (right)

The Chinese learned how to mine for salt by using bamboo poles with iron tips. The Chinese would drill thousands of feet underground to get salt water. Then they would use natural gas to heat these mines until the water evaporated, leaving the salt behind. They raised the salt to the surface in bamboo buckets.

113

One important scientific invention during the Han era was the *seismograph*. Do you know what a seismograph is? It is an instrument that is used to detect and measure earthquakes. The ancient Chinese seismographs were not like the ones that are used today, however. Instead, they were very decorative pieces of bronze.

Look at the pictures on this page. Inside the *urn*, or vase, is a pendulum. Whenever the earth moved, the pendulum would move, hitting a small ball that fell out of the dragon's mouth into the frog's mouth.

The Chinese determined the direction of the earthquake by which frog the ball fell into. Why do you think the ancient Chinese needed a seismograph? Why do we use seismographs today? Earthquakes often cause damage to buildings and land. The Chinese used the bronze seismograph to determine the general location of an earthquake. Then Chinese leaders sent out troops with food and supplies to help people— particularly the farmers, whose work supported the entire country.

114

Progress and inventions—Instruct the students to read pages 113-14 silently to learn in what three areas the Han people made special progress. *(writing, medicine, and science)*

Discussion Questions

➤ **What accomplishment from the Han era helped the Chinese to excel in writing?** *(a dictionary)*
➤ **How many words with their meanings were included in this dictionary?** *(about nine thousand)*
➤ **What aside from word meanings were included in the early Chinese dictionaries?** *(different ways to write each word)*
➤ **What medical treatments were common in this era?** *(acupuncture, herbs)*
➤ **What new mining techniques did the Chinese use during the Han era?** *(using bamboo poles with iron tips, drilling down to get salt water, evaporating water with natural gas so that salt could be collected)*
➤ **What important scientific tool was invented during the Han era?** *(seismograph)*
➤ **What is a seismograph used for?** *(detecting and measuring earthquakes)*
➤ **What device was placed in the center of the Chinese seismograph?** *(pendulum)*
➤ **How did an earthquake affect the seismograph?** *(The pendulum moved and hit a ball, which then fell out of the dragon's mouth and into a frog's mouth.)*

➤ **How could a person tell the direction of the earthquake from the seismograph?** *(by seeing which frog's mouth the ball fell into)*
➤ **What did the Chinese do with the information they learned from the seismograph?** *(After learning the location of the earthquake, they sent out troops with food and supplies to help the people in that area.)*

Use the clues below to complete the puzzle.

Across

3. the dynasty after the Ch'in
4. discovered a famous tomb
7. mined by bamboo drills
8. a "sticky" medical procedure
9. scholar whose writings were studied by mandarins
12. a Chinese official
14. placed in the center of a seismograph

Down

1. Mandarin is now a _____ in China.
2. a metal loved by artists
5. emperor buried with an army (two words)
6. a Han accomplishment that included nine thousand words
7. an invention to measure earthquakes
9. An entire army made of _____ guarded Shi Huangdi's tomb.
10. Writing, medicine, and _____ progressed under the Han dynasty.
11. dropped a ball from its mouth when shaken
13. Mandarins wore special _____.

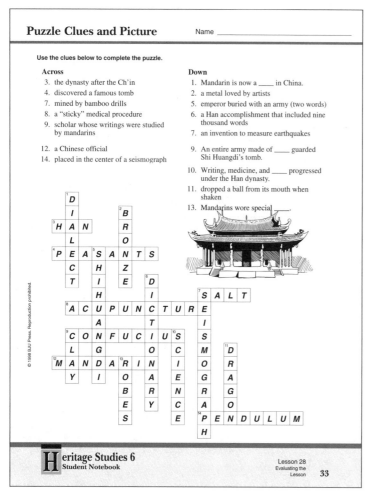

Crossword answers:
3. HAN
4. PEASANTS
7. SALT
8. ACUPUNCTURE
9. CONFUCIUS
12. MANDARIN
14. PENDULUM

Down answers:
1. DIALECT
2. BRONZE
5. SHIHUANGDI
6. DICTIONARY
7. SEISMOGRAPH
9. CLAY
10. ART
11. DRAGON

Think of an idea for an invention that, like the ancient seismograph, is both useful and decorative. Draw a picture of your invention below.

☐ Evaluating the Lesson

Puzzle Clues and Picture (Notebook pages 33-34)—Instruct the students to use the clues to complete the crossword puzzle. Then tell them to imagine an object that, like the bronze seismograph, is both useful and decorative, and to draw a picture of it.

═══ Going Beyond ═══

☐ Enrichment

Making clay models—Set up an AREA with modeling clay. Remind the students that much of what we know about ancient Chinese armies comes from the clay figures found in Shi Huangdi's tomb. Encourage each student to shape a clay item that demonstrates some aspect of life as we know it today so that if someone in the future were to find it, it would give that person information about our lifestyles. Possible items include vehicles, machines, furniture, and toys.

☐ Additional Teacher Information

The Chinese peasants first discovered the clay figures greatly in need of repair. Time had worn away their original coat of paint, but it was obvious that meticulous artistry had gone into their making. No two figures in the entire terra cotta army are exactly alike. Uniforms, hairstyles, and facial expressions are different. Today, many of the damaged figures have been restored and replaced in the tomb.

With the Han dynasty began the imperial era of China's history. The mandarins were a great administrative help to the emperors. There were different levels of authority among the mandarins. Some were actually part of the emperor's entourage, helping him make his most important decisions, while others held lower rank and managed smaller areas of business in the empire.

The ancient Chinese had great respect for literature. They valued not only the books themselves, but also the preservation of them. The Han dynasty kept archives of books even before paper was invented. By the first century B.C., they possessed ten thousand bamboo scrolls and three thousand rolls of silk covered with Chinese characters.

LESSON 29
A Land of Paper and Silk

Text, pages 115-18
Notebook, page 35

- Making Paper
- Paper
- The Silk Road
- China Today

━━ Preview ━━

□ Objectives
Given proper instruction, the students will be able to do the following:
- Make their own paper.
- Identify true and false statements about China.
- Correct false information about China.

□ Materials
Have available:
- 2 wide-mouthed tin cans (at least 12 ounces) for each pair of students.*
- A can opener.*
- An 8-ounce glass jar or plastic container with a lid for each pair of students.*
- Two 7" squares of window screen for each pair of students.*
- Newspapers.*
- A towel or a thick cloth for each pair of students.*
- 1 to 2 rolls of two-layered toilet tissue.*
- A slightly damp sponge for each pair of students.*
- A roll of paper towels.*
- 2 pieces of dry cloth for each pair of students.*
- An iron.*
- An ironing board.*
- Maps and More 8.
- Pitchers of water or access to a water supply.*

Prepare one of the two tin cans for each pair by cutting the bottom off with the can opener. (*NOTE:* If one of the cans is smaller than the other, cut the bottom off the smaller one.)

□ Notes
You could use different colors of toilet tissue in order to make the handmade paper more attractive.

◆ DISCOVERING HOW ◆

To Make Paper
1. Help your teacher prepare and set up the equipment for making paper.
2. Listen as your teacher reads the steps needed in making paper.
3. Work with your partner, completing each step as your teacher directs.

116

Day 49

━━ Lesson ━━

□ Introducing the Lesson
Making paper—Direct a *Discovering How* activity on page 116. Tell the students to work with their Heritage Studies partners to set up the two cans on a layer of newspaper, with one piece of window screen between them. (*NOTE:* The can with the bottom cut out should be on top.) Instruct each pair of students to fill the glass jar one-third full with water. Give each pair three sheets of toilet tissue, telling them to shred the tissue into small pieces and drop them into the jar. Instruct them to seal the jar tightly and shake it until they can no longer see the separate pieces of toilet tissue.

Now, tell each Heritage Studies pair to remove the lid of the jar and add more water to the solution until the jar is three-fourths full. Instruct them to dump the contents of the jar through the top tin can as quickly as possible without spilling, taking care to hold the screen in place. Point out that the tissue fibers have collected on the screen while the water has drained into the bottom can.

Instruct each pair of students to spread the towel or thick cloth on top of a desk or other hard, level surface. Tell them to remove the top can, carefully lift off the screen, and set it onto the towel or cloth, placing the other piece of screen over the top of the fibers to protect them. Instruct them to press firmly on the top screen with the damp sponge to soak up excess water, wring out the sponge, and repeat this process until they have removed as much water from the fibers as they can.

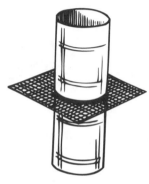

Instruct each Heritage Studies pair to lift the top screen slowly from the layer of fibers and to use the paper towels to soak up more water gently from the layer. Tell them to peel the layer carefully from the bottom screen without tearing it and to place it between two pieces of dry cloth.

Allow the Heritage Studies partners to take turns using the iron, pressing the layer of paper between the cloths until it is completely dry. When they remove the layer from the cloths, it will be a piece of paper strong enough to write on. Display the finished handmade paper in the classroom. (*NOTE:* In order for each student to have a portion to take home, you could cut the handmade paper samples in half.)

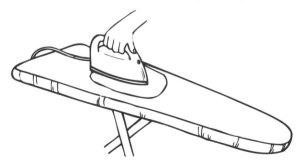

Paper

Imagine what our world would be like without paper. We use paper for many things. Can you name a few? Newspapers, textbooks, labels on cans, and money are just a few of the things we use that are made from paper.

Have you ever wondered who were the first people to use paper? The ancient Chinese were. During the Han dynasty, the Chinese made paper by using the hemp plant or the bark from a mulberry tree. They pounded these substances to a pulp and mixed them

Ancient Chinese paper-making process

with water. The mixture was then spread out flat. The dried pulp formed a coarse sheet of paper that was difficult to write on. This early paper was used merely as wrapping for different items or for clothing. Later, the Chinese used rags, rope, or fishing nets to make a smoother pulp.

What did people write on before paper was invented? The ancient Chinese used silk, bone, or turtle shell to keep written records. Other ancient peoples recorded information on clay tablets or on walls. After the Chinese invented paper, they used it to write on and eventually to make paper money. The paper you use today to do your homework is an "echo" of the ancient Chinese invention of paper. Can you think of any advantages or disadvantages of paper compared to the types of surfaces people wrote on earlier?

Rolls of paper being produced in a modern paper factory

115

Day 50

□ Teaching the Lesson

Paper—Instruct the students to read page 115 silently to learn who were the first people to make paper. (*the ancient Chinese*)

Discussion Questions

➤ **What types of plants did the people of the Han era make paper from?** (*hemp plant or bark from the mulberry tree*)

➤ **How did they make the paper?** (*pounded plant to a pulp, mixed it with water, spread it out flat to dry*)

➤ **What was this early paper like?** (*coarse, difficult to write on*)

➤ **What was it used for?** (*wrapping paper*)

➤ **What items did the Chinese later use to make their paper smoother?** (*rags, ropes, fishing nets*)

➤ **What did the Chinese write on before paper was invented?** (*silk, bone, turtle shell*)

➤ **What did other ancient peoples use to write on?** (*clay tablets, walls*)

➤ **What did the Chinese use paper for, other than something to write on?** (*money*)

➤ **What advantages does our modern paper have over ancient types of writing surfaces?** (*easier to write on, readily available for everyone*)

➤ **What disadvantages does our modern paper have that ancient writing surfaces did not have?** (*Modern*

The Silk Road

How did Chinese inventions, such as the seismograph or paper, reach other countries? Until the Han dynasty, China had remained a secluded country. Do you remember one reason? Natural barriers had hindered interaction with other peoples. The Han dynasty changed China in many ways. Perhaps one of the most important ways it changed China, and even the rest of the world, was by opening up a trade route that became known as the *Silk Road*.

How do you think the trade route received this name? The Chinese used this route to trade silk and spices for fruits and items that they did not have. The Silk Road crossed many of China's natural barriers, such as mountains and deserts. It stretched for over four thousand miles to the west.

Do you think the people who traded with the Chinese had any influence on China? They brought new products, such as different fruits and even horses from their own lands, to trade with the Chinese. Besides trading products, other countries eventually exchanged ideas and inventions with China.

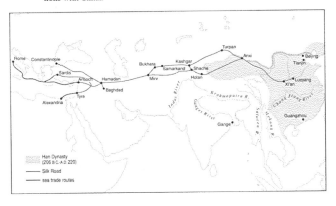

Han Dynasty
(206 B.C.–A.D. 220)
— Silk Road
— sea trade routes

117

The ancient Chinese were a great people. Under the early dynasties, China began to develop and grow, surpassing other countries of the time. The technology of the early Chinese stretches across the centuries to our own day as we use things such as paper and the seismograph.

It is amazing to think that thousands of years ago people secluded from other civilizations were creating inventions that would make our lives easier today. The ancient Chinese laid the foundation for future advances.

Today, traces of China's ancient past may be seen in its culture. The Chinese hold the family as one of the most important aspects of one's life, just as Confucius taught. Education is also important to the modern Chinese as it was centuries ago, and scholars are greatly admired.

Mao Zedong's portrait hangs above the Gate of Heavenly Peace, where he first declared the founding of Communist China in 1949.

Although these values are similar to the ideals held by the ancient Chinese, China's government has greatly changed since the early dynasties in seclusion. Communism strictly rules China, even to the point of limiting families to one child. Today the glory of the ancient Chinese seems dimmed by the reign of Communism. Perhaps someday China will shine once more.

118

---

paper tears and wrinkles easily and is less durable than ancient surfaces.)

➤ **Name some other ways in which we use paper today.** *(Answers will vary.)*

The Silk Road—Instruct the students to read page 117 to discover how Chinese inventions reached other countries. *(by means of a trade route, the Silk Road)*

Discussion Questions

➤ **Why had there been little trade before the time of the Han dynasty?** *(Natural barriers had cut China off from other countries.)*
➤ **How did the new trade route get its name?** *(It was called the Silk Road because China used it to trade silk and spices for fruits and other items they did not have.)*
➤ **How did the Silk Road solve the problem of natural barriers?** *(It crossed mountains and deserts.)*
➤ **How long was the road, and in what direction did it lead?** *(over four thousand miles long; west)*
➤ **How did the countries who traded with the Chinese influence China?** *(They brought new products, new ideas, and new inventions.)*

Display Maps and More 8 and give the students a few moments to examine the map. (*NOTE:* Another name for Chang Jiang River is the Yangtze River.) Explain that this is the route of the Silk Road. Point out that the Silk Road stretched as far as Persia and Arabia and that the sea routes extended it to Alexandria and Rome. Ask them how they

think people in other countries used the silk they traded for with China. *(Answers will vary.)*

China today—Instruct the students to read page 118 to find the names of two ancient Chinese inventions that we still use, in other forms, today. *(paper and the seismograph)*

Discussion Questions

➤ **In what ways can traces of China's past be seen in its modern culture?** *(The family is important, as Confucius taught; education is important; and scholars are greatly admired.)*
➤ **What new governmental system rules China today?** *(Communism)*
➤ **Name one way in which Communism places strict limits on the Chinese people.** *(limits their families to one child)*
➤ **Ask the students what they think the main need of China's people today is.** *(Answers will vary.)*

> Remind the students that no matter what problems nations or individuals may have, the fundamental need of all people is salvation through Christ. (BAT: 1b Repentance and Faith)

True or False?

Name _____

Write *T* in the blank if the statement is true. Write *F* in the blank if the statement is false. For each false statement, write a corrected statement on the line(s).

Wording will vary.

T 1. The ancient Chinese were the first people to use paper. _____

F 2. The people of the Han dynasty made paper from the bark of cherry trees.
   They used the bark of mulberry trees.

F 3. The pulp that formed from the bark was smooth. **The pulp was coarse.**

T 4. The Chinese later used rags and rope to make a smoother pulp. _____

T 5. Some Chinese wrote on silk before paper was invented. _____

T 6. Other peoples wrote on clay tablets and walls. _____

F 7. The Chinese never used paper money. **They used paper money.**

F 8. Before the Silk Road opened, China traded heavily with other countries.
   Before the Silk Road, China was isolated from other countries.

T 9. The Silk Road crossed many of China's natural barriers. _____

T 10. The Silk Road carried Chinese inventions to other countries. _____

F 11. The Silk Road was about two thousand miles long. **It was about four thousand miles long.**

T 12. Horses and certain fruits entered China as a result of the Silk Road. _____

Heritage Studies 6
Student Notebook

Lesson 29
Evaluating the Lesson   **35**

□ Evaluating the Lesson

True or False? (Notebook page 35)—Instruct the students to write a *T* in the blank if the statement is true and an *F* in the blank if the statement is false. Tell them to rewrite each false statement to make it true.

━━━ **Going Beyond** ━━━

□ Enrichment

Creating advertisements—Set up an AREA with pencils, crayons, felt-tip pens, and writing paper. Encourage the students to create imaginary "advertisements" for items that were traded along the Silk Road.

□ Additional Teacher Information

Communist rule in China officially began in 1949 with the leadership of Mao Zedong. Mao was brought up in a peasant family in Hunan Province and became interested in Communist ideas while he worked in a university library in Beijing. In 1921 he and eleven friends established the Chinese Communist Party. After years of struggle with the Chinese Nationalists, Mao's political party gained control of China soon after World War II. Mao's new policies included an alliance with the Soviets, agricultural and industrial expansion programs, and advances in nuclear research. He later broke his alliance with the USSR in the early 1960s. After his death, the country's economy was poor, and the government instituted some reforms. Private enterprise replaced collective farms, and an increase in foreign trade brought economic growth once again.

Communist control is still strong in China. In 1989 Chinese university students gathered in Tiananmen Square to demand democratic reforms and protest government corruption. The Chinese government sent soldiers and tanks to the square to crush the demonstration, and hundreds of protesters were killed. Many more were later arrested and executed.

Natural Barriers of the World

1. Name a mountain range that forms a barrier between two countries. Name the two countries it separates. _____

   _____

2. Name a large desert and the continent on which it is located. _____

   _____

   _____

   How might a desert be a natural barrier? _____

   _____

   _____

3. Name a jungle and the continent on which it is located. _____

   _____

   _____

4. Find one other type of landform that you think could be a natural barrier.

   _____

   Explain how this landform could create a barrier to the spread of culture.

   _____

   _____

   _____

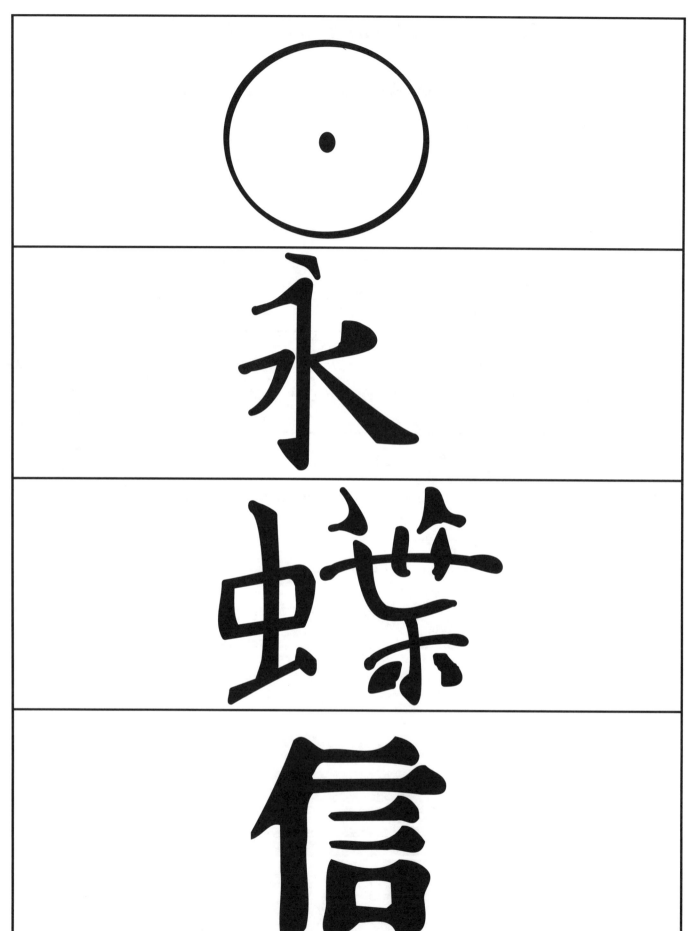

Use with Lesson 26.

6 LESSONS 30-36

A Glory by the Sea: Classical Greece

This chapter focuses on the land, people, and culture of classical Greece. The students will read about the contributions of each major city-state—from democratic Athens to militaristic Sparta. Monuments like the Parthenon on the Acropolis are memorials to Greece's sophisticated but lavish society. The legacies of Pericles and Alexander the Great are memorials to a culture that emphasized strength, power, and beauty. The ancient Greeks celebrated life by cultivating literature, art, and science. Grecian intellectuals, including Homer, Socrates, Aristotle, and Hippocrates, enjoyed world renown that endures to this day. Greece maintained its glory through the Persian Wars, but the Peloponnesian Wars between Athens and Sparta opened the way for foreign rule. The students will learn how classical Greece played an important part in history and continues to shape culture even today.

□ Materials

Lesson 34 requires certain items that must be obtained or prepared several days to several weeks before the presentation of the lesson. These items are labeled with an asterisk (*) in the lesson and in the Materials List in the Supplement. Occasionally, items not commonly found in the classroom as well as items needed in large quantities may also be labeled with an asterisk. For further information, see the individual lessons.

□ Chapter Bulletin Board

Display a map of ancient Greece, labeling Athens, Sparta, Peloponnesus, Salamis Bay, Olympia, and Macedonia. As key locations, people, or events are discussed, affix the corresponding Maps and More figures to the bulletin board map. (*NOTE:* See Maps and More 9 and 10.) Use a column design on the right and left sides.

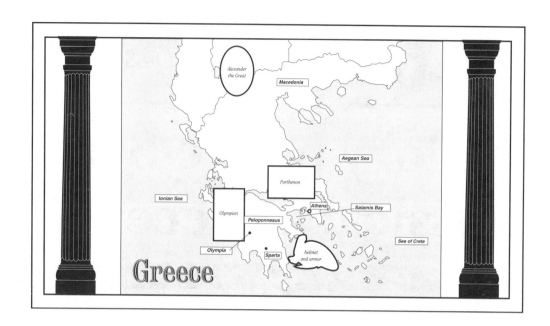

Greece

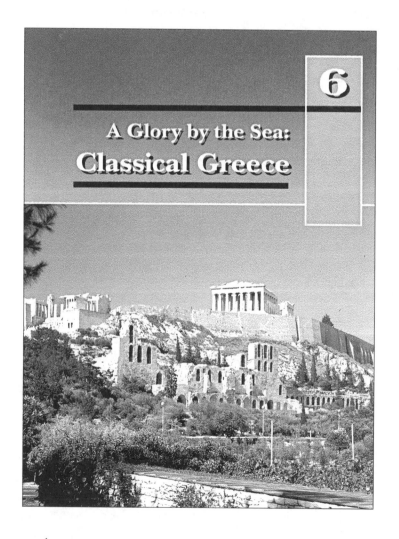

6

A Glory by the Sea:
Classical Greece

LESSON 30

"The Glory That Was Greece"

Text, pages 120-22
Notebook, page 36

- The Classical Age
- The Land and People
- Then and Now

Modern Greek seacoast

The poet Edgar Allan Poe once wrote of "the glory that was Greece." What do you think he meant? Was he describing the land of Greece itself—its steep white rocks towering above a sapphire blue sea? Was he thinking of its architecture—its magnificent marble buildings, its columned porches, its statues? Or was he speaking of the Grecian people, draped in their long, flowing robes or clad in their bronze armor—accomplished warriors, philosophers, mathematicians, poets, and artists?

Poe was clearly referring to the Classical Age of Greece, a period of time beginning about 500 B.C. and lasting nearly two hundred years. Why do we remember these centuries of history in Greece as glorious?

The Classical Age was a peak of human achievement. The culture of the Greeks in this time period made a lasting impact on the Western world. Over the centuries, people have looked back to the classical Greeks for patterns to follow in government, philosophy, and the arts.

120

▬ Preview ▬

□ Objective
Given proper instruction, the students will be able to do the following:
- Complete statements about Greece by identifying the missing words.

□ Materials
Have available:
- An overhead projector.
- A blank overhead transparency.

Prepare an overhead transparency of the poem excerpt. (*NOTE: See the reproducible material at the end of Lesson 36.*)

□ Notes
The Enrichment activity requires the following food items: grapes, olives, feta cheese, and samples of wheat, barley, and olive oil.

Day 51

▬ Lesson ▬

□ Introducing the Lesson
Poetry reading—Display the overhead transparency of an excerpt of Edgar Allan Poe's poem "To Helen." Explain that in Greek mythology, Helen of Troy was the most beautiful woman in the world. Tell the students that her beauty supposedly caused the Trojan War. Read the poem excerpt, explaining words that the students may not understand. Choose a volunteer to give Poe's description of Helen and what she symbolizes. (*Helen's hyacinth hair, classic face, and Naiad [water nymph] manner symbolize the glory of Greece.*) Explain that the glory of Greece was often honored in Greek myths and legends.

□ Teaching the Lesson
The Classical Age—Instruct the students to read page 120 silently to find when the Classical Age of Greece began. (*about 500 B.C.*)

Discussion Questions
➤ **In what ways does Greece seem glorious?** (*its steep white rocks towering above a sapphire blue sea; its magnificent marble buildings, columned porches, and statues; the accomplished warriors, philosophers, mathematicians, poets, and artists*)
➤ **How was the Classical Age of Greece a peak in human achievement?** (*The ancient Greeks set patterns to follow in government, philosophy, and the arts.*)
➤ **Do you think modern Greece is as glorious as it once was?** (*Answers will vary.*)

Remind the students that earthly glory is fading, but the Lord's majesty is eternal. Encourage the students to give the Lord the proper attention and worship that He deserves. (BATs: 7b Exaltation of Christ, 7c Praise)

The Land and Its People

The homeland of the Greeks was in the same place as the Greece of today. Situated in southern Europe, Greece is a land of mountains, valleys, natural harbors, and hundreds of tiny islands. Greece is a peninsula, bordered by the Ionian Sea on the west, the Mediterranean Sea on the south, and the Aegean Sea on the east. The southern portion of this peninsula is called the *Peloponnesus*.

Because of the mild Mediterranean climate, the Greeks spent much time outdoors. Greece's rugged coastline and island-strewn seas helped make its people seafarers and traders. Often it was easier to go by boat from one place to another than to try to cross the mountains.

Some Greeks were also farmers. The soil in Greece was poor, but farmers could grow crops such as barley, wheat, olives, and grapes. The Greeks often prepared simple meals from these native products even though they imported other types of food.

121

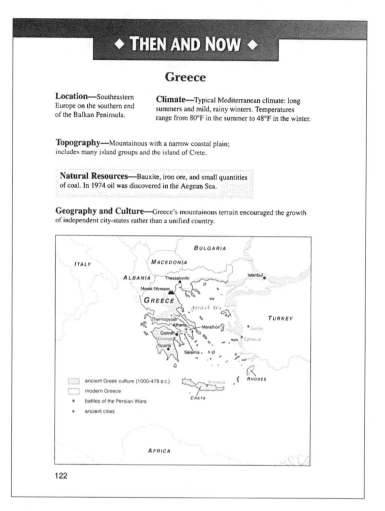

Greece

Location—Southeastern Europe on the southern end of the Balkan Peninsula.

Climate—Typical Mediterranean climate: long summers and mild, rainy winters. Temperatures range from 80°F in the summer to 48°F in the winter.

Topography—Mountainous with a narrow coastal plain; includes many island groups and the island of Crete.

Natural Resources—Bauxite, iron ore, and small quantities of coal. In 1974 oil was discovered in the Aegean Sea.

Geography and Culture—Greece's mountainous terrain encouraged the growth of independent city-states rather than a unified country.

122

The land and people—Instruct the students to read page 121 silently to find the names of the three seas that border Greece. *(the Ionian Sea, the Mediterranean Sea, and the Aegean Sea)*

Discussion Questions

➤ **What is a *peninsula*?** *(a piece of land surrounded by water on three sides and connected to a larger body of land)*

➤ **What is the southern part of the Grecian peninsula called?** *(the Peloponnesus)*

➤ **Why did the Greeks spend much time outdoors?** *(because of the mild Mediterranean climate)*

➤ **Why did the land help make the Greeks seafarers and traders?** *(The rugged coastline and island-strewn seas made it easier to travel by boat than to try to cross the mountains.)*

➤ **What crops did the Greek farmers grow?** *(barley, wheat, olives, and grapes)*

Then and Now—Instruct the students to read page 122 silently to find how Greece's mountainous terrain affected the unity of the country. *(The terrain encouraged the growth of independent city-states rather than a unified country.)* Direct the students' attention to the Then and Now map, noting ancient cities, changes in boundary lines, and so on.

Write the letters of the missing word in the spaces provided. The circled
letters form a word that describes the landform of Greece.

1. The poet _E_ _D_ _G_ _A_ _R_ _A_ _L_ _L_ _A_ _N_ (P)_O_ _E_ wrote of
"the glory that was Greece."

2. The terrain encouraged the growth of _C_ _I_ _T_ _Y_ - _S_ _T_ _A_ _T_ (E)_S_
instead of a unified country.

3. Greece has the typical _M_ _E_ _D_ _I_ _T_ _E_ _R_ _R_ _A_ (N)_E_ _A_ _N_ climate.

4. _O_ (I)_L_ is a natural resource found in the Aegean Sea.

5. The basic topography of Greece is _M_ _O_ _U_ _N_ _T_ _A_ _I_ (N)_O_ _U_ _S_ .

6. Because of the terrain, the people were traders and (S)_E_ _A_ _F_ _A_ _R_ _E_ _R_ _S_ .

7. _S_ (U)_M_ _M_ _E_ _R_ is the season in Greece when the average temperature is
around 80°F.

8. The southern part of Greece is called _P_ _E_ (L)_O_ _P_ _O_ _N_ _N_ _E_ _S_ _U_ _S_ .

9. _G_ _R_ (A)_P_ _E_ _S_ are one of the fruits grown in Greece.

10. The hidden word describing the landform of Greece
is _peninsula_ _____.

Heritage Studies 6
Student Notebook   Lesson 30
Evaluating the Lesson   **36**

□ Evaluating the Lesson

Missing Words (Notebook page 36)—Instruct the students
to write the missing words in the spaces provided. Tell them
that the answer to number ten may be found by using the
circled letters in their answers.

━━━ Going Beyond ━━━

□ Enrichment

Greek food—Set up a food display AREA with samples of
olives, grapes, and feta cheese. Allow students to taste these
Greek foods. Include for display, not for tasting, samples of
barley, wheat, and olive oil.

□ Additional Teacher Information

Ancient Greeks made porridge, cakes, and bread from
their main grains—wheat and barley. Other parts of their diet
included fruits, vegetables, eggs, poultry, and fish. The Greeks
used olive oil and honey to cook these foods. Modern Greek
food includes lamb, seafood, eggplant, feta cheese made
from goat's milk, and many herbs and spices. Olive oil is
still an important ingredient in preparing and seasoning
Greek food.

LESSON 31
With Your Shield or on It

Text, pages 123-26

- City-states
- Early Democracy
- The Spartan Life
- Grecian Women

Athens and Sparta

Before the Classical Age of Greece was a period we call the Dark Age. Few records were kept to tell us what life was like in Greece during this time. But we do know a little about how the people lived. How do you think we got this knowledge?

Because Greece's mountains and valleys divided the land, the people lived in independent groups in separate areas. These groups were called *city-states*. The people in a city-state were like a large family—they claimed common ancestors, practiced the same customs, and spoke the same Greek dialect. Rather than having one central government for the entire country, each city-state had its own government. During Greece's Dark Age, most city-states were ruled by a king. The Greeks called this type of government a *monarchy*.

The two most famous city-states were Athens and Sparta. Although they were once similar to one another, they ended up being very different. By the end of the Dark Age, both city-states had adopted a new type of government—an *oligarchy*. By now you might have guessed that the suffix *-archy* means "rule." The prefix *olig-* means "few." Can you guess what *oligarchy* means? It means "rule by the few," and usually the few who rule are the rich upper class.

123

━━ Preview ━━

□ Objective

Given proper instruction, the students will be able to do the following:
- Determine characteristics of Athens and Sparta.

□ Materials

Have available Maps and More 9.

Prepare:
- Maps and More 9 by cutting apart the two illustrations. (*NOTE:* The figure of the Parthenon will be used in Lesson 33.)
- Enough copies of the "Voting Roles" page for each student to have a role.

Day 52

━━ Lesson ━━

□ Introducing the Lesson

Voting activity—Choose a topic for the students to vote on, such as a longer recess period or a day for a class party. Write on the chalkboard the qualifications for voting in ancient Greece: a male, at least eighteen years of age, and a Greek citizen. Tell the students that they all will represent Greek citizens but will be of different sexes, ages, and professions. Randomly distribute the voting role slips, one per student. Tell those students whose role slip meets the three qualifications on the chalkboard to stand; allow only those students to vote. Ask the students whether they think it is fair that only certain people are allowed to vote. (*Answers will vary.*) Explain that America's method of democracy has its roots in ancient Greek practices. Point out that the ancient Greeks set up a democracy, but only those who met the three qualifications were allowed to vote. Discuss how these qualifications are similar to or different from voting requirements where the students live.

□ Teaching the Lesson

City-states—Instruct the students to read page 123 silently to find the name of the period before the Classical Age of Greece. (*the Dark Age*) Explain that because the Dark Age was a time when few records were kept, not much is known about how the Greeks lived. Ask the students how they think we know things about this time period. (*through oral stories and traditions, etc.*)

Discussion Questions

➤ **What are *city-states*?** (*independent groups in separate areas*)
➤ **What were the people like who lived in a city-state?** (*like a large family, with common ancestors and customs and the same Greek dialect*)
➤ **How did the land affect the city-states?** (*The mountains and valleys divided the land, causing the people to spread out into separate city-states.*)
➤ **What type of government did the city-states have during the Dark Age?** (*rule by a king—a monarchy*)
➤ **What were the two most famous city-states in Greece?** (*Athens and Sparta*)
➤ **Based on the meanings of *-archy* and *olig-*, what is an oligarchy?** (*"rule by the few"*)
➤ **What types of people usually made up the oligarchy?** (*the rich upper class*)

Early democracy—Instruct the students to read page 124 silently to find where the word *democracy* comes from. (*from the Greek words meaning "power of the people"*)

146

After the Dark Age, many city-states branched out and formed colonies along the Mediterranean Sea. People who had gained wealth and power from trading grew discontent with having an oligarchy ruling over them. Some city-states soon began to form new ideas about what type of government was best. Athens was one of these.

Individual men rose to power in Athens, supported by discontented people. These men were called *tyrants*. Some of them ruled well. Others ruled poorly. Most wanted the lower classes to have better living conditions and more say in government. Several of them passed laws in favor of the lower classes.

By 500 B.C. these laws had greatly changed the government of Athens. Athens became a democracy. The word *democracy* comes from the Greek words meaning "power of the people." Every male citizen over eighteen years old attended meetings of the *Assembly*, listened to leaders speak, and voted. Every male citizen now had a voice in the government of Athens.

The Athenian democracy became the most successful one in the ancient world. Democratic countries today look back to Athens as a model in some ways for government by the people.

124

Spartan warriors going into battle

Sparta, on the other hand, kept its oligarchy. The oligarchy had one aim—to have a strong army. What do you think life would have been like in a city-state with this goal?

Life in Sparta was much more rigid than life in Athens. For centuries, Sparta made no advances in art or literature as Athens and other city-states did. Such things were forbidden in Sparta. When a baby boy was born, his parents presented him to the rulers of the city. If the rulers thought he was strong, they allowed him to live. If not, they left him in the countryside to die. The Spartans did not want any weaklings in their army. A boy who was not put to death stayed at home until he was seven years old. Then the army took him and trained him to be a soldier.

During most of his young adult life, a Spartan boy lived with a group, or *pack*, of boys. Pack members had little to eat or wear. They were expected to steal food from farms. Every year some of the pack members were beaten in public as part of a ceremony to the gods. At age twenty, a Spartan man was allowed to marry. But he could not live at home with his wife. He had to live with the other men, training to be a soldier, for ten more years. The training a man received in the Spartan army was harsh and disciplined. Why do you think this was true? The Spartans felt that learning to suffer pain and hardship would make a man a good soldier.

125

Discussion Questions

➤ **Why were the people becoming discontented with the oligarchy?** *(Wealthy traders in newly-formed colonies did not want just a few people ruling over them.)*

Write the word *tyrant* on the chalkboard. Invite the students to suggest qualities associated with this word. *(Possible answers include mean, angry, and cruel.)* Explain that in ancient Athens a tyrant was a man who rose to power through the support of discontented people.

➤ **Were all tyrants bad?** *(No, some ruled well and some ruled poorly.)*

➤ **What did most tyrants want for the people?** *(the lower classes to have better living conditions and more say in government)*

➤ **How did democracy work in Athens?** *(Every male citizen over eighteen voted, participating in the government of Athens.)*

➤ **How is the democracy of the United States similar to or different from the Athenian democracy?** *(In America citizens can participate in government, but in Athens there were more restrictions determining who was eligible to vote.)*

Day 53

The Spartan life—Take the illustration of the helmet, sword, and shield from Maps and More 9 and affix it to the bulletin board map next to the city of Sparta. Instruct the students to read page 125 silently to find the goal of Sparta's oligarchy.

(to have a strong army) Select volunteers to describe how they think life would be in a society that had this goal. *(Answers will vary.)*

Discussion Questions

➤ **Which society was more advanced in art and literature—Athens or Sparta?** *(Athens)*

➤ **Why do you think that is so?** *(Sparta was focused on developing its army, not its culture.)*

➤ **How were baby boys treated in Sparta?** *(When a baby boy was born, he was presented to the rulers of the city to determine whether he should live or die.)*

➤ **Why do you think the Spartan government did not want any weaklings in its army?** *(They wanted to have the strongest army; weak boys would not help that cause.)*

➤ **How do you think you would feel if you had to leave home and join the army at your age or a little younger?** *(Answers will vary.)*

➤ **What was a *pack*, and what kind of conditions did pack members have to endure?** *(a group of boys; little to eat or wear, public punishment)*

➤ **When was a Spartan man allowed to marry?** *(at age twenty)*

➤ **What restriction was put upon the Spartan man after his marriage?** *(For ten years he had to live with other men, training to be a soldier.)*

➤ **Why did the Spartan men have to endure harsh and disciplined training?** *(The Spartans felt that learning to suffer pain and hardship would make a man a good soldier.)*

What was life like for the women in classical Greece? That depended on where they lived.

Athenian women led sheltered lives. An upper-class woman went out of the house only to festivals and plays and then only when accompanied by servants. Her slaves did the daily shopping and errands. Lower-class women, who did not have slaves, were not as protected, but they rarely shopped or worked outside the home. They stayed home and kept their households supplied with meals and clothing.

Spartan women received physical training much like that of their men. Their training was designed to make them strong mothers. Mothers taught their children to be loyal to the city-state and to uphold Spartan bravery. Women sent their husbands and sons into battle with the cry, "Return with your shield or on it!" Do you know what the women meant? They meant that the soldier should return as a living conqueror or a dead hero. The Spartan army had no room for cowards or quitters.

Women in Greece were not allowed to vote or participate in governmental meetings. But many were thinkers with ideas and talents of their own.

126

Remind the students that Christians should be spreading the gospel message and fighting against sin. Tell them that the Lord empowers His soldiers to do His work. (BATs: 8b Faith in the power of the Word of God, 8c Fight, 8d Courage)

Grecian women—Instruct the students to read page 126 silently to find what type of training Spartan women had. *(physical training much like that of their men)*

Discussion Questions

➤ **What determined what life was like for the women in classical Greece?** *(the city-state in which they lived)*
➤ **What kind of life did upper-class Athenian women have?** *(sheltered lives, going out of the house only for festivals and plays and then only when accompanied by servants)*
➤ **What was the purpose of physical training for Spartan women?** *(to make them strong mothers)*
➤ **What did Spartan mothers teach their children?** *(to be loyal to the city-state and to uphold Spartan bravery)*
➤ **Explain the meaning of the Spartan women's battle cry, "Return with your shield or on it!"** *(The soldier should return as a living conqueror or a dead hero. There was no room in the Spartan army for cowards or quitters.)*
➤ **How was the role of Grecian women different from the role of American women today?** *(Grecian women were not allowed to vote or to participate in governmental meetings.)*

➤ **How are American women similar to the women of classical Greece?** *(Many are thinkers with ideas and talents of their own.)*

☐ Evaluating the Lesson

Athens and Sparta—Group the students into two teams, Athens and Sparta. Instruct the students to listen as you read a statement that refers to Athens, Sparta, or both. Tell the students to stand and shout out their team name if the statement refers to the city-state represented by their team.

1. I was governed by tyrants. *(Athens)*
2. My chief goal was a strong army. *(Sparta)*
3. My government was an oligarchy. *(both)*
4. Here boys lived in packs. *(Sparta)*
5. I am a city-state. *(both)*
6. I had an early form of democracy. *(Athens)*
7. Here upper-class women left the house only when accompanied by servants. *(Athens)*
8. Here women received physical training so that they would become strong mothers of healthy babies. *(Sparta)*
9. Here male citizens attended meetings of the Assembly. *(Athens)*
10. Here women sent men off to war with the cry "Return with your shield or on it!" *(Sparta)*
11. Here women were not allowed to vote or participate in governmental meetings but were thinkers with ideas and talents. *(both)*

Going Beyond

☐ Enrichment

Military display—Set up an AREA where students can display military uniforms, medals, photographs, and so forth, of their relatives or friends. As time allows, permit the students bringing items for display to tell about them.

Invite a soldier to speak to the class, telling about his basic training and describing his uniform. (*NOTE:* Contact your local recruiting office to request a military representative to speak to your class.)

☐ Additional Teacher Information

The Athenian tyrant Draco created the first written law in Athens. His official codes were often harsh, including punishment by enslavement or death. Draco's laws allowed debtors to be enslaved by those from whom they borrowed. Many of the rich took advantage of this situation, enslaving the poor who could never repay these loans.

Solon, considered one of the seven wise men of Greece, became a leading figure in the government of Athens after Draco's rule. Solon, born into an aristocratic family, was a poet and a politician. He reformed Draco's harsh debt laws and changed the monetary system to make payments and foreign trade easier. He also set up the *Assembly,* a group of ordinary citizens who served as a governing body. With Solon's new system of government, every male citizen above the age of eighteen had the opportunity to rise from one class to another and to participate in the governing of his city-state.

LESSON 32
Restoring the Glory

Text, pages 127-29
Notebook, page 37

- **Fighting the Persians**
- **Pericles**
- **The Agora**

Preview

☐ Objective
Given proper instruction, the students will be able to do the following:
- Complete statements about ancient Athens.

☐ Materials
Have available the figure of Pericles (429 B.C.) from the History TimeLine Packet.

Day 54

Lesson

☐ Introducing the Lesson
The marketplace—Read aloud the following scenario, instructing the students to listen carefully.

Anphocles leaned against a marble column. The stone felt cool in the heat of the day. He stroked his chin, watching in amusement as a slave haggled with a merchant over some special cheese.

"Anphocles!" A voice floated over the busy hum of the marketplace. "There you are! Ah, my friend! You've come to hear the latest news, I see." A young man approached the column where Anphocles stood.

"And how are you, Demitris?" Anphocles asked, shading his eyes as the young man came and stood beside the column. "Where have you been?"

Demitris smiled. "Listening to the wise men of Athens," he said, motioning to the building that stood on the opposite side of the market square. "Many things are happening here, my friend." Demitris's dark brows crinkled with thought. "They are talking of war, Anphocles. War with the Persians."

Anphocles stared silently ahead. A slave in the next porch purchased olives and figs. A few schoolboys ran noisily through the open square to the building where they received lessons. "Xerxes," he said at last. "He will come. And Athens—" His voice dropped.

"And Athens?" Demitris said, staring at Anphocles.

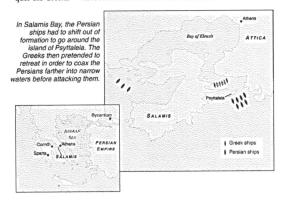

War and Restoration
In the fifth century B.C., the Greeks clashed with the mighty Persian Empire. The Persians were angered by the growth of Greek city-states. They wanted to conquer Greece and make it part of their own empire. But they soon found that defeating the Greeks would not be easy. For over ten years the Greeks fought the Persians and had many successes in battle.

In 480 B.C. the Greeks met the forces of Xerxes (zûrk´sēz), the Persian king, at the Battle of Salamis Bay. They burned 200 of the Persians' 350 ships. Following this defeat, the Persians tried only one more time to conquer the Greeks—without success. Greece was victorious.

In Salamis Bay, the Persian ships had to shift out of formation to go around the island of Psyttaleia. The Greeks then pretended to retreat in order to coax the Persians farther into narrow waters before attacking them.

Have you ever been a member of a team that beat a stronger rival? If you have, you can probably understand how the Greeks felt after their victory over the Persians. They felt as if they could accomplish anything.

However, war had taken its toll on Greece. Many of the country's buildings and temples lay in ruins. One of the first ways the Greeks put their new confidence to work was in restoring their cities.

127

"And Athens—she will be ready. But all this—" His arm swept the air, indicating the white columns, the haggling slaves, and the strength of the wise men. "All this may cease to be." The two men studied the activities of the marketplace as if seeing the place for the first time.

"Athens will live on," said Demitris, firmly nodding his head. "It shall always live."

Anphocles remained silent. How he hoped Demitris was right.

Discussion Questions
➤ **Where does this scene take place?** *(in an open market in Athens)*
➤ **What important news does Demitris bring to Anphocles?** *(Athens may go to war with the Persians.)*
➤ **What did Anphocles mean when he said, "All this may cease to be"?** *(There was a chance that war would destroy the city of Athens.)*

Explain to the students that the people in this scenario are fictional, but Xerxes, the Persians, and the marketplace in ancient Athens really *did* exist. Tell the students that they will learn more about ancient Athens as they study this lesson.

☐ Teaching the Lesson
Fighting the Persians—Instruct the students to read page 127 silently to find the name of the Persian king who waged war against the Greeks. *(Xerxes)*

Pericles

The most famous leader of the democracy in Athens was Pericles. Pericles is considered one of the greatest public speakers, or *orators*, of all time. The Greeks made him their leader because they respected his wisdom and his ability to reason.

Not only was Pericles a powerful speaker and politician, but he loved the city of Athens as well. He was born and reared in Athens, and he wanted it always to be a city that others would admire and love as he did. After the Persian Wars, he wanted to repair the damages caused when Xerxes burned the city. He wanted to restore to Athens all of its former beauty and more.

The *Acropolis,* a hill overlooking the city, was the center of religious life in Athens. Pericles encouraged the Athenians to rebuild the ruined temple and construct other sacred buildings on that hill. He hired talented architects, sculptors, and artists. Under his leadership Athens, as we remember it, took shape—the columns, the sculptures, the great Entrance Gate. He not only supervised reconstruction of buildings but also supported the growth of manufacturing and trade and helped build up the army.

Pericles so dominated Athens during the fifth century B.C. that this period is often called the *Age of Pericles.*

128

In the center of Athens was the *agora (ăg′ər ə),* a busy marketplace. The agora was made up of open-air buildings called *porches.* Every day, citizens gathered there to buy and sell. Athenians could buy fresh food that had been brought to the agora from local farms. But there was not enough good farmland around Athens to feed all of the people, so some foods, such as meats and cheeses, were imported. Shoppers could also find materials like iron, copper, timber, ivory, animal hides, wool, papyrus, furniture, and textiles.

A modern marketplace in Athens

Food and supplies were not the only things to be found at the agora. Schools, government buildings, courts, and private businesses were located there also. Sometimes people just gathered there, not to shop or conduct business but to discuss politics, philosophy, and the latest news. Would you like to have an agora where you live?

129

Discussion Questions

➤ **Why did the Persians want to wage war against Greece?** *(They were angered by the growth of Greek city-states. They wanted to conquer Greece and make it part of their own empire.)*

➤ **How long did the Persians and Greeks fight?** *(for over ten years)*

Point to Salamis Bay on the bulletin board map. Ask the students what happened there. *(The Greeks burned 200 of the Persians' 350 ships.)*

➤ **How do you think the Greeks felt when they defeated the Persians?** *(as if they could accomplish anything)*

➤ **How did the war affect Greece?** *(Many of the country's buildings and temples lay in ruins.)*

➤ **How did the Greeks put their new confidence to work?** *(by restoring their cities)*

Remind the students that Christians should place their confidence in God and not in man or self. Explain that trusting in the Lord requires humility. (BAT: 7e Humility)

Day 55

Pericles—Add the figure of Pericles to the History Time-Line at 429 B.C. Instruct the students to read page 128 silently to find who Pericles was. *(the most famous leader of the democracy in Athens)*

Discussion Questions

➤ **What talent did Pericles have?** *(He was one of the greatest orators of all time.)*

➤ **Why did the Greeks choose him as a leader?** *(because they respected his wisdom and ability to reason)*

➤ **How did Pericles feel toward Athens?** *(He loved it.)*

➤ **What did he want to do to Athens after the war with Persia?** *(repair the damages and restore Athens to all of its former beauty)*

➤ **What is the Acropolis?** *(a hill that overlooked the city and served as the religious center of Athens)*

➤ **What legacy did Pericles' reconstruction leave?** *(the columns, the sculptures, the great Entrance Gate)*

➤ **What other accomplishments did Pericles have?** *(He supported the growth of manufacturing and trade and helped build up the army.)*

➤ **When was this Age of Pericles?** *(fifth century B.C.)*

The agora—Instruct the students to read page 129 silently to find what the *agora* was. *(a busy marketplace made up of open-air buildings)*

Discussion Questions

➤ **What were *porches*?** *(open-air buildings in the agora)*

➤ **What kinds of things were sold at the agora?** *(fresh farm products, imported meats and cheeses, and materials like iron, copper, timber, ivory, animal hides, wool, papyrus, furniture, and textiles)*

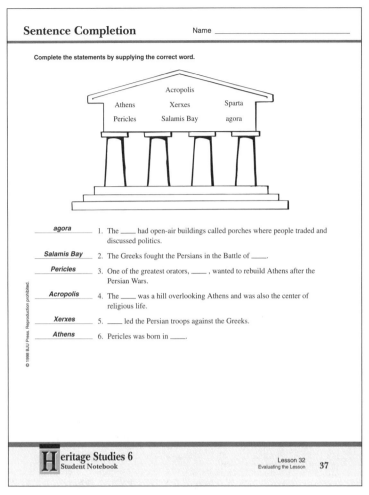

Sentence Completion   Name _____

Complete the statements by supplying the correct word.

Acropolis

Athens   Xerxes   Sparta

Pericles   Salamis Bay   agora

_____ agora _____   1. The _____ had open-air buildings called porches where people traded and discussed politics.

_____ Salamis Bay _____   2. The Greeks fought the Persians in the Battle of _____.

_____ Pericles _____   3. One of the greatest orators, _____ , wanted to rebuild Athens after the Persian Wars.

_____ Acropolis _____   4. The _____ was a hill overlooking Athens and was also the center of religious life.

_____ Xerxes _____   5. _____ led the Persian troops against the Greeks.

_____ Athens _____   6. Pericles was born in _____.

© 1998 BJU Press. Reproduction prohibited.

Heritage Studies 6
Student Notebook

Lesson 32
Evaluating the Lesson   **37**

Going Beyond

□ Enrichment

Be an orator—Instruct each student to write a brief speech in praise of his state or country. As time permits, allow each student to be an orator and make his speech to the class.

□ Additional Teacher Information

Sculptures of Pericles almost always depict the great leader wearing a helmet—probably to disguise the abnormal shape of his head. One of Pericles' greatest contributions was the establishment of a salary for government workers. Previously, only the rich were economically able to work for the government because those of the lower classes needed to earn wages to survive. By making government offices paid positions, Pericles enabled even the poor to participate in the Athenian democracy. He went on to lead Athens in the Peloponnesian Wars but was struck by the plague that spread among the Athenian people.

➤ **What modern place does this shopping aspect of the agora resemble?** *(grocery store, department store, or mall)*

➤ **What other kinds of buildings were found in the agora?** *(schools, government buildings, courts, and private businesses)*

➤ **For what reasons other than shopping did people go to the agora?** *(to discuss politics, philosophy, and the latest news)*

➤ **Would you like to have an agora near you?** *(Answers will vary.)*

□ Evaluating the Lesson

Sentence Completion (Notebook page 37)—Instruct the students to complete the statements by supplying the correct word.

LESSON 33
Myths and Marble

Text, pages 130-32
Notebook, page 38

- The Midas Touch
- The Building of the Parthenon
- The Paths of the Parthenon

━━━ Preview ━━━

□ Objective
Given proper instruction, the students will be able to do the following:
- Identify statements about myths and the Parthenon as being true or false.

□ Materials
Have available the figure of the Parthenon from Maps and More 9.

Prepare a copy of the "What's This?" page for each student. (*NOTE:* See the reproducible material at the end of Lesson 36.)

Day 56

━━━ Lesson ━━━

□ Introducing the Lesson
Perception activity—Give each student a copy of the "What's This?" page, telling him to look at it carefully without conferring with anyone. Allow five to ten minutes for the students to study the picture and write on the paper what they think the picture is. Invite the students to tell what they think this is a picture of. Accept all answers; then tell the students that the picture is an *optical illusion.* Write the phrase on the chalkboard, defining it as an image that is deceptive or misleading. When we look at printed material, we usually perceive the darker, smaller, more regular part of the picture as the object and the rest of the picture as the background; In the picture on the "What's This?" page, there is no clear figure or background, you can see either a vase or two faces. Since neither figure is better than the other, the two images seem to pop in and out of your perception. Tell the students that in this lesson they will learn about the use of optical illusions in the architecture of ancient Greece.

□ Teaching the Lesson
The Midas touch—Instruct the students to read page 130 silently to find what Greek *myths* are. *(stories about the lives of the Greek gods that attempt to explain life)*

Religion in Classical Greece
The Greeks believed in many different gods. Although they thought that their gods had supernatural powers, they did not believe the gods were much different from humans in other respects. Drawings and sculptures depicted the gods as having human bodies. In their character, too, the gods were like humans—they were jealous, vengeful, immoral, and childish. Do gods like these seem to you to be worthy of reverence?

The Greeks made up stories, called *myths,* about the lives of their gods. You are probably familiar with some of these myths. Have you ever heard the story of Midas, the king with the golden touch? Midas was granted a wish by the god Bacchus. He was told he could have any gift he desired. What would you have asked for? Midas requested that everything he touched might turn to gold. Do you think this was a wise request?

Midas soon came to regret his wish. Every time he tried to eat, his food would turn to gold before he could taste it. Some versions of the story say that he even turned his daughter to a gold statue when he touched her. Eventually, he had to ask Bacchus to take the gift back.

130

Discussion Questions
➤ **What did the Greeks believe about their gods?** *(The gods had supernatural powers but were not really much different from humans.)*
➤ **How were the Greek gods like humans?** *(They were depicted as having human bodies and as being jealous, vengeful, immoral, and childish.)*
➤ **How were the Greek gods different from the God of the Bible?** *(They were sinful and wicked, but the true God is holy and sinless.)*

Select a volunteer to explain the Midas myth.
➤ **Why was Midas's request unwise?** *(because everything he needed or loved was turned to gold when he touched it)*
➤ **What important lesson can be learned from the Midas myth?** *(Greed brings ruin.)*

Remind the students that Christians should be giving, not greedy. They should be good stewards of all that the Lord has given them. (BAT: 5b Giving)

On the Acropolis stands the *Parthenon,* an enormous temple made of white marble surrounded by forty-six columns. This temple is dedicated to Athena, the goddess of wisdom, for whom the city of Athens is named. A huge statue of her once stood in the Parthenon. The statue contained so much ivory and gold and so many jewels that it was worth more than the temple that housed it. Around A.D. 400, the statue was captured by the Romans and taken to Constantinople. Soon afterward it mysteriously disappeared.

The Parthenon is the ultimate example of Greek architecture. Several *optical illusions* have been included in its design. An optical illusion occurs when an object appears to take a shape it does not really have. Have you ever looked down a set of railroad tracks? The rails on each side of the tracks seem to come gradually closer together and meet in the distance. The only way to make the rails appear straight would be to place them farther apart as they get farther away from you.

The architects of the Parthenon created some clever illusions. They distorted their work on purpose to correct appearance problems. The steps leading up to the temple are humped in the center, but they appear perfectly level from a distance. The columns lean slightly inward and are thicker in the middle than at the top and base. But to the eye they appear straight and tall.

The Parthenon as it might have appeared in ancient times

131

The Parthenon

Parthenon ruins as they appear today

The Parthenon has been used in many different ways since it was first constructed by the Greeks over two thousand years ago. For many years it was a pagan temple dedicated to Athena. It is now believed to have been a place of human sacrifice. No one knows exactly what it looked like at that time. It was carved with designs and sculptures that told stories about the lives of Athena and the other gods.

In the Middle Ages, the Parthenon was used as a church. Christians met there, and the walls must have echoed with the notes of their hymns. Later, after Turkish Muslim forces captured Athens, the Parthenon became a Muslim mosque. The walls heard different echoes then—the hollow sounds of muttered prayers to Allah.

While the Turks ruled Athens, they stored gunpowder and ammunition in the Parthenon. During a battle with the Venetians in 1687, a shot landed in the Parthenon and set off an explosion. The building is now only an empty shell, but thousands of tourists travel to Athens each year to admire it. They can still see in its remains the beauty and intricacy of its architecture. Perhaps, too, they like to imagine they can hear "echoes" of voices that spoke there when it was the beautiful Greek temple of long ago.

132

Day 57

The building of the Parthenon—Affix the figure of the Parthenon from Maps and More 9 beside the city of Athens on the bulletin board map. Instruct the students to read page 131 silently to find what the Parthenon was. *(an enormous temple made of white marble and surrounded by forty-six columns)*

Discussion Questions

➤ **To whom was the Parthenon dedicated?** *(Athena, the goddess of wisdom)*

➤ **What happened to the statue of Athena?** *(It was captured by the Romans in A.D. 400 and taken to Constantinople; soon afterward it disappeared.)*

➤ **Why do you think the Romans wanted the statue of Athena?** *(probably because it was made of ivory, gold, and other jewels)*

➤ **When does an optical illusion occur?** *(when an object appears to take a shape it does not really have)*

➤ **Give an example of an optical illusion.** *(Answers will vary.)*

➤ **How does the Parthenon use optical illusions?** *(The steps are humped in the center, and the columns lean slightly inward and are thicker in the middle than at the top and base.)*

➤ **What does the architecture of the Parthenon tell us about Greek builders?** *(They were intelligent, sophisticated, and skilled craftsmen.)*

The paths of the Parthenon—Instruct the students to read page 132 silently to find how we know that the Parthenon was a temple. *(It was carved with designs and sculptures that told stories about the lives of Athena and the other gods.)*

Discussion Questions

➤ **How was the Parthenon probably used during the Middle Ages?** *(Christians met there and used it as a church.)*

➤ **What is a mosque?** *(a Muslim house of worship)*

➤ **When was the Parthenon used as a mosque?** *(after Turkish Muslim forces captured Athens)*

➤ **What else did the Turks use the Parthenon for?** *(to store gunpowder and ammunition)*

➤ **What happened to the temple in 1687?** *(A shot landed in the Parthenon and set off an explosion during the battle with the Venetians.)*

True or False

Name _____

Write *T* beside each true statement and *F* beside each false statement.

_T_ 1. In the Middle Ages, the Parthenon was used by Christians as a church.

_F_ 2. A myth is a true story passed from generation to generation.

_F_ 3. The Parthenon was destroyed in 1687 during a battle with the Spartans.

_T_ 4. An optical illusion occurs when an object appears to take a shape it does not really have.

_T_ 5. Greek gods were jealous, vengeful, immoral, and childish.

_F_ 6. The Parthenon was a temple dedicated to King Midas.

Write several sentences explaining how you would feel if everything you touched turned to gold. Explain why Midas's wish was harmful.

Answers will vary.

_____

_____

_____

_____

_____

_____

_____

_____

Heritage Studies 6
Student Notebook

Lesson 33
Evaluating the Lesson   **38**

□ Evaluating the Lesson

True or False (Notebook page 38)—Instruct the students to identify whether each statement is true or false. Then tell them to imagine being like King Midas. Instruct them to write several sentences explaining how they would feel if everything they touched turned to gold and why Midas's wish was harmful.

━━ **Going Beyond** ━━

□ Enrichment

Optical illusions—Set up a display AREA with samples of optical illusions. (*NOTE:* Check your local library for books about optical illusions.) Allow the students to examine these samples or books. You may choose to allow the students to try to create their own optical illusions.

□ Additional Teacher Information

Pericles hired the talented artist, Phidias, to construct the Parthenon. Phidias also designed the great statue of Athena as well as smaller statues, and the *frieze,* or decorative band, that runs along the upper wall of the temple. Historians speculate that Phidias may have used small clay models for the design of the frieze and statues. The Athenians were amazed at the grandeur of the temple, but they became angry with Phidias for carving a picture of himself and Pericles on Athena's shield. To the Athenians, this intermingling of humanity with deity was blasphemy. Phidias was tried and exiled for his crime. He sought refuge in Mount Olympia, where his art was well known and readily received.

LESSON 34
The Arts and Sciences

Text, pages 133-37
Notebook, page 39

- Knowledge
- The Arts
- The Olympics
- Lovers of Wisdom
- The Sciences
- Map Work
- Hippocratic Oath

Preview

□ Objective
Given proper instruction, the students will be able to do the following:
- Match people or items to their descriptions.

□ Materials
Have available:
- An overhead projector.
- A blank overhead transparency.
- Maps and More 10.
- A wire coat hanger.*
- A large empty thread spool.*
- Wire cutters.*
- A small plastic cup with a handle.*
- A globe or a wall map of the world.

Prepare:
- The overhead transparency of the Greek alphabet. (*NOTE:* See the reproducible material at the end of Lesson 36.)
- Maps and More 10 by cutting apart the two illustrations. (*NOTE:* The figure of Alexander the Great will be used in Lesson 36.)
- A pulley by cutting the hanger with the wire cutters and placing the spool on the hanger. Bend the hanger so that it forms a closed loop. Tie one end of the string to the cup handle. Place the other end of the string over the spool.

Knowledge in Classical Greece

Would you like to go to school with a servant who was there just to make sure you behaved? Wealthy boys in Greece had to do this. The servants who accompanied them were called pedagogues. Boys began school at age six and continued at least to age fourteen. At school they studied reading, writing, arithmetic, grammar, music, and sports. Boys from poorer families could not afford to go to school, and girls were not allowed to go at all.

Reading was much different in classical Greece from how it is at your school. The Greeks had an alphabet with only twenty-four letters. Some letters were the same as ours, and some were different. The Greeks used no punctuation or spacing between words.

Writing was different as well. Greek students wrote on wax-coated tablets with an instrument called a *stylus*. The stylus was pointed on one end to scratch letters into the wax and blunt on the other end to rub out mistakes.

The Greeks used a special instrument called an *abacus* to teach math. Perhaps you have seen one. It is a wooden frame with rows of movable beads on it.

133

□ Notes
Read the Hippocratic Oath. You may find a copy of this oath in an encyclopedia or in books dealing with Greek history.

Day 58

Lesson

□ Introducing the Lesson
The Greek alphabet—Display the overhead transparency of the Greek alphabet. Select volunteers to explain how the Greek and English alphabets are similar or different. Instruct each student to try to write his name using letters from the Greek alphabet. (*NOTE:* Not all letters of the English alphabet are represented in the Greek alphabet.)

□ Teaching the Lesson
Knowledge—Instruct the students to read page 133 silently to find out who *pedagogues* were. (*servants who accompanied wealthy boys to school*)

Discussion Questions
➤ **What was the task of the pedagogues?** (*to make sure the schoolboys behaved*)
➤ **How old were boys when they began school?** (*six years old*)
➤ **How long did they attend school?** (*until they were fourteen*)
➤ **What subjects were studied in school?** (*reading, writing, arithmetic, grammar, music, and sports*)

Do you take music lessons? The Greeks regarded music as the greatest of all the arts, more important than architecture, painting, sculpture, or literature. The Greek god Apollo was believed to be the god of music. Greek art often pictures Apollo entertaining the other gods with a *lyre,* or small harp, in his hands. The Greeks also believed that a group of nine goddesses called *the Muses* presided over the arts. Each goddess had a particular specialty, such as epic poetry or religious music. Can you guess where our word *music* comes from?

If you were a wealthy boy in classical Greece, you would be required to study music but probably not the type you are used to. Greek students learned to play the lyre and the *aulos (ou'läs),* a type of flute.

Singing was also an important part of a Greek boy's musical training. Students memorized the *Iliad* and the *Odyssey,* two great works by the poet Homer, who lived during the Greek Dark Age.

Playing the aulos

Instead of reciting these lengthy poems, the students put them to music and sang them. Some boys continued their studies with training in public speaking, hoping to become leaders in the democracy.

134

The Greeks believed that developing the body was as important as developing the mind. Our English word *athlete* comes from the Greek language. Schoolboys spent hours in the gymnasium running, jumping, wrestling, boxing, and throwing the javelin and the discus.

The Greeks held special festivals in which athletes took part. These festivals were held in honor of the gods. Athletes from all over Greece would travel to the city where the festival was being held to compete in various events. Does this sound familiar? What festival of games still takes place in our modern world?

The Greeks were the first to hold the Olympic Games. The games were held at the city of Olympia. Athletes competed in many of the same events as do athletes of today—sprints, long jumps, discus and javelin throwing, and wrestling. They also had chariot races and events for younger boys. The winners were given garlands of olive leaves to wear on their heads as crowns.

135

➤ **Who were not able to go to school in ancient Greece?** *(boys from poorer families and girls)*

➤ **How was Grecian reading different from reading English?** *(The Greeks have a shorter alphabet, different letters, and no punctuation or spacing between words.)*

➤ **What is a *stylus*?** *(a writing instrument that is pointed on one end and blunt on the other)*

➤ **How was a stylus used?** *(The pointed end was used to write letters in wax, and the blunt end was used to rub out mistakes.)*

➤ **What is an *abacus,* and what was it used for?** *(a wooden frame with rows of movable beads used to teach math)*

The arts—Instruct the students to read page 134 silently to find what the Greeks considered to be the greatest of all the arts. *(music)*

Discussion Questions

➤ **Who was Apollo?** *(the Greek god of music)*

➤ **Who were the Muses?** *(a group of nine goddesses who presided over the arts—each with a particular specialty, such as epic poetry or religious music)*

➤ **What is an *aulos*?** *(a type of flute)*

➤ **What was different about Grecian singing?** *(It usually involved poems or stories put to music and sung.)*

➤ **What were the *Iliad* and the *Odyssey*?** *(two great works by the poet Homer, who lived during the Greek Dark Age)*

The Olympics—Affix the Olympic figure from Maps and More 10 to the bulletin board map next to the city of Olympia. Instruct the students to read page 135 silently to find out how important athletic activities were to the ancient Greeks. *(They believed that developing the body was as important as developing the mind.)*

Discussion Questions

➤ **What types of athletics did Greek schoolboys participate in?** *(running, jumping, wrestling, boxing, and throwing the javelin and discus)*

➤ **What type of athletics do we have today?** *(baseball, soccer, football, basketball, etc.)*

➤ **Why do people participate in these sports?** *(exercise, competition, fun, etc.)*

➤ **Why did the Greeks hold certain athletic festivals?** *(in honor of the gods)*

➤ **What award did the winning athlete receive at the Greek Olympic Games?** *(a garland of olive leaves to wear on his head as a crown)*

➤ **What kinds of awards are athletes of today given at the modern Olympic Games?** *(medals and flowers)*

Do you know what the word *philosopher* means? It means "lover of wisdom." During the Classical Age of Greece, many thoughtful scholars lived in Athens. These men were called *philosophers.*

Socrates *(sŏk′rə tēz′)* taught by asking his students thought-provoking questions. "What is the meaning of life?" he would ask. "What is a good man?" The questions made his students think about what they really believed. How would you answer these questions? Socrates was also a firm believer in democracy, but he wanted to make the government a perfect one. He believed that right thinking would lead to right actions.

Plato was one of Socrates' students. Plato wrote books in the form of conversations. In these books, called *dialogues,* he said that the ideal government was ruled by a few of the most intelligent men. He also taught that there was a *spiritual world*—a world of the mind and of ideas—that was superior to the physical world.

Aristotle *(ăr′ĭ stŏt′l),* Plato's pupil, was a third great philosopher. Science, to him, was the most important academic subject. We give him credit for the *scientific method,* a method of study requiring careful observation and record keeping. He also taught that reason controls behavior.

School of Athens, Raphael's famous painting in the Vatican, depicts Plato and Aristotle (center back) with other Greek scientists and philosophers around them.

136

Not only philosophers but also other learned men lived in Greece. When you study math and certain types of science, you rely upon the discoveries of several Greek scholars. Archimedes *(är′kə mē′dēz)* was a mathematician who perfected the lever and compound pulleys, machines that make the moving of objects easier. Euclid wrote the first geometry book. The entire study of geometry was built around his teachings. Pythagoras *(pĭ thăg′ər·əs),* another mathematician, studied geometry and came up with an important *theorem,* or carefully tested idea, about triangles.

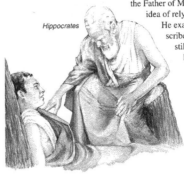

Pythagoras

Look at a map of the world. Did you know that a Greek named Eratosthenes *(ĕr′ə tŏs′thə·nēz)* was the first to draw the latitude and longitude lines on the map? He also calculated the circumference of the earth with reasonable accuracy.

An astronomer named Aristarchus *(ăr′ĭ stär′kəs)* was the first to suggest that the universe was sun centered rather than earth centered, as most people of those days believed.

Two other Greeks, Hippocrates *(hĭ pŏk′rə tēz′)* and Herodotus, *(hĭ rŏd′ə təs)* are famous today for their contributions. Hippocrates, called the Father of Medicine, did not agree with the idea of relying on magic to treat patients. He examined them carefully and prescribed treatment. Doctors today still take the Hippocratic Oath in honor of this man's wisdom and principles in the medical profession. Herodotus is called the Father of History. Much of what we know about life in classical Greece comes from the careful notes that he recorded during that time.

Hippocrates

137

Day 59

Lovers of wisdom—Instruct the students to read page 136 silently to find what the word *philosopher* means. *(lover of wisdom)*

Discussion Questions

➤ **Who was Socrates?** *(a teacher during the Classical Age of Greece who taught by asking thought-provoking questions)*

➤ **What were some of the questions Socrates asked his students?** *("What is the meaning of life?" and "What is a good man?")*

➤ **How did these kinds of questions help students learn?** *(They made the students think about what they really believed.)*

➤ **How did Socrates believe the government could become a perfect one?** *(through right thinking that would lead to right actions)*

➤ **Who was Plato?** *(one of Socrates' students)*

➤ **What were the *dialogues* and what did they say about government?** *(Plato's books written in the form of conversations; they said that the ideal government was ruled by a few of the most intelligent men.)*

➤ **What was the spiritual world according to Plato?** *(a world of the mind and of ideas)*

➤ **Who was Aristotle?** *(Plato's pupil)*

➤ **What subject did Aristotle think was the most important?** *(science)*

➤ **What is the scientific method?** *(a method of study requiring careful observation and record keeping)*

➤ **According to Aristotle, what controls behavior?** *(reason)*

Explain that no amount of thinking or reasoning can change man's sin nature. Remind the students that the only way to attain a pure life is through salvation. It is only through Christ's death on the cross that people can live a righteous new life. (BATs: 1a Understanding Jesus Christ, 7a Grace; Bible Promises: A. Liberty from Sin, Guiltless by the Blood, D. Identified in Christ, E. Christ as Sacrifice)

The sciences—Demonstrate how a pulley works by hanging the pulley you have prepared. Allow several volunteers to try the pulley. Invite the students to give another example of a common pulley on the school grounds. *(a flagpole)* Instruct them to read page 137 silently to find who Archimedes was. *(a mathematician who perfected the lever and compound pulleys)* Explain that people use items today that the ancient Greeks invented.

Discussion Questions

➤ **What is significant about levers and pulleys?** *(They are machines that make the moving of objects easier.)*

➤ **What contribution did Euclid make to science?** *(He wrote the first geometry book, providing the basis for the entire study of geometry.)*

Greek Letters

Name _____

Write the Greek letter of the correct answer beside each statement.

1. Greek students used this instrument to write on a waxed tablet.

2. The Greeks believed that these nine goddesses presided over the arts.

3. a lover of wisdom

4. ancient Greek festival of games

5. He wrote an oath that some doctors take even today.

6. servants who accompanied wealthy boys to school

7. the author of two famous works, the _____ and the _____

8. person who taught by using thought-provoking questions

9. mathematician who perfected the lever and pulleys

10. credited for first using the scientific method

11. Father of History

Olympics

Aristotle

pedagogues

Homer

Socrates

Herodotus

philosopher

the Muses

Archimedes

Hippocrates

stylus

© 1998 BJU Press. Reproduction prohibited.

Heritage Studies 6
Student Notebook

Lesson 34
Evaluating the Lesson **39**

➤ **What is a *theorem*?** *(a carefully tested idea)*
➤ **What was Pythagoras's theorem about?** *(triangles)*

Map work—Direct the students' attention to a wall map of the world or to a globe. Ask them what the lines running horizontally and vertically are called. *(latitude and longitude)* Explain that a Greek man named *Eratosthenes* was the first to draw these lines on a map.

Discussion Questions

➤ **What other important calculation did Eratosthenes make?** *(the circumference of the earth)*
➤ **What theory did Aristarchus suggest?** *(that the universe was sun centered rather than earth centered)*
➤ **Who was Hippocrates?** *(the Father of Medicine)*
➤ **What did Hippocrates believe about medical treatment?** *(It was not based on magic; patients needed to be carefully examined before treatment was prescribed.)*

Hippocratic Oath—Select a volunteer to explain what an *oath* is. *(a promise to tell the truth or act in a particular way, with God or some sacred object as witness)* Tell the students that Hippocrates wrote an oath for doctors to affirm. Explain that his oath is a code of *ethics,* or behavior for doctors to follow. Give the students some basic tenets of the Hippocratic Oath, such as the doctor's vow not to give deadly drugs and not to betray a patient's confidence.

Discussion Questions

➤ **Who was Herodotus?** *(the Father of History)*
➤ **What contribution to history did Herodotus make?** *(Much of what we know about life in classical Greece comes from his careful notes.)*

☐ Evaluating the Lesson

Greek Letters (Notebook page 39)—Instruct the students to write the Greek letter of the correct answer beside each statement.

━━━ Going Beyond ━━━

☐ Enrichment

A student's oath—Set up a writing AREA with notebook paper and pencils. Instruct the students to write several paragraphs of a student's oath, giving a code of behavior that a student should follow. Suggest to the students behavior such as completing assignments on time, never cheating, always paying attention, and so on. As time permits, allow the students to read aloud their oaths or display them on the bulletin board.

☐ Additional Teacher Information

The Olympic games were first held around 776 B.C. These festivals were considered sacred events. If two Greek city-states were fighting, a temporary truce was called for the duration of the games. Participants had to prove their Greek citizenship as well as swear that they would obey the rules of the games.

The winning athletes were honored for years after their victories. They were given meals paid for by the city, the best seats in the theater, and a special inscription of their names in Olympian records.

In 1875, a Frenchman, Baron Pierre de Coubertin, took the idea for the modern Olympics from the archaeological discovery of the Olympia Stadium. In 1896, the first modern Olympics occurred in Athens, Greece. Women did not participate until 1900. The Olympic games are designed to bring together countries in a peaceful situation. The five rings on the Olympic flag represent the continents of Asia, Africa, Australia, the Americas, and Europe.

LESSON 35
Ancient Artistry

Text, pages 138-40

> - Harmony and Beauty
> - Comedy and Tragedy

Preview

☐ Objective

Given proper instruction, the students will be able to do the following:

- Design a mask that conveys a particular emotion.

☐ Materials

Have available:

- A 9"×12" sheet of construction paper for each student.
- Crayons or felt-tip pens for each student.
- Scissors.

Day 60

Lesson

☐ Introducing the Lesson

Word origin—Write the Greek word *hupokrites* on the chalkboard. Ask the students what modern English word *hupokrites* resembles. *(hypocrite)* Select a volunteer to explain what a *hypocrite* is. *(a person who puts on a false appearance of being good, kind, honest, moral, or religious)* Explain that in ancient Greece, the word *hupokrites* referred to an actor. Ask the students how this meaning resembles the English meaning. *(Both mean someone who is pretending to be what he is not.)* Explain that many English words come from the Greek language. Tell the students that acting was an important part of Greek culture.

☐ Teaching the Lesson

Harmony and beauty—Instruct the students to read page 138 silently to find the goal of Grecian art. *(to create the ideal representation of an object or person)*

Discussion Questions

➤ **What were important qualities in Greek art?** *(balance, completeness, harmony, simplicity, and beauty)*
➤ **Where does our knowledge of Grecian life come from?** *(from the Greeks' art)*
➤ **Where did Greek art appear?** *(on plates, jugs, pots, jars, cups, bowls, perfume bottles, jewelry, wall murals, marble statues, coins, floor mosaics, and embroidery)*
➤ **What kinds of figures did the Greeks often portray in their art?** *(humans, gods or goddesses, mythological creatures)*

Art in Classical Greece

Greek artists wanted their work to be perfect. They strove to create the ideal representation of an object or person. Important qualities of Greek art were balance, completeness, harmony, simplicity, and beauty.

Much of what we know about how the Greeks lived and dressed comes from their art. The work of painters adorned plates, jugs, pots, jars, cups, bowls, and perfume bottles. Metal craftsmen decorated gold and silver cups and fashioned delicate jewelry. Sculptors' work appeared in marble statues and on coins. In wall murals, floor mosaics, and embroidery, Greek art flourished as well. Many artists portrayed human beings or gods and goddesses. Others depicted mythological creatures such as Pegasus, the winged horse, or animals and birds, such as goats, deer, bulls, lions, dolphins, and cranes.

Greek grave relief, 450-440 B.C.
The Metropolitan Museum of Art, Fletcher Fund, 1927
Photograph © 1997 The Metropolitan Museum of Art

Athenian jar, ca. 540 B.C.
The Metropolitan Museum of Art, Rogers Fund, 1917 (17.230.14a,b); Gift of J.D. Beazley, 1927 (27.16)
Photograph © 1999 The Metropolitan Museum of Art

Greek architecture, too, expresses the Greek love of beauty and harmony. Compare a Greek temple with an Egyptian pyramid or a Sumerian ziggurat. What differences do you see?

Greek Erechtheum (Porch of the Maidens), Acropolis, Athens

Compare the pyramid of Khafra in Egypt to Greek temples.

138

Explain to the students that Pegasus was a Greek mythological character that had the shape of a winged horse. Tell them that according to Greek legend, Pegasus carried lightning and thunderbolts for the chief god, Zeus.

➤ **What differences or similarities do you see between the Greek temple and the Egyptian pyramid?** *(Answers will vary.)*

> Remind the students that Christians should use their talents to glorify God, not themselves. (BATs: 3a Self-concept, 7c Praise, 7e Humility)

Comedy and tragedy—Instruct the students to read page 139 silently to find what an *amphitheater* is. *(a huge outdoor theater)*

Discussion Questions

➤ **What were most Greek plays about?** *(gods and heroes)*
➤ **What were the two types of Greek drama?** *(comedy and tragedy)*
➤ **What were the purposes of a comedy?** *(to make the audience laugh and to put them in a lighthearted mood)*
➤ **What was the purpose of a tragedy?** *(to instruct)*
➤ **What usually happened in a tragedy?** *(It usually ended with the downfall of the hero because of some character flaw, such as pride or jealousy.)*
➤ **How did audiences usually feel after watching a tragedy?** *(more sober and thoughtful about themselves and their failures)*

The Greeks perfected another art form as well—the art of drama. Crowds would gather in huge outdoor theaters called *amphitheaters* to watch the actors perform plays as part of religious festivals.

Most Greek plays were about gods and heroes. There were two types of Greek drama: *comedy* and *tragedy*. Comedies were meant to make the audience laugh and to put them in a lighthearted mood. Tragedies were meant to instruct. They usually ended with the downfall of the hero because of some character flaw, such as pride or jealousy. Tragedies left audiences feeling more sober. They often made people think about themselves and their failures. Which type of drama would you have preferred?

A modern Greek mask play

An ancient Greek dramatic mask

Greek plays were very different from the plays we are used to today. Imagine that you are sitting on a cool stone bench in a large amphitheater in ancient Greece, far away from the stage. How could you hear the actors' voices and see the expressions on their faces? You would probably have very little trouble because the actors would be wearing exaggerated costumes and large masks that would allow you to tell them apart. Some of them might exchange their masks for different ones when they were happy or sad or angry. The funnel-shaped mouthpieces inside the masks acted as megaphones that made actors' voices carry to everyone in the crowd.

139

To Make a Greek Mask

1. Decide what character quality or emotion you want to represent with your mask.

2. Practice several emotions as you hold a mirror in front of your face. Note the facial distinctions for each emotion.

3. Draw a face on construction paper, trying to show the quality or emotion you chose in Step 1.

4. Cut out holes for the eyes.

5. Hold your mask in front of your face, and allow the other students to guess what emotion you tried to illustrate.

140

➤ **Why do you think tragedies had this effect on audiences?** *(Tragedies encouraged people to think more seriously.)*

➤ **Which type of drama would you prefer?** *(Answers will vary.)*

Select volunteers to describe how Greek plays were different from the plays that are performed today. *(The audience sat outdoors, far away from the stage. The actors wore larger costumes and large masks with mouthpieces that had megaphones.)*

□ Evaluating the Lesson

Mask making—Direct a *Discovering How* activity on page 140. Read aloud the steps to make a Greek mask. Instruct each student to follow the steps, creating his own mask. Suggest different emotions, such as happiness, anger, sadness, or fear. When all masks are completed, allow each student to hold his mask in front of his face and challenge the other students to guess the emotion illustrated.

Going Beyond

□ Enrichment

Decorative painting—Set up an art AREA with one paper plate and paintbrush for each student, plastic disposable cups, and watercolors. Display photographs of Greek art as found on common objects, such as jugs or plates. (*NOTE:* You may find such photographs in the encyclopedia or books dealing with Greek history.) Instruct each student to paint a scene from his daily life on his plate. Tell the students that their paintings should be decorative and should also illustrate something about how they live.

□ Additional Teacher Information

Although hundreds of plays were written during Classical Greece, only about thirty-five have survived. Almost all of these remaining plays are tragedies, written by the three great tragedians: Aeschylus, Sophocles, or Euripedes. The most famous comedic playwright of Greece was Aristophanes, who often parodied Greek life.

The amphitheater was similar to modern stadiums in that the stone seats were situated in a curve around the open acting arena called the *orchestra*. Beyond the orchestra was a stage house, or *skene*, that was probably used as a dressing room. The theater, located on a hill below the Acropolis, held about fourteen thousand spectators.

LESSON 36
Gone Is the Glory

Text, pages 141-44
Notebook, page 40

- The Peloponnesian War
- Alexander the Great
- One Empire
- Mars' Hill

════ Preview ════

□ Objectives
Given proper instruction, the students will be able to do the following:
- Sequence events in chronological order.
- Give examples of Greek influences that occur in society today.

□ Materials
Have available:
- Bibles for several students.
- The figure of Alexander the Great from Maps and More 10.
- The figure of Alexander the Great (340 B.C.) from the History TimeLine Packet.
- A wall map of the world.

Day 61

════ Lesson ════

□ Introducing the Lesson
Governors and warriors—Write *Athens* and *Sparta* on the chalkboard. Select volunteers to give characteristics of each city-state. Write their answers in the correct column.

Discussion Questions
➤ **Which city-state would probably be more successful in a war?** *(Sparta would probably fight better than Athens.)*
➤ **Which city-state would be more successful at setting up a government after a war?** *(Athens)*
➤ **How do you think two such different cities would get along?** *(Answers will vary.)*

Explain that the two city-states had a war that led to the decline of glorious Greece. Ask the students why they think war would harm the development of culture. *(It destroys buildings and lives and can hinder growth.)*

□ Teaching the Lesson
The Peloponnesian War—Instruct the students to read silently the first two paragraphs on page 141 to find what the Peloponnesian War was. *(war between Athens and Sparta)*

The Spread of Greek Culture
In 431 B.C., a war began that was to change Greece forever. Following the Persian Wars, some of the city-states had joined with Athens in a league for protection from the Persians. Sparta and its allies began to see Athens and its allies as a threat, and soon war broke out between the two groups. This war was called the Peloponnesian War, and it lasted twenty-seven years. Who do you think won in the end?

Sparta, with its well-trained warriors, won the war. But it proved to be weak in ruling the democratic city-states it had conquered. Quarrels broke out between city-states. The weakened condition of Greece allowed Philip II of Macedonia to take control of its government in 338 B.C.

Philip died two years later, and his son Alexander took the throne of Macedonia. Alexander had been tutored by Aristotle, and he loved the Greek ways of life and philosophy. He took control of the army at the age of twenty and began to pursue his dream of uniting the entire world under one empire. He extended his rule eastward as far as India, spreading the Greek culture through much of the world. His military genius and unconquerable spirit have earned him the title "Alexander the Great."

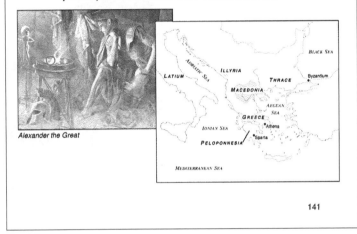

Alexander the Great

141

Discussion Questions
➤ **When did the Peloponnesian War begin?** *(431 B.C.)*
➤ **What was one reason the war broke out?** *(Sparta and its allies began to see Athens and its allies as a threat.)*
➤ **How long did the war last?** *(twenty-seven years)*
➤ **Who won the war?** *(Sparta)*
➤ **Why do you think the Spartans won?** *(Sparta had well-trained warriors.)*
➤ **How was Philip II able to conquer Greece?** *(Sparta was weak in ruling the democratic states it had conquered, and the city-states were quarreling.)*

Alexander the Great—Add the figure of Alexander the Great to the History TimeLine at the year 340 B.C. Affix the figure of Alexander the Great from Maps and More 10 to the bulletin board map next to Macedonia. Instruct the students to read silently the last paragraph on page 141 to find out who ruled after Philip II. *(his son, Alexander)*

Discussion Questions
➤ **Who tutored Alexander, and how did this affect his reign?** *(Aristotle tutored Alexander; Alexander loved the Greek ways of life and philosophy.)*
➤ **What did Alexander do when he was twenty years old?** *(took control of the army and pursued his dream of uniting the world under one empire)*
➤ **How does Alexander's dream differ from your goals?** *(Answers will vary.)*

Now people all over the Western world were becoming like the Greeks. They adopted the ideas of Greek philosophers. They used Greek inventions and learned the teachings of Greek scholars. The works of Greek artists appeared in all parts of the empire.

Most importantly, the spread of Greek culture brought a common language to the Western world. The Greek language was now the official language for all of Alexander's empire. It was understood by both the commoner and the nobleman. What were some advantages of having a common language?

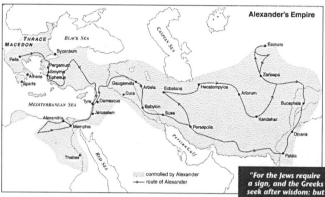

Alexander's Empire

controlled by Alexander
→ route of Alexander

The Greek language made communication throughout the empire much easier. Imagine the possibilities. People could travel for miles and still meet others who spoke their language. The written word could be read and understood throughout the region. In a few centuries, there would be a very important message to carry to the world—the message of Jesus Christ. The spread of the Greek language paved the way for the gospel to go into all the world.

> "For the Jews require a sign, and the Greeks seek after wisdom: but we preach Christ crucified, unto the Jews a stumblingblock, and unto the Greeks foolishness; but unto them which are called, both Jews and Greeks, Christ the power of God, and the wisdom of God."
> *I Corinthians 1:22-24*

142

Paul's Sermon on Mars' Hill

The Classical Greeks were some of the most well-educated, artistic, and talented people of all time. In the eyes of most of the world, the Greeks had everything. They were a successful people. But can you think of one important thing that was missing from their lives?

After Christ's work on earth was finished, Paul was called to be a missionary. He was called to the Jews first and then to the Greeks. During his travels, he spent some time in the city of Athens. Acts 17 tells us that one of the first things he noticed about the city was its widespread idolatry. The Greeks may have possessed knowledge of many different subjects, but they had no knowledge of God.

As Paul walked through the city, he found an altar with an inscription carved into it. "To the Unknown God," it read. When he stood up to speak to the Athenians on Mars' Hill, he told them about the one true God. He told them that God is not a statue made of gold or silver and not a name carved in stone. He is real, He is Creator and Lord, and He wants people everywhere to repent and seek Him.

Do you think the Athenians believed? Many made fun of Paul's message. Some left thoughtfully, wanting to hear more. But a few men and women grasped the truth of Paul's words and believed with all their hearts. Paul's mission trip to Athens had not been in vain.

View of the Acropolis from Mars Hill

143

Display a wall map of the world. Point out the area conquered by Alexander. Explain that he conquered land as far east as India, spreading the Greek culture as he went.

> **How did Alexander earn the title "Alexander the Great"?** *(through his military genius and unconquerable spirit)*

One empire—Instruct the students to read page 142 silently to find how people in the Western world were becoming like the Greeks. *(They adopted the ideas of Greek philosophers, used Greek inventions, learned teachings of Greek scholars, and possessed the works of Greek artists.)*

Discussion Questions

> **What was probably the most important influence of Alexander's empire?** *(a common language to the Western world)*
> **What are some advantages of having a common language?** *(It is easier to communicate, trade, and so on.)*
> **What did the spread of the Greek language pave the way for?** *(for the gospel to go into all the world)*

Day 62

Mars' Hill—Instruct the students to read page 143 silently to find how the rest of the world viewed the Greeks. *(The Greeks had everything. They were a successful people.)*

Discussion Questions

> **What was the one thing that the Greeks did not have?** *(They did not know the true God.)*

Select volunteers to take turns reading aloud from Acts 17:15-34.

> **What was one of the first things that Paul noticed when he first arrived in Athens?** *(The city had widespread idolatry.)*
> **What inscription did Paul find on an altar in Athens?** *("To the Unknown God")*
> **What did Paul say about the Unknown God?** *(He told the Greeks about the one true God—the God who is not a statue but is real. God is Creator and Lord and wants people to repent and seek Him.)*
> **How did the Athenians respond to Paul's message?** *(Many made fun of him, but some believed and wanted to hear more.)*
> **Do you think Paul's mission trip was useless? Why or why not?** *(No; answers will vary.)*

The glory of Greece could not last forever. After Alexander's death, his empire was divided into four parts. Most of this empire would later be conquered by Rome.

We owe a great deal to the Greeks. Look around you. Every time you see a column, you are seeing an example of Greek architecture. Every time you watch a play, you are enjoying the contributions the Greeks made to drama. Every time you admire a sculpture or read a lovely poem, you are appreciating the very arts that the Greeks perfected. And when you study literature, science, math, and history, you are reaping the benefits of Greek discoveries in those realms.

Open your Bible to the New Testament. Every word you see on all the pages was originally written in the Greek language. Aren't you glad that the Greeks had an alphabet and writing skills? The richness of their language gave us a detailed history of the Lord Jesus Christ and helped point the way to heaven.

A New Testament in the Greek language

144

Number the events in the order that they occurred.

6	Paul preached a sermon on Mars' Hill.
2	The Peloponnesian War began.
4	Alexander the Great conquered many lands.
1	The Age of Pericles began.
3	Philip II of Macedonia took control of Greece.
5	Greek culture spread to many nations.

Write one or two sentences describing things in our culture that we have borrowed from Greece.

Possible answers include columns, words, the New Testament, and foods.

_____

_____

_____

_____

© 1998 BJU Press. Reproduction prohibited.

Heritage Studies 6
Student Notebook

Lesson 36
Evaluating the Lesson   **40**

Remind the students that Christians should be spreading the gospel just as Christ did. Explain that no effort to spread God's Word is useless. (BATs: 5c Evangelism and missions, 8b Faith in the power of the Word of God, 8c Fight, 8d Courage)

Instruct the students to read page 144 silently to find what happened to Alexander's empire after he died. *(It was divided into four parts.)*

Discussion Questions

➤ **What eventually happened to Alexander's already divided empire?** *(It was later conquered by Rome.)*

➤ **What are some Greek influences still seen today?** *(columns, plays, sculptures, poems, literature, science, math, history, and the New Testament)*

□ Evaluating the Lesson

Sequencing Events (Notebook page 40)—Instruct the students to number the events in the order of occurrence. Then tell each student to write one or two sentences describing things in our culture that we have borrowed from Greece.

▬▬ Going Beyond ▬▬

□ Enrichment

Alexander's journal—Distribute the story starter to each student. (*NOTE:* See the reproducible material at the end of this lesson.) Encourage each student to pretend that he or she is Alexander the Great as a young boy. Read aloud the story introduction. Instruct each student to complete the journal entry that Alex began writing. As time permits, allow each student to share what he wrote with the class.

□ Additional Teacher Information

Alexander the Great was born to royal parents in Macedonia in 356 B.C. Olympia, his mother, was a Greek princess. She taught Alexander that he was the descendant of the *Iliad* hero Achilles. King Philip II, his father, taught him that all Macedonian kings were the descendants of Hercules, the son of Zeus.

In an attempt to build a world empire, Alexander and his troops crossed continents and forged through rivers, mountains, and deserts. In 323 B.C., at age thirty-two, Alexander was stricken with a fever. He was about to march into India to conquer the East, but weakened from exhaustion and battle wounds, the great Alexander fell ill with fever and died.

To Helen

Edgar Allan Poe

Helen, thy beauty is to me
Like those Nicean barks of yore,
That gently, o'er a perfumed sea,
The weary, wayworn wanderer bore
To his own native shore.

On desperate seas long wont to roam,
Thy hyacinth hair, thy classic face,
Thy Naiad airs have brought me home
To the glory that was Greece,
And the grandeur that was Rome.

Use with Lesson 30.

Voting Roles

a fifteen-year-old male	an eighteen-year-old female
a twelve-year-old female	an eighteen-year-old male
a thirty-year-old female	a twenty-five-year-old soldier
an old woman	an old man
a forty-year-old man	a fifteen-year-old female
a male merchant in his thirties	a female slave
a sixteen-year-old soldier	a female merchant in her thirties
a fifty-year-old male politician	an eighteen-year-old soldier
a twelve-year-old male	a fifty-year-old grandmother

What's This?

Use with Lesson 33. Heritage Studies 6 TE

Greek alphabet		English equivalent	
A	α	a	
B	β	b	
Γ	γ	g	
Δ	δ	d	
E	ε	e	(pronounced "ĕ")
Z	ζ	z	
H	η	e	(pronounced "ā")
Θ	θ	th	
I	ι	i	(pronounced "ī" or "ē")
K	κ	k	
Λ	λ	l	
M	μ	m	
N	ν	n	
Ξ	ξ	x	
O	ο	ŏ	
Π	π	p	
P	ρ	r	
Σ	σ, ς*	s	
T	τ	t	
Υ	υ	y	(pronounced "ū")
Φ	φ	ph	
X	χ	ch	(pronounced "k")
Ψ	ψ	ps	
Ω	ω	ō	

* Use this form when the letter appears at the end of a word.

Someday

Alex stretched over the terrace rail, straining to see as far in the distance as he could. He often liked to do that—to see how far the land extended from the palace. He imagined that it was all his kingdom and his alone. He wondered about those distant hills—what kind of people lived there? How he longed to see beyond the palace garden—to explore!

Alex heard footsteps on the garden path. He moved away from the terrace to a stone bench. He picked up the stylus and wax tablet that he had set aside to daydream. He began writing. "Someday, when I become a strong man, I shall . . ."

_____

_____

_____

_____

_____

_____

_____

_____

_____

_____

_____

Power of the Seven Hills: Roman World

This chapter is a survey of the history of Rome as a city, a republic, and an empire. Students will learn how the study of the Roman world is interwoven with the study of other cultures and people and how the Roman culture of power and practicality dominated for hundreds of years along the Mediterranean Sea, expanded to the regions beyond, and influenced life in modern times as well. Highlighted are the accomplishments of the Romans in military conquests, oratory, architecture, the Latin language, the republican form of government, road construction, and calendar format. In the *Discovering How* activity for Lesson 38, the students will experience the Roman legislative process and learn how individuals affect decision making among leaders. The supplemental lesson discusses the rights and responsibilities of citizenship.

☐ Materials

Lessons 37 and 39-40 require certain items that must be obtained or prepared several days to several weeks before the presentation of the lessons. These items are labeled with an asterisk (*) in each lesson and in the Materials List in the Supplement. Occasionally, items not commonly found in the classroom as well as items needed in large quantities may also be labeled with an asterisk. For further information, see the individual lessons.

☐ Chapter Bulletin Board

Place a background of colorful fabric on the bulletin board. Prepare twenty to thirty "building blocks" from white or gray construction paper. (*NOTE:* See the reproducible material at the end of Lesson 42.) Label the building blocks with names and terms from the chapter. Place the building blocks in a basket by the bulletin board. You may separate the blocks and place them in the basket according to the lesson in which they will be used. Prepare two foundations by joining two building blocks for each foundation. Label the foundations *Ancient Rome* and *Jesus Christ* and affix them to the lower corners of the bulletin board. Entitle the board *Building on the Foundations.* As you progress through the chapter, allow the students to choose building blocks from the basket, telling something about each name or term. Affix each building block above the *Ancient Rome* foundation. Lesson 42 emphasizes the solid foundation a person has when following the Lord. You may choose to allow the students to prepare building blocks to add to the foundation *Jesus Christ* (e.g., holiness, eternal life, joy).

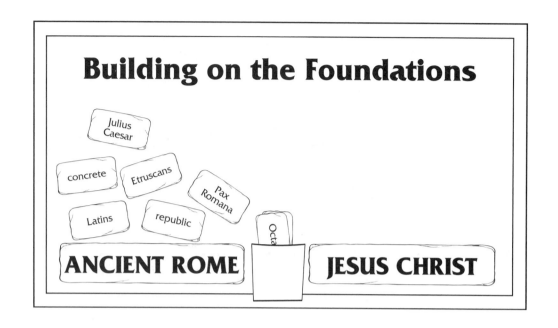

Building on the Foundations

Julius Caesar

concrete

Etruscans

Pax Romana

Latins

republic

Octa

ANCIENT ROME

JESUS CHRIST

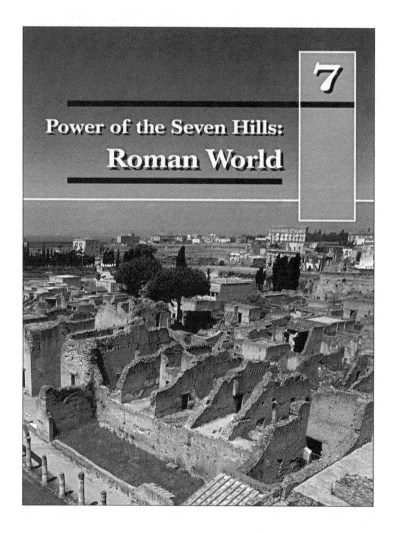

7

Power of the Seven Hills:
Roman World

LESSON 37
Rome: The City

Text, pages 146-48
Notebook, pages 41-42

- Roman Legend
- The City of Rome
- Then and Now

Preview

□ Objectives

Given proper instruction, the students will be able to do the following:
- Solve word puzzles relating to the founding and development of Rome.
- Recount the story of the founding of Rome and its first settlers.

□ Materials

Have available:
- A penny, nickel, dime, or quarter for each student.*
- The figure representing the founding of Rome (753 B.C.) from the History TimeLine Packet.

□ Notes

The pizza activity in the Enrichment section requires some preparation and planning prior to the lesson.

Day 63

Lesson

□ Introducing the Lesson

Language Link (Notebook page 41)—Distribute a coin to each student. Ask the students how all U.S. coins are alike. *(Each coin includes a date, a monetary value, the word* Liberty, *the words* United States of America, *the phrase* In God We Trust, *and the Latin motto* E pluribus unum.) Point out that some Latin phrases are still used today. Direct attention to the top of Notebook page 41. Select students to read aloud and complete each example.

Direct attention to the etymology section of Notebook page 41. Instruct the students to write each English word from its Latin root.

□ Teaching the Lesson

Roman legend—Instruct the students to read page 146 silently to find out why the brothers Romulus and Remus wanted to build a city. *(to remember the place of their rescue)*

Language Link   Name _____

Today we still use some of the Latin language as it was used years ago.
Complete the three examples below.

E pluribus unum   1. ____ is the Latin motto that appears on coins in the United States. It means "out of many, one," and it refers to the forming of the United States from the original thirteen colonies.

etc.   2. The Latin words *et cetera* mean "and the rest." Today we use the abbreviation ____ to mean "and so on."

letter   3. The abbreviation *P.S.* stands for *postscript* and comes from the Latin *postscribere*, which means "to write after." Today you would use this abbreviation to add a thought after signing a ____.

Etymology is the history of a word, including where it came from and how it got its present form and meaning. Many words in the English language have a Latin origin or influence. Write the English word derived from the Latin words below. You may use a dictionary to find the etymology and to check your work.

popular   vote   library   liberty
candidate   video   salary   vocal

English word	Latin background
popular	4. *popularis* means "of the people," from *populus* meaning "the people" and of Etruscan origin
vote	5. *votum*, from *vovere* meaning "to vow"
library	6. *librarium* means "bookcase," from *librarious* meaning "of books," from *liber* meaning "book"
vocal	7. *vocalis*, from *vox* meaning "voice"
video	8. *video*, from *videre* meaning "to see"
candidate	9. *candidatus* means "clothed in white"
salary	10. *salarium*, from *salarius* meaning "of salt," from *sal* meaning "salt"
liberty	11. *libertas* means "free"

Heritage Studies 6
Student Notebook

Lesson 37
Introducing the Lesson   **41**

Discussion Questions

➤ **According to the legend, who built the city of Rome?** *(Romulus)*
➤ **What location did Romulus prefer for the city of Rome?** *(the seven hills near the mouth of the Tiber River)*
➤ **Why were cities often built close to a river?** *(to provide water and transportation)*
➤ **Does your town have a river or lake nearby? How is this water source important to your town?** *(Answers may vary but could include to provide drinking water, electricity, transportation of goods and people, recreation, and irrigation for crops.)*
➤ **What is a negative reason for settling near a river?** *(flooding)*

Day 64

The city of Rome—Instruct the students to read page 147 silently to find out whether the people of Rome were always called Romans. *(no)* Ask the students in what year the city of Rome began. *(753 B.C.)* Add the figure representing the founding of Rome (Romulus and Remus) to the History TimeLine at 753 B.C.

Discussion Questions

➤ **What people settled in Rome first and what were they like?** *(Latins; farmers and herdsmen)*
➤ **How did the Etruscan people differ from the Latins?** *(The Etruscans were skilled at trading and architecture.)*

Long ago, in the land we now call Italy, twin brothers were born. Abandoned by their mother, they were left floating in a basket on the Tiber River. A wolf spied the basket from the shore and swam out into the river to investigate. Tiny cries came from inside the little vessel. The wolf dragged the basket to the safety of the shore and waited for help to come.

Soon a shepherd wandered by and found the two babies crying in the basket. "What is this?" he asked himself. "Orphans, no doubt. I will take them home with me."

The shepherd and his wife named the twin brothers Romulus and Remus. They reared them to be brave young men. When they were grown, the brothers decided to build a city on the Tiber River so that they would remember the place of their rescue.

But they could not agree on the exact spot. Romulus wanted to build on the seven hills near the river's mouth. Remus began marking out different boundaries. In anger, Romulus killed his brother, buried him, and built the city of Rome on top of Remus's grave. Later, as the ruler of Rome, he kept an empty throne next to his, in memory of Remus.

Do you believe that this story is true? It is a popular legend about the founding of the city of Rome.

146

Rome: The City

Rome has been a city, a republic, and an empire. Now it is once again a city in Italy. Rome began around 753 B.C. when a group of settlers from central Europe called *Latins* made their homes there. The Latins were farmers and herdsmen, and Rome was their city.

The Latins had been living in Rome for over one hundred years when another tribe, the *Etruscans,* conquered them. The Etruscans were from northern Italy, and their culture had been influenced by the Greeks. They were skilled at trading and architecture. The Etruscan kings were powerful, and Rome became the most respected city in the region. But the Latins did not like having the Etruscan kings ruling over them.

In 509 B.C., the nobles of the city drove the Etruscan king, Tarquin the Proud, from the throne. Rome no longer had kings. The republic of Rome had begun. From then on the Latins were known as *Romans.*

An Etruscan bronze sculpture of a warrior

147

➤ **When did the Latins become known as Romans?** *(in 509 B.C. when they conquered the Etruscans)*

➤ **Who was the last Etruscan king to rule?** *(Tarquin the Proud)*

➤ **Would you like to be ruled by a king? Why or why not?** *(Answers will vary.)*

Point out that some rulers were kind, while others only concerned themselves with power or wealth. Remind the students that God loves them and has paid the price to buy them from the slavery of sin. When a person accepts Christ as Savior, he becomes Christ's servant. There is no room for pride when people realize their sinfulness and God's mercy. Christians should serve the Lord with humility and love and then serve others with love and respect as unto the Lord. (Eph. 6:5-9) (BATs: 2a Authority, 2b Servanthood, 7e Humility; Bible Promise: I. God as Master)

Then and Now—Instruct the students to read page 148 silently to find out how the Mediterranean Sea influenced Italy. *(The people of Italy were seafarers; the central location in the Mediterranean area aided the building of an empire.)*

Direct the students' attention to the Then and Now map, noting changes in boundary lines and so on. Invite the students to describe the peninsula of Italy. *(boot-shaped)* Ask the students to tell in which direction they would have

to travel to get to Italy from where they live. Point out the vast domain of the Roman Empire. Invite the students to compare how being the mayor of a city (like Rome) might differ from being the president of a country. *(Answers will vary but could include accountability is more direct in a city or small community; decisions might affect more people in a country.)*

Discussion Questions

➤ **How is a peninsula different from an island?** *(An island is completely surrounded by water; a peninsula is surrounded by water on only three sides.)*

➤ **What main islands are also part of Italy?** *(Sardinia and Sicily)*

➤ **What are the two mountain ranges in Italy?** *(the Apennines and sections of the Alps)*

□ Evaluating the Lesson

Rome: Then and Now (Notebook page 42)—Direct the students' attention to the go-together puzzles. Point out that the letters they will use are in the box at the bottom of the page. Tell them to cross out each letter as it is used. If you wish, solve the first go-together as a class. Allow time for the students to solve the puzzles. When all students have completed this assignment, check the papers together for accuracy.

Choose a volunteer to recount the story about the first settlers of Rome, using the words from the first go-together. *(The Latins were farmers and herdsmen. The Latins were conquered by the Etruscans, who then were later ruled by*

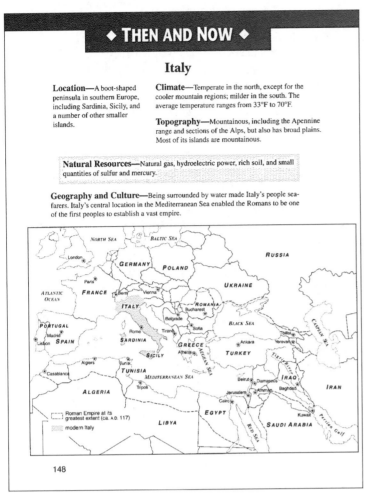

Italy

Location—A boot-shaped peninsula in southern Europe, including Sardinia, Sicily, and a number of other smaller islands.

Climate—Temperate in the north, except for the cooler mountain regions; milder in the south. The average temperature ranges from 33°F to 70°F.

Topography—Mountainous, including the Apennine range and sections of the Alps, but also has broad plains. Most of its islands are mountainous.

Natural Resources—Natural gas, hydroelectric power, rich soil, and small quantities of sulfur and mercury.

Geography and Culture—Being surrounded by water made Italy's people seafarers. Italy's central location in the Mediterranean Sea enabled the Romans to be one of the first peoples to establish a vast empire.

148

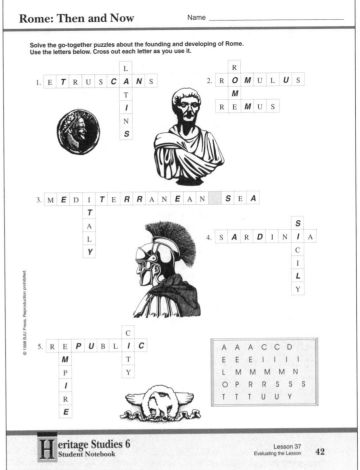

Solve the go-together puzzles about the founding and developing of Rome. Use the letters below. Cross out each letter as you use it.

© 1998 BJU Press. Reproduction prohibited.

Heritage Studies 6
Student Notebook

Lesson 37
Evaluating the Lesson   42

---

the Romans.) Call on a student to give a sentence about the founding of Rome, using the words from the second puzzle. *(Romulus and Remus were orphan twins who decided to build a city, called Rome.)*

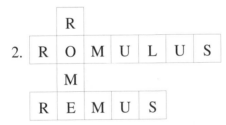

▬▬ Going Beyond ▬▬

□ Enrichment

Making pizza—Set up a food display AREA with olives, mozzarella cheese, pepperoni slices, green peppers, onions, mushrooms, bacon, and pizza sauce. Allow the students to taste any items with which they are unfamiliar. Tell the students that they will be making their own pizzas. Provide a refrigerated biscuit, a small piece of aluminum foil, and a name label for each student. Place a name label on the corner of the foil which has been folded back. Display a chart giving the steps for making pizza.

1. Flatten the biscuit onto the aluminum foil.
2. Add the pizza sauce.

3. Include any toppings of your choice.
4. Sprinkle on the cheese.
5. Follow the instructions on the biscuit container to bake the mini-pizzas. Lower the baking time by about five minutes for flattened biscuits.

A small toaster oven could be used in the classroom with supervision.

The activity could also be changed to make a fruit pizza which requires no baking. Use a baked sugar cookie for the crust, whipped topping for the sauce, various fruit selections as toppings, and decorative sprinkles for the top.

□ Additional Teacher Information

The Greek alphabet was used by the Etruscans and was further developed by the Romans. The letter *G* in the English language was added by the Romans. The present form of most capital letters in the English language is modeled closely after those in the Roman alphabet. The Roman alphabet also contributed to the roundness of the letters and the *serifs.* Many examples of ancient inscriptions in stone show these bold but elegant Roman letters. The thin strokes, called *serifs,* appear at the top and bottom of many letters in the Roman style of lettering even today.

The city of Rome is located among many hills in central Italy. The seven famous hills are the Aventine, Caelian, Capitoline, Esquiline, Palatine, Quirinal, and Viminal Hills. Palatine Hill overlooks the Tiber River and is the site of the ancient city.

LESSON 38
Rome: The Republic

Text, pages 149-52
Notebook, page 43

- Making Laws
- Equal Representation
- Military Strength
- Roman Republic

━━━ Preview ━━━

□ Objectives
Given proper instruction, the students will be able to do the following:
- Participate in a role-playing activity.
- Match characteristics and other facts with the appropriate terms.

□ Materials
Have available:
- A cassette player.
- *HERITAGE STUDIES Listening Cassette B.*
- Maps and More 11.
- A blank overhead transparency.
- An overhead projector.

Prepare:
- An overhead transparency of the song "Stand Up, Stand Up for Jesus." (*NOTE:* See the reproducible material at the end of Lesson 42.)
- A copy of the Senate/Assembly page or as many copies as the number of students requires. (*NOTE:* See the reproducible material at the end of Lesson 42. There should be an approximate ratio of three Senate members to every six Assembly members. The star identifies one student from each group of six Assembly members to be a tribune. These slips will be used as part of the *Discovering How* activity.)

□ Notes
You will need to know the names of your state's two senators and your district's representative. A short discussion in the lesson will explain representative government on the federal level.

The Enrichment activity calls for interaction with an elected official from the state or local level. You will need to either make arrangements to visit the office of an elected official or invite an elected official to come and address the class.

Day 65

━━━ Lesson ━━━

□ Introducing the Lesson
A standard—Tell the students that the words *banner* and *standard* are used in many hymns about the Christian's warfare. Point out that a *banner* is a piece of cloth used like a flag. Explain that the Roman *standard* was a flag that bore a design or figure and was carried on a pole. Each group of Roman soldiers had a standard with its own sign. The eagle was often used as a symbol of power. During battle the standard was raised like a flag to encourage the soldiers onward or to reassemble the troops. It was a disgrace for the standard to fall into enemy hands. Ask for a show of hands of the students who have played the game Capture the Flag. Explain that the object of the game is to capture your opponent's flag while also defending your own flag. Point out that winning the battle was important to the Romans, but keeping their standard meant keeping their pride as well. This lesson tells more about the Roman soldiers.

Soldiers of the cross—Display the overhead transparency of "Stand Up, Stand Up for Jesus." Play this song from *HERITAGE STUDIES Listening Cassette B.* Tell the students that this song was inspired by the last words of a dying man to admonish and challenge his friends. Direct the students to read the words silently to determine what challenge is given as you play the song again.

> Remind the students that Christians should continually fight against sin, pray, and rely on God for strength. Christians should not grow weary or be afraid when confronted with evil. One of their weapons is the Word of God. They must know the Scripture and meditate upon it. (BATs: 8b Faith in the power of the Word of God, 8c Fight, 8d Courage)

Rome: The Republic

Do you know what the word *republic* means? It comes from the Latin words that mean "belonging to the people." In a republic, the government is the people's responsibility.

In Rome, the citizens elected representatives to pass laws for all of Rome. But not everyone in Rome could vote at first. Only *patricians*, or members of the noble class, could vote. The common workers, small farmers, artisans, merchants, and foreigners were called *plebeians*, and they did not have the privilege of voting. Do you think everyone in Rome was satisfied with this arrangement?

The plebeians protested, and they were finally allowed to have their own governing body. It was called the *Assembly*, and their leaders were called *tribunes*. The patricians' body was the Senate, governed by *consuls*. The Assembly could not make official laws, but the Senate could. One of the first things the Assembly asked the Senate to do was to write down the law. The members of the Senate had the Roman law engraved on twelve bronze tablets and set into the temple wall where everyone could see it.

149

In this painting, the artist Macarra showed the Roman Senate as it might have looked in ancient times.

The plebeians were also given *veto power*. The Latin word *veto* means "I forbid." Tribunes stood in the Senate doorway during its meetings. The tribunes could stop the Senate's actions at any time by shouting, "Veto!"

Gradually, the plebeians gained more rights. They were allowed to marry patricians. They could be elected as consuls. At last, the Assembly was permitted to make laws that were just as official as those the Senate made. The plebeians and the patricians now had equal say in the government of Rome.

Would you expect a republic like this one to work? It worked very well for several hundred years. Most people in Rome worked hard and respected the law. And most lawmakers wanted to help and protect the citizens of Rome.

150

□ Teaching the Lesson

Making laws—Instruct the students to read page 149 silently to find what the Romans called their government. *(a republic)* Explain that this was a representative government because the people chose representatives to make laws for everyone in Rome.

Discussion Questions

➤ **Who is responsible for the government in a republic?** *(the people)*

➤ **What were the two groups of citizens in Rome?** *(the patricians or noble class, and the plebeians)*

➤ **In the beginning, which group of citizens could vote?** *(only the patricians)*

➤ **What was the governing body of the plebeians called, and who were the leaders?** *(Assembly; tribunes)*

➤ **How was the Senate different from the Assembly?** *(The Senate represented the patricians, made official laws, and voted.)*

➤ **What were the leaders of the Senate called?** *(consuls)*

➤ **What did the Assembly require of the Senate?** *(The Assembly requested that the Senate write down the law.)*

Explain that when the law was not written down, the law was not the same for all people. Point out that the judge could rule according to the lawbreakers' wealth and position.

Keeping the law was very important to the Romans. But God's Word says no one can keep the law perfectly. In fact, Paul wrote the book of Romans to tell the Roman people that the law only shows people their need of a Savior. Romans 3 explains that everyone is guilty of sin, but Jesus Christ paid the penalty by willingly giving His life. Point out that God will judge each person one day. People cannot earn salvation by wealth, power, fame, or good works. Ephesians 2:8-9 explains that it is only by accepting Christ through faith that a person can have eternal life. (BATs: 1a Understanding Jesus Christ, 7a Grace; Bible Promise: E. Christ as Sacrifice)

Day 66

Equal representation—Instruct the students to read page 150 silently to find out what rights the tribunes gained. *(They could marry patricians, veto laws of the Senate, become consuls, and make laws.)*

Discussion Questions

➤ **How could the tribunes stop the Senate's actions?** *(by shouting "Veto!" at the Senate doorway)*

➤ **What is the meaning of the word *veto*?** *("I forbid.")*

➤ **What was the final step for the plebeians to gain political equality with the patricians?** *(The Senate gave the plebeian Assembly the power to make laws.)*

What protects a republic? One factor that gave Rome strength was its military forces. Roman soldiers were disciplined and well trained. Rome's infantry was divided into *legions,* units of several thousand men. The soldiers in these units were called *legionaries.*

You have probably seen pictures of Roman legionaries in artists' portrayals of the crucifixion of Christ. These soldiers wore short wool tunics under leather jackets reinforced with metal strips. Bronze helmets protected all but their ears and faces. Centurions and other officers wore tall crests on top of their helmets so that they could be seen easily. Each legionary carried a short sword and a six-foot javelin that weighed about ten pounds.

In the early years of the republic, Rome's legions conquered the entire Italian peninsula. With all of Italy under its control, Rome turned next to the west. Over the next 125 years, Rome battled the North African city of Carthage for control of the Mediterranean Sea. The three major wars between Rome and Carthage are called the *Punic Wars.*

152

◆ DISCOVERING HOW ◆

The Roman Republic Worked

1. Find out from your teacher whether you will be a member of the Senate or of the Assembly.

2. Go to your appropriate place and follow the instructions as the meeting proceeds.

3. Discuss the meeting with your classmates. Did you feel as if your opinion was important? Was your decision respected by the other group? Do you think this method of making laws is a good one?

151

> **What kept the republic strong?** *(citizens who respected the law and lawmakers who served the interests of all people)*
> **How is the government of your country similar to or different from Rome's republic?** *(Answers may vary.)*

Review with the students the definition of *democracy* as learned in Chapter 6. Compare and contrast the idea of a democracy with that of a republic. *(In a pure democracy the people meet together to decide their laws. Pure democracy works best when people are few and live close together, as in the Greek city-states. Both forms of government provide citizens the opportunity to participate in the government, but a republic stresses the use of elected representatives whose duty is to serve the people.)* Tell the students that the United States is a democratic republic because citizens can elect representatives. The government of the United States was designed to prevent one man or group of men from gaining total control.

Remind the students that Jesus was a humble servant while on earth. Christians too should be humble as they seek to serve others daily. Their words and actions will reflect Christ when they allow the Holy Spirit to control them. (BATs: 2b Servanthood, 6c Spirit-filled, 7e Humility)

Military strength—Instruct the students to read page 152 silently to find another factor that kept the Roman republic strong. *(military forces)* Refer to the picture of the soldier on the page as you ask the following questions.

Discussion Questions
> **What did each legionary wear?** *(a short wool tunic under a leather jacket reinforced with metal strips, and a bronze helmet)*
> **What did each legionary carry?** *(a sword and a javelin)*
> **What made the Roman soldiers effective?** *(discipline and training)*
> **What was the first area of conquest for the Roman soldiers?** *(the Italian peninsula)*
> **Who was the enemy to the Romans in the Punic Wars?** *(Carthage)*

Locate Carthage on Maps and More 11. Explain that this map shows the Roman Empire around A.D. 117 as well as the lands conquered later. Point out Italy. Tell the students that the Alps to the north and the seas around Italy provided protection. Ask the students why Rome wanted to fight

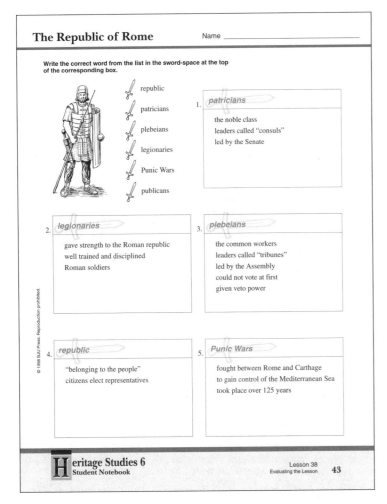

The Republic of Rome   Name _____

Write the correct word from the list in the sword-space at the top of the corresponding box.

🗡 republic
🗡 patricians
🗡 plebeians
🗡 legionaries
🗡 Punic Wars
🗡 publicans

1. 🗡 *patricians*
   the noble class
   leaders called "consuls"
   led by the Senate

2. 🗡 *legionaries*
   gave strength to the Roman republic
   well trained and disciplined
   Roman soldiers

3. 🗡 *plebeians*
   the common workers
   leaders called "tribunes"
   led by the Assembly
   could not vote at first
   given veto power

4. 🗡 *republic*
   "belonging to the people"
   citizens elect representatives

5. 🗡 *Punic Wars*
   fought between Rome and Carthage
   to gain control of the Mediterranean Sea
   took place over 125 years

© 1998 BJU Press. Reproduction prohibited.

Heritage Studies 6
Student Notebook

Lesson 38
Evaluating the Lesson   **43**

Carthage. *(for control of the Mediterranean Sea)* Explain that many trade routes connected people and supplies around the area. Tell the students that control of the Mediterranean Sea gave access to goods like gold, silver, marble, grain, silk, spices, pottery, and animals.

Day 67

Roman Republic—Direct the students' attention to the *Discovering How* activity on page 151. Give to each student a slip of paper, telling him whether he will be in the Senate or the Assembly. Tell the students that each Assembly member with a star on the slip of paper is also to be a tribune. Tell the students that they will be discussing a new classroom rule. Allow the Senate members to formulate the rule. Tell the Assembly members to decide whether they want their tribunes to veto the rule or not. Allow the tribunes to shout "Veto!" if they do not like the rule, and then tell the Senate to change the rule until the Assembly is satisfied.

Discussion Questions

➤ **What advantages and disadvantages are there for this method of making laws?** *(Advantages—the Senate is less likely to control the situation, the focus is on agreement, and all people have a say; disadvantages—people could be swayed by wealth or power of individuals, and a majority of people could oppose your view.)*

➤ **What can you do if there are laws in your country with which you disagree?** *(Write or contact your elected officials on the local, state, and national levels, stating the reasons for your disagreement with the law.)*

Point out that representation in the U.S. Congress focuses on equal representation in the Senate with two Senators from each state, but the population of each state determines the number of a state's representatives in the House of Representatives. Tell the students the names of the two senators from your state and the representative from your district. Explain that the Constitution provides guidelines for these offices.

☐ Evaluating the Lesson

The Republic of Rome (Notebook page 43)—Direct the students to write the correct word from the list on the sword at the top of the corresponding box.

━━━ Going Beyond ━━━

☐ Enrichment

Writing—Set up a writing AREA before the visit with an elected official. Instruct the students to write three or more questions for the elected official. Encourage them to think of personal or political questions. Read the questions to prepare a list of appropriate discussion questions.

Open forum—Invite an elected official from the state or local level to visit the classroom. *(NOTE:* You may choose to take a field trip to the office of the elected official instead.*)* As time permits, allow the students to ask questions. Ask the visitor what recent items of discussion have arisen in his office and how that information or decision directly affects the students. Point out that any elected official has a specific length of term before another election. Explain to the students that the Romans used a similar method of a representative government.

☐ Additional Teacher Information

Inscribed on many Roman standards are the letters *SPQR*, which stand for *Senatus Populusque Romanus,* or "The Roman Senate and the People." This phrase implied that the Senate ruled in partnership with the people rather than over the people.

During the republic most of the Roman soldiers were free citizens who were called to service in times of military need. At first, only landowners were called to fight in the army. An established army was in place when the Roman Empire began. The navy began during the time of the Punic Wars, when Rome was fighting for control of the Mediterranean Sea.

SUPPLEMENTAL
LESSON
Citizenship

- Citizens of Rome
- Citizens of the United States

Preview

□ Objectives

Given proper instruction, the students will be able to do the following:
- Answer questions about the history and government of the United States.
- Plan and implement a class project.

□ Materials

Have available:
- A Bible for each student.
- A sheet of notebook paper for each student.
- A blank overhead transparency.
- An overhead projector.

Prepare:
- An overhead transparency of the "Do You Know?" page. (*NOTE:* See the reproducible material at the end of Lesson 42.)
- A copy of the "Citizenship" page for each student. (*NOTE:* See the reproducible material at the end of Lesson 42.)

□ Notes

The Evaluating the Lesson section requires a service project for the entire class. Contact a community leader to find out needs or problems in the community that your class could address.

For the Enrichment activity, you will want to acquire postal or e-mail addresses for your state's representatives or senators. Provide postage stamps or tell the students to bring in a postage stamp if they will be mailing their letters.

You may choose to review or study the Constitution of the United States before or after presenting this lesson.

Lesson

□ Introducing the Lesson

Citizens of the Unites States—Display the overhead transparency of the "Do You Know?" page. Explain that the following questions are an example of the test an individual must take to become a U.S. citizen. Tell them that a person must answer at least twelve of these questions correctly to pass the test. Instruct each student to answer as many questions as he can on a separate sheet of notebook paper. Discuss the answers briefly.

1. *(fifty)*
2. *(the Constitution)*
3. *(July 4, 1776)*
4. *(Answers will vary.)*
5. *(Washington, D.C.)*
6. *(two)*
7. *(Answers will vary.)*
8. *(an amendment)*
9. *(citizens who have registered to vote and who are at least eighteen years old)*
10. *(George Washington)*
11. *(the Declaration of Independence)*
12. *(by birth or by naturalization)*
13. *(the War for Independence)*
14. *(New Hampshire, Massachusetts, Connecticut, Rhode Island, New York, Pennsylvania, Delaware, New Jersey, Maryland, Virginia, North Carolina, South Carolina, Georgia)*
15. *(two years)*
16. *(the Pilgrims)*
17. *(Answers will vary.)*
18. *(the Supreme Court)*
19. *(eighteen years old)*
20. *(Answers will vary.)*

Explain that it is a privilege and a responsibility to be a citizen of the United States. Tell the students that they will learn more about citizenship in this lesson.

□ Teaching the Lesson

Citizens of Rome—Call on students to explain what is meant by *citizenship. (the legal status of an individual with rights and responsibilities)* Remind the students that in the early days of Rome, peoples conquered and ruled by Rome were not granted citizenship. Explain that citizenship gave power to individuals. Only citizens could vote and hold public office. Point out that the Romans were proud and sometimes arrogant about their citizenship. Instruct the students to read silently the account of Paul and Silas in Philippi from Acts 16:19-21, 35-40.

Discussion Questions

➤ **What was Paul's citizenship?** *(Roman)*
➤ **What charge was given against Paul and Silas?** *(They were Jews and had offended the Romans by teaching contrary to the Roman customs.)*
➤ **Was this true?** *(no)*
➤ **Why were Paul and Silas treated this way?** *(Others thought they were foreigners.)*
➤ **What punishment did they receive?** *(They were beaten and jailed.)*
➤ **Did Paul tell them he was a Roman to be arrogant?** *(No, he stated that he was a citizen of Rome to remind them of his specific privileges according to the law.)*

As citizens of Rome, the people then gave glory and honor to Rome. As a Christian, Paul directed this glory and honor toward Christ. Christians remember God's grace and praise His name. (BATs: 7a Grace, 7c Praise)

Citizens of the Unites States—Distribute the "Citizenship" page to the students. Ask the students how an individual becomes a citizen of the United States. Tell them that a person is a citizen of the United States by birth or by naturalization. Explain that people born in the United States or in a territory of the United States are citizens. Point out that an individual born outside the United States boundaries may also be a citizen if his parents are citizens of the United States. Direct attention to the statements under the first question on the "Citizenship" page. Instruct the students to check each statement that applies to them.

Direct attention to the second section. Instruct the students to read silently to find out how a person who is not born in the United States becomes a citizen. *(by naturalization)*

Discussion Questions

➤ **What are the requirements for individuals seeking naturalization?** *(must be at least eighteen years old; must have lived in the state where they are applying for the last five years; must exemplify good character; and must possess the ability to speak, read, and write English)*
➤ **What conduct do you think might disqualify a person for citizenship?** *(Answers will vary.)*
➤ **Should these citizenship guidelines remain or change? Why or why not?** *(Answers will vary.)*
➤ **Do you think a naturalized citizen could be a senator?** *(yes, after being naturalized for nine years)*
➤ **Is a person seeking naturalization required to read, to speak, and to write English?** *(Yes, but those over age fifty may be exempted.)*

Choose a student to read the steps in the process of naturalization. *(taking a test, completing a form, paying a fee, appearing before a judge, taking the oath of allegiance, and receiving a certificate)* Emphasize that the oath is a promise to defend and to support the Constitution and laws of the United States. Point out that a naturalized citizen also promises to fight for his country if necessary.

Direct attention to the third section. Instruct the students to write some of the duties of a citizen. Call on volunteers to state their answers. *(to vote, to keep informed, to obey the laws, to pay taxes, to defend the country, to hold public office if desired and elected, and to serve on a jury if selected)*

Direct attention to the last section. Instruct the students to read silently to find out which amendment states the age at which they may vote. *(Twenty-sixth Amendment)*

Discussion Questions

➤ **Which amendment says that a person born in the United States is a citizen?** *(Fourteenth)*
➤ **What event in the history of the United States influenced the Fifteenth Amendment?** *(the Civil War)*
➤ **How old do you have to be before you can vote in the United States?** *(eighteen)*

> Call on volunteers to read aloud Philippians 1:27 and 3:20. Explain that the word *conversation* conveys the meaning of "citizenship." A Christian is a citizen of heaven. Time on earth is temporal, like visiting a foreign country. A Christian's eternal home is in heaven.

Discussion Questions

➤ **How should a Christian's actions be different from those of the unsaved?** *(Answers will vary but may include that a Christian is to be holy, honest, and loving.)*
➤ **What are some duties or responsibilities of the Christian?** *(to serve and obey God and to defend the faith)*
➤ **What privileges do Christians have?** *(Answers will vary but may include access to God through prayer and the power of the Holy Spirit.)*

> Sinners must be redeemed by the blood of Jesus Christ. It is by accepting His payment for sins and not by good works that people are saved. Christians should do things that bring glory to the Lord (I Tim. 4:12; I Pet. 1:15,18; I Pet. 2:12; II Pet. 3:11). God also expects believers to work together in service for Him. (BATs: 1b Repentance and faith, 1c Separation from the world, 3e Unity of Christ and the church, 4b Purity; Bible Promise: F. Christ as Intercessor)

☐ Evaluating the Lesson

Good citizenship—Remind the students that to become a naturalized citizen, an individual must reflect good conduct and loyalty. Point out that every citizen should strive for excellence in character, but Christians especially should be examples for Christ. Explain a community project that you have been told about in which the entire class can participate (e.g., cleaning up the school grounds or gathering, preparing, and serving food to the needy). Assist the students as they plan and implement the class project.

▬▬▬ Going Beyond ▬▬▬

☐ Enrichment

Writing—Set up a letter writing AREA with stationery and pens. Encourage each student to write a short letter to a congressional representative or senator, explaining why he is thankful to be an American or why he is glad to be living in his home state.

☐ Additional Teacher Information

For more information on naturalization, contact your county clerk for the nearest office of the Immigration and Naturalization Office.

A person may lose his U.S. citizenship by serving in a foreign country's armed forces, by holding public office in that country, or by being convicted of a major federal crime. An individual can also willingly give up his citizenship.

America recognizes September 17 as Citizenship Day. Individuals who have met the requirements for naturalization are often given the oath of allegiance on this day.

A person may have *dual citizenship*. A child has citizenship in the country of his birth as well as in the country where his parents are citizens.

LESSON 39
Rome's Expansion

Text, pages 153-55
Notebook, page 44

- Battle Strategies
- Conquests and Changes
- Road Construction

━━━ Preview ━━━

□ Objective

Given proper instruction, the students will be able to do the following:

- Complete a word puzzle about the growth of Rome.

□ Materials

Have available:

- A Bible for the teacher and each student.
- A large road map showing several states.*
- Maps and More 11.
- A blank overhead transparency.
- An overhead projector.
- An overhead transparency pen.

Prepare an overhead transparency of "The Romans Road" and a copy of the page for each student. (*NOTE:* See the reproducible material at the end of Lesson 42.)

□ Notes

Instructions for preparing a Roman road are included in the Enrichment section. Prepare your example in an old aquarium to make the layers visible.

Day 68

━━━ Lesson ━━━

□ Introducing the Lesson

Map reading—Display the road map of several states. Explain that the symbol for an interstate highway is a red, white, and blue shield with numbers. Call on volunteers to locate several interstate highways and to trace the path through several states. Write the numbers of the highways on the chalkboard. Circle the even numbers. Direct attention to the map. Ask the students what direction the even-numbered interstate highways go. (*east and west*) Point out that odd-numbered interstate highways go north and south. Challenge the students to estimate the number of interstate highway miles in the United States. (*about forty-three thousand miles*) Tell the students that the Romans had more than fifty thousand miles of roads without the modern machines and materials we have today. Tell them that this lesson shows the development and importance of Roman roads.

The Second Punic War

The Second Punic War is the most famous of the three wars because of a man named Hannibal. Hannibal was the general of the armies of Carthage and a brilliant soldier. He decided that, in order to defeat Rome, he would first invade Italy and win the support of the other Italian peoples against the Romans. He gathered his army in Spain. To avoid having the Romans see him, he planned to march his soldiers eastward into Italy across the cold, rugged Alps.

Hannibal left Spain with about forty thousand men and a group of war elephants. Elephants were often effective in ancient warfare. Enemy lines would break in fear when elephants charged them, and horses shied away from them because they disliked their smell. But Hannibal never got a chance to use his elephants against the Romans. The cold weather was hard on the elephants, and most of them died in the snowy Alps. Many of Hannibal's soldiers did not survive the journey either.

By the time Hannibal's army reached Italy, it was much smaller than the Roman army. But Hannibal's skill at planning strategies made up for the size of his army. He won battle after battle against the Romans. But he could not completely defeat them.

153

Bible study—Give each student a copy of "The Romans Road" page as you display the overhead transparency of the page. Explain that the verses listed are a useful tool in presenting the message of salvation. Call on volunteers to read or recite the verses in the order given. Challenge the students to determine which statements at the bottom of the page show God's plan of salvation. (*Numbers 1, 3, 5, 9, and 10 are correct.*) Mark the correct answers on the transparency. Point out that other religions may teach that man can earn his way to heaven or that Jesus is not the Son of God. Present other verses such as John 3:16, Ephesians 2:8-9, and I John 5:11-13, calling on students to read these aloud.

□ Teaching the Lesson

Battle strategies—Instruct the students to read page 153 silently to find out the plan of attack by the general of the armies of Carthage in the Second Punic War. (*to cross the Alps and attack Rome with elephants*)

Discussion Questions

➤ **Who was the general of the armies of Carthage?** (*Hannibal*)

➤ **What was Hannibal's purpose for the invasion?** (*to win support of the other Italian peoples against the Romans*)

➤ **How did Hannibal plan to enter Italy unnoticed?** (*by marching from Spain across the Alps into Italy*)

➤ **Why would elephants be used in battle?** (*Men were afraid of them; horses shied away because of their smell.*)

Finally, Rome's Senate found a commander who was equal in ability to Hannibal. This new general, Scipio, decided to win the war by ignoring Hannibal. He and his army left Italy and attacked Carthage. Hannibal immediately rushed home to protect his city. The battle that followed was hard fought, but Scipio gained the victory. Hannibal fled and committed suicide rather than die at the hands of Rome. Carthage made peace with Rome, and the Second Punic War ended.

Second Punic War

- Carthaginian territory
- Roman territory
- important Roman victories

Byzantium

Rome
Cannae

Syracuse

Carthage
Zama

MEDITERRANEAN SEA

While fighting Carthage, Romans conquered other lands. They marched eastward and conquered the remnants of Alexander the Great's empire. Then they conquered Greece itself and gained control over the eastern Mediterranean Sea. The great sea was now a Roman lake.

When the soldiers returned home, they discovered that more than just Rome's boundaries had changed. Citizen farmers who had left their farms to be soldiers now lost their property. They moved to the city to find work. But most jobs had already been filled by slaves taken from conquered territories. The rich class took advantage of the poor by buying their votes and filling the government with other rich men. How long would you expect this kind of republic to last?

154

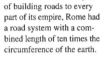

Building Roads

Have you ever heard the saying, "All roads lead to Rome"? Rome is famous for the system of roads it built to connect the lands it had conquered.

Many goods were taken along the Roman roads to other lands. Money, grain, slaves, and precious metals traveled back into Rome as *tribute*, or taxes paid to a ruler by conquered peoples.

Ideas also traveled along the roads. Visitors to Rome carried Roman philosophies away with them. Rome also borrowed knowledge from other lands. The Romans used and improved on the inventions and discoveries of others. They adopted religions from faraway places. Cultures from the East and the West blended, and each changed.

Eventually, the Romans learned how to cut through mountains and keep the roads straight. Roman roads were fast and easy to travel. After five hundred years of building roads to every part of its empire, Rome had a road system with a combined length of ten times the circumference of the earth.

The Roman road on the right had stepping stones placed so that people could cross on them and chariot wheels could go between them.

155

➤ **What went wrong with Hannibal's plan?** *(Many soldiers and elephants died in the Alps.)*

Point to Carthage and Rome on Maps and More 11. Tell the students that Hannibal's army reached Rome by way of the Alps. Explain that battleground terrain, weather conditions, and appropriate weapons are still important factors in warfare today.

Remind the students that Christians are engaged in spiritual warfare. Point out that God gives His children victory over sin and helps them to live holy lives through the power of the Holy Spirit. (BAT: 4d Victory; Bible Promise: A. Liberty from Sin)

Day 69

Conquests and changes—Instruct the students to read page 154 silently to find out the result of the Second Punic War. *(Rome defeated Carthage and gained new territory.)*

Discussion Questions

➤ **Whom did Rome send to fight Hannibal?** *(Scipio)*
➤ **What was Scipio's plan against Hannibal?** *(ignore him and attack Carthage)*
➤ **Where else did Roman soldiers fight?** *(in the remnants of Alexander the Great's empire and in Greece)*

➤ **Why was the Mediterranean Sea called a Roman lake?** *(The sea was surrounded on all sides by Roman territory.)*
➤ **What changes occurred in Rome as a result of the wars?** *(Rome had new boundaries, returning soldiers who needed work, fewer jobs as the captives became slaves, and a corrupt government.)*
➤ **Why did many poor people go to Rome?** *(to find work)*
➤ **How do you think the Roman government changed when only rich people were in power?** *(Decisions may have been based on who had the most money and not on what was right.)*

Direct the students' attention to the map on page 154 which shows Rome after the Punic Wars. Explain that the Alps to the north would seem to protect Italy from invasion, but there are several mountain passes through which many enemies came. Tell the students that high cliffs protect the southern coast of Italy.

Road construction—Instruct the students to read page 155 silently to find out why the Romans built a system of roads. *(to connect the lands that they had conquered)*

Discussion Questions

➤ **What did the roads bring to Rome that helped to unify the people?** *(goods and ideas)*
➤ **How are roads important to your community?** *(Answers will vary but should include bringing raw materials for manufacturing and industry, taking finished products to other people for sale, traveling for pleasure,*

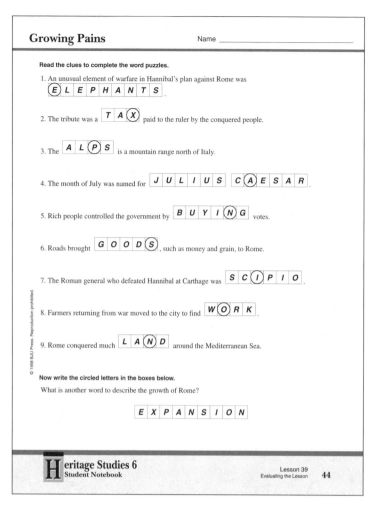

Growing Pains   Name _____

Read the clues to complete the word puzzles.

1. An unusual element of warfare in Hannibal's plan against Rome was
Ⓔ L E P H A N T S .

2. The tribute was a T A Ⓧ paid to the ruler by the conquered people.

3. The A L Ⓟ S is a mountain range north of Italy.

4. The month of July was named for J U L I U S C Ⓐ E S A R .

5. Rich people controlled the government by B U Y I Ⓝ G votes.

6. Roads brought G O O D Ⓢ , such as money and grain, to Rome.

7. The Roman general who defeated Hannibal at Carthage was S C Ⓘ P I O .

8. Farmers returning from war moved to the city to find W Ⓞ R K .

9. Rome conquered much L A Ⓝ D around the Mediterranean Sea.

Now write the circled letters in the boxes below.

What is another word to describe the growth of Rome?

E X P A N S I O N

H eritage Studies 6
Student Notebook

Lesson 39
Evaluating the Lesson   **44**

communicating with others, and making available public services such as hospitals, libraries, and schools.)

➤ **What new ideas came to Rome because of the roads?** *(inventions, discoveries, and religions from conquered lands)*

➤ **What was *tribute*?** *(taxes paid to a ruler by conquered peoples)*

> Read Romans 13:6-7 aloud to the students. Point out that God specifically told the Romans that it was right to pay the tribute and honor the leaders. Explain that God expects Christians to obey the laws, including the law to pay taxes. (BAT: 2a Authority)

□ Evaluating the Lesson

Growing Pains (Notebook page 44)—Direct the students to use the clues to complete the word puzzles. Then tell them to write the circled letters in the boxes at the bottom of the page to find another word to describe the growth of Rome.

Going Beyond

□ Enrichment

Building a road—Set up an AREA for each student to view a road segment. Prepare a section of a road in an old aquarium, using layers of soil, sand, pea-sized gravel, and rocks. Be sure to include a higher center, curbs, and ditches. You may provide the same materials for each student to assemble his own segment of road in a small, clear container.

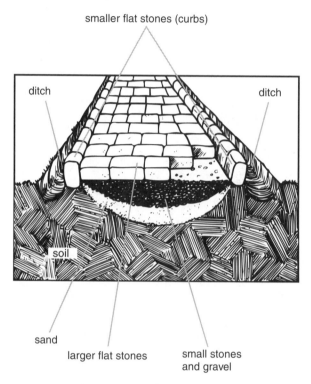

smaller flat stones (curbs)

ditch   ditch

soil

sand

larger flat stones   small stones and gravel

Mapping locations—Set up an AREA with an enlarged map of your city or community and a highlighting pen. Place an adhesive star at the location of your school. Instruct the students to place an adhesive dot on the approximate location of their residence. Tell each student to highlight the route he takes to school each morning.

□ Additional Teacher Information

The Roman roads often started with a foundation of small stones and gravel, followed with consecutive layers of larger stones that were cemented together, and ended with a layer of large stones on top. The Romans also used drainage ditches along both sides of the road. Some roads even had stepping stones for the people to use when crossing the road. Today, road builders still follow the Roman principles of preparing a solid foundation, using curbs, and making the center of the road higher to drain off water.

182

Heritage Studies 6 TE

LESSON 40

The Republic in Ruins

Text, pages 156-60

- ■ **Forsaking the Foundations**
- ■ **Caesar, the Conqueror**
- ■ **Reign's End**
- ■ **Calendar Change**

━━━ Preview ━━━

☐ Objective

Given proper instruction, the students will be able to do the following:
- • Identify statements about Julius Caesar and the calendar as either true or false.

☐ Materials

Have available:
- • A wall map of the world.
- • A 3"×5" card for each student.*
- • A calendar for each group of eight students.*
- • A small piece of magnetic tape or cellophane tape for each group of eight students.
- • A colored pencil for each group of eight students.

Prepare a copy of the "Gallons of Water" page for each student. (*NOTE:* See the reproducible material at the end of Lesson 42.)

☐ Notes

The "Gallons of Water" page assigned at the end of this lesson requires the students to evaluate their water usage for one day. You will want to assign and complete the survey before Lesson 41 if possible.

The Enrichment activity in Lesson 41 challenges the students to locate and photograph or sketch examples of classical architecture in your town or neighboring cities. You may want to complete the activity yourself and then prepare a list of sites to assign.

Day 70

━━━ Lesson ━━━

☐ Introducing the Lesson

Leadership qualities—Distribute a 3"×5" card to each student. Tell each student to think of someone he admires as a leader and to write that person's name on the card. Instruct the students to turn the cards over and to write some words or phrases that describe a good leader. Collect the cards and read aloud the names given. Place the cards on the chalkboard with the magnetic tape or cellophane tape. In the center of the chalkboard, write the phrase *leadership qualities* and

---

The Collapse of the Republic

As the plebeians of Rome gave up their right to rule, they became less and less concerned about how the government was run. They no longer studied the issues so that they could vote carefully. They cared only that the government fed and protected them.

Violence became common in Rome. Different men tried to rise to power with the support of the common people. Civil wars broke out between different leaders and their followers.

In 100 B.C., a child was born who would grow up to bring dramatic changes to the government of Rome. Julius Caesar was born in the month later named for him, July.

Roman statue of Julius Caesar

156

---

draw a circle around it. Call on volunteers to come to the chalkboard, select a card, and read the words or phrases that describe a good leader. As each word is given, write it above, below, or to the side of the phrase *leadership qualities* until you have made a word cluster. Discuss each description and erase any that the class decides does not accurately describe a good leader. Point out that a good leader seeks to serve others rather than seeking power, control, or fame for himself. Tell the students that the focus of this lesson is the rule of a famous Roman.

> Stress the importance of a leader who applies godly principles, such as honesty and humility. Tell the students that a Christian should be known as one who seeks to please God. A Christian should desire to be Christlike in his words and actions. A Christian receives power for victory through the power of the Holy Spirit. (BATs: 3d Body as a temple, 4b Purity, 4d Victory, 6c Spirit-filled; Bible Promise: D. Identified in Christ)

☐ Teaching the Lesson

Forsaking the foundations—Instruct the students to read page 156 silently to find out why the republic of Rome collapsed. *(unconcern of plebeians and civil wars)* Remind the students that the republic had been strong because citizens respected the law and because the lawmakers served

As a member of a patrician family in Rome, Julius Caesar received an excellent education in his youth. He married a patrician and was quick to make his voice heard in government. He had an eloquence and determination that made him popular with the people, and he rose early to high positions in the government.

He was also an outstanding military general. Leading a mighty army of fifty thousand men, he began conquering the land northwest of Italy, called Gaul. For nine years his soldiers defeated tribes in what is today Switzerland, France, Spain, Holland, Belgium, and parts of Germany. Caesar even attacked Britain, which until then had been an unknown land.

Caesar's next conquest came in Rome itself. His popularity as a conqueror threatened the power of the government leaders. The Senate ordered Caesar to disband his army and return to Rome. However, at the Rubicon River, Caesar made his decision to disobey and to return to Rome with his army. This action immediately plunged him into a civil war against the strongest Roman leader, Pompey. Caesar fought Pompey's army for four years before defeating it.

Roman bust of Pompey

157

In 46 B.C., the Senate proclaimed Caesar dictator of Rome. At first his term was to last only ten years, but he soon changed it so that he would be dictator for life. He made many changes in the government, hoping to solve the problems of the republic.

He limited the power of the corrupt Senate. He granted citizenship to people from Italian territories and even allowed them to have members in the Senate. He promoted colonization, schools, libraries, and public works in all of Rome and its surrounding territories. His actions helped to unify Rome and strengthen its bonds with its conquered peoples.

How do you think the Romans felt about Caesar's methods of governing Rome? Although many Romans liked Caesar and respected his accomplishments, many others were angry with him. They knew that as long as Caesar insisted on having absolute power, the government of Rome could be a true republic no longer.

158

---

the interest of all people. Point out that the republic of Rome existed for over four hundred years.

Discussion Questions

➤ **What did the plebeians desire from the government?** *(food and protection)*

➤ **What specific duties were given to the United States government by the Constitution?** *(The duty of the government is to protect the people and to uphold the Constitution.)*

➤ **In what year was Julius Caesar born?** *(100 B.C.)*

➤ **Which month of the year is named after Julius Caesar?** *(July)*

Day 71

Caesar, the Conqueror—Instruct the students to read page 157 silently to find out whether Caesar's conquests began at home or in the regions beyond Italy. *(in the regions beyond Italy)*

Discussion Questions

➤ **Why did the people like Julius Caesar?** *(He was eloquent, determined, well educated, and an outstanding military general.)*

➤ **Where did Julius Caesar begin his military conquest?** *(in Gaul, the land northwest of Italy)*

Direct attention to the wall map of the world. Point out Switzerland, France, Spain, Holland, Belgium, Germany, and Britain. Explain that Caesar's conquests in western

Europe affected the development of that region's culture. Later, the western European settlers extended this culture to America.

➤ **Who did not like Caesar's popularity? Why?** *(The government leaders did not like Caesar's popularity because they felt that he was a threat to their power.)*

➤ **What action did the Senate take?** *(They demanded that Caesar disband his army and return to Rome.)*

➤ **How did Caesar respond?** *(He disobeyed and brought the army back to Rome.)*

➤ **Who was Caesar's rival in the civil war when he returned to Rome?** *(Pompey)*

➤ **What was the outcome of this civil war?** *(Caesar defeated Pompey.)*

Stress that what Julius Caesar did in "crossing the Rubicon" was wrong. Governmental powers are ordained by God (Rom. 13:1), and He rules in the affairs of men and nations, accomplishing His purposes despite man's sinful intentions (Gen. 50:20). (BAT: 2a Authority; Bible Promise: I. God as Master)

Instruct the students to read page 158 to find out what victory Caesar won in his conquest for power at home. *(The Senate proclaimed him dictator of Rome.)* Tell the class that a dictator rules with absolute power, usually in a cruel and oppressive manner, to get what he wants.

The Ides of March

As Caesar's reign continued, angry Romans grew more and more desperate. They wanted the government of Rome to "belong to the people" again. Brutus and Cassius, two senators whom Caesar had considered his friends, met with a group of other Senate members. Secretly they plotted to kill Caesar.

On the fifteenth day of March, called the *ides* of March on the Roman calendar, these men hid in the Senate chamber with knives. When Caesar entered the room, they attacked him and stabbed him. Caesar fell dead at the foot of a statue of Pompey, his old enemy.

Do you think killing Caesar solved the problems of the republic? These senators had broken the law in trying to uphold the law. Their actions had weakened the laws of the republic. And now many other men were eager to take Caesar's place as ruler of Rome. From that time on, men, and not laws, would rule Rome.

Julius Caesar stabbed by Brutus in a scene from Shakespeare's Julius Caesar (Bob Jones University Classic Players)

160

Julius Caesar's Calendar

Have you ever wondered where the leap year got its start? Julius Caesar originated it when he was ruler of Rome.

One of the biggest problems facing Julius Caesar when he came to power was the calendar. In the past, Roman calendars had ignored the fact that the solar year lasts not just 365 days, but $365\frac{1}{4}$ days. By the time of Caesar's reign, the calendar was so far off that none of the seasons fell in the right place. Caesar had the idea to add an extra day every four years to balance out the calendar. The fourth year is called a leap year, and the extra day is added to February.

Before putting his new idea into practice, Caesar had to bring the calendar up-to-date. So, Caesar made the year 46 B.C. last 445 days! This extra-long year was often called the "year of confusion."

I don't care WHAT month you think it SHOULD be, Aras! If we don't all cooperate, we'll NEVER get this calendar thing straightened out!

Caesar's calendar, known as the Julian calendar, was used by Europeans for centuries. Today we use a reformed version of this calendar, called the *Gregorian calendar*. But "echoes" of Caesar's calendar can still be heard in the names of our months. Many of the months were named after Roman gods or rulers.

159

Discussion Questions

➤ **How long was Caesar initially to hold the position of dictator?** *(ten years, but he changed it to a lifetime term)*
➤ **What were some of Caesar's accomplishments?** *(limited power of the Senate; granted citizenship and representation to conquered peoples; promoted colonization, schools, libraries, and public works)*
➤ **How did Caesar's actions help Rome?** *(He brought unity to Rome.)*
➤ **Why did some people not like Caesar?** *(He took control of the government away from the people.)*

Day 72

Reign's end—Instruct the students to read page 160 silently to find out how Caesar's reign ended. *(He was killed by men in government whom he thought to be his friends.)*

Discussion Questions

➤ **On what day was Caesar killed?** *(on the fifteenth day of March, known as the "ides of March")*
➤ **How did the actions of Brutus and Cassius harm the republic?** *(They weakened the laws; there was a struggle for power.)*
➤ **What new problem faced the government?** *(Men would rule, not laws.)*
➤ **Why do you think it would be harmful to be ruled by men and not laws?** *(There no longer would be an absolute standard of what is right.)*
➤ **What are some laws which govern your life?** *(Answers will vary.)*

Remind the students that God says a person's heart is wicked (Jer. 17:9). Point out that one's actions may be right, but God sees the heart and knows the motive. Christians should obey God and those He puts in authority over them because they love Him. (BATs: 2a Authority, 5a Love)

Calendar change—Instruct the students to read page 159 to find out how leap year originated. *(Julius Caesar changed the calendar to add one day every four years to balance the calendar with a solar year.)*

Discussion Questions

➤ **How many days are in a solar year?** *(365¼ days)*
➤ **In what year was the calendar adjusted to bring it up to date?** *(46 B.C.)*
➤ **How long was the "year of confusion"?** *(445 days)*
➤ **What was Caesar's calendar called?** *(Julian calendar)*
➤ **How does the present calendar reflect the impact of the Julian calendar?** *(Many months were named after Roman gods or rulers; there are 365 days in normal years, and leap years have 366 days.)*

☐ Evaluating the Lesson

Calendar game—Assign the students to teams of eight or fewer to play the Calendar Game. Instruct the team members to arrange themselves in a line. Give a colored pencil and a calendar opened to January to the first member of each team.

Tell the students that they should listen carefully as you read aloud each statement. The first member of each team responds to the same statement by writing his answer (*T* or *F*) on the calendar month of January. For each correct answer, the team member turns the team's calendar page to the next month (February). After each statement, each team member passes the calendar and colored pencil to the next team member. The game continues as you read aloud the next statement and the next team member writes his answer on the calendar, and so on. The first team returning to the month of January wins the game. Use statements such as the following. (*NOTE:* For false statements, corrections are given here, but students are not required to give corrections in the relay.)

1. **Julius Caesar was born in 100** B.C. *(T)*
2. **At the Tiber River Julius Caesar decided to disobey the Senate and return to Rome with his army.** *(F; Rubicon River)*
3. **Caesar declared himself to be the dictator.** *(F; the Senate)*
4. **Leap year has 366 days.** *(T)*
5. **The year 46** B.C. **lasted 445 days and was called the "year of Caesar."** *(F; "the year of confusion")*
6. **We still use the Julian calendar today.** *(F; the Gregorian calendar)*
7. **Under Caesar's rule, the government no longer belonged to the people.** *(T)*
8. **Brutus and Cassius were two friends who warned Caesar of danger.** *(F; they killed him)*
9. **The ides of March was the name for the fifteenth day of March on the Roman calendar.** *(T)*
10. **The Julian calendar used the names of Roman gods and rulers to name the months.** *(T)*
11. **Caesar unified Rome by promoting citizenship, schools, and libraries.** *(T)*
12. **All Romans liked Caesar and respected his accomplishments.** *(F)*
13. **Pompey originated leap year when he was ruler.** *(F; Caesar)*
14. **Julius Caesar grew up as a poor, uneducated boy.** *(F; a well-educated patrician)*

Survey—Distribute the "Gallons of Water" page to the students. Challenge them to estimate how much water they use each day and to record it on the page. Instruct them to monitor how much water they use during the next twenty-four hours and to place a tally mark in the "occurrences" column to indicate how many times they do each activity. Direct the students to complete and return the survey for the next Heritage Studies lesson.

Going Beyond

□ Enrichment

Creating a calendar—Set up an AREA at the classroom computer with software for designing a calendar. Allow the students to design monthly or yearly calendars.

If your class does not have a computer, printer, or software available, you may provide paper, colored pencils, felt-tip pens, rulers, stencils, and clip art or other art supplies for the students to make their calendars.

□ Additional Teacher Information

Many sayings used in reference to the Romans are still familiar today. William Shakespeare portrays Caesar's conquest for power in the play *Julius Caesar.* You may want to read the following quotations from this play.

> **"Cowards die many times before their deaths, The valiant never taste of death but once."** (Julius Caesar)
> **"Friends, Romans, countrymen, lend me your ears!"** (Mark Antony)

Today the expression "crossing the Rubicon" refers to making a decision that cannot be changed.

Caesar's response to the Senate upon a particular victory was "Veni, vidi, vici," which means "I came, I saw, I conquered."

LESSON 41
Rome:
The Empire

Text, pages 161-64
Notebook, page 45

- **A Man of Many Words**
- **Peace and Prosperity**
- **Life in Rome**
- **A City of Marble**

Preview

□ Objective
Given proper instruction, the students will be able to do the following:
- Complete statements about the Roman Empire.

□ Materials
Have available:
- A Bible.
- "Gallons of Water" survey results from Lesson 40.
- A wall map of the world.
- Maps and More 11, 12, and 13.

Day 73

Lesson

□ Introducing the Lesson
Water survey—Compare the results from the "Gallons of Water" survey assigned in Lesson 40. Call on volunteers to tell how their estimated water use compared to their actual water use. *(Answers will vary.)* Ask the students what activity used the most water. Explain that many people in the world use less than thirteen gallons of water each day. Tell the students that the average daily water use for each person in America is about one hundred gallons. Ask the students how they think the Romans got water to their houses almost two thousand years ago. Explain that this lesson tells about the accomplishments of the Romans during the Roman Empire.

Cicero

Marcus Tullius Cicero was a member of the Roman Senate and a famous orator. He composed over one hundred speeches, all of them known for their exact language, creative descriptions, and clear statements of his ideas.

Cicero was born into a middle-class family of Arpinum, Italy, and received a good education. He studied *rhetoric* (persuasive language), philosophy, and Greek and Latin literature. He became an expert in the Latin language. He even thought of Latin words for technical Greek phrases and ideas.

Cicero became famous as a defense lawyer in Rome. In 63 B.C., he was chosen for the office of consul, Rome's highest elected position. That same year he spared Rome from a military takeover by Lucius Catiline, who wanted to establish a dictatorship.

Cicero was killed by Mark Antony in 43 B.C. because he opposed the heavy government control that Antony wanted to force on Rome. Yet Cicero is still remembered today as one of Rome's greatest patriots, a man who represented the true spirit of its republic.

161

□ Teaching the Lesson
A man of many words—Instruct the students to read page 161 to find out why Marcus Tullius Cicero is remembered. *(His speeches were known for their exact language, creative descriptions, and clear statements of his ideas.)*

Discussion Questions
➤ **What is another name for someone who gives a formal speech?** *(an orator)*
➤ **What is *rhetoric*?** *(persuasive language)*
➤ **How was the study of rhetoric helpful to Cicero?** *(helped him in presenting a case or argument as a defense lawyer, as a Senate member, and as the consul)*
➤ **How did Cicero demonstrate patriotism for Rome?** *(He kept Rome from a military takeover, and he opposed the heavy government control encouraged by Mark Antony.)*

Tell the students that Cicero said an individual must be of good character to make laws, to influence others in the right way, and to be a good orator. Read Psalm 19:14 aloud. Point out that what a person says begins in his mind. Christians should control what they say so that their words please God. (BATs: 3b Mind, 5d Communication)

Rome: The Empire

Caesar's death paved the way for the beginning of Rome's history as an empire. Rome had already conquered many territories and was technically an empire at the time of Caesar. But Rome's new leader, Octavian, was the first to hold the title *imperator,* from which we get our words *empire* and *emperor.*

Octavian, Julius Caesar's adopted son, came to power around 30 B.C., after a fifteen-year struggle with his rivals. He worked to restore honesty, diligence, and respect to the government of Rome. He restored power to the Senate and Tribal Assembly, reserving the office of tribune for himself. He could propose or veto new laws. He also reorganized the army and the governments of Rome's territories. He continued to promote trade and industry and to build roads throughout the empire.

Octavian had complete control of Rome, but he did not call himself a dictator as Caesar had done. He called himself by several different titles. One of these was *Princeps,* meaning "first citizen." Another was *Augustus,* or "revered one." Would you say that he lived up to this title?

Octavian's reign began a period of peace and prosperity that Rome enjoyed for the next two hundred years. This period is called *Pax Romana,* which means "Peace of Rome."

During the Pax Romana, Roman culture was similar to Greek culture in many ways. Like the Greeks, the Romans placed importance on learning, architecture, and religion.

This Roman coin displays the image of Augustus Caesar.

162

Learning in the Pax Romana

During the republic, children had been reared by their mothers. But during the empire period, many wealthy families left this job to *pedagogues.* Both boys and girls received an education outside the home. They studied reading, writing, and mathematics. After mastering these basics, most girls stayed home to learn the art of homemaking, but some studied further with a private tutor.

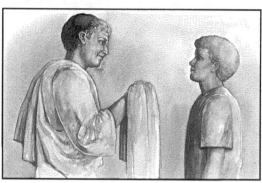

Boys continued their education by studying Greek, Latin, history, geography, astronomy, and literature. At sixteen a boy became a citizen, and a special citizenship ceremony was held at the *Forum,* the Roman marketplace. The boy was given an official citizen's garment—a loose, one-piece robe called a *toga.* He was also given a man's haircut and his first shave.

After becoming citizens, young men continued their studies or entered business or the army. Many Roman adults read a great deal. Some of Rome's best writers lived during Octavian's reign. Virgil wrote the *Aeneid,* an epic about the founding of Rome. Livy wrote a detailed history of Rome, including events from the day in which he lived.

163

Day 74

Peace and prosperity—Instruct the students to read page 162 silently to find out who was the first Roman to have the title *imperator. (Octavian)*

Display Maps and More 11 and a wall map of the world. Point out on Maps and More 11 the area conquered by Rome. Explain that the Roman Empire surrounded the Mediterranean Sea. This vast empire stretched from Britain in the West to areas beyond the eastern city of Jerusalem in Judea. Tell the students that the influence of the Roman culture still exists. Direct attention to the wall map, selecting volunteers to identify the modern countries that were once a part of the Roman Empire. *(Switzerland, France, Spain, Holland, Belgium, and parts of Germany)*

Discussion Questions

➤ **When did Octavian begin his reign of the Roman Empire?** *(around 30 B.C.)*
➤ **What titles did Octavian prefer?** *(Princeps, meaning "first citizen," or Augustus, meaning "revered one")*
➤ **In what two ways did Octavian change the government of Rome?** *(He worked to restore honesty, diligence, and respect; restored power to the Senate and Tribal Assembly; and reorganized the army and the territorial governments.)*
➤ **During what period did the Roman Empire experience peace and prosperity?** *(Pax Romana, Peace of Rome)*

➤ **How long did this peace of Rome last?** *(two hundred years)*

> Point out that knowing Christ as Savior brings everlasting peace. Remind the students that a Christian can also have peace by walking with the Lord daily, praying and focusing on God rather than on problems. (Bible Promise: H. God as Father)

Life in Rome—Instruct the students to read page 163 silently to find out in what way the training of the children was different among the wealthy families during the empire period. *(Pedagogues, not mothers, reared the children.)* Tell the students that the pedagogues of the empire period were well-educated slaves from Greece. Remind the students that the Greeks also had pedagogues, but their duty was to accompany wealthy boys to school to make sure they behaved. Point out that the Romans adopted many ideas from the lands they conquered.

Discussion Questions

➤ **At what age did a boy become a citizen?** *(sixteen)*
➤ **Where was the ceremony held when a boy became a citizen?** *(at the marketplace, called the Forum)*
➤ **What garment did Roman citizens wear?** *(a toga)*
➤ **Who were two of Rome's best writers?** *(Virgil and Livy)*

Architecture in the Pax Romana

Rome's greatest artistic achievements were in architecture. The Romans built for practical purposes rather than beauty, but their works are impressive. Before Octavian died, he claimed that he had found Rome as a city of brick and left it as a city of marble.

Romans were the first to use *concrete*, a mixture of gravel and sand in mortar. Rather than build in solid marble, Romans often built in concrete and covered the structure with a thin layer of marble. Not only did concrete help lower building costs, but it also made Roman structures so durable that many still exist today.

A Roman aqueduct in modern Turkey

After the fall of Rome, the process of making concrete was lost for many centuries. A British engineer rediscovered it in the 1700s. Concrete is widely used today. The sidewalks in your neighborhood are probably made of concrete. What other concrete structures are near you?

The Romans borrowed the idea of the *arch* from the Sumerians. Arches enhance most Roman structures, including temples, houses, and even *aqueducts,* raised troughs that carried water through the city. Sometimes the Romans put several arches back-to-back to make a tunnel called a *barrel vault*. And they were the first to put several arches together to make a *dome*. The largest domed building in Rome was a temple called the *Pantheon*. It still stands in Rome today, with a dome rising fourteen stories high.

A painting by Giovanni Paolo of the interior of the Pantheon

164

Read each sentence. Fill in the blanks with the correct words from the arch.

pedagogues	Pax Romana	Livy
rhetoric	aqueducts	Augustus
Aeneid vault	dome	Forum
concrete		orator
Octavian		Princeps

_____ **orator**   1. Cicero is remembered as a patriot and a famous _____.

_____ **rhetoric**   2. The study of persuasive language is called _____.

_____ **Pax Romana**   3. The period of peace and prosperity in Rome is known as the _____ _____, or the "peace of Rome."

_____ **Octavian**   4. The first leader in Rome with the title of imperator was _____.

_____ **Augustus**   5. A title used by Octavian was _____, which means "revered one."

_____ **pedagogues**   6. Wealthy families had _____ to train the children.

_____ **Forum**   7. The Roman marketplace was called the _____.

_____ **Livy**   8. A detailed history of Rome was written by _____.

_____ **Aeneid**   9. Virgil wrote about the founding of Rome in the _____.

_____ **concrete**   10. Roman structures were durable because they were made of _____.

_____ **dome**   11. A temple called the Pantheon was the largest building to use a _____

_____ **aqueducts**   12. The Romans built _____ to carry water through the city.

© 1998 BJU Press. Reproduction prohibited.

H eritage Studies 6
Student Notebook

Lesson 41
Evaluating the Lesson   **45**

➤ **Which Roman writer told about historical events?** *(Livy)*

Day 75

A city of marble—Instruct the students to read page 164 silently to find the focus of Roman architecture. *(practicality)*

Discussion Questions

➤ **What new building material did the Romans use?** *(concrete)*

➤ **What were two advantages in using concrete?** *(lowered building costs and made structures so durable that many still exist today)*

➤ **How did the Romans carry water through the cities?** *(by using aqueducts)*

➤ **What are some features of Roman architecture?** *(domes, arches, and barrel vaults)*

➤ **What building in Rome uses several arches together to make a dome?** *(Pantheon)*

Display Maps and More 12 and 13. Tell the students that today's architecture reflects the Roman use of concrete, domes, arches, and vaults. Explain that the arch and dome allow vast open areas in buildings as the support rests on the outer walls rather than on inside walls or columns. Point out and identify each example of Roman architectural influence on Maps and More 12 and 13.

☐ Evaluating the Lesson

The Roman Empire (Notebook page 45)—Direct the students to fill in the blanks with the correct words from the arch. Then tell them that they will use Notebook page 45 in the following building relay.

Divide the class into four teams named for cities—Rome, Venice, Florence, and Naples. Instruct each student to take Notebook page 45 with him as he lines up with the other members of his city. Direct each city-team to line up on opposite sides of the classroom. Tell the students that you will read aloud each question in turn from Notebook page 45, calling on a student to give the correct answer aloud. Instruct the students to raise their hands if they have the correct answer written on Notebook page 45. Count and record on the chalkboard the number of students from each city who have the correct answer for each question. When a city's total correct answers equal five, allow a student from that city to draw a brick on the chalkboard to build his city's arch similar to the arch on the Notebook page. Continue this procedure for each question on Notebook page 45. When all of the questions have been answered, the city with the most nearly completed arch wins the relay.

══ Going Beyond ══

□ Enrichment

Search for classical architecture—Set up an art AREA to display pictures of classical architecture. (*NOTE:* The Parthenon in Athens, Greece, and the Pantheon in Rome, Italy, are two examples of classical architecture.) Challenge the students to look in their town or city or neighboring towns or cities for buildings patterned after the classical style. Encourage them to photograph or sketch these buildings for display in the classroom. Label each picture with the name and location of the buildings and the name of the student who brought the sketch or photograph.

□ Additional Teacher Information

The Romans built aqueducts throughout the empire. The open troughs were raised above the ground on bridgelike structures. From its start in the mountains, an aqueduct gradually sloped toward the city, allowing the water to flow downhill. Over two hundred million gallons a day flowed through the aqueducts.

The Colorado River Aqueduct in Southern California is used today to take water to many people in the West and Southwest regions of the United States. Water from the Colorado River travels across the desert and provides water for crop irrigation, recreation, drinking, transportation, and industry.

The best-preserved building of ancient Rome is the Pantheon. Built as a temple for all the gods, the structure combines durability and beauty. The magnificent dome rises 142 feet above the floor and allows light in through a thirty-foot hole at the top. Concrete was poured over a wooden mold to make the dome. The walls of the Pantheon are twenty feet thick to support the weight of the dome. The sixteen supporting columns of the front porch are made of Egyptian granite, and each weighs forty-eight tons. The builders covered much of the concrete with marble. They also made bronze plates to cover the outside of the dome. Today, the Pantheon is a reminder of "the grandeur that was Rome" as well as the Romans' worship of many false gods.

The Forum, or the ancient Roman marketplace, was the center of activity in daily Roman life. Here the laws were discussed and formulated, legal actions were processed, ceremonies were given to present young men their citizenship, and goods were exchanged among merchants and customers. The Forum also served as a meeting place for people to discuss ideas, hear orators, and observe spoils from battles.

Julius Caesar developed the first public library in Rome. The idea then spread across the empire. Earlier libraries had served only an individual or the elite class of society.

Thomas Jefferson was one of many architects influenced by the Italian architect Andrea Palladio. Palladio used the dome and other elements of the classical Roman style. Thomas Jefferson fashioned his home, Monticello, and the buildings for the University of Virginia after the Roman style.

LESSON 42
Religion in Rome

Text, pages 165-68
Notebook, page 46

- ■ Diversity of Religions
- ■ Christ in the Roman World
- ■ Persecution of Christians
- ■ Rome Remembered

━━━━━ **Preview** ━━━━━

□ Objectives

Given proper instruction, the students will be able to do the following:

- • List examples of how the Roman influence exists today.
- • Number in order the stages of Rome's history.

□ Materials

Have available:

- • A Bible for each student and the teacher.
- • A sheet of notebook paper for each student.
- • Maps and More 11.
- • The figure representing the birth of Christ (c. 4 B.C.) from the History TimeLine Packet.
- • The figure representing the fall of Rome (A.D. 476) from the History TimeLine Packet.

Day 76

━━━━━ **Lesson** ━━━━━

□ Introducing the Lesson

Writing about ambitions—Give each student a sheet of notebook paper. Direct him to write the names of *Caesar* and *Paul* along with his own name across the top of the paper. Tell each student to write his three main goals or ambitions below his name. Direct the students to write below Caesar's name what they think motivated Caesar to rule Rome. *(Answers may include the desire for power, fame, or wealth.)* Explain that *ambition* is a strong desire to accomplish something and that ambitions can be good or bad. Select volunteers to read aloud Romans 1:15, Romans 15:20, I Corinthians 1:17, Philippians 3:10, and II Timothy 2:3-4. Instruct the students to write Paul's ambitions on their papers. Explain that Paul's desire was to please Christ, to portray Christ, and to preach the gospel. Point out that much of the New Testament was written during the Romans' rule.

> Remind the students that a Christian tells the message of the gospel by his words and actions. Christians should work with a happy, willing spirit as unto the Lord. (BATs: 2e Work, 2f Enthusiasm, 5c Evangelism and missions)

Religion in the Pax Romana

Like the Greeks, the Romans worshiped many gods. The Roman religion included many of the Greek gods, but the Romans called them by different names. The Romans worshiped with many rituals, offerings, and prayers.

To the Romans, an emperor was like a god. The Romans used the term *Augustus* for their gods, but every emperor during the time of the empire also carried this title. Some emperors demanded that the Roman people worship them.

The Romans accepted other religions from different parts of their empire. Religions from the Far East became popular.

Apollo, Roman god of prophecy, music, medicine, and poetry

Two Greek philosophies were also practiced as religions in Rome. *Epicureanism* was a belief that there is no God, that no life after death exists, and that the present is all that matters. Epicureans lived for pleasure alone and tried to keep their lives happy and free from pain. A very different Greek philosophy was called *Stoicism*. The Stoics believed that duty was all that mattered in life, and they emphasized bravery in battle and obeying laws. Stoicism was popular among the Roman soldiers.

Diana, Apollo's twin, Roman goddess of hunting and childbirth

165

□ Teaching the Lesson

Diversity of religions—Instruct the students to read page 165 silently to find out another way the Romans borrowed from the cultures of the people throughout the empire. *(in religion)*

Discussion Questions

➤ **What were some of the diversities in the religions of the Romans?** *(They worshiped the Greek gods, the emperors, religions from the Far East, and Greek philosophies.)*

➤ **Whom did the Romans follow in their worship of many gods?** *(the Greeks)*

➤ **What title did the Roman emperors use that was also used for the Roman gods?** *(Augustus)*

➤ **What did the Epicureans live for?** *(for pleasure and the present)*

➤ **What religious philosophy appealed to the Roman soldiers?** *(Stoicism)*

➤ **What one word summarizes the belief of Stoicism?** *(duty)*

> Point out that the Romans did not acknowledge the one true God. Today many people have similar attitudes to those of the Epicureans. They seek pleasure and have no hope. In contrast to this lifestyle, the Christian has the blessed hope of Christ's return and eternal life with Him (Titus 2:13). (BAT: 1c Separation from the world)

Christ in the Roman World

"But when the fulness of the time was come, God sent forth his Son, made of a woman, made under the law."
Galatians 4:4

What would you say is the most important event in all of human history? That question has only one true answer. The most important event took place during the Pax Romana. Christ was born into the world, lived, and died for the sins of all mankind.

God chose the Pax Romana as His perfect time for Jesus Christ to live on earth. His birth in Bethlehem instead of Joseph's home city of Nazareth was the result of Caesar Augustus's decree that everyone in the Roman Empire return to his birthplace to be taxed. God used this decree to fulfill the prophecy in Micah 5:2 that the Messiah would be born in Bethlehem.

During his life, Christ supported the Roman government by paying the required tax to Caesar. He encouraged the other Jews to do the same (Matthew 22:21).

The method of Christ's death reflected the era in which He lived. After His trials, he was condemned to death by crucifixion, a typical Roman means of execution. In this way God fulfilled Christ's words that the Messiah would be "lifted up" in death (John 12:32) and the Old Testament prophecy that none of His bones would be broken (Psalm 34:20).

Il Sodoma, Procession to Calvary, The Bob Jones University Collection

166

After Christ's death, His followers throughout the Roman Empire were hated. One Roman emperor, Nero, blamed the Christians for starting a fire that destroyed nearly two-thirds of the city of Rome. Without enough evidence to convict them, he ordered many Christians to be put to death by crucifixion or burning.

Through the empire's remaining years, the Romans continued to persecute and torture Christians in cruel ways. Because there was not enough work for everyone in Rome, the people had plenty of time for leisure activities, such as feasts, circuses, and the theater. Another favorite pastime was held in large arenas, such as the Colosseum. There Roman citizens would watch men called gladiators fight other men or animals to the death. During the reign of the emperor Diocletian, Christians, rather than *gladiators*, were released into the arena to be killed by lions.

Do you think these persecutions caused Christians to give up their faith? The Christians became even more determined to follow Christ when they saw the courage of others. They held secret worship services in underground tombs called *catacombs* and spoke out boldly when questioned about their faith in Christ.

"Blessed are ye, when men shall revile you, and persecute you, and shall say all manner of evil against you falsely, for my sake. Rejoice, and be exceeding glad: for great is your reward in heaven: for so persecuted they the prophets which were before you."
Matthew 5:11-12

Colosseum

Catacombs

167

Day 77

Christ in the Roman world—Instruct the students to read page 166 to find out what the most important event in all of human history was. *(Christ's life)* Add the figure representing the birth of Christ to the History TimeLine at approximately 4 B.C. Call on a student to write today's date with the year on the chalkboard. Point out that we recognize the fact of Christ's birth each time we write the date.

Remind the students that the system for numbering years from the birth of Christ began nearly fifteen hundred years ago. Point to the abbreviations B.C. and A.D. on the History TimeLine. Ask the students which abbreviation is used for the years *before Christ. (B.C.)* Ask the students when to use the abbreviation A.D. *(for years after Christ's birth)* Point out that A.D. stands for *anno Domini* which is Latin for "in the year of the Lord." Write the dates 753 B.C. and A.D. 476 on the chalkboard. Point out that B.C. is written *after* the year while A.D. is written *before* the year and that we usually include A.D. only when it is needed to avoid confusion. Explain that at the time of Christ's birth the Romans numbered the years from the founding of Rome.

Discussion Questions

➤ **During what period did Jesus Christ live on the earth?** *(during the Pax Romana, or the peace of Rome)*

➤ **How did Christ show he was supportive of the Roman government?** *(by paying the required tax to Caesar)*

➤ **What is the significance of Jesus' birth in Bethlehem?** *(It was the fulfillment of the prophecy that the Messiah would be born in Bethlehem.)*

➤ **What method of Roman execution was used to put Christ to death?** *(crucifixion)*

➤ **Why did Jesus Christ come to earth?** *(to die for the sins of mankind)*

Read I John 4:14-15 aloud. Tell the students that Jesus is the Son of God and that He was a willing sacrifice for the sins of each individual. Point out the TimeLine figure representing the crucifixion of Christ at A.D. 30. Explain that when a person repents and asks Jesus to be his Savior, he has the promise of eternal life. Point out that although the world was at peace under Rome's rule, men's hearts could not be at peace with God unless Christ died to provide a way of salvation. (BATs: 1a Understanding Jesus Christ, 1b Repentance and faith; Bible Promise: E. Christ as Sacrifice)

Persecution of Christians—Instruct the students to read page 167 silently to find out how Christ's followers were treated in the Roman Empire after His death. *(They were hated, persecuted, and tortured.)*

In A.D. 286, Diocletian decided that the Roman Empire was too large to be ruled by one man. He divided the empire in half, keeping the eastern part under his own control and appointing another ruler for the western part. He eventually appointed assistant rulers for each half, further dividing his power.

Later in Diocletian's reign, a struggle for power began and turned into civil war in the empire. The Pax Romana was only a memory. Soon the Roman Empire itself would collapse and fall to invading tribes from the north.

We remember Greece for its glory—its beautiful artwork, its elegant poetry, its athletic grace. But how do we remember the civilization of Rome? We uphold Rome for its practicality and its power. Massive domes, arched aqueducts, grand road systems, brave legionaries, and fiery patriots who lived and died for the republic—these are the things we think of when we remember Rome.

168

Discussion Questions

➤ **What two Roman emperors were especially known for their cruel treatment of Christians?** *(Nero, Diocletian)*

➤ **Why do you think the Christians were disliked?** *(Answers will vary but may include that they were different; they did not worship the gods and emperors; they told of man's sin and God's judgment for sin; emperors thought they were a threat to the empire, and wicked men hated God.)*

➤ **What were the gladiator contests?** *(Men fought other men or animals in an arena as other people watched.)*

➤ **Why did the people of Rome at this time seek amusements such as feasts, circuses, the theater, and gladiator contests?** *(There was not enough work in Rome.)*

➤ **What were the *catacombs*?** *(underground tombs where Christians held worship services)*

➤ **How did Christians react to the persecutions?** *(They held services in the catacombs and spoke boldly.)*

Read aloud the verses on page 167. Remind the students that Christians should not fear when they remember the importance and privilege of sharing Christ with others (Rom. 1:16, II Tim. 1:7-9). Point out that it is God's power that works in the heart of a person to bring him to salvation. (BAT: 8d Courage)

Day 78

Rome remembered—Instruct the students to read page 168 silently to find out what caused the end of the Pax Romana. *(civil war)*

Discussion Questions

➤ **Why did Diocletian divide the Roman Empire?** *(It was too large for one man to rule.)*

➤ **What specific accomplishments of the Romans were significant?** *(domes, aqueducts, road system, disciplined soldiers, patriots)*

➤ **What part of the divided empire did Diocletian rule?** *(eastern)*

Display Maps and More 11. Point out the dividing line between the western empire and the eastern empire on the the inset map, explaining that the western empire was conquered by invaders in A.D. 476, shortly after the division of the empire, while the eastern part remained until A.D. 1453. (*NOTE:* Diocletian eventually chose assistant rulers, or prefects, to govern each of the subdivisions of the empire. Point these out on Maps and More 11 inset map.) Add the figure representing the fall of Rome to the History TimeLine at the year A.D. 476. Tell the students that the republic of Rome lasted almost five hundred years but that the Roman Empire lasted over five hundred years. Ask the students how many years passed from the founding of Rome to the collapse of the Roman Empire. *(753+476=1229 years)*

Reflections of Rome

Name _____

Number in order the stages of Rome's history.

_1_   Rome is a city ruled by the Etruscan king Tarquin the Proud.

_6_   Diocletian divides the Roman Empire.

_4_   Christ was born into the world, lived a sinless life, and then died for the sins of all mankind.

_3_   Octavian's reign begins the Pax Romana, or the "peace of Rome."

_5_   Christians are persecuted by Nero.

_7_   The Roman Empire falls when conquered by invading tribes from the north.

_2_   Julius Caesar is proclaimed dictator by the Senate.

ITALY

Write five examples of how the Roman influence still exists today.

1. *Possible answers include language, architecture (dome, arch), republican form of government, roads, calendar adjustment, spread of the gospel, concrete,*

2. *laws, veto power, rhetoric, coins with Latin phrases, and Roman numerals.*

3. _____

4. _____

5. _____

Heritage Studies 6
Student Notebook

Lesson 42
Evaluating the Lesson   **46**

□ Evaluating the Lesson

Reflections of Rome (Notebook page 46)—Direct the students to number in order the stages of Rome's history. Then tell them to list five examples to show that the Roman influence still exists today.

━━━ Going Beyond ━━━

□ Enrichment

Story illustrations—Set up an AREA with drawing paper, colored pencils, and felt-tip pens. You may also include fabric scraps, buttons, and yarn. Instruct each student to illustrate his favorite story from the New Testament. You may extend this activity as you display the pictures and choose volunteers to tell the story to a group of children or to portray the story with charades.

Summary writings—Set up an AREA with a boot-shaped outline of Italy for each student. (*NOTE:* See the reproducible material at the end of this lesson.) Direct the students to write inside the outline what interested them most about the Romans.

□ Additional Teacher Information

Many reasons are given for the fall of Rome. However, it is clear that internal turmoil preceded the outward destruction of the Roman Empire. Within Rome a power struggle among the leaders allowed the army leaders to gain strength. Yet the army could not provide order and stability either. The government required heavy taxes to provide food, amusements, and military strength for the people. The people became apathetic about participating in the government and turned to the pursuit of pleasure. Eventually the Roman Empire experienced social, economic, political, and moral collapse.

The date for the fall of Rome is usually given as A.D. 476, when invading tribes conquered Rome. The Eastern Roman Empire continued as the Byzantine Empire until 1453. Constantinople, named by the Roman emperor Constantine, became the capital of the new empire.

The *Colosseum* was a famous arena used for amusements in Rome. This oval-shaped building was four stories high and held fifty thousand people. The people gathered here for games, contests, circuses, and other events. The Colosseum floor could also be flooded for performing mock sea battles. Now only a shell of the original building, the Colosseum depicts the durability of the Roman architectural ability.

The catacombs provided an effective place of refuge for the persecuted Christians because the Romans respected burial places. Many paintings and symbols of the early Christians have been found on the walls.

Stand Up, Stand Up for Jesus

Stand up, stand up for Jesus,
Ye soldiers of the cross;
Lift high His royal banner,
It must not suffer loss.
From victory unto victory,
His army shall He lead,
Till every foe is vanquished
And Christ is Lord indeed.

Stand up, stand up for Jesus,
The trumpet call obey;
Forth to the mighty conflict,
In this His glorious day.
"Ye that are men now serve Him"
Against unnumbered foes;
Let courage rise with danger
And strength to strength oppose.

Stand up, stand up for Jesus,
The strife will not be long;
This day the noise of battle,
The next, the victor's song.
To him that overcometh
A crown of life shall be;
He with the King of glory
Shall reign eternally.

Refrain

Stand up, stand up for Jesus,
Ye soldiers of the cross;
Lift high His royal banner,
It must not suffer loss.

Use with Lesson 38.

Senate	Assembly ✳	Assembly
Senate	Assembly	Assembly
Senate	Assembly	Assembly
Senate	Assembly ✳	Assembly
Senate	Assembly	Assembly
Senate	Assembly	Assembly

Do You Know?

1. How many stars are on the American flag?

2. What document provides the plan for the government of the United States?

3. What date marks the celebration of the independence, or birthday, of the United States?

4. Who currently holds the office of president of the United States?

5. What is the capital of the United States?

6. How many senators does each state elect to Congress?

7. Who is your district's representative (or congressman) in Congress?

8. What is a change to the Constitution called?

9. Who is given the privilege to vote in the United States?

10. Who was the first president of the United States?

11. What document declared freedom for Americans in 1776?

12. How does a person become a citizen of the United States?

13. In which war did the United States win independence from Great Britain?

14. What were the original thirteen states?

15. Is a member of the House of Representatives in Congress elected to serve for two, four, or six years?

16. Who came to America on the ship called the *Mayflower?*

17. In what year is the next presidential election in the United States?

18. What is the highest court in the United States?

19. What is the minimum age required for a person to vote in the United States?

20. Who is the chief justice of the Supreme Court?

Citizenship

1. **Who is a citizen of the United States? Check each statement that applies to you.**

   ____ I am a citizen of the United States.

   ____ I was born in the United States.

   ____ My parents are United States citizens.

   ____ I am a citizen of another country.

2. **Read about naturalization.**

   An individual may apply for citizenship by naturalization if he or she—
   —is at least eighteen years old,
   —has resided for five years in the state where he or she is applying,
   —exemplifies good character, and
   —possesses the ability to speak, read, and write English.

   The process of naturalization involves taking a test, completing a form (petition), paying a fee, appearing before a judge, taking the oath of allegiance for naturalization, and receiving a certificate.

3. **List some of the responsibilities of a U.S. citizen.**

   a. _____

   b. _____

   c. _____

   d. _____

   e. _____

   f. _____

   g. _____

4. **Read about some amendments to the Constitution that speak about citizenship.**

   • Citizenship is defined by the *Fourteenth Amendment.*

   • The *Fifteenth Amendment* says that a citizen may vote regardless of his race, color, or former servitude.

   • The *Nineteenth Amendment* grants women the right to vote.

   • Paying a tax is no longer a requirement for voting because of the *Twenty-fourth Amendment.*

   • The *Twenty-sixth Amendment* states that a citizen must be at least eighteen years old to vote.

The Romans Road

Romans 3:10

Romans 3:23

Romans 5:12

Romans 6:23

Romans 5:8

Romans 10:9-13

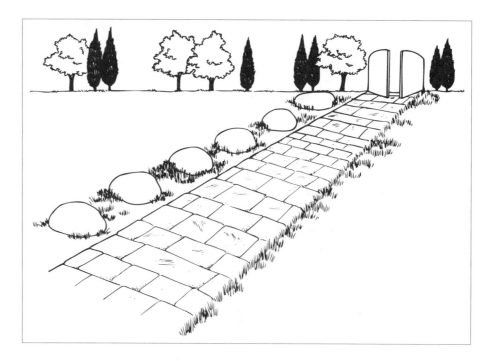

Which Way?

Put a check mark by the statements that show God's plan of salvation.

____ 1. I am a sinner.

____ 2. I will accept Christ as my Savior later.

____ 3. The penalty for sin is death.

____ 4. My good works are enough to get me to heaven.

____ 5. I must repent of my sins, believe that Jesus died and rose again, and ask Him into my heart.

____ 6. I do not deserve punishment.

____ 7. Jesus did not have to die.

____ 8. I am not that bad.

____ 9. Christ died for my sins so that I would not have to die.

____ 10. I must confess to others that I have accepted Jesus.

Gallons of Water

I estimate my daily water use is _____ gallons of water.

Record a tally mark in the "occurrences" column to show how many times you do each activity. Multiply the number of occurrences by the gallons to find the total gallons used.

Activity	Today occurrences × gallons =		
washing hands		0.25	
washing face		2	
flushing toilet		5	
showering		30	
taking a bath		40	
brushing teeth		1	
washing car		20	
washing dishes—by hand		10	
washing dishes—by machine		15	
washing laundry (one load)		30	
watering lawn (30 minutes)		240	
drinking water		0.1	
		Total	

Predict how much water you need for a week and for a month.

My projected water use for *one week* is _____ gallons.

I think I will use _____ gallons of water in *one month*.

Bonus question: How much water will *your family* use in the coming month?

_____ gallons

Read John 4:13-14. What did Jesus say to the woman about the water from the well?

_____

_____

Use with Lesson 42.

Of Jade and Stone: Ancient Mayas

This chapter carries the students back into the mysterious world of the ancient Mayas, one of the earliest Native American peoples. Students will discover the origins of a favorite modern drink—hot chocolate—and study an ancient ball game called pok-to-pok, which combined elements of several of today's popular sports. They will marvel at the Mayas' achievements in art, astronomy, and architecture. They will also learn about the strange Mayan ideal of beauty and the superstition that pervaded the Mayan way of life. Enrichment activities give the students opportunities to sample Mayan food and make accordion-fold books similar to Mayan codices. The *Discovering How* activity in Lesson 48 offers Heritage Studies partners the experience of studying Mayan archaeological finds and compiling observation notebooks. Although little is known about the exact religious practices of the Mayas, the evil, ritualistic nature of their worship is soberingly evident. This chapter emphasizes primarily the artistic and scholarly accomplishments of the Mayan society. Yet, as the students acquire appreciation for the rich culture of this land of jade and stone, they will also be asked to evaluate Mayan ideals and beliefs from a biblical perspective.

□ Materials

Lessons 43 and 45 require certain items that must be obtained or prepared several days to several weeks before the presentation of the lessons. These items are labeled with an asterisk (*) in each lesson and in the Materials List in the Supplement. Occasionally, items not commonly found in the classroom as well as items needed in large quantities may also be labeled with an asterisk. For specific information, see the individual lessons.

□ Chapter Bulletin Board

Affix the Mayan map from Maps and More 14 to the center of the bulletin board beneath the title *A Land of Jade and Stone*. Prepare the Mayan map and the figures of Mayan culture and architecture from Maps and More 14, 15, and 16 by cutting apart the charts and arranging them on the bulletin board.

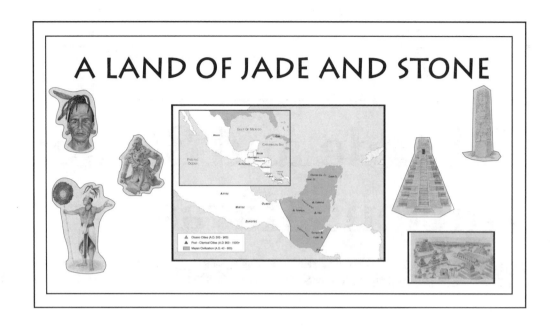

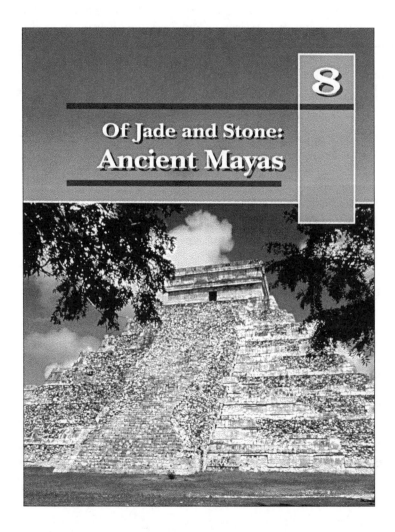

LESSON 43
A People with Taste and Talent

Text, pages 170-72
Notebook, page 47

- The Mayas and Their Inventions
- The Desire for Chocolate
- Mayan Eras

━━━ Preview ━━━

☐ Objectives

Given proper instruction, the students will be able to do the following:

- Determine whether sentences about the Mayas are true or false.
- Correct false information about the Mayas.

☐ Materials

Have available:

- Maps and More 14, 15, and 16.
- 25-30 cups of water.*
- A large, electric coffee urn (25-30 cups).*
- A Styrofoam cup for each student.*
- A plastic spoon for each student.*
- A packet of hot-chocolate mix for each student.*
- The figure of the Olmecs (3500 B.C.) from the History TimeLine Packet.
- The figure of Christopher Columbus (A.D. 1492) from the History TimeLine Packet.

Prepare water for hot chocolate by heating it in the urn.

Day 79

━━━ Lesson ━━━

☐ Introducing the Lesson

A special Mayan invention—Invite each student to tell what his favorite dessert is. Every time someone mentions the word *chocolate* or something made of chocolate (e.g., fudge, brownies) put a tally on the chalkboard. Count the tallies to see how popular chocolate is in your classroom. Ask the students how far back in history they think people have been enjoying chocolate. Give each student a cup of hot water, a packet of hot-chocolate mix, and a plastic spoon. While they are preparing and drinking their hot chocolate, explain that this drink was invented by an ancient Indian people called the Mayas, who lived several thousands of years before Christ. Allow the students to continue drinking their hot chocolate as you teach this lesson.

The Other Side of the World

Thousands of miles from Rome and Greece, there lived a people in what is now part of Mexico and Central America. They were accomplished artists, mathematicians, and builders. Their huge civilization was a secret from Europe until Columbus met one of their sailors on his voyage to the Americas. Even then, it was years before a European saw their cities. They were the Mayas, the dominant culture in the ancient Americas.

Mayan Inventions

Is there a zero in your telephone number or your street address? The ancient Mayas developed the idea of zero, an abstract idea that even the Greeks and Romans did not know about. The Babylonians and the Hindus of India also invented a zero, but the Europeans did not use the number until hundreds of years later. With their zero, the Mayas were able to do difficult calculations and keep detailed records.

Mayan Numbers 0–20

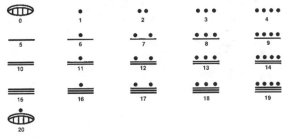

The Mayas also made calendars based on the cycles of the moon and the sun. Their solar year had the same number of days that ours does. The Mayas made their calendars after years of careful sky watching. Their observations were so accurate that they figured out the orbits of the planets and could predict an eclipse of the sun.

170

☐ Teaching the Lesson

The Mayas and their inventions—Instruct the students to read page 170 silently to find out where the Mayas lived. *(in what is now part of Mexico and Central America)*

Call the students' attention to Maps and More 14, displayed on the bulletin board. Point out the location of the Mayan area on the inset map. Ask the students what direction from the United States the Mayan civilization was located. *(south)* Ask the students what countries now make up what once was the Mayan area. *(parts of present-day Mexico, Guatemala, Honduras, and El Salvador and all of Belize)* Direct the students' attention to the enlargement of the Mayan civilization, pointing out the divisions between the Lowland Maya and the Highland Maya. Explain that the Highland Maya was located in the mountains.

Discussion Questions

➤ **How did Europe find out about this ancient civilization?** *(Columbus met one of their sailors on his voyage to the Americas.)*

Add the figure of Columbus to the History TimeLine at A.D. 1492.

➤ **What important mathematical accomplishment did the Mayas make?** *(They invented the idea of zero.)*
➤ **What did the zero enable the Mayas to do?** *(do difficult calculations and keep detailed records)*
➤ **What was another important Mayan invention?** *(a calendar)*

ECHOES FROM THE PAST

The Desire for Chocolate

Do you like hot chocolate? Many people do. It is a tasty "echo" from the tables of Mayan kings and noblemen. The Mayas invented the drink that, with some variations, has been popular for centuries. The Mayas made their hot drink from powdered cocoa beans.

Chocolate was so special to the Mayas that the cocoa beans were also used for money. In the Mayan society, a slave was worth one hundred cocoa beans. Because cocoa beans were so valuable, counterfeiters sometimes filled empty bean shells with dirt or sand and passed them off as real beans. If caught, the counterfeiter was made a slave. Poor people could rarely afford the extravagance of grinding up their money to make a hot drink.

Cocoa beans growing on the tree (above) and being harvested (left)

171

Mayan Eras

As early as 6000 B.C., groups of people in the Valley of Mexico and lands east had turned from hunting for food to growing squash and other foods. Some were growing cotton. By 3500 B.C., farming villages were planting corn and other crops as well. At this early date, there are mysterious evidences of an amazing civilization called the Olmecs. Six-foot stone sculptures of the heads of kings have been found scattered throughout the jungle. But little else is known about these people.

The earliest traces archaeologists have found of Mayan-speaking villages date from 2500 B.C. These villages contained groups of houses surrounded by fields. Some places had public buildings, possibly for religious and government reasons.

For twenty-five centuries the Mayas made farms and homes in the jungles, rain forests, and high plateaus. The Mayas prospered; the population increased. Villages grew large, containing many families and extended families. People spent more time building and decorating their houses; they built more and more public buildings. By A.D. 250, these people dominated the region. Instead of villages, they built complex cities.

Olmec head statue

172

➤ **How was the Mayan calendar like ours today?** *(It had the same number of days; it was based on the cycles of the moon and the sun.)*

➤ **What other observations did the Mayas make about astronomy?** *(They figured out the orbits of the planets and could predict an eclipse of the sun.)*

Day 80

The desire for chocolate—Instruct the students to read page 171 silently to find out what the Mayas used to make the first hot chocolate. *(powdered cocoa beans)*

Discussion Questions

➤ **What else did the Mayas use cocoa beans for?** *(money)*

➤ **How many cocoa beans did a slave cost?** *(one hundred)*

➤ **How did some people attempt to counterfeit cocoa beans, and what was their punishment?** *(They filled the empty shells with dirt or sand; they would be made a slave if caught.)*

➤ **Why could only rich people afford to drink hot chocolate regularly?** *(Only they could afford to grind up their money to make a drink.)*

➤ **Would you like to have a money system like the Mayas did?** *(Answers will vary.)*

Point out that the Mayas, who did not have the Bible, knew that cheating and deceit were wrong. Emphasize that even ancient people who did not know the true God recognized sin and knew that it deserved punishment. Remind the students of the reality of the sin nature and the need for God's forgiveness. (BATs: 6d Clear conscience, 6e Forgiveness)

Mayan eras—Instruct the students to read page 172 silently to find out how many years before Christ people were living in the Valley of Mexico. *(six thousand)*

Discussion Questions

➤ **What kinds of crops did these people grow?** *(squash, cotton)*

➤ **What civilization was thriving there around 3500 B.C.?** *(the Olmecs)*

➤ **What evidence do we have that the Olmecs existed?** *(large stone sculptures of the heads of their kings)*

Add the figure of the Olmecs to the History TimeLine at 3500 B.C. On Maps and More 14 point out the area where the Olmecs lived.

➤ **From what year do archaeologists trace the first Mayan-speaking villages?** *(2500 B.C.)*

➤ **By what year were the Mayas building complex cities instead of villages?** *(A.D. 250)*

True or False?

Name _____

Write *T* if the sentence is true; write *F* if the sentence is false. For each false sentence, write a corrected statement in the blank.

Wording may vary.

F 1. The Mayas lived in what is now Mexico and North America. *The Mayas lived in what is now Mexico and Central America.*

T 2. The Mayas were talented artists and builders. _____

F 3. Vasco da Gama was the first European to meet a Maya. *Columbus was the first European to meet a Maya.*

T 4. The Mayas developed the idea of zero. _____

T 5. The Mayas based their calendars on the cycles of the sun and moon. _____

F 6. Hot chocolate was a popular drink among the poor Mayas. *Hot chocolate was a popular drink among the rich.*

T 7. Cocoa beans were used to buy slaves. _____

F 8. Anyone who tried to counterfeit cocoa beans was put into prison. *Anyone who tried to counterfeit cocoa beans was made a slave.*

F 9. People lived in the Valley of Mexico as early as 8000 B.C. *People lived in the Valley of Mexico as early as 6000 B.C.*

F 10. The Mayas began building large cities around 2500 B.C. *The Mayas began building villages around 2500 B.C.*

□ Evaluating the Lesson

True or False? (Notebook page 47)—Tell the students to write a *T* if the sentence is true and an *F* if the sentence is false. Then tell them to correct each false sentence by writing a corrected statement in the blank.

——— Going Beyond ———

□ Enrichment

Observing the moon—Set up an AREA with books about the moon and a moon observation sheet for each student. (*NOTE:* See the reproducible material at the end of Lesson 48.) Remind the students that the Mayas were careful astronomers, basing their calendar on their observations of the sun and moon. Encourage the students to observe the moon for five days and to draw the moon's shape in the box for each night that they see it. (*NOTE:* Give the students about two weeks to complete this project. They might have difficulty observing the moon for five consecutive days because of weather conditions or their location.)

□ Additional Teacher Information

The name *Olmecs* means "the rubber people." The Olmecs are thought to have been neighbors of the Mayas and to have had some contact with them. It is not likely that they were on friendly terms with the Mayas. Archaeological studies have shown that the Olmecs were highly advanced in art, language, and mathematics. They probably developed many of the hieroglyphs later used by the Mayas.

Nearly all that is known of the Olmec civilization today comes from the artifacts they left behind. Terra cotta pottery, sculptures, and large basalt monuments reveal the Olmecs' artistic skill. Many of these sculptures and masks depict jaguars. The jaguar was probably an important creature in ancient Olmec mythology.

LESSON 44
Mayan Mysteries

Text, pages 173-76
Notebook, page 48

- Then and Now
- Mayan Legacies
- Mayan Books

Preview

□ Objective

Given proper instruction, the students will be able to do the following:

- Recognize incorrect answers to questions about the Mayas.

□ Materials

Have available:

- The figure representing the empty Mayan cities (A.D. 900) from the History TimeLine Packet.
- Maps and More 14.

Day 81

Lesson

□ Introducing the Lesson

Word association—Instruct the students to listen to the words that you are about to say. Tell them to say the first word that comes to mind when they hear that word. (*NOTE:* As an example, explain that if you say the word *cold,* someone might think of *ice cream,* while someone else might think of *winter.*) Say the following words, calling on two or three volunteers to respond after each one: *writer, artist, musician, architect, astronomer, mathematician, athlete, builder.*

When the activity is finished, point out that each of these words are associated with one word: *Maya.* The Mayas were skilled in each of these areas, as the students will see in this lesson.

◆ THEN AND NOW ◆

Mayan Lands

Location—125,000 square miles of Mexico and Central America contain much of what we recognize as ancient Mayan land.

Topography—The Yucatán Peninsula is a lowland with thin soil; the central Mayan lands are mainly rain forest; the southernmost land rises into mountains and plateaus.

Climate—The northern part of the Yucatán Peninsula is dry, receiving only 51 to 102 centimeters (20 to 40 inches) of rain per year. The southern part receives more. The temperatures in the peninsula range from 68°F to over 86°F. Lands farther south have temperatures averaging around 80°F and receive almost daily rain. The mountains in the southernmost region have a mild climate and get 51 to 76 centimeters (20 to 30 inches) of rain per year.

Natural Resources—The rain forest and highlands of the area offer rich sources of lumber and good places to grow coffee, cotton, rubber trees, spices, and bananas, among many other things. The northern part of the area provides the right conditions for growing cocoa, sugar cane, and other crops. Many minerals, natural lakes, and rivers can be found throughout the region.

Geography and Culture—The varied climate and topography allowed the people to develop many crops and eventually to establish large cities. The cities became the cultural centers of Mayan society. Today most people in the area are descendants of the Mayas.

173

□ Teaching the Lesson

Then and Now—Instruct the students to read page 173 silently to find out what kinds of crops are grown in the Mayan region. *(coffee, cotton, rubber trees, spices, bananas, cocoa, sugar cane)* Ask the students what the cultural centers of Mayan society were. *(cities)* Direct the students' attention to the Then and Now map, noting ancient cities, changes in boundary lines, and so on.

Mayan legacies—Instruct the students to read page 174 silently to discover in which three fields the Mayas made great advances. *(art, architecture, and literature)*

Discussion Questions

➤ **Name some of the activities which the Mayas spent their time doing.** *(writing books, sculpting, building palaces and temples, building irrigation systems, studying the stars, composing music, playing games, trading)*

➤ **What legacies have the Mayas left as evidence of their involvement in these activities?** *(ruins of buildings and statues, roads, music, irrigation systems, ball courts)*

➤ **Which important Mayan artifacts have been almost entirely lost?** *(their books)*

➤ **What makes books so important to our knowledge of the Mayas?** *(The books tell how the Mayas lived and thought.)*

Mayan ruins, Uxmal, Mexico (above and below)

Between A.D. 250 and 900, the Mayas made great advances in art, architecture, and literature. For six centuries, the Mayas wrote hundreds of books, made thousands of sculptures, constructed huge palaces and temples, built irrigation systems for their fields, studied the stars, composed music and songs, and played games. They traded regularly within the network of their own cities and with other peoples.

Today many of the buildings and statues lie in ruins. The roads the traders used can still be seen, and the music is still played by Mayan descendants. Irrigation systems lie unused; ball courts are waiting for players. But almost all the Mayan books are gone, and with them, much information about how the Mayas really lived and thought.

174

◆ THINGS PEOPLE DID ◆

Writing Books

Unlike any other people in the ancient Americas, the Mayas had a way of writing *sounds,* not just making pictures of objects or ideas. Thus, anything that could be spoken could also be written. Why is this ability significant? There is no limit to the amount or kind of information that can be recorded.

Furthermore, the Mayas made books of their writings. They wrote on long strips of bark from wild fig trees. To make this "paper," the Mayas pulled bark off the fig trees and soaked it in water to remove the sap, and then they beat the strips with ridged wooden hammers. In two or three days, the fibers in the bark stretched out, making a wide, flat surface. This material was then cut into strips about eight inches wide and up to several yards long.

The strips were coated for strength with a thin layer of a gummy substance and then painted over with lime to make a white surface. Scribes then wrote and drew on the paper with paints made from vegetables and minerals. When the strips were dry, they were folded in an accordion fashion and bound between wooden covers.

175

Point out that reading a book can tell a person how the author thinks. Point out that the Bible is vitally important to a Christian's knowledge of God. Encourage each student to have a personal time of studying the Bible every day. (BATs: 6a Bible study, 8b Faith in the power of the Word of God)

Day 82

Mayan books—Instruct the students to read page 175 silently to find out how the writing of the Mayas was different from that of the other peoples in ancient America. *(The Mayas had a way of writing sounds, instead of just making pictures of objects or ideas.)*

Discussion Questions

➤ **What did the Mayas use as paper?** *(long strips of bark from wild fig trees)*
➤ **How did they flatten the bark to make it a good surface on which to write?** *(After soaking it to remove the sap, they beat it with wooden hammers until its fibers stretched out.)*

➤ **What further treatment did the Mayas give these strips before writing on them?** *(They were coated with a gummy substance to strengthen them and then painted with lime to make them white.)*
➤ **What did the scribes use to write in the books?** *(paints made from vegetables and minerals)*

Instruct the students to read page 176 silently to find out how many Mayan books are in existence today. *(three)*

Discussion Questions

➤ **Describe what one of these books is about.** *(observations about the planet Venus and charts used to predict solar eclipses)*
➤ **What is the biggest Mayan mystery of all?** *(why the Mayas fled their cities around A.D. 900 and never returned)*

Add the figure representing the empty Mayan cities to the History TimeLine at A.D. 900. Draw attention to Maps and More 14 on the bulletin board, pointing out the Mayan cities in the north and telling the students that these were some of the early cities that the people fled.

Today only three Mayan books are known to exist. One is almost complete; it contains observations about the planet Venus and charts used to predict solar eclipses. But it does not tell anything about Mayan customs or history. Nor does it give any clues to the biggest Mayan mystery of all.

Mayan temple, Edzná, Mexico

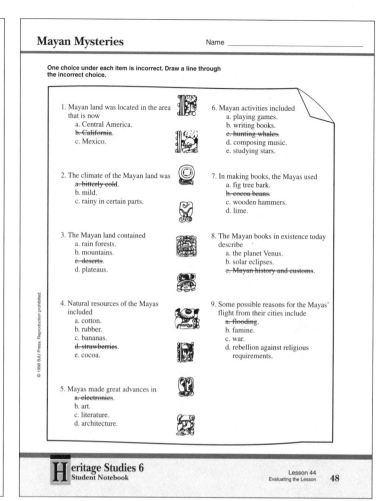

Around A.D. 900, the Mayas seem to have fled their cities. There are no carvings with dates after A.D. 889. No one knows what happened. Many places seem to have been left in a hurry. And the belongings left behind suggest that the people meant to return. But they never did—at least not to rebuild. For six hundred years, they lived in other cities and places, never regaining their former power.

Some archaeologists believe that a famine drove the people away. Others think that war may have ended the great civilization. Still others think that the way of life in Mayan cities—full of rituals and religious superstitions—may have caused the people to rebel. Perhaps a combination of all these reasons brought the society down.

176

One choice under each item is incorrect. Draw a line through the incorrect choice.

1. Mayan land was located in the area that is now
   a. Central America.
   b. California.
   c. Mexico.

2. The climate of the Mayan land was
   a. bitterly cold.
   b. mild.
   c. rainy in certain parts.

3. The Mayan land contained
   a. rain forests.
   b. mountains.
   c. deserts.
   d. plateaus.

4. Natural resources of the Mayas included
   a. cotton.
   b. rubber.
   c. bananas.
   d. strawberries.
   e. cocoa.

5. Mayas made great advances in
   a. electronics.
   b. art.
   c. literature.
   d. architecture.

6. Mayan activities included
   a. playing games.
   b. writing books.
   c. hunting whales.
   d. composing music.
   e. studying stars.

7. In making books, the Mayas used
   a. fig tree bark.
   b. cocoa beans.
   c. wooden hammers.
   d. lime.

8. The Mayan books in existence today describe
   a. the planet Venus.
   b. solar eclipses.
   c. Mayan history and customs.

9. Some possible reasons for the Mayas' flight from their cities include
   a. flooding.
   b. famine.
   c. war.
   d. rebellion against religious requirements.

© 1998 BJU Press. Reproduction prohibited.

Heritage Studies 6
Student Notebook

Lesson 44
Evaluating the Lesson   **48**

Discussion Questions

➤ **What evidence suggests that the Mayas meant to return to their homes?** *(They seem to have left in a hurry; they left belongings behind.)*

➤ **What reasons have been suggested for the Mayas' flight?** *(famine, war, rebellion against religion and superstition)*

➤ **What are other reasons that the Mayas might have fled?** *(Answers will vary.)*

➤ **Which reason seems most sensible to you?** *(Answers will vary.)*

☐ Evaluating the Lesson

Mayan Mysteries (Notebook page 48)—Tell the students that one choice under each item is incorrect. Instruct them to draw a line through each incorrect choice.

——— Going Beyond ———

☐ Enrichment

Making Mayan books—Set up an AREA with an ample supply of pencils, felt-tip pens, tape, scissors, glue, white paper cut into foot-long, 3-inch-wide strips, wrapping paper of various colors, and 4-inch squares of cardboard. Encourage each student to write a short message, such as a verse or a proverb, on a strip of white paper. He may want to decorate the paper using the felt-tip pens. Then instruct him to fold the paper accordion-style so that it will fit between two

cardboard squares. Encourage the students to cover two cardboard squares with wrapping paper to make decorative "covers" for their books. Tell them to glue one end of the paper to each square so that the book opens and closes like an accordion. Display finished books on a table in the classroom.

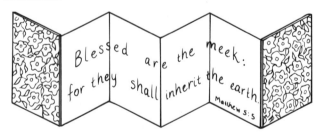

☐ Additional Teacher Information

The books that the Mayas made were called *codices.* (The word in its singular form is *codex.*) The codices were usually about eight inches high and several yards long when unfolded. Each page was called a *katun.* On the *katuns* were written records or religious prophecies in pictures and symbols. These symbols are usually read from top to bottom in columns and from left to right in pairs.

The Dresden Codex is the best example of a Mayan book still in existence. It was found in Vienna in 1739 and is now kept in the State Library at Dresden. The other two surviving books are called the Madrid Codex and the Paris Codex, named for the cities in which they are housed.

LESSON 45
The Quest for Beauty

Text, pages 177-79
Notebook, page 49

- Diego de Landa
- The Mayan Ideal
- Ornaments and Hygiene

The Mayan civilization continued in fragmented form in smaller towns and in cultures of other peoples. But then Spanish explorers arrived in 1520. Once the explorers found a few gold figures in the Mayan ruins, they believed that much more was to be had. From then on, the Spanish determined to overcome the Mayas with force and with religion—often with both.

One priest, named Diego de Landa, used every means to make the Mayas accept Roman Catholicism. He had those who refused his religion stretched on pulleys and burned with candles. He had an entire library of Mayan books burned on July 12, 1562, because they contained only "superstition and lies of the devil." In an effort to communicate with the Mayan people, Landa became a careful student of their ways and tried to translate their symbolic writing into Spanish. Landa's writings give us much of the information we have today about the Mayas of the 1500s and their ancient ancestors. The rest of the information must be painstakingly gathered from the stones and artifacts in Mayan lands.

Mayan stele (left) and carvings (below), Copán, Honduras

177

═══════════════ **Preview** ═══════════════

☐ Objectives
Given proper instruction, the students will be able to do the following:
- Evaluate the priority level of beauty and hygiene in magazine advertisements.
- Complete statements about the Mayan culture.

☐ Materials
Have available:
- A magazine with advertisements for each student.*
- A sheet of notebook paper for each student.
- The figure of Diego de Landa (A.D. 1562) from the History TimeLine Packet.

☐ Notes
You will want to look through the magazines and remove any offensive material before allowing the students to use them.

Day 83

═══════════════ **Lesson** ═══════════════

☐ Introducing the Lesson
Magazine search—Give each student a magazine and a sheet of notebook paper. Instruct the students to page through the magazines, looking only at the advertisements. Direct each student to keep a tally on his sheet of paper of all the ads that promote a product for beauty or hygiene, such as toothpaste, perfume or cologne, jewelry, soap, and so forth. When all the students have finished, invite them to count their tally marks and share the number with the rest of the class.

Ask the students what the number of advertisements devoted to beauty and cleanliness tells them about the value modern culture places on these things. *(Modern culture places a very high value on beauty and cleanliness.)* Explain that in this lesson, they will learn about the value that the Mayas placed on beauty and cleanliness.

Day 84

☐ Teaching the Lesson
Diego de Landa—Instruct the students to read page 177 silently to learn what brought many Spanish explorers to the land of the Mayas. *(Gold figures were found in the Mayan ruins in 1520.)*

Discussion Questions
➤ **In what form did the Mayan civilization continue after its major cities were abandoned?** *(The Mayas continued their civilization in smaller towns and in cultures of other peoples.)*
➤ **What did the newly arrived Spaniards decide to do about the Mayas?** *(overcome them with force and religion)*
➤ **Who was the most influential leader who wanted to convert the Mayas?** *(Diego de Landa)*
➤ **What religion did Landa want the Mayas to accept?** *(Roman Catholicism)*
➤ **What did he do to those who refused to accept his religion?** *(stretched them on pulleys and burned them with candles)*
➤ **What did he do to the Mayan books, and why did he take this action?** *(He burned them because he thought they contained only superstition and lies that would hinder the Mayas from accepting the Roman Catholic religion.)*
➤ **On what date did the book burning take place?** *(July 12, 1562)*

Add the figure of Diego de Landa to the History TimeLine at A.D. 1562.

Mayan People

According to Landa, the Mayan people were about five feet tall, the women being around four feet, ten inches tall and the men just slightly over five feet. They all had thick, dark hair. The men wore their long hair in braids around the crowns of their heads with one braid down the back. Women wore several hairstyles, most using braids with ribbons coiled around their heads.

The Mayas seem to have preferred long noses and sloping foreheads. They would improve their looks with clay, creating a ridge from the top of the forehead to the bridge of the nose. The true sign of beauty, the sloping head, had to be formed early in life. Parents bound newborns' heads between boards until the soft bones grew into a slanted, almost cone shape.

Mayas also thought crossed eyes were best, perhaps because one of their gods was cross-eyed. To achieve this look, parents hung a bead between the babies' eyes; after the babies looked at the beads for months, their eyes grew permanently crossed.

178

When older, the Mayas added other features to their appearances. Most young men shaved their foreheads to show off their slanting brows. They also tattooed symbols on their arms, legs, and faces. Many had their ears pierced—but not as people do today. The men wore earplugs in holes sliced into their lobes. They kept adding bigger and bigger plugs until the holes were the size of golf balls. Into these ear holes they placed disks of jade or shell.

Both men and women would often file their teeth to points and inlay them with jade. How do you think modern people know how these ancient Mayas looked? We can tell from sculptures and paintings that the Mayas made.

Mayas took frequent baths, a practice shunned and feared in Europe at the time. They liked perfume that they made from flowers and herbs. Most of the men carried mirrors to check their appearance from time to time.

This mural by Diego Rivera helps us see how the ancient Mayas may have looked and dressed.

179

➤ **What good things did Landa do?** *(made an effort to communicate with the Mayas, studied their ways, tried to translate their writing into Spanish)*

➤ **What other sources of Mayan information do we have today?** *(stones and artifacts from Mayan lands)*

Ask the students what was wrong with Landa's actions toward the Mayas. *(He was not kind and loving toward them; he used torture and cruelty to get his way.)* Remind the students that God expects Christians to treat others with love and that love is necessary to win others to Christ. (BATs: 5a Love, 5c Evangelism and missions)

The Mayan ideal—Instruct the students to read page 178 silently to find out how tall most Mayan men and women were. *(Men were slightly over five feet; women were around four feet ten inches.)*

Discussion Questions

➤ **Describe a typical Mayan man's hairstyle.** *(long, worn in braids around the crown of the head with one long braid down the back)*

➤ **How did Mayan women wear their hair?** *(many different styles, usually with braids and ribbons coiled around their heads)*

➤ **What kinds of facial features did the Mayas prefer?** *(long noses, sloping foreheads, and crossed eyes)*

➤ **Name three methods Mayan parents used to alter their own facial appearances and those of their children.** *(They used clay to form a ridge from the top of the forehead to the nose, bound newborns' heads between boards to slant the bones in the forehead, and hung beads between babies' eyes so that their eyes would become permanently crossed.)*

Day 85

Ornaments and hygiene—Instruct the students to read page 179 silently to learn what other ways the Mayas altered their appearances. *(shaved their foreheads to show off slanting brows; tattooed their arms, legs, and faces; pierced their earlobes and placed plugs inside until the holes were the size of golf balls and then placed disks of jade or shell into the holes; filed their teeth to points and inlaid them with jade)*

Discussion Questions

➤ **How do we know how the ancient Mayas looked?** *(from the paintings and sculptures they made)*

➤ **How do we know that the Mayas were concerned about hygiene?** *(They took frequent baths and wore perfume made from flowers and herbs.)*

➤ **What did the Mayan men do that reveals their concern with their appearance?** *(carried mirrors to check their appearance from time to time)*

➤ **How is modern culture like that of the Mayas when it comes to personal appearance?** *(Answers will vary but should include that physical beauty and cleanliness are greatly emphasized.)*

Fill in the blanks. Read the boxed letters to answer the question at the bottom of the page.

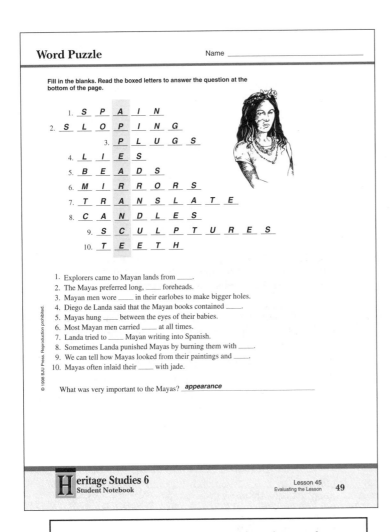

1. S P A I N
2. S L O P I N G
3. P L U G S
4. L I E S
5. B E A D S
6. M I R R O R S
7. T R A N S L A T E
8. C A N D L E S
9. S C U L P T U R E S
10. T E E T H

1. Explorers came to Mayan lands from ____.
2. The Mayas preferred long, ____ foreheads.
3. Mayan men wore ____ in their earlobes to make bigger holes.
4. Diego de Landa said that the Mayan books contained ____.
5. Mayas hung ____ between the eyes of their babies.
6. Most Mayan men carried ____ at all times.
7. Landa tried to ____ Mayan writing into Spanish.
8. Sometimes Landa punished Mayas by burning them with ____.
9. We can tell how Mayas looked from their paintings and ____.
10. Mayas often inlaid their ____ with jade.

What was very important to the Mayas? __appearance__

© 1998 BJU Press. Reproduction prohibited.

Heritage Studies 6
Student Notebook   Lesson 45
                                                    Evaluating the Lesson   **49**

Remind the students that even in cultures where the outward appearance is emphasized, Christians must realize that God is more concerned about the condition of the heart. (BATs: 4b Purity, 7e Humility)

□ Evaluating the Lesson

Word Puzzle (Notebook page 49)—Instruct the students to use the clues to fill in the blanks. Explain that the boxed letters will spell the answer to the question at the bottom of the page.

Going Beyond

□ Enrichment

Creating the Mayan Mona Lisa—Set up an AREA with pencils, felt-tip pens, and drawing paper. Encourage each student to draw a large picture of a Mayan face, either male or female, representing the Mayan ideal of beauty. Remind the students to study the details they have learned in this lesson in order to add as many as possible to their drawings. If desired, display the completed drawings.

□ Additional Teacher Information

Diego de Landa's writings reveal much of what is known today about Mayan culture. In a book written in 1566, he explained how to decipher the glyphs that the Mayas used to represent dates. This work has helped historians understand the Mayan calendar and has helped translators decode the writing of the Mayas. Although Landa's work is of great value, the amount of knowledge and history he destroyed in the Mayan book burning is inestimable.

Despite their small stature, most Mayas had strong, sturdy builds. They were a dark-skinned people with thick, black hair and dark brown eyes. They dressed colorfully, sometimes even painting their whole bodies a certain color. Warriors often painted themselves black and red, and sometimes young men painted themselves black until they were married. Human sacrifice to the gods was common, and the person to be killed was always painted blue.

The idea of crossed eyes as a form of beauty probably came from the Mayan representation of the sun god, who was always shown with crossed eyes.

LESSON 46
Levels of Mayan Society

Text, pages 180-83
Notebook, page 50

- **Kings and Priests**
- **Nobles, Peasants, and Slaves**
- **Mayan Clothing**
- **Home Life**

━━━━ Preview ━━━━

□ Objective

Given proper instruction, the students will be able to do the following:

- Match descriptions of people in Mayan society with the appropriate class.

□ Materials

Have available:

- 6 blank sheets of paper.
- A black felt-tip pen.
- 6 safety pins.

Prepare the sheets of paper by writing one of the following names on each one: king, priest, nobleman, noblewoman, peasant man, and slave girl.

Day 86

━━━━ Lesson ━━━━

□ Introducing the Lesson

A class act—Choose six students to represent the different characters in the story below. Pin the appropriate name tag to each character's shirt and then instruct all of them to listen carefully as you read the story and to silently act out their parts as each occurs.

Zintal, the king, sat alone, surveying the vast stretch of empty space in the courtyard of his palace. He took a long drink of hot chocolate and then stroked his chin for a few moments, deep in thought. "What we need," he said at last, "is a monument. A stone statue of my father, the last king. Right in the center of the courtyard. I must inform the royal artist immediately."

Near the palace was a well-built stucco house where a nobleman, Manuel, lived with his wife, Quinta. A few afternoons later, Manuel was seated outside the front entrance, bent over the drawing table he had made from a smooth, flat stone. He was carefully sketching a man's face on a square of fig-tree paper. Quinta sat nearby, watching and humming quietly to herself. Their slave girl, Nina, sat in the doorway of the house grinding corn, her face flushed in the heat.

"Whose face are you drawing?" Quinta asked, looking over her husband's shoulder.

"I'm sketching a monument by order of King Zintal," he said. He held the drawing up for her to see. "A picture of his father. Do you think it's a good likeness?"

Quinta tipped her head to one side and smiled. "Very good," she said. "No one draws better than you, Manuel. It is no wonder the king has chosen you for this important task."

Early the next week, Tazmel, a peasant builder, was hard at work building the monument. Dragging stone after heavy stone to the site and lifting it into place was a tiring job. Tazmel paused often to wipe his forehead with his arm. But he smiled to himself when he thought of how the monument would look when it was finished. How pleased King Zintal would be!

At last the monument was finished. All the people of the city came to watch the dedication ceremony—even Nina, though she had to stay on the outskirts of the crowd.

The people grew quiet as the priest, Kancha, stood up beside the statue. Everyone bowed and listened respectfully as Kancha offered a long prayer to the gods, asking their blessing on the monument and on King Zintal's departed father, wherever he might be. As soon as the prayer was over, all the people let out a loud cheer and then everyone feasted and sang songs and drank hot chocolate. No more work was done for the rest of the day.

Instruct the six actors to return to their seats and then discuss the following questions with the class.

Discussion Questions

➤ **What was the king doing in the story?** *(sitting and drinking hot chocolate)*

➤ **What kind of work did the nobleman do?** *(He was the artist who designed the monument.)*

➤ **Describe the house where the nobleman and his wife lived.** *(near the palace, well built, made of stucco)*

➤ **What kind of work did the peasant man do?** *(He built the monument.)*

➤ **How can you tell from the story that the priest held a high position of authority?** *(The people listened respectfully when he talked; he was responsible to offer the prayer to the gods.)*

➤ **What are some differences between the two women in the story?** *(Quinta, the noblewoman, did not have work to do; she could attend the ceremony with her husband. Nina, the slave, had to grind the grain and stay on the outskirts of the crowd at the ceremony.)*

The Mayan society had several levels. At the top was the ruler, the absolute king. He was called, in at least some Mayan cities, *makina*, the "great sun lord," and *halach uinic*, the "true man." Like the Egyptians, the Mayas believed that the kings were descended from the gods and that they should be obeyed without question. The kings, in return, would speak to the gods on behalf of the people.

Just below the kings in power were the priests. There were at least four classes of priests. The highest ranking priests were in charge of all the others. They taught writing, astronomy, mathematics, and all rituals associated with the Mayan religion.

Lower ranks included priests who treated sickness. Sometimes the cure was more dangerous than the illness. Nosebleeds, for example, required a priest to cut the foot of the sufferer to let him bleed freely. Other priests were fortune-tellers. They probably ate leaves and mushrooms that caused them to have hallucinations. And another group of priests had the duty of cutting the hearts from the people sacrificed to the gods.

180

Also high ranking were the nobles. It was from this class that all the priests came. The nobles, men and women, were educated, and they held important positions in the government. The man in charge of the armies, the *batab*, was a member of this class.

Lesser nobles included the artists and architects, traders and scribes, advisors and engineers. Although they did not have the high positions of the first class of nobles, they had many of the privileges. No nobleman or noblewoman had to do common work, such as grinding corn, planting crops, or cleaning. Such labors were left to the common people.

The peasants did the hard manual work of the Mayan society. They grew, harvested, and processed the food. They grew the cotton and produced the fabrics. They tended the buildings. They were the soldiers for the armies and the laborers for construction of the monuments and temples. They were the ordinary people who made the extraordinary visions of the architects, artists, and kings a reality.

At the bottom of society was the slave. Anyone who was in debt or who had committed a crime was considered a slave, the property of another. Sometimes prisoners of war were kept as slaves as well. Important prisoners were used for sacrifices; lesser ones were made to work.

181

Day ⁸⁷

□ Teaching the Lesson

Kings and priests—Instruct the students to read page 180 silently to find out who was the highest person in Mayan society. *(the king)*

Discussion Questions

➤ **What were some of the names given to the king?** *("the great sun lord," "true man")*

➤ **How were the Mayas like the Egyptians in their beliefs about the king?** *(They believed that the king descended from the gods and should be obeyed without question.)*

➤ **Could the people speak directly to the gods?** *(No, the king spoke to the gods in their behalf.)*

➤ **Who was next in rank to the kings?** *(the priests)*

➤ **What were the duties of the highest-ranking priests?** *(They were in charge of all the other priests and taught writing, astronomy, mathematics, and all rituals associated with the Mayan religion.)*

➤ **What were the responsibilities of the lower ranks of priests?** *(treating sickness, telling fortunes, cutting the hearts from human sacrifices)*

➤ **Would you like to have one of these priests treat an illness of yours? Why or why not?** *(Answers will vary but may include that often the "cures" used by these priests were more dangerous than the illness itself.)*

➤ **What did the priests who told fortunes probably do to get a glimpse of the future?** *(ate leaves or mushrooms that caused them to have hallucinations)*

Nobles, peasants, and slaves—Instruct the students to read page 181 silently to learn which class all of the priests came from. *(nobles)*

Discussion Questions

➤ **What sort of positions did the highest-ranking nobles hold?** *(important government positions or man in charge of the armies,* batab*)*

➤ **What did lesser nobles do for a living?** *(were artists, architects, traders, scribes, advisors, and engineers)*

➤ **What were the lives of noblewomen like?** *(They did not have to do common work.)*

➤ **What was the class beneath the nobles?** *(peasants)*

➤ **Name some of the jobs of the peasants.** *(growing, harvesting, and processing food; raising cotton and producing fabric; tending buildings; serving as soldiers; constructing monuments and temples)*

➤ **Why was the work of the peasants important to the Mayan society?** *(Without their efforts, the artistic and architectural visions of the nobles would never have become reality.)*

Most Mayas wore simple cotton clothes. The men wore tunics and breechcloths, sometimes with a short cape. The women wore straight, plain dresses or wraparound skirts and long blouses. Both men and women wore a lot of jewelry: earrings, rings, armbands, and necklaces, all made of shells, volcanic rock, animal teeth and bones, or jade. They either went barefoot or wore sandals of straw and rope.

The Mayas obtained feathers of many brilliant colors from native birds.

Rich people wore the same things, only with more embellishments, such as feathers woven into the fabric. Their shoes were made of deerskin. The kings wore jaguar skins and jade breastplates. The three-foot plumes in their headdresses and on their clothes came from the quetzal, a beautiful bird of the rain forests. The kings had jade bands on their wrists and ankles and gold rings on their toes. To the common Maya, a king's appearance must have been dazzling indeed.

182

A modern Mayan home

Mayan Life

The classes of Mayan society were reflected in places people lived. The kings lived in palaces, huge monuments covering many acres. Nobles lived in large houses near the center of the city—the closer to the center, the more impressive. The houses had stucco walls and many airy rooms. Rooms may have been divided with embroidered cotton draperies. Some houses even had plumbing and, possibly, fireplaces or ovens.

While the kings, priests, and nobility practiced their ceremonies, waged wars on neighbors, and planned huge building projects, the average Maya led a far quieter and simpler life. Most peasant families lived in small wooden houses with grass-thatched roofs.

Before four o'clock in the morning, women were awake and building fires. By five o'clock the men and boys had eaten breakfast—usually a warmed-up *tortilla*—and were tending to the crops. When planting corn in swampy places or on riverbanks, farmers made ridges in the soil and poked holes into the ridges with a planting stick. Another person came behind, dropping in corn kernels and covering the holes.

183

> Point out that for a Christian every job, including schoolwork, is important because it is an opportunity to prove oneself faithful in God's eyes. (BATs: 2c Faithfulness, 2e Work)

➤ **Who was at the bottom of Mayan society?** *(the slave)*
➤ **What was the slave's function in society?** *(He was the property of another, a prisoner for some crime that he had committed. He was either used for a sacrifice or put to work.)*

Day [88]

Mayan clothing—Instruct the students to read page 182 silently to find out what kind of fabric most Mayan clothes were made out of. *(cotton)*

Discussion Questions

➤ **What kind of clothing did men wear?** *(tunics and breechcloths, sometimes with a short cape)*
➤ **What kind of clothing did women wear?** *(straight, plain dresses or wraparound skirts and long blouses)*
➤ **What did they wear as ornaments?** *(earrings, rings, arm bands, and necklaces, all made of shells, volcanic rock, animal teeth and bones, or jade)*
➤ **What kind of footwear did the Mayas wear?** *(sandals of straw and rope)*
➤ **How did rich people's clothing differ from clothing of the common people?** *(The rich embellished their clothing with feathers and wore deerskin shoes.)*

➤ **How did the king distinguish himself by his dress?** *(He wore jaguar skins and a jade breastplate, quetzal plumes in his headdress, jade bands on his wrists and ankles, and gold rings on his toes.)*

Home life—Instruct the students to read page 183 silently to find out how the Mayan kings lived. *(They lived in huge palaces that covered many acres.)*

Discussion Questions

➤ **What were the homes of the nobles like?** *(large houses near the center of the city, each house having stucco walls, many rooms, cotton draperies, and sometimes plumbing, fireplaces, and ovens)*
➤ **How did most of the peasants live?** *(in small wooden houses with grass-thatched roofs)*
➤ **Who got up first in a Mayan household?** *(the women)*
➤ **What early-morning duty did women perform?** *(building the fires)*
➤ **What job did most peasant men do after breakfast?** *(tending the crops)*
➤ **Describe the process of planting corn.** *(One person made ridges in the soil and poked holes with a planting stick. Another person came behind, dropping in corn kernels and covering the holes.)*

Mayan Matchup

Name _____

Match each description with the correct Mayan class. Write the appropriate letter in each blank.

A. kings   D. peasants
B. priests   E. slaves
C. nobles

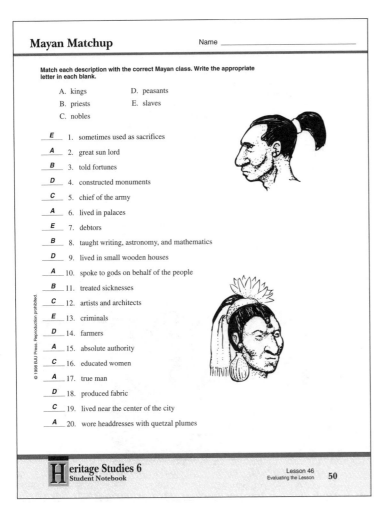

__E__ 1. sometimes used as sacrifices

__A__ 2. great sun lord

__B__ 3. told fortunes

__D__ 4. constructed monuments

__C__ 5. chief of the army

__A__ 6. lived in palaces

__E__ 7. debtors

__B__ 8. taught writing, astronomy, and mathematics

__D__ 9. lived in small wooden houses

__A__ 10. spoke to gods on behalf of the people

__B__ 11. treated sicknesses

__C__ 12. artists and architects

__E__ 13. criminals

__D__ 14. farmers

__A__ 15. absolute authority

__C__ 16. educated women

__A__ 17. true man

__D__ 18. produced fabric

__C__ 19. lived near the center of the city

__A__ 20. wore headdresses with quetzal plumes

Heritage Studies 6
Student Notebook

Lesson 46
Evaluating the Lesson   **50**

□ Evaluating the Lesson

Mayan Matchup (Notebook page 50)—Direct the students to match each description with the correct Mayan class by writing the appropriate letter in each blank.

■ Going Beyond ■

□ Enrichment

Mayan diaries—Set up an AREA with a blank sheet of paper and a pencil for each student. Encourage the students to choose one of the Mayan classes, make up a character who belongs to that class, and write several diary entries for that character's daily life.

□ Additional Teacher Information

Much of what we know about how the Mayas dressed comes from their sculptures. Tall stone panels called *stele,* carved between A.D. 300 and 900, have been found throughout the Mayan region. Most of the stele depict rulers wearing feather-and-bead capes and elaborate headdresses. The figures are often shown holding objects, such as a shield or a bar carved with the head of a snake. Inscribed on these monuments are important dates in the ruler's life, such as his birth, accession to the throne, and death.

Mayan children often wore distinctive ornaments. A mother braided a white bead into the hair of her son when he turned five, and for her daughter she made a belt with a red shell attached. The children wore these items until their initiation ceremony, when the ornaments were ceremonially removed by a priest. A girl's initiation usually occurred at age twelve, followed in a few years by her marriage. A boy was initiated at age fourteen and usually married around the age of eighteen.

LESSON 47
Work, Play, and Ritual

Text, pages 184-86
Notebook, page 51

- **Work and Leisure**
- **In the Plaza**
- **Mayan Religion**

─────── **Preview** ───────

☐ Objective

Given proper instruction, the students will be able to do the following:

- Answer questions about Mayan traditions and celebrations.

☐ Materials

Have available Maps and More 17.

Day 89

─────── **Lesson** ───────

☐ Introducing the Lesson

Mayan cures—Ask the students what treatments are used in their homes for common ailments, such as a sore throat or a headache. Allow several students to share their home remedies. Then instruct the students to listen as you read the following "cures" that the Mayas had for two common ailments.

> For toothache: Take soot that is left on the cooking stones, wrap it in wool, and apply it to the tooth. Or take a crocodile tooth and grate it with a fish skin, wrap it in wool, and apply it to the tooth.

> For sneezing: Boil orange leaves; then drain the liquid and rub it onto the body, particularly the foot.

Ask the students whether they think they would like to try these cures next time they have a toothache or a sneezing spell. *(Answers will vary.)* Ask them whether they think these cures worked. *(Answers will vary.)*

Explain that the Mayas used many herbs and other plants that had true healing value. Sometimes their cures really worked. But when a cure worked, the Mayas attributed the cure to magic and not to God's power.

In the dry seasons, farmers went into the rain forests and cut down trees. They burned the stumps and the underbrush. In the ashes they planted corn. The corn grew well for a year or two, but such soil wore out quickly. The only remedy was to move to a new place to cut and burn again. Farmers gave part of all they grew to the upper classes of people.

The women worked all day grinding grain in stone bowls or making thread from cotton for the looms. They wove cloth and made clothes, kept the houses, and tended the children. Even the little girls helped make tortillas and other food. The big meal of the day, which usually included beans, fruits, *tamales*, and, occasionally, meat, came in the late afternoon. A favorite drink, *pozole,* was made from corn paste and water, sometimes mixed with honey. Women and girls made the meal, served it to the men and boys, and ate later.

There were days when no one had to work, however, and favorite foods, like chocolate, abounded. Special celebrations were attended by everyone. The most popular event seems to have been a ball game called *pok-to-pok.* Every Mayan city had a ball court—one city had seven courts. Shaped like a capital I, a court measured 100- to 150-feet long and 25- to 50-feet wide. Players, allowed to use only their padded wrists, elbows, and hips, tried to hit a small rubber ball through a vertical hoop or onto a marker on the side of the wall.

Statue of a pok-to-pok player (above) and a ball court at Chichén Itza, Mexico (left)

184

☐ Teaching the Lesson

Work and leisure—Instruct the students to read page 184 silently to learn what the farmers did during the dry seasons. *(cut down trees and burned stumps and underbrush in the rain forests; then planted corn in the ashes)*

Discussion Questions

➤ **How often did the farmers need to move to a new place for planting?** *(every year or two years)*
➤ **Did the farmers get to keep all the corn that they grew?** *(No, they gave part of all they grew to the upper classes.)*
➤ **What kinds of jobs did the women do?** *(grinding grain, making thread from cotton, weaving cloth, making clothes, keeping house, tending children, preparing food)*
➤ **When was the big meal of the day?** *(late afternoon)*
➤ **What foods did a typical meal consist of?** *(beans, fruits, tamales, meat, and a drink called pozole)*
➤ **Who ate first?** *(men and boys)*
➤ **What special food was eaten on holidays?** *(chocolate)*
➤ **What special event took place on holidays?** *(a ball game called pok-to-pok)*
➤ **What was a pok-to-pok court like?** *(shaped like a capital I, 100-150 feet long, 25-50 feet wide)*
➤ **What was the object of the game?** *(to hit a small rubber ball through a vertical hoop or onto a marker on the side of the wall)*
➤ **What limitations were placed on how players could hit the ball?** *(could be hit only with padded wrists, elbows, and hips)*

Only the nobles could play pok-to-pok, but everyone in the city watched. Many nobles placed bets on the outcome, losing much property or many slaves when their wagers were wrong.

All such events took place in the plazas of the cities. Some cities had courts and markets made especially for buying, selling, celebrating, and playing games. The city centers were busy places when people came to trade vegetables, animals, jewelry, jade, pottery, honey, fabrics, and, of course, cocoa beans.

The plazas also saw slave trading. Mayas bought and sold people frequently. Some of the slaves were Mayas. Since Mayan cities had no jails, people who fell behind on their debts, stole, or committed other crimes were made slaves. So were orphans and the children of slaves. Other slaves were stolen, bought, or won in war from neighboring cities.

185

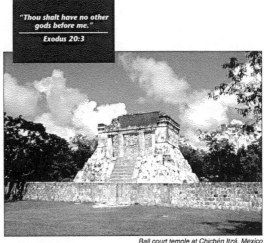

"Thou shalt have no other gods before me."
Exodus 20:3

Ball court temple at Chichén Itzá, Mexico

Mayan Religion

The whole Mayan society, even the popular ball game, was dominated by Mayan religion. Before and after the game, players had to make sacrifices to the gods. Some scholars believe that the players, perhaps the winners, were sacrificed. Everything the Mayas did, from cooking beans to attending ceremonies involving a solar eclipse, had to be done according to ritual. A man about to kill a deer had first to ask the deer to forgive him by saying, "I have need."

Everything, even pottery, was believed to have a spirit. Mayas talked to the objects around them and were always in fear of evil dwarfs who caused sickness and bad crops. To appease the dwarfs, Mayas put out food for them. If illness or bad crops came, a priest prescribed medicine or performed a ritual. Some of the medicines, made from herbs and other plants, were good and often cured the illnesses. Other "cures," however, were far worse than the disease.

186

Display Maps and More 17. Tell the students that the game of pok-to-pok was played on an *I*-shaped court with side markers or rings set twenty-seven feet high. Two teams, each with two or three players, used only their wrists, elbows, and hips—not hands or feet—to propel the ball from side to side on the court. Points were scored when the ball was forced into the opposing team's end zone or when the ball hit a marker or passed through a ring. Often the game varied according to the time and place it was played. Ask the students what modern games this ancient game reminds them of. (*Answers will vary but may include basketball, volleyball, football, and soccer.*)

Day 90

In the plaza—Instruct the students to read page 185 silently to find out who was allowed to play pok-to-pok. (*nobles*)

Discussion Questions

➤ **What made these ball games even more important to some spectators?** (*Some people placed bets on the outcome.*)
➤ **In what part of the city did pok-to-pok games take place?** (*the plaza*)
➤ **What other events took place in the plazas?** (*buying and selling at the markets, celebrating, playing games, trading*)
➤ **What items were traded?** (*vegetables, animals, jewelry, jade, pottery, honey, fabrics, cocoa beans, slaves*)

➤ **Since the Mayas had no jails, what did they do with people who committed crimes?** (*made them slaves*)
➤ **Who else besides Mayan criminals were made slaves?** (*debtors, orphans, children of slaves, conquered peoples*)

Mayan religion—Instruct the students to read page 186 silently to find out what took place before and after pok-to-pok games. (*The players made sacrifices to the gods.*)

Discussion Questions

➤ **What do some scholars believe about these sacrifices?** (*It may have been the players themselves, perhaps the winners, who were sacrificed.*)
➤ **Name three activities that had to be done according to a certain ritual.** (*cooking, attending ceremonies, hunting*)
➤ **What ritual was involved in killing a deer?** (*Before killing it, the hunter had to ask the deer's forgiveness by saying, "I have need."*)
➤ **What kinds of things were believed to have spirits?** (*everything*)
➤ **Who did the Mayas think caused sickness and bad crops?** (*evil dwarfs*)
➤ **What did they do to appease the dwarfs?** (*put out food for them*)
➤ **Who came to help in cases of illness or bad crops?** (*a priest*)
➤ **What were Mayan medicines made from?** (*herbs and other plants*)

Mayan Traditions

Name _____

Answer the following questions about Mayan traditions and celebrations.

Wording may vary.

1. Name four responsibilities of Mayan women. *Possible answers include grinding grain, making thread, weaving cloth, making clothes, keeping house, tending children, and cooking.*

2. Describe a typical Mayan meal. *beans, fruits, tamales, meat, pozole*

3. Describe a typical Mayan holiday. *No one worked; foods like chocolate abounded; pok-to-pok was a popular sport.*

4. Name three activities that took place in the city plazas. *Possible answers include pok-to-pok and other games, buying and selling at market, trading, and celebrating.*

5. Name five items that were traded among the Mayas. *Possible answers include vegetables, animals, jewelry, jade, pottery, honey, fabric, cocoa beans, and slaves.*

6. Name three activities that involved religious rituals. *Possible answers include pok-to-pok games, cooking, ceremonies, and hunting.*

Heritage Studies 6
Student Notebook

Lesson 47
Evaluating the Lesson   **51**

➤ **Were all the priests' medicines good?** *(No, some were far worse than the disease itself.)*

> Point out that Mayan rituals were based on superstition—a false trust. The Mayas placed their trust in their rituals and magic, things that had no power to help them. Remind the students that only God has power to heal people and to make crops grow. (Bible Promise I: God as Master)

□ Evaluating the Lesson

Mayan Traditions (Notebook page 51)—Direct the students to answer the questions about Mayan traditions and celebrations.

Going Beyond

□ Enrichment

Sampling Mayan food—Set up a food-sampling AREA with various foods, such as bite-sized pieces of bean tortillas and tamales, banana slices, chili peppers, and chocolate.

□ Additional Teacher Information

The Mayan religion dominated everything their society did, even their games and leisure time. Responding to the demands of the "gods" often led the Mayas to commit evil, violent acts—not only against their enemies but also among themselves. Even the pok-to-pok game had violent overtones. Some scholars believe that the players used the heads of their enemies for balls.

Farming was yet another Mayan activity that was dominated by religious ritual. Maize, the main crop of the Mayas, was considered a sacred food. Before clearing the land, the Mayas would make offerings to the gods. After planting, more offerings would be made, especially to the rain god. If rain were scarce, the Mayas resorted to offering human sacrifices, thinking that these would appease the wrath of the rain god.

The Mayas were fascinated with the medicinal value of plants, and many Mayas did extensive study on this subject. Herbs were often used in their "cures," along with ritualistic chants and prayers. Tobacco was an especially popular plant in Mayan society, grown both for medical and religious purposes.

LESSON 48
To Please the Gods

Text, pages 187-90
Notebook, pages 52-54

- **Mayan Gods**
- **Rituals of Death and Burial**
- **Mayas Today**

━━━━ Preview ━━━━

□ Objectives
Given proper instruction, the students will be able to do the following:
- Record observations and interpretations of archaeological items.
- Match Mayan beliefs with Bible verses that refute them.

□ Materials
Have available:
- A stapler.
- A Bible for each student.

Prepare copies of the archaeological items pages for each pair of students. (*NOTE:* See the reproducible material at the end of this lesson.)

◆ DISCOVERING HOW ◆

To Think Like an Archaeologist

1. Get Notebook pages 52 and 53, the papers your teacher gives you, a pen or pencil, and a stapler.

2. Form an archaeological team with your Heritage Studies partner. Make observations about the "finds" reported in the papers you have received from your teacher.

3. Produce a booklet based on your conclusions. Share your observations and opinions with other teams.

190

Day 91

━━━━ Lesson ━━━━

□ Introducing the Lesson
Observations and Interpretations (Notebook pages 52-53)—Direct a *Discovering How* activity on page 190. Read the steps aloud. Instruct the students to get with their Heritage Studies partners to form their archaeological "team." Distribute copies of the archaeological items pages to each team. Instruct each team to examine the finds, choose one that interests them, and complete Notebook pages 52-53 about that item. Instruct them to staple their Notebook pages and archaeological items pages together to form a booklet. Allow time in class for several or all of the teams to share their observations and opinions with the rest of the class.

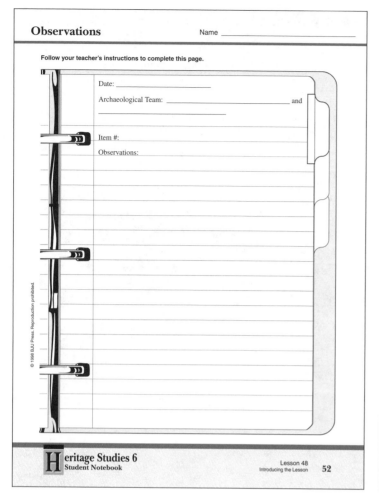

Name _____

Follow your teacher's instructions to complete this page.

Date: _____

Archaeological Team: _____ and
_____

Item #: _____

Observations:

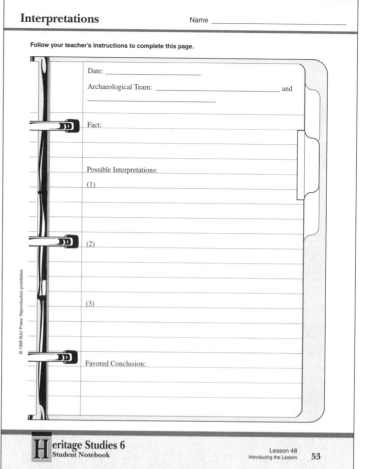

Name _____

Follow your teacher's instructions to complete this page.

Date: _____

Archaeological Team: _____ and
_____

Fact:

Possible Interpretations:

(1)

(2)

(3)

Favored Conclusion:

Day 92

□ Teaching the Lesson

Mayan gods—Instruct the students to read page 187 silently to discover what the Mayas believed about the world. *(that it was a flat square atop a giant crocodile god in a lily pond)*

Discussion Questions

➤ **According to the Mayan religion, what were the possible places a person could go after death?** *(to one of the nine underworlds or one of the thirteen heavens)*

➤ **Name several things that the Mayas believed were ruled by an individual god.** *(the sea, the moon, bees, medicine, corn, the sun, life, death, days of the calendar, each of the underworlds, each of the heavens)*

➤ **How did the Mayas try to please their gods?** *(by keeping rules)*

➤ **How did the Mayas remember all of the rules they were supposed to keep for each god?** *(The priests were in charge of keeping the rules in order.)*

➤ **What Mayan ritual is most often written about?** *(human sacrifice)*

➤ **What did the Mayas think the gods required from them to be satisfied?** *(human blood)*

➤ **What minor sacrifice did the king and his wife sometimes make to the gods?** *(They cut themselves and caught the blood on special paper.)*

➤ **What major sacrifice was required when times were especially hard?** *(A slave was killed and his blood put onto the statues of the gods.)*

➤ **Why do you think the Mayas felt this kind of sacrifice was necessary to make their gods happy?** *(Answers will vary.)*

The Mayas thought that the world was a flat square that was atop a giant crocodile god in a lily pond. When a person died, he was expected to leave the square and go to one of nine underworlds or thirteen heavens, each under the control of a separate god.

Mayas believed that almost everything had its own god: the sea, the moon, bees, medicine, corn, the sun, life, death, days of the calendar, and so on. Since there were so many gods and so many rules about how to please each god, the Mayas had to depend on the priests to keep everything in order.

Of all the rituals of the Mayan religion, the one most often written about is the human sacrifice. Like other ancient religions, such as that practiced by the priests of Baal, the Mayan religion taught that the gods must be satisfied with human blood. Sometimes the king and his wife would cut themselves and catch the blood on special paper. But on rarer occasions, when the king was gravely ill or the country had experienced a long famine, priests took slaves to the temple altars and killed them and put the blood on the statues of the gods.

Mayan corn god (left) and sacrificial altar (above)

187

For all their care to obey the priests and please the gods, the Mayas feared death greatly. Only priests, warriors who had died in battle, people who had hanged themselves, and people who had been sacrificed by the priests could be sure of getting into Mayan paradise. All others, no matter how well they had kept the rules, might—by the whim of some god—be condemned to the underworld.

When someone died, he was mourned for days. He was buried according to his station in life. The common people were often buried under their houses, which were then abandoned by the others who lived there. The rich could afford tombs with heavy stone coverings, elaborately engraved. Almost everyone, regardless of his class, had a piece of jade in his mouth so that he would have some money in the next life.

Kings were buried with great ceremony and wealth. One king, Pacal, was buried in a large room under a Mayan pyramid. Buried with him were six other people and a huge cache of jade jewelry and other treasures. This king had a jade mask over his face, perhaps to show his power in the afterlife.

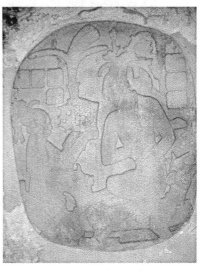

This relief carving, possibly depicting Pacal, is on a wall in Palenque, Mexico (Pacal's city).

188

Remind the students of Christ's sacrifice for our sins on the cross. Point out that Hebrews 9:27-28 says that Christ was offered once for sin, and this sacrifice was the only payment necessary in God's eyes. Invite any students who have questions about salvation to speak to you sometime soon. (BAT: 1a Understanding Jesus Christ; Bible Promise: E. Christ as Sacrifice)

Rituals of death and burial—Instruct the students to read page 188 silently to find out how the Mayas felt about death. *(They feared it greatly.)*

Discussion Questions

➤ **Who could be sure of getting into Mayan paradise?** *(priests, warriors who died in battle, people who hanged themselves, people sacrificed by the priests)*
➤ **What decided whether a person was condemned to the underworld?** *(the whim of a god)*
➤ **What ritual continued for days after someone died?** *(mourning)*
➤ **Where were common people buried?** *(under their houses)*
➤ **Where were the rich buried?** *(in tombs with heavy stone coverings)*
➤ **What burial practice was common to all the Mayan classes?** *(burying a person with a piece of jade in his mouth so that he would have some money in the next life)*

➤ **What was unique about King Pacal's burial?** *(He was buried with six other people, with a huge cache of treasures, and with a jade mask over his face.)*

Read aloud Deuteronomy 11:1. Ask the students whose rules the Bible says are important to keep. *(God's)* Remind the students that keeping God's rules is something Christians should do out of love for God, not out of fear of being punished. (BATs: 2a Authority, 2c Faithfulness)

Mayas Today

In 1960 a man exploring a cave came upon a series of rooms holding many Mayan artifacts and paintings. When he told about his find, a Mayan priest from a nearby village came and demanded that he be allowed to perform ceremonies to pacify the gods of rain whose cave had been violated. It had probably been a thousand years since anyone had been inside that cave. But after all that time, the Mayan way still held power over the Mayan descendants.

As many as two million descendants of the Mayas are living in the region today. A few still weave cloth, plant and harvest corn, and practice some rituals as the ancient Mayas did. Some still use the same calendars and speak languages quite close to what Pacal and his people may have spoken, although neither would probably be able to understand the other.

Mayan life is now a mix of Mayan, Roman Catholic, and modern ideas. Some farmers plant their fields with the same prayers that were said in ancient times. But in other places, the great-great-great-great-great-grandchildren of the Mayas are reading about their ancestors on their computers. What might an ancient Maya think of the hot chocolate those grandchildren are drinking, made from a packet of powder that even commoners can obtain?

189

Look up each Bible passage listed below and match it with the Mayan belief it provides an answer for. Write the correct letter in each blank. Then answer the question at the bottom of the page.

> A. Hebrews 7:26-27
> B. Deuteronomy 11:11-12
> C. Matthew 6:19-21
> D. Exodus 20:3
> E. Titus 3:4-7
> F. Romans 3:20
> G. Romans 8:15-16

__D__ 1. The Mayas believed that nearly everything had its own god.

__F__ 2. The Mayas believed that they had to follow certain rules to please the gods.

__A__ 3. The Mayas believed that they had to offer sacrifices—even human ones—to make peace with the gods.

__B__ 4. The Mayas believed that their gods controlled the weather and the crops.

__E__ 5. The Mayas believed that only certain people who did noble things would go to paradise.

__G__ 6. The Mayas lived in fear that the gods would, on a whim, condemn them to the underworld.

__C__ 7. The Mayas believed that if they put treasure into a dead person's tomb, he could carry those riches with him into the next life.

What would you tell someone who was not sure where he would go after death?

Answers will vary.

_____
_____
_____
_____

Heritage Studies 6
Student Notebook

Lesson 48
Evaluating the Lesson   **54**

Day 93

Mayas today—Instruct the students to read page 189 silently to find out what discovery was made in 1960. (*A man found rooms in a cave containing Mayan artifacts and paintings.*)

Discussion Questions

➤ **What did the Mayan priest want to do when he found out about the man's discovery?** (*perform ceremonies to pacify the gods of rain whose cave had been violated*)

➤ **What does this show about the Mayan religion?** (*It still held power over Mayan descendants after thousands of years.*)

➤ **How many Mayan descendants live in the region today?** (*about two million*)

➤ **What ancient traditions do modern Mayas still keep?** (*weaving cloth, growing corn, performing rituals, using the same calendars, speaking the same languages*)

➤ **What are some of the differences between the ancient Mayas and their modern descendants?** (*The modern Mayas mix the Mayan religion with Roman Catholicism and modern ideas; they use computers and drink hot chocolate made from packets of powder.*)

□ Evaluating the Lesson

Bible Verse Matching (Notebook page 54)—Instruct the students to look up each Bible passage on Notebook page 54 in order to match it with the Mayan belief it refutes. Tell them to write the letter of the correct Bible passage in each blank. Then instruct them to answer the question at the bottom of the page.

Going Beyond

□ Enrichment

Creative-writing activity—Set up an AREA with pencils and writing paper. Tell the students to imagine that a Maya from long ago could visit the world today and see how much it has changed since his time in history. Invite each student to write a brief letter from the Maya's perspective, expressing his thoughts and opinions on our world today.

□ Additional Teacher Information

Today most of the people in Central America are of mixed Spanish-Native American ancestry. But full-blooded Mayas still remain, and Maya is the most widely spoken native language in the region. Other surviving Native American groups in Central America include the Payas, the Jicaques, the Miskito, the Bribri, the Cabecar, the Guaymi, the Choco, and the Cuna.

The Mayan descendants are most numerous in the country of Guatemala. They live in small communities, each having its own traditional clothing styles and ways of life. Poverty and illiteracy are common in the native communities. The Mayas still worship some of the ancient gods of their ancestors.

Moon Observation Sheet

Date _____

Date _____

Date _____

Date _____

Date _____

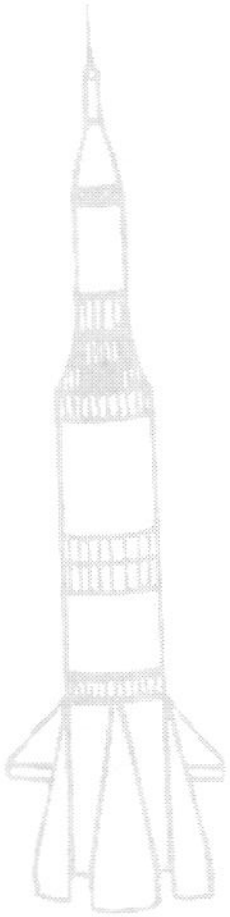

Mayan Archaeological Items

1. The feathered snake in this Aztec drawing looks much like the one in Mayan work. What might this drawing suggest about Aztec and Mayan religions?

2. This figure looks similar to an Aztec figure from nearly the same time. What does this figure suggest about Aztec and Mayan cultures?

Use with Lesson 48.

Mayan Archaeological Items

3. A figure like this one was found in a city in Mexico hundreds of miles from the Mayan city where it was made. What does this fact suggest about Mayan trade?

4. Stone heads such as this were found fifty miles from places where such stone exists. What does this fact suggest about the Olmec people?

Story Keepers and Kings: Ancient Africa

This chapter focuses on the empires of ancient Africa, tracing the kings and kingdoms that passed through the once Dark Continent. Oral history is a primary source for knowledge about these ancient kingdoms. Other sources of information are linguistics, botany, and archaeology. The students will read about the different peoples of Africa, from the camel-riding Tuareg to the Bushmen, who speak in Clicks. The empires are as varied as the people, prospering in trade and wealth, falling in wars and poverty. Africa, a land glittering with diamonds and gold, is rich not only in natural resources but also in tradition. Slowly, the darkness of this secret land was dispelled by other countries—some seeking the wealth of the land, others seeking the wealth of slave trading. Some came to Africa to trace the hidden passages coursing through the continent, and still others brought the gospel message. By studying this chapter, the students will gain an appreciation for the diverse culture and characteristics of Africa—a land of story keepers and kings.

□ Materials

Lesson 52 requires certain items that must be obtained or prepared several days to several weeks before the presentation of the lesson. These items are labeled with an asterisk (*) in the lesson and in the Materials List in the Supplement. Occasionally, items not commonly found in the classroom as well as items needed in large quantities may also be labeled with an asterisk. For further information, see the individual lessons.

□ Chapter Bulletin Board

Place a background of colorful fabric on the bulletin board. Display a silhouette of the continent of Africa made from a piece of black poster board big enough to make the continent on one sheet. At the top of the bulletin board, place the title *AFRICA: Story Keepers and Kings.* Affix Maps and More 18 beneath the title. You may choose to display pictures from post cards or travel brochures of different parts of Africa.

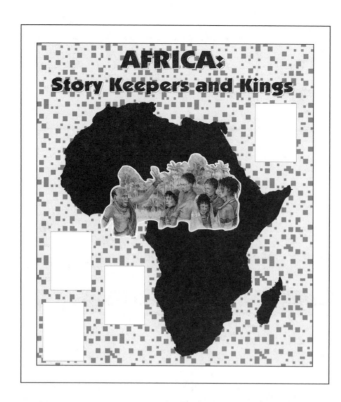

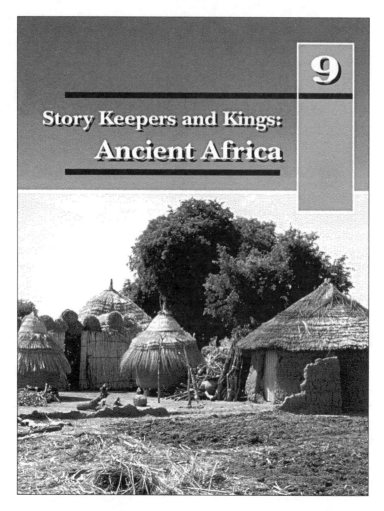

LESSON 49
The Dark Continent

Text, pages 192-95
Notebook, pages 55-56

- **Storytelling**
- **A Dry and Wet Land**
- **Then and Now**
- **Regions**

═══ Preview ═══

□ Objectives
Given proper instruction, the students will be able to do the following:
- Label the major landforms on a map of Africa.
- Answer questions about Africa's major landforms.

□ Materials
Have available:
- A Bible for each student.
- A wall map of Africa.

Prepare the chalkboard or a chart by writing the following African proverbs:

> No one tests the depth of the water with both feet.
>
> Knowledge is like a garden. If it is not cultivated, it cannot be harvested.

□ Notes
The Enrichment activity calls for a film about African wildlife that may need to be ordered in advance.

Day 94

═══ Lesson ═══

□ Introducing the Lesson
African proverbs—Select a volunteer to explain what a *proverb* is. *(a short saying with a practical lesson)* Explain that the ancient Africans had proverbs that they passed from generation to generation. Call attention to the proverbs on the chalkboard or chart. Select volunteers to explain what these two African proverbs mean. *(When trying something new, try little changes at a time. It takes time and effort to gain and use knowledge.)*

Ask the students whether there are any sayings, or proverbs, that their parents or grandparents use. As time permits, select a volunteer to read aloud Proverbs 17:17. Explain that one benefit of a proverb is that it is easy to remember and pass on to others.

Voices called from the rain forest—not human voices, but voices of birds and monkeys and insects. The sun blazed down on Namasha, warming her bare arms, and turned the distant river to gold. She glanced around her at the faces of the other village children. Their eyes were fixed on the storyteller.

"This is a tale of how the mountains came to be," said the old man seated before them. "Long, long ago, before any of us were born, the earth was smooth and flat like this river stone I hold in my hand. But one day, the earth decided to have a conversation with the sky. She rose up high, higher than birds fly, until she touched the sky. The earth and the sky told one another their secrets. When they finished talking, the earth bade the sky good-bye and started to return to her place. But on the way down, she became very tired. Parts of her became so tired that they stopped right where they were, before reaching the ground. Now we call these parts mountains and hills."

Namasha swatted at a fly and yawned. She liked the old man's stories, but she had heard this one before. She had heard most of his stories before. Stories about mountains and rivers and lakes and animals. Stories about the ancient people who had lived here before.

Namasha squinted beyond the old man toward the river. She remembered the old Congolese proverb her father often quoted: "No matter how full the river, it still wants to grow." She wanted to grow. She wanted to hear new stories. When would the storyteller give them something new?

192

□ Teaching the Lesson
Storytelling—Instruct the students to read page 192 silently to find an old Congolese proverb. *("No matter how full the river, it still wants to grow.")*

Discussion Questions
➤ **Where is Namasha?** *(in her village in an African rain forest)*
➤ **What is she doing?** *(listening to the storyteller)*
➤ **What is the storyteller describing?** *(how the mountains came to be)*
➤ **Do you think this is how the mountains truly were created?** *(No, it is just a story.)*

> Explain that people have different ideas about how the earth came into existence. Remind the students that the Bible gives the true account of Creation. (Bible Promise: I. God as Master)

➤ **What do you think the Congolese proverb means?** *(People naturally desire to grow and increase in knowledge.)*
➤ **What does Namasha want to do?** *(to grow, to hear new stories)*

The Dark Continent

For hundreds of years Europeans called Africa "the Dark Continent" because they knew almost nothing about Africa or its many people. After explorers visited Africa and told of their findings, however, the European world learned a great deal about the continent. They learned that Africa has large lakes, grand mountain ranges, mighty rivers, vast deserts, and lush rain forests.

Sand dunes, Sahara Desert

Africa is both a dry and a wet land. If you were to walk along the equator, you would be walking right through the heart of Africa. It is the only continent to have deserts both north and south of the equator. The Sahara, the largest desert in the world, almost completely covers the northern half of Africa. The Kalahari and Namib Deserts are in southern Africa. To the east, by the *Horn of Africa* where Somalia is today, lies another desert area. Somalia receives little rain because winds blow most of the water vapor into the mountains of Ethiopia before it reaches Somalia. What would you call an area like this? Somalia is called a *rain shadow.*

Africa is also home to many lakes and rivers. Lake Victoria, in East Africa, is the source of the Nile River, the longest river in the world. Lake Chad supplies water for four different African countries. Lakes Nasser and Volta, both manmade lakes, supply electricity.

Study the map of Africa on the next page. How many different rivers can you find?

Waterfall, Cameroon

193

Africa

Location—A large continent to the southwest of Asia; includes the islands of Madagascar, Comoros, Réunion, Mauritius, Canary, and Seychelles in the Indian Ocean. Africa is divided almost in half by the equator.

Climate—Much of the climate is tropical, with warm temperatures during the day and cool temperatures at night; other parts have a dry desert climate. Temperatures in the Sahara range from 50°F in the winter to 100°F in the summer. In northern Somalia, summer temperatures of 115°F or more are common.

Topography—Deserts cover about two-fifths of Africa's land. Africa also has mountain ranges, rivers, rain forests, beautiful lakes, and savannas.

Natural Resources—Rich in mineral resources, Africa has gold, petroleum, oil, copper, diamonds, and natural gas.

Geography and Culture—For many centuries, the Sahara kept Africa isolated from European culture because Europeans traded only along the coast, never venturing inland.

194

Day 95

A dry and wet land—Instruct the students to read page 193 silently to find why Africa was called "the Dark Continent." *(because Europeans knew almost nothing about Africa or its people for hundreds of years)*

Discussion Questions

➤ **What did explorers learn about Africa?** *(It has large lakes, grand mountain ranges, mighty rivers, vast deserts, and lush rain forests.)*

➤ **What runs through the heart of Africa?** *(the equator)*

➤ **What kind of climate exists along the equator?** *(hot)*

➤ **How is Africa different from other continents?** *(It is the only continent to have deserts both north and south of the equator.)*

➤ **What desert almost completely covers northern Africa?** *(the Sahara Desert)*

➤ **What two deserts are in the southern half of Africa?** *(the Kalahari and Namib Deserts)*

➤ **What country is located on the Horn of Africa?** *(Somalia)*

Point to Somalia and Ethiopia on a wall map.

➤ **What is a *rain shadow?*** *(an area that receives little rain because winds blow the water vapor into the mountains)*

➤ **What African country experiences the rain shadow effect?** *(Somalia)*

Point to the Nile River on a wall map. Trace the Nile River to its source.

➤ **What is the source of the Nile River?** *(Lake Victoria, in East Africa)*

➤ **What is unique about the Nile River?** *(It is the longest river in the world.)*

Then and Now—Instruct the students to read page 194 silently to find how the Sahara Desert affected African culture. *(It kept Africa isolated from European culture.)* Direct the students' attention to the Then and Now map, noting ancient empires, changes in boundary lines, and so on.

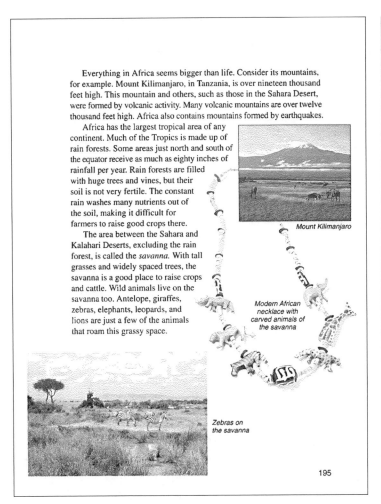

Everything in Africa seems bigger than life. Consider its mountains, for example. Mount Kilimanjaro, in Tanzania, is over nineteen thousand feet high. This mountain and others, such as those in the Sahara Desert, were formed by volcanic activity. Many volcanic mountains are over twelve thousand feet high. Africa also contains mountains formed by earthquakes.

Africa has the largest tropical area of any continent. Much of the Tropics is made up of rain forests. Some areas just north and south of the equator receive as much as eighty inches of rainfall per year. Rain forests are filled with huge trees and vines, but their soil is not very fertile. The constant rain washes many nutrients out of the soil, making it difficult for farmers to raise good crops there.

The area between the Sahara and Kalahari Deserts, excluding the rain forest, is called the *savanna*. With tall grasses and widely spaced trees, the savanna is a good place to raise crops and cattle. Wild animals live on the savanna too. Antelope, giraffes, zebras, elephants, leopards, and lions are just a few of the animals that roam this grassy space.

Mount Kilimanjaro

Modern African necklace with carved animals of the savanna

Zebras on the savanna

195

Map Activity   Name _____

Complete the following statements by filling in the blanks on this page or by labeling the map on page 56.

1. Label the Sahara Desert.

2. Label the Kalahari and Namib Deserts. On which coast is the Namib Desert?
   southwestern

3. Label the Nile River and the lake that is the source of the Nile. *Lake Victoria*

4. What country is Mount Kilimanjaro in? *Tanzania*

5. What two countries are on the Horn of Africa? *Somalia, Ethiopia*

6. What lake touches the countries of Niger, Chad, Nigeria, and Cameroon? Label it on the map. *Lake Chad*

7. Label the island off the coast of eastern Africa. *Madagascar*

8. Explain how the Sahara Desert has affected Africa's culture. *The Sahara Desert kept Africa isolated from European culture because Europeans traded only along the coast, never venturing inland.*

Heritage Studies 6
Student Notebook

Lesson 49
Evaluating the Lesson   **55**

Day 96

Regions—Instruct the students to read page 195 silently to find two ways that African mountain ranges were formed. *(by volcanic activity and earthquakes)*

Discussion Questions

➤ **How high is Mount Kilimanjaro?** *(over nineteen thousand feet)*

➤ **How much rain do some African rain forests receive?** *(as much as eighty inches per year)*

➤ **How does so much rain in the rain forests affect the soil?** *(The soil is not very fertile because the rain washes the nutrients out.)*

➤ **What is the area between the Sahara and the Kalahari Deserts called?** *(the savanna)*

➤ **What are the characteristics of the land in the savanna?** *(tall grasses and widely spaced trees)*

➤ **How is the land in the savanna useful?** *(It is good for raising crops and cattle.)*

➤ **What kinds of animals inhabit the savanna?** *(antelope, giraffes, zebras, elephants, leopards, and lions)*

□ Evaluating the Lesson

Map Activity (Notebook pages 55-56)—Direct the students to complete the map activity by filling in the blanks on Notebook page 55 and by labeling the map on Notebook page 56.

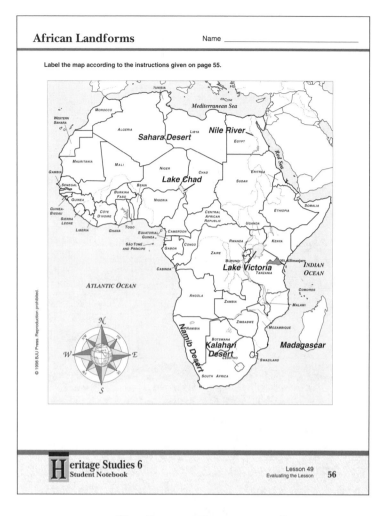
━━━ Going Beyond ━━━

□ Enrichment

African wildlife—Show a film about African wildlife on the savanna.

□ Additional Teacher Information

Any region receiving less than ten inches of rainfall a year, regardless of temperature, is considered a desert. The Sahara Desert, the largest desert in the world, covers almost the northern third of Africa. The deserts in southern Africa, the Namib and the Kalahari, are smaller than the Sahara. The Namib Desert is a coastal desert in the modern country of Namibia.

The forests of Africa are not thick jungles. They are tropical rain forests with fairly open floors. Some forest areas along the coast have thick bush and swamp land.

Africa has many rivers, the Nile being the most famous. In modern times, the Congo River has been used by explorers seeking ivory and gold. The river most closely associated with David Livingstone is the Zambezi River, which empties into the Mozambique Channel. This river has perhaps the most spectacular cataract in the world: Victoria Falls, named for Queen Victoria of England.

LESSON 50
Keys to Africa's Past

Text, pages 196-99

- Linguistics
- Botany and Archaeology
- Oral History

━━━━━━ **Preview** ━━━━━━

☐ Objective

Given proper instruction, the students will be able to do the following:

• Tell a story.

Day 97

━━━━━━ **Lesson** ━━━━━━

☐ Introducing the Lesson

A rememberer's story—Read the following fictional account of a village rememberer's story.

Shamaloh sat on a tree stump, shading his eyes against the morning sun. The village children came slowly today. He studied the children who gathered about his bare feet. He lifted a hand that was crooked with age. Two boys in the back stopped their scuffling and sat still. They listened.

"Mangawanni," Shamaloh said, greeting them with the "Good morning" that was his custom. He cleared his throat. "When I was this high—" He motioned just above the head of one of the sitting children. "A great change came to the village. It was the season when more corn is to be picked. My sister and mother worked in front of our hut, preparing sadza, our corn drink that you enjoy today." Shamaloh drew a bent finger through the air, pointing at each upturned face.

The old man licked his dry lips so that it seemed he could taste the sadza. He shook his head sadly. "That—that was the last sadza that we drank for many days. The great winds came, and the sun burned hot. There was not a drop of wet."

At the back of the group, the two boys swatted at each other. One covered his mouth to hide a laugh. "Do you know what that means?" Shamaloh's voice rose. The two boys jumped and stared at him with wide eyes.

"Shangwa!" whispered Shamaloh. He beat one fist into the other hand. "No food. And what happens to the people when there is no water or corn or sadza?" He shook his head. "We become no more. Many villagers died during the shangwa. Those who were still alive—my father and my father's father—prayed that the gods would

Keys to Africa's Past

We often learn about people and their history from what we read in books. We know that the Egyptians left written records on both stone and papyri. But most of the people of Africa did not have a written language. How then can we know anything about them? There are many ways of learning about people other than by reading written records.

Linguistics

One way is to study the spread of languages. Long ago the *Bantu,* an early African people, left their homes on the Benue River and traveled into central and eventually eastern and southern Africa. Moving to another region is called *migrating.* When the Bantu migrated, they took their language with them. After settling in a new area, they had to learn to speak with the people already living there. Both groups shared and borrowed bits of language—a word or two, or a new way of saying something. Slowly, each language changed.

Linguists, people who study languages and the ways they change, can discover where people went by the words and grammar that they lent and borrowed. Linguists helped trace the migration route of the Bantu.

196

be angry no more. It was many days, the shangwa, but soon, the gods sent rain, and the earth began to grow."

"You children," Shamaloh spread his hands. "You have not known shangwa like your fathers' fathers. But beware! Honor the gods or you will know shangwa."

Discussion Questions

➤ **What was the old man telling the children about?** *(about a drought and famine that had happened to their village a long time ago)*

➤ **What reason did Shamaloh give for the famine?** *(The gods were angry.)*

➤ **Why do you think Shamaloh told this story to the children?** *(to warn them about displeasing the gods)*

Remind the students that there is only one God, and He controls all. Explain that although Shamaloh attributed the drought and famine to the wrong causes, his story was valuable because it passed down information about the past to the children.

☐ Teaching the Lesson

Linguistics—Instruct the students to read page 196 silently to find ways to get information about some ancient people. *(through written records and languages)*

Discussion Questions

➤ **On what were Egyptian written records found?** *(on stone or papyri)*

Botany

Linguists follow people through changes in their language. *Botanists,* who study plants, trace the movements of people by their crops. When the Bantu farmers moved to new homes, they took seeds with them so that they could plant crops to feed their families. The whole Bantu migration took about fifteen hundred years and covered half of the continent of Africa.

By tracking the spread of their crops, botanists helped trace the migration routes of the Bantu.

African crops

Archaeology

Another important source of information comes from archaeology. In some areas of Africa, archaeologists have found caves with paintings on the walls. From these drawings we know about the weapons that the early African people used for fighting and hunting, as well as what animals they hunted. Some of the paintings are accompanied by symbols that may have been part of a written language. Unfortunately, no one has discovered what these symbols mean.

Ancient African rock painting

197

Oral History

Do you have an older friend or relative who tells stories about the times when he or she was a child? Such stories are called oral history because they are spoken and not written.

Most African villages, like Namasha's, had at least one person who was the official rememberer. It was his job to learn the village's history. He taught the children and reminded the adults of their past. He described the journeys of their ancestors when they looked for new farmland. He told of the deeds of past leaders and heroes. And he reminded the villagers of their ancient traditions.

The village rememberer told his stories at every opportunity. He wanted to keep the village's history from being forgotten. Modern historians know that oral history is important in learning about the past of Africa.

In Africa, jewelry can sometimes tell a person's tribe, age, marital or financial status, social standing, or accomplishments.

198

➤ **What do you think the Africans kept records about?** *(Answers will vary.)*

Explain that the word *linguistics* means "the study of language or speech." Select a volunteer to explain what a *linguist* is. *(a person who studies languages and the ways they change)*

➤ **How does studying the spread of languages reveal information about a culture?** *(Linguistics can show how cultures have combined, separated, migrated, and so on.)*

➤ **What does the word *migrating* mean?** *(moving to another region)*

➤ **Who were the *Bantu*?** *(an early African people who left their homes on the Benue River and traveled into central and eventually eastern and southern Africa)*

➤ **What kinds of things did the Bantu take with them when they moved?** *(their language, culture, and so on)*

➤ **How did the Bantu have to adjust to the new region?** *(They had to learn to speak with the people already living there.)*

➤ **How can linguists learn where people went?** *(by the words and grammar that they lent and borrowed)*

Day *98*

Botany and archaeology—Instruct the students to read page 197 silently to find what *botanists* do. *(study plants)*

Discussion Questions

➤ **How do botanists trace the movements of people?** *(by their crops)*

➤ **Why did the Bantu take seeds with them when they migrated?** *(so that they could plant crops to feed their families)*

➤ **How long did the Bantu migration take, and how far did it go?** *(about fifteen hundred years; half the continent of Africa)*

➤ **How do we know the migration spread that far and took that long?** *(Botanists tracked the spread of the Bantu's crops, revealing their migration routes.)*

➤ **How has archaeology revealed information about ancient Africa?** *(Archaeologists have found cave paintings that illustrate weapons for fighting and hunting as well as the animals that early Africans hunted. Some paintings include a written language.)*

➤ **Have archaeologists found out more from the writings with the paintings?** *(No, no one has discovered what these symbols mean.)*

Oral history—Instruct the students to read page 198 silently to find the job of an official rememberer. *(He had to learn the village's history, teach it to the children, and remind the adults of their past.)*

Discussion Questions

➤ **What is *oral history*?** *(stories about the past that are spoken and not written)*

➤ **What types of things did the official rememberer describe?** *(the journeys of his people's ancestors, the deeds of past leaders and heroes, and the ancient traditions)*

◆ DISCOVERING HOW ◆

To Preserve History Orally

1. Think of an important event in the history of your family, such as an adventurous experience or a meaningful accomplishment. It should be something you could tell about in less than three minutes.

2. In your group, tell your own story and listen to the stories of the other group members, trying to remember the details of each story.

3. Now find a student from another group. Tell him your own story and the stories of your group members. Listen as he tells you his story and the other stories from his group. Do you think you could remember all of these stories to tell to someone else?

199

➤ **How often did the village rememberer tell his stories?** *(at every opportunity)*

➤ **Why did the rememberer tell his stories this often?** *(to keep the village's history from being forgotten)*

➤ **Do you think being the village rememberer was an important job?** *(Answers will vary.)*

➤ **Do you think it was an easy job?** *(Answers will vary.)*

➤ **How is oral history viewed by historians today?** *(as an important part of learning the past)*

> Explain that one disadvantage of oral history is that it can change as it is passed from person to person. The Bible, however, never changes. Its truths will endure forever. (BAT: 8b Faith in the power of the Word of God)

Day ⁹⁹

□ Evaluating the Lesson

Practicing oral history—Direct a *Discovering How* activity on page 199. Read aloud the steps. Direct Heritage Studies partners to join together to form groups of four. Instruct each group to do Steps 2 and 3. As time permits allow the students to discuss the advantages and disadvantages of storytelling as a means of keeping records.

━━━ Going Beyond ━━━

□ Enrichment

Story time—Set up a rememberers' AREA at the back of the classroom. Invite some older people to each tell a story about some historical event that he or she has witnessed. (*NOTE:* Choose an event like the landing of the first man on the moon or the explosion of the *Challenger*—something not too far removed from the students' own time. Request that the storyteller give details about what that day was like, how people responded, how he or she first heard of or saw the event, and so on.) Tape record or videotape these accounts for the students to use in the rememberers' AREA.

□ Additional Teacher Information

Africa has more than eight hundred languages. Several languages, such as Swahili and Arabic, are more widely spoken than others. Swahili is one of the most common Bantu languages. In South Africa, the two major languages are English and Afrikaans, a Germanic language derived from the Dutch settlers. The numerous languages make interaction difficult among the various African groups.

LESSON 51
Africa's People

Text, pages 200-202
Notebook, page 57

- Desert People
- People of the Savanna
- People of the Rain Forest

Preview

□ Objective

Given proper instruction, the students will be able to do the following:

- Match African groups to the characteristics that describe them.

□ Materials

Have available a wall map of Africa.

Day 100

Lesson

□ Introducing the Lesson

Click words—Direct the students to get with their Heritage Studies partners. Instruct each set of partners to make up click sounds with their tongues to represent the greeting "hello." As time permits, allow each set of partners to share its click greeting with the other students. Ask the students whether they would like to speak with clicks, or noises, all the time. Explain that there is a group in Africa that speaks using the Click language.

□ Teaching the Lesson

Desert people—Instruct the students to read page 200 silently to find what kind of people the *Tuareg* were and where they lived. *(nomadic people, living in the Sahara Desert)*

Africa's People

Africa was home to many different people. In the north lived the nomads of the Sahara. The greatest of these nomadic people were the *Tuareg*.

Imagine seeing a group of warriors, dressed in loose, flowing garments and riding swift camels, coming toward you in a cloud of sand. As one of the men comes closer, you see that his head is wrapped with a long piece of dark blue cotton that acts as both a turban and a veil. His face is hidden except for a narrow slit for his eyes. The Tuareg frequently attacked caravans in bands. They even attacked towns built on the edges of the desert.

The camel helped the Tuareg become the most feared of the desert peoples. Camels had been introduced into northern Africa shortly after the birth of Christ. Though ill-tempered and stubborn, the camel was a necessity because of its ability to survive and work in the desert. With camels, the Tuareg could move freely across the Sahara. They also used camel hides to make their tents, and from camel milk they made butter and cheese.

200

Discussion Questions

➤ **How are the Tuareg described?** *(as warriors dressed in loose, flowing garments and riding swift camels)*
➤ **What did a Tuareg warrior wear on his head?** *(a long piece of dark blue cotton cloth that acted as both a turban and a veil, hiding his face except for the eyes)*
➤ **Why do you think he wore this kind of headgear?** *(Possible answers include to keep cool, to keep the sand out of his face, and to conceal his identity.)*
➤ **Why is the camel a good desert animal?** *(It is able to survive and work in the desert.)* (*NOTE:* Camels can go for weeks with little or no food or water. Long, curly eyelashes shade the camel's eyes and keep out the desert sand. The strong, muscular legs of the camel enable it to carry heavy loads for long distances.)
➤ **How did the camel help the Tuareg become the most feared of the desert peoples?** *(Camels enabled them to move freely across the Sahara.)*

In the grassy savanna and the forests southwest of the Sahara lived many prosperous people. Some farmed the fertile soil. Others built cities and sent their goods across the Sahara to the Mediterranean coast. These peoples formed great empires to protect themselves and their trade routes.

The Nilotic people originally lived in the area of the modern country of Sudan. Then they migrated to the shores of Lake Victoria and into the modern countries of Kenya, Tanzania, and Uganda. Perhaps the best known of these peoples are the tall and slender Masai. They measured their wealth and social standing by the number of cattle they owned.

A modern Masai tribesman

Much of the rest of Africa was settled by the Bantu, who migrated from the Benue River. They wandered south and settled in the Congo Basin. For perhaps two hundred years or more, the Bantu prospered and their numbers grew. Finally, the land could support no more villages, and some of the Bantu packed their belongings and moved southeast once more, all the way to the tip of Africa.

A Bantu carved figure

201

The Bantu were not the only ones living in the center of Africa. Pygmies, people of very small size, lived deep in the rain forest of the Congo Basin. The Bushmen and Hottentots lived there too. When these two groups lost their land to the Bantu, they moved to the south and west where they formed small family groups of hunters and gatherers.

The Bushmen spoke an unusual Click language. Think of all the noises you can make with your tongue, teeth, and lips that are not words at all. In a Click language, these sounds have meaning. Try talking to a friend and adding a few clicks and pops as you speak. It is not easy!

Europeans also lived in Africa. In the middle of the seventeenth century, the Dutch set up a station to provide water and food for ships on their way to India. The Dutch found a beautiful place on the southern tip of Africa and decided it would be a good place to live. Englishmen joined them about one hundred fifty years later. Both the Dutch and the English have lived there ever since.

A pygmy man

202

People of the savanna—Instruct the students to read silently the first two paragraphs on page 201 to find the name of some of the peoples who lived in the savanna. *(the Nilotic people or Masai)*

Discussion Questions

➤ **How were the people of the savanna and the southwest forests prosperous?** *(Some farmed the fertile soil; others built cities and exported goods, forming great empires to protect trade routes.)*

➤ **Who were the Nilotic people?** *(They originally lived in what is now Sudan but later migrated to the shores of Lake Victoria and into what are now the countries of Kenya, Tanzania, and Uganda.)*

Select a volunteer to point out on a wall map the general route of the Nilotic people.

➤ **Who are the Masai?** *(the best known of the Nilotic people)*

➤ **How did the Masai measure their wealth?** *(by the number of cattle they owned)*

➤ **How is this similar to or different from the way people measure their wealth today?** *(Some people measure their wealth by their possessions, viewing wealth in terms of money, cars, clothes, and houses.)*

Remind the students that Christians should not place their confidence in material wealth, but in the Lord. Instead of trying to accumulate possessions, Christians should focus on having a proper relationship with the Lord. (BAT: 7d Contentment; Bible Promise: G. Christ as Friend)

Day 102

People of the rain forest—Instruct the students to read silently the last paragraph on page 201 and all of page 202 to find the name of the people who migrated from the Benue River. *(the Bantu)*

Discussion Questions

➤ **Where did the Bantu migrate?** *(They wandered south and settled in the Congo River Basin.)*

Select a volunteer to point to the Congo River area on a wall map.

➤ **How long were the Bantu in this area?** *(about two hundred years)*

➤ **Why did the Bantu leave the Congo area?** *(The land could support no more villages, so they moved southeast.)*

➤ **What other groups of people lived in the rain forest of the Congo River?** *(pygmies, Bushmen, and Hottentots)*

➤ **What language did the Bushmen speak?** *(a Click language)*

239

Africa's People

On each line, write the letter(s) of the people being described. Choices can be used once, more than once, or not at all.

A. Bantu   D. Dutch   G. English
B. Tuareg   E. Nilotic   H. Hottentots
C. Bushmen   F. Pygmies   I. Masai

D   1. set up a station to provide water and food for ships on their way to India in the seventeenth century

E   2. migrated from Sudan to Lake Victoria and into the modern countries of Kenya, Tanzania, and Rwanda

B   3. were the most feared of the desert peoples

A, C, F, H   4. lived in the rain forest of the Congo Basin

I   5. measured their wealth and social standing by the number of cattle they owned

B   6. used camels as transportation as well as for making tents, butter, and cheese

A   7. migrated from the Forest States to the Congo Basin

C   8. spoke the unusual Click language

Heritage Studies 6
Student Notebook

Lesson 51
Evaluating the Lesson **57**

➤ **What is the Click language like?** *(It consists of noises made with the tongue, teeth, and lips.)*

➤ **What group of people came to Africa in the seventeenth century, and why did they come?** *(The Dutch set up a station to provide water and food for ships on their way to India.)*

➤ **Where in Africa did the Dutch settle?** *(on the southern tip)*

➤ **What group of people joined the Dutch there about one hundred fifty years later?** *(the English)*

☐ Evaluating the Lesson

Africa's People (Notebook page 57)—Instruct the students to match the description with the correct people or peoples by writing the letter(s) on the line provided.

══ Going Beyond ══

☐ Enrichment

Bead work—Set up an art AREA with multicolored beads, fishing line, and necklace clasps. Encourage each girl to string her own beaded necklace. Explain that Masai women wore many strings of beaded jewelry.

Veils—Set up an AREA with a dark blue sheet or towel for each boy. Encourage each boy to wrap the towel on his head like a turban. Explain that Tuareg warriors wore turbans and veils such as these.

☐ Additional Teacher Information

Each African group has unique customs. The Masai women of Tanzania adorn themselves with beaded necklaces that can weigh several pounds. Unlike the women, who shave their heads, Masai men wear long braids greased with clay and animal fat. In southern Algeria, the Tuareg men, not the women, wear veils. In the evening, the women sing and talk while the men listen in respect. Tuareg women discuss poetry and tell stories for the audience of men.

LESSON 52
African Empires

Text, pages 203-7
Notebook, page 58

- Aksum
- Ghana
- Mali
- Mansa Musa

━━━━ Preview ━━━━

☐ Objectives
Given proper instruction, the students will be able to do the following:
- Write about a travel experience.
- Complete statements about the African empires.

☐ Material
Have available:
- A wall map of Africa.
- A 4-foot piece of yarn.*
- Fabric remnants.*
- Several small bowls.*
- Costume jewelry.*
- Coins.*
- 2 sheets of construction paper.
- The figure of Mansa Musa (A.D. 1312) from the History TimeLine Packet.

Prepare a "Merchants" sign and a "Buyers" sign on the construction paper.

☐ Notes
Bring enough coins, bowls, jewelry, and fabric for each student to have at least one item. Those who have coins should not have fabric, bowls, or jewelry.

Day 103

━━━━ Lesson ━━━━

☐ Introducing the Lesson
African trading—Tell the students that this activity will be done without any talking. Place the students in two groups, positioned in opposite corners of the room. Place the "Merchants" sign with the first group and distribute the fabric remnants, bowls, and jewelry among them. Place the "Buyers" sign with the second group and give coins to each of these students. Place the yarn on the floor to form a line in the middle of the classroom. Tell the merchants to come forward, place their goods near the yarn, and then return to their corner. Instruct the buyers to go to the yarn, examine the goods, decide how many coins they think each object is

African Empires

Aksum

On the east side of Africa lies the modern nation of Ethiopia. Long before the birth of Christ, farmers settled in this area and eventually built the empire of Aksum. Aksum was a wealthy and powerful kingdom. It supplied precious

Stele of Aksum

stones, incense, gold, ivory, ebony, myrrh, and elephants to the Egyptian pharaohs. Archaeologists who have studied the ruins of Aksum tell us that walled castles dominated the capital city. Aksum's educated people spoke Greek. Linguists believe that the Aksumites visited the Greek city of Byzantium often, perhaps to trade.

King Ezana ruled the empire of Aksum. He wore gold jewelry and rich clothing, and he rode in a golden chariot drawn by four elephants. Under King Ezana, Aksum became the strongest country in East Africa, conquering neighboring kingdoms.

After Ezana conquered the people of Kush, he is recorded as giving thanks to the Lord for the victory. Ezana had become a Christian. Christianity was probably introduced into Aksum by Byzantine traders during the reign of Constantine. With Ezana's conversion, Christianity became Aksum's state religion.

After the fall of Rome, Aksum's trade dwindled. Then in the seventh century, Muslim armies conquered Egypt and cut Aksum off from its trade with the Mediterranean world. The power of the kings declined as the kingdom grew poorer. When the nobility rebelled and divided Aksum among themselves, the kingdom disappeared.

203

worth, leave the coins beside the goods, and return to their corner. Instruct the merchants to go to the goods and coins and decide whether the payment is sufficient. If the payment is sufficient, they should take the coins and return to their corner. If the payment is considered insufficient, the merchants should leave the coins, return to their corner, and wait for the buyers to make a better offer. After the payment has been accepted, instruct the purchasers to return to the yarn boundary and take their goods.

Explain that this method of trading was used by two ancient African groups. As time permits, discuss with the students the advantages and disadvantages of trading in this manner and how it is different from other methods of trading they have studied.

Day 104

☐ Teaching the Lesson
Aksum—Instruct the students to read page 203 silently to find the name of the king of the Aksum empire. *(King Ezana)* Select a volunteer to locate Ethiopia on a wall map.

Discussion Questions
➤ **What kind of empire was Aksum?** *(a wealthy and powerful kingdom)*
➤ **What kind of goods did Aksum supply to the Egyptian pharaohs?** *(precious stones, incense, gold, ivory, ebony, myrrh, and elephants)*
➤ **What language did educated Aksumites speak?** *(Greek)*

In the grassy savanna, Africans founded three great empires: Ghana, Mali, and Songhai. You can see the outlines of these empires on the map on page 194.

Ghana

No one knows who founded Ghana, but the kingdom probably appeared about three hundred years after the birth of Christ. By the eighth century A.D., Ghana was an empire. Ghana was governed by African kings, but many Arab merchants also lived in Ghana. Much of what we know about this empire comes from their accounts.

Gold mines were found on the land adjoining the king- dom of Ghana. Ghana did not own the gold mines, but their mer- chants traded for the gold in a unique way. The traders never saw

The ancient empire of Ghana was once located in present-day Mauritania.

one another. Great peoples of the Sudan, who lived on the land with the mines, set up a boundary that no one could cross. The merchants from Ghana would place wares and cloth on the boundary line and leave. Then the people of the Sudan would bring gold and leave it beside the merchan- dise before retreating. The merchants would then return to take the gold. If they were not satisfied with the amount of gold the Sudan people had left, they would go away again and wait for the people to add more gold until the price for the merchandise was acceptable.

204

The merchants of Ghana traded the gold—along with cola nuts, honey, and slaves—for copper, dried fruit, cowrie shells, and salt from the salt mines of the Sahara. They also traded for horses, cloth, swords, and books from North Africa and Europe.

Ghana had so much gold that the king was afraid its value would go down, so he decreed that the gold would always have a certain value. The king also taxed all trade. He was fabulously rich.

Ghana consisted of two towns. One town was Muslim. The other town, where the king lived, practiced a religion that involved sorcery. Between the two towns were all the houses of the kingdom's people.

Many African towns are still Muslim, with people worshiping in mosques such as the one above.

Ghana's army and cavalry protected its trade. When the Arabs heard of the wealth of Ghana, their leader sent his army across the Sahara to attack Ghana's capital city. After a ten-year siege, the Arabs conquered and destroyed the city. These wars interrupted trade and weakened Ghana's kings. When the army of Mali attacked, the empire could not fight back. The empire of Ghana ended in 1203.

205

➤ **How do linguists think the Aksumites learned to speak Greek?** *(The Aksumites probably visited Byzan- tium often to trade.)*

➤ **What did the city probably look like?** *(Walled castles dominated the capital city.)*

➤ **What was King Ezana like?** *(He wore gold jewelry and rich clothing, and he rode in a golden chariot drawn by four elephants.)*

➤ **How did King Ezana's rule affect Aksum?** *(Aksum be- came the strongest country in East Africa, conquering neighboring kingdoms.)*

➤ **What did Ezana do after he conquered the people of Kush?** *(He gave thanks to the Lord for the victory.)*

➤ **How did Christianity spread to Aksum?** *(Christianity was probably introduced into Aksum by Byzantine trad- ers during the reign of Constantine. Ezana probably made it Aksum's state religion.)*

➤ **What happened to Aksum after the fall of Rome?** *(Ak- sum's trade dwindled.)*

➤ **What happened to Aksum in the seventh century?** *(Muslim armies conquered Egypt and cut Aksum off from its trade with the Mediterranean world. This caused the kingdom to decline.)*

➤ **What caused the kingdom to disappear finally?** *(The nobility rebelled and divided Aksum among themselves.)*

Ghana—Instruct the students to read page 204 silently to find the name of three great empires founded in the grassy savanna. *(Ghana, Mali, and Songhai)*

Discussion Questions

➤ **When did the Ghanaian kingdom first appear?** *(about A.D. 300)*

➤ **What people lived in Ghana?** *(Africans and Arab mer- chants)*

➤ **What was found on the land adjoining the kingdom of Ghana?** *(gold)*

➤ **How did Ghanaian merchants trade with the peoples of the Sudan?** *(The merchants from Ghana placed their wares and cloth on the boundary line; the people of Su- dan would bring payment and leave it beside the mer- chandise. Neither group saw the other during this trading process.)*

➤ **Do you think this method of buying and selling would work today? Why or why not?** *(Answers will vary.)*

Day 105

Instruct the students to read page 205 silently to find what the merchants of Ghana traded. *(gold, cola nuts, honey, and slaves)*

Discussion Questions

➤ **What did the Ghanaian merchants receive in return for their goods?** *(copper, dried fruit, cowrie shells, salt from the salt mines of the Sahara, horses, cloth, swords, and books from North Africa and Europe)*

➤ **What did the king of Ghana do to the economy?** *(de- creed that gold would always have a certain value and taxed all trade)*

Mali

The empire of Mali included all of Ghana and much more land besides. No one knows who founded Mali, but by 1225 its ruler, Sundiata, had conquered Ghana. In just a few years, Sundiata gained control of the gold and salt trade and built his capital on the main trade route across the Sahara.

Ibn Battuta, a traveler from Tangier, visited Mali from 1352 to 1353. He described the people of Mali as lovers of justice and honesty. Travelers in the kingdom felt completely free from fear of harm by robbers. Although the people of Mali did many good deeds, they did not follow Christ. The Islamic religion dominated the kingdom.

This great empire was weakened by quarrels over who would become the next ruler. The fighting inside the empire encouraged enemies on the outside to attack. After four hundred years, Mali was once again a small village on the banks of the Niger River.

Muslim school in modern Mali

206

Mansa Musa

The most famous of all the Mali emperors was Mansa Musa. Mansa was his title; Musa, his name. He ruled from 1312 to 1337. He became famous, not because he was a brave general or a wise lawgiver but because he was rich.

Mansa Musa was a Muslim. In 1324 he made a pilgrimage to Mecca. At the front of his caravan marched five hundred slaves, each carrying a six-pound staff of gold. One hundred camels followed behind Mansa Musa, each carrying three hundred pounds of gold. If the value of an ounce of gold is $375, the total value of Musa's gold was about $200 million.

Mansa Musa wore gold jewelry and dressed extravagantly in velvet tunics. He had a large silk tent in the palace yard, where he met with members of his court. Slaves and musicians surrounded him during public appearances, making a great ceremony of everything he did.

In spite of his love of pomp and extravagance, Mansa Musa was very generous. He gave money freely to officials, shopkeepers, and charities everywhere he went.

207

➤ **Why did the king do this?** *(He was afraid that the value of gold would go down.)*

➤ **What were the religions of the two towns of Ghana?** *(One was Muslim, and the other practiced sorcery.)*

Explain that *sorcery* is a form of witchcraft. Remind the students that sorcery is evil and that Christians should have nothing to do with it. Instead, Christians should focus on God and His Word. (BATs: 6a Bible Study, 6b Prayer; Bible Promise: H. God as Father)

➤ **What happened when the Arabs heard of the wealth of Ghana?** *(Their leader sent his army across the Sahara to attack Ghana's capital city.)*

➤ **How long did the Arabs and the Ghanaians fight?** *(for ten years)*

➤ **How did these wars affect Ghana?** *(They interrupted trade and weakened Ghana's kings.)*

➤ **Why did the empire of Ghana finally collapse?** *(Ghana was weakened by the fighting and collapsed under the attack of another empire, Mali, in 1203.)*

Mali—Instruct the students to read page 206 silently to find the name of the ruler of Mali. *(Sundiata)*

Discussion Questions

➤ **What land made up the empire of Mali?** *(all of Ghana and more)*

➤ **Where was the capital of Mali?** *(on the main trade route across the Sahara)*

➤ **Why do you think Sundiata wanted the capital in this location?** *(so that he could make the most of trading gold and salt and make more money)*

➤ **Who was Ibn Battuta?** *(a traveler from Tangier who visited Mali from 1352 to 1353)*

➤ **How did Ibn Battuta describe Mali and its people?** *(as lovers of justice and honesty)*

➤ **What was the religion of Mali?** *(Islam)*

Explain that Muslims worship a god named Allah and his prophet, named Muhammad. Remind the students that only the God of the Bible is worthy of worship. (Bible Promise: I. God as Master)

➤ **What weakened the empire of Mali?** *(quarrels over who would become the next ruler)*

➤ **What happened to Mali?** *(The fighting encouraged enemies to attack. Eventually, Mali was only a small village.)*

Day 106

Mansa Musa—Add the figure of Mansa Musa to the History TimeLine at A.D. 1312. Instruct the students to read page 207 silently to find who Mansa Musa was. *(the most famous of all the Mali emperors)*

Discussion Questions

➤ **When did Mansa Musa rule?** *(from 1312 to 1337)*
➤ **Why was Mansa Musa famous?** *(because he was rich)*

Explain that *Mecca* is the most sacred city of Islam because it is Muhammad's birthplace. Even today, Muslims journey to Mecca to worship. (*NOTE:* Muslims are required to go to Mecca at least once during their lifetime.)

➤ **What did Mansa Musa take on his journey to Mecca?** *(a large amount of gold)*
➤ **How did Mansa Musa use his wealth?** *(He wore gold jewelry and dressed extravagantly in velvet tunics. He had a large silken tent and many slaves and musicians. He gave money freely to officials, shopkeepers, and charities everywhere he went.)*

> Remind the students that Christians should be generous with what they have, whether they have a lot or very little. Christians should be good stewards of their money and possessions, helping others who are in need. (BATs: 5a Love, 5b Giving)

□ Evaluating the Lesson

African Empires (Notebook page 58)—Instruct the students to complete each statement by supplying the correct word(s). Then tell each student to write a paragraph explaining which African empire he would have liked to live in.

━━ Going Beyond ━━

□ Enrichment

Travel journal—Tell the students that some of the information about ancient Africa that we have today comes from descriptions in the travel journal of Ibn Battuta. Give each student a travel journal page, instructing him to write a brief journal entry about a trip he has taken or about a place he has visited. Encourage the students to describe the people and activities that they have seen on these trips. (*NOTE:* See the reproducible material at the end of Lesson 53.)

□ Additional Teacher Information

One particular city in Mali, Timbuktu, became the learning center of the empire. It was in this city by the Niger River that knowledge flourished, ushering in a golden age. Timbuktu, also the center of Muslim culture, had many mosques that were great buildings made with solid gold domes and intricate carvings. During Timbuktu's golden age, Europe was going through the Hundred Years War. The Mali empire flourished in this city for several hundred years. The first African university was founded in Timbuktu around this time.

LESSON 53
Eastern and Central Africa

Text, pages 208-12
Notebook, page 59

- Songhai
- Zimbabwe
- Coastal Cities
- Central Africa

Preview

☐ Objectives

Given proper instruction, the students will be able to do the following:

- Identify true or false statements about eastern and central Africa.
- Correct false statements by making them true.

☐ Materials

Have available:
- Maps and More 19.
- A wall map of Africa.

Day 107

Lesson

☐ Introducing the Lesson

Stanley and Livingstone—Show Maps and More 19, explaining to the students that David Livingstone was a great missionary and explorer in Africa. Another man, Henry Morton Stanley, was sent as a reporter to locate Dr. Livingstone in the heart of Africa. Explain that Stanley searched a long time for the doctor. Read the following account of their first encounter in an African village.

> When they were about three hundred yards from the village, Stanley heard someone call, "Good morning, sir." Looking around, he saw a smiling native dressed in a long white shirt and a turban of American sheeting coming toward him.
>
> "Who are you?" Stanley asked.
>
> "I am Susi, the servant of Dr. Livingstone," he replied with a smile.

> "What! Is Dr. Livingstone here?"
>
> "Yes, sir."
>
> "In this village?"
>
> "Yes, sir."
>
> "Are you sure?"
>
> "Sure, sure, sir. Why, I leave him just now."
>
> "Well, Susi, run and tell the doctor I am coming."

> Stanley forgot to say who he was, and Susi did not think to ask him. Presently he came running back to say that Dr. Livingstone would like to know the white man's name.

> They were close to the village now, and suddenly Selim, a guide, tugged at Stanley's coat sleeve and said, "I see the doctor, sir. Oh, what an old man he is! He has a white beard."

> Turning in the direction toward which Selim pointed, Stanley saw for the first time the man he had been sent to Africa to find. He called the caravan to a halt and stood for a few moments looking intently at Livingstone. The doctor was standing under a mango tree a little apart from a group of Arabs. He wore a blue cloth cap with a faded gold band on a red background, a red woollen cardigan, and gray tweed trousers. And, yes, he looked old and weary and pale.

> Stanley struggled to control his emotions. He wanted to rush up to Livingstone and embrace him. But that would not be proper, he thought. With so many people around he had to act with dignity. Also, he did not know yet whether the doctor would welcome him.

> Slowly, Stanley began to walk forward from the rear of his caravan. The crowd moved back, and the ranks of his men parted to make a lane for him. There was absolute silence now, and all eyes were upon the short, compact man in the sun helmet and white flannel suit.

> He went on deliberately until he came face to face with the doctor. Removing his helmet, Stanley said gravely, "Dr. Livingstone, I presume?"

> "Yes," the doctor replied with a kind smile, lifting his cap slightly. The two men shook hands.

Discussion Question

➤ **Why do you think this was such a great moment for Stanley?** *(After much searching, he had finally found the famous Dr. Livingstone.)*

Explain that Stanley's words, "Dr. Livingstone, I presume?" became famous throughout the world. Remind the students that Livingstone and Stanley's exploration opened the door for other missionaries and explorers to go to Africa.

Songhai

Songhai had been an important town in the empire of Mali. Like Mali, it depended on trade and sent merchants to Spain, Tunis, and Egypt. In the fifteenth century under the leadership of Sunni Ali, Songhai won its independence.

Sunni Ali was a man of war, and he was never defeated. Some people believed that he was a magician who could change himself, his horses, and his soldiers into other creatures or even make them invisible. Sunni Ali fought Mali for twenty-eight years. Eventually he controlled all of the trade routes and the best farmland. Sunni Ali built a fleet of canoes to patrol the Niger River. He also built several capital cities to rule his empire better.

Timbuktu

The ancient city of Timbuktu became Songhai's center of Islamic faith and learning. It looked as though no one would ever be able to defeat the empire of Songhai.

Finally Morocco, one of Songhai's neighbors to the north, attacked Songhai. The Moroccan army had muskets, and its soldiers were better disciplined than Songhai's. The army of Songhai was defeated, and its government was destroyed.

Now other enemies attacked Songhai over and over again. Famine struck and then plague. Soon the empire of Songhai disappeared. In its place appeared many smaller states that constantly fought each other over land and trade.

208

Mwene Mutapa

Far to the south of Ghana, Mali, and Songhai in the modern country of Zimbabwe lie many ruins of stone walls and buildings—the ruins of the kingdom Mwene Mutapa. Archaeologists believe these ruins date from the eighth century.

The first settlers in ancient Zimbabwe were ancestors of the Shona, or Mashona, as they were called. They moved across the Zambezi River to have more room to live and plant crops. They organized themselves into clans and built *zimbabwes*, or big stone houses.

One zimbabwe is a huge fortress with intricate passageways and numerous rooms. It may have been the king's house. In the valley nearby is a stone ruin that may have been a temple. All of these buildings were built of stone without any mortar.

The Shona worshiped their kings as gods. Anyone who wanted to talk with the king had to come into his presence creeping and clapping his hands. Because the king was taught to be a god, he had to be perfect. If he fell ill or was deformed in any way, he was expected to commit suicide.

The Shona were farmers, but they also raised cattle. They found gold along the rivers and streams and traded it for textiles, glass beads, and Chinese porcelain. When the empire grew too big for the land to support, the Shona abandoned their zimbabwes. Archaeologists believe the Shona moved away during the fifteenth century.

The Wall (left) and Shona Village (above), parts of the Zimbabwe National Monument

209

Day 108

□ Teaching the Lesson

Songhai—Instruct the students to read page 208 silently to find who led Songhai to independence. *(Sunni Ali)*

Discussion Questions

➤ **Where did Songhai send merchants?** *(to Spain, Tunis, and Egypt)*
➤ **What did some people believe about Sunni Ali?** *(that he was a magician)*
➤ **Why do you think people thought that?** *(because he was powerful and undefeated)*
➤ **What was important about controlling the trade routes and the best farmlands?** *(They provided important income and provisions, such as food.)*
➤ **Where was Songhai's center of Islamic faith and learning?** *(Timbuktu)*
➤ **Who was finally able to defeat Songhai, and how did they do it?** *(Morocco attacked Songhai with muskets and a more disciplined army.)*

Zimbabwe—Instruct the students to read page 209 silently to find who the first settlers in ancient Zimbabwe were. *(ancestors of the Shona or Mashona)*

Discussion Questions

➤ **Why did the Shona move across the Zambezi River?** *(to have more room to live and plant crops)*
➤ **What is a *zimbabwe*?** *(a big stone house)*
➤ **How did the Shona view their kings?** *(as gods)*
➤ **How did the people have to approach the king?** *(creeping and clapping their hands)*
➤ **What happened if a king became ill or was deformed?** *(He was expected to commit suicide.)*
➤ **Why was this death expected of the king?** *(because he was supposed to be perfect, without any faults)*

> Remind the students that no man is perfect and that it is only by the blood of Christ that anyone can be acceptable to God. (BAT: 1a Understanding Jesus Christ; Bible Promises: B. Guiltless by the Blood, D. Identified in Christ)

The Coastal Cities of East Africa

The Shona traded their gold on the east coast of Africa in cities built especially for trade. No one knows who founded these cities. But by the fourth century they were governed by the Omani, Arab kings who lived far away in Oman. Mogadishu was the northernmost city, and Sofala was the southernmost city.

All along the coast, the weather was warm and the waters were full of fish. Farmers raised sheep and grew rice, millet, sorghum, cucumbers, coconuts, sugar cane, oranges, lemons, pomegranates, and bananas.

Omani merchants traded at these cities for ivory and tortoise shells. As the cities grew, more items became available for trade. By the tenth century the Africans were trading timber, gold, iron, amber, saffron, and leopard skins. To Chinese merchants they sent slaves, rhinoceros horns, pearls, incense, myrrh, and *ambergris,* a waxy substance obtained from whales and used in perfumes. One fifteenth-century Chinese emperor even traded with the Africans for a giraffe, which he thought was a unicorn. If you had been able to trade with these coastal cities, what items would you have wanted?

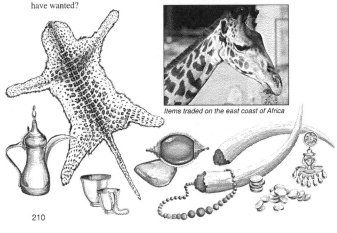

Items traded on the east coast of Africa

210

Central Africa

The peoples of central Africa had no written language. And few artifacts remain because of the hot, wet climate. We do not know much about the ancient history of these peoples, but we know that they later formed important trading empires. The Nyamwezi controlled the trade routes to the east coast of Africa for hundreds of years. Their *porters,* or men who carried goods to market, were the best in central Africa.

The culture and customs of Africa had remained unchanged for centuries. But as trade and exploration increased, the Western world gained greater interest in this land they called "the Dark Continent." More and more Europeans came to Africa to trade for slaves and to explore. And some came to preach the gospel.

Missionary David Livingstone, right, and meeting Stanley, below

"And this gospel of the kingdom shall be preached in all the world for a witness unto all nations; and then shall the end come."

Matthew 24:14

211

Day 109

Coastal cities—Instruct the students to read page 210 silently to find who governed the African cities on the coast. *(Omani, or Arab kings who lived in Oman)*

Point to Oman, Mogadishu, and Sofala on a wall map.

Discussion Questions

➤ **Do you think it was difficult to rule the coastal cities from Oman?** *(Answers will vary.)*

➤ **What did farmers raise along the coast?** *(sheep and crops of rice, millet, sorghum, cucumbers, coconuts, sugar cane, oranges, lemons, pomegranates, and bananas)*

➤ **What did Omani merchants trade for in the coastal cities?** *(ivory and tortoise shells)*

➤ **What other items did they trade as the cities grew?** *(timber, gold, iron, amber, saffron, leopard skins, slaves, rhinoceros horns, pearls, incense, myrrh, and ambergris)*

➤ **What is *ambergris,* and what is it used for?** *(It is a waxy substance obtained from whales. It is used in perfumes.)*

➤ **Why do you think the Chinese emperor thought the giraffe was a unicorn?** *(probably because it was tall and different from anything he had ever seen)*

➤ **What types of items would you want from these coastal cities?** *(Answers will vary.)*

Central Africa—Instruct the students to read page 211 silently to find why there are few artifacts from central Africa. *(because the climate is hot and wet)*

Discussion Questions

➤ **Who were the Nyamwezi?** *(They controlled the trade routes to the east coast of Africa for hundreds of years.)*

➤ **Who were the *porters?*** *(men who carried goods to market)*

➤ **Who are porters today?** *(The term usually refers to people who carry luggage at hotels or airports.)*

➤ **Why did the world gain more interest in the Dark Continent?** *(People wanted to trade for goods and slaves, to explore, and to preach the gospel.)*

Namasha watched the face of this new storyteller. His eyes were kind. His stories did not come from his head—they came from the thick book with the black cover that he carried everywhere.

"In the beginning, God created the world—the sky, the trees, the mountains, the hills, the rivers. And then He created man and woman. He walked on the earth and talked with them and loved them. But then they disobeyed Him. He still loved them, even after they had sinned, so He gave them a gift—His only Son. Jesus Christ came to earth to walk and talk with men and women. He came to die for them because He loved them just as His Father did."

Ever since this new storyteller had come to the village, something had changed. Monkeys and parrots still called from the forest. Light still slanted through the bamboo trees and made crisscrossed shadows on the village paths. The river still rippled in the distance. But something was different.

These stories were new. They were not like the old man's stories that Namasha knew so well. Namasha leaned closer as the missionary held up a picture of a man, torn and bleeding, hanging on a wooden cross. Her throat felt tight. She wanted to hear more of these new stories about Jesus.

212

True or False   Name _____

Write *T* if the statement is true. Write *F* if the statement is false.
Rewrite each false statement to make it true.

Wording may vary.

___F___ 1. Under the leadership of Mansa Musa, Songhai won its independence in the fifth century. *Under the leadership of Sunni Ali, Songhai won its independence in the fifth century.*

___T___ 2. By the fourth century, the coastal cities of east Africa were governed by the Omani, Arab kings living in Yemen. _____

___F___ 3. A zimbabwe was a Shona god who was thought to be perfect. *A zimbabwe was a big stone house.*

___F___ 4. The ambergris were men of central Africa who carried goods to market. *The porters were men of central Africa who carried goods to market. OR Ambergris is a waxy substance from whales that is used in perfumes.*

___T___ 5. Europeans came to Africa to trade for slaves, to explore, or to preach the gospel. _____

___T___ 6. The ancient city of Timbuktu was Songhai's center of Islamic faith and learning. _____

Heritage Studies 6
Student Notebook

Lesson 53
Evaluating the Lesson   **59**

Day 110

Instruct the students to read page 212 silently to find what book the new storyteller held. *(the Bible)*

Discussion Questions

➤ **How is the new storyteller's account of Creation different from the story at the beginning of the chapter?** *(The new storyteller gives the biblical account of Creation and the gospel.)*

➤ **Who was the new storyteller?** *(a missionary)*

> Remind the students that Christians should share the gospel wherever they are. (BAT: 5c Evangelism and missions)

□ Evaluating the Lesson

True or False (Notebook page 59)—Instruct the students to write *T* if the statement is true and *F* if the statement is false. Then tell them to rewrite the false statements, making them true. (*NOTE:* There may be several ways to make the false statements true.)

━━━ Going Beyond ━━━

□ Enrichment

Missionary story—Set up a reading AREA with an ample supply of 4"×6" index cards. Also have available several copies of Patricia St. John's book *Star of Light* or other missionary stories or biographies about Mary Slessor, Lillian Trotter, or any other missionary to Africa. Instruct the students to read these stories during any free time, and to write on the index card the missionary's name, the book title, and any elements of African culture presented in the story. As time permits, allow the students to discuss the different stories they have read.

□ Additional Teacher Information

The missionary David Livingstone was also an explorer. He knew exploration of Africa was necessary before missionaries could begin their work. Everywhere Livingstone went he told the Africans of God's love for all people. On one of his last trips, Livingstone discovered the Zambezi River and named its magnificent waterfalls for Queen Victoria. He thought the river might be a highway to carry God's Word to Africans who lived in the interior. Finally, he returned to England to call for missionaries to go to Africa. In one of his lectures at Cambridge, Dr. Livingstone encouraged others to carry on his work, saying of his work in Africa, "I know that in a few years I shall be cut off in that country which is now open; do not let it be shut again. I go back to Africa to try to make an open path for Christianity. Do you carry out the work which I have begun? I leave it for you."

10 LESSONS 54-61

Golden Age of the Orient: China, Japan, India

This chapter focuses on life during the golden days of classical China, Japan, and India. Students will learn about the inventions, art, music, and literature that developed in these countries during this time and how they have influenced life in modern times. The students will also learn about the rulers of these countries and about the way of life for the people who lived within the court as well as those who lived outside the court. The chapter discusses the prominent religions during the golden age and how they continue to have an influence today. The students will gain a greater understanding of the ancient culture and lifestyles of the people and how ancient traditions relate to modern traditions.

□ Materials

Lesson 59 requires certain items that must be obtained or prepared several days to several weeks before the presentation of the lesson. These items are labeled with an asterisk (*) in the lesson and in the Materials List in the Supplement. Occasionally, items not commonly found in the classroom as well as items needed in large quantities may also be labeled with an asterisk. For further information, see the individual lessons.

□ Chapter Bulletin Board

Prepare the bulletin board with a blue background, a gold border, and the title *Golden Age of the Orient* in gold letters. Place the outlines of India, China, and Japan on the board. (*NOTE:* See the reproducible material at the end of Lesson 61.) Surround each country with pictures of artwork, inventions, and so on which were developed by the countries during the golden age of the Orient. (*NOTE:* See the reproducible material at the end of Lesson 61.)

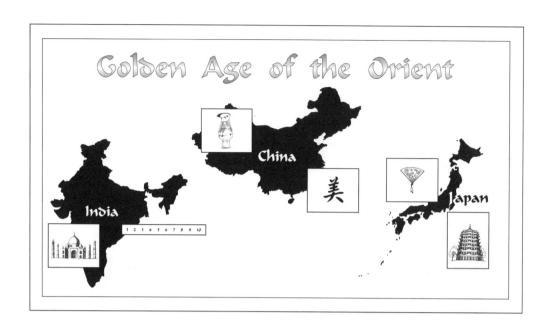

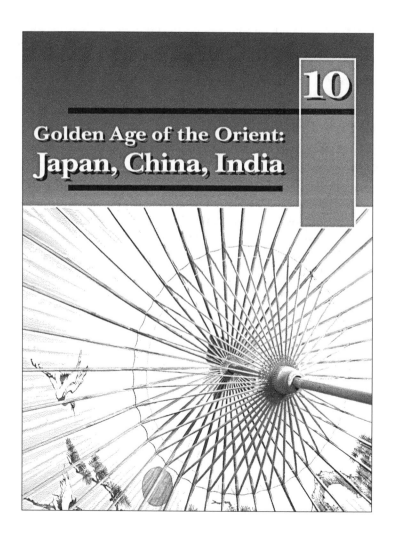

10

Golden Age of the Orient: Japan, China, India

LESSON 54
China's Golden Age of Literature

Text, pages 214-19
Notebook, page 60

- **The Golden Years**
- **The Tang and Song Dynasties**
- **Chinese Writers and Literature**
- **Printing Then and Now**

━━━━ Preview ━━━━

□ Objective

Given proper instruction, the students will be able to do the following:

- Identify terms relating to China's golden years by completing sentences.

Day 111

━━━━ Lesson ━━━━

□ Introducing the Lesson

Word association—Write the word *golden* on the chalkboard. Invite the students to tell what items come to mind when they see this word. Write the names of the items on the chalkboard as the students name them. *(Possible answers include jewelry, coins, and sunshine.)* Tell the students that in this chapter they will learn about the ancient Orient.

□ Teaching the Lesson

The golden years—Instruct the students to read page 214 silently to find out the term used to describe a country at its peak. *(the golden age)*

What do you think of when you hear the word *golden*? Do you think of rich kings and glittering palaces? Or do you think of shiny coins in a treasure chest? We use the word *golden* to refer to such things, but it can also be used to describe a time when a country is at its best. We say that a country at its peak is in its *golden age.*

Listen closely. In the distance you can hear the gongs vibrate in a mysterious melody. Inside, scholars are bent over tables, brushing fine strokes onto paper in a delicate writing of symbols and lines. Outside, in a small building, people in robes and sashes are kneeling before a stone statue. Farther out—out in the fields—are rows and rows of tea plants. You are visiting the Orient.

The Orient refers to countries in the Far East, such as China, Japan, and India. Each of these countries enjoyed a golden age when its culture, art, and literature flourished. These golden periods in the Orient produced many inventions, works of art, and intriguing stories. As you make this journey into the golden age of the Orient, you will meet a people who, though they lived thousands of years ago, made contributions to the modern world.

214

Discussion Questions

➤ **What sights and sounds might someone see and hear in the Orient?** *(Answers will include gongs vibrating, scribes writing, people dressed in robes and sashes, and rows of tea plants.)*

➤ **What did the golden age of these countries produce?** *(many inventions, works of art, and intriguing stories)*

China's Golden Years

Do you remember what a dynasty is? A *dynasty* is a line of kings and rulers who belong to the same family. In A.D. 618, the Tang rulers came to power in China. For nearly three hundred years, they ruled China. The Song dynasty replaced the Tang dynasty and ruled for about three hundred years. The six hundred years of these two dynasties make up what is called China's golden age (A.D. 618-1279).

During both of these dynasties, trade was an important part of China's economy. The Han dynasty began trade with other countries by opening the Silk Road. The Silk Road was the trade route between China and countries to the west, such as ancient Persia. Through this route, the Chinese traded their famous silk, spices, and fine pottery. How do you think China's trading with other countries affected its culture? The Chinese not only traded their goods with other countries but also shared their ideas and inventions. The golden age in China produced some great pieces of literature and art as well as some important inventions.

A Tang dynasty tomb figure

215

The Written Word

Writers of the Tang and Song dynasties produced some of China's finest literature. All scholars had to be good writers of both poetry and prose. The test for becoming a government worker required skill in both

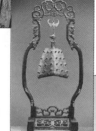

A Chinese bell and stand

The Metropolitan Museum of Art, The Crosby Brown Collection of Musical Instruments, 1889 (89.4.2077) Photograph, all rights reserved, The Metropolitan Museum of Art.

Some of nearly fifteen thousand stone tablets at Yunju Temple on which Buddhist monks engraved scriptures for preservation

writing styles. Often scholars spent hours in conversation, making up and exchanging poems. Their poems spoke of life, nature, home, friendship, and romance. One collection of forty-eight thousand poems from the Tang dynasty names twenty-two hundred different poets.

China's most famous poets lived during the golden age. Often poets wrote poems to be put to music, especially to the music of common folk tunes. One tune might have several sets of words. Singers performed these songs accompanied by chimes, bells, drums, flutes, and lutes. The scholar did not just write words for music; he also had to be able to play his song on the lute.

A modern Chinese girl playing a pipa

216

The Tang and Song dynasties—Instruct the students to read page 215 silently to find out what a dynasty is. *(a line of kings and rulers who belong to the same family)*

Discussion Questions

➤ **What rulers came to power in China in A.D. 618?** *(the Tang rulers)*

➤ **How long were the Tang rulers in power?** *(for nearly three hundred years)*

➤ **What dynasty came to power after the Tang dynasty?** *(the Song dynasty)*

➤ **What were the years of China's golden age?** *(A.D. 618-1279)*

➤ **What was an important part of China's economy during the Tang and Song dynasties?** *(trade)*

➤ **What started trade between China and other countries?** *(the opening of the Silk Road)*

➤ **What goods did China trade with other countries on the Silk Road?** *(silk, spices, and fine pottery)*

➤ **What did China also share with other countries?** *(their ideas and inventions)*

Chinese writers—Instruct the students to read page 216 silently to find out what was required of all Chinese scholars. *(They had to be good writers of poetry and prose.)*

Discussion Questions

➤ **What were the subjects of many Chinese poems?** *(life, nature, home, friendship, and romance)*

➤ **What was expected of a scholar who wrote a song?** *(He had to be able to play his song on the lute.)*

Another type of writing, the writing of history, also became important during the golden age of the Orient. The Tang rulers began a tradition in which each new dynasty wrote the official history of the last dynasty. Historians had to examine piles of court records. Then they decided which events were important and should be included in the history. Scholars who volunteered or were appointed to the task spent several years at this work. Chinese historians prided themselves on keeping accurate, detailed histories. From these records we know much about Chinese life.

Other golden age literature included philosophy, religion, politics, stories, and fables. Writers produced many "how-to" books, giving instruction in painting, handwriting, and gardening. Gardening was important to the Chinese. They created different shapes in their gardens by trimming the bushes to look like miniature mountains and by building small pools to look like lakes and rivers.

All the written works of the Orient, whether in scroll or book form, were kept in government and private libraries. Reading was a favorite pastime for many Chinese people.

An Oriental garden

217

The Printed Word
Block Printing

One reason that writing and libraries were so common in China was that the Chinese knew how to print books. The Chinese of the Tang dynasty already knew how to make paper. During the golden age, they developed *block printing.*

In block printing, the printer carved a whole page of symbols, or characters, into a block of wood. The characters had to be backwards, much like those on a rubber stamp. Next, he rolled ink onto the raised letters, carefully laid a piece of paper onto the block, and then removed the paper after it was printed. A fast printer could print two thousand pages a day. The oldest known printed book is a block-printed scroll dating from A.D. 868. It is the *Diamond Sutra,* a book sacred to Buddhists.

The Diamond Sutra

During the Song dynasty, the Chinese began to use movable-type printing. In movable-type printing, individual characters or letters were carved onto individual wood blocks. The printer then arranged these characters to form a whole page. The blocks could be used again to form a new page. The major problem the Chinese had in using movable type was organizing the more than forty thousand characters of the written Chinese language.

218

Day 112

Chinese literature—Instruct the students to read page 217 silently to find out what other type of writing became important during the golden age. *(the writing of history)*

Discussion Questions
➤ **What tradition did the Tang rulers begin?** *(Each new dynasty wrote the official history of the last dynasty.)*
➤ **What other types of literature were included in the golden age of literature?** *(philosophy, religion, politics, stories, and fables)*
➤ **What subject matter was included in Chinese "how-to" books?** *(instruction in painting, handwriting, and gardening)*
➤ **Where were all written works of the Orient kept?** *(in government and private libraries)*
➤ **What was a favorite pastime of the Chinese?** *(reading)*

An early form of printing—Instruct the students to read page 218 silently to find out what type of printing the Chinese developed. *(block printing)*

Discussion Questions
➤ **How did the characters have to be carved into a block of wood in order to be used for block printing?** *(backwards)*
➤ **With this method and with the printer working quickly, how many pages could be printed in a day?** *(two thousand)*
➤ **What is the name of the oldest block-printed scroll?** *(the Diamond Sutra)*
➤ **What did the Chinese begin to use in printing during the Song dynasty?** *(movable type)*
➤ **What major problem did the Chinese have in using movable type?** *(organizing the more than forty thousand characters of the written Chinese language)*

The Chinese printed all types of literature, such as dynastic histories, religious books, almanacs, pamphlets, dictionaries, and prose and poetry collections. Do you remember who Confucius was? He taught the values of having strong character and being responsible. Many of his teachings were printed as a collection of rules and standards of behavior, the Confucian *Classics*.

Movable type, invented by the Chinese of the golden age, was not used in Europe until about four hundred years after it had first been used in China. Today printing is a big part of our lives. Think about the newspapers you read, the words on a cereal box, or even the words on this page. Can you imagine how hard it would be to print everything we need using the Chinese block-printing method?

While we may not print like the early Chinese, our methods still echo their early methods. Computers and electronic devices do much of the work that the ancient printers had to do by hand. What do you think are some of the advantages or disadvantages of the progress we have made in printing methods?

Modern printing

219

China's Golden Age   Name _____

Complete each sentence with the appropriate word(s) from the lesson.

dynasty	1. A line of kings who belong to the same family is called a ___.
Tang	2. In A.D. 618, the ___ rulers came into power in China.
Silk Road	3. The ___ ___ opened trade between China and other countries.
poetry _prose_	4. All scholars in China's Golden Age had to be good writers of ___ and ___.
music	5. Poets often wrote poems to be set to ___.
"how-to"	6. Literature written in China's Golden Age included philosophy, religion, poetry, prose, and ___ books.
libraries	7. All written works of the Orient were kept in ___.
block	8. The Chinese developed ___ printing, a system of printing that involved carving a sheet of characters into a block of wood.
Diamond Sutra	9. The ___ is the oldest-known block-printed book.
Classics	10. The ___ were a collection of Confucius's rules and standards of behavior.

大苦芳梁多黃醎粢
臑肥之甘些若行辛腱

© 1998 BJU Press. Reproduction prohibited.

Heritage Studies 6
Student Notebook

Lesson 54
Evaluating the Lesson   **60**

Day 113

Printing then and now—Instruct the students to read page 219 silently to find out what types of literature the Chinese printed. *(Answers include dynastic histories, religious books, almanacs, pamphlets, dictionaries, and prose and poetry collections.)*

Discussion Questions

➤ **Who was Confucius?** *(a teacher of the values of having strong character and being responsible)*

➤ **What was the collection of Confucian rules and standards of behavior called?** *(the Confucian* Classics*)*

> Explain that the Chinese followed Confucius's writings as a guide which taught them how to live. Ask the students what book Christians have as a guide to show them how to live. *(the Bible)* Remind them that Christians should read the Bible daily to learn more of God. (BAT: 6a Bible study)

Invite the students to name several examples of printing that they see every day. *(Possible answers include textbooks, cereal boxes, and newspapers.)* Explain that printing methods have improved. Invite the students to name ways modern printing is different from old printing methods. *(Possible answers include faster method and advanced technology.)*

□ Evaluating the Lesson

China's Golden Age (Notebook page 60)—Instruct the students to complete each sentence with the appropriate word(s) from this lesson.

■ Going Beyond ■

□ Enrichment

Potato stamp printing—Set up an art AREA with several ink pads as well as a half potato, a serrated plastic knife, and paper for each student. Explain to the students that they will be experimenting with a type of printing similar to Chinese block printing.

Invite the students to carve whatever words or pictures on their potato halves that they wish. Point out that words must be carved backwards. When the students have finished carving, instruct them to stamp the potato onto the ink pad and to stamp on paper. When they have finished, display the samples of the students' printings around the classroom.

□ Additional Teacher Information

The *Diamond Sutra* was printed on May 11, 868, by Wang Chieh who intended for the book "to perpetuate, in deep reverence, the memory of his parents." In 1907, Sir M. Aurel Stein uncovered the *Diamond Sutra* in a walled-up chamber of a Buddhist monastery in Tun-huang. Today, the *Diamond Sutra* is on display in the British Museum.

256   Heritage Studies 6 TE

LESSON 55
China's Golden Age of Invention

Text, pages 220-23
Notebook, page 61

- The First Use of Gunpowder
- The Magnetic Compass
- Other Chinese Inventions
- Chinese Porcelain

━━ Preview ━━

□ Objective

Given proper instruction, the students will be able to do the following:
- Match Chinese innovations with their definitions.

□ Notes

For the Enrichment activity, the students will be making a magnetic compass. (*NOTE:* See the reproducible material at the end of Lesson 61.) If you choose to do this activity, you will need to purchase a cork stopper for each student and several bar magnets. These items can be purchased from Bob Jones University Press, craft stores, or discount stores.

Day 114

━━ Lesson ━━

□ Introducing the Lesson

The new invention—Read the following story to the students.

Li Qing *(lē kǐng)* worked quickly, hurrying about the room as fast as her tiny feet would allow her. In a few hours, the dinner guests would be arriving, and there was still so much to do. Qing sighed and looked at her small brown hands as she carefully chopped up raw vegetables. She was barely twelve years old, yet ever since her mother's death two years ago, she had taken on the responsibilities of a woman. Although she was quite adept at taking care of the house and the younger children, she sometimes missed her mother's kindness and wisdom.

Qing heard men's voices as her father and brothers entered the house. They had come in early from the rice fields to make themselves presentable for receiving guests. Qiang, her older brother, smiled as he passed by her. Qing smiled back. Qiang, unlike her younger brother, Wei, treated her with respect. Wei, on the other hand, believed that women were inferior and treated her with disdain.

The guests arrived just as Qing set out the last dish. The Xiang family had been friends of the Li family for a long time. Quite often they had dinner together. Xiang Xia, the youngest daughter, and Qing were close friends. Qing looked forward to talking with Xia. The family sat down at a low table and began to eat. Qing knew that she would not be allowed to speak much at the dinner table, but she listened carefully to the men's conversation.

"And they have discovered a new device," Mao, Xia's father, was explaining to Qing's father. "When they put a piece of iron on a piece of wood or cork and float it on water, it always points to the south."

"This is indeed remarkable," Qing's father said. "How, I wonder, do they plan to use this new device?"

Mao shrugged. "Someone remarked to me that they may use it to help make up the calendar and to set up the New Year."

The conversation then began to drift to other topics, but Qing did not pay much attention to the discussion any longer. A new device made simply from wood and iron that always pointed south when it floated on the water! It was truly remarkable! Qing wished that she could see such a device. Several other remarkable discoveries had already been made, and Qing was sure that the diligent scholars would come up with more remarkable inventions. It was wonderful to be able to see and hear about all the advances her countrymen were making. Qing could not know for certain, but she did believe that someday China would be one of the greatest countries in the world.

Explain that the remarkable device mentioned in the story was the magnetic compass, invented by the ancient Chinese. Tell the students that they will learn more about the magnetic compass and other inventions of the Chinese in this lesson.

An Age of Invention

Printing was not the only invention of China's golden age. Chinese scholars put their minds to work on several other practical matters. Did you know that gunpowder was first used by the Chinese during the golden age?

The Chinese did not use gunpowder in warfare until the Song dynasty. But earlier, they used it for another purpose. In religious and government celebrations, the Chinese set off firecrackers made with gunpowder. Most Americans associate firecrackers with the Fourth of July, but the Chinese use them to celebrate the New Year. On the first day of the year, every person and animal in China becomes one year older. How would you like to celebrate your birthday this way?

The Chinese New Year falls somewhere in January or February of each year, depending on the moon's position in its yearly cycle. Even today, the Chinese celebrate the New Year with parades, costumes, and firecrackers.

Man, these party favors are really a blast!

220

The Chinese also discovered the magnetic compass. They found that when a piece of magnetic iron ore was attached to a piece of wood or cork floating in water, it always pointed north-south. The magnetic compass was most useful for guidance on land or navigation at sea.

The Chinese, however, did not use the compass for navigating at first. Instead, they used it for religious and superstitious purposes. The compass aided astrologers in making up the yearly calendar and setting the date of the New Year. Years later, in the Song dynasty, the Chinese began to use the compass for navigation.

Although the early Chinese compasses indicated south rather than north, they operated on the same principle as modern ones.

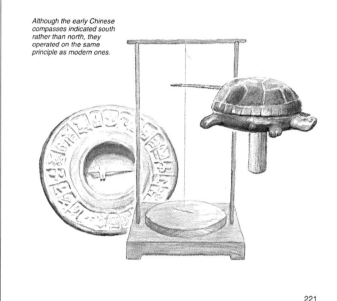

221

□ Teaching the Lesson

The first use of gunpowder—Instruct the students to read page 220 silently to find out for what purpose the Chinese first used gunpowder. *(to set off fireworks)*

Discussion Questions

➤ **On what occasions did the Chinese use fireworks?** *(religious and government celebrations and the Chinese New Year)*

➤ **What happens on the Chinese New Year?** *(Every person and animal turns a year older.)*

➤ **What determines when the Chinese New Year will be celebrated?** *(the moon's yearly cycle)*

➤ **When did the Chinese first begin using gunpowder in warfare?** *(during the Song dynasty)*

The magnetic compass—Instruct the students to read page 221 silently to find out what useful navigational tool the Chinese discovered. *(the magnetic compass)*

Discussion Questions

➤ **How did the Chinese first use the magnetic compass?** *(for religious or superstitious purposes)*

➤ **How did the compass aid Chinese astrologers?** *(It helped them make up the yearly calendar and set the date for the Chinese New Year.)*

➤ **When did the Chinese begin using the compass for navigation?** *(during the Song dynasty)*

The Chinese produced other practical devices too. They built highly accurate clocks run by water. They made rain and snow gauges that helped them with flood control. To connect the regions of the empire, they built a system of roads, bridges, and canals. They also made maps. The oldest printed map existing today shows China in 1155.

In medicine, the Chinese studied diseases and recommended treatments. Acupuncture, a medical practice developed during the Han dynasty, continued to be used during the golden age. It is still being used today in some parts of the world.

The Chinese of this period also used various herbs as medicine. In the early twelfth century, the government published the *Imperial Medical Encyclopedia*, a volume listing medical problems with their symptoms and treatments.

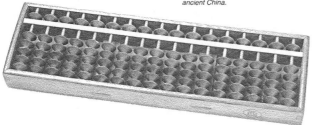

The abacus was one of many practical devices developed in ancient China.

222

Making Porcelain

The Chinese invented a way of making *porcelain*, a thin, but strong, translucent pottery. Porcelain, or "china," is made from a mixture of white clay and the mineral feldspar. The Chinese tried many combinations to get just the right mixture. The potter worked with this clay mixture, using a potter's wheel or a mold. Once the pottery dried, it was decorated with paint, carvings, or a glaze of liquid glass. Pale green and blue gray were two favorite colors used in porcelain designed by the Chinese in the golden age.

After the artist finished his decorating, the pottery was fired in a very hot oven. After the firing, the clay, or porcelain, was hard, shiny, and translucent. Porcelain has a clear, bell-like ring when tapped lightly on the edge. By the

A Song dynasty vase with pale green glaze

end of the Tang period, the Chinese had learned to make beautiful porcelain. Today, old Chinese porcelain is rare and extremely valuable.

The Chinese used porcelain for both practical and decorative purposes. Many families served their daily tea in porcelain cups. The emperor was a major buyer of porcelain goods. He occasionally ordered several thousand pieces of porcelain at a time. Some provinces sent porcelain to the emperor's court as their required *tribute*. A tribute was a payment made to ensure protection or to show submission to the emperor.

223

Day ¹¹⁵

Other Chinese inventions—Instruct the students to read page 222 silently to find out what other things the Chinese invented or developed. *(Possible answers include clocks run by water; rain and snow gauges; a system of roads, bridges, and canals; and maps.)*

Discussion Questions

➤ **What does the oldest existing printed map show?** *(China in 1155)*
➤ **What medical practice was developed during the Han dynasty?** *(acupuncture)*
➤ **What was the name of a volume that listed medical problems with their symptoms and treatments?** *(the* Imperial Medical Encyclopedia*)*

Explain that during its golden age, China achieved much through its inventions. Remind the students that when Christians achieve something great, they should give the glory to God. (BAT: 7b Exaltation of Christ)

Chinese porcelain—Instruct the students to read page 223 silently to find out what two materials were mixed to make porcelain. *(white clay and the mineral feldspar)*

Discussion Questions

➤ **What were the two favorite colors used in porcelain?** *(pale green and blue gray)*
➤ **Who was a major purchaser of porcelain?** *(the emperor)*
➤ **For what purpose did some Chinese provinces use porcelain?** *(to pay their required tribute to the emperor)*

Chinese Innovation Match   Name _____

Match the innovations with their definitions by writing the correct letter beside each description.

A. acupuncture   F. gunpowder
B. rain gauge   G. maps
C. *Imperial Medical Encyclopedia*   H. clock
D. magnetic compass   I. porcelain
E. road, bridge, and canal system

__F__ 1. The Chinese used this invention to make fireworks.

__D__ 2. This invention consisted of a piece of iron attached to a piece of wood or cork that could float in water.

__B__ 3. This invention helped to prevent flooding.

__A__ 4. This medical practice was used in ancient China and is still used today.

__C__ 5. This volume lists medical problems with their symptoms and treatments.

__E__ 6. This network connected the regions of the empire.

__G__ 7. The oldest of these in existence today was made in China.

__I__ 8. This is a thin but strong translucent pottery.

__H__ 9. This invention was highly accurate and was run by water.

Heritage Studies 6
Student Notebook

Lesson 55
Evaluating the Lesson   **61**

□ Evaluating the Lesson

Chinese Innovation Match (Notebook page 61)—Instruct the students to match the innovations with their definitions by writing the correct letter beside each description.

━━━ Going Beyond ━━━

□ Enrichment

Magnetic compass construction—Set up an art AREA with a cork stopper, a pin, a large sewing needle, glue, a plastic cereal bowl, and a copy of the instruction sheet for each student. (*NOTE:* See the reproducible material at the end of Lesson 61.) Also have available several bar magnets and a compass. Instruct each student to construct a magnetic compass as directed on the instruction sheet. When the students have finished, encourage them to be sure their compasses point in a north-south direction while floating in water.

□ Additional Teacher Information

Although most of the medical practices used in ancient China do not have basis in modern medical sciences, some treatments probably did work. For instance, willow bark, used in one of the ancient treatments, contains salicylic acid, which is the chemical basis for aspirin. Another example is foxglove, which contains digitalis, a powerful drug used for heart problems.

The most famous Chinese medical treatment was acupuncture. In this treatment, fine needles were stuck into a person at various places on his body. The patient did not experience any pain through this treatment. Modern medical science has recognized acupuncture as an effective method of rendering temporary insensitivity to pain and temporary improvement in some nervous-system diseases.

Although doctors in China are trained to practice modern methods of treatment, many still practice some of the effective treatments of traditional medicine. Traditional Chinese medicine is also becoming popular in other parts of the world.

LESSON 56
China's Golden Age of Art

Text, pages 224-25
Notebook, pages 62-64

- **Chinese Paintings**
- **Other Art Forms**

Preview

□ Objective
Given proper instruction, the students will be able to do the following:
- Identify words in a crossword puzzle and use the words to complete sentences about ancient China.

□ Materials
Have available:
- A sheet of white drawing paper for each student.
- A felt-tip pen for each student.

Day 116

Lesson

□ Introducing the Lesson
Landscape drawing—Allow the students to go outside for a few minutes to find something of the landscape that they want to draw. Instruct them to study this object for a few minutes. When the allotted time has passed, lead the students back into the classroom and give them each a piece of paper and a felt-tip pen. Tell the students to draw a picture of what they saw outside as accurately as they can remember it. After they have finished and as time allows, invite them to discuss whether they thought it was hard to draw a scene from memory.

Explain that in ancient China, artists would paint a landscape from memory. Tell the students that they will learn more about Chinese artists and the different forms of Chinese art in this lesson.

An ancient Chinese landscape painting

An Age of Art
The Chinese distinguished between artists and craftsmen. For example, in making porcelain, only the potter and the decorator were considered artists. The other men who helped were considered crafts-men. The Chinese considered painters to be true artists. Painters usually trained for at least twenty years before they were considered good artists. Like writing poetry, painting became a requirement on the exams that had to be passed before a person could work for the government.

The most common type of painting was landscape painting. A Chinese artist did not paint while he looked at a scene. Instead, he studied the scene for several hours. Then, in his studio, he put down his thoughts of the scene on a silk or paper scroll, using ink and brushes made from animal hairs. Once he had made a stroke, it could not be erased, covered up, or changed. Painters worked quickly, before their thoughts of the view faded.

In China, paintings did not hang on the walls but were on rolled-up scrolls that were stored in cases. The owners of the scrolls displayed the paintings only on special occasions. Visitors and family members enjoyed these works of art that honored nature.

A Chinese calligraphy set

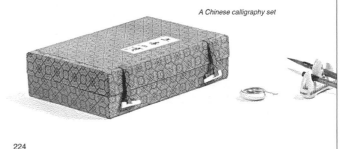

224

□ Teaching the Lesson
Chinese paintings—Instruct the students to read page 224 silently to find out whom the Chinese considered the true artists in the making of porcelain. *(the potter and the decorator)*

Discussion Questions
➤ **How long were painters trained before they were considered good artists?** *(twenty years)*
➤ **What was the most common type of painting?** *(landscape painting)*
➤ **How did a Chinese artist paint a scene?** *(He studied a scene for hours and then painted it from memory back in his studio.)*
➤ **Where were paintings kept?** *(in cases)*
➤ **When were paintings displayed?** *(only on special occasions)*

Calligraphy, from the Greek words meaning "beautiful writing," is an art similar to painting. The Chinese did not simply "write" words, but created a series of beautiful symbols. Calligraphers practiced many years, first to learn and then to improve their art. The government even had a special college that taught calligraphy. An excellent calligrapher received great honor and praise in China. Where do you see examples of calligraphy today?

Architecture was also an important art in the golden age. The Chinese believed their buildings should blend into the landscape. They built houses low and long. Wooden pillars and beams supported the roofs of the houses, while the walls were simply screens decorated with carvings, paintings, or lacquer, a clear and shiny coating.

Pagoda temple, Hong Kong

Roofs having curved eaves came into use during the Tang dynasty and soon became typical of Chinese architecture. Another Chinese building style begun during this age was the *pagoda*. Pagodas were first used as Buddhist temples. Soon, however, the pagoda was just another type of building used for many purposes.

225

Chinese Crossword Clues   Name _____

Use the following clues to solve the crossword puzzle on page 63.

Across

4. strong, translucent pottery
5. rulers who came into power in A.D. 618
9. oldest block-printed book (two words)
11. comes from Greek words meaning "beautiful writing"
13. The Chinese produced many _____, such as gunpowder.
14. These rulers came to power after the rulers in 5 Across.

Down

1. a building once used as a Buddhist temple
2. a type of printing developed in China
3. lines of kings and rulers from the same family
6. Writers during the time of the Tang dynasty produced fine _____.
7. A country at its peak is in its _____ _____. (two words)
8. art involving building construction
10. These people celebrate the New Year with fireworks.
12. a popular form of Chinese painting

Heritage Studies 6
Student Notebook   Lesson 56
Evaluating the Lesson   **62**

Other art forms—Instruct the students to read page 225 silently to find out where the word *calligraphy* originated. *(from the Greek words meaning "beautiful writing")*

Discussion Questions

➤ **Rather than just writing words, what did the Chinese create?** *(a series of beautiful symbols)*
➤ **How was an excellent calligrapher treated?** *(He received great honor and praise.)*
➤ **What other art form was important in the golden age?** *(architecture)*
➤ **What did the Chinese believe about their buildings?** *(that they should blend into the landscape)*
➤ **What were the walls in a Chinese house like?** *(screens decorated with carvings, paintings, or lacquer)*
➤ **For what were pagodas first used?** *(as Buddhist temples)*

Remind the students that God has given Christians special talents, whether it be in art, music, or another area. Tell the students that Christians should give God the glory for their accomplishments and should always be humble, knowing that men's praise on earth will not matter in eternity. (BATs: 7b Exaltation of Christ, 7e Humility)

☐ Evaluating the Lesson

Chinese Crossword (Notebook pages 62-64)—Instruct the students to complete the puzzle on Notebook pages 62-63 and then to use the puzzle words to complete the paragraph on Notebook page 64.

Use the clues on page 62 to complete the puzzle below.

```
        ¹P      ²B          ³D
         A       L           Y
         G       O           N
       ⁴P O R C E L A I N     A
         D       K          ⁵S
         A              ⁵T A N G
                            I
        ⁶L      ⁷G      ⁸A
       ⁹D I A M O N D S U T R A
         T       L           C
         E       D           H      ¹⁰C
         R       E    ¹¹C A L L I G R A P H Y
         A       N       A    T      I
         T       A    ¹³I N V E N T I O N S
         U       G       D    C      E
         R       E       S    T     ¹⁴S O N G
         E               C    U      E
                         A    R
                         P    E
                         E
```

Heritage Studies 6
Student Notebook   Lesson 56
Evaluating the Lesson   63

Use the words from the puzzle on page 63 to complete the following paragraph.

Under the ___**Tang**___ and ___**Song**___ ___**dynasties**___,
      5 Across   14 Across   3 Down

the ___**Chinese**___ people enjoyed a time when their country was at its best. This
     10 Down

time is often referred to as China's ___**Golden Age**___. During this period, writers
      7 Down

produced some of China's finest ___**literature**___. Their writing included poetry,
      6 Down

prose, histories, and fables. The Chinese also printed books. The style of printing they

developed was ___**block**___ printing. The ___**Diamond Sutra**___ is the
     2 Down   9 Across

oldest-known book printed in this fashion. Art was also important. ___**Calligraphy**___,
      11 Across

or beautiful writing, was a valuable skill. People gifted in this ability were well respected.

Painting, too, was a form of art. ___**Landscape**___ painting was especially popular.
      12 Down

The Chinese also invented ___**porcelain**___, a strong, translucent pottery, and some
      4 Across

objects made from this material are considered art today. ___**Architecture**___ was yet
      8 Down

another important art form. A type of building constructed was the ___**pagoda**___.
      1 Down

These were at first used as Buddhist temples. Other ___**inventions**___, such as gun-
      13 Across

powder, the magnetic compass, and maps, first came into use during China's days of splendor.

Heritage Studies 6
Student Notebook   Lesson 56
Evaluating the Lesson   64

Going Beyond

□ Enrichment

Calligraphy project—Set up an art AREA with white drawing paper, a calligraphy pen or felt-tip pen, and a copy of the Bible verse in calligraphy for each student. Display the calligraphy handwriting chart. (*NOTE:* See the reproducible material at the end of Lesson 61.) Instruct the students to follow the strokes for forming the letters in calligraphy to write the verse. When they have finished, encourage them to draw pictures to frame the verse. Display the students' copies of the verse around the classroom.

□ Additional Teacher Information

Chinese painting today is much like ancient Chinese painting. There are five subjects depicted: humans, landscapes, flowers, birds, and animals. Many accomplished Chinese artists specialize in one of these subjects.

Art critics often give much attention to the brush strokes in a Chinese painting. The strokes are important to the painting, and critics judge how the strokes contribute to the painting's texture. Brush strokes have fancy names such as "raindrops," "ax cuts," or "wrinkles on a devil's face."

One form of Chinese painting, finger painting, was developed during the Tang dynasty. In this form of painting, the artist's fingernails are his main tools. A broken fingernail is a great hindrance to the painter.

LESSON 57
The Land of the Rising Sun

Text, pages 226-29
Notebook, page 65

- Two Japanese Religions
- The Rule of the Yamato Clan
- The Heian Age
- The Japanese Language

━━━ Preview ━━━

☐ Objective

Given proper instruction, the students will be able to do the following:
- Identify words relating to ancient Japan by unscrambling them and using specific letters from the words to solve a riddle.

☐ Notes

The Enrichment activity in Lesson 58 requires the students to use shoeboxes. If you choose to do this activity, instruct each student to bring a shoebox to class several days before the activity is to be done.

Day 118

━━━ Lesson ━━━

☐ Introducing the Lesson

Japanese greetings—Write the words *Ohayo otaka onna* (*Ohīō ōtäkə ōnə*) on the chalkboard. Encourage the students to guess what the words mean. Say the words aloud and tell the students that the words mean "Hello, boys and girls" in Japanese. Invite the students to repeat the words as you say them slowly. Write another word, *sensei (sĕn′ sā)*, on the chalkboard. Tell the students that this is the Japanese word for teacher. Encourage the students to practice saying the phrase *Ohayo sensei*. Invite them to say this phrase in reply when you say "Ohayo otaka onna."

Explain that when the Japanese language was first developed, scholars spent many years learning how to speak it. Tell the students that even today the Japanese language is difficult to learn. Explain that they will be learning more about the Japanese language in this lesson.

Japan's Golden Years

China's Influence

Who do you think causes more changes in a country—people who trade with the citizens of the country or people who come to live there? During China's golden age, Buddhist missionaries were sent to neighboring countries. Many of these missionaries went to live in Japan, bringing new styles of clothing, new ideas, new customs, and a new religion.

The Buddhist missionaries had a great influence on Japan. Many Buddhist missionaries were scholars and teachers. Besides teaching the Japanese about Buddhism, these missionaries also taught the Japanese how to read and write Chinese, study Chinese literature, and create art in the Chinese style. Later, many Japanese traveled to China to study in the Buddhist schools. This travel between China and Japan caused Chinese ideas and customs to influence Japan greatly.

Buddhism was not the only religion in Japan, however. Shintoism was, and still is, the main religion of Japan. Shinto means "the way of the gods" and teaches that every object or creature in nature has a god. So, in Shintoism, many gods are worshiped. How is this type of worship different from what the Bible teaches? A big part of Shintoism is emperor worship. The Japanese believed that the emperor descended from the sun goddess's grandson, *Jimmu Tenno,* and so deserved to be worshiped.

Stone Buddha, Kyoto

A torii marking the entrance to a Shinto shrine in Miyazima

226

☐ Teaching the Lesson

Two Japanese religions—Instruct the students to read page 226 silently to find out who brought Buddhism to Japan. *(Buddhist missionaries from China)*

Discussion Questions

➤ **What other things did the missionaries teach the Japanese?** *(how to read and write Chinese, to study Chinese literature, and to create art in the Chinese style)*
➤ **Where did the Japanese go to study in the Buddhist schools?** *(to China)*
➤ **What other religion was prominent in Japan?** *(Shintoism)*
➤ **What does the word *Shinto* mean?** *("the way of the gods")*
➤ **What does Shintoism teach?** *(that every object or creature in nature has a god)*
➤ **What did Shintoists believe about the emperor?** *(that he descended from the sun goddess's grandson, Jimmu Tenno, and deserved to be worshiped)*

Ask the students how Shintoism differs from what the Bible teaches. *(The Bible teaches that there is one true God who controls all things; Shintoism teaches that there are many gods to be worshiped.)* Remind the students that God is sovereign, and He orders the lives of His people for His glory and their good. (Bible Promise: I. God as Master)

Early Japanese society was made of *clans*. A clan is a group of people who claim to have a common ancestor. The many clans of Japan fought among themselves for control of other clans and land. Finally, the *Yamato* clan gained the most power. The leader of the Yamato clan claimed to be related to Jimmu Tenno, the legendary grandson of the sun goddess. This supposed ancestry allowed the leader of the Yamato clan to claim the title of emperor. Chinese culture first entered Japan in the fourth century A.D., during the early centuries of the Yamato rule.

In the seventh century, the Yamato rulers started a new program in Japan. This program was aimed at making Japan much like Tang China by improving the government system. The Japanese admired the achievements of the Chinese and wanted this progress in their own land.

The first Japanese capital was set up in *Nara*. It was the capital of the Yamato rule and also the center of Japanese Buddhism. The Yamato wanted to lessen the power of the Buddhists because that religious movement kept getting stronger. The Yamato moved the capital to a new location, Heian-kyo. This city became the center of culture and the arts, opening the doors to Japan's golden age.

Seventh-century carving, Nara Prefecture

Monuments on a mountain trail, Nara Prefecture

227

The Heian Age

Soon after the capital was moved to Heian-kyo, another family, the *Fujiwara,* came into power. The Chinese continued to influence Japan under the Fujiwara rule. The Japanese looked to China as a model to follow. However, the Japanese changed the Chinese patterns and made them part of their own Japanese culture. Much of the typical Japanese culture had its start in the court life at Heian.

Chinese learning greatly influenced Japanese learning at Heian. Japanese students learned to read and write Chinese and to memorize Chinese poetry. In Japan, however, only the nobility attended school. Government positions were open only to nobles. The Japanese government did not emphasize education as much as the Chinese government did. Family background, wealth, and social position were more important than ability in holding government positions.

In addition to teaching Chinese culture, Japanese education also included much instruction in court *etiquette,* or manners. Life at the Heian court demanded strict rules of behavior. Every situation had a proper action and response, from accepting a piece of food to meeting the emperor. Above all, a person at the court must have *composure* and not show his emotions at any time. If someone did not follow these rules, he was not welcome at court.

This fragment of Japanese poetry is from the Ise Shu, an anthology of poems by Lady Ise, composed during the Fujiwara period (early 12th century, ink on decorated paper; collection Osaragi Jiro, Japan).

228

Day *119*

The rule of the Yamato clan—Instruct the students to read page 227 silently to find out when Chinese culture first entered Japan. *(in the fourth century A.D. during the early centuries of the Yamato rule)*

Discussion Questions

➤ **What made up early Japanese society?** *(clans)*

➤ **What is a *clan*?** *(a group of people who claim to have a common ancestor)*

➤ **To whom did the leader of the Yamato clan claim to be related?** *(to Jimmu Tenno, the legendary grandson of the sun goddess)*

➤ **What did this claim allow the leader of the Yamato clan to do?** *(to claim the title of emperor)*

➤ **How do you think rival clans felt when the Yamato clan's ruler claimed the title of emperor?** *(Possible answers include jealous and angry.)*

➤ **What new program did the Yamato start in the seventh century?** *(a program to make Japan much like Tang China)*

➤ **How did the Japanese people respond to this program?** *(They admired the Chinese achievements and wanted the same progress in their own land.)*

➤ **Where was the first Japanese capital established?** *(at Nara)*

➤ **Why did the Yamato clan move the capital to a new location?** *(to lessen the power of the Buddhists)*

➤ **Where was the new capital located?** *(in Heian-kyo)*

The Heian Age—Instruct the students to read page 228 silently to find out what family came to power shortly after the Japanese capital was moved to Heian-kyo. *(the Fujiwara)*

Discussion Questions

➤ **Where did much of the typical Japanese culture have its start?** *(in the court life at Heian)*

➤ **Who could attend school?** *(only the nobility)*

➤ **Who could hold government positions?** *(only the nobles)*

➤ **What things were more important to the Japanese than education and the ability to hold government positions?** *(family background, wealth, and social position)*

➤ **In addition to Chinese culture, what else did Japanese education include?** *(instruction in court etiquette)*

➤ **What happened if a person did not follow the rules of court etiquette?** *(The person was not welcome at court.)*

The Spoken Word

The Japanese had their own language; however, Chinese was the official language of the court. Japanese scholars spent many years learning Chinese. Often, how far a man was promoted at court depended upon how well he spoke Chinese. For centuries, all the official writing in the Japanese court was done in Chinese. Histories, diaries, and poetry were all written in Chinese by nobles at court.

Although the Japanese had a spoken language, they had no written language. Japanese differed greatly from Chinese, but the Japanese adopted Chinese characters and made them fit their own language. This process took place over many years during the Heian period. Even today, Japanese is a difficult language to master.

Japanese character for "house"

229

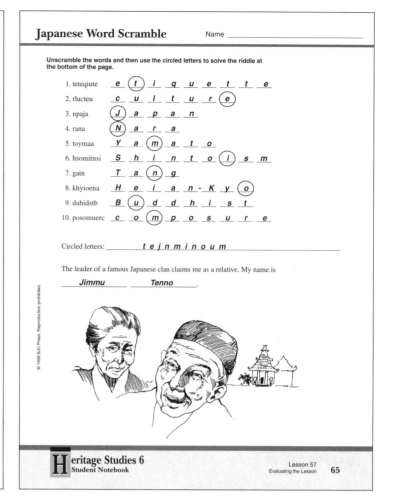

Japanese Word Scramble   Name _____

Unscramble the words and then use the circled letters to solve the riddle at the bottom of the page.

1. teteqiute   e (t) i q u e t t e
2. rlucteu   c u l t u r (e)
3. npaja   (J) a p a n
4. rana   (N) a r a
5. toymaa   Y a (m) a t o
6. hsomitnsi   S h i n t o (i) s m
7. gatn   T a (n) g
8. khyioena   H e i a n - K y (o)
9. duhidstb   B (u) d d h i s t
10. posomuerc   c o (m) p o s u r e

Circled letters: _____ t e j n m i n o u m _____

The leader of a famous Japanese clan claims me as a relative. My name is

Jimmu   _Tenno_   .

© 1996 BJU Press. Reproduction prohibited.

Heritage Studies 6
Student Notebook

Lesson 57
Evaluating the Lesson   **65**

Day 120

The Japanese language—Instruct the students to read page 229 silently to find out the official language of the court. *(Chinese)*

Discussion Questions

➤ **What often determined how far a man was promoted at court?** *(how well he spoke Chinese)*

➤ **How did the Japanese solve the problem of not having a written language?** *(They adopted characters from the Chinese and made them fit their own language.)*

☐ Evaluating the Lesson

Japanese Word Scramble (Notebook page 65)—Instruct the students to unscramble the words and then to use the circled letters to solve the riddle.

Going Beyond

☐ Enrichment

Research activity—Set up an AREA with a copy of the "Three Major Religions" page for each student. (*NOTE:* See the reproducible material at the end of Lesson 61.) Instruct the students to use their texts and encyclopedias to find the information requested. Answers are as follows:

1. Answers include reincarnation, ancestor worship, and the Eight Fold Path.

2. Answers include a god for every creature or object in nature, nature worship, emphasis on moral standards, and emperor worship.

3. Answers include that there is only one God, that everyone is born a sinner, that Christ died to save mankind and rose again, and that Christians will live in heaven with Christ.

4. Answers include that Shintoism teaches the worship of more than one god, that Buddhism teaches that when a person dies he is reincarnated as a different form of life on earth, and that the Bible teaches that when a person dies he will go directly to heaven if he is saved or to hell if he is unsaved.

☐ Additional Teacher Information

The Japanese capital was moved from Nara to Heian-kyo toward the end of the eighth century. Heian-kyo, "the City of Peace and Tranquility," was later called simply Kyoto, which means "capital." It was the seat of imperial government through most of the nineteenth century.

Kyoto was much like the Chinese capital. Soon, however, the Japanese government became concerned about the immense influence of the Chinese culture in Japan. In an attempt to lessen the strong impact of the Chinese, the government did not allow anyone except priests to go into China. Any relations between China and Japan were limited to trade.

Although Japan has drawn away from China's influence, the Chinese heritage is not lost, nor is the Japanese culture without similarities to Chinese culture. China's influence was too great to be forgotten.

LESSON 58
Japanese Literature and Art

Text, pages 230-34
Notebook, page 66

- **Court Literature**
- **Japanese Poetry**
- **Japanese Art and Architecture**
- **Then and Now**

━━━━━ Preview ━━━━━

□ Objective
Given proper instruction, the students will be able to do the following:
- Write one or more haiku.

□ Materials
Have available:
- A wall map of the world.
- Crayons for each student.

Day 121

━━━━━ Lesson ━━━━━

□ Introducing the Lesson
Haiku reading—Read the following haiku to the class.

> Skies change to violet
> Red-gold sphere slowly descends
> Day turns into night.

Discussion Questions
➤ **What type of picture do you imagine with this poem?** *(the sun setting)*
➤ **What type of mood does the poem convey?** *(Possible answers include peaceful, quiet, and thoughtful.)*

Explain that this type of poem is called a *haiku*. Tell the students that haiku was a popular form of poetry during the Heian period of Japan and that it continues to be popular today. Explain to the students that they will learn more about haiku in this lesson and will be given an opportunity to write some haiku of their own.

The Written Word

Japan's Golden Age of Literature
The Japanese language became common during the Heian period; it was used for unofficial writing. In fact, the Heian period is known as the golden age of literature in Japan. Japanese literature was written mainly by ladies who were wealthy. They wrote in Japanese because women were not thought capable of learning Chinese; therefore, they were never taught the Chinese language. These women often spent their leisure time writing about their experiences in the emperor's court.

These writings provide a complete picture of life for the wealthy. One Heian woman wrote the first Japanese novel. Her six-volume *Tale of Genji* tells the story of Prince Genji and his life at court.

230

□ Teaching the Lesson
Court literature—Instruct the students to read page 230 silently to find out what the Heian period is sometimes called. *(the golden age of literature)*

Discussion Questions
➤ **Why did the Japanese language become common during the Heian period?** *(It was used for unofficial writing.)*
➤ **Who wrote most of the Japanese literature?** *(wealthy women)*
➤ **Why did the women write in Japanese?** *(The Japanese thought women were incapable of learning Chinese.)*
➤ **What did these women mainly write about?** *(their experiences in the emperor's court)*
➤ **What is the name of the first Japanese novel?** *(Tale of Genji)*

Poetry was an important part of Japanese culture. A person was judged by how well he could create a poem. One special type of Japanese poem that is still popular today is the *haiku,* a poem with only three lines. The words are chosen according to meaning and syllables. There are only seventeen syllables in the entire poem. A Japanese poet tries to create a mood and a picture with his words. Here are some modern examples of haikus that follow the ancient Japanese form.

Celebration
Leaves sprinkle the grass
Confetti tangled in hair.
Fall hosts a party.

Playground
Sloping string of grass
Droplets quiver at the top
To ride the green slide.

Japanese wood sculpture of Jizo Bosatsu created during the Heian period

231

The Arts

Even today, Japanese art and architecture resemble those of China. This influence began before the Heian period. The Japanese looked to China for models in painting, calligraphy, sculpture, and music.

Gradually, the Japanese left the Chinese models and developed their own artistic patterns. One characteristic of Japanese art was brilliant color. Bright colors made paintings full of life and activity. Colors decorated houses and temples as well. A second characteristic of Japanese art is its use of everyday objects. Boxes, baskets, furniture, combs, and fans were painted and carved. These objects were beautiful as well as useful.

Ikebana was a special Japanese art form that involved arranging flowers. Colors and types of flowers were chosen carefully to match the occasion and the season. Chrysanthemums, for example, were used in the month of May. Every year a Chrysanthemum Festival was held in which the emperor inspected the flower gardens at the palace. In celebration, the Japanese drank wine that was made from chrysanthemums, believing that the wine would give them a long life.

All the arts were important at court. Painters and sculptors represented court life in their works. Architects designed new buildings, and calligraphers recorded the writings of the court with their beautiful penmanship. Elegant music and graceful dancing entertained the people.

233

Japanese poetry—Instruct the students to read page 231 silently to find out how many lines a haiku has. *(three)*

Discussion Questions

➤ **What determines which words are used in a haiku?** *(the meaning and the number of syllables)*
➤ **What does a Japanese poet try to achieve with his poem?** *(He tries to create a mood and a picture with his words.)*

Day 122

Japanese art and architecture—Instruct the students to read page 233 silently to find out from what country Japan modeled its art and architecture. *(China)*

Discussion Questions

➤ **What were the two characteristics of Japanese art?** *(brilliant colors and the use of everyday objects)*
➤ **What effect did the bright colors have on Japanese art?** *(They made Japanese paintings full of life and activity.)*
➤ **What were some of the ordinary objects which the Japanese made into works of art?** *(boxes, baskets, furniture, combs, and fans)*
➤ **What was a special form of Japanese art that involved arranging flowers?** *(ikebana)*
➤ **What type of flower was used in the month of May?** *(chrysanthemum)*
➤ **What did the emperor do during the Chrysanthemum Festival?** *(inspected the flower gardens at the palace)*

➤ **What arts were important in the Japanese court?** *(all of them—painting, sculpting, architecture, calligraphy, music, and dance)*

Remind the students that just as all of the artists' abilities were important in the Japanese court, God has given every Christian special abilities with which to serve Him. God will reward Christians who use their talents to serve Him. (BAT: 3a Self-concept)

Japan

Location—A chain of islands in the Pacific Ocean east of China and Korea.

Climate—Varies from north to south. Average temperatures range from winter lows of 21°F in the north to summer highs of 79°F in the south. Annual precipitation is an average of fifty inches.

Topography—Four main islands and a large number of smaller islands that are really the peaks of submerged mountains. The Japanese Alps on the island of Honshu include Mount Fuji, Japan's highest mountain (12,388 feet). Many of the island mountains are volcanoes.

Natural Resources—Few natural resources. The mountainous terrain leaves less than 15 percent of land that can be farmed. Small deposits of coal, zinc, copper, lead, and gold may be found. The many short, swift rivers are used to provide electricity and to irrigate rice paddies.

Geography and Culture—Living on islands encouraged the Japanese people to use the sea for transportation and food. Japan's closeness to China allowed Chinese culture to influence Japan's art and religion.

234

To Write a Haiku

1. Get Notebook page 66, crayons, and a pencil.

2. Go to the playground and look at the things around you. What do you see? Select an object or scene. Describe it using a few creative words.

3. On Notebook page 66, describe your object or picture, using five syllables in the first line of the poem, seven syllables in the second line, and five syllables in the last line. The middle line should describe your scene, using a *metaphor*, a type of word symbol. Choose another object or scene. Write a haiku about it.

4. Illustrate one of your haikus.

232

Day 123

Then and Now—Instruct the students to read page 234 silently to find the name of Japan's highest mountain. (*Mount Fuji*) Direct the students' attention to the Then and Now map, noting previous capitals and so on.

□ **Evaluating the Lesson**

Haiku (Notebook page 66)—Direct a *Discovering How* activity on page 232. Select a volunteer to read the steps aloud to the class. Allow the students to go outside to find a scene or object to write about. After the allotted time, instruct them to return to the classroom to write and illustrate their haiku on Notebook page 66. (*NOTE:* If some students experience difficulty in writing haiku, limit their writing to just one haiku or allow them to copy a haiku from a book of poetry.)

Haiku

Name _____

Write some haiku in the spaces below. When you have finished, illustrate one of them.

_____

_____

_____

_____

_____

_____

Heritage Studies 6

▬▬▬ Going Beyond ▬▬▬

□ Enrichment

Painted boxes—Set up an art AREA with a shoebox, several sheets of colored construction paper, felt-tip pens, glue, and scissors for each student. Instruct the students to use construction paper to cover the boxes completely. Tell them to use the remaining construction paper to draw and cut out pictures of things in nature (birds, flowers, etc.) to glue within their boxes.

□ Additional Teacher Information

Although no one is sure what the real name of the author of *Tale of Genji* is, Murasaki Shikibu has been the name given to her throughout history. Murasaki was born about A.D. 978. She belonged to a minor branch of the powerful Fujiwara clan. Her father, Tametoki, held several government positions and became the governor of Echizen. He later served as governor of Echigo.

Like her father, Murasaki had a love of learning. She was familiar with both Chinese and Japanese literature. Her father was grieved that such abilities had been wasted on a girl. Warned that such a love of learning would make her unpopular, Murasaki carefully concealed the fact she could write in Chinese.

Shortly after the death of her husband, Murasaki became a lady-in-waiting to Princess Akiko, who enjoyed academic pursuits. Exposure to court life gave Murasaki the background for her novel, *Tale of Genji*. The date of writing is disputed, but many believe it was written in A.D. 1004. *Tale of Genji* gave Murasaki fame as the creator of the Japanese "prose epic of real life."

LESSON 59
India's Golden Age of Learning

Text, pages 235-36
Notebook, page 67

- The Glory of the Guptas
- Indian Student Life

Preview

□ Objective
Given proper instruction, the students will be able to do the following:
- Identify key terms about India by making false statements true.

□ Materials
Have available:
- A decorative, braided cord, such as those worn on some military dress uniforms.*
- A wall map of the world.

□ Notes
The U.S. Army infantry uniform includes a blue braided cord. Some uniforms for members of marching bands also include a decorative, braided cord.

If you do not have access to a braided cord, show an encyclopedia or magazine picture of a uniform that includes this type of cording.

Day 124

Lesson

□ Introducing the Lesson
Ceremonies and symbols—Make two columns on the chalkboard. Label one column *Ceremonies* and the other column *Symbols*. Invite the students to name different types of ceremonies. *(Possible answers include wedding, graduation, and awards.)* If there is a symbol which signifies that a person has gone through a ceremony, encourage the students to name it. *(NOTE:* For example, a wedding band signifies that a person is married.)

Explain that just as we hold special ceremonies today, the people of ancient India also had ceremonies. Show the decorative, braided cord, telling the students that braided cord similar to this was used in an ancient Indian ceremony. Explain that life for a Hindu boy changed between the ages of eight and twelve when he received the sacred cord at a special ceremony. The sacred cord, made from a triple-strand string, was ceremoniously placed over the boy's left

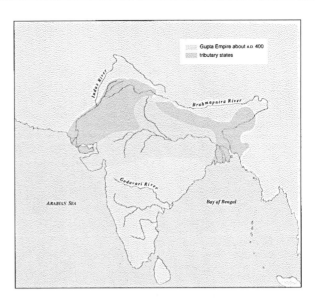

India's Golden Years
Do you remember where Buddhism first started? In India. Look at a globe. It is easy to see how India, China, and Japan shared ideas, religions, and trade. India, like China and Japan, had its own golden age too. India's golden years were from A.D. 320 to 540.

In these years, India was ruled by a dynasty called the Gupta. The Gupta dynasty began in A.D. 320 under King Chandragupta. Beginning with a small kingdom, Chandragupta built an empire in northern India. Under his grandson, Chandragupta II, the Gupta Empire reached the peak of its golden age. During the Gupta dynasty, the Indians made great advances in science, art, and literature.

235

shoulder and under his right arm and was to be worn throughout the boy's life. Explain to the students that in this lesson they will learn more about this initiation ceremony and the significance of the sacred cord.

□ Teaching the Lesson
The glory of the Guptas—Instruct the students to read page 235 silently to find out where the Buddhist religion first started. *(India)*

Discussion Questions
➤ **What were the years of India's golden age?** *(A.D. 320 to 540)*

Direct the students' attention to the wall map, pointing out India, Japan, and China. Ask them why it would have been easy for India to share ideas, religions, and trade with Japan and China. *(The countries are close to each other.)*
➤ **What dynasty ruled in India during its golden age?** *(the Gupta)*
➤ **Who was the first ruler of this dynasty?** *(King Chandragupta)*
➤ **Under whose rule did India reach the peak of its golden age?** *(Chandragupta II)*
➤ **In what areas did the Indians make advances during the golden age?** *(science, art, and literature)*

Student Life

The Gupta period was India's golden age of learning. A Hindu boy began his education at home where he learned the alphabet and *Sanskrit,* the Indian language. Once a boy reached a certain age, his family held a special *initiation* ceremony. A priest placed a special sacred cord on the boy's left shoulder and fastened it under his right arm. The cord had three strands, each one woven from nine threads. Throughout the rest of his life, the boy would wear the sacred cord as the symbol of his place in Hindu society.

Once this ceremony of the sacred cord was performed, the Hindu boy went to live with his teacher, who was called a *guru.* The guru began by teaching the student the ritual phrases he would repeat every day for the rest of his life.

A guru usually worked with several students at a time. They spent several hours a day learning the *Vedas,* sacred Hindu texts that were written in Sanskrit. In order to learn the *Vedas* perfectly, the boys memorized small phrases or verses. They repeated them forward and backward for the guru. Once the students had memorized the passages, the teacher lectured about the students' duties in society and the rules for living according to their *caste,* or social class.

The guru also taught his students Hindu rituals. Every activity from cooking a meal to fighting a battle followed a ritual. The Hindus believed that the correct performance of these rituals was necessary to please the Hindu gods.

236

© 1998 BJU Press. Reproduction prohibited.

False into True   Name _____

All of the following statements are false. Make the statements true by crossing out the words which make the statements false and replacing them with words from the list.

Chandragupta	India	ten times
Sanskrit	A.D. 770	guru
Japan	*Vedas*	forward and backward
A.D. 540	emperor	Gupta

1. Buddhism first started in ~~China.~~ **India**

2. India's golden age was from A.D. 320 to ~~A.D. 600.~~ **A.D. 540**

3. The dynasty that ruled India during this time was the ~~Vedas.~~ **Gupta**

4. ~~Genghis Khan~~ came to power in India in A.D. 320. **Chandragupta**

5. As part of his education at home, a Hindu boy learned ~~calligraphy.~~ **Sanskrit**

6. After his initiation ceremony, a Hindu boy went to live with his teacher, who was called ~~The Wise One.~~ **guru**

7. The sacred Hindu text a Hindu boy learned was called the ~~Koran.~~ **Vedas**

8. In order to learn the sacred text, a Hindu boy would repeat verses to his teacher while ~~standing on both feet, then on one foot.~~ **forward and backward**

Heritage Studies 6
Student Notebook

Indian student life—Instruct the students to read page 236 silently to find out what the Gupta period was sometimes called. *(India's golden age of learning)*

Discussion Questions

➤ **Where did a Hindu begin his education?** *(at home)*

➤ **What was the Indian language?** *(Sanskrit)*

➤ **What happened to a Hindu boy during the initiation ceremony?** *(A priest placed a special sacred cord on the boy's left shoulder and fastened it under his right arm.)*

➤ **What did the sacred cord symbolize?** *(the boy's place in Hindu society)*

➤ **With whom did a Hindu boy live once the initiation ceremony was performed?** *(a guru)*

➤ **What did a guru first teach his students?** *(ritual phrases that a student would repeat every day for the rest of his life)*

➤ **What were the sacred Hindu texts that were written in Sanskrit?** *(the* Vedas*)*

➤ **How did students learn the *Vedas*?** *(by memorizing short phrases or verses and repeating them backward and forward for the guru)*

> Ask the students what sacred text Christians have. *(the Bible)* Tell them that just as the Hindus were dedicated to learning the *Vedas,* Christians should be dedicated to learning the Bible. (BAT: 6a Bible study)

➤ **What types of activities involved a Hindu ritual?** *(every activity from cooking a meal to fighting a battle)*

➤ **What did Hindus believe about the correct performance of these rituals?** *(They were necessary to please the Hindu gods.)*

☐ Evaluating the Lesson

False into True (Notebook page 67)—Instruct the students to make the false statements true by crossing out the words which make the statements false and replacing them with words from the list.

═══ Going Beyond ═══

☐ Enrichment

Bible memorization—Set up an AREA for Bible memorization. Encourage the students to choose one or two verses to memorize in the coming week. Explain that at the end of the week, the students will quote the verses to their Heritage Studies partners.

□ Additional Teacher Information

The caste system in India is always changing and has begun to lose its importance in some areas. Originally, there were four castes of people. The *brahmans* were priests and scholars, *kshatriyas* were warriors and rulers, *vaisyas* were tradespeople and farmers, and *sudras* were servants and ordinary workers.

Sometimes a person's occupation defined the caste he was in. At other times, a particular religious belief held by a group of people defined a caste. During the Aryan Period (c. 1500 B.C.), a fifth class of people was added to the four original classes. This group, called a "non-caste," performed duties considered too demeaning for even the sudras to perform. Such tasks included tanning animal hides and sweeping the grounds where the dead had been cremated.

The people who were part of this "non-caste" were called the "untouchables." They were not allowed to mingle with other members of Hindu society. They could not even live in the same neighborhoods. Some Hindu people thought that if a shadow of an untouchable fell on them, they were contaminated. In recent years, however, untouchability has been declared illegal by the government. Although it still exists in remote parts of rural India, feelings toward untouchables are changing.

L E S S O N 6 0
India's Academic Achievements

Text, pages 237-39
Notebook, pages 68-69

- **Development of Arabic Numerals**
- **Scientific Discoveries**
- **Indian Literature**

Preview

□ Objective

Given proper instruction, the students will be able to do the following:

- Write a journal entry about some of the achievements in ancient India.

Day 126

Lesson

□ Introducing the Lesson

Arabic or Roman Numerals? (Notebook page 68)—Direct the students to solve the math equations. When they have finished, check the answers together. Ask the students which set of equations they thought was easier to solve. Tell the students that the Indians developed Arabic numerals during the Gupta age. Explain that in this lesson they will learn more about the Arabic number system and other discoveries the Indians made.

Arabic or Roman Numerals?   Name _____

Solve these math equations and then be prepared to discuss which set of equations was easier to solve.

A. Roman math—Use the table of Roman numerals to complete these math equations.

I. I+III= ___*IV*___

II. IX−V= ___*IV*___

III. II×III= ___*VI*___

IV. IX÷III= ___*III*___

Roman Numeral Table	
Arabic Numbers	Roman Numerals
1	I
2	II
3	III
4	IV
5	V
6	VI
7	VII
8	VIII
9	IX
10	X

B. Arabic math—Use Arabic numbers to complete these math equations.

1. 4+3= ___*7*___

2. 10−4= ___*6*___

3. 3×5= ___*15*___

4. 16÷8= ___*2*___

© 1998 BJU Press. Reproduction prohibited.

Heritage Studies 6
Student Notebook

Lesson 60
Introducing the Lesson   **68**

□ Teaching the Lesson

Development of Arabic numerals—Instruct the students to read page 237 silently to find out who developed Arabic numerals. *(the Hindus)* Explain that these numerals are called "Arabic" because Arabs took them from Asia to Europe.

Discussion Questions

➤ **In what three subject areas did the Indians make accomplishments in the Gupta age?** *(mathematics, science, and medicine)*

➤ **What type of numerals do we use today?** *(Arabic numerals)*

➤ **What numeral did the Indians use first?** *(zero)*

➤ **What other mathematical concepts did the Indians use?** *(the decimal system, place values, and positive and negative numbers)*

➤ **In the area of more advanced mathematics, what concepts did the Indians use?** *(square and cubic roots, an accurate value for* pi, *and elementary algebra)*

ECHOES FROM THE PAST

Our Number System

Write the numerals one to ten on a piece of scrap paper. Think about the numerals around you—prices in the grocery store, the numerals on street signs, or the numerals in your textbook. Did you ever wonder where the numbers we use came from?

The Gupta age was the golden age of mathematics, science, and medicine. Many of these subjects that we use today echo the Indian achievements. What we call *Arabic* numerals were really invented by the Hindus. Arabic numerals are the numerals we use every day, such as *1, 2, 3,* and *4.* How are these numerals different from *Roman* numerals?

The Indians were also one of the first peoples to use a zero. Several hundred years before, the Mayas had invented zero, but the Indians discovered it independently. It is the zero invented in India that spread into Europe in the 1400s. The Indians also used the decimal system, place values, and positive and negative numbers. In more advanced mathematics, the Indians learned how to find square and cubic roots, figured an accurate value for *pi,* and used elementary algebra.

237

In science, Indian students studied chemistry, physics, and astronomy. Far ahead of other people living at this time, the Gupta Indians described the principle of gravity. They even had an idea of how atoms make up all matter.

Through their careful observations and calculations, they discovered that the earth and all planets are spheres. They also found that the earth rotates, and they calculated a nearly correct value for the earth's diameter. Many centuries passed before the Europeans accepted these ideas from the Indians.

In medicine, Indian students learned from dissecting human corpses. They also performed some surgeries and applied first aid.

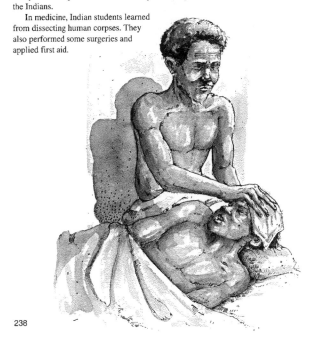

238

Scientific discoveries—Instruct the students to read page 238 silently to find out what three branches of science the Indians studied. *(chemistry, physics, and astronomy)*

Discussion Questions

➤ **What scientific principle did the Indians understand before the other people living at this time?** *(the law of gravity)*

➤ **What did the Indians discover about the shape of the earth and other planets?** *(They are spheres.)*

➤ **What else did the Indians find out about the earth?** *(that it rotates; a nearly correct value for its diameter)*

➤ **What did the Indians learn to do in the field of medicine?** *(perform some surgeries and apply first aid)*

The Age of Literature

Besides science and math, Indian students studied the language arts: grammar, writing, and literature. They polished their writing of Sanskrit. They also studied the literature of India's finest dramatists and poets. Many excellent writers lived during the Gupta age. Their writings made this the golden age of Sanskrit literature.

Two types of literature that were popular during the Gupta age were the fable and the fairy tale. Indian fables and fairy tales were popular not only in India but also in other countries. How do you think other countries first came in contact with Indian literature? Trade had a big part in spreading the stories that Indian writers created.

Many of the traditional stories that we have today are based on the early fables of India. One such story is that of Sinbad the Sailor in *A Thousand and One Nights*. Indian poetry, on the other hand, did not spread like the fables. The poetry of this time was complex and a favorite pastime of the people of the court. The ability to create poetry was very important; competitions were often held to see who could write the best and most complicated poem.

239

Day 127

Indian literature—Instruct the students to read page 239 silently to find out the two types of literature that were popular during the Gupta age. *(fable and fairy tale)*

Discussion Questions

➤ **What had a big part in exposing other countries to Indian literature?** *(trade)*

➤ **What fable from early India is now part of a collection called *A Thousand and One Nights*?** *(the story of Sinbad the Sailor)*

➤ **What type of writing did not spread to other countries as quickly?** *(poetry)*

➤ **How can we tell that the ability to write poetry was important in India?** *(Competitions were often held to see who could write the best and most complicated poems.)*

Tell the students that just as the ancient Indians accomplished many things, Christians can achieve much through abilities God has given them. Remind the students that God has given Christians special abilities to do different types of work for Him and that Christians should praise God continually for what He accomplishes through them. (BATs: 3a Self-concept, 7c Praise)

Journal Entry   Name _____

Imagine that you were living in India when all of the accomplishments you read about in this lesson were being made. Write a journal entry describing some of these achievements. Include your reactions and others' reactions to the new innovations.

Heritage Studies 6
Student Notebook

Lesson 60
Evaluating the Lesson   **69**

☐ Evaluating the Lesson

Journal Entry (Notebook page 69)—Instruct each student to write a journal entry describing some inventions in ancient India and reactions to these innovations.

▬▬ Going Beyond ▬▬

☐ Enrichment

Story activity—Set up an art AREA with books containing stories about Sinbad the Sailor, felt-tip pens, and drawing paper. Instruct each student to select one of the Sinbad stories to read and then to draw a picture of a character or event in the story. As time allows, encourage each student to write a brief summary of the story under his picture. When the students have finished, display the pictures in the classroom.

☐ Additional Teacher Information

Poetry during the Gupta period took on several different forms. For instance, one poet never used any *s* sounds. It is believed that he wrote this type of poetry for a young prince who had a speech impediment. Other poems were written so as to have one meaning if read from left to right and another meaning if read from right to left.

Poetry competitions were common at the Gupta court. A dignitary presented a topic, and the competitors used techniques such as puns, speeches, and short poems to vie for the prize. To some competitors, winning was so important that they bribed a judge beforehand.

LESSON 61
The Classical Age

Text, pages 240-42
Notebook, page 70

- A Gentleman's Interests
- Gupta Art
- A Look at the Present

Preview

□ Objective
Given proper instruction, the students will be able to do the following:
- Identify terms about the Orient by matching them with their appropriate countries.

□ Materials
Have available:
- Maps and More 20.
- A cassette player.
- HERITAGE STUDIES Listening Cassette B.

Day 128

Lesson

□ Introducing the Lesson

Indian music—Show the students Maps and More 20. Explain that the sitar has been a popular instrument in India for several hundred years. Play the Indian music from HERITAGE STUDIES Listening Cassette B, inviting the students to describe the music. Explain that in ancient India, a knowledge of music was well respected. Tell the students that they will learn more about Indian music in this lesson.

□ Teaching the Lesson

A gentleman's interests—Instruct the students to read page 240 silently to find out what two areas an Indian gentleman had to have a knowledge of. *(art and music)*

Gentlemanly Pursuits

During the Gupta period, a gentleman had to have a knowledge of art and music. If he showed any ability in this area, he tried to develop it. The Indians of the Gupta period produced such excellent works that this age is called the *Classical Age* of Indian art or music. Indian music was not like the music we hear today. It was not even like what we call classical music. Most Indian music was not written down. A performer began with a familiar tune and then improvised, or made changes in the melody as he played. The main instrument that the Indians used was called a *vina*. The vina was a type of lute similar to a guitar. They also played flutes and other reed instruments. Drums, bells, cymbals, and gongs were other common Indian instruments. Trumpets, made from large conch shells, were used only for battle or other special occasions.

Playing the vina

240

Discussion Questions

➤ **In relation to art or music, what is the Gupta period sometimes called?** *(the Classical Age)*
➤ **What was a main difference between the music of the Gupta period and the music of today?** *(The music of the Gupta period was not written down.)*
➤ **How did a performer play music which was not written down?** *(He began with a familiar tune and then made changes in the melody as he played.)*

Ask for a show of hands of students who play a musical instrument. Ask them how the Gupta method of playing music could be more difficult. *(Possible answers include difficulty in playing a tune the same way more than once and other musicians playing the song in a different way.)*

➤ **What was the main instrument that the Indians used?** *(the vina)*
➤ **What was the vina like?** *(It was a type of lute similar to a guitar.)*
➤ **What other instruments did the Indians play?** *(flutes, reed instruments, drums, bells, cymbals, and gongs)*
➤ **What instrument was used only for battle or other special occasions?** *(trumpet)*

Gupta Art

The art of the Gupta appears peaceful and happy. Many of the best examples of Indian sculpture come from this period. The wealthy enjoyed painting. Most gentlemen and ladies knew how to paint. Many people had their own private galleries of both their own works and the works of others. In the cities, public galleries displayed artwork for the poorer people.

The best examples of Gupta paintings that we have today are found in the caves at *Ajanta*. These paintings were done by Buddhist artists. Although they are primarily scenes from the life of Buddha, the paintings include details of Indian life. From these paintings we can learn something of how the people lived, such as what they wore and what plants and animals they raised.

This detail shows two seated Buddhas from a wall painting found in the Ajanta Caves, Maharashtra, India (Gupta period, 5th-6th century).

241

During the golden age of the Orient, life for the people of China, Japan, and India was changing and improving. New inventions and ideas affected all areas of society—medicine, mathematics, literature, poetry, art, architecture, and even religion.

Time tests the success of man, however. As the years slipped by, these great societies began to lose their glitter. Wars and fightings caused the great dynasties to crumble and fall.

Today China is governed by Communism. The Chinese people suffer great restrictions under its rule. In India there is fighting between the Hindus and Muslims. The Indian people suffer many hardships from drought and poverty. Of the three countries, Japan is the most successful. The Japanese economy is prospering with the manufacturing of cars, machines, and electronic devices. Japan's trade with other countries has greatly added to this success, but the people must deal with stress, overcrowded cities, and pollution.

Throughout history, the civilizations of the Orient moved in cycles of failure to success to failure. Perhaps the modern countries of China, Japan, and India will reach a golden peak once more in the course of time; yet, without God, neither they nor any other nation can ever reach true success.

"Verily every man at his best state is altogether vanity."

Psalm 39:5

242

Gupta art—Instruct the students to read silently page 241 to find out how Gupta art appears. *(peaceful and happy)*

Discussion Questions

➤ **Who enjoyed painting during the Gupta period?** *(the wealthy)*

➤ **Where did the wealthy often keep their works of art and those of others?** *(in private galleries)*

➤ **Where could the poor people go to enjoy works of art?** *(to the public galleries in the cities)*

➤ **Where can the best examples of Gupta paintings be found?** *(in the caves at Ajanta)*

➤ **Other than scenes of Buddha's life, what do the paintings show?** *(details of Indian life)*

➤ **What can one learn from the Gupta paintings?** *(how people lived, what they wore, and what plants and animals they raised)*

Remind the students that the ancient Indians accomplished some of their finest works of art and music during the Gupta period. Explain that Christians, too, by using the talents that God has given them, have made great accomplishments in these areas. (BAT: 7b Exaltation of Christ)

A look at the present—Instruct the students to read silently page 242 to find out what areas of Oriental society have been affected by new inventions and ideas. *(medicine, mathematics, literature, poetry, art, architecture, and religion)*

Discussion Questions

➤ **What caused the great dynasties to fall?** *(wars and fightings)*

➤ **What type of government now exists in China?** *(Communism)*

➤ **What are conditions like today in India?** *(fighting between Muslims and Hindus, drought, and poverty)*

➤ **Of all the countries studied in this lesson, which is the most successful today?** *(Japan)*

Ask the students whether they think China and India will ever rise to be the great countries they once were. *(Answers will vary.)* Ask them who must be in control in order for countries to be successful. *(God)*

Match the following terms with the countries to which they are associated.
Write *C* for China, *J* for Japan, *I* for India, or *A* for all the countries.

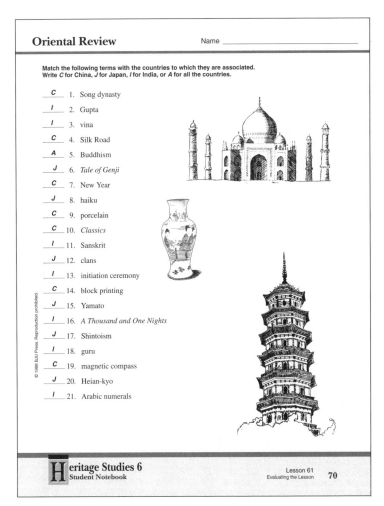

_C_ 1. Song dynasty

_I_ 2. Gupta

_I_ 3. vina

_C_ 4. Silk Road

_A_ 5. Buddhism

_J_ 6. *Tale of Genji*

_C_ 7. New Year

_J_ 8. haiku

_C_ 9. porcelain

_C_ 10. *Classics*

_I_ 11. Sanskrit

_J_ 12. clans

_I_ 13. initiation ceremony

_C_ 14. block printing

_J_ 15. Yamato

_I_ 16. *A Thousand and One Nights*

_J_ 17. Shintoism

_I_ 18. guru

_C_ 19. magnetic compass

_J_ 20. Heian-kyo

_I_ 21. Arabic numerals

Heritage Studies 6
Student Notebook

Lesson 61
Evaluating the Lesson   **70**

□ Evaluating the Lesson

Oriental Review (Notebook page 70)—Instruct the students to match the terms with either China, Japan, or India.

━━━ Going Beyond ━━━

□ Enrichment

Religious art—Set up an art AREA with drawing paper and felt-tip pens for each student. Remind the students that much of the art in ancient India reflected their religion. Instruct each student to draw a picture of an activity that occurs in a normal Sunday service at their church. (*NOTE:* Examples include collecting the offering, singing, and praying.)

□ Additional Teacher Information

The sitar, a stringed instrument similar to the guitar, was developed in either India or Persia in the 1200s. The instrument is still used today in the classical music of southern India. A sitar has a long wooden neck and a pear-shaped body made from a gourd. There are seven main strings that the performer plucks with a wire pick. Twelve other strings, called sympathetic strings, vibrate when the seven main strings are played.

The sitar is usually played as a solo instrument and is often accompanied by a drum called a tabla and a lute. Recently, musicians in the West have begun to use the sitar in their music.

CHINA

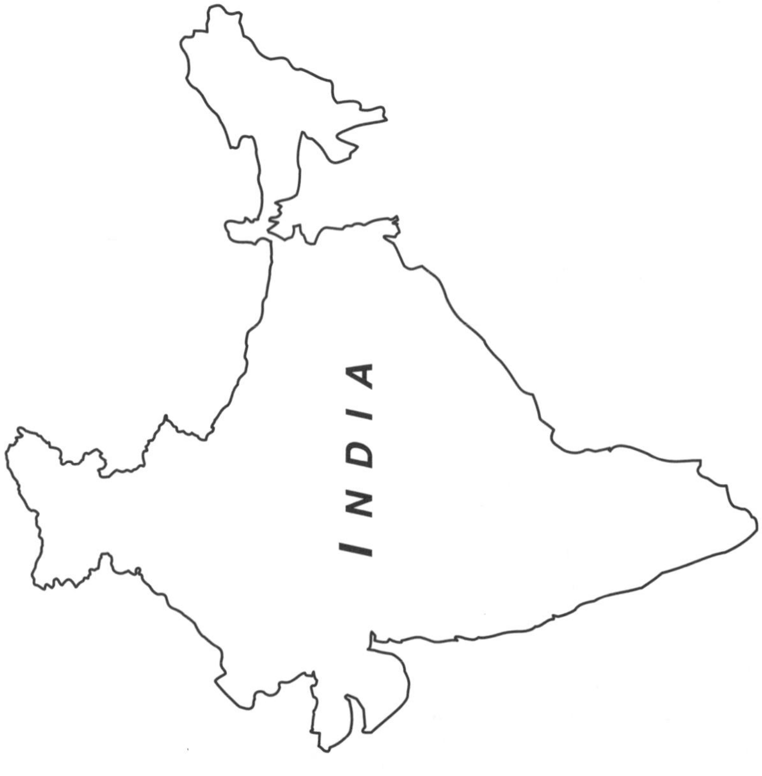

INDIA

Use with the chapter bulletin board.

Heritage Studies 6 TE

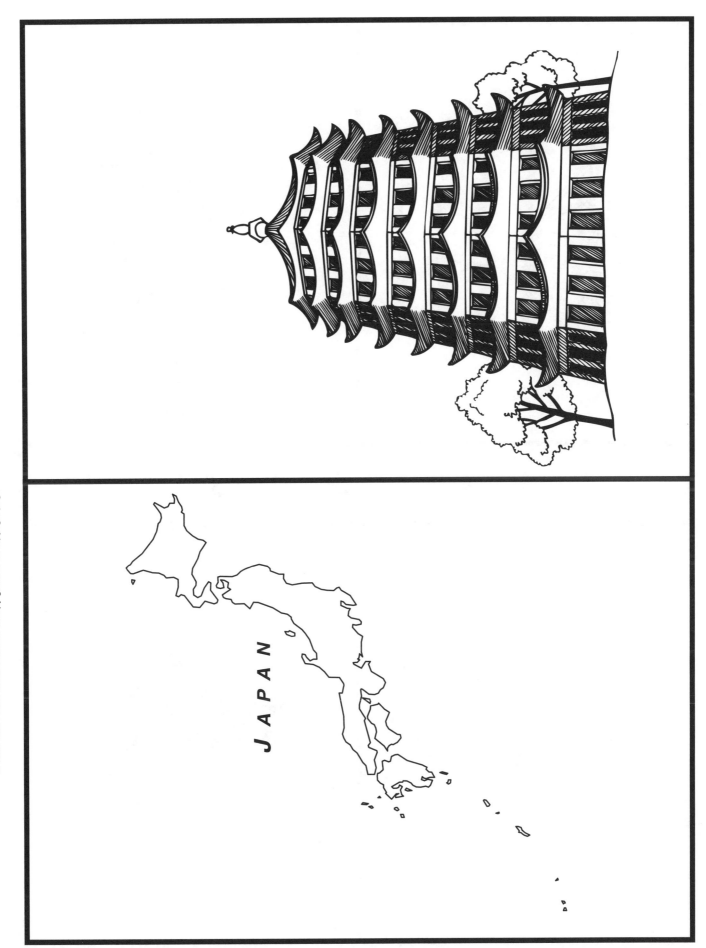

J A P A N

1 2 3 4 5 6 7 8 9 10

Use with the chapter bulletin board.

Making a Magnetic Compass

1. Fill the plastic bowl with water.

2. Put the pin through the bottom of the cork stopper as shown.

3. Put the stopper into the bowl of water. The stopper should float on the water evenly and turn easily.

4. Magnetize the needle by stroking it in the *same* direction about fifty times with a bar magnet.

5. Put a small drop of glue on the needle. Place the needle carefully onto the cork stopper. Observe what the cork and the needle do.

6. Use the compass supplied by your teacher to check whether your compass needle points in a north-south direction.

Calligraphy Chart

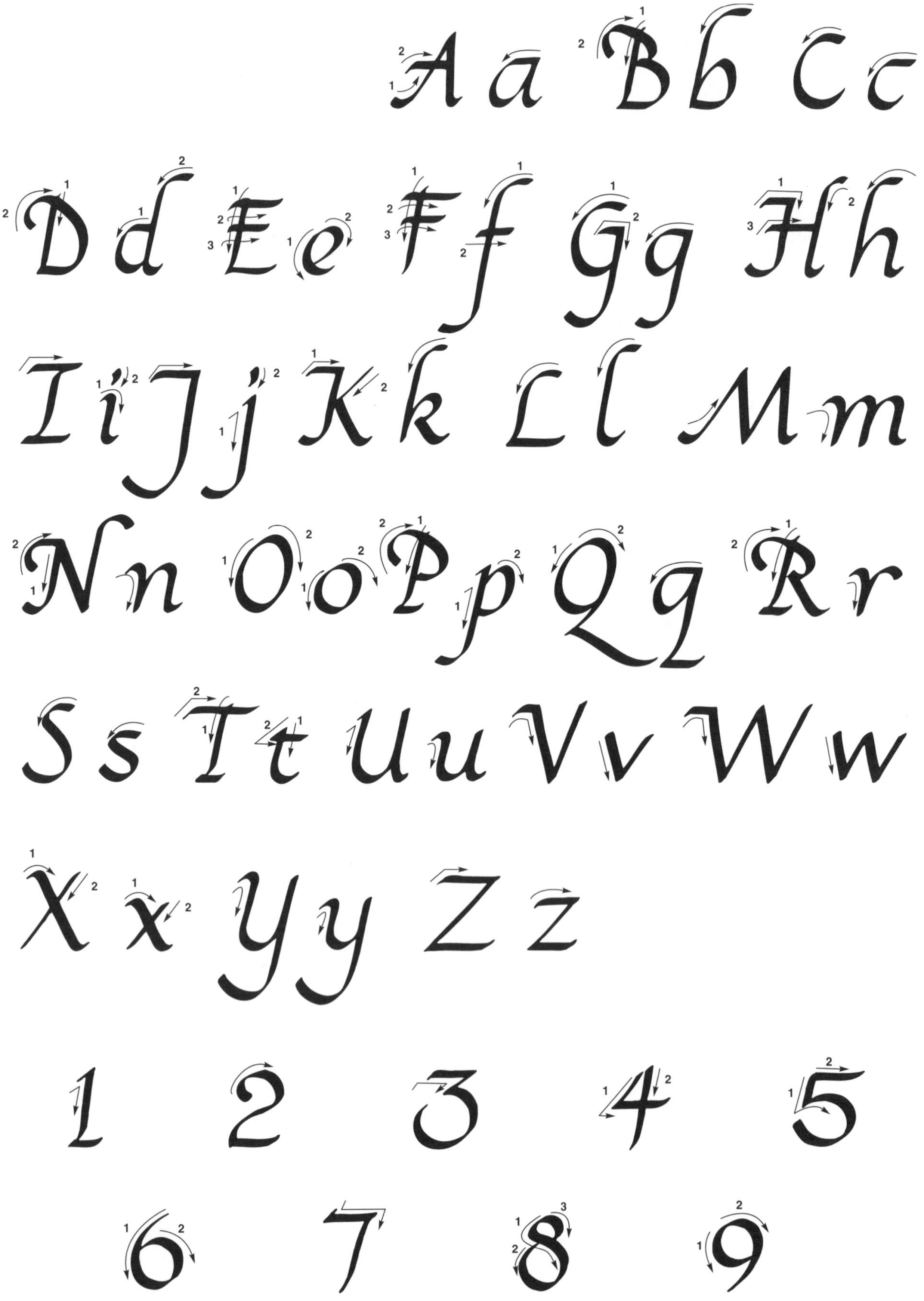

A a B b C c

D d E e F f G g H h

I i J j K k L l M m

N n O o P p Q q R r

S s T t U u V v W w

X x Y y Z z

1 2 3 4 5

6 7 8 9

Use with Lesson 56.

Heritage Studies 6 TE

I will praise thee; for I am fearfully and wonderfully made: marvellous are thy works; and that my soul knoweth right well.

Psalm 139:14

Three Major Religions

Using your text and encyclopedias, answer the following questions about Buddhism, Shintoism, and Christianity.

1. Name one major teaching of Buddhism. _____

   _____

   _____

   _____

2. Name one major teaching of Shintoism. _____

   _____

   _____

   _____

3. Name one major teaching of Christianity. _____

   _____

   _____

   _____

4. The religions of Buddhism and Shintoism teach principles that contradict what

   the Bible teaches. Name some ways in which these two religions go against the

   teachings of the Bible. _____

   _____

   _____

   _____

   _____

   _____

11 LESSONS 62-69

Mosaics and Minarets: Byzantium

This chapter introduces students to the Byzantine Empire, tracing it from its settlement by Greek colonists in the centuries before Christ to the fall of the Empire in 1453. The Byzantine Empire was a continuation of the Roman Empire, which fell to barbarian invasion in the fifth century. Although never reaching the geographical greatness of the Roman Empire, the Byzantine Empire played a major role in the preservation of ancient learning, in the advancement of the arts and architecture, and in the religious climate of Eastern Europe. Highlighted topics include Constantine and Justinian, the rise of Islam as a major religious and political force, and the Crusades.

□ Materials

Lessons 62 and 65 require certain items that must be obtained or prepared several days to several weeks before the presentation of the lessons. These items are labeled with an asterisk (*) in each lesson and in the Materials List in the Supplement. Occasionally, items not commonly found in the classroom as well as items needed in large quantities may also be labeled with an asterisk. For further information, see the individual lessons.

□ Chapter Bulletin Board

Entitle the bulletin board *Byzantine Empire Exclamations!* Cut out exclamation points from construction paper. Encourage the students to draw pictures or write explanations or stories about some of the topics covered in the chapter. Affix the student work to colored paper and place the papers between the exclamation points on the bulletin board.

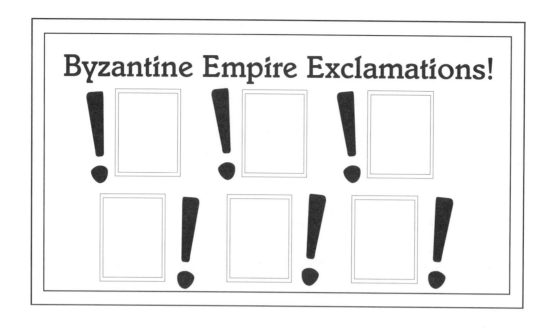

Byzantine Empire Exclamations!

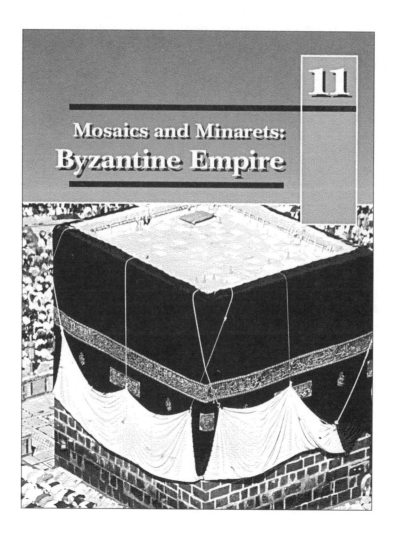

11

Mosaics and Minarets:
Byzantine Empire

LESSON 62
City by the Sea

Text, pages 244-46

- Seacoast Trading
- Then and Now

"Who cares about this old empire?" Dan rested his head on his hands.

"I don't know, but I'm out of here in an hour," said Troy. He punched the inside of his baseball glove. "Coach wants me to set up the bases for practice. So let's get this report over with. What's the first question? Give it to me—I like fast balls."

Dan tossed the baseball across the table. He picked up the sheet of paper as the ball slapped into Troy's glove. "How did the Byzantine Empire get its name?"

Troy pulled his book over. He ran his finger down the paragraph. "Here it is. The empire was named after the village Byzantium. Write that down, Dan."

"We'd better find that on the map. You know how Miss Hayden is about geography." Dan studied his textbook. "Here it is. Right there by the southwest corner of the Black Sea . . . on the Straits of the Bosporus, that real narrow body of water right there." He pointed and held the book under Troy's nose.

244

▬▬▬▬ Preview ▬▬▬▬

☐ Objective
Given proper instruction, the students will be able to do the following:
- Use clues to identify events and items about Byzantium.

☐ Materials
Have available:
- A shish kebab skewer or party pick for each student.*
- 4 or 5 small fruit pieces for each student.*
- A sheet of notebook paper for each student.
- A wall map of the world.
- Maps and More 21.

Prepare a shish kebab platter with skewers and small fruit pieces.

Day 130

▬▬▬▬ Lesson ▬▬▬▬

☐ Introducing the Lesson
Shish kebabs—Give each student a skewer and four or five small pieces of fruit. Direct the students to make a shish kebab by running the skewer through the middle of each fruit piece. Tell the students that they will be learning about the area of the world that is now called Turkey. Point out Turkey on the wall map. Shish kebabs are a favorite Turkish food and are usually made with lamb meat and vegetables. Allow the students to eat their fruit shish kebabs.

☐ Teaching the Lesson
Seacoast trading—Instruct the students to read pages 244-45 silently to find out what advantages Byzantium's location offered to merchants. *(Various sea routes provided for trade with the Greeks, Romans, and North Africans.)* Point to the large map on Maps and More 21. Invite the students to identify this area. *(Europe and part of Asia and Africa)* Call on a student to point out this area on the wall map. Point out the location of Byzantium (Constantinople). Explain that the smaller map telescopes a larger representation of the city of Byzantium. Trace with your finger the Wall of Theodosius. Ask the students why the people might have built a wall here for Byzantium. *(to keep out invaders from other lands)*

Discussion Questions
➤ **Who settled in the village of Byzantium?** *(Greek colonists from Athens)*
➤ **Why do you think the Athenians moved from Athens to Byzantium?** *(Answers will vary.)*
➤ **What did they build for protection from enemies?** *(a wall)*
➤ **What items were offered for sale in Byzantium?** *(furs, amber, grain, gold, ivory, silk, spices)*

The Village by the Sea

Greek colonists from Athens built the village of Byzantium where the Black Sea flows into the Straits of the Bosporus across from Asia Minor. This was an ideal place for a village. The triangle-shaped piece of land had water on two sides, and the Athenians built a wall across the land side to make their village safe.

This location was also good for trade. A fine harbor lay just north of the village. Villagers could travel around the Black Sea to trade with Asian merchants who had brought furs and amber down the Dnieper and Don Rivers, or they could sail west into the Aegean and Mediterranean Seas. There they could trade with the Greeks, Romans, and North Africans for grain, gold, and ivory.

Merchants came overland from India and China with silks and spices to sell. Their caravans traveled through Asia Minor and crossed the straits at the narrowest point, right where Byzantium had been built. The Byzantine villagers saw almost everything anyone had to sell.

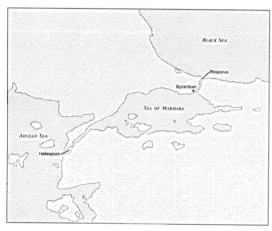

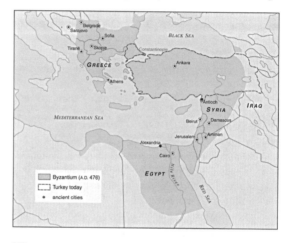

◆ THEN AND NOW ◆

Turkey

Location—Turkey, once part of the Byzantine Empire, is in southeastern Europe and Anatolia (Asia Minor).

Climate—Temperate along the coast; harsh and dry on the plateau; snowy or icy in the mountains. Average temperatures range from 13°F to 80°F.

Topography—Has an inland plateau formed by the Taurus and Pontic mountain ranges. In eastern Turkey, where these two chains meet, is Mount Ararat.

Natural Resources—Has large mineral deposits, but most have not been mined. Oil has been discovered and is now being produced.

Geography and Culture—Situated on the southern bridge between Europe and Asia, the region has been conquered many times and has a mixed cultural heritage.

246

Day 131

Then and Now—Instruct the students to read page 246 silently to find out what kind of climate Turkey has. *(temperate along the coast; harsh and dry on the plateau; snowy or icy in the mountains)* Direct the students' attention to the Then and Now map, noting ancient cities, changes in boundary lines, and so on.

> Remind the students that God chose Mount Ararat as the resting place of Noah's Ark. Tell them that many people have searched the mountains looking for the Ark, but so far no one has been able to positively identify it. Explain that the Ark saved Noah's family from destruction just as Jesus Christ keeps His people safe from the eternal judgment of God. (BAT: 1a Understanding Jesus Christ)

☐ Evaluating the Lesson

Identification activity—Direct the students to number a sheet of paper from one to ten. Tell them to listen as you read clues and to write the answers on their papers.

1. I am a small village at the corner of the Black Sea. What is my name? *(Byzantium)*
2. I am a large country in Asia. Merchants purchased silk from me to sell all over the world. What is my name? *(China)*
3. We are the people who came from Athens to settle Byzantium. Who are we? *(Greek colonists)*
4. I was built to provide protection to the small village. What am I? *(a wall)*
5. I am an empire built up from the small village. What is my name? *(Byzantine Empire)*
6. I am a narrow body of water connecting the Black Sea to the Sea of Marmara. What is my name? *(Bosporus)*
7. I am an item of trade that was sold in the small village. What is my name? *(any of the following: silk, spices, grain, gold, ivory, furs, or amber)*
8. I am a range of mountains that forms an inland plateau. What is my name? *(Taurus or Pontic)*
9. I am a mountain. A famous boat rested on me. What is my name? *(Mount Ararat)*
10. I am a modern country built where the small village of Byzantium was. What is my name? *(Turkey)*

Going Beyond

□ Enrichment

Mapmaking—Set up an art AREA with scissors, glue, and felt-tip pens. Also have available a frame page and a land-form page copied on blue construction paper for each student. (*NOTE:* See the reproducible material at the end of Lesson 69.) Cut each map apart, putting the pieces of each map into a separate envelope so that each student has an envelope of map pieces. Tell the students to glue their map pieces on the map frame when they have the appropriate configuration. You may want to display Maps and More 21 as a guide for the students. Encourage them to label the major bodies of water.

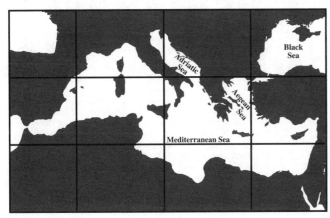

□ Additional Teacher Information

The Byzantine Empire forms a bridge between the ancient Roman Empire and the Italian Renaissance. Spanning the "Dark Ages" of supposed cultural dearth, the Byzantine Empire preserved ancient manuscripts, erected churches of artistic splendor, and developed the Eastern Orthodox Church, firmly establishing this arm of Christianity in a previously pagan area.

In A.D. 324, Constantine I chose Byzantium as his capital. The city officially became the capital in A.D. 330, and the name was changed to Constantinople, meaning "city of Constantine." Today, the name of this city is Istanbul. It is the largest city in Turkey. Ankara is the capital of Turkey.

LESSON 63

Constantinople: An Emperor's City

Text, pages 247-49
Notebook, page 71

- **Constantine's City**
- **Beginning of the Byzantine Empire**
- **The Body of Law**

Preview

□ Objective

Given proper instruction, the students will be able to do the following:

- Answer questions about the early Byzantine Empire.

□ Materials

Have available:

- A wall map of the world.
- Maps and More 21.

□ Notes

For Lesson 64, you might request that one-half of the class members wear blue and that the rest of the class members wear green.

Day 132

Lesson

□ Introducing the Lesson

Required by law—Invite students to tell laws (rules) that they are required to obey. *(Answers will vary but will include civil laws, scriptural laws, and rules set by their parents and by school authorities.)* Tell the students that during the Byzantine Empire, Emperor Justinian assigned a man to organize five hundred years' worth of laws into one law code.

> Remind the students that they should obey any laws that do not force them to violate God's word. Read Mark 12:17: "And Jesus answering said unto them, Render to Caesar the things that are Caesar's, and to God the things that are God's. And they marvelled at him." (BAT: 2a Authority)

"Wish I'd been there," said Dan. "Just think of all that neat stuff you could trade for. Wonder what they'd give you for baseball cards? I'd get rich and live like a king."

"Not at first." Troy kept reading. "It says here that Byzantium did not grow rapidly. When the Roman emperor Constantine saw the village, he knew it could become a great city, so he built a new city right where the old village had been. He named it Constantinople, after himself."

Constantinople during the Byzantine Era, around 1493

Constantine's new city became one of the greatest cities of the world. It was a secure place, far away from the wars and invasions among the barbarians in other parts of Europe. *Barbarian* was a name given by the Romans to nomadic peoples who had not adopted Roman culture and who did not speak Latin or Greek. The Romans considered these people primitive and crude. By A.D. 470 the Roman emperors had moved to Constantinople. Now the emperors were too far away to protect the western half of their empire. The barbarians soon controlled all of western Europe.

247

□ Teaching the Lesson

Constantine's city—Instruct the students to read page 247 silently to find out why the village of Byzantium was renamed Constantinople. *(The Roman emperor Constantine built a city at the location of the old village and named it for himself.)* Explain that the suffix *-ople* means "city." Tell the students that Emperor Constantine is sometimes referred to as Constantine the Great.

Discussion Questions

➤ **Why did Constantinople become a great city?** *(It was securely positioned, far from wars and safe from invasion by barbarians.)*

➤ **Who were the barbarians?** *(nomadic peoples who had not adopted Roman culture and who did not speak either Latin or Greek)*

➤ **Why did the barbarians soon control all of western Europe?** *(The Roman emperors moved to Constantinople by 470, leaving Rome open to invasion.)*

Point out both Rome and Constantinople on the large map on Maps and More 21 and on the wall map of the world. Call on students to give reasons that Rome was vulnerable after the government moved to Constantinople. Ask them what happened to the city of Rome when the army became unable to defend it. *(It was captured.)*

Early Years of the Byzantine Empire

Justinian I, the first great emperor of Byzantium, reigned from 527 to 565. But he wanted to rule more than the eastern half of the old Roman Empire. He sent his best warrior, General Belisarius, to reconquer the western provinces.

Belisarius first conquered Egypt, an important grain-producing province. Then he marched his army across North Africa to the city of Carthage. A barbarian people called the Vandals ruled there. They were fierce fighters, but Belisarius's army defeated them and destroyed their kingdom.

Next, Belisarius's men built ships so that they could cross the Mediterranean Sea and invade the island of Sicily. Before long, the general led his army through Italy and claimed it for Emperor Justinian. Justinian now controlled land on what three continents?

Compare the map of the old Roman Empire with the map of the new Byzantine Empire. Did Justinian get his wish to rule all of the old Roman Empire? What parts of the Roman Empire did Belisarius not conquer?

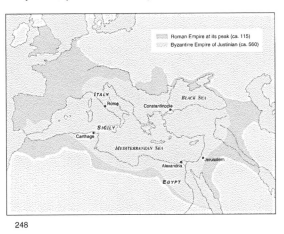

248

Corpus Juris Civilis

Justinian believed that a reunited, well-governed empire needed a good system of law. He adopted all the laws of the old Roman Empire. Imagine how many laws had been passed in the last five hundred years! When you add to that all the lawyers' opinions about the laws, there must have been enough books to fill a city library. No one could learn all the law.

Tribonia, a member of the court, was chosen to simplify the law and to make it easy to understand. In just four years, he and his committee finished their work.

The new, much shorter law code was called the *Corpus Juris Civilis,* or *The Body of Civil Law.* Because of this work, we know a great deal about Roman law. And some modern European countries, such as France and Italy, base their legal systems on this law code.

249

Roman emperors thought their empire would last forever. However, internal moral decay and the loss of military strength within the Roman Empire worked to the advantage of the invaders. The Roman Empire collapsed in A.D. 476. Remind the students that Christians have the assurance of God's help and protection no matter what political situation may exist. (Bible Promise: I. God as Master)

Day 133

Beginning of the Byzantine Empire—Instruct the students to read page 248 silently to find out what empire began after the end of the Roman Empire. *(the Byzantine Empire)* Remind the students that the capital of the new empire was Constantinople.

Discussion Questions

➤ **Who was the first great Byzantine emperor?** *(Justinian I)*
➤ **Why did Justinian choose Belisarius to fight in the West?** *(Belisarius was his best warrior.)*
➤ **What were General Belisarius's most important achievements?** *(He captured territories in Africa and Europe.)*

The body of law—Instruct the students to read page 249 silently to find out what the Latin phrase *Corpus Juris Civilis* means. *(The Body of Civil Law)*

Discussion Questions

➤ **Why was it considered necessary for someone to organize the laws of the Roman Empire?** *(There were thousands of laws, too many for anyone to learn.)*
➤ **Who was Tribonia, and how did his work progress?** *(He was in charge of the committee that organized the laws. The work was finished in four years.)*
➤ **How has Tribonia's work influenced later centuries?** *(His law code is the basis for the legal systems of some modern European countries.)*

Write the letter of the correct answer in each blank.

__B__ 1. Constantine was the

    A. first Roman emperor.
    B. emperor who built a city at Byzantium.
    C. emperor at the time of Christ.

__C__ 2. People who did not speak Latin or Greek were called

    A. invaders.
    B. infidels.
    C. barbarians.

__A__ 3. To gain security, the Roman emperors

    A. moved to Constantinople.
    B. burned Rome.
    C. drove their enemies into Asia.

__B__ 4. The first great emperor of the Byzantine Empire was

    A. Belisarius.
    B. Justinian.
    C. Byzantium.

__C__ 5. The Byzantine general who conquered Egypt was

    A. Justinian.
    B. Barbarius.
    C. Belisarius.

__B__ 6. The people conquered in Egypt by the Byzantines were the

    A. Berbers.
    B. Vandals.
    C. Pharaohs.

__A__ 7. The new law code was called the

    A. Body of Civil Law.
    B. Byzantine Law Code.
    C. Corpus Tribonius.

Heritage Studies 6
Student Notebook

---

8. Describe the victories of Belisarius.

Belisarius conquered Egypt. Then he conquered Carthage in northern Africa. He

also defeated the island of Sicily and all of Italy.

_____

_____

_____

9. Explain why the emperors at Constantinople were unable to rule Rome.

They were too far away from Rome to be able to defend it or to enforce laws.

_____

_____

_____

_____

71a

☐ Evaluating the Lesson

Early Byzantine Empire (Notebook page 71)—Direct the students to write the letter of the correct answer in each blank. Then tell them to write two or three sentences to answer the questions on the back.

━━━ Going Beyond ━━━

☐ Enrichment

Coloring activity—Remind the students that Justinian's men organized thousands of laws. Ask the students whether anyone could keep those laws perfectly. *(no)* Provide copies of "The Penalty of the Law Paid" page. (*NOTE:* See the reproducible material at the end of Lesson 69.) Encourage the students to color the page neatly. Choose a student to tell what is pictured on this page. *(the figure of Christ on the cross and the words of the Ten Commandments)* Explain that this page symbolizes the fact that Christ's sinless life fulfilled the law of God, and His death paid the penalty of the broken law for those who trust Christ as their Savior. Encourage the students to think about the wonderful gift of salvation God has granted to those who have trusted Him. (BAT: 1b Repentance and faith)

☐ Additional Teacher Information

The term *barbarian* was applied by the Romans to peoples who were unlike them in language and culture and who lived outside the Roman Empire. The term *Vandal*, on the other hand, was the actual name of a people who were sometimes in conflict with the Roman Empire and, later, the Byzantine Empire. It was not pejorative as was *barbarian*.

In the year 311, Constantine, one of the rulers of the Roman Empire, said he had seen a vision of a burning cross and the command "In this sign conquer." Constantine, thereafter, fought as a Christian, and in a short time he defeated his rivals to the throne and became Constantine I, Roman emperor. Constantine used Christianity as a unifying force within his kingdom. He outlawed the persecution of Christians and gave Christian clergy the same benefits that were enjoyed by pagan priests. He legalized the celebration of Christian holidays and built a number of Christian churches. Although he had his children trained in the Christian faith, he himself was not baptized until just before his death.

Constantine chose Constantinople as his capital because of its strategic location. Lying on the Bosporus, Constantinople could control all sea traffic, both military and merchant.

The cluster of buildings that formed the emperor's palace in Constantinople contained reception halls, churches, storerooms, kitchens, stables, guardrooms, dungeons, servants' quarters, as well as living quarters for the emperor and his family. In addition, the palace area had pavilions, fountains, gardens, swimming and bathing pools, a private stadium, and even an indoor riding school.

LESSON 64
Hagia Sophia: Holy Wisdom

Text, pages 250-52
Notebook, page 72

- The Riot of the Blues and Greens
- The Hagia Sophia
- Making Mosaics

Preview

□ Objectives
Given proper instruction, the students will be able to do the following:
- Match descriptions to the correct Byzantine person or term.
- Make a mosaic.

□ Materials
Have available:
- The figure of the Hagia Sophia (A.D. 537) from the History TimeLine Packet.
- Glue for each student.
- Scissors for each student.
- A sheet of construction paper for each student.
- Various colors of construction paper for each student to make mosaics.

Day 134

Lesson

□ Introducing the Lesson
Relay race—Tell the students that the Blues and the Greens were sports clubs in Constantinople during the Byzantine Empire. These clubs held chariot races in the *hippodrome*, a large arena. Divide the class into two teams, the Blues and the Greens. Take the students outside and allow them to run a relay race.

Not everything went smoothly for Justinian. Two great sports clubs in the city of Constantinople were the cause of his problems. These clubs were called the Greens and the Blues. Almost everyone in the city belonged to one of these clubs. At sporting events, they cheered their favorite teams to victory.

These clubs also served as the city guard and helped keep the city walls in repair. When they disagreed with the government, they rioted. In 532, the Greens and the Blues protested the emperor's high taxes. During these *Nika Riots*, the club members looted and burned much of the city.

Justinian would have run for his life had it not been for his wife, Theodora. She had been a circus performer before she married Justinian. She told her husband that she preferred to die an empress and that royal purple made a fine shroud. Justinian found enough courage to stay and sent Belisarius out to fight the rioters.

Belisarius waited until the Blues and the Greens were holding a meeting in the *hippodrome*, a large open-air stadium, and then he led his army in. At the end of the battle, thousands of rioters lay dead in the huge arena.

The Hippodrome in Constantinople

Troy leaned across the table. "Can you believe that? Sports clubs leading riots! Coach would make us do pushups for fifty years if we acted that way."

Dan tapped his book with the eraser of his pencil. "And that part about Theodora. An emperor marrying a *circus performer?*"

"I didn't believe it, either. But Miss Hayden says that Theodora was a circus performer, and Justinian was the son of a peasant."

"How'd they get to be the rulers?"

"Justinian's uncle was emperor before him and made Justinian his heir."

"No wonder Justinian was scared—he was brand-new at this emperor thing. Let's see what else he did."

250

Day 135

□ Teaching the Lesson
The riot of the Blues and Greens—Instruct the students to read page 250 silently to find out what job Theodora had before she became an empress. *(circus performer)* Allow the students to discuss their ideas about a circus performer becoming an empress.

Discussion Questions
➤ **What did the Blues and the Greens do when they were not rioting?** *(They cheered for their teams, served as the city guard, and kept the city walls repaired.)*
➤ **Why did the Blues and the Greens riot during Justinian's reign?** *(They did not want to pay high taxes.)*
➤ **What did Theodora mean by her statement that she preferred to die an empress and that royal purple made a fine shroud?** *(She would rather die than give in to the rioters.)*
➤ **How did Justinian respond to the rioters?** *(He sent General Belisarius to fight the rioters. The rioters were defeated.)*

> Discuss with the students how a Christian should respond when faced with opposition. *(A Christian should do right and trust God to help him and protect him.)* (BAT: 8a Faith in God's promises)

Taxes went up even more after the Nika Riots because so much of the city needed to be rebuilt. Justinian took advantage of the opportunity to make Constantinople more beautiful than it had ever been. The emperor set his architects to work, planning and building new public baths, government buildings, churches, and aqueducts and cisterns for carrying and storing water.

The most famous of all these structures was the *Hagia Sophia,* or the Church of Holy Wisdom. The Hagia Sophia was the most important and most beautiful church in the empire. It still stands today.

The church was built in the form of a Greek cross, which is a cross that has arms of equal length. Over the center of the church, the builders erected a magnificent dome that reached 184 feet above the floor. The Ottoman Turks added the *minarets,* the four surrounding towers, to the Hagia Sophia after 1453.

The inside of the Hagia Sophia was brilliantly decorated. A picture of God the Father surrounded by angels and archangels looked down from the highest part of the dome. Pictures of the saints covered the walls of the church. Many of these pictures were *mosaics.* Mosaics are pictures made of small stones or pieces of glass set in mortar. Have you ever seen a mosaic?

Hagia Sophia (below) and a mosaic from its interior (right)

251

To Make a Mosaic

1. Get glue, scissors, and several different-colored sheets of construction paper.

2. Cut the construction paper into small squares or shapes of varying sizes.

3. Apply a thin layer of glue to a small portion of a sheet of construction paper.

4. Arrange the small pieces of paper close together, side by side on top of the glue. Keep working, applying glue and arranging pieces to form a picture, until the entire sheet of paper is covered and no more glue can be seen.

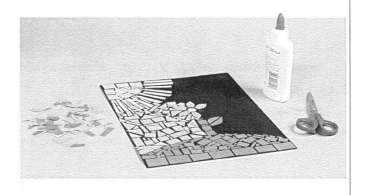

252

The Hagia Sophia—Instruct the students to read page 251 silently to find out what form was used as the design for the Hagia Sophia. *(a Greek cross—all four arms of equal length)*

Discussion Questions

➤ **What is the meaning of the name *Hagia Sophia?*** *(Holy Wisdom)*

➤ **How did Justinian raise the money to build the Hagia Sophia?** *(He raised taxes to rebuild the city of Constantinople after the riots.)*

Place the figure of the Hagia Sophia on the TimeLine at A.D. 537, the year the building of Hagia Sophia was completed. Tell the students that the Hagia Sophia had already stood for 1,239 years when the Declaration of Independence was signed. Choose a student to tell how many years the Hagia Sophia has been standing now. *(Subtract 537 from the current year.)*

➤ **What is a *mosaic?*** *(a picture made of small stones or pieces of glass set in mortar)*

➤ **What did some of the mosaics in the Hagia Sophia represent?** *(God the Father surrounded by angels and archangels, saints)*

➤ **How does the Hagia Sophia differ from the church you attend?** *(Answers will vary.)*

Day 136

Making mosaics—Direct a *Discovering How* activity on page 252. Select a student to read aloud the steps on the page. Remind the students that the walls of the Hagia Sophia were covered with mosaics. Explain that they will be making mosaics by following the directions given on page 252. Distribute the materials, allowing time for the students to make their mosaics. Display the completed mosaics in the classroom.

Byzantium Match   Name _____

Write the letter of the correct description in each blank.

A. "Holy Wisdom"   F. pictures made with bits of colored tile
B. former circus performer   G. powerful emperor
C. army general   H. caused by angry Blues and Greens
D. increased after the riots   I. open-air stadium
E. sports clubs   J. built by the Ottoman Turks in the 1400s

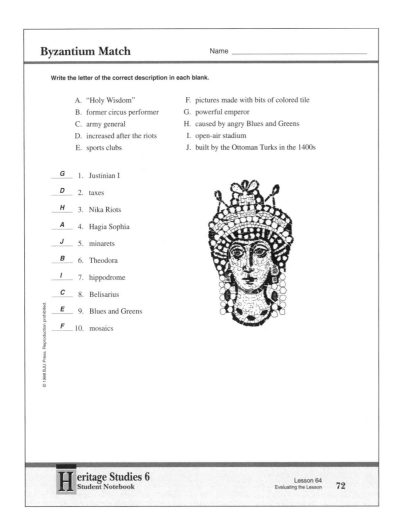

_G_ 1. Justinian I

_D_ 2. taxes

_H_ 3. Nika Riots

_A_ 4. Hagia Sophia

_J_ 5. minarets

_B_ 6. Theodora

_I_ 7. hippodrome

_C_ 8. Belisarius

_E_ 9. Blues and Greens

_F_ 10. mosaics

Heritage Studies 6
Student Notebook

Lesson 64
Evaluating the Lesson   **72**

☐ Evaluating the Lesson

Byzantium Match (Notebook page 72)—Direct the students to write the letter of the correct description in each blank.

▬▬ Going Beyond ▬▬

☐ Enrichment

Circus activity—Set up an AREA with construction paper, felt-tip pens, and books about circuses. Encourage students to look through the books and decide what type of circus performance interests them most. Allow each student to draw and color a picture of himself as a circus performer.

☐ Additional Teacher Information

Theodora's father was a bear keeper for the circus.

The hippodrome was modeled after the Roman Colosseum. However, because the population of Constantinople was largely Christian, the events held in the hippodrome were different from those held in the Colosseum. Plays, chariot races, and even public political forums were held in the hippodrome.

Minarets were added to the Hagia Sophia after Constantinople was conquered by Muslims in 1453. Today, the Hagia Sophia is a museum.

LESSON 65
An Army's Struggle

Text, pages 253-56

- Unhappy Soldiers
- The Lombard Invasion
- Emperor Heraclius's Victories
- Byzantine Culture

——— Preview ———

□ Objective

Given proper instruction, the students will be able to do the following:

- Identify statements about the Byzantine army as either true or false.

□ Materials

Have available a pocket-sized New Testament.*

Day 137

——— Lesson ———

□ Introducing the Lesson

Conduct a smuggling activity—Prior to class, select a student to "smuggle" a pocket-sized New Testament into the room in his pocket. Instruct the student to arrange his shirt so that the New Testament does not show. Call ten students, including the "smuggler" to the front of the room. Tell them to turn all the way around. Challenge the other students to guess which student has smuggled the New Testament into the room. Explain that many courageous Christians have smuggled Bibles into lands that are closed to the gospel. (BAT: 5c Evangelism and missions) Tell the students that today they will be learning about another kind of smuggling.

The Empire's Struggle for Existence

After rebuilding the city, the emperors had no money left in the imperial treasury. To save money, they decreased their soldiers' pay.

The soldiers in the Byzantine army were foreigners hired by the government. They came from many countries, were paid to fight, and were loyal only to their generals. Such soldiers were called *mercenaries*. If you were a mercenary, what would you do if the Byzantine emperor paid you only half of what he had promised?

The Persian emperor thought this would be a good time to attack the Byzantine Empire and take Syria for himself. He wanted Syria because it was rich from trade and could afford to pay high taxes. The Byzantine emperor did not want to lose Syria. Because the mercenary armies would not fight for half pay, the Persians won the war.

253

□ Teaching the Lesson

Unhappy soldiers—Instruct the students to read page 253 silently to find out why the soldiers in the Byzantine army were unhappy. *(Their pay was cut in half.)*

Discussion Questions

➤ **Why did the emperor have to cut the pay of the soldiers?** *(Too much money had been spent on rebuilding the city; there was no money in the treasury.)*

➤ **How did decreasing the soldiers' pay affect the outcome of the next war?** *(The mercenary soldiers would not fight on half pay. The Persian army was able to defeat the Byzantine army.)*

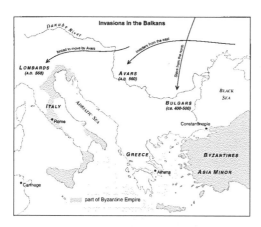

The Byzantine armies did not fight well in the Balkans either. Can you find the Balkan region on the map? Line a ruler up from the north end of the Adriatic Sea to the northwest corner of the Black Sea. All the land to the south, including Greece but not Asia Minor, is the Balkan Region.

Two barbarian tribes from Asia were migrating into this area. They were called the Avars and the Bulgars. They were strong enough to take the land away from Byzantium and settle in it.

Then the emperor received news of another tribe of barbarians called the Lombards. They had invaded Italy and had successfully attacked the empire there. In just one hundred years, Byzantium lost nearly all the land conquered by Justinian's general, Belisarius. The Byzantine Empire seemed to be disappearing from the map.

254

Heraclius

Heraclius began his reign in A.D. 610. Without him the Byzantine Empire might have disappeared. He reformed the army, reconquered the land taken by Persia and the barbarians, and made the roads safe for commerce.

To reform the army, Heraclius fired the mercenary soldiers and trained Byzantine peasants for the army. Heraclius did not have enough money to pay his new citizen-soldiers, so he gave each one enough land to support himself and his family.

With his new army, Heraclius drove the Persians from Asia Minor and conquered Syria, Palestine, and Egypt. Then he marched the army to the Balkans and defeated the Avars. Why do you think these citizen-soldiers were more successful than the mercenaries?

Heraclius added so much land to the empire that he had to find a new way to organize it. He divided the land into provinces called *themes*. Each theme was a military zone with many peasant soldiers living in it. These soldiers were responsible for the theme's defense. This system lasted almost until the fall of the Byzantine Empire in 1453.

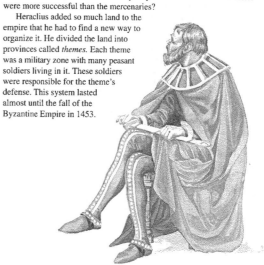

255

The Lombard invasion—Instruct the students to read page 254 silently to find out who the Lombards were. *(a barbarian tribe that was attacking Byzantine territory in Italy)*

Discussion Question

➤ **Why do you think the barbarian tribes were able to take land from the Byzantine Empire?** *(The Byzantine army was weak, and the territory was widely scattered.)*

Day 138

Emperor Heraclius's victories—Instruct the students to read page 255 silently to find out what Heraclius did to save the Byzantine Empire from total defeat. *(reformed the army, reconquered land, made roads safe)*

Discussion Questions

➤ **How did Heraclius motivate the peasant soldiers to fight since he had no money to pay them?** *(He gave each soldier enough land to support himself and his family.)*

➤ **Why did these soldiers fight harder than the mercenary soldiers had fought?** *(They were defending their own land.)*

➤ **How did Heraclius organize all the land he had gained for the Byzantine Empire?** *(He divided the land into provinces called* themes.*)*

Trade flourished under the government of Heraclius. Special groups called *guilds* united moneychangers, goldsmiths, and notaries, who oversaw the writing of legal documents. In the cities, other guilds supplied meat, fish, and bread to the populace. Foreign merchants traveled throughout Byzantium selling furs, leather, slaves, wax, ointments, spices, and grain.

One of the most important items of trade was silk. Silk was worn only by the members of the government. Each government official had his insignia of office woven into the fabric. Silk was extremely expensive because it came all the way from China, and the Persians controlled much of the silk trade route.

Byzantine spies discovered how the Chinese made silk. They stole some silkworms and smuggled them out of China. Silk production became one of the most important industries in the empire, especially in the cities of Constantinople, Antioch, Tyre, and Beirut.

Chinese workers collecting silkworm cocoons to use in making silk

Heraclius also changed the language of the empire. Though the people of Byzantium believed their empire was a continuation of the old Roman Empire, very few Byzantines in the seventh century spoke Latin. Almost everyone spoke Greek, so Heraclius decreed that the language of the empire would be Greek. He even stopped using Roman titles for emperor and used the Greek title *Basilius*.

Dan rubbed his eyes. "I didn't think I'd like studying the Byzantine Empire very much. Heraclius was some emperor!"

"Look at the next question," Troy said. "'What new empire threatened the Byzantine Empire during the seventh century?' Seems like this empire was always getting into fights with somebody! Man, all this competition stuff is putting me in the mood for baseball!" He tossed the ball to Dan.

256

Byzantine culture—Instruct the students to read page 256 silently to find out what secret the Byzantine spies learned in China. *(how to make silk)*

Discussion Questions

➤ **Do you think it was right for the Byzantine spies to smuggle the silkworms out of China? Why or why not?** *(Answers will vary.)*

> Tell the students that although the Byzantine spies profited by smuggling the silkworms out of China, the Bible instructs Christians to behave honestly and not to steal. (BAT: 4c Honesty)

➤ **What purposes did the *guilds* serve?** *(The guilds brought supplies to be bought and sold; they helped the moneychangers, goldsmiths, and notaries work together.)*

➤ **Why did Heraclius make Greek the official language of the Byzantine Empire?** *(He wanted people to think of the Byzantine Empire as the continuation of the Roman Empire, but since no one spoke Latin, he decided to pattern his empire after the Greek Empire.)*

□ Evaluating the Lesson

Direct an oral evaluation—Tell the students that you will read aloud statements related to this lesson. If the statement is true, they should salute with the right hand. If the statement is false, they should raise the left hand in the air. After each false statement, select a volunteer to correct the statement, making it true. Use the following statements.

1. Soldiers who fight for pay are called merchants. *(false; mercenaries)*
2. The Persian army defeated the Byzantine army. *(true)*
3. Belisarius was Justinian's best general. *(true)*
4. Trade groups were called unions. *(false; guilds)*
5. Most people in the Byzantine Empire spoke Italian. *(false; Greek)*

══ Going Beyond ══

□ Enrichment

Observing caterpillars—Set up an AREA with books about silk making. Encourage the students to read the books and to collect caterpillars to keep in jars in the classroom. Remind them to poke holes in the lids of the jars to let in air in order to keep the caterpillars alive. Encourage the students to draw pictures of the caterpillars at different life stages.

□ Additional Teacher Information

For centuries, only the Chinese knew the secret of making silk. Knowing how important having a monopoly on the silk trade was, the Chinese carefully guarded the secret of weaving cloth from the threads of silkworm cocoons. The punishment for revealing the silk-making process to a foreigner was death.

Emperor Justinian wanted to expand Byzantine trade by producing silk. He sent two monks to China with the express purpose of finding out how to make silk. The monks learned how to make silk and were able to smuggle silkworms out of China. They also smuggled out mulberry leaves, the food of the silkworms. When the monks returned home and told of their discoveries, the Chinese monopoly on making silk ended.

In A.D. 622, Emperor Heraclius wanted to recapture Asia Minor, which had been taken by the Arabs. By 626, he had retaken Asia Minor, Syria, Egypt, and Palestine. However, these outer provinces became a drain on the imperial treasury. It was difficult to maintain an army large enough to defend the far-flung territories. By the end of the seventh century, the Byzantine Empire was a small fraction of what it had been.

LESSON 66

Islam: Religion of Conquest

Text, pages 257-59
Notebook, pages 73-74

- Muhammad's "Vision" and the Koran
- Hegira
- Jihad

━━━ Preview ━━━

□ Objective
Given proper instruction, the students will be able to do the following:
- Complete a word-search puzzle about the beginnings of Islam.

□ Materials
Have available:
- A Bible for each student.
- An overhead projector.
- 2 blank overhead transparencies.
- An overhead transparency pen.
- A wall map of the world.

Prepare:
- An overhead transparency of "Jesus Christ—'True Prophet' or Son of God?" (*NOTE:* See the reproducible material at the end of Lesson 69.)
- An overhead transparency of "Christianity and Islam Contrasted." (*NOTE:* See the reproducible material at the end of Lesson 69.)

Day 139

━━━ Lesson ━━━

□ Introducing the Lesson
Bible activity—Display the overhead transparency of "Jesus Christ—'True Prophet' or Son of God?" Choose a student to read the sentence at the top of the transparency. *(Islam teaches that Jesus Christ is a "true prophet" but is not the Son of God.)* Select students to look up each of the first four verses listed. Write in the blank what the verse says about the divinity of Jesus Christ. *(Matthew 27:43—People at the crucifixion quoted Jesus as saying He was the Son of God. John 9:35-37—Jesus tells a man He has healed that He is the Son of God. John 10:36—Jesus claims to be the Son of God. John 19:7—The Jews accuse Jesus of claiming to be the Son of God.)* Read and discuss the three sentences in the center of the page. Emphasize that the Bible clearly

---

A New Enemy and a New Faith

Far to the south, in the city of Mecca, a merchant named Muhammad was concerned for his people, the Arabs. They had no government or system of law to guarantee peace.

Muhammad traveled throughout the Middle East. Along the caravan routes, he met people from all over the world. Persians told him of the greatness of their empire and its laws. Jewish merchants explained their faith in the *Torah.* The Torah gave them the laws they lived by. The Christian merchants declared that God had given all people the Bible to tell them of the freedom offered in Christ.

Muhammad wanted his people to have a holy book of their own. One day, he claimed that he had received a special message from the angel Gabriel. Gabriel told Muhammad that Allah had chosen him to be his prophet. Through Muhammad, Allah would give the Arab people a holy book that would tell them how to live without fighting.

Allah's holy book was called the *Koran.* Muslims believed that the Koran contained the messages given to Muhammad from Allah. The new religion was called *Islam. Islam* means "submission to Allah." Anyone who followed Islam was called a *Muslim,* or one who submits to Allah. Those who did not believe were called *infidels.*

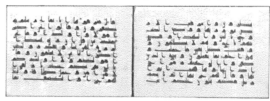

An eighth- or ninth-century copy of the Koran

257

---

teaches that Jesus is the Son of God. Read and discuss the related verses at the bottom of the page as desired.

Day 140

□ Teaching the Lesson
Muhammad's "vision" and the Koran—Instruct the students to read page 257 silently to find out why Muhammad wrote the Koran. *(He wanted the Arab people to have a holy book of their own.)*

Discussion Questions
➤ **What is the religion of Muhammad, and what are the followers of that religion called?** *(Islam; Muslims)*
➤ **What did Muhammad say was included in the Koran?** *(instructions from Allah for living without fighting)*

> Remind the students that the Bible is the only book that God inspired to reveal Himself. Read Revelation 22:18-19 aloud, pointing out what the Bible says about adding to or taking away from the Holy Scriptures. (BAT: 8b Faith in the power of the Word of God)

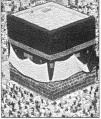

The Kaaba

This craftsman is working on part of a gold- and silver-embroidered cloth to cover the Kaaba. A new cover is made each year at a cost of several million dollars.

Muhammad preached this new religion on the street corners of Mecca. What do you think the people of Mecca thought of these new ideas? The Meccans did not like the new religion because it had only one god. Their old religion had many gods. And in Mecca stood a temple where many of the idols of those gods were kept. Every year thousands of Arabs came to worship at this temple called the *Kaaba.* If the Arab people accepted Muhammad's new religion, the merchants of Mecca were afraid they would lose all the money that came from the yearly *pilgrimage.*

In the year 622, the non-Muslim Meccans forced Muhammad to leave his home. He led his followers two hundred miles north to the city of Medina. Their flight from Mecca was called the *Hegira.* The year of the Hegira, 622, is the first year of the Islamic calendar.

The city of Medina welcomed Muhammad because he helped settle serious disagreements between some of the city's families. The Medinans soon made Muhammad their governor, but Muhammad was still thinking of Mecca. He wanted the Meccans to accept the new religion of Islam. He also believed that the Kaaba was the sacred temple of Allah. He and his followers wanted to worship there. How do you think he accomplished these goals?

In the year 630, Muhammad led his army to Mecca. When an Islamic army fights for its faith, the war is called a *jihad,* or holy war. The Muslims conquered the city and went directly to the Kaaba. There Muhammad removed all the idols and declared it the temple of Allah. The jihad against Mecca had been successful, and the city accepted Islam.

258

The Conquests of the Muslims

The men who led the Muslims after Muhammad's death were called *caliphs* or successors. Many of them were fine generals. The first was Abu-Bakr. He led the Muslim army into the Arabian Peninsula. In only two years he conquered the whole peninsula and converted its people to Islam.

No one could stop the Muslim army. Caliph Omar's best general, Khalid ibn al-Walid, led the army into Persia. After defeating one of the Persian armies, Caliph Omar sent his army against Syria and Egypt and captured both from Heraclius, emperor of Byzantium. How could Omar's army succeed against the two powerful empires of Persia and Byzantium?

Persia had been fighting Byzantium for a long time, and by the time Omar's army reached Persia, the Persian soldiers were exhausted. The Byzantine soldiers were weary too. In addition to fighting the Persians in the southeast, Heraclius's army had been fighting the Avars and Bulgars in the Balkans. The Byzantine army simply was not large enough to fight the Arabs at the same time.

During these battles, Khalid conquered Jerusalem, where the Muslims wanted to worship at a sacred rock. The Dome of the Rock, an Islamic mosque, stands over the rock today.

The Dome of the Rock is built on the spot in Jerusalem believed to be the site of Muhammad's ascension into heaven.

259

Hegira—Instruct the students to read page 258 silently to find out why Muhammad wanted to go back to Mecca. *(He wanted to worship at the Kaaba, which he believed to be the sacred temple of Allah.)*

Discussion Questions

➤ **Why did the merchants of Mecca force Muhammad to leave their city?** *(They feared their business would be adversely affected if Islam became a popular religion.)*
➤ **What was the *Hegira*?** *(Muhammad's withdrawal from Mecca)*
➤ **Why is the year 622 important to Muslims?** *(It was the year of the Hegira and is the first year of the Muslim calendar.)*

Display the overhead transparency "Christianity and Islam Contrasted." Discuss each point as desired.

Day 141

Jihad—Instruct the students to read page 259 silently to find the name of the first caliph. *(Abu-Bakr)* Point out the Arabian Peninsula on the wall map. Choose a student to tell how long it took the Islamic army to conquer this area. *(two years)*

Discussion Questions

➤ **How do the actions of the Muslim generals compare to the Koran's teaching of how to live without fighting?** *(The actions are inconsistent with the teaching.)*

➤ **Did the Muslims succeed against the Byzantine armies?** *(Yes, Omar's armies defeated both Persia and Byzantium.)*
➤ **What important religious city was conquered by the Muslims?** *(Jerusalem)*

Emphasize that any religion that offers salvation through good works is a false religion. Many forms of Christianity have become false religions because they encourage their followers to trust in the works that they do for salvation rather than in the work of Christ on the cross. Even a person in a Bible-believing church may fail to comprehend that he must trust Christ as his Savior. Attending Sunday school, giving money to the church, or doing any other good works cannot save anyone. Read aloud Titus 3:5 and Ephesians 2:8-9. (BATs: 1a Understanding Jesus Christ, 1b Repentance and faith)

Islam Word Search Clues   Name _____

Write the answer on the blank. Then find the answer in the word search.

Answer		Clue
Mecca	1.	The Kaaba is located in this city.
Muhammad	2.	the prophet of Islam
Arabs	3.	some people who live in the Middle East
Khalid ibn al-Walid	4.	Caliph Omar's best general
Dome of the Rock	5.	a famous mosque in Jerusalem
caliphs	6.	the successors of Muhammad
Persia	7.	Middle Eastern country conquered by Khalid ibn al-Walid
Muslims	8.	people who follow Muhammad's religion
Torah	9.	holy book of the Jews
Abu-Bakr	10.	the first caliph
Kaaba	11.	temple in Mecca dedicated to Allah
Heraclius	12.	Byzantine emperor who fought Avars and Bulgars
infidels	13.	Muslim term for Christians and others who do not believe in Islam
Medina	14.	city Muhammad fled to from Mecca
Jerusalem	15.	Jewish city conquered by Khalid
Allah	16.	the god of Islam
Koran	17.	Islam's "holy book"
Jewish	18.	Muhammad met Christian and ____ people on his travels.
caravan routes	19.	Muhammad met many people along these. (two words)
Hegira	20.	Muhammad's flight from Mecca
Christian	21.	a person who trusts Jesus Christ for salvation
Islam	22.	Muhammad's religion
Middle East	23.	area of the world populated mostly by Arabs
jihad	24.	Islamic "holy war"
Gabriel	25.	Muhammad claimed this angel spoke to him.

Heritage Studies 6
Student Notebook

Lesson 66
Evaluating the Lesson **73**

Islam Word Search   Name _____

Find the answers from page 73 in the puzzle below,

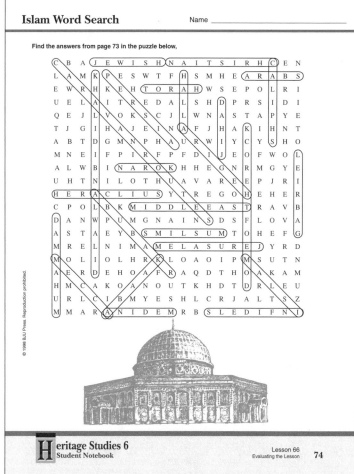

Heritage Studies 6
Student Notebook

Lesson 66
Evaluating the Lesson **74**

□ Evaluating the Lesson

Islam Word Search (Notebook pages 73-74)—Direct the students to write the answer in each blank on Notebook page 73 and then to find each answer in the word search on Notebook page 74.

■■■ Going Beyond ■■■

□ Enrichment

Classroom visit—Invite a pastor or missionary who has ministered among Muslims to visit your class to talk about his work. Encourage the students to ask questions about the Muslim people.

□ Additional Teacher Information

As part of the religion of Islam, each Muslim performs five duties, called the *Five Pillars of the Faith, that he believes will earn him salvation.*

The first Pillar is belief. To become a Muslim, one must repeat the Islamic statement of belief: "There is no god but Allah, and Muhammad is his Messenger."

The second Pillar is prayer. A Muslim must pray five times a day: morning, noon, midafternoon, sunset, and night. The prayer must be in Arabic and must be prayed toward Mecca. It is preferable to pray in a mosque, but prayers may be said anywhere. On Fridays at noon, there is a special time of prayer and teaching in the mosque.

The third Pillar is giving. A Muslim gives voluntary alms as well as a tax to his government. He believes that his giving is a good work that will help him earn salvation.

The fourth Pillar is fasting. During the month of Ramadan, the ninth month of the Muslim calendar, all Muslims are to fast. From dawn to dusk Muslims may not eat, drink, or smoke. The Muslims fast to show their belief in Allah and as a good work.

The fifth Pillar is a pilgrimage. Each Muslim should, if he can, visit the city of Mecca once during his lifetime. There he should perform the rites and rituals of the pilgrimage of *hajj.*

Islamic cultural distinctives include a strict code of separation of men and women. Men and women do not mix in social or business settings. Women wear very modest clothes and focus on family responsibilities. Some Muslim countries are more strict in enforcing these codes than others. In Saudi Arabia, for example, women are not permitted to drive cars. In other Islamic countries, women are allowed to wear Western clothes, drive, hold jobs, and so on.

The Saudi Arabian flag is a green ground with the *shahada*—"There is no god but Allah, and Muhammad is his messenger"—written in Arabic over a sword.

LESSON 67
Greek Fire

Text, pages 260-63

- Leo the Isaurian
- Greek Fire
- A Split Church
- A New Alphabet

━━━ Preview ━━━

□ Objective

Given proper instruction, the students will be able to do the following:
- Write a newspaper article.

□ Materials

Have available:
- A Bible.
- A cassette player.
- *HERITAGE STUDIES Listening Cassette B.*
- An overhead projector.
- A blank overhead transparency.
- A sheet of notebook paper for each student.

Prepare an overhead transparency of John 3:16 in Russian. (*NOTE:* See the reproducible material at the end of Lesson 69.)

Day 142

━━━ Lesson ━━━

□ Introducing the Lesson

Russian reading—Display the overhead transparency of John 3:16 in Russian without revealing the English pronunciation. Ask whether anyone can read the words. Tell the students that this is the verse John 3:16 in Cyrillic letters. Play the Russian reading of John 3:16 from *HERITAGE STUD-IES Listening Cassette B.* Display the English pronunciation and play the recording again, allowing students to try to read along with the tape. Explain that they will learn about the origin of the Cyrillic alphabet in this lesson.

Conflict Continues

To provide soldiers for all their wars, the Byzantine emperors gave more and more land to peasants who joined the army. The nobility especially disliked this practice. They thought only noblemen should own land. The wars also brought a rise in taxes and angered the Byzantines. Often rebellion resulted, and the current emperor was murdered.

For twenty years civil war tore the empire. Seven emperors tried to rule during this time. Most were assassinated after only a few months on the throne. The empire needed a powerful ruler to save it.

Leo the Isaurian was the man they needed. He could handle all the problems of the empire. He had lived among the Arabs when he was a boy. He even spoke Arabic. When he was older, his family had moved to the Balkan area, so he was familiar with the barbarians there.

As an adult, Leo had served as an administrator and a general in the Byzantine government. Soon he was more powerful than the emperor. With his army, Leo captured the emperor and all his household. In A.D. 717 he named himself Emperor Leo III.

260

□ Teaching the Lesson

Leo the Isaurian—Instruct the students to read page 260 silently to find out why the Byzantines thought Leo the Isaurian would be able to deal with the Arab threat to Byzantine power. (*He had grown up among the Arabs and spoke Arabic.*)

Discussion Questions

➤ **Why were the nobles unhappy?** (*The emperors were giving more and more land to the peasants who joined the army.*)

➤ **How did Leo rise to power?** (*He worked in the Byzantine government, raised an army, and seized the imperial power, deposing the previous emperor.*)

Muslim ships burning from Greek fire

Just six months after Leo became emperor, Muslim armies camped outside the walls of Constantinople. The Muslim navy closed off the city by sea. They were trying to starve the citizens into surrendering.

Leo III sent his ships out against the Muslims. The Byzantines had only a few ships, but they had something even more important—a secret weapon. They had invented an explosive mixture called *Greek fire* that burst into flames when it touched water. When the Muslim ships drew close enough, the defenders of Constantinople threw their Greek fire toward the ships. The Muslim ships burned to the water line. Then Leo could bring supplies into his city by ship so that no one would starve.

The following winter was so cold that many of the Muslim soldiers encamped around Constantinople froze to death. The next summer a large number died of a plague. Finally, the Muslims withdrew. Leo led his army into Asia Minor and took it back from the Muslims.

Leo had proved his ability to lead the empire. However, he believed that he ruled not only the empire but also the church. Claiming to have authority over both the state and the church is called *caesaropapism.* Can you see the two parts of this word? A *caesar* rules the state. A pope, or *papal* government, rules the church. Leo III was a caesaropapist.

Troy shoved his book across the table. "Look at that picture. That's an actual picture of Greek fire. I wonder what it's made of?"

Dan shrugged and frowned. "I'm confused," he said. "Are Muslims the same as Arabs?"

Troy was still looking at the picture of the burning ships. "Huh? Oh, it's simple. The Arabs were the people of Muhammad. Islam is the religion Muhammad invented for the Arabs. Arabs who believed in Islam were called Muslims."

"So the Arab army and Muslim army are the same army."

"Yeah." Troy turned back to his book. "I want to find out more about this Greek fire."

261

Iconoclasm

Icons are sacred pictures and statues of Jesus and the saints. When an earthquake shook Constantinople in 726, Leo believed it was a judgment from God against the use of icons. He ordered the destruction of all sacred statues and pictures in the churches.

Hatred of icons is called iconoclasm. Throughout the empire, those who disliked icons, called *iconoclasts,* broke statues and painted over pictures.

Many people, however, tried to protect the icons. These people appealed to Pope Gregory III in Rome. The pope believed that he, not Leo, was the head of the church. He thought it was right to use icons in worshiping God. The pope condemned what Leo had done.

Leo was not going to allow the pope in faraway Rome to tell him how to govern the Byzantine Empire. He imprisoned those who tried to protect the icons, including some messengers from the pope.

Neither Leo III nor Pope Gregory III was going to give in. Finally, the church divided between Byzantium in the East and Rome in the West. This same division exists today. The eastern part is called the Eastern Orthodox Church. Its leader is called the *patriarch.* The western part is called the Roman Catholic Church and is controlled by the pope.

Iconoclasm ended in the year 843. But the division of the church between the East and West remained.

Byzantine 13th Century, Madonna and Child on a Curved Throne, Andrew W. Mellon Collection, Image © 2006 Board of Trustees, National Gallery of Art, Washington.

> "Thou shalt not make unto thee any graven image, or any likeness of any thing that is in heaven above, or that is in the earth beneath, or that is in the water under the earth."
>
> Exodus 20:4

262

Greek fire—Instruct the students to read page 261 silently to find out how the Muslim navy hoped to force the Byzantines to surrender. *(They tried to starve them by closing off the city from the sea.)*

Discussion Questions

➤ **How did Leo's navy defeat the Muslim navy?** *(They waited until the ships were close together and attacked them with Greek fire, a mixture that exploded when it hit the water.)*

➤ **How was the Muslim army defeated?** *(Most of the soldiers froze to death during the winter, and many who remained died of a plague.)*

➤ **Was Leo content to stay in Byzantium when the Muslims left?** *(No, he went into Asia Minor and recaptured it from the Muslims.)*

➤ **What is *caesaropapism*?** *(the belief in having one ruler of both church and state)*

Day 143

A split church—Instruct the students to read page 262 silently to find out what happened when Leo ordered all icons destroyed. *(Many icons were destroyed. Others were protected by people. Some people appealed to Pope Gregory III to protect the icons.)*

Discussion Questions

➤ **Did Leo obey Gregory's order to save the icons?** *(No, he imprisoned those who tried to protect the icons.)*

➤ **What happened when neither Emperor Leo nor Pope Gregory III would give in to the other's authority?** *(The church split into two sections, the Eastern Orthodox Church and the Roman Catholic Church.)*

Explain that the Great Schism (split) happened because there was an argument about which man would control the Christian church, Leo or Gregory III. Tell the students that Christians are instructed by the Bible to follow Christ and not to take the word of any man as the Word of God. Read Acts 17:11 aloud. Tell the students that the Christians of Berea searched the Scriptures to make sure that the words of the apostles were consistent with what the Bible taught. Encourage the students to be followers of Christ, not of men. (BAT: 8b Faith in the power of the Word of God)

The Golden Age of the Byzantine Empire

The empire had its best and most powerful years between 843 and 1025. The emperors successfully fought their enemies in the Balkans and the Middle East. Michael III reorganized the University of Constantinople. Basil I oversaw the revision of the law. The empire became more and more wealthy from its trade throughout Asia, Europe, and Africa.

Missionaries traveled throughout eastern Europe. Two missionaries, Cyril and Methodius, translated the Bible into Slavic. Because the Slavic people did not have a written language, the missionaries had to invent a new alphabet. They called it the Cyrillic alphabet. Because of the work of these two missionaries, thousands of people learned of the gospel of Christ.

The most unusual emperor during the golden age was Basil II. He never married, and he devoted his life to making the empire stronger. His army was well trained, and he made the nobles collect his taxes. He kept the church from taking land from the peasants. Though Basil was somber and suspicious, he was one of the fairest and best rulers the Byzantine Empire ever had.

Basil II, often called "the Bulgar Slayer," was a great warrior. When the Bulgars attacked the empire, Basil not only defeated them but also captured fourteen thousand of their soldiers. To intimidate the Bulgar king, he blinded all the captured soldiers and sent them back home in groups of a hundred. Each group had a one-eyed man to lead the way. When the Bulgar king saw his soldiers blinded and stumbling, he reportedly fell over dead. How many other kings do you suppose would challenge Basil after they heard this story?

Cyrillic Alphabet

Russian		Roman equivalent
А	а	a
Б	б	b
В	в	v
Г	г	g
Д	д	d
Е	е	ye
Е	ё	yo
Ж	ж	zh
З	з	z
И	и	i
Й	й	y
К	к	k
Л	л	l
М	м	m
Н	н	n
О	о	o
П	п	p
Р	р	r
С	с	s
Т	т	t
У	у	u
Ф	ф	f
Х	х	kh
Ц	ц	ts
Ч	ч	ch
Ш	ш	sh
Щ	щ	shsh
Ъ	ъ	
Ы	ы	y
Ь	ь	
Э	э	e
Ю	ю	yu
Я	я	ya

263

A new alphabet—Instruct the students to read page 263 silently to find out why the Cyrillic alphabet was devised. *(so that the Bible could be translated into Slavic)*

Discussion Questions

➤ **What successes did the Byzantine Empire see during the golden age?** *(The law was revised, the university was reorganized, enemies were defeated, the empire became wealthy, and missionaries traveled extensively.)*

➤ **What good things did Basil II accomplish?** *(He strengthened the empire's military force, increased the government's income, and limited the power of the church over the peasants.)*

➤ **What did Basil do that earned him the title "Bulgar Slayer"?** *(He captured fourteen thousand Bulgar soldiers, blinded them, and sent them home.)*

Day 144

□ Evaluating the Lesson

Writing—Direct the students to write on notebook paper an "on the scene" newspaper article for one of the events discussed in this lesson. Remind them to provide a headline for their article. Encourage them to include "quotations" from people who participated in the event as well as the facts of time and place. Display the newspaper articles in the classroom.

━━━ Going Beyond ━━━

□ Enrichment

Cyrillic alphabet—Set up a penmanship AREA with paper and pens. Display a copy of the Cyrillic alphabet. *(NOTE: See the reproducible material at the end of Lesson 69.)* Allow the students to try to write their names or other words using Cyrillic letters.

□ Additional Teacher Information

We do not know for sure how the Byzantines formulated their "Greek fire." Modern scientists believe that it was probably a combination of ingredients that included naphtha, sulfur, and saltpeter.

Most Byzantine art portrayed Christ, saints of the early church, or scenes from the Bible. Many of these pictures were intended to inspire worshipers to greater devotion. By reminding the people of biblical characters and events, they were intended to help turn worshipers' thoughts toward God and His Word. However, these images, called icons, came to be misused. People made them objects of worship, prayed to them, and expected miracles of them.

The Eastern Orthodox and Roman Catholic Churches had disagreements for hundreds of years before the final split in 1054. Pope Leo IX excommunicated the patriarch of the Eastern Orthodox Church. The patriarch responded by excommunicating the pope.

Symbolism in sacred art has developed through the years to communicate the message of the painting. Mary is typically pictured wearing blue, Paul is bald, and Peter has a rounded white beard. This symbolism made it easy for people—many of whom could not read—to identify the person being represented.

The missionaries Methodius and Cyril were brothers. They traveled to the Slavic tribes at the request of Emperor Michael III. Within a few years, the Slavic tribes had been converted to Christianity.

LESSON 68
Taking Up the Cross

Text, pages 264-67
Notebook, page 75

- The First Crusade
- The Fourth Crusade
- Constantinople Sacked by Crusaders
- The New Byzantine Empire

Preview

□ Objective
Given proper instruction, the students will be able to do the following:
- Answer questions about the Crusades.

□ Materials
Have available:
- A wall map of the world.
- A Bible.

Day 145

Lesson

□ Introducing the Lesson
Robin Hood—Ask the students whether they have heard the story of Robin Hood. Allow students to discuss the main characters and events of the story of Robin Hood.

Discussion Questions
➤ **How did Robin Hood get money to give to poor people?** *(He stole from rich people.)*
➤ **Who was the wicked ruler who wanted to kill Robin Hood?** *(Prince John)*
➤ **What good king returned from a far journey at the end of the story?** *(King Richard the Lion Heart)*

Tell the students that Prince John ruled England while his brother Richard the Lion Heart was in Palestine trying to capture cities from the Muslims. Explain that these missions were called the *Crusades*.

The Crusader Kingdom of Constantinople
After Basil II's death, no one was strong enough to run the government the way he had. The empire weakened, both inside and out. Venice, an Italian city, took over much of the trade. New enemies appeared: the Normans from northern Europe, the Patzinaks from Russia, and the Seljuk Turks from central Asia. All of them attacked the empire. The Byzantines hated the Turks most of all because the Turks had captured the holy city of Jerusalem.

In 1096, Emperor Alexius Comnenus I sent a message to the pope in Rome, asking for help to fight the Turks. He needed a well-trained army of professional soldiers. Instead, Pope Urban II called all the knights in Europe to a crusade against the Turks. Their effort was called the First Crusade.

Thousands of knights prepared for the long march to Constantinople. They were going to rescue Byzantium, but it would be even better, they thought, to rescue Jerusalem. The crusaders forgot about helping the emperor and went right on to Jerusalem.

Alexius never did get the army for which he had asked. Neither he nor the emperors who ruled after him could win back the territory that had been lost. By the year 1200, the Turks controlled the Middle East from Egypt to Syria.

264

□ Teaching the Lesson
The First Crusade—Instruct the students to read page 264 silently to find out who the crusaders were. *(knights called by the pope to fight against the Turks)*

Discussion Questions
➤ **Why did Emperor Alexius Comnenus I ask the pope to send soldiers?** *(He needed help against the Turks who were attacking the Byzantine Empire.)*
➤ **Did the crusaders help Alexius?** *(No, they decided to go to Jerusalem to recapture it from the Muslims.)*
➤ **What happened to the Byzantine Empire when the crusaders would not help?** *(The emperor was unable to recapture his lost land.)*

Display the wall map of the world. Point out England, France, Germany, and Italy. Explain that many of the crusaders came from these areas. Point out Jerusalem. Remind the students that most of the crusaders were peasants who traveled on foot the long distance from Europe to the Holy Land.

About one hundred years later, in the year 1202, Pope Innocent III called for a special crusade. He told the knights they would be going to Egypt to fight the Turkish leader Saladin. But he really wanted the crusaders to fight Byzantium. He wanted to reunite the Eastern Orthodox Church with the Roman Catholic Church. This was called the Fourth Crusade.

The Venetians provided ships to take the knights across the Mediterranean Sea. During the voyage they told the knights about the wealth of Constantinople. "You'll become rich," they told the crusaders. "And after you help us in Constantinople, you can go on to Egypt and fight Saladin if you'd like."

The knights argued for several weeks. Finally, they agreed to help. The Venetians sailed their ships into the Aegean Sea toward Constantinople. Many historians wonder whether the Venetians ever meant to take the crusaders to Egypt at all. What do you think?

265

When the ships reached Constantinople, they broke the great floating barrier that barred the entry to the city's harbor, the *Golden Horn*. The Venetian ships attacked from the sea while the crusaders attacked the city walls from the land.

Constantinople fell. The emperor fled, taking with him the imperial treasure and the crown jewels. On April 13, 1204, the crusaders and Venetians took over the government. For three days, the soldiers and sailors killed thousands of people and destroyed many priceless treasures. A Byzantine writer said that even the Turks were more merciful and kind than the men "who bear the cross of Christ on their shoulders."

"I wonder what happened during the other crusades." Troy stretched and yawned. "This book says there were about a dozen."

"These two are enough for me . . . the way the crusaders and Venetians destroyed so much of Constantinople. They both claimed to be Christian, but they sure didn't act like it. I wonder what Saladin, the Muslim leader, thought about that."

"Yeah." Troy turned the baseball over and over in his hand. "It's kind of the same way in sports. The other teams know we're a Christian school. Wonder what they think of us?"

266

Day 146

The Fourth Crusade—Instruct the students to read page 265 silently to find out the purpose of the Fourth Crusade. *(to reunite the Eastern Orthodox Church with the Roman Catholic Church)* Ask the students whether they think such a union could be accomplished by force. *(probably not)*

Discussion Questions

➤ **How was Pope Innocent III's real purpose for the Fourth Crusade different from what he told the knights?** *(He told the knights he wanted them to fight Saladin in Egypt, but he really wanted to fight Byzantium.)*

➤ **Why did Pope Innocent III lie to his troops?** *(Perhaps he thought they would not be willing to fight against Byzantium.)*

➤ **How did the Venetians convince the knights to fight against Constantinople?** *(They told them they would become wealthy when Constantinople was defeated.)*

Remind the students that it is never right to lie. Nor is it right to try to manipulate someone into doing what you want him to do. (BAT: 4c Honesty)

Constantinople sacked by Crusaders—Instruct the students to read page 266 silently to find out how the Venetians and crusaders defeated Constantinople. *(The Venetians attacked from the sea, and the crusaders attacked from the land.)* Ask them what the emperor took when he left Constantinople. *(the imperial treasure and the crown jewels)*

Discussion Questions

➤ **How did the crusaders treat the people of conquered Constantinople?** *(They killed thousands of people.)*

➤ **Compare the "Christian" crusaders to the Muslim soldiers.** *(The crusaders were more cruel than the Muslims.)*

Remind the students that the crusaders were fighting for worldly goals—more land and better trade routes. Tell the students that Jesus never taught His people to pursue victory by force of arms. Read aloud John 18:36. Explain that God has ordained preaching, not fighting, as His means of bringing men to Christ. (BAT: 8b Faith in the power of the Word of God)

The Recovery of Byzantium

The crusaders never did go on to Egypt to fight Saladin. From 1204 to 1261 the Venetians and crusaders ruled Constantinople. It looked as if the Byzantine Empire had come to an end.

But the real government of Byzantium had not been destroyed. The Byzantines fled to Asia Minor where they organized a new empire. Nicaea was its capital. For over fifty-seven years the new empire fought the armies of both Constantinople and the Turks.

The emperors at Nicaea worked hard to strengthen their new state. One emperor, John III, banned evil practices in government and the courts. He helped the poor by founding hospitals and charitable institutions. His government built churches and gave land to its citizen-soldiers. The government also encouraged the improvement of agriculture and raising stock. To protect his people, the emperor had a system of fortifications and frontier defenses built.

By 1261, Emperor Michael VIII had strengthened his army enough to attack and capture Constantinople. He entered the old capital of Byzantium on August 15, 1261, and was recrowned emperor in the Hagia Sophia the following September. Michael VIII spent vast sums of money to rebuild and beautify his capital.

Lost by 1092
Lost by 1350
Lost by 1453

267

Crusade Questions   Name _____

Answer each question.

1. Why did the Byzantines hate the Turks? __because the Turks had captured__ __Jerusalem__

2. Which emperor asked for help to fight the Turks? __Emperor Alexius Comnenus I__

3. What was the goal of Innocent III's crusade? __He wanted to unite the Eastern__ __Orthodox Church with the Roman Catholic Church.__

4. How did the Venetians persuade the crusaders to fight against Constantinople?
__They told the crusaders they would become rich if they helped defeat__ __Constantinople.__

5. What happened on April 13, 1204? __The crusaders and Venetians took control__ __of the Byzantine government.__

6. What improvements did John III make while he was Byzantine emperor at Nicaea?
__He built hospitals, churches, and charitable institutions. He gave land to__ __citizen-soldiers. He built up the country's defenses.__

Heritage Studies 6
Student Notebook

Lesson 68
Evaluating the Lesson **75**

Day 147

The New Byzantine Empire—Instruct the students to read page 267 silently to find out where the Byzantine government moved after the crusaders conquered Constantinople. *(Nicaea in Asia Minor)*

Discussion Questions

➤ **What things did John III do to strengthen the new empire?** *(banned evil practices in government and the courts, founded hospitals and charitable institutions, built churches, gave land to citizen-soldiers, improved agriculture, encouraged the raising of stock, fortified defenses)*

➤ **What Byzantine emperor was able to defeat the crusaders and move back to Constantinople?** *(Michael VIII)*

☐ Evaluating the Lesson

Crusade Questions (Notebook page 75)—Direct the students to answer each question, using their books if necessary.

━━━ Going Beyond ━━━

☐ Enrichment

Robin Hood research—Set up an AREA with books about Robin Hood and the time period of the Crusades (1096-1270). Allow the students to draw and color pictures of different events of the Crusades.

☐ Additional Teacher Information

People had many different reasons for setting out on a crusade. Some peasants believed that the taking of Jerusalem paved the way for the Second Coming of Christ. Others believed that killing Muslims would further the "Christianization" of the region. Some nobles, merchants, and churchmen wanted to extend the authority of the church and expand trade.

Crusaders sewed the symbol of the cross onto their clothing and said they were "taking up the cross" of Christ. The word *crusade* comes from the Latin word for cross.

The Children's Crusade of 1212 was a particular disaster. Thousands of children between the ages of six and eighteen left their homes in Europe with the objective of defeating the Muslims in Jerusalem. They believed that the adults who had gone crusading before them had done so in the strength of the flesh and not of the spirit. They believed that God would use them because they were weak and faithful. Without weapons and with only a few supplies, they believed that God would part the Mediterranean Sea as He had parted the Red Sea for the Israelites. Most of the children starved or froze to death. The few who survived were captured and sold into slavery.

LESSON 69
The Fall of Byzantium

Text, pages 268-70
Notebook, pages 76-77

- Dividing the Empire
- End of the Empire

Preview

□ Objective
Given proper instruction, the students will be able to do the following:
- Complete a crossword puzzle about the Byzantine Empire.

□ Materials
Have available a Bible.

□ Notes
The board game Mosaics to Minarets is introduced in the Enrichment section. If you choose to use the game, refer to Lesson 12 for instructions to assemble the game pieces. (*NOTE:* See the reproducible material at the end of this lesson.)

Make a copy of the game markers. (*NOTE:* See the reproducible material at the end of this lesson.) Cut out the figures and the bases and affix them to tagboard backing. After laminating the figures, cut a slit along the dark cutting line and slide each figure onto a base.

Day 148

Lesson

□ Introducing the Lesson
Charades—Direct Heritage Studies partners to join together to form groups of four. Instruct each group to think of one event from this chapter and to spend a few minutes devising a charade to illustrate this event. Allow the students to perform their charades for the class. Encourage the class to guess which event has been represented.

The Decline and Fall of the Byzantine Empire
Michael VIII tried to win back the rest of the land held by the former Byzantine Empire. But a new group of Turks, called the Ottomans, had invaded the Middle East. The Ottoman Turks conquered the Seljuk Turks, adopted Islam as their religion, and moved north to attack Byzantium.

The Ottomans threatened the empire in Asia Minor, and the Serbs attacked in the Balkans. Since Michael VIII did not have enough money to go to war, he divided the empire among his family members, hoping that each would protect his share. But his relatives all wanted to make their parts of the empire independent little countries. They each hired mercenaries and were soon fighting each other instead of protecting the empire.

Meanwhile, Venetian and Genoese merchants gained control of Constantinople's trade. They collected the profits and taxes from commerce that had once belonged to the emperor. The emperors became so poor that they had to sell their gold and silver dishes and the palace decorations to pay their bills.

By 1371 the Turks had conquered all of the Byzantine Empire except the city of Constantinople. Some Byzantine emperors visited Europe, hoping to find a king who would send an army to fight the Ottoman Turks. The leaders of the Eastern Orthodox Church begged the pope in Rome for help for the empire. Do you think he was willing to help them?

This silver plate showing David's being anointed by Samuel is one of a series of David Plates from Constantinople (A.D. 613-629/30).

The Metropolitan Museum of Art, Gift of J. Pierpont Morgan, 1917 (17.190.398) Photograph © 1990 The Metropolitan Museum of Art

268

Day 149

□ Teaching the Lesson
Dividing the empire—Instruct the students to read page 268 silently to find out why Michael VIII divided the Byzantine Empire among his family members. (*He did not have enough money to defend the entire empire; he hoped that each family member would protect his share of the empire.*)

Discussion Questions
➤ **Were Michael VIII's relatives able to protect the empire?** (*No, they raised armies and began to fight each other.*)
➤ **How did the Venetian and Genoese merchants impoverish the Byzantine emperors?** (*They gained control of Constantinople's trade and collected taxes that had once belonged to the empire.*)
➤ **Where did the Byzantine emperors go for help when the Ottoman Turks threatened Constantinople?** (*They asked the pope for help.*)

No one in Europe could help the Byzantines, even if he had been willing. All of Europe was suffering from the Black Death, a horrible disease that we now call the bubonic plague. The disease killed at least one-third of all the people in Europe. And England and France had been at war for over one hundred years. No ruler had an army or even money to help Byzantium.

After the Ottomans completed their conquest of Asia Minor, they crossed into the Balkans. The city of Adrianople and the country of Bulgaria fell to them, and then they conquered Greece. By March 1453 the Ottomans surrounded Constantinople. The last emperor, Constantine XI, died defending his city. After the battle his body could be identified only by the purple boots he wore.

Muhammad II's Muslim army destroyed or stole the priceless works of art, icons, and precious manuscripts of Constantinople, and then the Sultan solemnly entered the city and made it the capital of the Ottoman Empire. The beautiful Hagia Sophia became an Islamic mosque. The Byzantine Empire had come to an end.

Why was the Byzantine Empire important? The Byzantines kept Roman law from disappearing. The scholars of the empire preserved Greek literature, learning, and philosophy. Without the Byzantine Empire, much of what we study today about the ancient world would have been lost.

269

"Hey, Troy, look at the time!" Dan said.

"I can't believe it! I sure never thought studying the Byzantines would go that fast."

"Remember how all those Byzantines played sports? It said they had archery, javelin throwing, wrestling, and chariot racing. I'll bet if there were Byzantines around today, they'd love baseball."

"Yeah, too bad." Troy slammed his book shut. "Our team could use some more good players."

"You know what Coach would say about that. Good is an attitude."

"Yeah. You're right. Coach is always saying attitude's the hardest part." He studied his glove for a minute. "If all those crusaders had had better attitudes, things would have turned out better for the Byzantines."

Dan grabbed his glove. "I never thought something Coach said would turn up in our history books. Come on, let's go set up those bases."

270

End of the empire—Instruct the students to read pages 269-70 silently to find out why no European country could come to the aid of the Byzantine emperor against the Muslims. *(The Black Death had devastated Europe. Also, no one had any money; they were worn out by years of war.)*

Discussion Questions

➤ **Who conquered Constantinople to end the Byzantine Empire?** *(the Ottoman Turks)*

➤ **Who was the last Byzantine emperor?** *(Constantine XI)*

➤ **The Byzantine Empire began at the end of the Roman Empire in 476. How many years passed between the fall of the Roman Empire and the fall of the Byzantine Empire?** *(977 years)*

➤ **If the United States were to survive for only 977 years, in what year would it fall?** *(2753)*

Remind the students that kingdoms and rulers are set up and taken down by God. Read Daniel 4:17 to the students. A Christian can trust God to preserve him and protect him through any political upheaval. (Bible Promises: H. God as Father, I. God as Master)

Byzantine Clues   Name _____

Use the clues to complete the crossword puzzle on page 77.

Across

2. The Islamic mosque Dome of the Rock is in this city.
3. This village later became Constantinople.
9. This group split from Roman Catholicism in 1054. (3 words)
10. These sports clubs rioted. (three words)
13. These people caused the final defeat of the Byzantine Empire in 1453. (two words)
14. A church built in the 530s is now an Islamic mosque called _____ Sophia.
16. This book is considered holy by Muslims.
17. He started the false religion of Islam.

Down

1. This emperor married a former circus performer.
4. The purpose of these was to conquer Jerusalem.
5. This chemical mixture exploded when it hit water. (two words)
6. These missionaries developed the Cyrillic alphabet to take the gospel to Russia. (three words)
7. His armies used Greek fire against their enemies. (three words)
8. This was the capital of the Byzantine Empire.
11. This church is led by the pope. (two words)
12. He moved the capital of the Roman Empire from Rome to Byzantium.
15. This conflict was over the use of images as objects of worship.

Byzantine Puzzle   Name _____

Use the clues on page 76 to complete the puzzle.

```
                              J
              ²J E R U S A L E M
                              S
          ³B Y Z A N T I U M
                              I
              ⁴C               N
    ⁵G        R               I       ⁶C
    R         U    ⁷L         A       Y        ⁸C
    ⁹E A S T E R N O R T H O D O X C H U R C H
    E         A    O          I        N
    K         D    T      ¹⁰B L U E S A N D G R E E N S
    F         E    H          A        T        O
    I         S    E          N        A        M
    R              I          D        ¹²C      A
    E              S          M      ¹³O T T O M A N T U R K S
                   A          E        I        C
                   U          T        N      ¹⁴H A G I A
    ¹⁶K O R A N              H        S        T    C
                   I          O        T        H    O
              ¹⁷M U H A M M A D        A        O    N
                   N          I        N        L    O
                              U        T        I    C
                              S        I        C    L
                                       N             A
                                       E             S
                                                     M
```

Day 150

□ Evaluating the Lesson

Byzantine Puzzle (Notebook pages 76-77)—Direct the students to use the clues to complete the crossword puzzle.

▬▬ Going Beyond ▬▬

□ Enrichment

Set up an AREA in which students can play the Mosaics to Minarets game. First, show the students the game board. Trace the direction of "traffic" on the game board with your finger, showing the students the possible added loops (detours). Point out the Greek Fire Factory, Crusader's Corner, Theodora's Circus, Hagia Sophia, the Hippodrome, Icon Island, and the Silk Shop.

Next, call attention to a space that has a star. Tell the students that whenever a player lands on a starred space, he should draw one card, follow the directions on the card, and then place the card at the bottom of the pile.

Give directions for playing the game. Explain that the object is to move a game marker to the *Ottoman Empire* space. All players begin with the game markers at *Start*. Each player spins once, and the player with the highest number goes first. Then, in turn, each player spins again. Each player moves his marker ahead as many spaces as the spinner indicates, drawing the appropriate card if he lands

on a starred space. Play continues until a player reaches the Ottoman Empire by the exact number on the spinner.

□ Additional Teacher Information

The Byzantine Empire was a continuation of the Roman Empire. Though it never gained the land area of the Roman Empire, the Byzantine Empire was a leader in culture, art, religion, and education. Ancient books that were discarded or burned in Western countries were preserved and copied in the Byzantine monasteries and universities.

The Ottoman Empire, which followed the Byzantine Empire, lasted until World War I, at which time many national boundaries were redrawn.

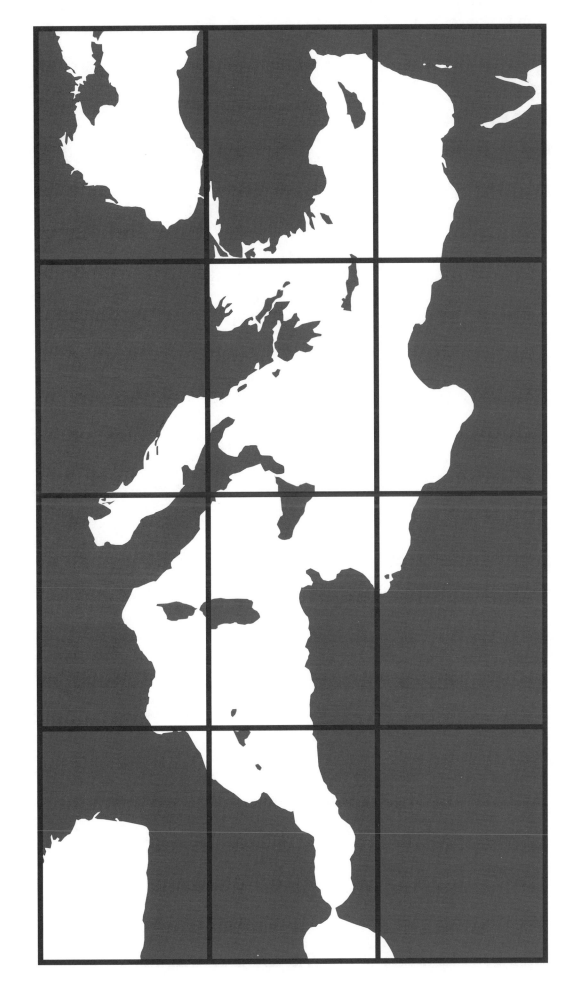

Use with Lesson 62.

THE PENALTY OF THE LAW PAID

Thou shalt have no other gods before me.

Thou shalt not make unto thee any graven image. . . . Thou shalt not bow down thyself to them, nor serve them.

Thou shalt not take the name of the Lord thy God in vain.

Remember the Sabbath day, to keep it holy.

Honour thy father and thy mother.

Thou shalt not kill.

Thou shalt not commit adultery.

Thou shalt not steal.

Thou shalt not bear false witness against thy neighbor.

Thou shalt not covet.

"Think not that I am come to destroy the law, or the prophets: I am not come to destroy, but to fulfill." (Matthew 5:17)

Jesus Christ—"True Prophet" or Son of God?

Islam teaches that Jesus Christ is a "true prophet" but is not the Son of God. What does each verse teach?

Matthew 27:43 _____

_____

John 9:35-37 _____

_____

John 10:36 _____

_____

John 19:7 _____

_____

Jesus said He was the Son of God.
If He is truthful, then He must be the Son of God.
If He is not the Son of God, then He was not truthful.

The Bible teaches that Jesus Christ is the Son of God.

Other related verses—

Testimony of the angel to Mary

Luke 1:35 _____

Testimony of the unclean spirits

Matthew 8:29 _____

Mark 3:11 _____

Luke 4:41 _____

Luke 8:28 _____

Testimony of John the Baptist

John 1:34 _____

Christianity and Islam Contrasted

Christianity	Islam
The Bible was given by God; it comprises Genesis through Revelation.	Islam teaches that Muhammad's sayings are the words of God and that the Koran is the final revelation of God's Word.
Jesus Christ is the Son of God. His death ransomed His people from their sins. He arose from the dead and bodily ascended into heaven.	Muhammad died in 632. He is buried in Medina, Saudi Arabia.
The Bible teaches that man is saved by trusting in the finished work of Christ. Those who trust Christ for salvation will go to heaven when they die.	Islam teaches that at the Day of Judgment a man's good works will be weighed against his evil works. If he has more good works, he will go to paradise. If he has more evil works, he will go to hell.
The Bible teaches that the sacrifice of Christ was the propitiation for the sins of His people. No other sacrifice can reconcile man to God.	A Muslim sacrifices a sheep or a goat as part of his pilgrimage to Mecca.

"If any man shall add unto these things, God shall add unto him the plagues that are written in this book."
(Revelation 22:18)

"For by grace are ye saved through faith; and that not of yourselves: it is the gift of God: not of works, lest any man should boast."
(Ephesians 2:8-9)

John 3:16 in Russian

Ибо так возлюбил Бог
мир, что отдал Сына
Своего единородного,
дабы всякий, верующий
в Него, не погиб, но
имел жизнь вечную.

Pronunciation

ébo täk vozlyubíl Bog

mir, shto otdäl Syna

Svoyevo yedinoródnovo,

daby vsyákiy, vyeruyushshiy

b nyevo nye pogib, no

imyél zhizn vyéchnuyu.

Russian		English equivalent
А	а	a
Б	б	b
В	в	v
Г	г	g
Д	д	d
Е	е	ye
Ё	ё	yo
Ж	ж	zh
З	з	z
И	и	i
Й	й	y
К	к	k
Л	л	l
М	м	m
Н	н	n
О	о	o
П	п	p
Р	р	r
С	с	s
Т	т	t
У	у	u
Ф	ф	f
Х	х	kh
Ц	ц	ts
Ч	ч	ch
Ш	ш	sh
Щ	щ	shsh
Ъ	ъ	__
Ы	ы	y
Ь	ь	__
Э	э	e
Ю	ю	yu
Я	я	ya

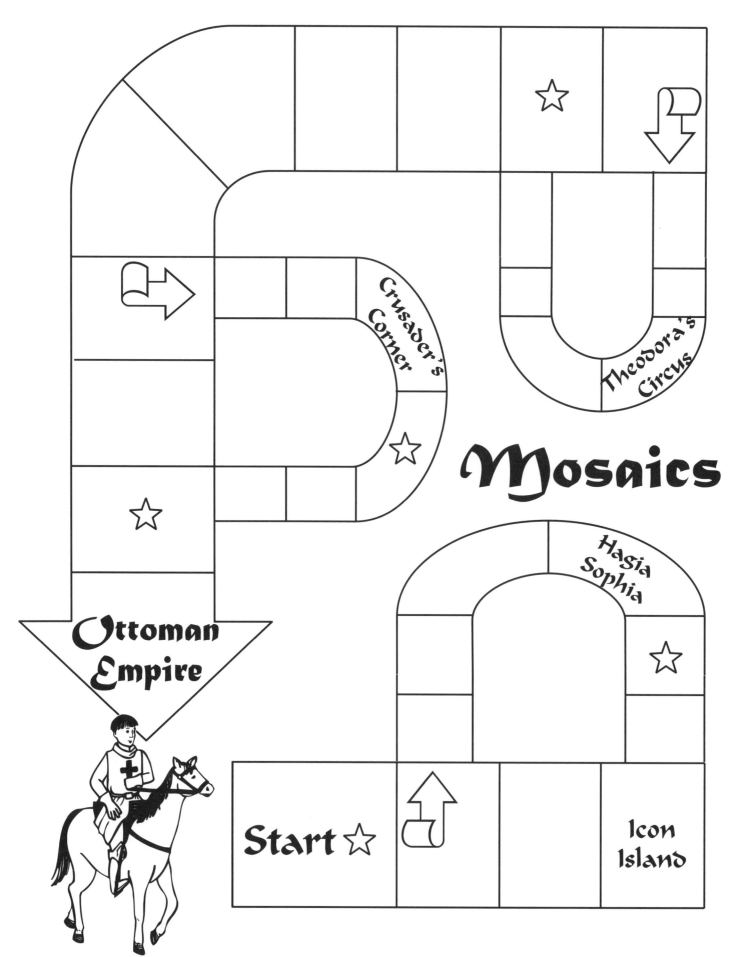

Mosaics

Crusader's Corner

Theodora's Circus

Ottoman Empire

Hagia Sophia

Start ☆

Icon Island

Use with Lesson 69.

Heritage Studies 6 TE

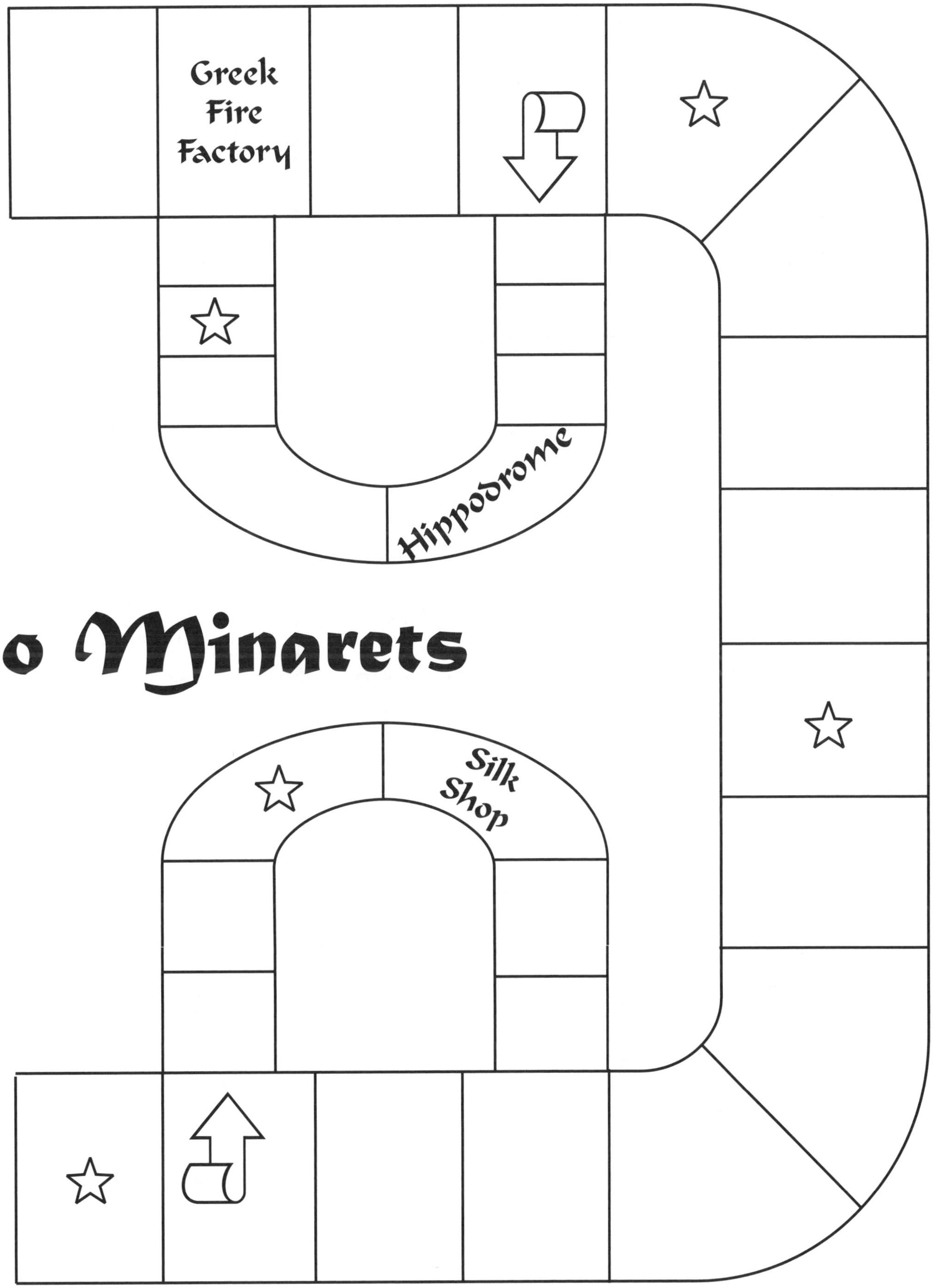

Greek Fire Factory

Hippodrome

to Minarets

Silk Shop

Go to Crusader's Corner.	The Hagia Sophia was built by Justinian in the 530s. Go to the Hagia Sophia.	Greek fire was a secret weapon that ignited when it hit water. Go to the Greek Fire Factory.
Empress Theodora's father was a bear trainer. Go to Theodora's Circus.	The Blues and the Greens were trapped in the hippodrome. Go to the hippodrome.	A fight arose over whether to use icons in worship. Go to Icon Island.
Go to the Silk Shop.	You are attacked by Turks. Go back 3 spaces.	You are arrested for smuggling silk worms. Go back 2 spaces.
Your silk wins first prize at the guild meeting. Go ahead 3 spaces.	You are wounded while attacking a Muslim village. Go back 3 spaces.	Your pay has been reduced by 50 percent. Go to the Greek Fire Factory to get a job.
You worked on compiling the Body of Civil Law. Go ahead 1 space.	You helped clean up Constantinople after the Nika Riots. Go ahead 2 spaces.	You are a mosaic maker. Go to Icon Island to complete your latest icon.
You fight for Emperor Heraclius and are rewarded with 100 acres of land. Lose a turn while you plant crops.	Congratulations! You have been accepted into your father's goldsmith guild. Take another turn.	You teach a Muslim family the true way of salvation through Christ. Take another turn.
You decide to join a crusade to the Holy Land. Go to Crusader's Corner.	The soldiers under your command have died of the plague. Go to the Hagia Sophia to pray.	You are an iconoclast. Lose a turn while you paint over the pictures in your church.
You travel with missionaries to the Slavic tribes. Go ahead 4 spaces.	You receive word that your family home has been attacked by Bulgars. Lose a turn.	General Belisarius awards you a bonus in pay for your fine work. Go to the Silk Shop to buy a fine gift for your mother.

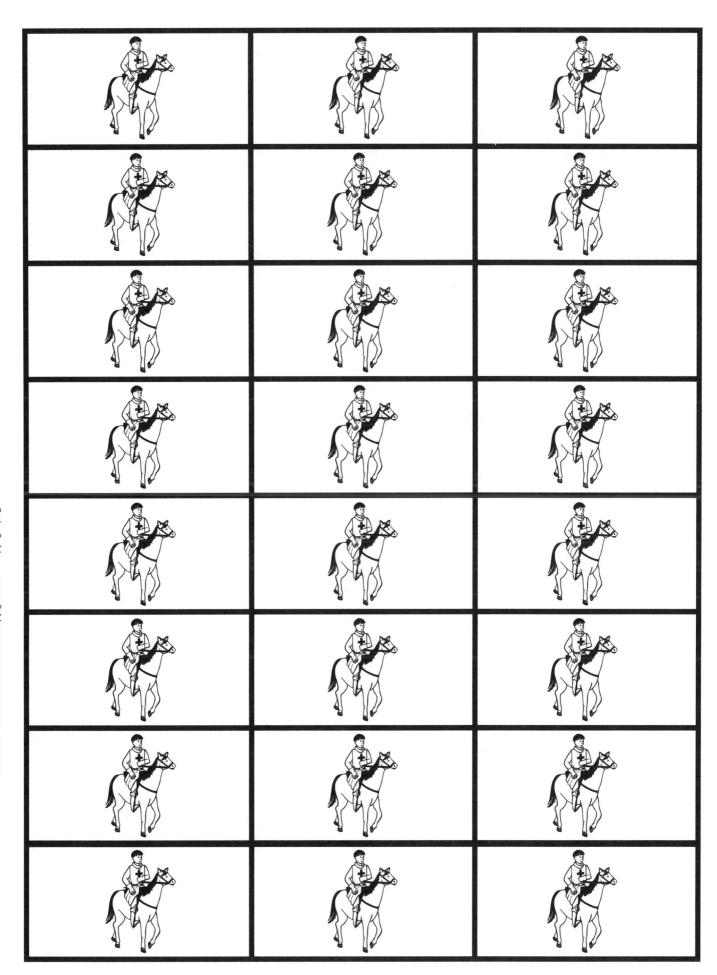

Mosaics to Minarets

Use with Lesson 69. Heritage Studies 6 TE

12 LESSONS 70-76

Shadow of the Castle: Middle Ages

This chapter presents life during the Middle Ages with focus on several people who made great achievements during this period of history. It also explains the social system that existed during the Age of Feudalism and compares Henry II's legal system to the old method of trial by ordeal. Students learn what life in a castle was really like and how a medieval boy received his training to be a knight. By learning about the Middle Ages, students will gain a greater understanding of medieval customs and entertainments. They will also learn more about the lifestyles of the wealthy, the middle class, and the poor during medieval times.

□ Materials

Lessons 70 and 72 require certain items that must be obtained or prepared several days to several weeks before the presentation of the lessons. These items are labeled with an asterisk (*) in each lesson and in the Materials List in the Supplement. Occasionally, items not commonly found in the classroom as well as items needed in large quantities may also be labeled with an asterisk. For specific information, see the individual lessons.

□ Chapter Bulletin Board

Prepare Maps and More 22, 23, and 24 by cutting out the pictures to put on a bulletin board entitled *The Middle Ages*. Use different coats of arms around the edge of the board as a border. (*NOTE:* See the reproducible material at the end of Lesson 76.)

THE MIDDLE AGES

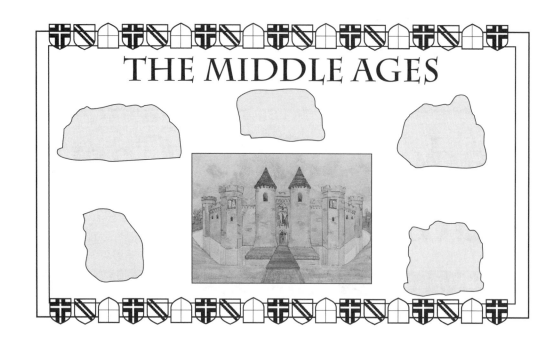

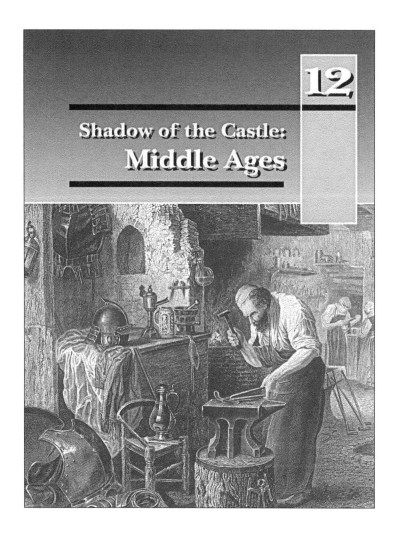

12

Shadow of the Castle:
Middle Ages

LESSON 70
The Dawn of a New Era

Text, pages 272-76
Notebook, page 78

- A Different World
- The End of the Roman Empire
- Then and Now
- The Pope and Priests
- Monks and Nuns

Preview

□ Objective
Given proper instruction, the students will be able to do the following:
- Define terms about the Middle Ages by matching them with their definitions.

□ Materials
Have available:
- A copy of Mark Twain's *A Connecticut Yankee in King Arthur's Court.**

□ Notes
The Enrichment activity requires Bible concordances. If you choose to do this activity, have available several concordances so that several students can work on the activity at one time.

Day 151

Lesson

□ Introducing the Lesson
Story reading—Read aloud the first chapter of Mark Twain's *A Connecticut Yankee in King Arthur's Court.* (*NOTE:* You may want to keep one or two copies of the book available for the students to read for themselves.)

Discussion Questions
➤ **How did the townspeople react to the narrator's appearance?** *(They stared at him and talked about him.)*
➤ **What type of clothing were the people wearing?** *(sandals and coarse tow-linen robes that came below the knees)*
➤ **Where did the townspeople live?** *(in windowless stone houses or in thatched cabins)*
➤ **Where did the noble cavalcade go?** *(into a castle)*

On a hill in France stands a deserted castle, its massive stone towers lifting to the sky. It seems to be listening for old sounds. The rustle of a lady's silk dress. The clank of a shield against a breastplate. Distant echoes of horses' hooves cantering off to battle. The hoarse voice of a serf, humming as he works out in the lord's field. Sounds that belonged to a different world.

After the fall of the Roman Empire, Europe was known for more than ten centuries as the medieval world. The word *medieval* comes from two Latin words—*medius,* meaning "middle" and *aevum,* meaning "age." Many people also call this time period between the fall of Rome and the Renaissance the Middle Ages.

Haut Konigsbourg, France

272

Explain that although this story is fictitious, people did at one time live and look like the people described in the story. Tell the students that in this chapter they will be learning about the Middle Ages and the people who lived then.

Day 152

□ Teaching the Lesson
A different world—Instruct the students to read page 272 silently to find out what Europe was called after the fall of the Roman Empire. *(the medieval world)*

Discussion Questions
➤ **From what two Latin words did the word *medieval* originate?** *(from the word* medius, *meaning "middle," and* aevum, *meaning "age")*
➤ **What other name is given to this period of time?** *(the Middle Ages)*

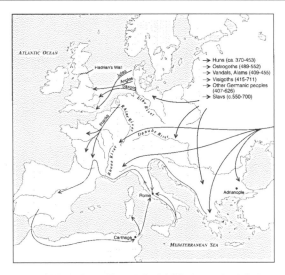

By A.D. 476, the Roman Empire had ended. What happened to the lands that had been part of Rome? The eastern half of this fallen empire eventually became the Byzantine Empire.

The western half was taken over by Germanic peoples from Scandinavia. A tribe called the *Visigoths* fought their way into Spain. The *Ostrogoths* set up a kingdom in Italy. The Franks conquered Gaul; and the Angles, the Saxons, and the Jutes invaded the British Isles.

When Rome fell apart, civilized life in most of Europe disappeared. Roads became overgrown with weeds, trade stopped, and cities stood in ruins. People built isolated villages and worked hard to grow enough food to feed their families. Disorder and destruction by invaders were constant threats to the people. No one had much time or money for education.

The people of the former Roman Empire needed a place to turn for leadership. Without an emperor to guide them, many turned to the church.

273

Scandinavia

Location—A group of countries surrounding the Baltic Sea in northern Europe: Denmark, Finland, Norway, and Sweden. The island of Iceland is also considered part of Scandinavia.

Climate—Temperate in the south to icy in the north, with temperatures ranging from 0°F to 60°F.

Topography—Low and flat in Denmark; mountainous in Norway and Sweden; low hills and mountains in Finland, with many lakes and rivers. Deep fjords, narrow inlets from the sea, are found along Norway's coast.

Geography and Culture—Because of the lack of farmland, most early Scandinavians either left their homeland or became seafarers.

Natural Resources—Forests cover much of Scandinavia's land, and large quantities of iron ore are buried beneath it. Oil and natural gas have been found in the North Sea.

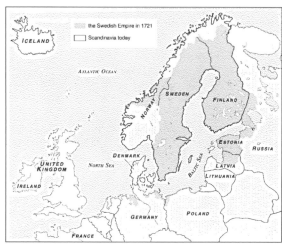

274

The end of the Roman Empire—Instruct the students to read page 273 silently to find the year the Roman Empire ended. *(A.D. 476)*

Discussion Questions

➤ **What empire developed out of the eastern part of the former Roman Empire?** *(the Byzantine Empire)*

➤ **What people took over the western part of the former Roman Empire?** *(Germanic people from Scandinavia)*

➤ **What group of people settled in Spain?** *(the Visigoths)*

➤ **What group of people set up a kingdom in Gaul?** *(the Franks)*

➤ **What three groups of people invaded the British Isles?** *(the Angles, the Saxons, and the Jutes)*

➤ **What threatened civilized life in most of Europe after the Roman Empire had fallen?** *(disorder and destruction from invaders)*

➤ **Where did many people turn for guidance?** *(to the church)*

Select several volunteers to tell how people might have felt living in a time when there was no emperor to guide them. *(Possible answers include afraid, confused, and helpless.)*

Remind the students that those who have authority over us work diligently to keep order and to protect the people they govern. Encourage the students to honor and respect elected officials and to obey the laws that have been established. (BAT: 2a Authority)

Day 153

Then and Now—Instruct the students to read page 274 silently to find what effects the lack of farmland had on the early Scandinavians. *(They either left their homeland or became seafarers.)* Direct the students' attention to the Then and Now map, noting changes in boundary lines and so on.

The bishop of the church of Rome was called the *pope,* a word that comes from the Latin word for "father." He soon extended his leadership over the whole Roman Church in Europe, not just the church in Rome. Europeans everywhere followed his teachings.

The pope directed the activities of the *clergy,* the religious leaders, during the Middle Ages. Two types of clergy worked in the Roman Church.

Some clergymen lived among the people. They ministered as priests in the churches. They led the services and instructed the people in how to live and worship. The priests of the Roman Church taught the people that they could not receive God's grace without the help of a priest. They also taught that people had to participate in certain ceremonies, called *sacraments,* in order to be saved. How do the priests' teachings compare to what the Bible says?

Medieval priests of the Roman Church

> "For there is one God, and one mediator between God and men, the man Christ Jesus."
>
> **I Timothy 2:5**

> "For by grace are ye saved through faith; and that not of yourselves: it is the gift of God: Not of works, lest any man should boast."
>
> **Ephesians 2:8-9**

275

Other clergymen, called *monks,* lived together in large quarters, or *monasteries,* and rarely had contact with the outside world. They vowed never to marry but instead to devote their lives to serving the Roman Church. What do you think made men want to live this sort of life?

A monk copying the Scriptures and a hand-copied page of the Latin Vulgate

Monasteries were among the few places where education was valued during the early Middle Ages. Literature, science, mathematics, and medicine were not often taught, but monks learned to read and write. Then they spent hours copying the Scriptures and the writings of the early churchmen. They copied by hand, bent for hours at a time over their writing desks, checking each word of the original manuscripts against the scratchings of their quill pens. Our word *clerical,* describing office work, can be traced back to this duty of clergymen in the Middle Ages.

Women also devoted their lives to the church. Those who took these vows were called *nuns.* Monks, nuns, priests, and popes still exist today. The Roman Catholic Church carries on these traditions from the Middle Ages.

276

The pope and priests—Instruct the students to read page 275 silently to find what the bishop of the church of Rome was called. *(the pope)*

Discussion Questions

➤ **How far did the pope's leadership extend?** *(over the whole Roman Church in Europe)*

➤ **What was one of the pope's functions during the Middle Ages?** *(directing the activities of the clergy)*

➤ **What type of clergy led the church services and instructed the people in how to live and worship?** *(priests)*

➤ **According to the priests, who had to help people receive God's grace?** *(a priest)*

➤ **According to the priests, in what ceremonies did people have to participate to be saved?** *(sacraments)*

Remind the students that salvation is a gift from God. No one can earn salvation. Tell them that for a person to be saved, he must confess his sins and have faith that God will forgive him. (BAT: 1b Repentance and faith)

Monks and nuns—Instruct the students to read page 276 silently to find out where monks lived. *(in monasteries)*

Discussion Questions

➤ **What did monks vow never to do?** *(marry)*

➤ **What task did the monks do in the monasteries?** *(copied Scripture and the writings of early churchmen)*

➤ **What word originated from this duty of clergymen in the Middle Ages?** *(clerical)*

➤ **What was the name given to women who devoted their lives to the church?** *(nuns)*

Medieval Matching

Name _____

Match each word with its definition.

A. Saxons	E. Visigoths	I. baptism	M. Franks
B. pope	F. sacraments	J. Ostrogoths	N. A.D. 476
C. monasteries	G. nuns	K. priests	O. clerical
D. A.D. 770	H. Byzantine	L. medius	P. monks

_N_ 1. the year the Roman Empire ended

_E_ 2. the tribe that settled in Spain

_A_ 3. one of the three groups of people who invaded the British Isles

_B_ 4. the bishop of the Roman Church

_F_ 5. ceremonies believed to bring salvation

_C_ 6. where monks lived

_G_ 7. women who devoted their lives to the Roman Church

_L_ 8. Latin word meaning "middle"

_H_ 9. the empire that developed out of the eastern part of the former Roman Empire

_J_ 10. group of people who settled in Italy

_K_ 11. clergymen who lived among the people

_O_ 12. a word which originated from clergymen's duties

© 1998 BJU Press. Reproduction prohibited.

Heritage Studies 6
Student Notebook

Lesson 70
Evaluating the Lesson   **78**

□ Evaluating the Lesson

Medieval Matching (Notebook page 78)—Match each word with its definition.

═══ Going Beyond ═══

□ Enrichment

Research activity—Set up an AREA with several Bibles and Bible concordances. Remind the students that when things were not going well after the fall of the Roman Empire, people turned to the church for guidance. Instruct each student to look up the words *guide* and *teach* in a concordance and write down at least five Scripture references that tell where and to whom one should go for guidance. As time permits, allow the students to read aloud some of the verses they have found.

□ Additional Teacher Information

When the Roman Empire collapsed in A.D. 476, the one institution strong enough to remain was the Roman Catholic Church. One of the main reasons for the church's strength was that the most capable people in the Roman Empire chose to serve the church rather than the state. As a result, the church had the strong leadership that the state lacked.

During the Middle Ages, the church's power was recognized by rich and poor alike. The church took care of the people's needs by setting up poorhouses and homes for orphans. It also settled marriages and wills.

The church reached the height of its power during the reign of Pope Innocent III (1198-1216). After Innocent III's rule, people began questioning the laws of the church. King Edward I of England and King Philip IV of France began to tax members of the clergy and their lands. Criticism of the church increased toward the end of the Middle Ages. Corruption in the church led to the Reformation in the sixteenth century.

LESSON 71
The Frankish Kings

Text, pages 277-79
Notebook, pages 79-80

- Clovis and Charles
- Pepin the Short
- Charlemagne

Preview

☐ Objective
Given proper instruction, the students will be able to do the following:
- Identify the names of major people in the Frankish kingdom by solving a crossword puzzle.

☐ Materials
Have available one-half sheet of notebook paper for each student.

Day 154

Lesson

☐ Introducing the Lesson
Name activity—Give each student one-half sheet of notebook paper. Instruct him to make up a nickname for himself that reflects his personality or the way he looks. (*NOTE:* For example, a boy with red hair named Jack might call himself Jack the Red.) As time permits, allow the students to make up similar titles for several of their classmates. (*NOTE:* Caution the students to be positive and complimentary, not derogatory or hurtful.) Take time for each student to tell the nickname he made up for himself.

Explain that in the Middle Ages a king was often given a title reflecting either his appearance or his personality. Tell the students that they will be learning about some of these kings in this lesson.

The Franks
The Franks, a Germanic people, invaded Europe after the fall of Rome. Over the next several centuries, the Franks formed a kingdom. Their first king was Clovis, who conquered the last of the Romans in Gaul. A large portion of western Europe fell under his control.

Clovis divided his kingdom among his four sons just before his death. His sons and their descendants were called the *Merovingian* kings. They struggled and plotted against one another, each wanting greater control. The Merovingians' authority weakened until most of the government work was done by their palace officials.

In 732, a new leader rose up to unite the Franks. Charles was not a king but a high official in a Frankish palace. He led an army against the Muslims and defeated them at the city of Tours. This victory kept the rest of Europe free from Muslim rule. Charles was given the name *Martel*, which means "the Hammer." What type of soldier and leader would be given a name like Martel?

After Charles Martel died, his son, Pepin the Short, became the new king of the Franks. He and his descendants were called *Carolingian* kings, from the Latin word for *Charles*.

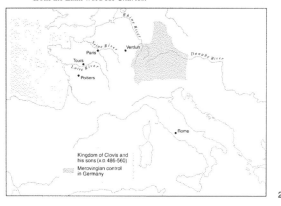

Kingdom of Clovis and his sons (A.D. 486-560)
Merovingian control in Germany

277

☐ Teaching the Lesson
Clovis and Charles—Instruct the students to read page 277 silently to find the name of one of the Germanic tribes that invaded Europe after the fall of Rome. (*the Franks*)

Discussion Questions
➤ **Who was the first king of the Franks?** (*Clovis*)
➤ **What were the sons of Clovis and their descendants called?** (*the Merovingian kings*)
➤ **Who did most of the government work while the Merovingian kings ruled?** (*the palace officials*)
➤ **What position did Charles hold before becoming king?** (*He was a high official in a Frankish palace.*)
➤ **Where was the battle fought that kept the rest of Europe free from Muslim rule?** (*the city of Tours*)
➤ **What name was given to Charles?** (*Martel*)
➤ **What does the name *Martel* mean?** (*"the Hammer"*)
➤ **Who ruled the Franks after Charles's death?** (*his son, Pepin the Short*)
➤ **What did Pepin call himself?** (*a Carolingian king*)

Pepin is best known for making an alliance with the church of Rome. Twelve years after Pepin became king, Pope Stephen II asked him to help defend Rome against an invader, the Lombards. In exchange for his help, the pope would officially approve Pepin's taking the Frankish crown away from the Merovingians.

In a public ceremony, Frankish bishops anointed Pepin with oil, and Pepin received the pope's blessing as king of the Franks. He went on to defeat the Lombards and to give part of their conquered land to the church leaders. The church called these lands the *Papal States,* and they remained part of Rome for centuries.

Pepin's son, Charlemagne, was the greatest of the Carolingian kings. The Latin word *magnus* means "great." Can you guess what the name *Charlemagne* means? It comes from the Latin words *Carolus Magnus,* meaning "Charles the Great."

278

Charlemagne

According to tradition, Charlemagne was praying beside Pope Leo III at the church service on Christmas Day in 800. The pope turned and placed a crown on Charlemagne's head, calling him emperor of the western Roman Empire.

Charlemagne had extended the Frankish kingdom to be greater in size than ever before. It was now an empire that included most of western Europe. Charlemagne divided his lands into small districts, each having several *manors,* or farms. Each manor sent Charlemagne a yearly report on its workers, production, and resources. Charlemagne regularly checked on local officials to make sure that their methods of rule were just.

Under Charlemagne's rule, the empire awakened to learning. Believing in the value of education, Charlemagne began schools for boys from both noble and poor families. These scholars studied reading, writing, mathematics, and astronomy. Charlemagne even struggled to teach himself how to read and write. He kept a tablet and a pen beneath his pillow and practiced often. Charlemagne never mastered these subjects, but he was an excellent speaker, even in the Latin language, and he learned how to make calculations.

Charlemagne even reformed handwriting in his empire. When scholars discovered that the writing in the monastery's books was hard to read, Charlemagne ordered a monk named Alcuin to develop a new style. Alcuin's writing style, which used both small and capital letters, is the basis for our handwriting today.

Charlemagne and II Timothy 2:15 written in the style he directed Alcuin to develop

Study to show thyself approved unto God, a workman that needeth not to be ashamed, rightly dividing the word of truth.

279

Day 155

Pepin the Short—Instruct the students to read page 278 silently to find out what Pepin is best known for. *(making an alliance with the church of Rome)*

Discussion Questions

➤ **What did Pope Stephen II ask Pepin to do?** *(to help defend Rome against the Lombards)*

➤ **What did the pope promise in exchange for Pepin's help?** *(official approval of Pepin's taking the Frankish crown from the Merovingians)*

➤ **What did Pepin do with part of the lands he conquered from the Lombards?** *(He gave them to the church leaders.)*

➤ **What did the church name the lands that Pepin gave it?** *(the Papal States)*

➤ **Who was the greatest Carolingian king?** *(Pepin's son, Charlemagne)*

Charlemagne—Instruct the students to read page 279 silently to find out what happened on Christmas Day in 800. *(Charlemagne was crowned emperor of the western Roman Empire.)*

Discussion Questions

➤ **According to tradition, who crowned Charlemagne emperor of the western Roman Empire?** *(Pope Leo III)*

➤ **What did Charlemagne accomplish for the Frankish kingdom?** *(He extended the kingdom to include most of western Europe.)*

➤ **What did each of Charlemagne's districts have several of?** *(manors, or farms)*

➤ **What became important during Charlemagne's rule?** *(education)*

➤ **What did Charlemagne attempt to teach himself to do?** *(read and write)*

➤ **What did Charlemagne reform?** *(the handwriting style in his empire)*

Remind the students that although Charlemagne could not read and write, he still accomplished great things. Tell the students that God created people with different abilities. Point out that God blesses Christians who use their abilities for Him. (BAT: 3a Self-concept)

Use the clues to solve the puzzle on page 80.

Across

1. monk who developed a new system of handwriting
3. a tribe which settled in Gaul
5. the greatest Carolingian king
8. Martel's son and successor (three words)
9. first Frankish king
11. name of Clovis's descendents
13. farms for Charlemagne
14. lands belonging to the church (two words)

Down

2. Martel was called a _____ king.
4. Latin for Charles the Great (two words)
6. crowned Charlemagne emperor
7. "the Hammer" to some (two words)
10. Martel defeated the Muslims at the Battle of _____.
12. invaders who were defeated by Pepin

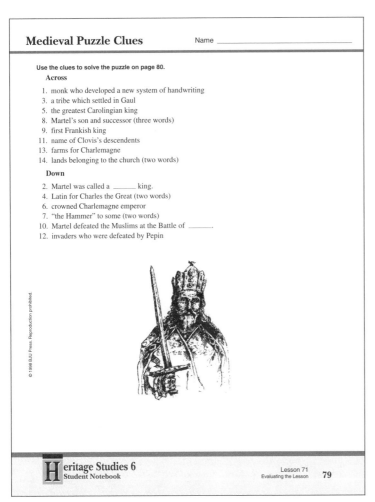

Heritage Studies 6
Student Notebook

Lesson 71
Evaluating the Lesson   **79**

Use the clues on page 79 to complete the puzzle.

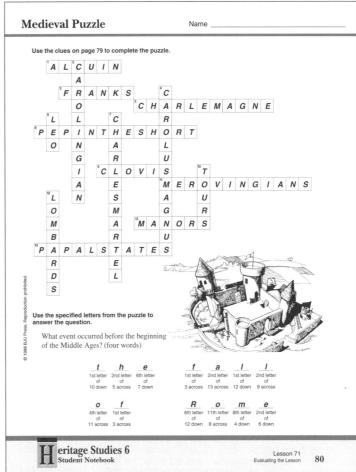

Use the specified letters from the puzzle to answer the question.

What event occurred before the beginning of the Middle Ages? (four words)

t   h   e   f   a   l   l
1st letter 2nd letter 6th letter   1st letter 2nd letter 1st letter 2nd letter
of   of   of   of   of   of   of
10 down   5 across   7 down   3 across   13 across 12 down   9 across

o   f   R   o   m   e
4th letter 1st letter   6th letter 11th letter 8th letter 2nd letter
of   of   of   of   of   of
11 across 3 across   12 down   8 across   4 down   6 down

Heritage Studies 6
Student Notebook

Lesson 71
Evaluating the Lesson   **80**

☐ **Evaluating the Lesson**

Medieval Puzzle (Notebook pages 79-80)—Direct the students to solve the puzzle. Explain that they will answer the question at the bottom of Notebook page 80 by using letters from the puzzle.

▬▬ Going Beyond ▬▬

☐ **Enrichment**

Research activity—Set up a research AREA with paper, colored pencils, several sets of encyclopedias, and any other available books about this time period. Instruct the students to choose one of the Frankish rulers discussed in this lesson. Direct each student to do some research about the ruler he has chosen and to write a paragraph or two about the ruler. Instruct each student to draw a picture of the ruler he has researched.

☐ **Additional Teacher Information**

Although his official title was the Mayor of the Palace, Charles Martel was the Frankish king in everything but name. Under his rule, the Franks became a powerful cavalry force. Martel was known for dealing hard blows to his enemies during warfare. This strategy earned him the name *Martel,* or *the Hammer.* Martel's best-known victory is the Battle of Tours, where he defeated the Muslims. As a result of this victory, the section of Europe north of the Pyrenees was never again threatened by Muslim attacks.

LESSON 72
The Manor Dwellers

Text, pages 280-81
Notebook, page 81

- The Manor
- A Serf's World

Preview

□ Objective
Given proper instruction, the students will be able to do the following:
- Identify differences between lords and serfs.

□ Materials
Have available:
- A mixing bowl.*
- A fork for each student.*
- 6 eggs.*
- ¼ teaspoon salt.*
- 6 tablespoons of butter or margarine.*
- A small onion.*
- 2 tablespoons dried parsley.*
- A 10- or 12-inch skillet with flared sides.*
- Access to a stove.*
- A spatula.*
- A small plate for each student.*

Prepare enough omelettes for each student to have a small portion.

□ Notes
If your school has a kitchen, it would be ideal to invite some of the students' parents to help in preparing the omelettes while the students observe.

You may use your own recipe or the recipe that follows to prepare the omelettes.

Simple Omelette

6 eggs

3 tablespoons water

¼ teaspoon salt

6 tablespoons butter or margarine

1 small onion, chopped

2 tablespoons dried parsley

In a mixing bowl, combine eggs, water, and salt. Beat eggs with a fork until combined but not frothy. In a 10- or 12-inch nonstick skillet with flared sides, melt butter over medium heat; add onion and parsley. Sauté until onion is tender. Add egg mixture to skillet; cook over medium heat. As eggs set, run a spatula around the edge of the skillet, lifting eggs and letting uncooked portion flow

Life on the Manor

People lived on manors during the Middle Ages. The owner of a manor was called a *lord*. In the early Middle Ages, the lord lived in the manor house, usually a large house made of logs. From about the ninth century on, lords lived in castles. The lord's home was safe and strong and offered a place of protection during attacks.

The manor was like a large farm. It had woods and fishing ponds and fields where grain was grown. It also had little villages where the peasants lived.

Every manor had a church building. The people living on each manor attended the church. No one worked on Sundays. Sometimes the church celebrated other special days to honor saints or certain seasons of the year. People were released from their work for a time of feasting, dancing, and relaxation. The church called these special occasions *holy days*. What word in our language comes from this medieval term? How has the meaning of this word changed over the centuries?

280

underneath. When eggs are set, but still shiny, remove from heat. Fold in half to serve. Yield: 3 servings. (*NOTE:* These servings are portions for a meal. You can probably get nine to twelve student servings if the students are just sampling. Make as many omelettes as are necessary.)

Day 156

Lesson

□ Introducing the Lesson
Medieval feast—Invite the students to sample some omelette. Explain that this type of omelette was sometimes served during medieval feasts. Tell the students that holy days were great occasions for feasts. Explain to them that they will be learning more about medieval holy days and holy-day traditions in this lesson.

□ Teaching the Lesson
The manor—Instruct the students to read page 280 silently to find where people lived during the Middle Ages. *(on manors)*

Discussion Questions
➤ **What was the owner of a manor called?** *(a lord)*
➤ **Where did the lord of the manor live in the early Middle Ages?** *(in the manor house)*
➤ **Where did peasants live on the manor?** *(in little villages on the manor)*
➤ **What were the days called on which no work was done?** *(holy days)*

The peasants who lived on the lord's land were called *serfs*. They paid rent to the lord and worked part-time for him. They farmed his land, cleared new lands, built and repaired buildings, dug ditches, and fixed roads. The lord even expected extra gifts from them at Christmas and Easter.

The serfs did not have many possessions of their own. They had to use the lord's mill to grind their grain into flour. They had to bake their bread in the lord's oven. Often the lord made them pay to use these items.

The homes of the serfs were very small. Some were only about fifteen feet long and six feet wide. Entire families ate, slept, and lived in the same room. Most serfs shared their homes with their sheep, cows, or pigs. The animals usually stayed in a separate room, partitioned off from the living area.

Serfs were bound to the same land all of their lives. They could leave only if they paid the lord. However, some peasants on manors were called *freemen* instead of serfs. They paid less rent, worked fewer hours for the lord, and were allowed to move from the manor if they wanted to.

Serfs are shown working on their lord's land in this early 15th century French illustration.

281

Sentence Completion   Name _____

Complete the following sentences.

manors	1. People lived on ____ during the Middle Ages.
lord	2. A person who owned a manor was called a ____.
logs	3. The lord lived in a manor house, a large house made of ____.
farm	4. The manor was like a large ____.
church	5. Every manor had a ____ building.
holy days	6. No one worked on special occasions that were called ____ ____.
serfs	7. Peasants who lived and worked on the lord's land were called ____.
mill	8. If a peasant wanted to grind grain or bake bread, he had to use the lord's ____ and oven.
six	9. Some of the serfs' homes were only about fifteen feet long and ____ feet wide.
freemen	10. Peasants who paid less rent, worked fewer hours, and were allowed to move from the manor if they wished were called ____.

Day 157

A serf's world—Instruct the students to read page 281 silently to find out what the peasants who lived on the manor were called. *(serfs)*

Discussion Questions

➤ **What were some of the things the serfs did for the lord?** *(farmed the land, cleared new lands, built and repaired buildings, dug ditches, and fixed roads)*

> Explain to the students that in exchange for the serfs' work, the lord offered the serfs protection. The lords expected the serfs' work to be satisfactory. Those who did slovenly work were punished. Remind the students that Christians should be willing servants for Christ. God will reward busy, dependable workers. (BATs: 2c Faithfulness, 2d Goal setting, 2e Work)

➤ **What did the serfs have to do when they wanted to grind their grain or bake their bread?** *(They had to use the lord's mill and oven; sometimes they had to pay for these privileges.)*
➤ **What was the size of some of the serfs' houses?** *(about fifteen feet long and six feet wide)*
➤ **With what did most of the serfs share their homes?** *(with their sheep, cows, or pigs)*
➤ **What was the only way that serfs could leave the manor?** *(by paying the lord)*

➤ **What were the peasants called who worked fewer hours and who were free to leave the manor?** *(freemen)*

☐ Evaluating the Lesson

Sentence Completion (Notebook page 81)—Instruct the students to complete the sentences.

▬▬▬ Going Beyond ▬▬▬

☐ Enrichment

Holy-day tradition—Tell the students that sometimes at medieval feasts small flat platters made of porcelain or stiff paper were passed around during the last course of the feast. Each platter, called a *roundel,* had a poem, text, or verse written on the bottom. Once the guests had eaten the food served on the roundels, they turned them over. Each guest was required to sing whatever was written on the bottom of his roundel. Plan to have a medieval feast in the classroom, complete with food and roundels. Invite the students to sing the songs on the roundels.

☐ Additional Teacher Information

In medieval times, feasts were often accompanied by music. Sometimes music was performed by professional musicians. At other times the feasters themselves performed. Every well-educated man and woman was expected to be able to sight-read simple musical scores.

LESSON 73
The Vikings Are Coming!

Text, pages 282-84
Notebook, pages 82-83

- Division of an Empire
- The Northmen
- Names of Our Days

Division of Charlemagne's Empire

Charlemagne's son, Louis the Pious, inherited his father's empire. But the empire was too large for one man to rule successfully, and it soon weakened. Wars among Louis and his three sons led to a division of Charlemagne's empire into three parts. Each of Louis's sons—Lothair, Charles the Bald, and Louis the German—received a share.

Two of these three parts formed the basis for two of our modern European countries. Compare the map on this page with a map of modern Europe. Can you guess which two modern countries came from these kingdoms?

Charles the Bald's section of the empire would one day become France. Louis the German's territory would be the nation of Germany. Lothair's part of the empire, located between the territories of his brothers, would be a source of strife between France and Germany for centuries.

At the time of the division, the languages spoken in the western and eastern parts of the empire were very different from one another. Western Frankish was changing into French, and eastern Frankish was developing into German.

282

Preview

☐ Objective

Given proper instruction, the students will be able to do the following:

- Identify key names in the lesson by unscrambling them.

☐ Materials

Have available:

- A wall map of the world.
- A folder.

Prepare the answer sheet for the enrichment activity by putting it inside the folder. (*NOTE:* See the reproducible material at the end of Lesson 76.)

☐ Notes

Eric the Red's name has been spelled at least two other ways in other sources. The alternate spellings are Eirik and Erik. For the purpose of consistency in this curriculum, his name will be spelled Eric the Red.

Day 158

Lesson

☐ Introducing the Lesson

Letter reading—Read the following letter to the class.

April, A.D. 845
Paris

My dear Robert,

I am much grieved as I write these words to you. They were here—the invaders from the North. Charles, our king, made a courageous attempt to defend us against the Vikings. My beloved husband, your brother, was among those who gallantly fought. Yesterday word came to me of the battle.

The king had divided his army into two groups. The reason for this, I am told, was so that the army could guard both banks of the Seine. With the army divided, the Vikings had little trouble defeating them. Over one hundred of our soldiers were taken captive. My husband, Henry, was among those taken. That is not the most horrible thing which occurred. In a sacrifice to one of their gods, the Vikings hanged every one of their captives.

On Easter, the Vikings came into the city. More bloodshed; these men know no mercy. Many of our friends have had valuable jewels and money stolen from them. My two children and I had to flee from our home. There is no saying what these savages would have done to an unprotected woman and her children.

The king gave the Vikings an enormous amount of silver to get them to leave the city. The Vikings accepted. Thankfully, they are gone. Such losses though! My house, along with so many others, has been looted. All of our money is gone, and much of our furniture has been broken beyond repair. If only Henry were here with us! Our losses could be easier to bear. I long to leave Paris and join you and Margaret in England.

May the Lord keep you and your family, Robert. If the Lord so wills, my children and I may travel to your country next winter.

Yours devotedly,

Madeleine

Explain that the events described in the letter actually occurred. Tell the students that in this lesson they will learn more about the Vikings, cruel invaders who were much feared by the people during the Middle Ages.

Vikings!

The bells in the church at Tours began to ring wildly, a shrill warning to villagers. "I've seen their ships!" cried one of the monks. "Coming down the Loire River! It's the Northmen—the Vikings! May God help us!"

Long wooden boats with curved ends sailed toward the village. Some villagers caught glimpses of the boatmen's faces. Beneath their thick, blond hair, their expressions were fierce. Even when seated, they looked tall. Strong hands gripped long oars. Fifty warriors must have been in each boat.

The attack was swift. Armed with spears, the Vikings invaded the village. They killed people, stole gold and expensive jewelry, and destroyed homes and buildings. Then, as quickly as they had come, they shoved off shore and were gone. Behind them the village lay in ruins.

This scene was a common one in Europe in the 800s. Viking raiders attacked Britain and then struck at the Franks in western Europe. They often attacked small villages, one at a time. Their attacks were always sudden and merciless, and they were feared by all.

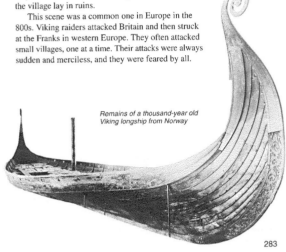

Remains of a thousand-year old Viking longship from Norway

283

The Names of the Days

The Vikings, often called *Norsemen* or *north men* by the Franks, were a fierce warrior people from Scandinavia. We remember them not only as raiders but also as explorers. They were the first to discover Iceland, Greenland, and the North American Atlantic coast.

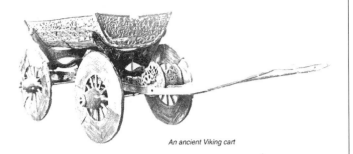

An ancient Viking cart

The Norse worshiped many gods, just as the Greeks and Romans had. Their chief god was named Odin (or Wodan). They believed that Odin was the one-eyed god of war, the god of creation, and the god of the dead. Under Odin was Thor, the giant-killing god. The Norse believed that Thor had authority over the wind and rain and acted as a guardian of justice. A third god, Frey, and his twin sister, Freya, were believed to be the god and goddess of love.

Almost every day, we "echo" the names of these gods from the Norse myths. Think about that the names of the days in our week. Wednesday comes from the name for the chief god, Odin (*Wodan's Day*). Thursday is named for Thor (*Thor's Day*). Can you guess where the name Friday comes from?

284

□ Teaching the Lesson

Division of an empire—Instruct the students to read page 282 silently to find who inherited Charlemagne's empire. *(Louis the Pious)*

Discussion Questions

➤ **Why did Charlemagne's empire weaken under Louis's rule?** *(The empire was too large for one man to rule successfully.)*

➤ **What led to a division of Charlemagne's empire into three parts?** *(wars among Louis and his three sons)*

Direct the students' attention to the map on page 282. Instruct the students to compare the map of Charlemagne's empire to the wall map of the modern world. Ask the students whether they can guess what two modern European countries developed out of the divisions within Charlemagne's empire. *(France and Germany)*

➤ **What country would develop from Charles the Bald's section of the empire?** *(France)*

➤ **What country would develop from Louis the German's section of the empire?** *(Germany)*

➤ **Whose part of the empire would be a source of strife between France and Germany for centuries?** *(Lothair's section, which was between the territories of his brothers)*

➤ **What language were people beginning to speak in the western Frankish empire?** *(French)*

➤ **What language were people beginning to speak in the eastern Frankish empire?** *(German)*

Day 159

The Northmen—Instruct the students to read page 283 silently to find out who the Northmen were. *(the Vikings)*

Discussion Questions

➤ **What did the Vikings look like?** *(They were tall, had thick blond hair, and had fierce facial expressions.)*

➤ **About how many men were in each Viking boat?** *(fifty)*

➤ **What effects did the Viking attacks have on villages?** *(People were killed, gold and jewelry were stolen, and homes and buildings were destroyed.)*

➤ **Why were Vikings feared by all?** *(Their attacks were sudden and merciless.)*

Names of our days—Instruct the students to read page 284 silently to find what other names the Franks called the Vikings. *(Norsemen or north men)*

Discussion Questions

➤ **Where were the Vikings from?** *(Scandinavia)*

➤ **How are Vikings remembered?** *(as raiders and explorers)*

➤ **What areas did the Vikings discover?** *(Iceland, Greenland, and the North American Atlantic coast)*

➤ **Who was the chief god of the Norse?** *(Odin, or Wodan)*

➤ **What did the Norse believe about Odin?** *(that he was the one-eyed god of war, the god of creation, and the god of the dead)*

Viking Word Scramble

Name _____

Unscramble the words below; then use the words to fill in the blanks in the paragraphs on page 83.

Vikings	1.	ignvski
Odin	2.	nodi
Louis	3.	solui
Freya	4.	erayf
Aquitaine	5.	naqauitei
Frey	6.	eyfr
Norsemen	7.	reosnemn
Germany	8.	raemngy
Lothair	9.	hrotila
Charles	10.	larsehc
Thor	11.	hrto
France	12.	afrecn

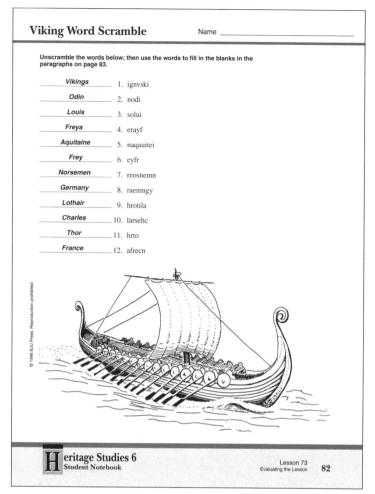

Word Scramble Paragraph

Name _____

Use the words from page 82 to complete these paragraphs.

When Charlemagne died, his son _____Louis_____ of _____Aquitaine_____ ascended to the throne. Unfortunately, the empire was too large for one man to rule alone. Wars broke out among the emperor and his three sons (_____Charles_____, _____Lothair_____, and Louis the German). The empire was divided into three parts. Two of the sections became the modern countries of _____France_____ and _____Germany_____.

In these days, Europeans feared attacks from _____Vikings_____. These invaders, also called _____Norsemen_____, worshiped several gods. There was _____Odin_____, the one-eyed god of war. Another god was _____Thor_____, the giant-killing god. A third god _____Frey_____ and his twin sister _____Freya_____ were the god and goddess of love.

➤ **What authority did the Norse believe that Thor had?** *(authority over the wind and rain and was a guardian of justice)*

➤ **Who were the Norse god and goddess of love?** *(Frey and his twin sister Freya)*

➤ **What three days of our week come from the names of Norse gods?** *(Wednesday, Thursday, and Friday)*

Explain that the Vikings, Greeks, and Romans were eager to please their gods. Some of them were afraid to commit any act which might anger the gods. Remind the students that Christians worship the one true God and should continuously glorify Jesus Christ. (BAT: 7b Exaltation of Christ)

☐ **Evaluating the Lesson**

Viking Word Scramble (Notebook pages 82-83)—Instruct the students to unscramble the words on Notebook page 82 and then to use those words to complete the sentences in the paragraphs on Notebook page 83.

═══ Going Beyond ═══

☐ **Enrichment**

Viking alphabet—Set up a code AREA with a copy of the encoded verse and Runic alphabet for each student. *(NOTE: See the reproducible material at the end of Lesson 76.)*

Explain that these symbols were the letters the Scandinavians used in the days of the Vikings. The alphabet was called a Runic alphabet, and the letters were often carved into stone. Encourage the students to decode the Bible verse using their copies of the Runic alphabet. Direct the students' attention to the answer sheet in the folder labeled "answer." *(NOTE: See the reproducible material at the end of Lesson 76.)* Instruct each student to check the answer sheet when he has completed decoding.

☐ **Additional Teacher Information**

Eric Thorvaldsson Raudi, otherwise known as Eric the Red, was a Viking explorer who seems to have had a fiery temperament to match his red hair. His explosive temper resulted in his being exiled from Iceland three times before he was thirty-five years old.

During his exile, Eric explored the area west of Iceland in search of land that had been sighted in A.D. 900 by a Norwegian named Gunnbjorn Ulfsson. Eric found the land and named it Greenland, arguing that a good name would attract people to it.

Eric later planned to lead an expedition west from Greenland to discover more land. Shortly before the expedition was to begin, however, Eric fell from his horse. He then refused to go, believing the fall was a bad omen. Later, in A.D. 1000, Eric's son, Leif, led what was probably the first expedition to North America.

LESSON 74
The Age of Feudalism

Text, pages 285-88
Notebook, page 84

- **Feudal Days**
- **Men in Shining Armor**
- **Coats of Arms and Chivalry**
- **Hastings**

Preview

□ Objectives

Given proper instruction, the students will be able to do the following:

- Identify weapons and armor by matching words with pictures.
- State opinions on how a knight would use a particular weapon or piece of armor.

□ Materials

Have available Maps and More 25, 26, and 27.

Day 160

Lesson

□ Introducing the Lesson

Weapons and armor guessing game—Write the words *battle-ax, helmet, breastplate, sword, mace,* and *shield* on the chalkboard. Display Maps and More 25, 26, and 27 (armor). Invite the students to guess the names of the pieces of weapons and armor. As time permits, allow each student to choose either a piece of armor or a weapon and give an opinion on how a knight would have used that particular weapon or piece of armor.

Feudalism

Life in Europe during the centuries after Charlemagne's death has been called the *Age of Feudalism*. Feudalism was the name for the type of government that developed during this time period.

Under the system of feudalism, two nobles entered into an agreement. One of them agreed to be the *vassal*, or servant, of the other. The vassal had to perform certain duties for the other noble, or the lord. Some of these duties included fighting for the lord in battle and providing lodging for the lord when he traveled on the vassal's land. In a special ceremony, the vassal knelt before the lord and took an oath of *fealty*, or faithfulness, promising to be loyal to the lord.

In exchange for these favors, the lord gave the vassal a *fief*, or a fee, which was usually a piece of land. Although the fief still belonged to the lord, the vassal could use it freely.

Being asked to become a vassal was considered a great honor. Vassals could, in turn, divide up their own land and become lords over lesser vassals. Divisions of land and loyalties often continued until the fief was the size of an average manor. A piece of land this size was large enough to support one knight.

285

□ Teaching the Lesson

Feudal days—Instruct the students to read page 285 silently to find out what life in Europe was called during the centuries after Charlemagne's death. *(the Age of Feudalism)*

Discussion Questions

➤ **What was the name of a noble who performed certain duties for the lord?** *(vassal)*

➤ **What did some of these duties include?** *(fighting for the lord in battle and providing lodging for the lord when he traveled on the vassal's land)*

➤ **What was the name of an oath the vassal gave to show his loyalty to the lord?** *(an oath of fealty, or faithfulness)*

➤ **What did the lord give the vassal in exchange for his services?** *(a fief, or fee)*

Have you seen pictures or read stories about knights? The knight was a mounted soldier who defended the manor during the Middle Ages. He wore a suit of metal armor from head to foot, and his horse was also heavily armored. He carried a sword, a lance, and sometimes a battle-ax as weapons. He wielded a heavy shield to protect himself in battle.

Nearly any nobleman could become a knight if he proved himself worthy. He had to be faithful and skilled in warfare. A young boy who wanted to be a knight could take the first step at the age of seven by becoming a *page*. As a page, a boy went to live in the castle of another noble to learn horsemanship and fighting skills. He also did chores for the lord and lady of the castle. At fourteen, he became a *squire*. His responsibilities then included helping his master dress, accompanying him on hunts or into battles, and caring for his warhorse. He continued his lessons in bow, sword, and lance fighting. When he was twenty-one, he could become a knight.

An elaborate ceremony was necessary for a man to become a knight. Before this ceremony, the man spent the entire night in church, praying that he would be worthy of the honor.

The next morning, other knights solemnly dressed him in his armor. The knight knelt before his lord, who touched him on the shoulder with a sword and said, "I dub you knight."

286

Sometimes new knights went immediately into battle. When there were no battles going on, knights often planned mock battles called *tournaments*. Rival groups of knights met to have *jousting* contests. The goal of a joust was for one knight to knock the other off his horse with a blunt lance. Great honor went to the winning jouster.

While a knight was fighting, the only way to identify him was by his coat of arms. The coat of arms was the emblem painted on his shield, and each knight had a different coat of arms.

What kind of person do you imagine when you think of a knight? How would he act in danger, or how would he treat a lady? Knights of the Middle Ages lived by a code of behavior called *chivalry*. This code taught a knight to be generous, loyal to his lord, skillful and brave in battle, faithful to the Roman Church, and protective of women. Do you think many knights lived up to these standards of chivalry?

287

Men in shining armor—Instruct the students to read page 286 silently to find out what name referred to mounted soldiers who defended the manor in the Middle Ages. *(knights)*

Discussion Questions

➤ **What did knights wear for protection in battle?** *(suits of metal armor from head to toe)*
➤ **What weapons did a knight carry?** *(a sword, a lance, and sometimes a battle-ax)*
➤ **What other thing did knights use for protection in battle?** *(a shield)*

Explain to the students that just as the knights in the Middle Ages wore suits of armor, Christians are protected with a suit of armor in their battle with Satan. The Bible calls this the armor of God. (Eph. 6:11-19) Christians have weapons also. They are armed with God's strength and the Word of God. When Christians faithfully use their protection and weapons, they can successfully stand against Satan. (BATs: 8c Fight, 8d Courage)

***Day** 161*

➤ **What qualifications did a noble need to have to be considered worthy of knighthood?** *(He had to be faithful and skilled in warfare.)*
➤ **At what age could a boy begin training to be a knight?** *(at age seven)*

➤ **What did a page do in the castle of a noble?** *(He learned horsemanship and fighting skills and did chores for the lord and lady of the castle.)*
➤ **What responsibilities did a squire have?** *(He helped his master dress, accompanied him on hunts and battles, cared for his warhorse, and continued his lessons in bow, sword, and lance fighting.)*
➤ **At what age could a noble become a knight?** *(twenty-one)*
➤ **What did a young noble do the night before his knighting ceremony?** *(prayed all night in the church.)*

Coats of arms and chivalry—Instruct the students to read page 287 silently to find out what mock battles were called. *(tournaments)*

Discussion Questions

➤ **What was the goal of a joust?** *(to knock the rival knight off his horse with a blunt lance)*
➤ **How was a knight identified when fighting?** *(by his coat of arms)*
➤ **Where was the knight's coat of arms displayed?** *(on his shield)*
➤ **What code of behavior did knights live by?** *(chivalry)*
➤ **What did the code of chivalry teach a knight?** *(to be generous, loyal to his lord, skillful and brave in battle, faithful to the Roman Church, and protective of women)*

Hastings—Instruct the students to read page 288 silently to find out what year the king of England died without an heir. *(in 1066)*

The Battle of Hastings

In 1066, the king of England died without an heir. Two powerful nobles, Harold Godwinson and Duke William of Normandy, both claimed the throne. Harold set himself up as the next king of England. William called upon his vassals to provide him with men and supplies to form an army. William and his army met Harold's forces on a field near the town of Hastings.

Harold, wanting to force William to attack first, placed his men along the top of a ridge. Standing side-by-side, Harold's men formed a *shield wall*. William knew his men would have to break through this wall to win the battle.

William and the Norman army surged up the hill toward Harold's men. Shouts rang out and metal clanged as the two armies clashed. William's army attacked the shield wall again and again. Late in the afternoon, the Norman army finally broke through. Harold was killed in the fierce struggle, and soon afterward his army fled.

William was now the king of England. He chose some of his own men to be lords, replacing the ones who were not loyal to him. All of England became a feudal kingdom. William was called "William the Conqueror."

One of many scenes on the Bayeaux Tapestry depicting the Battle of Hastings

288

Sword or Shield?   Name _____

Read the following statements. Circle the sword if the statement is true. Circle the shield if the statement is false. If the statement is false, cross out the incorrect word(s) and write the correct word(s) on the blank.

1. To be worthy of knighthood, one had to be ~~of noble birth~~.
   faithful and skillful in battle

2. A boy could begin training to be a knight at age ~~twelve~~. **seven**

3. A squire learned to fight with a bow, a sword, and a lance. _____

4. The night before the dubbing ceremony, a man spent the night praying in the church. _____

5. The way to identify a knight in battle was by ~~the color of the plume (feather) in his helmet~~. **his coat of arms**

6. Duke William of Normandy won the Battle of ~~Tours~~. **Hastings**

7. The way a knight was supposed to behave was called the code of ~~courtly behavior~~. **chivalry**

8. Harold Godwinson fought the Norman army. _____

9. Knights used swords, lances, and ~~bows and arrows~~ as weapons.
   battle-axes

10. Duke William was called "William the ~~Brave~~." **Conqueror**

Heritage Studies 6
Student Notebook

Lesson 74
Evaluating the Lesson   **84**

Discussion Questions

➤ **What two nobles disputed over the throne of England?** *(Harold Godwinson and Duke William of Normandy)*
➤ **What battle was fought by Harold Godwinson and Duke William of Normandy?** *(the Battle of Hastings)*
➤ **Who won the Battle of Hastings?** *(Duke William of Normandy)*
➤ **What was William called after his victory?** *(William the Conqueror)*

☐ Evaluating the Lesson

Sword or Shield? (Notebook page 84)—Instruct the students to circle the sword if the statement is true and to circle the shield if the statement is false. Tell them to cross out the incorrect word(s) in each false statement and to write the correct word(s) on the blank.

Going Beyond

☐ Enrichment

Catapult construction—Set up a model-construction AREA for each student to make a model catapult. Explain that knights used catapults in battle to hurl objects at the enemy. Display a completed model catapult and the Catapult Construction Sheet. (*NOTE:* See the reproducible material at the end of Lesson 76.) Have available the following materials for each student: a small cardboard carton or box, scissors, a hole puncher, a rubber band, two pencils, a small twig, a

small matchbox-sized box or piece of cardboard (approximately 2"×1"), and tape.

Instruct the students to construct their catapults by following the instructions given on the Catapult Construction Sheet. As time permits, divide the students into two teams. Give each student several marshmallows and allow them to fire marshmallows at the opposing team.

☐ Additional Teacher Information

Little is known about the legendary King Arthur, but many historians believe that this medieval ruler actually lived. For nearly a thousand years, authors have written of Arthur and his knights. Most of the accounts are fictional, not historical.

The most well known account of King Arthur was written by Sir Thomas Malory around 1470. His book *Morte D'Arthur* is the basis for many other accounts. Malory's book is entertaining, but he had another purpose—to portray Arthur and his knights as ideal, chivalric gentlemen. The last lines of *Morte D'Arthur* show that Malory wanted to set up Arthur as a legend.

> Yet some say in many parts of England that King Arthur is not dead, but had by the will of our Lord Jesus into another place; and men say that he shall come again, and he shall win the Holy Cross. Yet I will not say that it shall be so, but I rather would say: here in this world he changed his life. And many men say that there is written upon the tomb this: "Here lies Arthur, the once and future king."

LESSON 75
Life at the Castle

Text, pages 289-91
Notebook, pages 85-86

- Inside the Castle
- At a Medieval Banquet Table
- The Castle Under Siege

════ Preview ════

□ Objective

Given proper instruction, the students will be able to do the following:

- Name important people and events of the Middle Ages by answering questions while playing a human chess game.

□ Materials

Have available Maps and More 28.

□ Notes

Students will participate in a human chess game as part of the Evaluating the Lesson section. Each student will have a label identifying the game piece he will represent. (*NOTE:* See the reproducible material at the end of Lesson 76.) There will be two kings, two queens, two knights, two bishops, and two rooks. All other players will be pawns.

The board game A Medieval Whodunit is introduced in the Enrichment section. If you choose to use this game, prepare the game pieces as you did for the game in Lesson 12.

Day 162

════ Lesson ════

□ Introducing the Lesson

A page goes to the castle—Display Maps and More 28 (castle and surroundings). Read the following story to the students, pointing out different parts of the castle and its surroundings on Maps and More 28 when necessary.

The sun had been up for only a few hours when the two travelers set off on their journey. One traveler was a man about thirty years old. He was dressed in a suit of blue velvet, richly trimmed with ermine. He sat straight and tall on a beautiful white charger. In front of him, on the same horse, sat a young boy about seven years old. The boy looked eagerly ahead, his blue eyes wide with anticipation. It was hard to sit still in the saddle, but the boy forced himself to sit quietly. He did not want his father to scold him today. It was a day the boy had looked forward to for a long time. He was going to the castle of Duke William to begin his training to become a knight! Despite his best efforts, the boy squirmed excitedly at the thought of being a knight just as his father had been. The castle was just a

few miles from the inn where he and his father had spent the night. Soon they would be there!

The father and son had traveled in silence for most of the journey. The boy, not wanting to disturb his father's reverie, looked around at the landscape surrounding them. He started when his father said, "Up yonder, Edmund, is Duke William's castle." The boy's heart beat faster as he looked ahead. There, surrounded by a moat, stood a magnificent stone castle. As they drew nearer, Edmund could see people moving on top of the castle walls. Looking at them more closely, Edmund saw that the people had swords. They must be knights! Edmund could hardly make himself sit still as he and his father crossed the drawbridge and entered the gatehouse. Once inside the outer bailey, a handsome young knight on a shining black steed approached them. "Good morning, Duke Anthony," the knight said. "I trust you are well?"

"I am, thank you, Sir Percival," Edmund's father replied.

"This is your son, Edmund, then?" asked Sir Percival. Edmund's father nodded.

"And Duke William is awaiting you," Sir Percival said. "He will see you in his chambers inside the keep."

Edmund's father dismounted and lifted Edmund off the horse. A servant led away the horse, and Duke Anthony, placing his arm around his son's shoulders, led him through the inner gatehouse to a large building.

Edmund was awed by the simple beauty of the keep's interior. Rich tapestries hung on the walls, and soft carpets lay on the floor to help keep away the cold drafts and to dispel the dreariness of the castle's rooms.

A servant approached Edmund and his father. "Duke William is expecting us," Edmund's father explained.

The servant nodded and led the way up a winding staircase. Edmund looked around him as he and his father walked to the duke's chambers. He had never been in Duke William's castle before. He hoped that the duke would allow him to explore the castle.

Duke William smiled and rose from his chair as Edmund and his father entered his chamber. Like the other castle rooms that Edmund had already seen, the room was furnished simply, but the coverings on the furniture were made of the finest fabrics. Duke William clasped Edmund's father's hand. "It has been a long time since we met, Anthony," he said.

"Aye," Edmund's father said. "A very long time."

The duke looked fondly at Edmund. "And this is young Edmund! I can see already that he will make a fine page and later a fine knight."

Edmund's father laid a hand on Edmund's head. "Yes, he is a fine lad."

"You will stay for a while, Anthony?" the duke asked. "I had hopes of playing a game of chess with you this afternoon. There is no better player than you. I am also having a banquet this evening and would be honored for you to attend."

Edmund's father nodded. "I thank you, William. Yes, I will stay."

The Castle

Castles had become common in Europe by the eleventh century. The castle in the Middle Ages was both a home and a military fortress.

Castles were surrounded by strong walls. Some castles in the later Middle Ages had stone walls over thirty feet thick. Inside the walls were towers, halls, and the courtyard.

The lord and his family had their living quarters in the keep. The keep, an inner castle tower, was the safest place in the castle. Often the keep stood on a hill. Inside it were the great hall, where meetings and banquets were held; the kitchen; the family's bedrooms and sitting rooms; and a few other rooms, such as offices or a chapel. Servants often slept in the rooms where they worked, rather than having private bedrooms.

Castles were cold and dark inside. Lords tried to brighten them by painting the walls and ceilings with bright colors and placing burning torches in the rooms. They put mats on the floors and hung large woven tapestries on the walls to keep out the cold.

Medieval tapestry, ca. A.D. 1500

The Metropolitan Museum of Art, Gift of John D. Rockefeller Jr., 1937
Photograph © 1988 The Metropolitan Museum of Art

289

◆THINGS PEOPLE DID◆

Giving Medieval Banquets

Wealthy people liked to give large banquets during the Middle Ages. Lords would invite many guests, and they would eat at long tables in the great hall of the castle. Pages waited on tables. Squires were often responsible to carve the meat for the guests.

Many different foods were served at these banquets. One meal might have included soup, cheese made from a pig's head, puddings, baked fish, pork, venison, pheasants, larks, and other birds. Dessert was usually a pie filled with fish or fowl. Have you ever heard the nursery rhyme that tells of "four and twenty blackbirds baked in a pie"? One medieval custom was to insert live birds into a pie and release them in front of the guests when dessert was served.

Banquet guests used large, flat pieces of bread as plates. Forks were never used until the 1600s, so the guests used their fingers to eat most foods. But they still observed certain rules about table manners. No one was supposed to gnaw on the bones, and it was considered rude to dip food into the common salt bowl.

290

"Good," the duke said. He extended his hand toward Edmund. "Come, Edmund. We shall go see where you will be staying here. I think that you will enjoy your stay."

Edmund smiled. Already he knew that the duke was right.

Explain that in the Middle Ages, wealthy people like Duke William and Edmund's father lived in castles with their families, knights, and servants. Tell the students that in this lesson they will be learning more about castles and the way of life within them.

Day 163

□ Teaching the Lesson

Inside the castle—Instruct the students to read page 289 silently to find out two purposes a castle served. *(as a home and a military fortress)*

Discussion Questions

➤ **Where was the safest place in the castle?** *(the keep)*
➤ **What rooms were in the castle keep?** *(the great hall, the kitchen, the family's bedrooms, the sitting rooms, offices, and a chapel)*
➤ **What purpose did the great hall serve?** *(Banquets and meetings were held here.)*
➤ **Where did the servants sleep in the castle?** *(often in the same rooms in which they worked)*
➤ **How did lords try to make living in their castles more comfortable?** *(by painting walls in bright colors, plac-*

ing burning torches in the rooms, putting mats on the floors, and hanging tapestries on the walls)

At a medieval banquet table—Instruct the students to read page 290 silently to find out what type of people liked to give banquets during the Middle Ages. *(wealthy people)*

Discussion Questions

➤ **Who usually waited on tables during the banquet?** *(pages)*
➤ **What types of food were served at a banquet?** *(Possible answers include soup, cheese made from a pig's head, puddings, baked fish, and venison.)*
➤ **What unusual dish was served during the Middle Ages?** *(a pie into which live birds were inserted and then released when the dessert was served)*
➤ **What was food served on at the banquet?** *(large, flat pieces of bread)*
➤ **How did medieval people eat most of their food?** *(with their fingers)*
➤ **What things were considered rude at the table?** *(gnawing on bones and dipping food into the common salt bowl)*
➤ **How might people have looked on someone with bad table manners?** *(Possible answers include with disgust, disrespect, and annoyance.)*

Early castles were made of wood. By the twelfth century, most castles were made of thick stone. Builders dug *moats*, wide trenches filled with water, around the castle to keep attackers from reaching it easily. A *drawbridge* crossed the moat to the castle gate. During an attack, the castle guards raised the drawbridge to cover the gate, cutting off the entrance to the castle.

If attackers got safely across the moat, they had to face the *gatehouse*. The gatehouse was a large stronghold in the castle wall. If the attackers entered the gatehouse, castle defenders could lower a large screen to trap them inside.

Soldiers attacked castles in different ways. Sometimes they used a *battering ram*, a long log tipped with iron, to knock down the gate or part of the castle wall. Sometimes they built tall towers, rolled them up against the wall, and climbed over into the castle. Sometimes they threw rocks and burning rags into the courtyard. And sometimes they dug tunnels beneath the castle, started fires in the tunnels, and tried to burn away the foundation so that the castle would collapse.

Human Chess Questions   Name _____

Use the words listed to complete the following.

pope	Clovis	holy days
Franks	Charlemagne	A.D. 476
Visigoths	Merovingian	lord
priests	sacraments	monasteries
nuns	Pepin the Short	A.D. 770

<u>A.D. 476</u> 1. In what year did the Roman Empire fall?

<u>Visigoths</u> 2. What tribe settled in Spain?

<u>Franks</u> 3. What group conquered Gaul?

<u>pope</u> 4. The bishop of Rome was called the ____.

<u>sacraments</u> 5. What ceremonies were believed necessary for salvation?

<u>priests</u> 6. Monks and ____ were clergy who worked for the Roman Church.

<u>monasteries</u> 7. Monks lived in ____.

<u>nuns</u> 8. Women who devoted their lives to the Roman Catholic Church were called ____.

<u>Clovis</u> 9. Who was the first king of the Franks?

<u>Merovingian</u> 10. The descendants of Clovis were the ____ kings.

<u>Pepin the Short</u> 11. What Frankish king made an alliance with the Roman Church?

<u>Charlemagne</u> 12. Who was crowned emperor of the western Roman Empire on Christmas Day, A.D. 800?

<u>lord</u> 13. A ____ was the owner of a manor.

<u>holy days</u> 14. What were special occasions called during the Middle Ages?

© 1996 BJU Press. Reproduction prohibited.

Heritage Studies 6
Student Notebook

Lesson 75
Evaluating the Lesson **85**

The castle under siege—Instruct the students to read page 291 silently to find out what castles were made of by the twelfth century. *(thick stone)* Show Maps and More 28 again, pointing out the parts of the castle and its surroundings as you direct the following discussion.

Discussion questions

➤ **What was built around the castle to keep attackers from reaching it too quickly?** *(a moat)*

➤ **How could a person get to the castle?** *(by crossing a drawbridge over the moat to the gate)*

➤ **What was the *gatehouse*?** *(a large stronghold in the castle wall)*

➤ **What could happen to attackers who entered the gatehouse?** *(The castle defenders could lower a large screen and trap the attackers inside the gatehouse.)*

➤ **How did soldiers use a battering ram in attacking the castle?** *(to knock down the gate or part of the castle wall)*

➤ **What other methods did soldiers use to attack castles?** *(Possible answers include building tall towers and climbing over the castle wall, throwing rocks and burning rags into the courtyard, and building tunnels beneath the castle and starting fires inside them.)*

Explain that knights who guarded the castle were expected to fight bravely when the castle was under attack. Remind the students that Christians are also expected to fight valiantly against sin and the Devil. (BATs: 1c Separation from the world, 8c Fight, 8d Courage)

Day 164

☐ Evaluating the Lesson

Human Chess Game (Notebook pages 85-86)—Direct the students to fill in the blanks with the correct words. Show the chess identification labels and allow each student to choose one. (*NOTE:* See the reproducible material at the end of Lesson 76.) Divide the students into two teams. All the white playing pieces will be on one team, and the black playing pieces will be on the other team. Instruct the team members to line up in front of the classroom facing one another. Each team member should bring with him Notebook pages 85-86 and a pencil.

Explain that in the Middle Ages chess was a popular game, especially among the wealthy. Tell the students that the object of chess is to capture the opposing team's king. Explain that they will be playing a game similar to chess. Each student will be given opportunities to ask questions to members of the opposing team. When a player has missed the maximum number of questions he is allowed to miss, he

Use the words listed to complete the following. After your teacher has checked your work, use your answers to participate in the Human Chess game.

vassal	battering ram	Vikings	1066
1030	William of Normandy	Age of Feudalism	courtyard
fief	moats	France	drawbridge
page	serfs	knight	keep
gatehouse	siege	Spain	

serfs   1. Peasants who lived on manors were called ____.

France   2. Germany and ____ developed from the division of Charlemagne's empire.

Vikings   3. Who were the invaders from Scandinavia?

Age of Feudalism   4. What was life in Europe called after Charlemagne's death?

vassal   5. A person who performed certain duties for a lord was called a ____.

knight   6. A mounted soldier was called a ____.

fief   7. A fee paid to a vassal was called a ____.

page   8. A seven-year-old boy in training to be a knight was called a ____.

1066   9. In what year did the Battle of Hastings take place?

keep   10. The ____ was the safest place in the castle.

moats   11. What were often built around castles to keep invaders from attacking castles easily?

gatehouse   12. The ____ was a large stronghold in the castle wall.

battering ram   13. A ____ was a long log tipped in iron that was used to knock down a gate or castle wall.

William of Normandy   14. Who won the Battle of Hastings?

Heritage Studies 6
Student Notebook

Lesson 75
Evaluating the Lesson   **86**

is out of the game and will return to his desk. Explain that the number of questions that may be missed is indicated on each chess name tag. Tell each student to tally on his name tag his number of incorrect answers. Explain that once a question has been asked and answered correctly, that question must be marked off Notebook pages 85-86 and not be asked again. Students from one team may ask a player from the opposing team as many questions as they wish; however, an individual player may ask only one question per turn and may not ask the same player a question every time it is his turn to ask a question. (*NOTE:* For instance, a player who has asked a king a question on one turn must ask another player a question on his next turn.) Tell the students that whatever team is the first to "capture" the opposing team's king as well as three other players wins the game. If all the questions have been asked and answered correctly or if time runs out before either team has won, the game ends in a stalemate with neither team winning.

Going Beyond

☐ Enrichment

A medieval whodunit—Set up a game AREA with the board game A Medieval Whodunit. Tell the students that this is a mystery game which takes place in a medieval castle. Show the students the game board of a castle's different rooms. Tell them that the object of the game is to solve the mystery by collecting clues from different rooms in the castle. The player who solves the mystery first wins the game.

Show the students the game markers. Each player selects a game marker to travel through the different rooms of the castle on the game board. Each student will also be given a clue sheet to write down the clues as he collects them. Tell the students to select one player to read aloud the directions for playing the game. (*NOTE:* See the reproducible material at the end of Lesson 76.)

☐ Additional Teacher Information

A well-known medieval castle is the Chateau Gaillard in France, which was built by Richard I of England in the 1190s. Richard wanted to protect his lands in France with a well-fortified castle. Richard was quite knowledgeable about defending castles and used his knowledge to oversee personally the castle's construction.

Chateau Gaillard was built within a year, a short time for a castle to be constructed. The keep of the castle was constructed in a different way. It was round, making it more difficult to destroy in a siege.

Although Gaillard seemed invincible, Philip Augustus of France lay siege to the castle in 1204. His soldiers used towers to scale the walls of the castle. One soldier climbed up a lavatory chute and helped the other soldiers gain access to the inside of the castle by opening a window. The English defended Gaillard from the French for nearly a month but were forced to surrender in the end.

LESSON 76
The Twilight of an Era

Text, pages 292-94

- A Reformed Legal System
- Bridges to the Modern Era

Preview

☐ Objective

Given proper instruction, the students will be able to do the following:
- Explain courtroom activities by participating in a mock trial.

☐ Materials

Have available:
- 5 sheets of white construction paper.
- A pencil for each juror.
- Tape.
- Safety pins.
- 2 suit coats and/or briefcases for each attorney (optional).

Prepare:
- Name cards using half of a sheet of white construction paper for each title. Label the name cards for the Prosecuting Attorney, Defense Attorney, Suspect, and Jurors.
- A badge for each juror. Write the word *Juror* inside a three-inch circle.
- A copy of the "Jurors Decision" page for each juror. (*NOTE:* See the reproducible material at the end of this lesson.)
- A copy of the evidence, rebuttal, and question cards. (*NOTE:* See the reproducible material at the end of this lesson.)

☐ Notes

Attach a badge to each juror. Position the desks so that the attorneys and the suspect face the front of the classroom if all of the students are involved in the activity. You may want the desks facing the back of the classroom for other students who are observing. Place desks for the jurors to the left. Tape the name cards to the desks.

Lesson

☐ Introducing the Lesson

Story reading—Read the following story to the students.

Sir Andrew Wythe slowly opened his eyes as the morning sun found its way through the open window. His eyes widened as he awoke. He did not wake up to the interior of a tent as he had done so many times before but to the rich furnishings of his own room. He was home—in England! Sir Andrew stretched then winced as a twinge of pain in his left leg reminded him of the two years he had been away from all the comfort and peacefulness of home.

Was it 1192 already? It seemed as though it had been only a few days ago that the news had swept through England that the Muslims had captured the holy city of Jerusalem. No Christians were allowed to enter the city. Not long after that, the king had begun a Third Crusade. Sir Andrew had been among those who had traveled to the Holy Land. He had seen many close friends fight bravely and die valiantly in an attempt to capture Jerusalem from the Muslims. Sir Andrew had not personally seen the end of the Crusade, but word had reached him that Jerusalem was still under Muslim control. However, Christians could now enter the city. Sir Andrew was glad that the blood spilt on the battlefield had not been entirely in vain.

A polite knock interrupted Sir Andrew's reverie. A servant entered, carrying a large pitcher of water. A bath, Sir Andrew thought, would be refreshing. He had lived for nearly two years with nothing but a basin of cold water in which to wash his face and hands.

"Good morning, Sir Andrew," the servant said. "I trust you slept well on your first night here."

"I vow I have not rested better for nearly two years, Guy," Sir Andrew said. "There, I thought that if the Saracens did not kill me first, the fleas that shared my bed every night would have eaten me alive."

"And yet you have returned by the grace of God," Guy said. "Her ladyship is glad indeed to have you with us again. She feared for a while that you had died."

"And I nearly did," Sir Andrew said.

Guy set down the pitcher of water. "You, sir?"

Sir Andrew nodded. He was silent for a few minutes, and then he spoke. "It was during a time when the spirits of the men under my command were quite low. Our food supply had diminished, and a mere loaf of bread cost a gold piece, which few of us had. We were forced to eat tree leaves or the flesh of horses and donkeys to stay alive. Then the Saracens attacked."

Sir Andrew closed his eyes. For a few moments, the room in his castle and his servant did not exist. He was back on a field, several miles away from Jerusalem. He could almost feel the intense heat of that day and hear the cries from knights who had been wounded. He could almost see the sweaty, dark faces of the Arabs as they rushed toward him and the other knights. They thrashed at the knights with their scimitars. Sir Andrew could see again their dark eyes, flashing with hate.

"The Saracens' attack was unexpected, and they were ruthless," Sir Andrew continued. "Most of my men panicked as they watched their comrades dropping dead beside them. I shouted at them to defend themselves, but they were either too weak from hunger or too frightened by the suddenness of the attack to fight well. I fought almost continuously for days, and then I fell ill with a high fever."

Sir Andrew paused. He picked up a silver goblet that was sitting on a table beside the bed. He took a drink of water and then went on with his tale. "For weeks I was delirious. When I finally regained my senses, I found myself in the home of a wealthy Arab named Khalid. He had found me several feet away from the camp. At first he thought that I was dead, but when he looked at me more closely, he realized that I was still alive. One of my men must have taken me away from the battle and hidden me, hoping that the Saracens would not find me. Khalid, who spoke English fluently, told me that most of the men had been brutally killed. Others had escaped somehow. A pain in my left leg told me that I had not escaped injury.

" 'Your leg was badly cut with a scimitar,' Khalid said. I then asked how he had learned English.

" 'I was an orphan,' he replied. 'A rich English merchant took pity on me and took me into his household as a son. I grew up in England. It was not until I was older that I returned to my homeland.'

" 'Yet you are Muslim?' I asked.

"Khalid shook his head. 'No, I am a Christian,' he said. 'Life here is not easy, but I have chosen to remain to help fellow converts who have suffered much.'

"Khalid and I became close friends. My wound began to heal slowly, and my health returned. With my men gone, I had no choice but to return to England. Khalid provided me with transportation, and after a regretful farewell we parted company."

Guy had been listening intently. "A truly remarkable story. Had it not been for this Arab convert, you surely would have died. God has looked after your welfare."

Sir Andrew nodded. Yes, God had protected him. He hoped that his friend Khalid would also be protected.

Explain to the students that the Crusades were often referred to as the Holy Wars. Tell them that although the Muslims were indeed fierce fighters, the crusaders themselves were in reality the aggressors. The church, greedy for more land, convinced the crusaders that they were helping do the work of God by fighting in the Crusades. Tell the students that they will learn about the major part the Crusades played in the Middle Ages.

Henry's Legal System

In 1154, after many years of civil war, Henry II came to power in England. He developed England's legal system, extending the king's power into new areas.

The courts of Henry's day tried people suspected of crimes by *ordeal*. A common method of trial by ordeal was to tie an accused person's hands and feet with rope and throw him into deep water. The people believed that if he floated, the pure water had "rejected" him because of his sin, and he was considered guilty; if he sank, he was innocent. What do you think usually happened to the "innocent" person?

After the civil wars, many land claims had to be settled, and the courts that tried by ordeal could not be used for this purpose. Henry II developed new procedures. He issued *writs*, or royal orders, to the local sheriffs, instructing them to decide who actually held each piece of disputed land. Even though someone else may have owned the land, the person who actually lived on it got to keep it. The sheriffs' decisions required *juries*. Jury members were local people who came to the court to tell what they knew about who had the best claim to the land.

If the sheriff gave a writ to someone who disagreed with the land settlement, that person could return the writ to the sheriff. A new court case then decided whether the first decision of the sheriff was correct. When a particularly difficult case came up, it was sent directly to Henry II for his decision. Over time, such decisions were written down and enforced throughout England, becoming England's common law.

292

Day 166

□ Teaching the Lesson

A reformed legal system—Instruct the students to read page 292 silently to find out who came to power around the middle of the twelfth century. *(Henry II)*

Discussion Questions

➤ **In what system of government did Henry II make reforms?** *(the legal system)*

➤ **How were people tried for crimes before Henry's time?** *(by ordeal)*

➤ **What was a common method of trial by ordeal?** *(tying an accused person's hands and feet with rope and throwing him into water)*

➤ **By what title did Henry's new legal system come to be known?** *(English common law)*

Tell the students that a jury in Henry's day could be made up of one hundred jurors. Today's courts have twelve-member juries. Several crimes were tried at once during a court session during Henry II's time while modern courts try one crime at a time. Jurors of Henry II's time as well as jurors of today still decide whether an accused person is guilty or innocent.

Henry II's family, called the *Plantagenets*, ruled England until the end of the 1400s. A family called the *Capets* ruled France during this time. Germany and most of Italy made up the Holy Roman Empire, an empire under the joint control of an emperor and the pope of the Roman Catholic Church. The Byzantine Empire was thriving in Eastern Europe.

The Crusades did much to weaken the system of feudalism. Fighting in Crusades was expensive, and most of the money was furnished by individual lords. Some lords even had to sell or mortgage their properties to pay for their Crusade expenses. Also, many serfs left their manors to fight in the Crusades. Most who left, having tasted freedom, never returned.

> "The Lord is my rock, and my fortress, and my deliverer; my God, my strength, in whom I will trust; my buckler, and the horn of my salvation, and my high tower."
>
> **Psalm 18:2**

By the year 1500, central governments all over Europe were run by kings. England and France were well on their way to becoming strong nations. The medieval world was no more. The modern era of history was about to begin.

The scepter (above) and orb (below) of the Holy Roman Emperors

294

A Jury Works

1. Listen as your teacher tells you which role you will play in the mock trial.

2. Follow your teacher's instructions as the trial proceeds.

3. Discuss the trial with your classmates. Was enough evidence given? Was the jury fair in its decision? How is this kind of trial superior to a trial by ordeal?

293

Bridges to the modern era—Instruct the students to read page 294 silently to find out the name of Henry's family. *(the Plantagenets)*

Discussion Questions

➤ **What family ruled France at the time the Plantagenets ruled England?** *(the Capets)*

➤ **What two countries made up the Holy Roman Empire?** *(Germany and most of Italy)*

➤ **What empire was thriving in Eastern Europe at this time?** *(the Byzantine Empire)*

➤ **How did the Crusades weaken the system of feudalism?** *(The lords lost money; many serfs refused to return to the manors after the Crusades.)*

➤ **Who ran the central governments in Europe by the year 1500?** *(kings)*

Remind the students that systems of government, just like everything else on earth, will not last forever. Tell them that Christians, however, can rely on and trust in something that will never change. Explain that the power of God's Word lasts forever because God, who gave the Bible to Christians, is eternal. (BAT: 8b Faith in the power of the Word of God)

Day 167

□ Evaluating the Lesson

A mock trial—Direct a *Discovering How* activity on page 293. Select a volunteer to read aloud the steps. Assign one student the role of the prosecuting attorney, another the role of the defense attorney, and a third student the role of the suspect. Explain to the other students that they will be jurors. Give the prosecuting attorney the evidence cards, question cards, and rebuttal cards labeled "Against the Suspect" or "Prosecutor"; give the defense attorney the evidence cards, question cards, and rebuttal cards labeled "For the Suspect" or "Defense Attorney." Give each juror a juror badge and a copy of the "Juror's Decision" page.

Explain that the suspect is accused of stealing a cola-scented eraser from his neighbor's desk. Tell the jurors that they will probably want to take notes on the backs of their decision sheets. Begin the trial by inviting the prosecuting attorney to state the evidence against the suspect. When he is finished, instruct the defense attorney to read the evidence in favor of the suspect. Once the evidence has been presented, give the defense and prosecuting attorneys an opportunity to give rebuttals either to strengthen their evidence or to argue against the evidence of the other attorney. After the rebuttals have been given, each attorney will be given a turn to ask the suspect the questions on his question cards. The suspect may answer the questions however he wishes. When the jury has heard all the evidence for and against the suspect, instruct the jurors to write the verdict of *Guilty* or *Not Guilty* and the reasons for choosing that verdict on the "Juror's Decision" pages. Tell each juror to sign his name at the bottom of the page. (*NOTE:* If the members of the jury do not all agree on the decision of guilty or not guilty, explain that this is what is now referred to as a hung jury. Give the jurors a certain amount of time to discuss the case among themselves in an attempt for all to agree on one verdict.) When the jury has made its decision, select one of the jurors to collect all of the "Juror's Decision" pages. This juror will count the number of *Guilty* and *Not Guilty* decisions and will tell the court whether the jury has found the suspect guilty or not guilty, giving the main reasons for that decision.

Once the verdict has been given, invite the students to discuss whether they thought that enough evidence was given, whether the jury was fair, and how trial by jury is much better than the old method of trial by ordeal.

Going Beyond

□ Enrichment

Medieval Word Search—Set up an AREA with a copy of the Medieval Word Search puzzle for each student. (*NOTE:* See the reproducible material at the end of this lesson.)

```
N P O P E D L M S U C I L C V U
L N S G S T R T D O Y K N R W I
O C T N U S E I W N T C R U Y F
O R R U W H K Y C N F R E S T U
C T O H T I R N L E Y C R A F R
U P G L E T H N I K I L K D L N
T R O N A M R F U G E Y O E U R
T H T E O N Y U N I H W T S E W
Y C H N T W E I J S T T D T E I
M N S T U G K L Y R U W R E D A
B T M I Y I A G E I T H T U O F
P L E W V L D N T M H N D I D N
O A N D I O K N W S A M E O N E
W K O M R D L A Y M S N S X Y R
S N N G R T N C A S T L E S S H
E A S T H R A R D E I O L Y T O
N R A H F Y R S Y B N T W N U S
I F T H S I S A L T G H T S H L
D N G U B K U R O L S O F A M N
T H N I G V U C H R D T F O R I
N T H E N R Y P L C E B Y M D S
```

□ Additional Teacher Information

Thomas à Becket was perhaps one of the closest friends of King Henry II. In 1162, Henry made Becket archbishop of Canterbury. Under his newly acquired title, Becket indulged in a rich lifestyle, and he often enjoyed the king's company. Later, when Henry appointed him chancellor of England, Becket reached a turning point in his lifestyle. He now lived more simply and opposed any of Henry's attempts to control the church.

Henry wanted to tax church lands and try church officials who were accused of serious crimes. Becket adamantly opposed Henry's attempts and was forced to leave England. Becket returned, however, and continued his hostile opposition to the king.

Henry became more irritated by Becket and asked, in the presence of his knights, whether anyone dared to take the life of Thomas à Becket. Four knights undertook the mission. On the evening of December 29, the knights seized and murdered Becket in the Canterbury Cathedral while he was at his evening prayers.

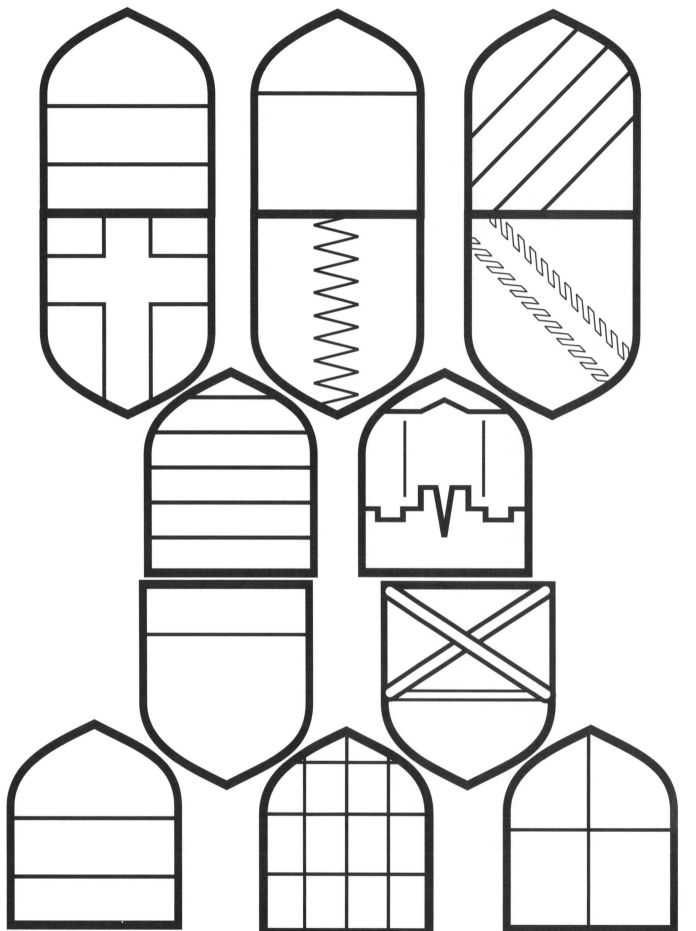

Use with the chapter bulletin board. Heritage Studies 6 TE

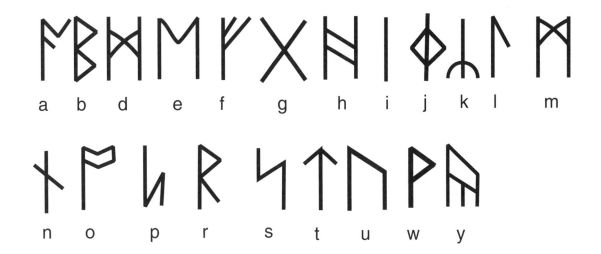

a b d e f g h i j k l m

n o p r s t u w y

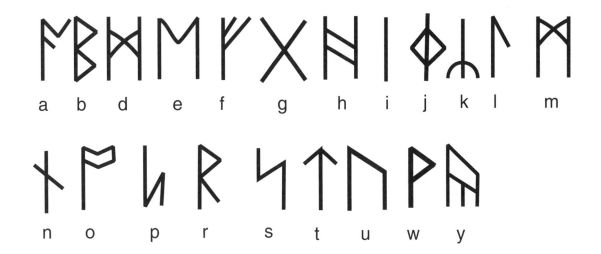

Answer Sheet

The answer is found in Exodus 34:14.

"For thou shalt worship no other god: for the Lord, whose name is Jealous, is a jealous God."

CATAPULT CONSTRUCTION

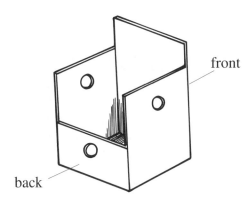

1. Cut the top off the carton and then cut it into the shape shown. Punch a hole in each side and one in the back.

front

back

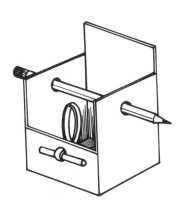

2. Thread the rubber band through the hole in the back and use the twig to keep the rubber band in place.

3. Push one of the pencils through the holes in the sides of the carton.

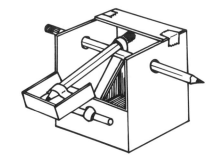

4. Cut the bottom of the small box in half and tape it to the end of the second pencil. Loop the rubber band underneath the first pencil and over the opposite end of the second pencil. Fold down the front flap of the carton and tape it down.

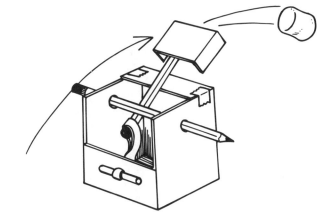

5. Put a marshmallow into the small box, pull back, and fire at the "enemy."

White King — May miss 4 questions	White Queen — May miss 3 questions	White Knight — May miss 2 questions
White Bishop — May miss 2 questions	White Rook — May miss 2 questions	Black King — May miss 4 questions
Black Queen — May miss 3 questions	Black Knight — May miss 2 questions	Black Bishop — May miss 2 questions
Black Rook — May miss 2 questions	White Pawn — May miss 1 question	White Pawn — May miss 1 question
White Pawn — May miss 1 question	White Pawn — May miss 1 question	White Pawn — May miss 1 question
White Pawn — May miss 1 question	White Pawn — May miss 1 question	Black Pawn — May miss 1 question
Black Pawn — May miss 1 question	Black Pawn — May miss 1 question	Black Pawn — May miss 1 question
Black Pawn — May miss 1 question	Black Pawn — May miss 1 question	Black Pawn — May miss 1 question

Use with Lesson 75.

A MEDIEVAL WHODUNIT
DIRECTIONS
4-6 PLAYERS

SETTING UP THE GAME

1. Place the clue cards facedown on the game board in the rooms in which they belong.

2. Place the solution card facedown beside the game board and near the Banquet Hall.

3. Place the game markers in the Outer Gatehouse square.

PLAYING THE GAME

1. One player will read the crime scenario to the other players.

2. Each player will spin once. The player who spins the highest number will go first.

3. Each player will move the number of spaces indicated on the spinner. If a player lands on a space directly in front of a room's entrance, he may enter the room and read the clue card silently. He will then write the clue on his clue sheet and return the clue card, keeping it facedown.

4. When a player thinks that he has enough clues to solve the mystery, he must go to the Banquet Hall. Once the player is in the Banquet Hall, he must state who stole the necklace, why the necklace was stolen, and where the necklace is hidden. He will then read the solution card silently. If he is right, he will read the card aloud to the other players. If he is wrong, he is automatically out of the game. The other players will continue until someone guesses correctly.

THE RULES OF THE GAME

1. A player may refer to the Crime Scenario at any time during the game.

2. Once a player has left a room, he may not read the room's clue card again unless he returns to the room.

3. If a player guesses incorrectly, he is automatically out of the game. The other players will continue until someone correctly guesses the solution.

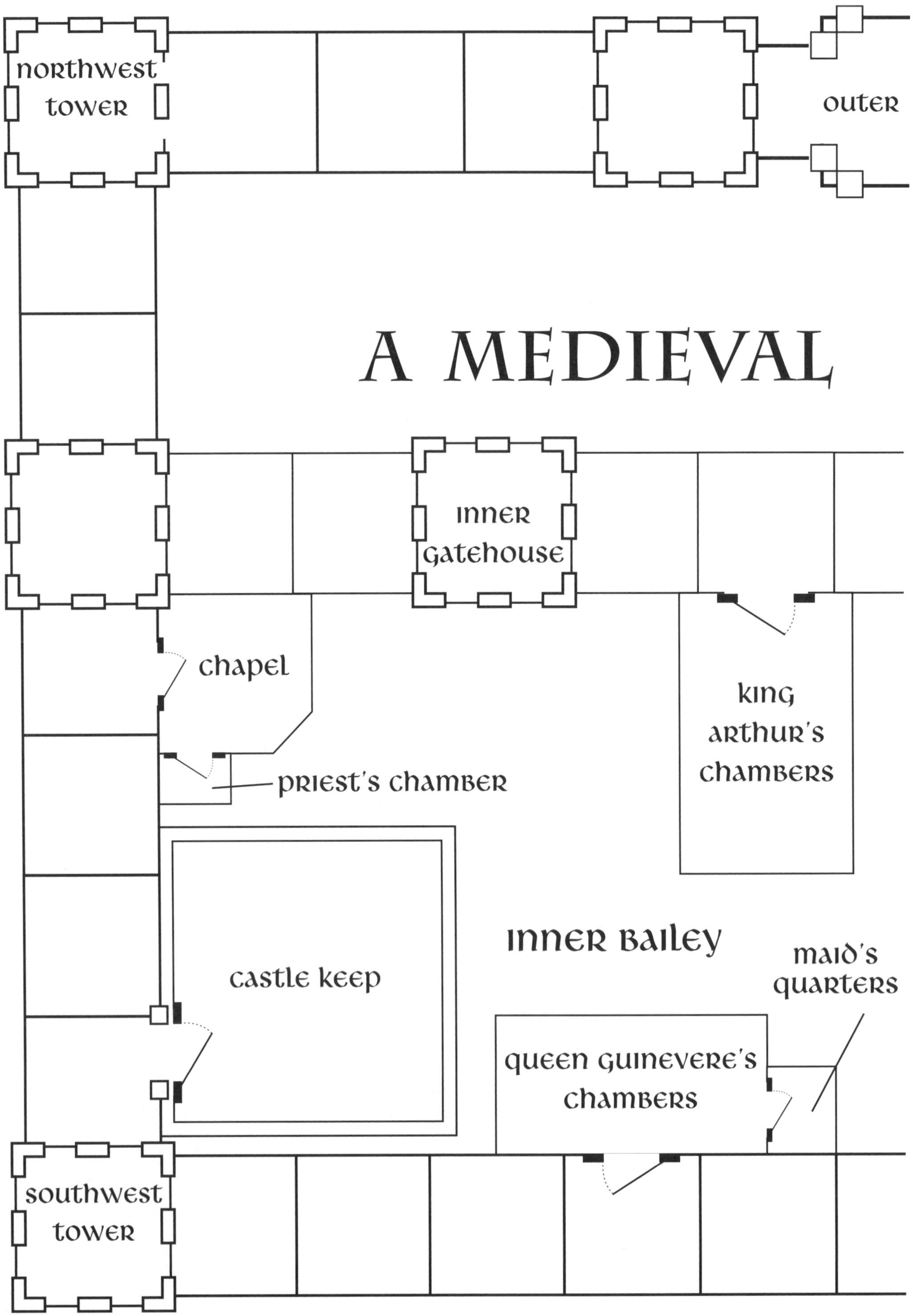

northwest
tower

outer

A MEDIEVAL

inner
gatehouse

king
arthur's
chambers

chapel

priest's chamber

inner bailey

maid's
quarters

castle keep

queen guinevere's
chambers

southwest
tower

Use with Lesson 75.

Heritage Studies 6 TE

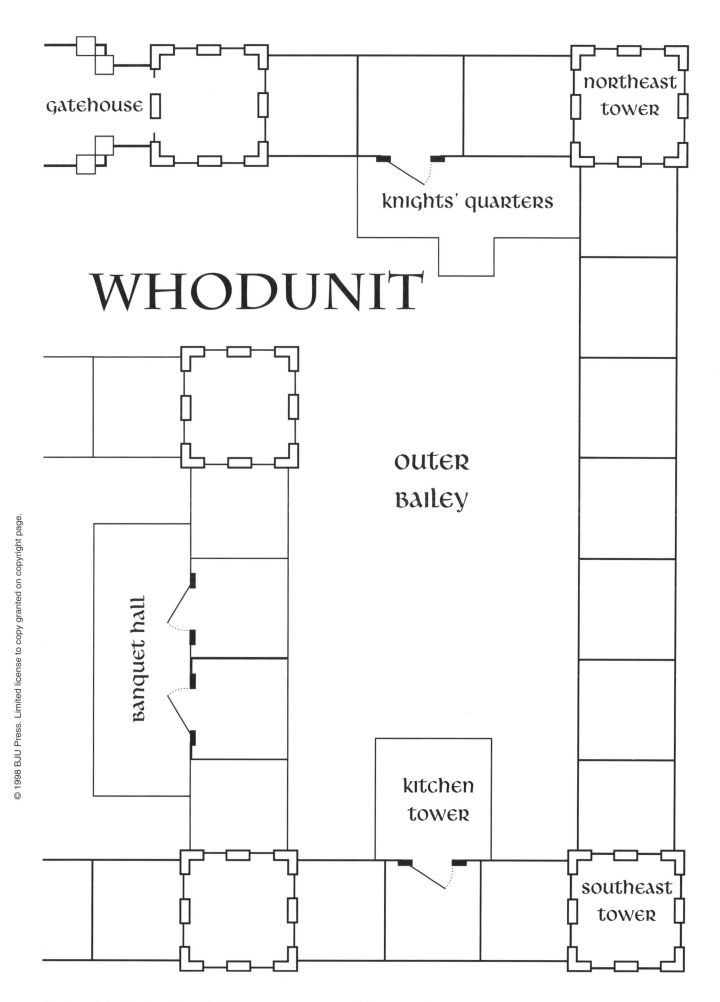

WHODUNIT

gatehouse

knights' quarters

northeast tower

outer bailey

banquet hall

kitchen tower

southeast tower

A MEDIEVAL WHODUNIT

CRIME SCENARIO

Queen Guinevere is quite distraught. A valuable necklace of precious jewels has been stolen from her chambers. The queen last saw her necklace when she was showing it to her friend Lady Elinore. The next morning the maid noticed that the queen's jewelry case had been moved from its normal place, so she put the case into its proper place. That afternoon, while preparing to attend a banquet with her husband and guests, Guinevere discovered that the necklace was missing. A thorough search was made of the room, but the necklace could not be found anywhere. Guinevere's chamber door is never locked, so anyone might have stolen the necklace. Guinevere must find the necklace before a banquet next week celebrating her husband Arthur's birthday. Arthur expects her to wear the necklace to the banquet. You must find out who has taken the necklace, why it was stolen, and where it is.

A MEDIEVAL WHODUNIT

SOLUTION

Lady Elinore was jealous of her friend for owning a necklace more magnificent than any of her own. Not wanting even the queen to outshine her at the upcoming banquet, Lady Elinore plotted with her suitor Sir Eldred to take the queen's necklace. That evening, Elinore, complaining that she was not well, stayed in her chambers while the king, queen, and the other guests dined in the Banquet Hall. Elinore quietly entered Guinevere's chambers and stole the necklace. Later Elinore told her maid that she was feeling better and asked her to send for a fruit tart. When the tart arrived, Elinore sent her maid away. Alone, Lady Elinore carefully cut off the top crust of the tart and hid the necklace inside. She then called her maid into the room and told her that the tart contained cherries, which she disliked. She instructed her maid to send the tart to Sir Eldred. Sir Eldred hid the necklace in his chambers at the Outer Gatehouse.

Use with Lesson 75.

CLUE SHEET

1. OUTER GATEHOUSE _____
_____
_____

2. KNIGHTS' QUARTERS _____
_____
_____

3. KITCHEN TOWER _____
_____
_____

4. INNER GATEHOUSE _____
_____
_____

5. NORTHWEST TOWER _____
_____
_____

6. KING ARTHUR'S CHAMBERS _____
_____
_____

7. MAID'S QUARTERS _____
_____
_____

8. QUEEN GUINEVERE'S CHAMBERS
_____
_____

9. CHAPEL _____
_____
_____

10. PRIEST'S CHAMBER _____
_____
_____

11. BANQUET HALL _____
_____
_____

CLUE SHEET

1. OUTER GATEHOUSE _____
_____
_____

2. KNIGHTS' QUARTERS _____
_____
_____

3. KITCHEN TOWER _____
_____
_____

4. INNER GATEHOUSE _____
_____
_____

5. NORTHWEST TOWER _____
_____
_____

6. KING ARTHUR'S CHAMBERS _____
_____
_____

7. MAID'S QUARTERS _____
_____
_____

8. QUEEN GUINEVERE'S CHAMBERS
_____
_____

9. CHAPEL _____
_____
_____

10. PRIEST'S CHAMBER _____
_____
_____

11. BANQUET HALL _____
_____
_____

CLUE SHEET

1. OUTER GATEHOUSE _____
_____
_____

2. KNIGHTS' QUARTERS _____
_____
_____

3. KITCHEN TOWER _____
_____
_____

4. INNER GATEHOUSE _____
_____
_____

5. NORTHWEST TOWER _____
_____
_____

6. KING ARTHUR'S CHAMBERS _____
_____
_____

7. MAID'S QUARTERS _____
_____
_____

8. QUEEN GUINEVERE'S CHAMBERS
_____
_____

9. CHAPEL _____
_____
_____

10. PRIEST'S CHAMBER _____
_____
_____

11. BANQUET HALL _____
_____
_____

A MEDIEVAL WHODUNIT GAME CARDS

NORTHWEST TOWER

Lady Elinore's maid says that Lady Elinore sent the cherry tart to Sir Eldred.

MAID'S QUARTERS

The queen's friend, Lady Elinore, had greatly admired the necklace.

ARTHUR'S CHAMBERS

The cook would never knowingly send food to a guest if a guest disliked the dish.

PRIEST'S CHAMBER

Lady Elinore says she dislikes cherries.

INNER GATEHOUSE

Someone noticed that the crust of the tart appeared to have been cut off and replaced.

KITCHEN TOWER

Lady Elinore ordered a fruit tart to be delivered to her room in the Northwest Tower last evening.

GUINEVERE'S CHAMBERS

A guard saw Lady Elinore enter the queen's chamber that evening.

OUTER GATEHOUSE

Sir Eldred lodges in the Outer Gatehouse.

KNIGHTS' QUARTERS

Sir Eldred tells the other knights that at the upcoming banquet Lady Elinore will be more beautiful than the queen.

CHAPEL

The knight, Sir Eldred, is courting Lady Elinore.

BANQUET HALL

Lady Elinore did not join the king and queen for dinner because she had not been feeling well.

A MEDIEVAL WHODUNIT

A MEDIEVAL WHODUNIT

A MEDIEVAL WHODUNIT

A MEDIEVAL WHODUNIT

A MEDIEVAL WHODUNIT

A MEDIEVAL WHODUNIT

A MEDIEVAL WHODUNIT

A MEDIEVAL WHODUNIT

A MEDIEVAL WHODUNIT

A MEDIEVAL WHODUNIT

A MEDIEVAL WHODUNIT

A MEDIEVAL WHODUNIT

Against the suspect

Witnesses saw the suspect standing near the eraser owner's desk while the owner was away.

Evidence

For the suspect

The desk has no lock. Anyone could have gained access to the eraser.

Evidence

Against the suspect

The suspect's desk is near the eraser owner's desk. He has easy access.

Evidence

For the suspect

There were no fingerprints from the suspect on the eraser owner's desk.

Evidence

Against the suspect

There were brown eraser crumbs on the suspect's desk.

Evidence

For the suspect

The suspect owns a brown, chocolate-scented eraser. The brown eraser crumbs came from his own eraser, not the missing cola-scented eraser.

Evidence

Against the suspect

The suspect stayed indoors at recess because he said he had a cold.

Evidence

For the suspect

The missing eraser was not found in the suspect's desk or on the suspect's person.

Evidence

Against the suspect

The suspect could have hidden the eraser while the other students were still at recess.

Rebuttal

For the suspect

The teacher and the suspect's parents have confirmed that the suspect really did have a cold.

Rebuttal

Against the suspect

The suspect had sufficient time to wipe away his fingerprints before the rest of the class returned from recess.

Rebuttal

For the suspect

Certainly no student would steal an eraser and then use that eraser in the classroom where he might be seen.

Rebuttal

Defense Attorney	Prosecutor
Did anyone else enter the room during the recess period?	Did you remain in the classroom all through the recess period?
Defense Attorney	**Prosecutor**
How did you occupy your time in the classroom while everyone else was at recess?	When did you purchase the chocolate-scented eraser?
Defense Attorney	**Prosecutor**
Were you and the owner of the eraser on good terms?	Were you alone in the classroom for most, if not all, of the recess period?

JUROR'S DECISION

I believe that the suspect, _____,

is _____ of the crime for which

he/she has been charged.

Reasons for the verdict

_____

_____

_____

_____

_____

_____

_____

_____

_____

_____

_____

Signature of juror

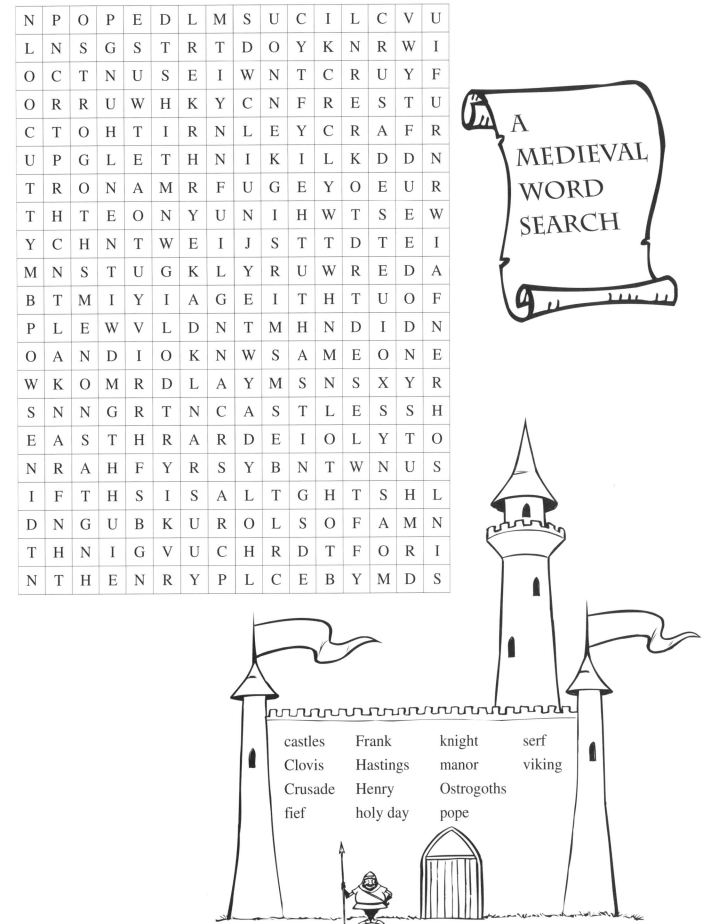

N	P	O	P	E	D	L	M	S	U	C	I	L	C	V	U
L	N	S	G	S	T	R	T	D	O	Y	K	N	R	W	I
O	C	T	N	U	S	E	I	W	N	T	C	R	U	Y	F
O	R	R	U	W	H	K	Y	C	N	F	R	E	S	T	U
C	T	O	H	T	I	R	N	L	E	Y	C	R	A	F	R
U	P	G	L	E	T	H	N	I	K	I	L	K	D	D	N
T	R	O	N	A	M	R	F	U	G	E	Y	O	E	U	R
T	H	T	E	O	N	Y	U	N	I	H	W	T	S	E	W
Y	C	H	N	T	W	E	I	J	S	T	T	D	T	E	I
M	N	S	T	U	G	K	L	Y	R	U	W	R	E	D	A
B	T	M	I	Y	I	A	G	E	I	T	H	T	U	O	F
P	L	E	W	V	L	D	N	T	M	H	N	D	I	D	N
O	A	N	D	I	O	K	N	W	S	A	M	E	O	N	E
W	K	O	M	R	D	L	A	Y	M	S	N	S	X	Y	R
S	N	N	G	R	T	N	C	A	S	T	L	E	S	S	H
E	A	S	T	H	R	A	R	D	E	I	O	L	Y	T	O
N	R	A	H	F	Y	R	S	Y	B	N	T	W	N	U	S
I	F	T	H	S	I	S	A	L	T	G	H	T	S	H	L
D	N	G	U	B	K	U	R	O	L	S	O	F	A	M	N
T	H	N	I	G	V	U	C	H	R	D	T	F	O	R	I
N	T	H	E	N	R	Y	P	L	C	E	B	Y	M	D	S

A MEDIEVAL WORD SEARCH

castles   Frank   knight   serf
Clovis   Hastings   manor   viking
Crusade   Henry   Ostrogoths
fief   holy day   pope

Photograph Credits

The following agencies and individuals have furnished materials to meet the photographic needs of this textbook. We wish to express our gratitude to them for their important contribution.

Carl Abrams
Ward Andersen
Aramco World Magazine
Art Resource
Austrian Press and Information Service
Gary Balius
Chris Barton
Bowater, Inc.
The British Library
The British Museum
Cadbury Ltd.
B. W. Carper
Christie's Images
Christine Osborne Pictures
George R. Collins
Corbis-Bettmann
Corel Corporation
Stewart Custer
Terry M. Davenport
Egyptian Tourist Authority
Gene Fisher
J. A. Franklin
Freer Gallery of Art
French Government Tourist Office
Friends of Free China
Greek National Tourist Organization

Greenville Public Library
Grace Collins Hargis
Peggy E. Hargis
India Tourist Office
Annie Lee Jones
Lyndia Jones
Sivasankar Kumar Kande
Mary Kraus
Kunsthistorisches, Museum Vienna
Library of Congress
Mary Evans Picture Library
Metropolitan Museum of Art
Mexican Government Tourism Office
National Archives
National Gallery of Art
Norwegian Tourist Board
Science and Society Picture Library
Stock Montage
Turkish Ministry of Tourism
Unusual Films
Vatican Museum
Harry Ward
West Point Museum
World Bank
Xinhua News Agency

Cover
World Bank (farmer, sheep); Ward Andersen (cistern, Parthenon)

Title Page
Aramco World Magazine

Chapter 1
John Feeney/Aramco World 1; Metropolitan Museum of Art 2 (left); Unusual Films 2 (right), 4 (right), 8 (top left), 10 (both), 11, 15 (both), 17 (all), 21; Aramco World Magazine 4 (left), 8 (top right); The Bob Jones University Collection and the Bowen Bible Lands Museum 4 (inset); Annie Lee Jones 5 (all); World Bank 8 (bottom); Wendy Levine/Aramco World 13 (top); Corel Corporation 13 (bottom); Corbis-Bettmann 14; Scala/Art Resource, NY 16

Chapter 2
Aramco World Magazine 23, 34, 48; Corel Corporation 25, 26 (bottom), 42 (bottom left, top right), 43 (middle, right); Torben B. Larsen/Aramco World 26 (top); Kunsthistorisches, Museum Vienna 30; Gene Fisher 32; Unusual Films 33 (top), 36; Harry Ward 33 (bottom); The British Museum 35 (top); Tor Eigeland/Aramco World 35 (bottom); Metropolitan Museum of Art 37; David Melody/Aramco World 40; Egyptian Tourist Authority 42 (top left, bottom right); Unusual Films 43 (left); Corbis-Bettmann 45

Chapter 3
Ward Andersen 49, 70 (inset), 72 (all); Corbis-Bettmann 53; Unusual Films 55, 59, 62 (both), 64, 71; Lyndia Jones 56, 69

Chapter 4
Peggy E. Hargis 73, 87, 89 (bottom); Christine Osborne Pictures 75, 80; World Bank 79 (photo by Kay Muldoon), 90 (bottom photo by Witlin); Unusual Films 83, 89 (top); National Archives 88; Greenville Public Library 90 (top); Sivasankar Kumar Kande 91 (all), 92 (both); Christie's Images 94; Government of India Tourist Office 95

Chapter 5
Mary Kraus 97, 98 (right), 100 (left), 109 (left); Gary Balius 98 (left), 100 (right), 105, 118 (both); Freer Gallery of Art, Smithsonian Institution, Washington, DC; Purchase, F1960.18 101(left); Freer Gallery of Art, Smithsonian Institution, Washington, DC; Purchase, F1938.5 101(right); Freer Gallery of Art, Smithsonian Institution, Washington, DC; Gift of Eugene and Agnes E. Meyer, F1961.30 107 (top right); Unusual Films 103, 107 (bottom), 113, 116 (both); Library of Congress 104; Metropolitan Museum of Art 107 (top left); Corel Corporation 109 (right); Xinhua News Agency 110; Science Museum/ Science and Society Picture Library 114; Aramco World Magazine 115 (top); Bowater, Inc. 115 (bottom)

Chapter 6
Ward Andersen 119, 143; Greek National Tourist Organization 120; West Point Museum 125; Library of Congress 128, 141; Corel Corporation 129, 139 (left); Unusual Films 132 (both), 140, 144; Vatican Museum 136; Metropolitan Museum of Art 138 (top both); Harry Ward 138 (bottom left); Stewart Custer 138 (bottom right); Christie's Images 139 (right)

Chapter 7
Ward Andersen 145, 155 (both), 168 (all); Christie's Images 147; Corbis-Bettmann 150, 156, 157, 161, 164 (bottom); Unusual Films 151, 160, 162, 166; Aramco World Magazine 153; Greenville Public Library 164 (top); Corel Corporation 165 (both); Grace Collins Hargis 167 (left); Mary Evans Picture Library 167 (right)

Chapter 8
Mexican Government Tourism Office 169, 172, 174 (both), 176, 179, 183, 184, 186, 188, 189; Unusual Films 171 (top left), 190; Cadbury Ltd. 171 (bottom left, right); Corel Corporation 177 (both); Library of Congress 187 (right)

Chapter 9
J. A. Franklin 191, 193 (bottom), 204 (both); Corel Corporation 193 (top), 195 (top right), 197 (top), 198 (both), 209 (both), 212; Unusual Films 195 (bottom right); Carl Abrams 195 (left), 201 (top), 205; Aramco World Magazine 197 (bottom); B. W. Carper 199 (top); Terry M. Davenport 199 (bottom); Chris Barton 201 (bottom), 208; Graphic House/Corbis-Bettmann 203; Brynn Bruijn/Aramco World 206; George R. Collins 210; Library of Congress 211

Chapter 10
Unusual Films 213, 219 (all), 222, 224-25 (bottom), 229, 230, 232 (all), 233 (both); Freer Gallery of Art, Smithsonian Institution, Washington, DC; Purchase, F1960.29 215; Mary Kraus 216 (top); Metropolitan Museum of Art 216 (middle); Gary Balius 216 (bottom); Corel Corporation 217, 225 (top), 226 (both), 227 (both); by permission of The British Library, Reference Number OR8210/P2 218; Freer Gallery of Art, Smithsonian Institution, Washington, DC; Gift of Charles Lang Freer, F1919.90 223; Friends of Free China 224 (top); Werner Forman/Art Resource, NY 228; Christie's Images 231; Borromeo/Art Resource, NY 241; Peggy E. Hargis 242

Chapter 11
Aramco World Magazine 243, 257, 258 (both); Turkish Ministry of Tourism 251 (both); Unusual Films 252; Library of Congress 256; Stock Montage 247, 250; Ward Andersen 259; National Gallery of Art 262; Metropolitan Museum of Art 268

Chapter 12
Library of Congress 271; Corel Corporation 272; Unusual Films 276, 293; Corbis-Bettmann 281, 290; Norwegian Tourist Board 283; French Government Tourist Office 288; Metropolitan Museum of Art 289; Austrian Press and Information Service, New York 294 (both)

SUPPLEMENT

Managing the Classroom for Group Activities

Many lessons in *HERITAGE STUDIES 6 for Christian Schools* suggest the use of groups. For clarification, the term *demonstration group* refers to any group of randomly selected students who come to the front of the class for a teacher-supervised activity while the other students watch.

The term *Heritage Studies groups* is used to designate small groups of students who work together on an independent activity. Consider the following suggestions in order to make Heritage Studies group activities purposeful and orderly.

- Although the number of students in the groups may vary according to the purpose of the activity or the supplies available, begin by assigning each student a Heritage Studies partner. Since these partners will work together regularly, give careful thought to the pairing, trying to balance differences in behavior and ability. This system of fixed partners will allow the lesson to proceed smoothly without the disruption of grouping the students each time. If the activity calls for larger groups, simply assign sets of partners to work together.
- You may reassign partners anytime during the year at your discretion.
- Devise a desk plan that the students themselves can quickly arrange for group activities. Assign each pair of partners to a permanent location within the arrangement so that the transition into group activities may be smooth and efficient.
- After giving instructions, allow the students to begin working independently as you move among them to answer questions and lend assistance.
- Since group activities require student interaction, clearly establish your expectations for behavior. If the students speak softly and raise their hands when asking for your help and if you circulate among the students, the classroom atmosphere should remain quiet and controlled.

Heritage Studies AREAs

When not involved in a Heritage Studies lesson, students can continue reviewing Heritage Studies concepts and facts by being involved in an individual or small group project. Many suggestions for these projects appear in the Enrichment section of the lessons. You can put the instructions and materials needed for AREAs (Additional Reinforcement/Enrichment Activities) in large folders, envelopes, or shoeboxes and arrange them in special locations around the room. Label the outside of each folder, envelope, or shoebox with the project name. Teach the students to go to these AREAs independently and to choose a variety of AREAs throughout the year. Often you may want an entire Heritage Studies group to participate in a selected project.

MATERIALS LIST

□ Chapter 1

Lesson 1
- A Bible
- Maps and More 1*
- A *HERITAGE STUDIES 6 Student Notebook* for each student*
- A three-ring binder for each student*

Lesson 2
- Items that the students have brought from home*

Lesson 3
- An overhead projector
- A blank overhead transparency
- Modeling clay for each student*
- A wooden craft stick for each student*

Lesson 4
- Either a potter with a potter's wheel and clay or a video showing the use of a potter's wheel*

Lesson 5
- A Bible for each student

Lesson 6
No materials are needed for this lesson.

□ Chapter 2

Lesson 7
- Maps and More 2
- The figure representing the Early Egyptians (3800 B.C.) from the History TimeLine Packet*

Lesson 8
- A tray
- An overhead projector
- A blank overhead transparency
- Watermelon slices for each student*
- Cantaloupe slices for each student*
- Cucumber slices for each student*
- A date for each student*
- A fig for each student*

Lesson 9
- Maps and More 3
- A roll of bathroom tissue for each group of four students*
- Small prizes for four students*
- The figure representing Egypt United (3100 B.C.) from the History TimeLine Packet

Lesson 10
- A sheet of notebook paper for each student
- Maps and More 4
- The figure of the Rosetta stone (A.D. 1799) from the History TimeLine Packet

Lesson 11
- A Bible for each student
- The figure of Joseph (1897 B.C.) from the History TimeLine Packet

Lesson 12
No materials are needed for this lesson.

Lesson 13
- A tape measure for each group of four students*
- A sheet of construction paper for each student
- A ruler for each student
- Scissors for each student
- Glue for each student
- Several staplers*
- Enough black yarn for each student to have 5-6 yards*
- A circle of black felt (about 9 inches in diameter) for each student*

□ Chapter 3

Lesson 14
- A wall map of the world
- The figure of Abraham (2000 B.C.) from the History TimeLine Packet

Lesson 15
- Maps and More 5
- An overhead projector
- A blank overhead transparency
- A Bible for each group

Lesson 16
- An overhead projector
- A blank overhead transparency

Lesson 17
- An overhead projector
- 2 light-colored overhead transparency pens
- 2 blank overhead transparencies

Lesson 18
- A cassette player
- *HERITAGE STUDIES Listening Cassette B*
- An overhead projector
- 2 blank overhead transparencies
- A Bible

Lesson 19
- A Bible
- An overhead projector
- A blank overhead transparency
- The figure representing the crucifixion of Christ (c. A.D. 30) from the History TimeLine Packet

□ Chapter 4

Lesson 20
- *Just So Stories* by Rudyard Kipling (optional)
- Crayons or colored pencils for each student: blue, green, orange, and purple

- A hand mirror*
- A Bible
- A globe or a wall map of the world
- Maps and More 6
- The figure representing the Indus Valley civilization (2500 B.C.) from the History TimeLine Packet
- 4 stickers for each student*

Lesson 21
- A triangular-bladed mason's trowel (optional)
- Several soft-bristled utility brushes (optional)
- A camera (optional)
- A sheet of paper for each student
- A permanent marking pen for each student*
- A self-adhesive label for each student*
- A resealable plastic bag for each student*
- A meter stick or metric ruler for each student*
- A postal scale*
- An artifact for each student*
- A box of sand (optional)
- An overhead projector
- A blank overhead transparency

Lesson 22
- Maps and More 1 and 6

Lesson 23
- A Bible for each student
- An overhead projector
- A blank overhead transparency

Lesson 24
- A Bible for each student and the teacher
- A red crayon, colored pencil, or felt-tip pen for each student
- A green crayon, colored pencil, or felt-tip pen for each student
- The figure of the Rig-Veda (1500 B.C.) from the History TimeLine Packet

☐ **Chapter 5**

Lesson 25
- A penny
- A tin can*
- A lead pipe or a mechanical pencil*
- An object made of bronze or of a metal that looks like bronze*
- The figure of the Shang art (1176 B.C.) from the History TimeLine Packet

Lesson 26
- An overhead projector
- A blank overhead transparency
- A blank sheet of paper for each student
- A black felt-tip pen for each student

Lesson 27
- A cassette player
- *HERITAGE STUDIES Listening Cassette B*
- Maps and More 7

Lesson 28
- A dictionary
- A small piece of paper for each student
- A container in which to collect the paper
- A sticker or small trinket for one student

Lesson 29
- 2 wide-mouthed tin cans (at least 12 ounces) for each pair of students*
- A can opener*
- An 8-ounce glass jar or plastic container with a lid for each pair of students*
- Two 7" squares of window screen for each pair of students*
- Newspapers*
- A towel or a thick cloth for each pair of students*
- 1 to 2 rolls of two-layered toilet tissue*
- A slightly damp sponge for each pair of students*
- A roll of paper towels*
- 2 pieces of dry cloth for each pair of students*
- An iron*
- An ironing board*
- Maps and More 8
- Pitchers of water or access to a water supply*

☐ **Chapter 6**

Lesson 30
- An overhead projector
- A blank overhead transparency

Lesson 31
- Maps and More 9

Lesson 32
- The figure of Pericles (429 B.C.) from the History TimeLine Packet

Lesson 33
- The figure of the Parthenon from Maps and More 9

Lesson 34
- An overhead projector
- A blank overhead transparency
- Maps and More 10
- A wire coat hanger*
- A large empty thread spool*
- Wire cutters*
- A small plastic cup with a handle*
- A globe or a wall map of the world

Lesson 35
- A 9"×12" sheet of construction paper for each student
- Crayons or felt-tip pens for each student
- Scissors

Lesson 36
- Bibles for several students
- Maps and More 10
- The figure of Alexander the Great (340 B.C.) from the History TimeLine Packet
- A wall map of the world

☐ Chapter 7

Lesson 37
- A penny, nickel, dime, or quarter for each student*
- The figure representing the founding of Rome (753 B.C.) from the History TimeLine Packet

Lesson 38
- A cassette player
- *HERITAGE STUDIES Listening Cassette B*
- Maps and More 11
- A blank overhead transparency
- An overhead projector

Supplemental Lesson
- A Bible for each student
- A sheet of notebook paper for each student
- A blank overhead transparency
- An overhead projector

Lesson 39
- A Bible for the teacher and each student
- A large road map showing several states*
- Maps and More 11
- A blank overhead transparency
- An overhead projector

Lesson 40
- A wall map of the world
- A 3"×5" card for each student*
- A calendar for each group of eight students*
- A small piece of magnetic tape or cellophane tape for each group of eight students
- A colored pencil for each group of eight students

Lesson 41
- A Bible
- "Gallons of Water" survey results from Lesson 40
- A wall map of the world
- Maps and More 11, 12, and 13

Lesson 42
- A Bible for each student and the teacher
- A sheet of notebook paper for each student
- Maps and More 11
- The figure representing the birth of Christ (c. 4 B.C.) from the History TimeLine Packet
- The figure representing the fall of Rome (A.D. 476) from the History TimeLine Packet

☐ Chapter 8

Lesson 43
- Maps and More 14, 15, and 16
- A large, electric coffee urn (25-30 cups)*
- A Styrofoam cup for each student*
- A plastic spoon for each student*
- A packet of hot-chocolate mix for each student*
- The figure of the Olmecs (3500 B.C.) from the History TimeLine Packet
- The figure of Columbus (A.D. 1492) from the History TimeLine Packet

Lesson 44
- The figure representing the empty Mayan cities (A.D. 900) from the History TimeLine Packet
- Maps and More 14

Lesson 45
- A magazine with advertisements for each student*
- A sheet of notebook paper for each student
- The figure of Diego de Landa (A.D. 1562) from the History TimeLine Packet

Lesson 46
- 6 blank sheets of paper
- A black felt-tip pen
- 6 safety pins

Lesson 47
- Maps and More 17

Lesson 48
- A stapler
- A Bible for each student

☐ Chapter 9

Lesson 49
- A Bible for each student
- A wall map of Africa

Lesson 50
No materials are needed for this lesson.

Lesson 51
- A wall map of Africa

Lesson 52
- A wall map of Africa
- A 4-foot piece of yarn*
- Fabric remnants*
- Several small bowls*
- Costume jewelry*
- Coins*
- 2 sheets of construction paper
- The figure of Mansa Musa (A.D. 1312) from the History TimeLine Packet

Lesson 53
- Maps and More 19
- A wall map of Africa

☐ Chapter 10

Lesson 54
No materials are needed for this lesson.

Lesson 55
No materials are needed for this lesson.

Lesson 56
- A sheet of white drawing paper for each student
- A felt-tip pen for each student

Lesson 57
No materials are needed for this lesson.

Lesson 58
- A wall map of the world
- Crayons for each student

Lesson 59
- A decorative, braided cord, such as those worn on some military dress uniforms*
- A wall map of the world

Lesson 60
No materials are needed for this lesson.

Lesson 61
- Maps and More 20
- A cassette player
- HERITAGE STUDIES Listening Cassette B

☐ Chapter 11

Lesson 62
- A shish kebab skewer or party pick for each student*
- 4 or 5 small fruit pieces for each student*
- A sheet of notebook paper for each student
- A wall map of the world
- Maps and More 21

Lesson 63
- A wall map of the world
- Maps and More 21

Lesson 64
- The figure of the Hagia Sophia (A.D. 537) from the History TimeLine Packet
- Glue for each student
- Scissors for each student
- A sheet of construction paper for each student
- Various colors of construction paper for each student to make mosaics

Lesson 65
- A pocket-sized New Testament*

Lesson 66
- A Bible for each student
- An overhead projector
- 2 blank overhead transparencies
- An overhead transparency pen
- A wall map of the world

Lesson 67
- A Bible
- A cassette player
- HERITAGE STUDIES Listening Cassette B
- An overhead projector
- A blank overhead transparency
- A sheet of notebook paper for each student

Lesson 68
- A wall map of the world
- A Bible

Lesson 69
- A Bible

☐ Chapter 12

Lesson 70
- A copy of Mark Twain's *A Connecticut Yankee in King Arthur's Court**

Lesson 71
- One-half sheet of notebook paper for each student

Lesson 72
- A mixing bowl*
- A fork for each student*
- 6 eggs*
- ¼ teaspoon salt*
- 6 tablespoons of butter or margarine*
- A small onion*
- 2 tablespoons dried parsley*
- A 10- or 12-inch skillet with flared sides*
- Access to a stove*
- A spatula*
- A small plate for each student*

Lesson 73
- A wall map of the world

Lesson 74
- Maps and More 25, 26, and 27

Lesson 75
- Maps and More 28

Lesson 76
- 5 sheets of white construction paper
- A pencil for each juror
- Tape
- Safety pins
- 2 suit coats or briefcases for each attorney (optional)

Index